CANON LAW AND THE LAW OF ENGLAND

CANON LAW AND
THE LAW OF ENGLAND

R.H. HELMHOLZ

THE HAMBLEDON PRESS
LONDON AND RONCEVERTE

Published by The Hambledon Press, 1987

102 Gloucester Avenue, London NW1 8HX (U.K.)

309 Greenbrier Avenue, Ronceverte WV 24970 (U.S.A.)

ISBN 0 907628 93 1

British Library Cataloguing in Publication Data

Helmholz, R.H.
    Canon law and the law of England:
    historical essays
    1. Law – England – History and criticism
    I. Title
    344. 2   KD610

Library of Congress Cataloging-in-Publication Data

Helmholz, R.H.
    Canon law and the law of England.

    Includes bibliographical references and index.
    1. Canon law – History.
    2. Ecclesiastical law – Great Britain – History.
    I. Title
    LAW   262.0'09   87-28950

Printed and bound in Great Britain
by Billing & Sons Limited, Worcester.

CONTENTS

ACKNOWLEDGEMENTS

The articles in this volume initially appeared in the following places. They are here reprinted by kind permission of the original publishers.

1   Published separately by the Selden Society, London (1983).

2   *Traditio* 25 (1969), 386-404.

3   *Proceedings of the Fourth International Congress of Medieval Canon Law.* Biblioteca Apostolica Vaticana, Monumenta Iuris Canonici, Series C (1976), 283-99.

4   *Mediaeval Studies* 43 (1981), 297-314.

5   *Minnesota Law Review* 60 (1976), 1011-33.

6   *Zeitschrift der Savigny-Stiftung für Rechtsgeschichte* 99 Kan. Abt. 68 (1982), 202-18.

7   *Law and History Review* 1 (1983), 1-26.

8   *The Jurist* 32 (1972), 80-90.

9   *The History of Childhood Quarterly* 2 (1975), 379-90.

10   *Virginia Law Review* 63 (1977), 431-48.

11   *American Journal of Legal History* 13:4 (1969), 360-83.

12   *Tulane Law Review* 52 (1978), 223-57.

13   *University of Illinois Law Review* (1984), 659-74 (Copyright by the Board of Trustees of the University of Illinois).

14   *Law Quarterly Review* 91 (1976), 406-32.

15   *Missouri Law Review* 48 (1983), 415-29 (Copyright by the Curators of the University of Missouri).

16   *American Journal of Legal History* 23:1 (1979), 68-82.

17   *Speculum* 61 (1986), 364-80 (Copyright by the Medieval Academy of America).

18   *Columbia Law Review* 79 (1979), 1503-13 (Copyright c. 1979 by the Directors of the Columbia Law Review Association, Inc. All rights reserved).

PREFACE

The papers published here, although concerned with some quite disparate aspects of legal history, all deal with one or more of three themes. The first is the relationship between the formal canon law and the law as put into practice in the English ecclesiastical courts. The second is an examination of the role the ecclesiastical courts played in areas of human life which the temporal law reached incompletely or not at all. The third is the exploration of the possibility that the canon law influenced the growth and development of the English common law.

Of these three, the first would seem to allow the most straightforward exposition. In fact it does not. Difficulties inherent in using record sources to draw conclusions about the law that was being applied and the considerable room which the canon law itself left for judicial discretion and local variation make it hard to sum up the relationship neatly. Nevertheless, something of a pattern does emerge. Much of the scope of the jurisdiction exercised by the English Church was based immediately upon local custom and synodal legislation. In fact this appears to have been true in many parts of Western Europe. The ecclesiastical courts did not enforce all the law found in the *Corpus iuris canonici*. However, this use of local custom did not mean that the canonical texts were irrelevant to legal practice. Far from it, the canon law and the academic commentary upon it determined a very large part of the legal rules applied.

Testamentary law, dealt with in several of these essays, provides an accessible example of this pattern. The English Church exercised a probate jurisdiction that was different in some quite fundamental ways from that found in the canonical texts and that applied in most Continental countries. The English Church's jurisdiction was not limited to charitable bequests, rather covering the whole of succession to chattels, and it included no control over the devolution of land at death save an indirect one. On the Continent, where the system of universal heirship based upon Roman law largely prevailed, testamentary jurisdiction followed more closely the model found in the canon law texts. The courts normally occupied the subsidiary role of ensuring correct application of charitable gifts, in which role they were not limited to jurisdiction over chattels.

Despite the distinct and customary nature of English ecclesiastical practice, the courts in England nevertheless made regular use of the academic law. Canonical and civilian principles were applied in formulating the duties of executors and other fiduciaries. The law of guardianship was taken from the canon and Roman law texts. Even many of the rules relating to bankrupt estates were found in the same sources. There was thus a clear and close connection between law and practice, even if the overall jurisdiction varied from the European pattern, and even if not every rule found in the texts was relevant to English probate practice.

The second theme in these papers, relating to the important role the ecclesiastical courts played in areas of the law not filled by the temporal law, seems, and in reality was, more straightforward. The essays dealing with it also make a point of significance for historians who have no particular interest in the canon law. Jurisdiction in medieval and early modern England was dispersed among different court systems. The common law courts had no monopoly. Rather, the king's courts assumed the enforcement of much law outside its boundaries. Where the judges declined to act, they did so as often because of these jurisdictional assumptions as they did because they were making a judgement about the merits of a rule of substantive law.

The law relating to illegitimate children, treated directly by two of these essays and indirectly by two others, shows this most immediately. At common law, jurisdiction over illegitimacy belonged largely, though not invariably, to the Church. The common law judges regularly deferred to the certificates of the episcopal tribunals when illegitimacy was pleaded in bar to a claim of inheritance. They also declined to force parents to support their illegitimate children, not because they considered the children to be without rights, but instead because they knew the ecclesiastical courts would do so. What seems to be an arbitrary or heartless decision is actually only a reflection of a jurisdictional boundary. What the ecclesiastical courts did in early ages, therefore, is sometimes essential knowledge for historians tracing the development of substantive rules of English law. The history of the common law of England without the history of the ecclesiastical courts must be incomplete.

The third theme found in these essays, that of possible influence of the canon law on the growth of the common law itself, is easily the most controversial of the three. Not all legal historians, perhaps even not many, would agree that except in rare circumstances did the English common lawyers have anything but antipathy for the law of the Church. Whatever coincidence in legal rule and practice existed is, in this view, better explained by coincidence, social forces, or the paucity of ways in which legal doctrine can be expressed than it is by conscious emulation.

The contrary argument is made in several of these essays, most directly in the first. It contends that although there were enduring and essential differences between the canon law and the English common law, nevertheless the men who practised in the two court systems knew something of the other's law and drew from it when their interests, or those of their clients, made borrowing appear desirable. Bracton's use of Roman and canon law in the thirteenth century to describe and thereby to shape English law and institutions was not an isolated incident in English history. He had successors. In several areas of the law, from advowsons and assumpsit to usury and wills, common lawyers made use of language and principles they found in ecclesiastical law. This use, these essays argue, has been one source of the development of English law.

No essay here argues that the borrowing was complete or that it ever happened as a matter of course. Indeed the influence suggested in these essays is consistent with express rejection of canonical rules that seemed wrong or inconsistent with existing common law principles, as many of them in fact did. It is also consistent with the common lawyers' rapid forgetting of the original source of many a rule. They rarely felt themselves bound to canonical rules. However, the independence of the common lawyers does not necessarily negate the possibility of interaction and influence between the two legal systems. That at least is the argument that several of the essays collected here make in specific areas of legal practice.

Reading through these eighteen papers, written over the course of twenty years, has not proved an entirely congenial task for their author. There are so many things that might have been said better, and some that probably should not have been said at all. Still, the evidence drawn from the manuscript records of the ecclesiastical courts continues to seem worth presenting. The three themes still seem worth pursuing. I am grateful for the opportunity. Particularly is this so for the articles which originally appeared in American law reviews. They almost inevitably escape the notice of all but the most assiduous of historians. For material help in preparing this volume, I am also grateful to the American Bar Foundation, the Sawyier Fund for Studies in Jurisprudence, and the Morton C. Seeley Fund.

Chicago
April 1987

R. H. Helmholz

TABLE OF CASES

YEAR BOOK (BLACK LETTER) CASES

CANON LAW AND
THE LAW OF ENGLAND

CANON LAW AND THE ENGLISH COMMON LAW

THE appearance of the volume *Select Canterbury Cases* is one in which we can all rejoice.(1) It is a magnificent addition to our series, and it brings to fruition painstaking and perplexing work both by the editors, Professors Adams and Donahue, and by our Literary Director, Professor Milsom. But for those of us interested in the history of the canon law, the appearance of this volume is more than a merely welcome event. It signals a recognition of the intrinsic importance to the development of the law of England of the jurisdiction once exercised by the courts of the Church. It implies that we should not be content with a legal history which dismisses the ecclesiastical courts as archaic and unpopular institutions. *Select Canterbury Cases* shows how little archaic they were, how in diverse aspects of procedure and proof they employed much that modern lawyers can admire. And as for unpopularity—although it seems unlikely that any system of courts has ever been, or ever will be, the subject of sustained popular enthusiasm— the maintenance of the Church's jurisdiction in important areas of human life through centuries shows that they were not widely thought to be disreputable or iniquitous institutions.

Still, even with the recognition of the intrinsic import- ance of the canon law, it is by reference to the common law that the Church courts must exercise any considerable hold on the imagination of legal historians. Legal history is winner's history, and at the end of the day the ecclesiastical courts were losers. Doctors' Commons is gone. This

---

(1)   *Select Cases from the Ecclesiastical Courts of the Province of Canterbury c. 1200–1301*, eds. Norma Adams and Charles Donahue, Jr., Selden Society, Vol. 95 (1981 for 1978–79).

Honourable Society survives and indeed flourishes. It would be foolish, and even contrary to my views, to treat this fact of life as cause for lament. Nor should it deter detailed studies of canonical rules and ecclesiastical institutions.(2) However, there is no disguising that these studies, worthwhile as they are, inevitably will have limited appeal to the person interested in the growth and development of modern law. His focus of attention will remain on those places where the canon law intersected with the common law. Therefore, the subject of my talk this afternoon: the relationship between the canon law and English common law.

There are three evident ways of approaching the subject: first, to examine areas where there was a clash—a difference of legal principle—between the two systems; second, to look at areas of cooperation—necessary mutual aid—between the courts of Church and State; and third, to investigate areas of possible reciprocal influence—lawyers using ideas drawn from the other system—between the canon and the common law. In each good work has already been done.(3) But there is still much that is unknown or imperfectly understood, and I want to take them up, treating the first two briefly and then dealing more specifically with the topic relating to reciprocal influence. In each instance, the essential evidence comes from the manuscript records of the Church courts, and of the royal courts as well. It is largely the exploration of these records which, in recent years, has permitted us to see more fully something of the realities, the complexities, and the possibilities to be found in each area.

(2)   Two recent and well done studies of the history of specific ecclesiastical courts may be noted: Ralph Houlbrooke, *Church Courts and the People during the English Reformation 1520–1570* (1979); Richard M. Wunderli, *London Church Courts and Society on the Eve of the Reformation* (1981).

(3)   The recent survey of William W. Bassett, 'Canon Law and the Common Law' *Hastings Law Rev.*, Vol. 29 (1978) 1383–1419, is useful and complete.

I

For the first, areas of conflict, probably the most important discovery of recent years has been the complexity of the subject. Where once it seemed natural to assume that wherever there was a conflict in legal rule, the royal court rule prevailed, now it seems clear that the evidence warrants no such reflexive assumption. At least during the Middle Ages, for every writ of prohibition or every threat of praemunire, there was a counterbalancing sanction of excommunication to defend the Church's position.(4) And although it seems strange to be forced to conclude that spiritual sanctions could have matched corporal and financial penalties in effectiveness, yet that conclusion fits the evidence better than the natural modern assumption that the secular sanctions must always have been the stronger. The spiritual sanctions seem in practice to have been as effective over all, or at least no more ineffective, than were the threats of the King's ministers. When one recalls that no sanctions, spiritual or secular, were terribly effective in the Middle Ages, it becomes a little less difficult to accept that the relationship between the common law rules and what happened in actual litigation is less susceptible of clear or consistent analysis than it seemed thirty years ago.

Perhaps the most promising area for research in this area lies in the post-Reformation period. How far did the Church courts conform to the rules of the common law in their internal organization after the breach with Rome in the sixteenth century? In some matters, the obvious case being that of appeals to the papal court, the English Church courts quickly and voluntarily conformed to secular law. But it by no means follows necessarily from this that the Church courts immediately accepted all common law rules wherever there was potential disagreement. It is well to

(4)   Evidence on the point is collected in my 'Writs of Prohibition and Ecclesiastical Sanctions in the English Courts Christian,' *Minnesota Law Rev.*, Vol. 60 (1976) 1011–33 : infra, 77-99.

recall how uncertain was the question of the common law's authority outside its traditional sphere during this period. The Coke–Ellesmere dispute was a live controversy. It may be as wrong to anticipate the outcome in these detailed points of law as it is on questions of State.

For example, there is the subject of tithe litigation during the reign of Elizabeth I. To judge from the King's Bench plea rolls, which contain hundreds of prohibition cases involving tithes, the royal courts were considerably restricting the freedom of the ecclesiastical courts to apply their own law. One would suppose that a prudent litigant would have had quick recourse to the royal courts, and that suing for tithes in the Church courts would have been an increasingly fruitless exercise, inevitably ending in a sentence which would later be overturned in the King's Bench.

However, when we look at the records of the Church courts themselves, a different picture emerges. Not only do those records show the ecclesiastical judges hearing and determining tithe causes in full, along traditional lines, they also show no diminution in numbers of tithe causes in the last half of Elizabeth's reign. In fact the act books show the reverse. There was a growing volume of litigation brought to recover tithes.(5) It is evidently false to conclude that rising numbers in the royal courts meant concomitant decline in the Church courts, and it is therefore at least an open question how the ecclesiastical officials responded to the rules developed in the prohibition cases. What we know so far suggests that in 1600 the day in which the ecclesiastical

(5)   Figures from the Act books of the diocese of Hereford are typical. In 1520, 26 causes to recover tithes or ecclesiastical dues (*cause subtractionis decimarum* or *cause subtractionis iurum ecclesiasticorum*) were introduced in the Consistory court. In 1585, the comparable figure for the same court had risen to 79. (Comparing Act book I/5 with Act book I/12, Hereford County Record Office, Hereford.) See also the figures in Ronald A. Marchant, *The Church under the Law: Justice, Administration and Discipline in the Diocese of York 1560–1640* (1969) 62. The City of London may well have been an exception; see Susan Brigden, 'Tithe Controversy in Reformation London,' *Journal of Ecclesiastical History*, Vol. 32 (1981) 285–301.

courts would obediently follow all the dictates of royal court rules still lay in the future.

That day ultimately arrived. English treatises on ecclesiastical law would come in time to be collections of the decisions of the royal courts, scarcely distinguishable in their choice of authorities from treatises on secular topics. But this was not yet so in 1600. The pages of Swinburne are dominated by references to canonists and civilians, though he clearly knew, and used, common law works as well.(6) He had not traded his copy of Panormitanus for Fitzherbert's *New Natura Brevium*. It may be that the legal historian does wrong to write too early a *finis* to the history of a separate and independent body of canon law enforced in the English Church courts. Here there is much work, and perhaps even some re-thinking, left to do.

II

For the second area, that of cooperation, it can be said that there is now a consensus that the area was broader than historians once thought. Even during the Middle Ages when the power and independence of the Church were great, the history of legal relations between Church and State ought more often to be seen more in terms of mutual assistance than in terms of struggle.(7) Routine royal caption of persons certified as excommunicate by the courts of English

(6)　Henry Swinburne, *Brief Treatise of Testaments and Last Wills* (1590–91); on Swinburne's authorities, and for useful discussion of the general problem, see J. Duncan M. Derrett, *Henry Swinburne (?1551–1624) Civil Lawyer of York* (1973). See also Helmut Coing, 'Das Schriftum der englischen Civilians und die Kontinentale Rechtsliteratur in der Zeit zwischen 1550 und 1800,' *Ius Commune*, Vol. 5 (1975) 1–55; Daniel R. Coquillette, 'Legal Ideology and Incorporation I: The English Civilian Writers, 1523–1607,' *Boston University Law Rev.*, Vol. 61 (1981) 1–89.

(7)　See the useful survey by W. R. Jones, 'Relations of the two jurisdictions: Conflict and Cooperation in England during the thirteenth and fourteenth centuries,' in *Studies in Medieval and Renaissance History*, Vol. 7, ed. William M. Bowsky (1970) 77–210.

bishops,(8) and ecclesiastical excommunication of those
who infringed the provisions of Magna Carta(9) are two
prominent and obvious examples of cooperation on both
sides of the jurisdictional boundary. There are many others.

Yet the subject yields unexpected complexity when
looked at in detail, and of this a good example is the so far
uninvestigated subject of episcopal collection of debt
judgments rendered against clerics in the royal courts.(10) It
is an obscure subject, raising (except by implication) no
issues of great moment. But it is the sort of practical
problem which often reveals a great deal about legal reality.
Briefly, the early practice was that when a cleric without lay
fee had been held liable for a debt in the royal courts, a writ
in execution would be issued to the bishop of the cleric,
ordering the bishop to raise the sum owed from the cleric's
ecclesiastical possessions. This sum the bishop was to
transmit to the royal court, together with the writ. He was,
as it were, acting as an ecclesiastical sheriff.

On the surface this practice is a notable example of
ecclesiastical cooperation with secular law, notable because
according to the letter of the canon law, the bishop's
obedience to the royal writ was illegal. It violated the
canonical principle that clerics had the privilege of being
sued in personal matters before their own tribunals.(11)
But the English prelates cooperated with the secular courts.
They violated, or at least they blinked at, the canonical
prohibitions, evincing in their responses to the royal writs

(8)   F. Donald Logan, *Excommunication and the Secular Arm in Medieval
        England* (1968).

(9)   See the references in *Councils & Synods with other Documents
        relating to the English Church II, A.D. 1205–1313*, eds. F. M. Powicke
        and C. R. Cheney (1964) Pt. 2, Index pp. 1428–9.

(10)   There is a brief mention of the practice in Robert E. Rodes, Jr.,
        Ecclesiastical Administration in Medieval England (1977) 96. Appar-
        ently, some vestiges remain in modern law; see E. Garth Moore,
        An Introduction to English Canon Law (1967) 121.

(11)   Hostiensis, *Summa Aurea* II, tit. *de foro competenti*, no. 13 (Venice,
        1574) col. 462. The fundamental modern study is R. Génestal, *Le
        Privilegium Fori en France*, Bibliothèque de l'Ecole des Hautes
        Etudes, Sciences Religieuses, 2 vols. (1921 & 1924).

an apparently fulsome desire to comply with the dictates of justice as determined by the king's ministers.(12)

The reality, however, was slightly more complicated than this picture of compliant cooperation implies. In fact the bishops seem often to have made a quasi-independent decision about the advisability of complying fully with the directions of the writ. The episcopal register of Simon Islip, Archbishop of Canterbury between 1349 and 1366, for instance, contains a collection of such royal writs.(13) To many of these the Archbishop has returned answers which a neutral observer might be tempted to describe as evasive, as that in which he has asserted the impossibility of finding buyers for the cleric's goods.(14) In some, it is evident that the Archbishop has interposed his own judgment about the underlying debt, as that in which he answered that the cleric had only goods which, properly understood, belonged to the Church, adding a little presumptuously that he 'did not believe the Lord King would wish to be answered from these'.(15) The Register appears almost like a model of forms for avoiding exact compliance with the royal court orders.

Much of the evidence from other ecclesiastical sources is similar. The cleric is poor and cannot pay,(16) or the benefice will support only a fraction of the amount claimed

(12)   E.g., in an ecclesiastical formulary of the fifteenth century, the direction by the bishop to his official to collect the debt is represented to the Crown as being made 'cum omni celeritate possibili.' British Library, Harl. MS. 2179, f. 41.

(13)   London, Lambeth Palace Library, fols. 343–46v.

(14)   Ibid., f. 346r: 'Et ea fecimus sub arto sequestro sed aliquos emptores eorundem hucusque non potuimus invenire et ideo nullos denarios levavimus.'

(15)   Ibid., f. 343v: '...de quibus sic mere spiritualibus ad ecclesiam et non ad personam tam pertinentibus et sic sub nostra custodia ad utilitatem ipsius ecclesie ut premittitur pertinentibus non credimus quod dominus noster Rex velit sibi responderi.'

(16)   Canterbury Cathedral, Library of the Dean and Chapter, Register Q, f. 152 (1328), in which the return is that the cleric 'pauper est et nichil habet ultra sustentacionem suam necessariam.'

by the royal court officers.(17) Moreover, at least a
preliminary examination of the plea rolls suggests that
Archbishop Islip's style of cooperation was the rule, not the
exception. Time after time, the bishop's return excuses his
failure to take the action demanded.(18) The apparent
automatic obedience to royal wishes masked a more
independent episcopal attitude. In other words, the
examination of an area of cooperation between the two
court systems leads, as does the study of conflicts, to
complex conclusions—conclusions which reveal something
about the nature of the enforcement of both canon and
common law.

III

The third area of legal relations between Church and
State relates to reciprocal influence. It is the most controversial area of the three, and perhaps it is no accident that
there is no emerging consensus. I hold to the view that there
was reciprocal influence, and that it was more than a trivial
and superficial thing. It may well be, I readily concede, that
my opinions are coloured by every researcher's inclination
to exaggerate the importance of his particular subject, an
inclination which is as natural as it is pathetic. But almost
everyone will agree that the position for reciprocal influence
deserves statement and illustration, and for this purpose two
concrete examples of legal development during the six-

(17)   Lambeth Palace Library, Reg. Reynolds, f. 303v (1321), in
which the sum of 5 marks was returned in lieu of the 18 marks
awarded by the judgment, the Archbishop noting, 'Et non sunt
plura bona in dicto beneficio ipsius magistri Johannis ad presens
inventa.'

(18)   E.g., *Cosyn* v. *Blunt*, P.R.O. CP 40/223, m. 213 (1318). Judgment
had been given in the amount of 66s. 8d. against the defendant,
parson of Harrietsham, but no sum was forthcoming from the
process described in the text: 'Et archiepiscopus nichil inde fecit set
mandavit quod predictus Thomas non habet aliqua bona ad
presens unde aliqui denarii fieri possunt. Et testatus est quod satis
etc. unde etc. Ideo sicut pluries.'

teenth century well serve to illustrate the point. The one, defamation, provides an instance of clear and direct influence. The other, bankruptcy, provide an instance of partial and less clear influence. Then follows a brief treatment of two objections to the conclusions drawn from these examples, the object being to bring into sharper focus the precise nature of the influence suggested by the record evidence.

The first example is taken from recently completed work on the history of the law of defamation. Much of this has appeared with full discussion and documentation in a Selden Society volume. But some of its conclusions may be conveniently summarized. The courts of the Church exercised exclusive jurisdiction over defamation in the fifteenth century and before, this on the basis of a Provincial Constitution of 1222 which defined defamation as the malicious imputation of a crime.(19) Rather than the expansive *actio iniuriarum* of Roman law, which treated defamation simply as one kind of actionable wrong, without requiring that any specific offence have been imputed to the plaintiff, the ecclesiastical courts in England enforced a more restricted version of defamation, excluding language which we today take to be slanderous, like imputations of professional unfitness, as well as mere abusive language.

The beginnings of royal court jurisdiction over defamation can be traced on the plea rolls to the early years of the sixteenth century, though the first cases were preceded by attempts to deprive the Church of its jurisdiction over imputations of secular crimes like theft and murder.(20) From the very start it is evident that the common lawyers were consciously using the remedy of the canon law. The earliest pleading found on the rolls was in fact copied from an ecclesiastical formulary; it is identical in language to that

(19)   *Councils and Synods with other Documents relating to the English Church, II A.D. 1205–1313*, Pt. 1 (1964) 107.

(20)   J. H. Baker, Introduction to *The Reports of Sir John Spelman*, Selden Society, Vol. 94 (1978) 66–70, esp. 67 note 2.

the Church courts used.(21) And throughout the sixteenth century, it was the imputation of a crime which largely defined the remedy in the royal courts. There was, from at least the middle of the century, some opinion among common lawyers in favour of expanding the remedy to cover slander of a man in his profession. Occasionally the attempts succeeded, but at least from the perspective of the plea rolls it was the limited remedy taken from the ecclesiastical courts which determined the scope of the secular action for slander. The notorious *mitior sensus* rule, for instance, according to which words would be given a lenient, non-actionable interpretation if this were possible, or even conceivable, was simply a rigorous application of the canonical rule that to be actionable, the defamatory words must tend to subject the victim to criminal prosecution.

The canonical influence in the early years of common law libel and slander is therefore clear. It is not, I think, unexpected, and it has been suggested by several legal historians. The more unexpected and exciting possibility suggested by research into the subject is the discovery that a connection continued *after* the years of origin. That is, it appears that well into the sixteenth and seventeenth centuries there continued to be interchange between the common law and the canon law, even that practice in one jurisdiction may illuminate apparent darkness in the other. For instance, in details of pleading: in the sixteenth century the ecclesiastical lawyers copied some of the forms used in the royal courts. The *innuendo* form appears in the Church court records, evidently copied from contemporary usage in the courts at Westminster.(22) Even the *mitior sensus* rule

(21)   The first entry so far found on the plea rolls is *Owughan* v. *Baker* (1507), CP 40/981, m. 596, to be printed in the forthcoming Selden Society volume.

(22)   E.g. *Wall* c. *Plummer*, Diocese of Coventry and Lichfield, Joint Record Office, Lichfield B/C/5/1593: '...publice predicavit videlicet that she (innuendo et accusando dictam Editham Wall) ys a whoore.'

was found tempting to some ecclesiastical lawyers.(23) Or, in a question of law of more moment: the role of malice, express or implied, in the common law action, long a subject of uncertainty and dispute among historians, is in fact illuminated by looking at contemporary practice in the sixteenth-century ecclesiastical courts. The manner of pleading the existence of malice and the evidence adduced in support of the pleading were very similar in both court systems.(24) Malice played a roughly equivalent role in both jurisdictions.

The conclusion suggested by the records, in other words, is that when men in the sixteenth and seventeenth centuries thought about defamation, they made a definite division of jurisdiction according to the matter imputed. But on many points of practice and even substantive law they assumed that underlying principles were no different. If this is so, the importance of the canon law for the development of English law is not simply one of the absorption into the royal courts of a remedy once offered by the Church, but a source of continued interchange of thought and practice.

A second example of possible canon law influence on the growth of the common law comes from the law of bankruptcy. The case is not so strong. The evidence here is more ambiguous and the parallels less exact. If there is a connection, it consists of the common lawyers' taking principles and practices from the ecclesiastical courts and adapting them to different needs, while leaving ecclesiastical practice substantially intact.

(23)   E.g., *Colsonsocke* c. *Worroll* (1567), Diocese of Chester, Cheshire Record Office EDC 5/1560–68, s.d. 1567. The words imputed were, 'Get thee whome and kepe thye bastards.' The question argued, on the basis of authority from both the canon and Roman law, was whether the words accused the plaintiff in the case of any actual complicity in the birth of the illegitimate children. They might, it was maintained, have belonged to her husband alone.

(24)   The evidence on this point is collected in my 'Civil Trials and the Limits of Responsible Speech,' in *Community Judgment and Freedom of Speech* (William Andrews Clark Memorial Library, 1983).

What is currently known about the history of the English law of bankruptcy is as follows. Prior to the sixteenth century, there was no law other than that which allowed all creditors to enforce their debts against the person and the property of their debtor. In 1542, however, the first, and in 1571 the principal, bankruptcy statutes were enacted.(25) They were as much creditor-protection statutes as they were the foundations of bankruptcy in the modern sense. No discharge of the bankrupt was allowed, and only merchants and traders were covered. Under these statutes there was also no such thing as a voluntary bankrupt. Only the petition of a creditor, after an imperfectly defined act of bankruptcy by the debtor, could initiate the process. But these differences apart, most of the basic features of bankruptcy law are found in these two statutes and the other statutes which followed under James I.(26) That is, the sequestration and valuation of the debtor's assets by appointed commissioners, the prevention of preferences among creditors, the invalidation of fraudulent conveyances, and the sale of the assets and distribution of the proceeds *pro rata* among the creditors.

The origins of the Tudor bankruptcy acts are obscure, to judge from the standard authorities. The Index to Holdsworth's great work contains this entry: 'Bankruptcy, Sixteenth Century: Not known in England before.'(27) And that is essentially the view taken by W. J. Jones's recent treatment, *The Foundations of English Bankruptcy*.(28) No bankruptcy procedure was known prior to the Tudor period. At that time it was invented. Coke is generally cited as contemporary authority for this view, and he held the opinion that the need for this invention could be laid almost

(25)   34 & 35 Hen. VIII, c. 4; 13 Eliz. I. cc. 5 & 7.

(26)   1 Jac. I, c. 15; 21 Jac. I, c. 19.

(27)   Edward Potton, *Tables and Index* to *A History of English Law* (1932) 76. For Holdsworth's substantive treatment, see *HEL*, Vol. 1 (7th ed. 1956) 470–73; Vol. VIII 229–245.

(28)   The full title is *The Foundations of English Bankruptcy: Statutes and Commissions in the Early Modern Period* (1979).

entirely to an alarming contemporary increase in numbers of fraudulent debtors, who were both seduced by the luxurious habits of Italian merchants and misled by the reprehensible spendthrift habits of his era.(29) Coke took the part of the *laudator temporis acti* in discussing the subject. He supposed an English past without bankrupts in any number that the law would have had to take into account. Modern writers have rejected the chauvinistic aspects of his treatment, but they are at one with Coke in ascribing the institution of English bankruptcy to the needs and to the invention of the sixteenth century.

The story is difficult to believe, and it may be that we will do better to think in terms of adaptation of certain aspects of Church court practice in discussing the foundations of English bankruptcy. It is at any rate true that the basic elements of bankruptcy are found in the probate records of the Church courts before 1542. By the sixteenth century, bankruptcy had already a considerable ecclesiastical pedigree. The story as shown by the Church court records is essentially this. It not infrequently happened that a man died with more debts outstanding than he had assets. It then fell to the courts of the Church to deal with the resulting probate problems. When this happened, the ecclesiastical practice was to sequester the decedent's goods, to cite persons who had received goods from the decedent prior to his death so that they could be required, under pain of excommunication, to restore those assets for which they had not given consideration, and for the court, or the executors acting under its supervision, to make a ratable award of the decedent's assets among the creditors.(30) In other words, what happened was very like the system inaugurated by the Tudor bankruptcy legislation.

The procedure could be initiated by a creditor, but

(29)   4 Co. Inst. 276–77.

(30)   Actions to protect against fraudulent alienations were under-
          taken under a Canterbury Provincial Constitution of 1343, *Cordis
          dolore*. See W. Lyndwood, *Provinciale (seu Constitutiones Angliae)*
          (1679) 161–65.

normally (at least to judge by the surviving act books) it emerged naturally as part of the collection of assets and registration of creditors' claims which were essential parts of probate practice in the ecclesiastical courts. Thus, to take only one example, when William Whaleys died insolvent at Winchester in 1527 the diocesan court was informed that there was a likelihood of insolvency when his testament was offered for probate. The court then deputed Jane his widow and John Lichfield to take custody of his goods. They were required to make an inventory of what was left of his assets and to record what claims there were against his estate. Once this had been completed and the account rendered, the judge awarded the creditors 8*d.* for each £1 of their claims,(31) a small enough percentage to be sure, although a small share is surely the normal fate of the unsecured creditor, then as now. Certainly most of the ratable distributions found in the remaining act books do not show creditors emerging with more than a small percentage of their full claim.

In view of this evidence from the Church court records, the standard accounts of the development of English law should be amended to show that bankruptcy was not a wholly new thing in the sixteenth century. There was a canonical antecedent. Of course, the parallels between canon law practice and the development of the common law are less clear in the case of bankruptcy than for defamation. It may be well to underline some of the differences. Not only did the Church provide bankruptcy proceedings only as a part of probate whereas the secular system dealt with living bankrupts, but quite a few differences in detail also existed. In ecclesiastical practice, for example, no provision for collecting double or treble damages from gratuitous trans-ferees of the bankrupt's property existed. They had merely to disgorge the property alienated. And of course the sanction against the intentionally fraudulent bankrupt was different. At common law he was subject to imprisonment. In canonical procedure he (or rather his corpse) was subject

(31)   Hampshire Record Office, Winchester, Act book C B 5, f. 34v.

to being dug up and cast out of consecrated ground.(32)

In this instance, therefore, it would be incautious to speak of the secular courts wholly taking over part of a jurisdiction that had once belonged to the Church. Instead, it may be justifiable only to think that the rules of the Church courts provided background and perhaps inspiration for some features of the Tudor bankruptcy legislation. The problem for the common law was manifestly different from that faced by the Church courts, and it would not have been appropriate to copy ecclesiastical procedure *in toto*. However, that does not rule out creative use of the canon law, adapted and augmented to fit a different situation. At the very least, the records of the Church courts make manifest one thing about the subject: it is wrong to suppose that the principles of bankruptcy law were unknown in England before the Tudor legislation. They were in frequent use before the courts of the Church.

The law of bankruptcy, then, as well as that of defamation, provide the legal historian with links between the canon law and the English common law. They show the possibility of influence by the one system on the other, influence which did not run always in the same direction and which could take quite different forms depending on the nature of the legal problem involved. These examples are not unique. The same point could be made as well for the laws of usury, aspects of criminal and civil procedure, guardianship, contracts, filiation, trusts, mortgages (perhaps), and several others.

IV

The argument for reciprocal influence can probably be made convincing only by the multiplication of examples. This task needs more time, and indeed more investigation of

(32)   In at least one case, exhumation of the insolvent's corpse was threatened; Archdeaconry of St. Alban's, Hertfordshire Record Office, Hertford, Act book ASA 7/1, f. 24r (1520).

the court records. However, even without this, there is good
reason to deal with two common, and sensible, objections
to the argument. The first is the lack of direct proof that
common lawyers really knew enough about the canon law
to be influenced by it. The second is that the suggestion of
connection is apparently contradicted by the insular habits
of mind of English lawyers as we see them exposed in the
Yearbooks and early Reports. English lawyers show no
indication of being slavish copiers of foreign ideas.

The premise of the first of this objections is open to
doubt. There are suggestions of a wider familiarity with the
learned laws among English common lawyers than has often
been said. Their frequent use of Latin maxims, perhaps
drawn from the *Regulae Iuris* found in the canon and civil
law texts is one example.(33) But even so, surely there is
something to the objection. Expertise in the canon law came
only after a course of study, and not a very short course of
study, in texts and learned commentaries. No one would
argue that common lawyers normally possessed this sort of
training, and therefore the first condition for influence
appears lacking: that is, knowledge.

The answer to this objection requires that we look at the
canon law not as an elaborate forest of texts, but as a living
legal system, one which had impact on the lives of most
Englishmen. An English common lawyer may have known
little of intricate points of canonical learning about the
sacraments or even about the scope of papal power, but he
would naturally have known something of the ecclesiastical
law of wills, because he would very likely have inherited
personal property or even have been an executor himself.
The same may be said for most of the areas of the Church's
jurisdictional competence: defamation, marriage, tithes,
and criminal jurisdiction. They touch most men's lives at
some point. The only kind of familiarity which my argument
requires is familiarity that grew out of every day life. It is

(33)   See, e.g., *Hotot* v. *Rychemund*, Y.B. Mich. 4 Edw. II, no. 88
        (1310), Selden Society, Vol. 22 (1907) 199–200. And see generally,
        Peter Stein, *Regulae Iuris* (1966) 154–62.

the practice of England's ecclesiastical courts, not the folios of Joannes Andreae, that provide the foundation for my argument.

The point is particularly important because the law enforced by the ecclesiastical courts was determined very often by customary practice as well as by the texts of the Decretals. There was often a divergence between canon law theory and practice, and it is essential that we look at the subject from the point of view of what actually occurred in the courts. For instance, the suggestion that the English law of guardianship, first in Chancery and then in Statute, was affected in any measure by the canon law seems unlikely if we look to the law of the texts. The canonists took the law of *cura* and *tutela* from the Roman law and endorsed it. Its division into two distinct sorts and its complexity raise a genuine stumbling block. But when we look at what English ecclesiastical courts were doing in fact as opposed to theory, we see a much simplified form of guardianship and a virtual consolidation of *cura* and *tutela*.(34) It looks much closer to some varieties of English guardianship. There are harmonies if we look at the practice, thus opening the possibility that English lawyers might have seen possibilities for change in the common law of wardship based on canonical principles.

This argument does not necessarily disparage the 'internationalism' of the medieval Church. That is a separate point. Indeed, the canon law was one of the influences which helped link the laws of different parts of Europe. But, throughout Latin Christendom, practice in local Church courts often took a direction different from that which one would suppose by looking at the canonical texts alone, and since it is fair to assume that the English common lawyer would have known of practice more immediately than he would have known of canonical theory, it is from the vantage point of the law actually administered in the Church courts that the problem of

(34)   See my article, 'The Roman Law of Guardianship in England, 1300–1600,' *Tulane Law Rev.*, Vol. 52 (1978) 223–57 : infra 211-45.

possible connections must be addressed. Once we do so, the fair objection that the common lawyers were no canonists can be put into perspective. It becomes less formidable.

The second objection is that the suggestion of possible connections between the canon law and the development of English common law ascribes too little freedom and toughness to English law and particularly to English lawyers. Everything we know about common lawyers argues against a habit of mind which would have endorsed a wholesale 'reception' of foreign law. English law, they evidently held, was not derivative, and it was not identical to the law on the Continent. This objection is almost self-evidently true, and indeed if my argument implied that the canonists were calling an Italianate tune to which the common lawyers danced, this would be a telling objection.

However, this is not my argument. I hold no brief for the view which would reduce common lawyers to receptacles for an alien and sophisticated system of law. The argument is rather that the canon law, as enforced in the Church courts, was one of the sources from which English lawyers could and did willingly draw ideas.(35) Sometimes this happened on the humble level of the lawyer drafting pleadings. Sometimes it occurred on the more elevated plane of decision by the Justices or by the Chancellor. But lawyers are seldom great inventors; they like to make use of other men's ideas and even other men's words. We call that creativity in a lawyer and we do not denigrate it as mere copying on that account. It is the essence of the lawyer's craft. What the argument for reciprocal influence requires, therefore, is entirely compatible with the objection that the common lawyers were the actors in the process of adapting some principles drawn from the canon law to English usage. They did the picking and the choosing.

In many areas of English law, there would have been no

(35)   Very suggestive on this point is Franz Wieacker, 'The Importance of Roman Law for Western Civilization and Western Legal Thought,' *Boston College International and Comparative Law Rev.*, Vol. 4 (1981) 257–81.

influence, or even any opportunity for influence, what-soever. The law of negotiable instruments or the rules relating to conveyancing, for instance, seem unlikely to have had any direct connection with the canon law. But this is not an 'all or nothing' proposition. What the argument denies is that the common lawyers' undoubted control over their law allows the legal historian automatically to assume the irrelevance of outside influence. This seems contrary to the evidence. It should not be enough to say that the English common lawyers were in control, and to leave it at that, dismissing the possibility that they carried out their work open to ideas drawn from contemporary developments in the Romano-canonical world.

V

It may be appropriate to conclude by recalling Mait-land's description of the areas of law and life where both Church and State made a claim. He called it 'that debatable land which is neither very spiritual nor very temporal'.(36) He went on to map the 'debatable land' in a way which only the exploration of the records of the ecclesiastical courts has made it necessary to resurvey. But still it is a valid and even a wonderful description. It is deservedly quoted by the editors of *Select Canterbury Cases*.(37) It gives just the right feel for the complexity and the fluidity which the records have since shown to have characterized relations—friendly and not so friendly—between the courts of the two legal systems. What this talk has meant to suggest is that the 'debatable land' of Maitland's phrase was not just one of shifting and uncertain boundaries. Certainly it was that. But it was also a land over which regular and fruitful journeys took place. There was movement back and forth, to the enrichment (I think) of both the canon and the English common law.

(36)   'Church, State and Decretals,' in *Roman Canon Law in the Church of England* (1898) 56.

(37)   See *Select Canterbury Cases*, 99.

2

CANONISTS AND STANDARDS OF IMPARTIALITY
FOR PAPAL JUDGES DELEGATE

In Act II, scene iv of Shakespeare's *Henry VIII*, Queen Catherine is confronted by the start of divorce proceedings against her. One of the two cardinals delegated as judges by the pope is Henry's faithful servant, Cardinal Wolsey, a man little likely to be an impartial judge of the legal merits of the famous case. And so the Queen says to him:

> I do believe
> Induced by potent circumstances, that
> You are mine enemy, and make my challenge
> You shall not be my judge.

Shakespeare does not today enjoy a wide reputation as a canonist, but he has here described with some correctness the canonical *recusatio*. This is the right, under certain circumstances, to challenge and remove a papal judge delegate for interest, prejudice, or unfitness for office.

The problem has exercised the intelligence of professional canonists since the thirteenth century.[1] Nor has it lost its interest today. The writer of a recent note on judicial disqualification in modern courts can state positively that 'the right to a trial before an impartial judge is an unquestioned part of our concept of due process of law.'[2] Modern jurists devote considerable thought to defining what circumstances warrant disqualification, and much the same can be said of the medieval canonists. Working from canon and Roman Law texts, they evolved strict requirements of judicial impartiality. Examination of their treatment of this question of recusation of papal judges delegate shows something of the ideals of medieval legal thought, and in addition it gives the

---

[1] I wish to thank Professor John T. Noonan, Jr. of the University of California Law School, Berkeley, for suggesting the general subject of this article and for several helpful comments in its preparation.

[2] Note, 'Disqualification of Judges for Bias in the Federal Courts,' 79 *Harvard Law Rev.* (1965) 1435. It ought to be noted, however, that at the time of Henry VIII's divorce, the English Common Law courts did not admit recusation of judges. Before the nineteenth century, disqualification of a judge for bias or for any other reason than direct financial conflict of interest was not a part of English Law. Cf. Coke's *Institutes* II 156; Blackstone's *Commentaries* III 361. Mr. H. G. Richardson has touched on the problem in his recent treatment of Bracton, showing that recusation was not possible in thirteenth-century English Law. *Bracton: the Problem of his Text* (London 1965) 89. But cf. *Fleta* 6.37, where it is said, 'Persona iudicis ex sola suspitione recusari potest.'

historian some glimpses of the realities of litigation in the courts of the medieval Church.

It seems best to preface examination of the standards with a short word about procedure. The principles of judicial qualification developed by the canonists were always part of a working legal system, and we should not disregard the practical context in which they arose. There is no need, of course, to stress the importance and the frequency of appeals to the papal court in the twelfth and thirteenth centuries. Those appeals, coming in greater and greater number, were in turn delegated to local churchmen, armed with apostolic authority, so that the case could be heard where the dispute had arisen in the first place.[3] Because of this dominant practice of delegation, the actual trial of cases appealed to Rome was not necessarily very different from that of cases handled solely by the local church. The constitutional significance of the routine recourse to the apostolic see and the growth and definition of the canon law it helped foster would, no doubt, have seemed of lesser importance to the litigants themselves than it does to historians. For the parties the chief result was usually delay.[4]

But there was one practical difference, important here. The judges delegate were selected individually for each case, and, insofar as any dignitary could escape judging causes in the Middle Ages, they were men who were not necessarily judges in the ordinary course of affairs. Instead of the official of the diocesan bishop, for instance, who sat to hear disputes in scheduled terms of a regular court, the judges delegate might be a bishop, an abbot, and a cathedral canon, or their substitutes,[5] expressly delegated to interrupt their normal work to hear and determine the dispute.

This individual selection of judges meant, among other things, that the problem of judicial impartiality was posed in special fashion. To some extent, at least, the party applying for delegation had the choice of who the judges delegate would be. It was customary for parties applying at the papal court for letters of justice to suggest judges acceptable to them.[6] As such, it was

---

[3] For a general treatment of the system of delegated papal jurisdiction, see George Pavloff, *Papal Judge Delegates at the Time of the Corpus Iuris Canonici* (Washington 1963) and the useful and brief introduction to *Papal Decretals relating to the Diocese of Lincoln in the Twelfth Century*, eds. Walter Holtzmann and Eric Kemp (Lincoln Record Society 47 1954).

[4] See the remarks of W. A. Pantin, 'The Fourteenth Century,' *The English Church and the Papacy in the Middle Ages*, ed. C. H. Lawrence (New York 1965) 177. He suggests that the incidence of delegation, in England at least, declined after the thirteenth century because of the frequent delays and because of improvements in procedure at the papal court itself.

[5] The right of the principal judge to subdelegate the hearing of the case to another cleric was well established (X 1.29.3, 27). The privilege was frequently exercised, and, to judge from the formularies for papal judges delegate which have survived from the thirteenth century, no excuse was required other than the general assertion that for urgent reasons the principal judge was unable to attend. Cf. Jane Sayers, 'A Judge Delegate Formulary from Canterbury,' *Bulletin of the Institute of Historical Research* 35 (1962) 205-06.

[6] E.g. William of Drogheda, *Summa Aurea* (Quellen zur Geschichte des römisch-kanonischen Processes im Mittelalter, ed. Ludwig Wahrmund [Innsbruck 1906-28] 2.2) 8; Johannes Bononiensis, *Summa Notaria*, ed. L. Rockinger, *Briefsteller und Formelbücher des elften bis vierzehnten Jahrhunderts* (Munich 1863) II 607, 609; and see Archbishop Pecham's

possible to try to secure the selection of favorable judges delegate in a way impossible in ordinary local litigation. To secure an interested group of judges gave a litigant at least an initial advantage. It was perhaps this feature, more than any other, which caused the canonists to devote particular attention to delegated cases, setting higher standards of impartiality for them than for ordinary litigation. Recusation of ordinary judges was also possible in canon law, but only under rather more restrictive conditions.[7]

In practice the question of suitability of these prospective judges delegate could be raised in two ways: at the time of their appointment in Rome or, later on, once the actual court was sitting. As to the first, in ordinary cases the matter was dealt with most often in the *audientia litterarum contradictarum*, where projected rescripts were read out, to be subjected to challenge and revision.[8] When only one party to a dispute was represented at the papal court, and this certainly was sometimes the case, the contradiction process was necessarily less effective than when both sides were there.[9] Only the judgment of the officials and the desire to avoid a later challenge to the person of one of the named delegates stood against the appointment of biased judges. How serious the latter was we shall examine below. Given the incompleteness of the curial officials' knowledge of local conditions, the papal court had sometimes to act, in the appointment of judges as in other things, as Professor Cheney has said, 'in complete ignorance of the facts.'[10]

However, it is also true that important people and religious corporations, the likely parties to delegated cases, were coming more and more in the thirteenth century to have proctors in Rome.[11] Regular proctors were very often

---

instructions to his proctors in Rome, 'Mittimus vobis in quadam cedula praesentibus inclusa nomina locorum et judicum in quae debeatis, et non alia, convenire . . .': *Registrum Epistolarum Fratris Johannis Peckham, Archiepiscopi Cantuariensis*, ed. C. T. Martin (Rolls Series 77.1) 279.

[7] E.g. Willielmus Durantis, *Speculum Judiciale* t. *de recusatione* § 5 (Lyons 1543) I 117ʳ; Hostiensis, *Summa Aurea* t. *de officio et potestate iudicis delegati* § 3 (Venice 1574) 283. Cf. X 2.1.18.

[8] On this court and its procedure see Geoffrey Barraclough, 'Audientia Litterarum Contradictarum,' DDC 1.1387; and Peter Herde, *Beiträge zum päpstlichen Kanzlei- und Urkundenwesen im dreizehnten Jahrhundert* (2nd ed. Kallmünz 1968). The elaboration of procedure is also usefully discussed by Herde in 'Papal Formularies for Letters of Justice (13th-16th Centuries),' *Proceedings of the Second International Congress of Medieval Canon Law* (Monumenta iuris canonici, *Subsidia* 1; Vatican City 1965) 321. Relevant documents can be found in Michael Tangl, *Die päpstlichen Kanzleiordnungen von 1200-1500* (Innsbruck 1894).

[9] An interesting case, illustrating the possibility of one party's acting without the other despite the desire for equal representation, grew out of the dispute between Archbishop Hubert Walter and the monks of Christ Church, Canterbury, over a college the archbishop had built, allegedly in violation of the monks' rights. Both sides agreed to seek papal intervention, but covenanted not to seek it *alteri parte inconsulta*. The monks sent a proctor anyway and got initial support for their case. *Epistolae Cantuarienses*, ed. William Stubbs (Rolls Series 38.2) xcvi.

[10] 'England and the Roman Curia under Innocent III,' *Journal of Ecclesiastical History* 18 (1967) 184.

[11] See the interesting discussion in Robert Brentano, *Two Churches, England and Italy*

more a necessity than a luxury, and when there was equal representation, the *audientia litterarum contradictarum* served as the forum for discussion and agreement on the persons to serve as judges delegate. One of the auditor's tasks was to bring the parties to agreement over the judges appointed. If they could not agree, procedural rules called for each party to nominate one judge and for the auditor to name a third, insuring at least one theoretically neutral judge. One possible obstacle, however, to the smooth working of this procedure was that there was considerable confusion in the *audientia*. Proctors had to be able to hear the letter touching their clients, but this was not always easy. The reading was carried on in a loud and unintelligible voice, and the proctors whistled and shouted to keep their opponents from hearing.[12] Repeated papal legislation designed to improve things was apparently of little effect.[13]

Even admitting the worst, however, a party's rights were not necessarily compromised if the letter had slipped by his proctor because of the noise, or if he had not been represented at all at the papal court. Recusation of prejudiced judges could always be sought at trial. A litigant was barred from objecting against only those judges he had specifically agreed to. And this was waived if the objectionable impediment arose after selection had been made, as for example would have been true in most cases of bribery.[14]

The recusation procedure at the trial level was fairly simple. One demanded the removal of one or more of the judges delegate in a more or less standard form, although this had normally to be done before the *litis contestatio*.[15] Deci-

---

in the Thirteenth Century (Princeton 1968) 25-52; Jane Sayers, 'Canterbury Proctors in the Court of the Audientia Litterarum Contradictarum,' *Traditio* 22 (1966) 331.

[12] Barraclough, 'Audientia' 1390.

[13] One example from the Constitutions known as *Qui exacti* from the reign of John XXII reads: 'Quod procuratores in eadem audientia sine strepitu maneant, lecturam predictam bene pacifice attente atque modeste audiant sine rumoribus cachinationibus superfluis, ne lectura seu lectores prefati in executione ipsius lecture seu alii audientes ibidem in audiendo valeant quomodolibet impediri,' Tangl, *op. cit.* 118 n. 8. Archbishop Pecham was apparently thinking of the same thing when he wrote to his Roman proctors, urging them to vigilance 'ne aliquae literae generales audientiam sub quacumque forma transeant sine contradictione, nec literae speciales sine convenientia judicum et locorum.' *Registrum Epistolarum* I 320.

[14] For discussion cf. Durant, *Spec. Iud.* t. *de rec.* § 5 ; *Glossa ordinaria* ad X 1.29.25 s.v. *postmodum*; Johannes Andreae notes that the judge delegate can be removed though previously agreed to 'superveniente inimicitia'; *Novella Commentaria in libros Decretalium* ad X 1.29.25 (Trent 1512) I 137. A more difficult problem was raised when the cause had existed all along, but it came to the attention of the aggrieved party only after he or his proctor had consented to the judges at the papal court or at trial after the *litis contestatio*. To allow recusation under these circumstances opened the door to particularly fraudulent delays, and as a result the canonists usually held that ignorance of the pre-existing impediment had to be proved as 'probabilis.' Cf. the discussion by Petrus de Ancharano, *Commentaria in quinque libros decretalium* ad X 2.29.36 (Bologna 1581) 352.

[15] 'Quia periculosum est, coram suspecto iudice litigare, idcirco ego M. intendens vestrum declinare examen, excipiendo propono, quod vos habeo suspectum in causa, quam mihi coram vobis F. movere intendit, cum ipse F. sit vester consanguineus vel vester familiaris vel quia estis dominus eius, propter quod vos tamquam suspectum recuso. Et hoc me offero probaturum coram arbitris ad hoc eligendis, quem pro parte mea eligo in continenti do-

sion on the issue of impartiality was then handed over to arbiters chosen by both parties or, after the reign of Boniface VIII, in certain circumstances to the judges who had not been challenged.[16] Either way, the arbiters' decision was appealable back to Rome, even where the rescript contained the usual supposed prohibition of appeal, *appellatione remota*. This clause was said to be limited to the principal case, and not to cover appeals of decisions as to recusation of judges.[17] William of Drogheda suggests that recusation and appeal were even possible if the rescript contained the words *recusatione remota*; in an argument not untypical of his approach he argues that the words forbid only 'frustratory' recusation; they have no application to legitimate causes of recusation.[18]

The effect of recusation was to suspend the case pending the arbiters' decision, including the power of the suspect judge to sub-delegate his powers. This is an important point, because it meant that if the outcome went against the suitability of the challenged judge, the rescript under which the case had been delegated was invalidated. New letters of justice had to be obtained at the papal court, unless the parties could agree to another solution. The recusing party could no longer be compelled to litigate under the rescript of delegation.[19]

As a practical matter, it was this rule more than anything else which made recusation of a judge an ideal weapon for delay. If the arbiters rejected the *recusatio*, the party could appeal that decision without regard for any *appellatione remota* clause. If they accepted it, the party would have forced the case back to Rome. The problem could have been resolved by allowing sub-delegation after recusation, but neither that solution nor any other was adopted.[20] Incidentally, we should note that the severity of this rule must have greatly limited the usefulness to one side of procuring biased judges at the papal court. If the rescript of delegation were to be anything more than a way of harassing one's enemies, if it were to serve as a means for an actual court hearing, it was essential that no excuse be given for challenge to the judges' impartiality. Every such challenge could mean recourse back to the papal court. A party

---

minum G. canonicum Bononiensem.' This is taken from Aegidius de Fuscarariis, *Ordo Iudiciarius* (Wahrmund, Quellen 3.1) 42. And see the case printed in the appendix. Use of the formula was not apparently necessary. In a French case from 1372, for example, the party simply objected: 'Vos non teneo pro judice meo pro certo'; *Registre de l'officialité de Cerisy*, ed. M. G. Dupont, *Memoires de la Société des Antiquaires de Normandie* (3rd Series 10.470).

[16] X 1.29.39; X 2.28.61; Sext. 1.14.4.

[17] This clause was generally ineffective as a weapon against obstructionist appeals, since there were many exceptions to it. As remarked in the *glossa ordinaria* ad X 2.28.53 s.v. *expresse*: 'Multa exempla posses assignare in quibus recipitur appellatio licet sit remota in rescripto.' And see C. R. Cheney, *From Becket to Langton* (Manchester 1956) 64.

[18] 'Si autem ex iuxta causa fuerit appellatio vel recusatio, est admittenda non obstante predicta clausula: appellatione remota vel recusatione': *Summa Aurea* 381-82.

[19] *Gl. ord.* ad X 2.28.61 s.v. *de recusatoris assensu*; Durantis, *Spec. Iud. t. de rec.* §5.

[20] Durantis, *ibid.* suggested that the arbiter should take over the recused judge's place, but he admitted that the majority view was against him: 'Alii autem fere omnes, ut Vincentius, Tancredus, Joannes, et Bernardus dicunt quod secundum canones probata suspitione evanescit jurisdictio delegati, . . . necesse est aliud de novo impetrari rescriptum.'

anxious for a final judicial decision would necessarily be careful to avoid it.[21]

With this procedure as background, we turn to the reasons for recusation, the qualifications required of papal judges delegate. For purposes of analysis, they are divided into three classes. The first consists of those grounds for disqualification based on the judges' personal status. They are largely predictable, although extensive.[22] Excommunicates, schismatics, heretics, Jews, and slaves could not be judges delegate. Neither could madmen, perjurors, grave robbers, adulterers, or other criminals. Minors under twenty years old were likewise disqualified, though there was some support for allowing judges over eighteen to serve by special agreement of the parties. Illiteracy was said to be a disqualification, although there was some opinion that if the unlettered man had experience in deciding cases, he could validly receive a mandate as a judge delegate. It was generally held that the deaf and dumb could not serve, Hostiensis excepting.

It must have been a rare occasion when these were tested. Judges subject to challenge on these grounds were not often appointed in the first place. Few litigants would suggest the appointment of a man known to be insane. An exception is the excommunicate, especially as it would sometimes have been within the power of one of the litigants to procure the excommunication of one of the judges. But apart from that, they present neither problem nor particular interest, and so it must have seemed to the canonists, who waste little time in citing Roman or Decretal law support for them.[23] They were, perhaps, too obvious. There is one other personal disqualification worth mention: no woman might be a judge delegate. Hostiensis gives a reason for this prohibition, the explanation that from their conception women are removed from all manly actions (*virilibus actibus*). But he adds that the pope, acting for special cause, could delegate the hearing of a case to a woman, perhaps an indication of the strength of Hostiensis' belief in the plenitude of papal power.

Official qualifications make up a second class of standards for papal judges delegate. A canon incorporated from the 1148 Synod of Rheims forbade laymen from acting as judges in spiritual matters.[24] This text, strangely enough, was glossed in the *glossa ordinaria* to say that laymen could in fact serve as judges

---

[21] This argument assumes, of course, that litigants were in the later Middle Ages interested in settling their disputes by judicial decision rather than by exhausting their opponents with trouble and expense. This is perhaps a dangerous assumption. But still it ought to give at least a moment's pause before accepting the argument that parties always sought prejudiced judges. The question is, of course, impossible to prove one way or the other, as there is no way of taking a statistical sample, and even where there was recusation of a judge delegate, we cannot usually find out whether it was justified. The comment in the *glossa ordinaria* seems to me to cut in both directions: ad X 2.28.61 s.v. *de recusatoris*: '... nam pro modica causa quandoque traheret eum ad Papam, ut illum fatigaret laboribus et expensis et sic posset saepe contingere quod potius renunciaret liti quam vellet taliter laborare.'

[22] Hostiensis, *Summa* t. *de off. et pot. iud. del.* §3; *Ordo judiciarius 'Scientiam'* (Wahrmund, Quellen 2.1) 34-35; Drogheda, *Summa* 400-403; Durantis, *Spec. Iud.* t. *de iudice delegato* §7.

[23] With the exception of William of Drogheda, who contrives to argue out several of them.

[24] X 2.1.2; Tangl, *op. cit.* 56.

delegate.[25] Johannes Andreae, noting this apparent contradiction, solved it to his satisfaction. The *glossa* must refer only to situations where no competent cleric could be found, and in all others holy orders were a prerequisite for papal judges delegate.[26] Examination of a fair number of documents involving delegated cases has, however, turned up no cases where laymen served as judges.

A second official qualification was that only men who held ecclesiastical dignities were eligible.[27] This meant, in practice, bishops, abbots, deans, archdeacons, and so forth, as opposed to ordinary clerics. Here again, documents show that this rule was generally adhered to.[28] The rule is worth noting, especially when we consider that there was no requirement that a judge delegate have any specific legal training. Apparently, it was considered more important that the judge be a highly placed churchman than that he have a substantial background in canon law. The most that the canonists added to the law on this subject was general language to the effect that it was proper for judges delegate to be familiar with the law. It was never required.[29]

The reason for requiring that only dignitaries might serve as judges delegate is, of course, that it seemed inappropriate for men to be judged by their inferiors in status.[30] Delegated cases normally involved important people, so that there was special reason for making certain of the status and prestige of the judges. No doubt some judges delegate, like the well known Abbot Samson in the twelfth century, were also careful to seek instruction in canon law as soon as they found themselves being appointed to hear delegated cases.[31]

---

[25] *Gl. ord.* ad X 2.1.2 s.v. *non praesumant.*

[26] Marginal gloss to *gl. ord. ibid.* s.v. *possunt.*

[27] For discussion see Hostiensis, *Summa* t. *de off. et pot. iud. del.* §3; 'Hodie etiam requiritur, quod delegatus a sede Apostolica sit in dignitate constitutus, vel ad minus canonicus cathedralis, vel alterius collegiatae ecclesiae.' This rule would seem to exclude most regular clergy, but as Hostiensis observed, if it did, it was not followed, since '. . . de facto tamen committitur religiosis causae cognitio tota die.'

[28] Two qualifications should be made to this rule. First, there are some instances in the twelfth century of cases delegated to men styled simply as *magister*, and even a few from the thirteenth, when the rule, on the whole, seems to have been better followed. H. E. Salter, *Cartulary of Oseney Abbey* (Oxford 1936) III 338, where the editor has listed the names of the judges delegate that appear in the cartulary. And see Herde, 'Papal Formularies' 331 n. 45. Second, cases were probably more often subdelegated to clerics who held no dignity. It does not appear to have been possible to challenge a judge delegate for this reason.

[29] '. . . oportet enim quod is cui committuntur iura canonum non ignoret': Hostiensis, *Summa* t. *de off. et pot. iud. del.* §3; Drogheda, *Summa* 182. It is true, however, that a significant portion of these dignitaries would have had some experience and training in canon law, and often in secular law as well. Cf. Cheney, *From Becket to Langton* 24.

[30] E.g. Hostiensis, *Summa* t. *de iudiciis* §5: 'Iudex minor maiorem iudicare non debet.' It was not, however, apparently required that the judges delegate hold a dignity superior to the parties. Cf. for example Philippus Decius, *Commentaria in Decretales* ad X 2.1.18 (Venice 1577, fol. 124r): 'Secundo nota honestum esse ut causa committatur iudicibus non habentibus dignitatem inferiorem ipsis partibus, non tamen necessarium est.'

[31] 'Nondum transierant vii. menses post electionem suam, et ecce offerebantur ei litere domini pape constituentes eum iudicem de causis cognoscendis, ad que exequenda rudis

On the other hand, it is not easy to be confident that all would have; and that Samson was appointed a judge delegate without any training whatsoever in the law points to the lack of the requirement. One cannot read through any substantial section of medieval canon law without being struck by its intricacy, especially on procedural matters. It was a complicated, sophisticated system, calling, so it would seem, for both ability and experience. Especially in light of the strict requirements of impartiality we shall examine below, it seems strange that the canon law did not strictly require legal expertise in judges delegate.

It may be objected that, unlike ordinary litigation, a delegated case had the legal side of the case already determined and set out in the rescript. The court had merely to find the facts. There is doubtless something to this, but there was no guarantee that new legal points would not be raised at the hearing. Indeed they very often were. Especially as litigants in these cases were well supplied with lawyers, cases appealed to Rome and delegated back probably raised more hard points of law than day-to-day proceedings in the consistory courts. It may be correct to say that the canon law in requiring the status of dignitary, and not legal training, was recognizing that attributes other than knowledge of the law made up the essential part of the judges' function. Legal advice could be had from assistants and assessors. Status that commanded respect and helped persuade disputants to agree to a decision could not.

The third, and most important, class of qualifications for judges delegate covers cases of personal prejudice or interest. If the other two arose seldom, this class came up with more frequency, and canonists devoted considerable energy and ingenuity to the elaboration of proper standards for recusation. For this, they found ample resources in canon and civil law. Hostiensis listed thirteen specific cases where a judge delegate could be disqualified for bias. William of Drogheda enumerated sixteen, and William Durant, by expansion and distinction, found room for thirty-six separate grounds for recusation.[32] These lists, with the authorities from both laws given in profusion by the canonists, were the stuff of which litigation, then as now, could be made. As found in these handbooks of practice in the Church courts, such lists supplied both ideas and authority for the medieval lawyer who thought his client would be best served by the removal of one or more of the judges. How the canonists evolved these grounds for objection and the nature of standards can be appreciated by examining their handling of the most common situations of prejudice as set out in the Decretals.

The first situation, defined in the decretal *Causam quae* (X 1.29.17), arose when the judge delegate was the lord (*dominus*) of one party. Even if the situation set out in the decretal had not been expanded, the case could have occurred frequently. Medieval churches often held extensive and widely scattered

---

fuit et inexercitatus . . .': *The Chronicle of Jocelin of Brakelond*, ed. H. E. Butler (London 1962) 33. St. Hugh of Lincoln was another frequent judge delegate unversed in the law (*quasi legum nescius*). *Magna Vita Sancti Hugonis*, eds. Decima Douie and Hugh Farmer (London 1962) II 150.

[32] Hostiensis, *Summa* t. *de recusatione iudicis delegati* §3; Drogheda, *Summa* 374; *Spec. Iud.* t. *de iud. delegato* §7. Durantis was bested, however, by the fifteenth-century canonist Philippus Francus, who listed forty grounds for recusation, marg. gloss to *gl. ord.* ad X 2.28.36 s.v. *septimum*.

property, so that it would not have been rare for a churchman involved in litigation to have held land or a benefice of a bishop delegated to decide the case, and since the word *dominus* was taken in a wide sense, this meant, for example, that if two clerks were beneficed in different dioceses, neither of their bishops could avoid recusation. Whether this sort of relationship would in most cases have created the personal bond of loyalty and interest that destroys impartiality is open to question, though certainly it was theoretically implied in the lord-vassal bond. But the canonists drew no distinctions between types of holdings or ecclesiastical benefices. It is hard to see where they could have drawn a line. Here, as elsewhere, they attached the disqualification firmly to the judge's status.

The movement was in the other direction, towards broadening the grounds for recusation under this heading. *Causam quae* was glossed to include the situation where the judge was the vassal, not the lord, of the party, on the apparent theory that the rationale of the decretal covered the reverse situation as well.[33] Petrus de Ancharano included all sureties for the obligations of the parties in the ban;[34] and it makes some sense to think that a judge will not look with entire disinterest on the fortunes of one whose obligations he is bound to meet in case of default. Hostiensis, again citing this decretal, extended it to include the case where the judge delegate was an enemy of the litigant's lord.[35] The reason is obvious, if perhaps a little flimsy in many cases: the judge will be tempted to strike at the lord who is his enemy in the person of the lord's vassal. Tancred and others included subordinates of any sort to the litigant in the disqualification under this heading.[36] It is also interesting to note that Panormitanus was later to use this decretal to suggest that a student could disqualify any examiner he could show to be suspect or prejudiced against him.[37]

A second instance involves consanguinity. The decretal *Postremo* (X 2.28.36) grew out of a case where it was pointed out that one of the parties was related by consanguinity to a judge delegate. Reasonably enough, the judge was disqualified. And, much as *Causam quae* was extended to cover the reverse situation, this decretal was said by canonists to cover relation by affinity as well as consanguinity.[38] Johannes Andreae also included under this title the case where the judge had been created the presumptive heir of one party, either in whole or in part.[39] Durantis added that it covered stepsons and daughters as well.[40] Combining this situation with that of lord and vassal, Innocent IV and others held that all the lord's kinsmen were equally subject to challenge,

---

[33] *Gl. ord.* ad X 1.29.17 s.v. *dominus*; Innocent IV, *Apparatus ad libros decretalium* ad X 1.27.17 (Cambrai 1525) fol. 49ʳ.

[34] *Commentaria ad idem.*

[35] *Summa t. de rec. iud. del.* §3.

[36] *Ordo Iudiciarius,* t. 6 §6 in *Pilii, Tancredi, Gratiae Libri de Iudiciorum Ordine,* ed. Friedrich Bergmann (Göttingen 1842) 148. Cf. also *gl. ord.* ad X 2.6.2 s.v. *accedens:* 'Nota quod iudex subditus actoris, potest legitime recusari.'

[37] *Commentaria in quinque decretalium libros* ad X 1.29.17 (Lyons 1578) I 91.

[38] Hostiensis, *Summa Aurea,* t. *de rec. iud. del.* §3; *gl. ord.* ad X 2.6.2 s.v. *subesse.*

[39] *Novella Commentaria* on the *Liber Sextus* ad 2.15.2 (Trent 1512) fol. 66ʳ.

[40] *Spec. Iud. t. de iud. del.* §7.

although a distinction was sometimes drawn between male and female branches of a family.[41]

The *glossa ordinaria* has a good discussion of the problem under this heading. The real issue, it says, is just how far *affectio* of the family extends, since it is affection which here destroys impartiality.[42] Decision on this point was more than an academic exercise; it was necessary to determine the degree of consanguinity which warranted recusation. Was it the seventh degree, as defined in the old law? Or did the Fourth Lateran Council's decision in 1215 to reduce the prohibited degrees to four apply to recusation of judges delegate as well? The conclusion as to the state of the law is cautious, but the *glossa* leaves no doubt on what the better view is. The affection that warps and distorts a man's judgment extends to the higher degree, no matter what the new law about marriage says.[43] In cases of doubt, it is always dangerous to litigate before a judge whose family or feudal position might normally give rise to pre-judgment. Surely here the canonists were adopting sensible standards in interpreting and enlarging on the decretal law.

A third instance, or set of instances, for recusation involved cases where other legal activity by the judge had warranted his disqualification. If the judge delegate had been the advocate of one party, a decretal (X 2.28.36) specifically stated that he could be removed, although canonists usually specified that the advocacy must have been in the same cause. Advocacy in a different, prior action would probably not disqualify the judge, though the question, like so many of the points raised by the canonists, was arguable.[44]

Hostiensis puts a similar case when he says a judge can be disqualified because of his position in another action. Suppose X was judge of a case involving Y. And suppose Y was delegated to hear a case involving X. The opposing party in each case could validly object, since both X and Y would be tempted to decide in favor of each other, in hopes of like treatment in the other action. Hostiensis had apparently seen just such a case and heard the objection made. 'Bona la mi fai, bona la ti farai,' the proctor had said.[45]

Still another situation occurred when the judge was involved in an action involving nearly the same issues (*similis paene causa*). Recusation was again allowed, it being reasoned that if a judge had an interest in seeing a legal issue resolved in one way in his own case, he would naturally have his mind made

---

[41] *Apparatus* ad X 1.29.25. The canonists are not very clear on how real a family relationship there had to be, and perhaps kinship of a lord without actual social connection was not enough. At any rate, the point could be debated. Petrus de Ancharano (*Commentaria* ad X 2.29.61) suggests, for example, that the outcome should depend on *mores regionis*, as family affection is stronger in some areas than others.

[42] '. . . cum remaneat affectio, potest recusari usque ad illum gradum in quo posset ei succedere. Nam familiaritatis affectio veritatem impedire solet. . .': *gl. ord.* ad X 2.28.36 s.v. *consanguineus.*

[43] *Ibid.*: '. . . sed certe honestius reputo, quod in superioribus adhuc repellatur, quia semper affectio et dilectio prima remanent.'

[44] Hostiensis, *Summa* t. *de rec. iud. del.* §3; Tancred, *Ordo* 148. Here Drogheda makes an argument, though he admits opinion is against it: 'Et illud est dictum Aristotelis: quod semel est verum, semper erit verum': *Summa* 386.

[45] 'Hoc est quod dicebat frater Gin. hospitaliorum procurator contra peregrinum subdelegatum domini V. Ebrudunen. archiepiscopi . . .': *Summa loc. cit.*

up in advance in a similar case.[46] This makes some sense. But what was a similar case? Did it include, for example, every dispute over episcopal rights to visit monastic houses, or only disputes raising exactly the same issues? Would, in this case, no bishop at all be competent to judge if he were also engaged in a controversy over visitation with a monastery in his diocese? If he had ever been? The *glossa ordinaria* says that such cases of exemption are covered in the prohibition. Bishops would have favored the right of episcopal visitation as an almost invariable rule. Abbots and priors would presumably have held the opposite prejudice just as often, even if they had never been involved in litigation over it.[47] The *glossa* goes on to say that too strict a view of the matter should not be taken in every case.[48] But it is difficult to know just where in all cases a line could be drawn. Innocent IV and Johannes Andreae suggested that the close cases should be left to the decision of a good judge (*boni iudicis arbitrium*), but that is not very helpful.[49] One may guess that it was open to litigation, a question which could be argued on both sides by an able proctor in each individual case.

A fourth situation where recusation was allowed is that of bribery. Estimates of how widespread bribery was are difficult to make. There were certainly some complaints about it, but this hardly proves that widespread buying of judges was the normal practice. And the canonists devoted less attention to it than to other sorts of prejudice, perhaps suggesting that we can easily exaggerate the problem. It was probably usual for both parties to give the judge some gift or payment as a matter of course. Judges delegate, to all appearances, were not paid for their work,[50] and not every gift is necessarily a bribe. Canonists generally recognized and accepted the practice. Hostiensis and Durantis, speaking of judicial corruption, both state that a judge delegate can be challenged if he is corrupted, *pecunia interveniente*. But the fault lies in the corruption of the judge through a bribe, not on the simple fact that money had changed hands.[51] William of Drogheda expressly says that only large gifts are forbidden to judges, small ones are all right.[52] The same attitude is evident in the so-called statutes of Robert of Winchelsey, Archbishop of Canterbury from 1294 to 1313, which, although not correctly ascribed to that

---

[46] X 2.1.18; Durantis, *Spec. Iud.* t. *de iud. del.* §7; *gl. ord.* ad X 2.1.18 s.v. *similis paene.*

[47] An illustrative case, apparently involving this situation, is the litigation over the right of the bishop of Worcester to visit the Abbey of Evesham, in 1202-03. Three abbots were appointed judges delegate, and the bishop successfully challenged them, but perhaps only because all three were black monks. *Chronicon Abbatiae de Evesham*, ed W. D. Macray (Rolls Series 29) 123. A similar problem occurs in the course of Grosseteste's attempt to visit the chapter of Lincoln, *Roberti Grosseteste Epistolae*, ed. H. R. Luard (Rolls Series 25) 253.

[48] *Gl. ord. loc. cit.*: 'Non tamen extendas hanc similitudinem ad omnes causas nam si iudex habeat causam decimarum et alia causa, puta iurispatronatus vel electionis ei committatur, illud ei non nocet.'

[49] *Apparatus* ad X 2.1.18; *Novella Commentaria* ad *idem.*

[50] Cheney, *From Becket to Langton* 72ff.

[51] '. . . quia per eum corruptus est, pecunia interveniente.' Hostiensis, *Summa* t. *de recusationibus* §1; Durantis, *Spec. Iud.* t. *de rec.* §5.

[52] 'Et intelligatis de magnis exhenniis, nam de parvis non obstat . . .': *Summa* 378.

archbishop, were accepted as authoritative in the later Middle Ages.[53] After laying down strict standards of judicial abstinence from presents and gifts, the statute adds, 'except those presents and gifts which neither offend the prohibition of the law nor generate scandal of any kind.'[54] Compared to modern notions of judicial impartiality, these standards seem lax and uncertain indeed. But we need not conclude that they were therefore unworkable. If both sides give small gifts to the judges, those gifts do not have any necessary influence on the outcome of the case, though it would be foolish not to acknowledge that they may easily lead to that.

The canonists' treatment of bribery furnishes an interesting contrast to the other three situations we have looked at. In them, the existence of a specific relationship or office is enough to disqualify a judge. The emphasis is on what lawyers today would call an objective standard: all first cousins or feudal lords are subject to recusation, whatever the actual state of their minds. Here, in dealing with bribery, the commentators abandoned the objective standard in favor of the trickier inquiry into the judge's state of mind. Even if Drogheda's standard were used, where do you draw the line between a large and a small gift? It may be that in a society where gratuities were the normal form of paying officials for services done, the canonists had to retreat to this subjective test. To disqualify a judge delegate for doing what was an accepted fact of life would have been impossible, perhaps even inconceivable. The canonists were here taking a practical approach to the subject of recusation.

These four sources of possible disqualification and their expansion are probably enough to indicate something of the nature of recusation and the methods of contemporary canonists. A few more are worth mentioning to show the width of the standards. William of Drogheda cites the master-pupil relationship as warranting disqualification, though it is not entirely clear whether he thought it continued to be objectionable after the pupil had left the master's school.[55] Hostiensis, remembering his difficulties in England, speaks with conviction in favor of recusation when the judge and one (but only one) of the litigants were from the same country.[56] A pre-existing enmity between the judge and

---

[53] Cheney, 'So-called Statutes of John Pecham and Robert Winchelsey,' *Journal of Ecclesiastical History* 12 (1961) 21.

[54] '. . . exceptis duntaxat donariis vel exenniis, quae nec juris prohibitionem offendant, nec scandalum generent quoquo modo': Wilkins, *Concilia* II 212. There is also an interesting passage in Bracton on the subject, which Maitland believed came from a canonical source, though he did not suggest which. See *Bracton and Azo*, Selden Society 8 (1894) 198. A large part of it comes ultimately from the Digest (Dig. 1.16.6.3), which serves here to interpret a scriptural text. The passage, fol. 106b, reads: 'Beatus qui excutit manus suas ab omni munere [Isai. 33.15]. Ab omni munere non est abstinendum, quia licet ab omnibus et passim avarissimum sit accipere et vilissimum, a nemine tamen accipere erit inhumanum, ut si amicus recipiat ab amico solo intuitu amicitiae et amoris.' An interesting comment on the medieval attitude is also to be found in two English statutes. 8 Ric. II c.3 enacted that justices might not take any 'robe fee pension gift or reward' of any but the king. The next year 9 Ric. II c.1 in effect nullified that statute 'because it is very hard and needeth declaration.'

[55] *Summa* 389-90.

[56] 'Consuevit etiam livor invidiae regnare inter indigenas et alienigenas, . . . ad decorem haec causa et quaedam aliae fecerunt me Angliam elongare': *Summa* t. *de rec. iud. del.* §3.

one party, as in the case of Shakespeare's Catherine of Aragon and Cardinal Wolsey, is almost universally mentioned as a proper ground for disqualification.[57] And there are others, verging on the bizarre, such as: the judge has not God before his eyes, or he has 'fraternal love' for the other side, or justice is not in him.[58] It is difficult to know what to make of these last, beyond speculating that phrases like 'not having God before one's eyes' may have concealed a more exact form of corruption than is apparent and noting that they introduce further a subjective test. All together, these grounds do show the extremely broad range of possibilities the canonists made available for attacking a judge delegate whose presence on the bench one side thought undesirable.

Nor do the canonists pretend that their lists of grounds for recusation are exhaustive. Hostiensis added to his: 'These causes and similar ones, which the diligent reader will be able to gather for himself, can be proposed against judges delegate.'[59] Such statements appear as well in other commentaries on the canon law. Given the broadness of the standards, the open-ended quality of the remedy, and the small number of men eligible by position and person for judging delegated cases in the first place, it is not hard to believe that the range of candidates who could be forced on unwilling litigants was restricted. It must, in fact, have sometimes been the case that few or no men fulfilled all the requirements. But we must remember that these were not mandatory standards. The parties could always agree to particular judges whether or not they fitted the ideal pattern. Recusation was a tool in the hands of a litigant, to be used as he thought best.

Disqualification of judges delegate thus offers another example of the canon law's extreme reluctance to force important litigation to a conclusion without the acquiescence of both parties to a dispute.[60] If the medieval Church law erred at all — and it is difficult to think that it was not a mistake to allow prolongation of these cases to the extent it did — that mistake lay not in forcing biased judges with all the authority of the distant and uninformed bishop of Rome down the throats of protesting litigants. It was rather in providing too wide a range for objecting to the judges. Recusation was a broadly framed remedy, one which could be used to defend justice by the dismissal of corrupted or biased judges, or to delay and defeat justice by frivolous and time-consuming objections. It had both these characteristics, which must exist under any

---

Hostiensis mentions that this was not in general use, but cf. X 2.6.4. And Durantis, *Spec. Iud.* t. *de iud. del.* §3, remarks in support: 'Puta in scolaribus vel mercatoribus qui se diligunt velut fratres.'

[57] C.3 q.5 c.15; Drogheda *Summa* 389-90; *gl. ord.* ad X 2.6.2. s.v. *nimis favens*; Tancred, *Ordo* 149.

[58] Durantis, *Spec. Iud.* t. *de iud. del.* §3 ('Item, non habet Deum pre oculis'); Drogheda, *Summa* 377 ('si fraterna caritate diligatur'); Durantis, *ibid.* ('quod non est in eo iustitia, unde nec iudex vocari meret').

[59] 'Hae causae et consimiles, quas diligens lector per se recolligere poterit, possunt proponi contra iudices delegatos.' *Summa* t. *de rec. iud. del.* §3. Panormitanus later wrote of possible reasons for recusation (*Commentaria* ad X 2.28.61): '. . . non sunt omnes in iure expressa, nec possunt de facili exprimi.'

[60] For an interesting article on this subject see Robert E. Rodes, Jr., 'The Canon Law as a Legal System — Function, Obligation, and Sanction,' *Natural Law Forum* 9 (1964) 45.

system allowing challenge of judges, in a measure seemingly more extreme than modern law.

The breadth of recusation did not come exclusively from canonical texts. Decretals left many questions open, and for assistance in dealing with them and in posing new questions the canonists relied here as they did elsewhere on Roman law. Citation from the *Corpus juris civilis* appears constantly in their work as authority for grounds for disqualification. Quite often only civil law was cited to support a proposition. At first glance, it seems that Roman law very largely shaped canonistic thinking on the disqualification of judges.

Closer examination calls for qualification of this appearance. Recusation of judges delegate was an established part of later Roman law. The usual statement that the canon law found its model in Roman law procedure is partly justified here.[61] But, on the other hand, canonists used citation from the *Corpus juris civilis* most frequently to supply reasons for recusation. Here the appearance is deceptive, for time after time the Roman law authority used has only the most tangential relevance to the rule proposed. Although this fact is not in itself unusual, it does in this instance warrant looking further into the canonists' use of the civil law.

Take some examples of that use. Durantis is trying to show that enmity in a general sense is sufficient reason for recusation of a judge delegate. His support is an excerpt from Ulpian allowing removal of a tutor if his conduct works fraud on the rights of the child.[62] William of Drogheda provides another: to show that a judge can be successfully challenged if he has 'fraternal love' for one of the parties, he adduces a Roman law citation that allowed a man to create another his heir, despite the absence of blood ties, if he loved the other man as his brother. Hostiensis used the same authority to show that a judge born in the same country as one of the litigants could be recused. These cannot be said to be very concrete authority, although we may recognise an analogy of sorts.[63] Sometimes the analogy is close. An imperial rescript denying to one accused of a crime the right to serve as a proctor is used to support recusation of a judge delegate similarly charged.[64] Sometimes the analogy is far-fetched. There is in the Code a law that a son could withhold inheritance from his (widowed) mother if she engaged in dishonest deeds, indecent machinations, or sexual relations with her son's enemies. This was said by one canonist to authorize recusation of a judge who was the friend of a 'capital enemy' of one of the litigants.[65]

It is hardly startling, of course, that these Roman law texts were being used out of context by the medieval commentators. But the fact is worth noting here for one reason, namely that the civil law, as found in the texts and as developed by the medieval civilians, required no cause to be shown or proved in order to remove a judge delegate. It was enough to allege suspicion.[66] Canon

---

[61] Cod. 3.1.16, 18.

[62] *Spec. Iud.* t. *de rec.* § 5; Dig. 26.10.3.

[63] *Summa*, 377; Dig. 28.5.58. For Hostiensis cf. *supra* n. 56.

[64] *Ordo jud.* 'Scientiam' 35; Cod. 2.13.6.

[65] *Ibid.*; Cod. 3.28.28.

[66] *Gloss* ad Cod. 3.1.16 s.v. *recusare* and marg. gl. s.v. *sufficit*: 'De iure civili sufficit allegare suspicionem, tametsi non exprimatur causa suspicionis.' Or cf. *gloss* ad Dig. 36.1.4 s.v. *neque illud*; Azo, *Summa Codicis* t. *de iudiciis* (Venice 1596) 162: 'Non est necesse probare

and civil law were in this matter quite different and the canonists could not here simply follow civilian procedure. The two laws on recusation diverged at other points as well.[67] Recusation of ordinary judges was allowed at canon law, rejected by civil law. More important here, the civilians held that a judge delegate could subdelegate his powers after he had been challenged. We saw above that a papal judge delegate could not, and that a new rescript had to be issued, absent agreement to the contrary. Perhaps this rule discouraged the canonists from moving towards adoption of civilian procedure in this area. Certainly to have done so would in practice have invited unlimited and uncontrolled delay through recusation.

At any rate, the difference on requiring cause for suspicion to be proved meant that the canonists could not find direct support for their arguments from civil law sources. For this support they had to go further afield. The results, as above, are not always convincing. Even in normal cases, they had to look for analogy, not absolute authority. If it were necessary to characterize shortly their treatment, it could be said that the *Corpus juris civilis* provided laws showing situations where a special relationship of interest or affection had arisen between two parties. With these, the canonists provided arguments that a similar relationship had grown up between judge and litigant, from which it could be said that a particular judge would naturally be biased. But the canonists did not in this area adopt the same rules as the civilians. We have not a case of a sophisticated Romanism shaping and overly developing the canon law. The canonists were doing the shaping.

To look through the thirteenth-century glosses and treatises one would not immediately guess that their authors were applying abstract principles of fairness in formulating their arguments for recusation. They seem to be mostly compilers of authorities. But as was the case, for example, in the extension of the decretal *Causam quae* to include others besides feudal lords, the use the canonists made of Roman law texts indicates that they were doing more than piling up relevant authority. They were holding to high standards of impartiality and fairness as a necessary part of the judicial office.

There are not many overt signs in their work on recusation of the intrusion of abstract principle. But there are some. William of Drogheda writes, answering a possible objection, 'To this I say, a slight offence repels a judge.' Or in the *glossa ordinaria*: 'But it is apparent that a small cause removes a judge.'[68] There are other instances. But more persuasive is the extensive widening, except in the case of gifts to judges, of the categories for recusation provided in Decretal and Roman law. The canonists worked with generally high, possibly exaggerated, ideas of what fairness and impartiality meant. Litigants had the right, if they chose to assert it, to judges delegate of exemplary disinterest.

---

causam suspicionis': Cino da Pistoia, *Lectura super Codice* ad Cod. 3.1.16 (Strasburg 1475).

[67] The most extensive discussion of the differences between Roman and canon law on recusation I have seen is Panormitanus, *Commentaria* ad X 2.2.4. He explained the necessity of showing cause in the church courts as arising from the need to avoid the all too frequent delays ('cum saepe fraudulenter et causa dilatandi talis recusatio fiat').

[68] *Summa* 376; *gl. ord.* ad X 2.6.2 s.v. *subesse*.

How these high standards of fairness worked in practice in the later medieval period is, however, not easy to say. The inadequate state of preservation and publication of the records of the medieval Church courts make judgments of this sort risky. We have an indication that recusation of judges delegate was a fairly frequent occurrence. The *glossa ordinaria* notes that one of the chapters allowing recusation was 'daily much alleged.'[69] But, by itself, what does this prove? That it was important and always possible to secure unprejudiced judges? Or that partiality was so standard that it was an insoluble problem? Perhaps, as may be suggested by the case printed in the appendix, recusation was mostly used as another tool in the canon lawyers' well-stocked bag of dilatory tactics. William of Drogheda says as much in his treatise: if you have a weak case and all else fails, try recusation of the judges.[70] The grounds for challenging the judge were broad enough and arguments for it so readily available that if a party wanted to delay, as Professor Cheney says, in the 'hope that something would turn up,' an easy way to do it was to seek recusation of the judge.

It is important, however, to see the recusation of papal judges delegate within the framework of the later medieval pattern of litigation. Most disputes ended in compromise.[71] Legal proceedings often served not so much to define rights by legal reasoning as they did to allow a chance for arbitration between the parties and eventual amicable settlement. Even where the trial has gone through to a conclusion, the judges delegate try to get the parties to agree to a compromise. Sometimes the judges hand down a final sentence, only to have the parties discard it in favor of a settlement in which both sides get something.[72] Thus, recusation which allowed wide grounds for rejection of prejudiced judges was another way of bringing the litigants to agreement.

It would surely be wrong to think that the canonists regarded the process of the law as mere window-dressing for the realities of compromise and settlement. Had this been so they could have followed the civil-law rule which allowed recusation of a judge delegate without regard to an objective standard

---

[69] *Gl. ord.* ad X 2.28.61 s.v. *cum speciali*: 'Et est capitulum multum allegiabile et quotidianum.'

[70] *Summa* 88: 'Si malam, differat eam et intendat componi. . . . Si contingat quod non possit in pace profiscere, ut habeat cum amicis suis colloquium. Et item mittat ad curiam Romanam super litterarum revocatoriarum impetratione, et hoc ad removendos iudices plus iusto favorabiles, ob aliquam causam optimam a iure approbatam.' Or, at p. 89, he advises his reader with a weak case: 'proponat dilationes et cavillationes et recusationes.' Matthew of Paris' comment, in connection with a case delegated to the bishops of Salisbury and Ely, says much the same: 'Quibus perlectis et intellectis, surrexerunt clerici Dunelmensis episcopi, quasdam recusationes frivolas et fallaces allegantes contra executores praedictos atque, ne procederent in inquisitione praedicta, praesentiam domini Papae appellarunt.' *Chronica majora* ed. H. R. Luard (Rolls Series 57.3) 63. And Johannes Andreae, *Commentaria* ad Sext. 2.15.2, '. . . reus enim qui tendit ad subterfugiam proponeret recusationem probabilem sed falsam, electis arbitris, appellabit et . . . sic impediet principalem.'

[71] Cf. Brentano, *Two Churches* 150.

[72] E.g. *Cartulary of Oseney Abbey* II 532-33; *The Records of Merton Priory*, ed. Alfred Heales (London 1898) 74; *Codice Diplomatico Barese* (Commissione provinciale di Archeologia e Storia patria, Bari 1899) II 34-38.

of impartiality. But they do point out that one of the important functions of a good judge is to bring the parties to an amicable agreement.[73] Viewed in this light, the requirement that a judge delegate hold a church dignity and the lack of insistence on legal training makes good sense. Important clerics would no doubt have been better able to promote the agreement that was the norm than legally well-versed, but officially unimpressive, judges delegate. No one could safely assert that smoothing the way to compromise was the primary thought of the canonists, but it does seem fair to say that such was among their aims. In the creation of the requirements for service as papal judges delegate, the canonists not only operated with and in some sense created high standards of judicial impartiality, they also had their glance fixed more firmly on the realities of medieval litigation than we sometimes assume.

APPENDIX

I have transcribed below the record of that part of a case heard before judges delegate in the Italian city of Bisignano in 1278 which illustrates the subject of this article. It deals with the attempt by the proctor of the archbishop of Rossano to disqualify the precentor of Bisignano, one of the three judges delegated at the *audientia litterarum contradictarum* to determine the dispute between the archbishop and the Abbey of Matina. The dispute concerned alleged invasion of the abbey's rights to grange land; it is more fully discussed in Professor Brentano's recent book, *The Two Churches* (pp. 140-46).

The value of printing this extract is that it illustrates in the concrete case the formation of an argument for recusation. The proctor has produced an impressive string of citations, although it may be noted that he has omitted two which bear perhaps most directly on his argument (X 1.29.17 and C.3 q.5 c.15). It is also interesting to note the introduction of an argument for recusation of the bishop because the abbey's advocate was the son of his brother; this was said by Hostiensis not to warrant recusation.[1] But as used by this proctor, it is developed by argument *a similibus ad similia*, the characteristic form of expansion used by the canonists in this and other areas. Here it seems quite reasonable. However, the proctor's case for recusation is disposed of by the judges on procedural grounds. We cannot tell what the outcome of proof before arbiters would have been.

This transcription was made from a photostatic copy of the manuscript which was kindly lent to me by Professor Brentano. The document is today in the Vatican Archives, *Archivio Aldobrandini, Documenti Storici, abbadie,* 4, no. 47. The original punctuation and capitalization have not been retained, but abbreviations have been extended only when the full reading was relatively sure, and the document's spelling is retained or noted.

Sequenti die Martis viiii° predicti mensis Augusti idem dominus P. presentavit se cum litteris procuratoris predicti domini archiepiscopi sufficientibus

---

[73] E.g. 'Pacis compositioni semper debet intendere . . .': Drogheda, *Summa* 181.

[1] Hostiensis, *Summa* t. *de rec. iud. del.* §3

in ipso negotio coram nobis et obtulit exceptiones infrascriptas. Dixit periculosum est et tristes solet sortiri eventus coram iudice litigare suspecto. Ideo
ego P. primicerus et canonicus ecclesie Ross' tanquam procurator domini archiepiscopi Ross' ad recusandum vos iudicem et ad quedam alia capitula constitutus in causa quam habet vel habere intendit cum abbate et conventu monasterii Matin' audientiam vestram domine cantor Bis' ecclesie ei suspectam
rationibus sive causis subscriptis[2] recuso, ceteris exceptionibus iuribus et obiec-
tionibus meis in omnibus et per omnia mihi salvis. Verum quia exceptio recusationis probanda est coram[3] arbitris et non coram iudice, ne forte provocatus
obesset, idcirco ego P. predictus me dictam exceptionem recusationis coram
arbitris ad hoc eligendis offero probaturum; arbitrum autem pro parte domini
archiepiscopi eligo episcopum Gerentinum, ut probatur C. de iudiciis, l. cum
specialis (Cod. 3.1.18), et l. apertissimi (Cod. 3.1.16), Extra, de appellationibus,
c. secundo requiris (X 2.28.41), et c. cum speciali (X 2.28.61), et de officio et
potestate iudicis delegati, c. suspicionis (X 1.29.39), et VI[4] de appellationibus,
c. legittima (Sext. 2.15.2). Causam autem recusationis asigno quia estis vos
domine cantor amicus sive familiaris abbati Matine et conventui litigatoribus,
cum in omnibus factis suis assistatis, et faveatis eisdem tanquam adiutor con-
sultor et protector, propter quod plurima dona et beneficia habuistis ab eo
et a monasterio et adhuc habeatis, que familiaritas sive amicitia suspiciones
inducit, Extra, de officio et potestate iudicis delegati, c. insinuante (X 1.29.25),
et Extra, ut lite non contestata, c. accedens (X 2.6.2), Extra de appellationibus,
ex[5] insinuatione (X 2.28.50). Familiaritatis enim[6] sive affectio amicitie veritatem impedire solet, ut iii. q.v., acusatores (C.3 q.5 c.12) et familiaritas sive
amicitia repellit iudicem, ut ff. de verborum significatione, 1. late § amicos
(Dig. 50.16.223). Assigno et aliam causam recusationis, quod dominus G. advocatus adverse partis est consangι 'neus vobis, scilicet filius fratris vestri,
per decretalem preallegatam, Extra, de appellationibus, ex[7] insinuatione (X 2.28.
50), ubi dicitur quod iudex videbitur fovere causam alterius adversarii ex eo
quod advocatus eius est iudici commensalis et consanguineus, ergo fovebit
iudex causam adversarii si advocatus eius fuerit iudici consanguineus vel affinis. Que exceptiones recepte fuerunt cum protestatione adverse partis, qui
dicebat non esse admittendas eo quod terminus iam erat clappsus.

[There follows in the record more argument and delay, largely unrelated to the archbishop's proctor's attempt to have the *recusatio* submitted to arbiters, and in any case
summed up in what follows. The court reconvened ten days later, on August 18th, where
the record takes up a more developed statement of the abbey's case against allowing recusation than its proctor had apparently had time or ingenuity for in the earlier sitting.]

Item ex parte monasterii Matin' allegationes proposite fuerunt in hunc modum: Frater P. procurator monasterii Matine allegat et dicit quod cum datus
fuisset terminus domino archiepiscopo Ross' ad proponendas omnes declina-
torias iudicii et omnes alias dilatorias usque per totum xxv^m diem a die Jovis

---

[2] MS add. *causo* underscored

[3] MS *coram coram*

[4] MS *vel*

[5] MS *et*

[6] MS add. *affectio* underscored

[7] MS *pro eo quod mittatur*

xiiii° Julii in antea numerando, nec oblate fuerint vel prestite exceptiones huiusmodi in termino nec etiam infra terminum, quoniam procurator dicti domini
archiepiscopi obtulit illas die Martis viiii° presentis mensis Augusti cum iam
terminus expiraverit; quod ad modo non est admittendus ad ipsas exceptiones,
nec sunt recipiendas exceptiones huiusmodi ut probatur Extra, de exceptionibus, c. pastoralis (X 2.25.4). Et licet procurator domini archiepiscopi com-
paruisset precedenti die Lune viii° presentis mensis Augusti, nullum procura-
torium obtulit sed tantum quoddam instrumentum excusationis ostendit contra
quod fuit oppositum quod non erat admittendum quia medici qui testifica-
bantur in ipso instrumento de infirmitate archiepiscopi deponebantur non iurati
et ideo non erat adhibenda fides predicto instrumento, ut Extra, de testibus,
c. nuper (X 2.20.51) et c. tuis (X 2.20.39). Quo etiam die si obtulissent exceptiones huismodi, cum nullo modo obtulerint, admittende non essent cum
predicto die Lune iam terminus expirasset, computato die quo terminus datus
est qui de iure computari debet, ut ii. q.vi, c. biduum (C.2 q.6 c.29), argu-
mentum ad hoc Extra, de sponsalibus ex parte (X 4.1.9). Item alia ratione
non est admittendus predictus archiepiscopus vel procurator eius ad recusandum iudicem, quia ipsi iudices electi fuerunt de consensu procuratoris domini
archiepiscopi ut constat per litteras testimoniales auditoris contradictarum
domini pape, et quod non sit admittendus probatur Extra, de causa posses-
sionis et proprietatis, c. cum olim (X 2.12.7). Item ex quo in termino non
prestiterunt nec exhibuerunt exceptiones, nullo modo postea admittendi sunt,
licet forte dicant voluntatem habuisse prestandi exceptiones predictas, quia
ubi facto opus est non sufficit sola voluntas, ut Extra, de eo qui mittitur[7] in
possessionem, c.1 (X 2.15.1), et ut alibi notatur. Nos igitur, visis allegationibus
utriusque partis, interlocutoriam pronuntiavimus die Sabbati xx° predicti mensis Augusti ante mediediem in hora tertia exceptiones dilatorias porrectas per
procuratorem domini archiepiscopi Ross' non esse admittendas quia non fuerunt
in termino presentate et quia plene constitit nobis quod de consensu procuratoris domini archiepiscopi fuimus electi in curia Romana. Quare procurator
domini archiepiscopi appellavit ab huiusmodi interlocutoria in hunc modum.
Ego P. Mediabarba primicerus ecclesie Ross' et procurator domini archiepiscopi Ross' sentiens me gravatum ab interlocutoria vestra, qua interlocuti
estis predictum archiepiscopum non comparuisse in termino et propterea contumacem, appello in scriptis ad apostolicam sedem et apostolos instanter peto.

3

ETHICAL STANDARDS FOR ADVOCATES AND
PROCTORS IN THEORY AND PRACTICE

The lawyers who served in the medieval Church courts have never enjoyed a good press. In fact, it is difficult to think of a body of men whose profession combined higher standards of ethical conduct with a lower reputation in living up to those standards. Contemporary literary critics[1] and even fellow lawyers[2] testify to the grasping and unethical conduct of medieval advocates and proctors. Modern commentators have taken this testimony as a fair characterization of the lawyers as a class. But is the criticism justified? Is it an accurate representation of reality? Much of the contemporary criticism was written for purposes of satire or of moral instruction. The criticism is not necessarily incorrect for that reason. But it was not intended to be morally neutral. Its purpose was not purely descriptive. The closest a modern historian can come to morally neutral evidence is, in my view, that given by the records of the Church courts themselves. The testimony of the English records on the subject of the ethical standards of practicing lawyers is the subject of this short paper.

The evidence these records provide is not systematic in a quantitative sense. Nor is it free from ambiguity. But it neither purposely hides nor deliberately emphasizes unethical conduct by the lawyers. Unprofessional conduct came to be recorded in the court records in several ways. One was open correction by the judge, as in a suit heard at Canterbury in 1420, where the Commissary General rebuked a proctor for his 'idleness and negligence'.[3]

---

[1] E.g. Lyndwood, *Provinciale (seu Constitutiones Angliae)* (Oxford 1679) 74 s.v. *advocatos*: 'supple infideles, et cavillosos, quorum malitiis justicia deperit, et litium processus innumeris subterfugiis impeditur'. See also William of Drogheda, *Summa Aurea (Quellen zur Geschichte des römisch-kanonischen Processes im Mittelalter*, ed. Ludwig Wahrmund [Innsbruck 1906-28] II:2) 58ff.

[2] For some of the anti-lawyer writings see A.H. Thompson, *The English Clergy and their Organization in the later Middle Ages* (Oxford 1947) 60-63; J.A. Yunck, 'The Venal Tongue: Lawyers and the Medieval Satirists', *American Bar Association Journal* 46 (1960) 267-70; Courtney Kenny, 'Bonus jurista malus Christa', *Law Quarterly Rev.* 19 (1903) 326-34; J.W. Baldwin, *Masters, Princes and Merchants: the Social Views of Peter the Chanter and his Circle* (Princeton 1970) I 192-8.

[3] Canterbury [Library of the Dean and Chapter] Act book Y.1.4, f. 33v: 'propter desidiam et negligenciam procuratoris'.

Another was objection by the opposing party, as in a case from 1293 in which one proctor was challenged as 'infamis et periurius'.[4] A third was dismissal of a proctor by his own client, although in some of these cases, the action may stem from the client's own unethical demands rather than from improper behavior by the lawyer.[5] The positive observance of the law's ethical standards, as will be seen below, was also sometimes incorporated in the Church court Act books. The surviving records are incomplete. And they were not compiled for purposes of evaluating the conduct of the lawyers. But they do show both sides. They contain good evidence to supplement, if not to supplant, the testimony of literary and social commentators. And, the records show that there is some reason for moderating the harsher criticism which has been levelled against the proctors and advocates of the ecclesiastical courts.

For purposes of this paper, advocates and proctors are considered together. For some purposes this would be unjustified. The two offices were, both in education and function, theoretically quite distinct.[6] And the advocate's position was a more honorable one than the proctor's.[7] But for an examination of ethical standards in the English Church courts, lumping the two together is a fair way to proceed. Proctors and advocates were bound by the same oaths to observe the same standards of conduct in their practice.[8] Iden-

---

[4] Canterbury Sede Vacante Scrapbook III no. 346: 'in procuratorem nullatenus posse nec debere admitti quia est infamis et periurius'.

[5] One interesting example of dismissal of a proctor and a subsequent change of mind is found in York [Borthwick Institute of Historical Research] Act book Cons. A B 5, f. 16v (1503): 'Isto die Ricardus Handson revocavit potestatem procuratoris sui. Et postea de novo constituit eundem.'

[6] The division, something like that between English barristers and solicitors, confined the advocate to giving legal advice, to framing the pleadings, and to arguing points of law before the judge. The proctor was a representative of his client who acted in his stead during the course of the suit. See P. Gillet, 'Advocate', DDC 1.1524-35 and R. Naz, 'Procureur', DDC 7.324-29 for convenient summaries of these offices. There is also discussion of the role of the two sorts of ecclesiastical lawyers in England in Roscoe Pound, *The Lawyer from Antiquity to Modern Times* (St. Paul 1953) 62-9.

[7] See *Constitutiones Legatinae sive legitimae regionis anglicanae . . . cum subtilissima interpretatione domini Johannis de Athon* (Oxford 1679) 70 s.v. *advocati officium*. See also the post-Reformation English canonist John Ayliffe, *Parergon Juris Canonici Anglicani* (London 1726) s.v. *advocates*: 'The Office of the former is difficult and honourable, but the Duty of the latter is easy, and of no honour at all.' He does say, however, that the proctor 'ought to be perfectly well acquainted with the Practice [of the law]'.

[8] Gregory X extended the oaths of advocates to proctors at the Second Council of Lyons (1274) c.19. See Mansi 11.986. English diocesan statutes also enforced the same oaths on advocates and proctors. See the Exeter oath in *Councils and Synods with Other Documents Relating to the English Church II, A.D. 1205-1313*, eds. F.M. Powicke and C.R. Cheney (Oxford 1964) II 1030-31.

tical ethical problems were faced by both. Also, the division between the two offices was blurred in English practice.[9] Some courts, those at Canterbury, Rochester, Lichfield, and Hereford for instance, did not employ advocates at all.[10] Here the proctors apparently served the same function as advocates. That is, they gave legal advice and argued points of law. Even where advocates made up a regular part of the court staff, as at York and Ely, the proctors apparently had a hand in formulating legal issues.

The criticism which has been levelled against the practicing proctors and advocates can, I think, be accurately put under one of two headings. First, the lawyers were excessively greedy. They refused to act for their clients unless they were paid large, often unconscionable, fees. Money alone made the lawyers serve their clients. Second, the lawyers used unethical tactics and legal subtleties to pervert the course of justice. They took and argued causes they knew to be unjust, using all the resources of canonical procedure, the dilatory exceptions and frustratory appeals, to secure victory. In other words, they preferred the narrow interests of their client to the larger goal of the attainment of justice.

The canon law, it should be stressed, obliged proctors and advocates to abstain from both these practices. In theory, the lawyers were bound to observe high ethical ideals. The formal law required them to meet certain standards. They were, for instance, to be sufficiently trained in the law and free from *infamia*.[11] More importantly, the advocates and proctors took an oath on admission to the court where they were to practice which, to judge from the surviving examples, required a degree of impartiality of a sort beyond what most modern lawyers would probably think necessary.[12] They were

---

[9] See Lyndwood, *Provinciale* 74 s.v. *advocatus*: 'Generaliter intelligendo, advocatus dicitur, qui controversiis agendis quoquo studio operatur. Unde et in hoc casu forsan dicerent aliqui quod procuratores advocati dicuntur . . . , stricte tamen loquendo, . . . procuratores licet assistant causae non dicantur advocati.'

[10] *The Ecclesiastical Courts: Principles of Reconstruction* (London 1954) 15; Brian Woodcock, *Medieval Ecclesiastical Courts in the Diocese of Canterbury* (Oxford 1952) 42; R.A. Marchant, *The Church under the Law* (Cambridge 1969) 17-18; for the other dioceses this conclusion is based on examination of the surviving pre-Reformation Act books. See below *passim*.

[11] See C. 3 q. 7 c. 2; Sext. 1.19.5; on the various persons disqualified see generally Hostiensis, *Summa Aurea* (Venice 1574, repr. 1963) I tit. *de postulando* no. 3.

[12] Several examples of the oaths sworn by English advocates and proctors have been printed. See D. Wilkins, *Concilia Magnae Britanniae et Hiberniae* (London 1737) II 27; II 204; *Councils and Synods* II 1030-31. For the diocese of Ely the *Registrum Primum*,

sworn to take only moderate fees, to deal honestly in all things with their clients, and to serve poor litigants without taking any fee at all.[13] They were to accept only cases they believed to be rightfully brought and to make no plea they did not believe in their conscience to be right. Rather significantly, if they had accepted a case they later learned to be without foundation, they were sworn to give it up, even during its prosecution. No distinction between initial acceptance and later withdrawal was made.[14] The law and their oaths enjoined them not to suborn witnesses, not to propose unnecessary delays, not to make frivolous appeals. And during the course of litigation, proctors had often to swear the oath of calumny, to the effect that their client was acting in good faith. In short, the canonical ideal was that the practicing lawyer should always act in the interests of justice; he was an instrument in the law's search for objective fact, rather than a servant of his client's wishes.[15]

All this is, of course, only theory. The lawyers renewed their oaths annually, so that the theory was put before them in concrete form at least once every twelve months. And they had sometimes to swear the oath of calumny during litigation. But this does not prove that the provisions of the oaths were observed in practice. Lawyers may forget, or ignore, their duty to the court even if it is set before them yearly. They may swear the oath of calumny falsely. How far were the standards of ethical conduct observed in actual practice?

The two basic criticisms of conduct by the ecclesiastical lawyers are worth examining separately. The evidence on the first point, the allegedly excessive greed of the lawyers, is ambiguous in many respects. The records provide

the earliest surviving Act book [Cambridge University Library EDR D/2/1] records the oath at f. 62v. See also the summary in Irene Churchill, *Canterbury Administration* (2 vols. London 1933) I 450-51, and the oath for lawyers at the papal *Audiencia Litterarum Contradictarum* in M. Tangl, *Die päpstlichen Kanzleiordnungen von 1200-1500* (Innsbruck 1894, repr. 1959) 47.

[13] On this subject see G. Post, K. Giocarinis, and R. Kay, 'The Medieval Heritage of a Humanistic ideal: Scientia donum Dei est, unde vendi non potest', *Traditio* 11 (1955) 195.

[14] E.g. *Councils and Synods* II 1030: 'Et si causam, quam in sua fide susceperunt improbam scirent vel penitus disperatam, vel certamine procedente talem eam cognoscerent, amplius eidem minime patrocinarentur, sed a tali communione sese totaliter seperarent.' This standard is somewhat different from that of modern ethical standards, which allow a lawyer to withdraw from a case he has once undertaken only in exceptional circumstances. See generally Henry S. Drinker, *Legal Ethics* (New York 1953) 140-41.

[15] A recent consideration of this subject for modern advocates is Piero L. Frattin, 'The Role of the Advocate in Church Courts', *The Jurist* 26 (1966) 194-203. And see John T. Noonan, Jr., 'From Social Engineering to Creative Charity', *Knowledge and the Future of Man*, ed. Walter J. Ong (New York 1968) 179-98.

evidence on both sides of the question. It is certainly possible to find examples of the profit motive in the court records. Richard Burgh, advocate and then examiner-general at York complained in a 1421 suit that 'he was in debt, and the court and his office were worth very little in those days'.[16] This obviously is the remark of a man who regards service in the ecclesiastical courts as a source of profit. As the comment implies, proctors and advocates were routinely paid for their services. The few schedules of expenses that have survived all contain provision for their salaries;[17] this without regard for the idea, endorsed by a number of canonists and taken from Roman Law, that proctors were to serve their patrons without payment.[18] The ideal was not observed in practice. But the proctors who served in the English courts were professionals, men who devoted their careers to representing clients before those courts. And they performed tasks which required training and skill. The records show them producing articles in court,[19] formulating exceptions,[20] making interrogatories,[21] taking appeals after definitive sentences,[22] providing their clients with legal counsel.[23] Even visiting a client who

---

[16] York [Cause papers] C.P. F 129: ' . . . quod fuit indebitatus et etiam quod curia Ebor' et officium suum modicum valuerunt illis diebus'.

[17] See Churchill, *Canterbury Administration* II 203; Woodcock, *Medieval Ecclesiastical Courts* 135-37; York C.P. F 190 (1454) is the only set of Cause papers I have seen to include a schedule of expenses; see below n. 26.

[18] See Cod. 2.13.15; Hostiensis, *Summa Aurea* I tit. *de proc.* no. 1: 'Is qui negotium domini gratuito administrat, . . . gratuito autem, ideo dicitur in descriptione, quia si interveniat merces, locator dicitur operarum, non procurator.' But cf. Guillelmus Durantis, *Speculum Iudiciale* I tit. *de salariis* § *de salariis procuratorum et tabellionum*: 'Hodie autem procurator in quacumque causa non potest nomine salarii ultra xii libras turonenses recipere.' There is much interesting material on this subject generally in William Forsyth, *Hortensius the Advocate* (Jersey City, N.J. 1882) 353-67.

[19] Rochester [Kent County Record Office, Maidstone] Act book DRb Pa 2, f. 87v (1448) : 'Et dictus procurator ministravit articulos in scriptis.'

[20] Canterbury Sede Vacante Scrapbook III no. 17 (1271): ' . . . quod procurator dictorum abbatis et conventus proposuit quandam excepcionem'. In Canterbury Act book Y.1.7, f. 61r (1460) the proctor protested 'de appellando quia ut asseruit non habuit tempus sufficiens ad scribendum excepciones in causa'.

[21] In Canterbury Act book Y.1.1, f. 46v (1373) the lawyer 'dicit quod liberavit huiusmodi interrogatorias tempore competenti advocato'. This is one of the few mentions of the availability of advocates at the Canterbury court, and it is difficult to reconcile with their absence from the fifteenth century records.

[22] Canterbury Act book Y.1.3, f. 52r (1417): ' . . . , a qua sentencia dictus David Mareys illico apud acta ad curiam Cantuar' directe appellavit et peciit apostolos sibi tradi sive assignari. Et commissarius dixit quod vellet deliberare super assignacione apostolorum.'

[23] Canterbury Act book Y.1.7, f. 42r (1460), in which proctors were assigned to be 'in consilio prefati A. Bower'.

had been imprisoned was among the duties of one York proctor in 1418.[24] Without regular provision for fees, this class of professional lawyer simply could not have existed. And the canon law, like any other sophisticated legal system, required a body of professionally competent lawyers. It is idle to pretend that the courts could have dispensed with fees for the services of proctors.

But were the fees received by the practicing lawyers reasonable in light of the services they rendered? That surely is the important question. It is impossible to judge with any assurance the quality of the services performed by the proctors and advocates. But the records do show that the size of the fees they took was not inconsiderable. Four shillings were paid to the proctor in a case appealed to the court at Ely in the 1370's, a time when the daily wage of an average carpenter was only six pence.[25] Two court appearances by an advocate in a York defamation suit cost a litigant 6s. 6d. in 1454, a year in which a mason was paid only 5½d. for a day's work.[26] The fee for the proctor in a suit heard in 1492 before the Consistory court at Hereford was 8s.[27] And twelve court appearances by a proctor at Canterbury in 1498 were taxed at 6s.[28] All of these represent substantial sums of money.

That the practicing lawyers regarded their work as a source of profit is also indicated by the fairly tight rein they kept on the number of men who could practice before each court. In the diocesan court at Canterbury, for example, only four men served as proctors at any one time during the fifteenth century.[29] At Hereford, in the 1490's, there were again only four proctors who monopolized the practice, and hence the fees, before the Consistory court. At Lichfield in the 1460's, the figure is four or five. Even in the more important Provincial court at York, only twelve advocates and eight proctors were authorized to practice at one time. And in fact the actual

---

[24] York Act book Cons. A B 1, f. 194r: 'Prefatus J. Willyng dixit ut prius quod predictus Ricardus dominus suus fuit et adhuc est apud abbathiam beate Marie extra muros Ebor' incarceratus et ibidem in carceribus detentus quia ut asseruit cum ipso in huiusmodi carcere loquebatur.'

[25] Registrum Primum EDR D/2/1, f. 114v. For the carpenter's wage, see J.E. Thorald Rogers, *A History of Agricultural Prices in England* (7 vols. Oxford 1866, repr. 1963) I 318-19.

[26] C.P. F 190; the proctor in the same suit received 5s. 6d. For the mason's wage, see Rogers, *History* IV 517.

[27] Act book [County Record Office, Hereford] I/1 p. 55.

[28] Woodcock, *Medieval Ecclesiastical Courts* 126; in Rochester Act book DRb Pa 1, f. 330v (1443) the total expenses were taxed at 20s., and the proctor had to swear 'quod ille sunt vere expense'.

[29] These figures and those which follow were compiled by counting the proctors whose appearance was recorded in the Act books for the dates given.

number of advocates employed seems to have been kept at an even smaller figure, perhaps five or six at one time. The steady way in which these small numbers were maintained over the course of time suggests that the practicing lawyers were excluding other lawyers in order to maintain the size of their own practice. It seems clear that one proctor or advocate had to die or leave before another was admitted to take his place. The record of the admission of William Morland, a new proctor at York in 1427, in fact explicitly states that he was filling the position of a man recently deceased.[30]

All this suggests that the practicing lawyers acted out of self interest to safeguard the size of their fees. It is not true, on the other hand, that they never agreed to act without being paid. The court books contain the admission of litigants *in forma pauperum*, the assignment of advocates and proctors to these litigants, and subsequent action in their causes.[31] There is no sign that these suits were handled in a more perfunctory manner than other suits. The formal entries of these cases give no indication of casual or inattentive behavior by the lawyers involved. It should be said, however, that admissions of poor litigants were not particularly frequent. One or two per year is the average for the Act books I have examined.[32] Far more frequent, in practice, was the *causa salarii*, brought by the lawyer against a client who had refused to pay a fee due and owing.[33] There are enough of these to suggest that proctors often had real difficulty in collecting for their services. And they show clearly that the lawyers were not reluctant to go to law to secure their fees. This too must be counted a sign of the greed of the Church court lawyers. The fees were large enough to be worth litigating about. And the lawyers acted to collect them.

However, the numbers of the *cause salarii* surely does not itself prove that the lawyers were deserving of criticism. Laymen often have trouble

---

[30] York Act book Cons. A B 2, f. 98v: 'Isto die venerabilis vir magister Ricardus Arnall' curie Ebor' officialis pro tribunali sedens Willelmum Morland clericum notarium publicum in procuratorem generalem dicte curie magistro Roberto Scurneton' eiusdem curie procuratore generali dum vixit noviter defuncto iudicialiter admisit.'

[31] Canterbury Act book Y.1.7, f. 122v (1462): 'Iudicialiter facta fide per mulierem, dominus commissarius admisit eam in forma pauperum.' And see York Act book Cons. A B 1, f. 97r (1418), where a proctor said 'publice et allegavit quod predicta Foxholes domina sua fuit et est pauper et modicum habens in bonis'. He asked that an advocate be assigned to her, which was granted.

[32] See for example London [Greater London Council Record Office] Act book DL/C/1, f. 42v (1500), f. 81v (1501), f. 128v (1502), f. 105v (1502); York Act book Cons. A B 5, f. 70v (1504), f. 78r (1504).

[33] For example, in Canterbury Act book Y.1.18, there were six different *cause salarii* for the year 1499, recorded at fols. 11r, 29v, 33r, 35r, 38r, and 39r; in Hereford Act book I/3 for 1500 there were three, at pp. 43, 52, 68, while there was only one admission *in forma pauperum* recorded at p. 58.

understanding why it is that lawyers are worth paying. They can see or feel what a merchant provides; a lawyer's services are necessarily intangible. After the suit is over, and particularly if it is lost, a party naturally finds it hard to part with all but the most nominal fee. Although the evidence shows that the advocates and proctors took action to secure and protect their fees, it does not prove that they were inordinantly greedy. Their fees were sizable, that is clear. But they had a legitimate right to collect them. That they sometimes had difficulty in doing so does not necessarily prove that they were greedier than most men.

This is by way of apology for the proctors and advocates. There is also more positive evidence, evidence which argues against the criticism that the medieval lawyers were interested exclusively in the profit to be derived from service in the courts. The Act books show clearly that the lawyers did not commonly protract litigation to increase the size of their fees. Those fees depended, so far as we can tell, largely on the amount of work the lawyer did for each suit, the number of court appearances, documents prepared, and so forth. What few schedules of fees have remained make this pretty clear.[34] To run up the size of their fees, the lawyers had only to insist on the full observance of the libellary procedure and make use of all the dilatory exceptions available under it. And this, the court records show plainly, they did not do.

A concrete illustration is provided by the use made in English practice of articles and positions. In theory, these documents served quite distinct functions in litigation. Both were submitted by the petitioner, the *pars actrix*, and both contained a series of assertions stating the separate factual elements of his case.[35] But positions were to be submitted first, and each assertion answered separately by the defendant. Then, after this had been done, the articles were submitted. They were then used in examining the witnesses. The theory was that the defendant would admit some of the positions, and so cut down on the number and range of articles which had to be submitted to the witnesses for proof.[36] I say theory, because that is not the way it worked

---

[34] In York C.P. F 190 (1454), for example, the advocate's fee was stated to be for appearances 'in duabus instanciis cause predicte'. In Lichfield [Joint Record Office, Lichfield] Act book B/C/1/1, f. 193r (1468) the proctor was given 8d. 'pro duabus procurationibus.' In Woodcock, *Medieval Ecclesiastical Courts* 136 there is recorded a fee of 12d. 'to owr proctor of the Corte for ii days'. And see Ely EDR D/2/1, f. 56v (1376): 'Inspecto labore taxamus salarium suum ad iiii s.' But in York [Minster Library] Act book M 2(1) a, f. 9v (1316) the sum of 2s. was said to be owing as a fee 'pro salario suo, merito et convento'.

[35] Both could, of course, also be submitted by the *pars rea* in presenting an affirmative defense.

[36] See Durantis, *Speculum Iudiciale* II tit. *de positionibus* no. 2:2: 'Grave est onus probandi per testes, . . . , et facilius fiunt confessiones quam testium productiones.'

in practice. Defendants routinely denied *seriatim* all of the petitioner's positions. 'Non credit ut ponitur' was the normal response.[37] Thus, while keeping
positions and articles distinct and requiring a separate term for each made
good sense in theory, in actual litigation it served only to waste time and
increase expense. No reduction in the scope of articles required was accomplished through the use of positions. What the lawyers did in response to
this problem was to combine the two documents, and to introduce them in
one court term.[38] By the early years of the fifteenth century, the joining of
positions and articles into a single document was the normal, though not
quite the invariable, practice in the English courts. Sometimes, in fact, the
libel was made to serve for both.[39] These combinations saved the parties on
document and one court appearance, with the fees that necessarily went
with them.

It may be suggested that this convenient practice was forced on the lawyers
by the judges. That is certainly possible. I would not want to exclude the
influence of the officials on the lawyers. But it is clear that the combination
of articles and positions was not made in every case.[40] There was apparently
an element of choice in actual litigation. The judge did not force all suits
to be introduced in the same way. It seems most likely, therefore, that
a large part of the decision was, in practice, left to the lawyer. And it is clear
that the lawyers usually (but not invariably) refused the choice which would
have artificially increased their fees.

There is other evidence to support the assertion that the proctors did not
normally prolong litigation to increase the size of their fees. For one thing,
proctors were sometimes recorded as asking specifically for the acceleration
and final expedition of their causes.[41] For another, the Act books record

---

[37] See Ayliffe, *Parergon* s.v. *answers*, objecting to this form of answer because of its 'great
uncertainty'.

[38] The combined document thus begins: 'Item ponit ac intendit probare quod. . .',
the former verb being the ordinary form for introducing positions, and the latter for articles.

[39] Examples: Lichfield Act book B/C/1/2, f. 50r (1472); Canterbury Act book Y.1.6,
f. 150r (1466); Hereford Act book 0/3, p. 78 (1446). See also Durantis, *Speculum Iudiciale*
II tit. *de positionibus* no. 5:1: 'In plerisque locis non fiunt positiones.'

[40] Compare, for example, York C.P. E 111 (1372), where the positions were combined
with the articles, with C.P. E 109 (1370) where they were not. I am indebted to Professor
Knut W. Nörr for raising the subject of this paragraph with me and for a good discussion
of the matter.

[41] E.g. Rochester Act book DRb Pa 1, fols. 248r-248v (1442): 'Et magister Henricus
Wilkhous affectans acceleracionem et finalem expedicionem eiusdem cause in iudicio apud
acta substituit nomine suo Gremond ad interessendum nomine suo productione et admis-
sione quarumcumque testium.' Other examples: DRb Pa 1, f. 270v (1442); Canterbury
Act book Y.1.7, f. 84r (1461); Ely Registrum Primum EDR D/2/1, f. 51r (1376).

many instances where the proctors actually renounced the normal procedural terms so that the case could move more quickly through the court.[42] Often in fact, where the substance of a case was before the judge in the first or second term, a day was at once set for hearing definitive sentence.[43] All intermediate terms were renounced. A third example is the continuance of a suit *sub spe concordie* and without further formal procedure.[44] This too was very often done. It served to save the parties the expense of documents and court appearances by proctors and advocates. Miss Sayers has recently reminded us in her *Papal Judges Delegate in the Province of Canterbury, 1198-1254* how ubiquitous compromise in litigation was.[45] Certainly this is true for the ordinary instance cases found in the remaining Act books. And normally the cases were settled by agreement short of full hearing. It is hard to tell whether the initiative for compromise came most often from the litigants or from the lawyers. But the lawyers represented almost all parties in contested litigation, and I think it is unreasonable to assert that the compromises were usually arranged against the objections of the lawyers. In fact, I have even found three cases where the proctors apparently agreed on what seemed to be a fair compromise during litigation, only to have both their clients later dissent and insist on continuing the original action.[46] These clients did so, however, without the services of their original proctors. Perhaps they had lost confidence in these lawyers. But in any event these attempted compromises, along with the many others in the Act books, do show that the proctors did not normally drag out the hearing of their cases in order to increase the size of their fees.

In all, then, on this first point, the records show that the practicing lawyers were protective of their professional fees. And they suggest that those

---

[42] It is for this reason that definitive sentences often noted specifically the renunciation of terms; e.g. Canterbury Act book Y.1.5, f. 47r (1455): '... ceterisque iuris solempniis in hac parte de iure requisitis in omnibus observatis seu saltem renunciatis'.

[43] E.g. Lichfield Act book B/C/1/2, f. 20v (1471): '... in termino ad respondendum libello; quo die datus est terminus ad audiendum sentenciam de consensu parcium'.

[44] E.g. Rochester Act book DRb Pa 1, f. 298r (1442); '... in termino ad libellandum, continetur causa sub spe pacis de assensu procuratorum'. York Act book Cons. A B 1, f. 124v (1419): '... ad deliberandum super libello; prorogatur ad idem sub spe pacis et concordie reformande'.

[45] (Oxford 1971) 239-42.

[46] Hereford Act book I/3, p. 18 (1499): 'In causa illa ad publicandum, partibus per procuratores suos comparentibus, procurator partis actricis dicit quod sunt concordes et illud eciam asserit Willelmus Bowley, ... et Jacobus Aveley alter executor asserit quod ipse vult defendere causam suam et peciit processum et publicationem. Et iudex asserit quod ipse vult deliberare usque ad proximum.' Other examples: York C.P. F 169 (1427-28); Canterbury Act book Y.1.6, f. 105r (1465).

fees were worth protecting. But they do not show the lawyers using the intricacies of canonical procedure to run up unnecessarily large fees. Quite the reverse, in fact. They embraced practices which saved litigants both time and money.

* *
*

The three cases of attempted compromise by the proctors against the wishes of their clients raise the second theme of this paper: consideration of how far the practicing canon lawyers went in advocating the interests of their clients. The criticism, to repeat, is that they took and argued cases they knew to be unjust, that they raised objections they knew to be without merit, that they used the intricacies of the law to frustrate justice in pursuit of victory for their clients.[47] From a lawyer's point of view this is surely the more interesting problem. How far the lawyer should be a servant of his client, and how far an officer of the court is a question which is neither settled nor academic. The question is difficult. Many lawyers argue that justice is better served by the presentation for each side of every argument available under the law. Lawyers should shun outright unethical practices, but they should not set themselves up as independent arbiters of the justice of their client's claim.[48] Other lawyers hold the opposite view. They insist that the lawyer's first duty is to justice. He must subordinate the wishes of his client to that duty.[49]

This dilemma for the individual lawyer in the medieval Church courts is well illustrated by a concrete case, one which was heard before the Provincial court at York in 1378. But it is only one of many which could be chosen. This particular suit was brought to enforce a marriage contract. It came before the York court on appeal. The lower court, which had been held by special commission, had given sentence in favor of enforcing the contract. On appeal the lawyer for the losing party in the first instance discovered that the first judge did not have the notary public or other 'two suitable men' with him to record the *acta* of that case, as required by the Fourth Lateran Council's decree *Quoniam contra falsam*.[50] But that was all he could say

---

[47] E.g. Baldwin, *Masters, Princes and Merchants* 195: 'The lawyer's principal temptation, however, was to defend causes which he knew to be unjust.'

[48] See for example L.D. Brandeis, 'The Opportunity in the Law', *American Law Rev.* 39 (1905) 555; E. Wayne Thode, 'The Ethical Standard for the Advocate', *Texas Law Rev.* 39 (1961) 575.

[49] See for example Frattin, 'The Role of the Advocate in Church Courts', *supra* n. 15.

[50] York C.P. E 138 (1389): 'Dictus dominus Johannes iudex sive commissarius pretensus in huiusmodi coram ipso ut predicitur facto et habito notarium publicum aut duos viros

against the process below. He had no other grounds for challenging the sentence. Should that lawyer have argued that the first hearing was void and of no effect? If so, and if he prevailed, the case would have to begin again. And the original petitioner might not want to. Or he might not be able to afford another suit. If so, an apparently good cause would be lost.

On the other hand, the decree which required proper recording of judicial process was not an unwarranted or a pointless rule. One of the real problems in marriage litigation in medieval England was that cases were too often judged by men who had neither the training nor the proper personnel to hear them properly. How else could the Lateran Council's decree be enforced if proctors and advocates did not insist on appeal that it be followed? What should the lawyer in the York case have done? It is hard to be sure, and there are doubtless many facts behind the case which the surviving documents do not reveal. But it is surely wrong to condemn this lawyer outright for bringing forth this exception, as he in fact did in the case. By doing so, he certainly opened himself to the charge of using frustratory tactics to delay justice. But it is not certain that the charge is warranted. Much good can come from a rigid insistence that proper procedure be followed.

No one who examines the court records would deny that some of the exceptions made by proctors and found there must have been meant only to delay. Challenging the instrument appointing the opposing proctor towards the end of a full hearing and against one of the regular court staff, for instance, can hardly have been anything but an attempt to drag out the case in hopes of compromise.[51] Objecting to the testimony of witnesses because they had been examined on a feast day was probably a similar attempt to delay.[52] But most of the exceptions made in litigation cannot easily be put in this category.[53] It is at least arguable that they reflect an insistence on the observance of important rules of procedure. In practice, lawyers must insist

---

ydoneos ad scribenda acta in dicto processu seu iudicio coram eo habito nullatenus adhibuit, set hoc facere contra constitutionem quoniam contra falsam [omisit].' For the constitution see X 2.19.11.

[51] Canterbury Act book Y.1.8, f. 286v (1472), in which M. Thomas Ramsey challenged the credentials of M. Thomas Notyngham. Notyngham produced the necessary letters during the next session, but the case was inhibited, perhaps also suggesting that Ramsey was seeking to impede the progress of the case.

[52] York C.P. E 1 (1303); there were other procedural objections in this case, however.

[53] E.g. Canterbury Act book Y.1.15, f. 71r (1488) in which the proctor 'allegavit quod pars sua non est legitime citatus (*sic*) quia infra locum exemptum'. Or Rochester DRb Pa 1, f. 277v (1442) where the petitioner's proctor 'proposuit excepciones contra testes viva voce. Et procurator partis ree peciit terminum sibi precludi ulterius proponendi eo quod non proposuit in scriptis in debita forma.'

that those rules be enforced, even at the risk of laying themselves open to the charge of using frustratory tactics or acting to delay justice.

This is by way of apology for the conduct of advocates and proctors. But there is also more positive evidence. The records sometimes show unwillingness by the lawyers to participate in the frustration of justice. Most striking is the refusal to undertake an unjust cause. Only rarely, of course, do the records give any clue to the way in which lawyers were hired. But they do occasionally. One such description can be taken from the deposition of John Ragenhill, a proctor at York in the early fifteenth century: It comes from a case where John Harwood sought to enforce a marriage contract with Margaret le Scrope. He sought, in other words, to prove that there was such a contract. She contended that there had been none. Ragenhill was contacted to serve as proctor for her. He told this story:

> Admitted, sworn, and diligently examined on the material contained in the aforesaid articles, Ragenhill says that about six or seven days before the last Michaelmas Synod, he was present in the cathedral church of York with the rector, as he said, of the Church of Wensley in the archdeaconry of Richmond . . . , who asked him if he would act for lady Margaret le Scrope in a certain matrimonial cause which a certain John Harwood, knight, intended to move and prosecute against lady Margaret. And Ragenhill said that he would do so, as long as he first had information on the merits of the said cause. And he asked the rector to give him true and just information. And the rector then informed him that John Harwood had once contracted marriage with the said lady Margaret before a certain venerable doctor of theology, and another time before another whose name the rector did not then declare.[54]

---

[54] York C.P. F 16 (1405): The full deposition, containing some words omitted from the translation is: 'Magister Johannes Ragenhill curie Ebor' procurator generalis etatis xxx annorum et amplius nulli parcium consanguineus affinis aut procurator, testis admissus iuratus et super materia in articulis predictis contenta diligenter examinatus, dicit quod quasi per vi aut vii dies proximo ante Synodum Sancti Michelis ultimo preterit' presens fuit iste iuratus in ecclesia cathedrali Ebor' cum quodam Tybbay cuius nomen proprium ignorat rectorem tamen ecclesie parochialis de Wenselawe archidiaconatus Richmondie se dicente presente ibidem magistro Thoma Otrington vicario de Pokelyngton, ubi et quando dictus Tybbay rogavit istum iuratum quatinus voluerit occupare pro domina Margareta le Scrope in quadam causa matrimoniali quam quidam Johannes Harwod' armiger contra dictam dominam in curia Ebor' ut asseruit movere et prosequi intendebat. Et tunc iste iuratus respondit quod voluit, primitus per ipsum habita informacione de meritis dicte cause et rogavit eundem Tybbay quatinus veram et iustam informacionem in dicta causa sibi voluerit ministrare. Et adtunc prefatus Tybbay informavit et retulit isti iurato quod dictus Johannes Harwod' cum dicta domina Margareta coram quodam venerabili viro doctore in theologia unica vice et altera vice coram altero quorum nomina adtunc non exposuit nec declaravit isti iurato quatenus recolit matrimonium contraxit ut dicit.'

Ragenhill had, in other words, just been told that the cause he was being asked to take was unjust. And, in the event, he refused to take it. The rector of Wensley was doubtless more circumspect in approaching the next proctor he tried. But the important fact is that Ragenhill would not act in a case he believed to be unjust. It is, of course, only rarely that such initial refusals would find their way into the official records. But there are a few other Act book entries where, by chance, we see initial refusals by proctors or advocates.[55] They are examples of real ethical concern by the lawyers. They refused to become personally involved in a cause they believed to be unjust.

The most frequent example of this ethical concern given in the court records is the dismissal by a proctor of a cause shown to be without foundation during the course of its hearing. It was a *causa desperata*, one the proctor could no longer defend in good conscience. The canon law and the proctor's own oath required him to dismiss as *desperate* any case he learned was wrongfully brought, even after he had once undertaken it.[56] The records sometimes expressly point to the element of injustice as the reason for dismissal by a proctor or advocate.[57] It cannot be said that examples of renunciation of such cases appear in every folio of every English Act book. Lawyers normally reach their decision about the justice of a cause before taking a case in the first place. But dismissal of a *causa desperata* was not at all unusual in English practice. At Canterbury I found thirty of them in the late medieval records.[58]

---

[55] York Act book Cons. A B 1, f. 30r (1417) in which proctor John Willyngham said he would not act unless the rights were clear to him; York C.P. F 78 (1410) in which the advocate Robert Ragenhill refused to take a case assigned to him 'quia et asseruit . . . , ipsa Mathilidis fovebat et defendebat causam iniustam'. Two other examples are found in York Act book Cons. A B 4, f. 157r (1488) and Rochester Act book DRb Pa 4, f. 170r (1480).

[56] E.g. Hostiensis, *Summa Aurea* I tit. *de postulando* no. 5: 'Item ad officium suum pertinet, ne causam suscipiat contra conscientiam et quamcito sentiet, quod desperata sit causa omnino recedere debet, alioquin dolo est advocatus.' Durantis, *Speculum Iudiciale* I tit. *de salariis procuratorum et tabellionum* no. 3: ' . . . qui etiam debet iurare quod quam cito causam malam esse noverit ipsam deseret'. The operative part of the Exeter oath is given *supra* n. 14. The Roman Law source for the phrase *causa desperata* and for the above oath is Cod. 3.1.14.4.

[57] Canterbury Act book Y.1.6, f. 133r (1466): 'Tunc Ramsey dimisit causam tanquam desperatam et iniustam.' But cf. York Act book Cons. A B 5, f. 72v (1504), where the proctor alleged as the reason for dismissal 'necligenciam domini sui qui non est diligens in productione testium'. And Ely Registrum Primum EDR D/2/1, f. 23v (1375): 'Allegatum per dictum Ricardum procuratorem partis actricis quod habet causam desperatam pro eo quod domina sua noluit consulere cum eo post productionem testium.'

[58] Act books Y.1.1, f. 12r (1373); Y.1.3, f. 152r (1420); Y.1.4, fols. 28r (1420), 29v (1420) (two cases), 78v (1422); Y.1.6, fols. 3r (1464), 133r (1466), 177r (1466); Y.1.7, f. 11r (1459); Y.1.8, fols. 234v (1471), 314r (1472); Y.1.12, fol. 96r (1475), 105v (1475), 115v (1476); Y.1.13, fols. 161r (1481), 209v (1481), 414v (1484); Y.1.14, f. 34r (1485); Y.1.15,

At Hereford I found twenty-nine.[59] Doubtless, a more determined search would have produced even more. And the Act books of the other dioceses for which Act books remain, York, Lichfield, Ely, Bath and Wells, and Rochester, also all contain examples of such dismissals.[60]

A modern lawyer may find the frequency of this practice disquieting. Only under extreme circumstances can he renounce a case during its prosecution. The effect such renunciation had on the client's chances for victory in the Church courts can well be imagined. Theoretically, the party was not hindered by dismissal of a *causa desperata*. He was summoned to continue his case personally if he chose.[61] But the records show that litigants rarely did so. It is hard to blame them. Their own lawyer had himself declared their cause to be unjust. There is something to be said for the proposition that the public renunciation of a case by a lawyer was itself unethical. Something like the same objection might be raised against the York proctor who refused to undertake lady Margaret le Scrope's case. What business had he testifying to information given him in confidence by the agent of a potential client? And how could the lawyers, mentioned earlier, agree to what *they* thought was a fair settlement, and then withdraw from the case when the parties whose interests were actually at stake disagreed with their opinion? Were not all of these ethically objectionable?

They were not, I think, by canonical standards. The lawyers had sworn an oath on admission not to associate themselves with causes they believed to be unjust. The canon law placed a much greater emphasis on their personal responsibility to the ideal of fairness and justice than on their duty to represent a client's interests. They were not to be associated with a cause they believed to be without merit. In dismissing a hopeless cause, a proctor

---

fols. 98v (1488), 131v (1489), 249v (1490), 326v (1491), 353r (1491); Y.1.16, fols. 7r (1492), 91r (1493), 110r (1493), 137r (1493); Y.4.3, f. 42v (1501) (archdeacon's court).

[59] Act books I/1, pp. 76 (1493), 163 (1494), 176 (1494), 178 (1494) (two cases), 179 (1494), 208 (1495), 237 (1496), 245 (1496), 252 (1497), 269 (1497), 295 (1498), 328 (1498), 344 (1499), 366 (1500); I/2, pp. 11 (1497), 32 (1497), 88 (1499), 106 (1499), 110 (1499), 112 (1499); I/3, pp. 2 (1499), 13 (1499), 46 (1500) (two cases), 54 (1500), 61 (1500), 64 (1500), 65 (1500).

[60] York Act books Cons. A B 1, f. 175v (1420); Cons. A B 2, fols. 20r (1424), 29v (1424); Cons. A B 5. fols. 43r (1503), 68v (1504), 72v (1504); and C.P. F 169 (1427-28); Lichfield Act books B/C/1/1, f. 109r (1466); B/C/1/2, f. 125v (1473); Ely Registrum Primum EDR D/2/1, f. 23v (1375); Bath and Wells [Somerset Country Record Office, Taunton] Act book D/D/C A 1, pp. 157 (1481), 161 (1485); Rochester Act books DRb Pa 1, fols. 23v (1437), 205v (1441), 218v (1443); DRb Pa 4, f. 195r (1486); DRb Pa 5, f. 64v (1500).

[61] E.g. Hereford Act book I/1, p. 163 (1494): 'Ideo decretum est quod dictam partem actricem principalem fore citandam ad proximum ad prosequendam causam suam si voluerit.' There is no sign, however, that the party did so. Canterbury Act book Y.1.6, f. 133r (1466): 'Tunc dominus decrevit partem principalem fore vocandum erga proximo ad procedendum.'

was living up to the terms of his oath. If this meant sacrificing the interests of his client, that had to be accepted. And I might suggest that in the ecclesiastical courts, where spiritual values were not irrelevant, the proctor who dismissed a *causa desperata* could easily see himself as acting in the long-term best interest of his client. No man's lasting advantage can be secured by a victory built on perjury or false swearing.

The dismissal of a *causa desperata* is perhaps the most striking evidence of a proctor's observance of his duty to the court. But the records also provide other instances of this same unwillingness to violate the canon law's ethical standards. One is a proctor's simple refusal to swear the oath of calumny when he was unsure enough of the merits of a cause or a plea to risk the onus that went with the oath. The Act books show a number of instances of this.[62] Another is the admission by a proctor that he was not fully informed on a question before the court. The proctor suggested that his own client be summoned personally to clear up the matter. Several examples of this action appear in the surviving records.[63] A third is the waiver of a seemingly valid objection to the admission of witnesses in order to get at the truth of the case.[64] All of these actions are indications of a lawyer's preference for justice over mere advocacy.

The records do, on the hand, produce some examples of unethical conduct. A proctor in one Canterbury case apparently 'coached' his party's

---

[62] London Act book DL/C/1, f. 67v (1501) in which the proctor was asked 'quod prestaret juramentum de malicia et de lite non differendo, qui huiusmodi prestare recusat'. Canterbury Act book Y.1.3, f. 193v (1421) in which 'Pars dicti magistri Jacobi [Burbaych] recusavit iurare de calumpnia. Igitur dominus commissarius continuavit causam.' Other examples: Canterbury Act book [Chartae Antiquae] A 36 II, p. 12 (1329); Hereford Act book I/3, p. 5 (1499); see also Canterbury Act book Y.1.6, f. 150v (1466), in which the proctor only agreed to answer the libel 'metu excommunicationis'.

[63] E.g. York C.P. F 16 (1405-6) in which the proctor 'dixit se non habere plenam informationem ad aliter respondendum eisdem positionibus'. Canterbury Act book Y.1.3, f. 189v (1421): 'Rea vero per magistrum David Marys dicentem se non habere informacionem a parte rea. Igitur dominus commissarius decrevit dictum Ricardum citandum ad personaliter respondendum libello in proximo consistorio.' Other examples: Canterbury Act book Y.1.18, f. 13v (1499); Y.1.6, f. 154r (1466).

[64] Rochester Act book DRb Pa 1, f. 17v (1437): 'Pars dicti Johannis Hegstapill dixit unum alium testem in causa predicta sibi necessarium et dixit quod voluit uti eodem teste supplicando iudici ut admitteret et examinaret eundem. Et iudex interrogavit partem dicti Johannis Calche an vellet consentire admissioni eiusdem, qui asseruit quod bene placuit sibi de eodem.' The entry does not make clear that the proctor's consent was involved, but Calche was represented by Henry Wilkhous, and the marginal note to the case is 'placuit pro'. York Act book Cons. A B 5, f. 2v (1502): 'Dictus Evers expresse renunciavit omnibus excepcionibus et probacionibus contra testes.' And see *supra* n. 41.

witness in answering the articles.[65] Another lawyer was challenged as having acted both as an advocate and as examiner-general.[66] This was inconsistent and unethical, since the examiner was required to hear and record all the testimony in a case. The judge gave his sentence on the basis of the examiner's formulation. But, in all, the number of recorded instances of unethical conduct is very small. They are far outweighed by cases in which the proctors and advocates are shown observing their oath to refrain from unethical conduct.

There is a word to be said in conclusion. No one would pretend that the evidence presented here proves that the lawyers practicing in the medieval church courts deserved none of the criticism which has been levelled against them. The court records are not always easy to evaluate with confidence. Their evidence is not statistically overwhelming. They will not convince anyone that all the criticism of the lawyers has been wide of the mark. But the evidence of the English court books does show clearly that there is a brighter side to the gloomy picture painted by literary and legal critics. The brighter side predominates in those records, although they clearly do not exclude instances of unethical or negligent conduct on the part of proctors and advocates. They indicate that, in the main, the lawyers did not use every means available to them to increase the profits of litigation. And at least some of the practicing lawyers did not forget their oath to act as servants of justice, as well as advocates of a private cause.

---

[65] Sede Vacante Scrapbook III no. 35 (1293).
[66] Canterbury Ecclesiastical Suit no. 297 (1293).

4

THE WRIT OF PROHIBITION TO COURT CHRISTIAN BEFORE 1500*

T HE English writ of prohibition was the principal tool used during the Middle
Ages to restrain what the seventeenth-century Protestant controversialist
William Prynne called the 'daring contempts of the ecclesiastical courts'.[1] A
royal writ available to any person who had been sued in an ecclesiastical court
over a secular matter, a prohibition could be directed both against the person
who had wrongfully brought suit in a Church court and against the judge in
that court. It required them to desist from prosecuting and from hearing a suit
which fell outside ecclesiastical competence. Its broad purpose was to enforce,
through the powerful self-interest of private litigants, the secular position on the
proper jurisdictional boundaries between the courts of Church and State.
Because the Church held a more expansive view of the permissible scope of its
jurisdiction than did the royal courts, prohibitions were a necessary judicial
remedy.

The fundamental work on the history of the writ of prohibition was
done thirty years and more ago by G. B. Flahiff in a series of articles which appeared in *Mediaeval Studies*.[2] As works of scholarship, Flahiff's articles were
meticulous, original, comprehensive and trustworthy. But we now know that

* An earlier version of this article was read at the Ninth Annual Meeting of the American
Society for Legal History, on 26 October 1979. The author would like to thank the following
scholars for valuable help of various sorts in the preparation of this article: Professor M. S.
Arnold, Dr. J. H. Baker, Mr. J. L. Barton, Professor Charles Donahue, Jr., Professor Stanley
Katz, Professor William McGovern, and Dr. Robert Palmer.

[1] William Prynne, *Exact Chronological Vindication and Historical Demonstration of the
Supreme Ecclesiastical Jurisdiction of our ... Kings*, 3 vols. (London, 1665-68), 3. 580 [hereinafter
cited as Prynne's *Records*].

[2] 'The Writ of Prohibition to Court Christian in the Thirteenth Century' (part 1), *Mediaeval
Studies* 6 (1944) 261-313, and (part 2) 7 (1945) 229-90 [hereinafter cited as Flahiff 1 and 2]. See
also G. B. Flahiff, 'The Use of Prohibitions by Clerics against Ecclesiastical Courts in England',
Mediaeval Studies 3 (1941) 101-16; Norma Adams, 'The Writ of Prohibition to Court Christian',
Minnesota Law Review 20 (1936) 272-93.

his assessment of the ultimate effectiveness of the writ of prohibition was mistaken. He concluded that the study of actual procedure permits us 'to see how the ecclesiastical courts found themselves constantly disadvantaged and just how the constant pressure of prohibitions was rendered so effective.'[3] Recent study of the records of the Church courts themselves has shown the contrary. The Church courts were able to maintain their jurisdiction in many areas theoretically outside their competence throughout the medieval period. The writ of prohibition was not decisive in determining the actual scope of ecclesiastical jurisdiction.[4]

This discovery has raised the obvious question: how can this have been? What can explain the apparent anomaly that the peremptory commands and penalties of the royal writ failed in practice to restrain the ecclesiastical courts? This article addresses that question by carrying Flahiff's investigation of the plea rolls of the royal courts through the end of the medieval period. He stopped in 1285. It concludes that the answer lies, at least in part, in examination of the seemingly straightforward question: how did the royal courts determine whether a suit brought in a Church court belonged there or not? What mechanisms were available, what were used, to decide whether or not a prohibition lay?

The evidence of the plea rolls shows that there were three different periods, each with a different fundamental way of making this decision. During the earliest, the predominant means of proof was by wager of law. That is, in a typical case the plaintiff alleged that the defendant had sued him in Court Christian over a secular matter. The defendant denied this in general terms, swore an oath to that effect, and found eleven oath helpers who swore that they believed he had sworn truly. That is, wager twelve-handed. During the second period, trial was predominantly by jury. The defendant typically denied that he had sued a lay plea contrary to a prohibition, and that question then went to the jury under the general issue. During the third period, the predominant method of decision was removed from the trial court almost entirely; argument and

[3] Flahiff 2. 283.

[4] See Brian Woodcock, *Medieval Ecclesiastical Courts in the Diocese of Canterbury* (Oxford, 1952), pp. 89-92; J. W. Gray, 'The Ius Praesentandi in England from the Constitutions of Clarendon to Bracton', *English Historical Review* 67 (1952) 481-509; M. M. Sheehan, 'Canon Law and English Institutions' in *Proceedings of the Second International Congress of Medieval Canon Law*, ed. Stephan Kuttner and J. Joseph Ryan (Vatican City, 1965), pp. 391-97, especially pp. 393-94; Charles Donahue, Jr., 'Roman Canon Law in the Medieval English Church: Stubbs vs. Maitland Re-examined after 75 Years in the Light of Some Records from the Church Courts', *Michigan Law Review* 72 (1974) 647-716; R. H. Helmholz, 'Assumpsit and Fidei Laesio', *Law Quarterly Review* 91 infra 263-89 and 'Debt Claims and Probate Jurisdiction in Historical Perspective', *American Journal of Legal History* 23 (1979) 68-82 : infra 307-21.

decision about the propriety of prohibiting a suit in the Church courts occurred in Chancery, largely on the basis of the ecclesiastical libel. Rarely was there more trial than this.

The adoption of each method of trial did not happen suddenly. Change from one to another occurred gradually. There was much overlapping. Likewise, the apparent definiteness of each method conceals what seems to have been more complex procedure in practice. Judges and litigants had more choice than this scheme suggests. There was room for dispute and variation in methods of decision. But with these caveats, the three-part division is useful and valid. Above all, when looked at in detail, each stage helps to understand the reasons for the failure of the medieval writ of prohibition effectively to determine the scope of ecclesiastical jurisdiction.

I

WAGER OF LAW

The earliest method of proof in prohibition cases was defendant's wager of law. Flahiff found that it was the exclusive method for trial of the general issue before the reign of Edward I (1272-1307).[5] Juries were used only to answer specific factual questions.[6] Thus, in a typical case, the plaintiff's formal count alleged that the defendant had sued him in an ecclesiastical court over a lay debt not touching marriage or testaments. It further specified the amount of the debt, the ecclesiastical court and judge before whom the suit had been brought, the place and date of the delivery of the writ of prohibition, the witnesses to the delivery, the refusal of the party prohibited to comply with the writ and the action taken against the plaintiff by the Church court judge. A suit against the judge contained similar allegations *mutatis mutandis*.[7] To this, the defendant's general denial (and this is the important point) alleged that never after receipt of

---

[5] Flahiff 2. 267.

[6] ibid.

[7] Although there is not absolute regularity of form, most Edwardian entries contain these elements; e.g., Croke v. Ros and Wygeyn, CP 40/57, m. 49d (1285): 'Et unde queritur quod cum Hugo le Estraunge implacitasset ipsum Rogerum in curia christianitatis coram predictis archidiacono et officiali exigendo ab ipso decem solidos qui non sunt de testamento vel matrimonio et idem Rogerus die lune proxima post festum sancti Michaelis anno regis nunc duodecimo detulisset eis regiam prohibitionem in ecclesia extra portam sancti Augustini London' in presencia decani London' et Johannis Oysel et aliorum ne predictum placitum ulterius tenerent in curia christianitatis predicti archidiaconus et officialis spreta prohibitione predicta tenuerunt predictum placitum in curia christianitatis ita quod fecerunt ipsum ab ingressu ecclesie suspendi et postea excommunicari ....' This plea roll, and all other citations to MS. sources not otherwise indicated, are found in the Public Record Office, London.

any writ of prohibition had he sued such a plea concerning a lay debt not touching marriage or testaments, and he then offered to deny this against the plaintiff and his suit as the court should award. The court awarded that the defendant should wage his law twelve-handed, and the defendant was ordered to come personally with his law on a later day.

Such, in its barest form, was the earliest method of proof in prohibition cases. It was simple. It was direct. And it put the proof of the central question – had the defendant sued over a matter outside ecclesiastical competence? – into the hands of the defendant and his oath helpers. That is, the responsibility for proof was placed not on the plaintiff who had been harmed, but on the party who had allegedly broken the Crown's jurisdictional rules and who would pay damages and suffer an amercement unless he could swear that he had not been guilty of illegitimately invoking spiritual jurisdiction, and find eleven of his fellows to take an oath that he swore truly.

What exactly did the defendant, and his oath helpers, swear to? What, that is, did the general denial put in issue? Normally, one cannot say with assurance; by nature the general issue was a blank denial.[8] But in this case we do know from cases in which the king was a party that the general denial could be based on any one of several possible defenses, for where the king was one of the plaintiffs it was disputed whether one could plead the general issue at all, and the specific objection raised against it was, as a 1295 case put it: 'the answer is *multiplex* and can have several causes of truth.'[9] It might signify that the defendant had never sued the plaintiff before an ecclesiastical court. It might signify that the defendant had sued but had discontinued the action once he received the writ. Or it might signify that the defendant had sued but over a matter properly within ecclesiastical competence.[10]

All this means, of course, that the earliest system of proof allowed a defendant to base his denial on any one of a number of legitimate defenses, that it drove no defendant to specify exactly which of them he relied on except where the king was a party, and that it tested the veracity of that defense by a

---

[8] See generally S. F. C. Milson, 'Law and Fact in Legal Development', *University of Toronto Law Journal* 17 (1967) 1-19.

[9] Rex v. Wallys et al., CP 40/109, m. 27 (1295), in which the plaintiff's argument was 'quod predicti prior et alii ad huiusmodi verificationem admitti non debuerunt quia dixit quod predicta responsio sua quam pretenderunt verificare multiplex fuit et plures causas veritatis habere potuit ....'

[10] idem, CP 40/106, m. 16d (1294): 'Predicta responsio ... plures causas veritatis habere potest videlicet quod predicti prior et Robertus nullum placitum ibidem inde tenuerunt nec predictus Galfridus de Wallys idem placitum secutus fuit vel quod iidem prior et alii idem placitum tenuerunt ibidem et secuti sunt set non attingit ad quartam partem advocationis predicte ecclesie vel quod ipsi tenuerunt idem placitum et secuti fuerunt ibidem ante prohibitiones eis porrectas sed non post unde petit per dominum regem quod certam inde dent responsionem.'

system of oath and compurgation largely within the defendant's control. It was, in short, a system of proof which favored defendants.

On the other hand, the plea rolls do show that the realities of proof in prohibition cases could be more complex. The possible unfairness of wager led to efforts to restrict the cases in which wager was allowed. There was, in the first place, the necessity for award of wager by the court. Some reality evidently lay behind this formal award. Bracton wrote that the oath helpers must be 'trustworthy and of good repute',[11] so that there must have been an initial determination of whether to allow compurgation to go forward with the men the defendant had brought. Several Yearbook cases where the availability of wager was argued also show the exercise of some control by the judges.[12] Moreover, in two specific situations, wager was excluded by rule: where the king's interest was directly involved, and where there had been a prior plea involving the same prohibited case in the Church courts. If the king was a party to a prohibition case,[13] or if a prior plea in his court had allegedly been disregarded by the defendant,[14] no defendant could be permitted to wage his law. He must put himself on the country.[15]

[11] Henry Bracton, *De legibus et consuetudinibus Angliae*, fol. 410, ed. and trans. G. Woodbine and S. E. Thorne, 4 vols. (Cambridge, Mass., 1968-77), 4. 276: 'Sufficit enim si fideles sint et bone opinionis.'

[12] See. e.g., *Baret* v. *Sparewe* (1310), Y.B. 3 Edw. II (Selden Society 20; London, 1905), p. 134; *Gras* v. *Houghton* (1312), Y.B. 5 Edw. II (Selden Society 33; London, 1916), p. 118. suggesting a judicial reluctance to deny defendants a right to wager. In St. George v. Prioress of Easebourne, CP 40/113, m. 58 (1296), the defendant argued 'quod predicta priorissa per legem suam se defendere non potest in hoc casu etc. cum huiusmodi prosecutiones placitorum de transgressionibus contra pacem regis factis et advocationibus etc. in lesionem corone et dignitatis regis manifeste redundent.' The case was tried by the country. See also *Brevia placitata* (Selden Society 66; London, 1951), pp. 171-72.

[13] Staunton et al. v. Pykeryng, London, British Library Add. MS. 31826, fol. 118r (c. 1301) *per* Warr': 'Mes ore se plainent il que vous avez play tenu de lor lay fe queu chose le rey ad playnement retenu a la dignete de sa coroune.' Dr. Robert Palmer called my attention to this case. See also *Butiller* v. *Le Wronge* (1311), Y.B. 5 Edw. II (Selden Society 63; London, 1944), pp. 121-23. in which the same argument was successful as to trespass by battery; St. George v. Prioress of Easebourne, above, n. 12.

[14] Compare the two entries of Lucy et al. v. St. Elena, CP 40/158, m. 231 (1306), a case tried by wager, with CP 40/163, m. 84 (1307), a second attachment on a writ of prohibition between the same parties, involving the same ecclesiastical plea which had been continued after the first action. The second was consequently tried by the country. Another example is furnished by Boheler et al. v. Nicholas parson of L., CP 40/171, m. 193d (1308), in which the defendant was summoned specifically for continuing suit pendente lite in the royal court, and was compelled to answer 'tam domino Regi quam predictis [plaintiffs] de contemptu et malicia predictis etc.'

[15] Thus the importance of the development of the writ brought by the king *ex relatu plurium* was specifically that it allowed the king to be made a nominal party and so excluded wager. See *Historical Papers and Letters from the Northern Registers*, ed. J. Raine (RS 61; London, 1873), pp. 70-71.

Initial determination of the availability of wager is also suggested by plea roll cases which contain more detailed pleading of facts than was necessary for the general denial appropriate in wager cases. In a case of 1286, for example, a woman was impleaded for having sued before an ecclesiastical court over lay debts and chattels. The entry in her defense states that 'the day he espoused her, her husband granted the aforesaid chattels to her as a *maritagium* and afterwards in his last will he left the aforesaid chattels to her, wherefore she sued [the plaintiff] in Court Christian for the aforesaid chattels as of those touching testaments, ... and she is ready to deny [etc.] as the court should award.'[16] The court then awarded wager. In a case from Easter term 1306, the defendant's denial specified both that the case in the ecclesiastical court had involved tithes. not lay chattels, and that a writ of consultation had previously been issued allowing him to proceed. Then wager was awarded.[17] It may be that such deviations from a simple denial were ways of justifying wager to the court, a means of making a plausible case for having sued which the court could pass on before admitting the defendant to wager. Some of the stories placed on the rolls by defendants were quite elaborate, obviously intended for some sort of scrutiny,[18] and where wager followed it is hard to see any reason for such pleading except as part of a preliminary discussion on the availability of wager.

However, none of these exceptions ever swallowed the ordinary rule. The king's interest was not invoked indiscriminately for the benefit of all litigants, and the pattern of blank denial and wager was the norm.[19] Even with such

---

[16] Fraunceys v. Grysun. JUST 1/578. m. 11: the defendant's full answer was 'quod quidam Hugo quondam vir suus die quo ipsam disponsavit concessit ei predicta catalla nomine maritagii et postea in ultima voluntate sua legavit ei predicta catalla unde dicit quod ipsa implacitavit predictum Rogerum de predictis catallis in curia christianitatis tanquam de illis que sunt de testamento et quod aliter ipsum non implacitavit et parata est defendere contra ipsum et sectam suam sicut curia consideraverit.'

[17] Tresel v. Nicholas parson of Hasalor. CP 40/159, m. 5: the defendant made his law at once.

[18] E.g., Bentele v. Lacy. JUST 1/1089, m. 17 (1293), in which the defendant pleaded the real nature of the underlying suit, his obedience to the original writ of prohibition, his successful attempt to secure a writ of consultation from the Chancellor Bishop Burnell. He also produced the writ of consultation before being allowed to wage his law. In Patemere v. Baldok and Graveshende. CP 40/155, m. 159 (1305), involving alleged suit over lay chattels in Court Christian, the defendant pleaded the tithing custom of the parish, alleging that the plaintiff had refused to comply with it. The plaintiff attempted to take issue on the custom and asked that this question be tried by the country. The court, however, refused to admit this form of issue, and forced the defendant to plead the general issue instead, i.e., 'non fuit secutus predictum placitum in eadem curia christianitatis etc.', and to wage his law.

[19] E.g., Rex v. Archbishop of Canterbury and Sardene. CP 40/121, m. 285 (1297): '... et super hoc iusticiarii interloquentes de forma querele domini regis in hac parte videtur curie quod huiusmodi querela potius ad predictas heredes ad quarum prosecutionem predicte prohibitiones impetrate fuerunt pertinet quibus directe competit actio in hoc casu versus predictum archiepiscopum et eius officialem quam ad dominum Regem etc.'

checks as there were, therefore, proof by wager of law in prohibition cases was naturally weighted in favor of defendants. In the end, proof was within their control. This was not necessarily because they and their oath helpers perjured themselves. We do not yet know enough to say that. It was rather because it was a good defense to a prohibition action that the underlying plea was properly within ecclesiastical competence. Mere disobedience to a writ was not enough to allow the plaintiff to recover. And it is undeniable that the same underlying facts might seem different when seen through ecclesiastical glasses than when seen through secular ones. What seemed to secular eyes a suit for trespass might legitimately seem sacrilege or even defamation from an ecclesiastical point of view.[20] What appeared to one person as a lay debt or contract might appear to another as a suit over usury or for correction of the soul of the debtor.[21] What looked to some like a suit over an advowson or lay chattels might look to others like one for tithes or spoliation.[22] Wager's weakness lay in allowing defendants to choose the glass through which the nature of the underlying facts would be seen.

Figures taken from the rolls confirm this weakness. In an overwhelming majority of cases wager was successful. Flahiff himself remarked on the 'somewhat disconcerting ease and regularity' with which defendants successfully made their law.[23] Searches in the post-1285 plea rolls amplify this suspicion. Of the ninety wager cases found on the rolls between 1285 and 1335 which show a result, fully eighty-four ended with the defendant successfully making his law.[24] In other words, in a meagre 7 % of the cases where the rolls

[20] Roger v. Abbot of Oseney, CP 40/69, m. 28 (1287), in which the defendant pleaded 'quod super spoliatione illa predictum Ingeranum implacitavit etc. Et si hoc non sufficit dicet aliud.' Manham v. Wyke, JUST 1/1100, m. 23 (1292), in which the defendant admitted 'quod ipse implacitavit ipsum ibidem de quadam diffamacione quam ei imposuit de qua nichil inde recuperare optinuisset in curia laycali.' See also Y.B. Hil. 14 Edw. II, fol. 416 (1321).

[21] Rex v. Executors of Peter of Middelton, KB 27/354, m. 99d (1348), in which the defendants justified 'quod ipsi prosequebantur versus prefatum Willelmum de Popelton in curia christianitatis pro lesione fidei sue in correctione anime ipsius Willelmi absque hoc quod ipsi prosequebantur ....' An interesting example comes from the manor court of Boxley, SC 2/180/9, m. 10 (1322), a prosecution against Richard Suton for having sued wrongfully in Court Christian; he justified 'quod racione usure hoc fecit et non aliter.' He was allowed to go without day.

[22] Danner v. John parson of Thurlaston, CP 40/208, m. 289d (1315): 'Et bene concedit quod ipse secutus fuit placitum in curia christianitatis de quibusdam decimis ... per viam spoliacionis.' See generally Donahue, 'Stubbs vs. Maitland' (above, n. 4), 661-62.

[23] Flahiff 2. 269. And see generally W. R. Jones, 'Relations of the Two Jurisdictions: Conflict and Cooperation during the Thirteenth and Fourteenth Centuries', *Studies in Medieval and Renaissance History* 7 (1970) 79-210, especially 82-83.

[24] Cases counted for the defendant were found on the following CP 40 rolls: Nos. 57, m. 49d; 58, m. 29; 60, m. 121d; 62, m. 1; 64, mm. 61, 64d; 68, mm. 24, 65; 73, m. 14d; 78, m. 82; 80, m. 19d; 100, mm. 53d, 111d; 103, m. 57; 104, mm. 131d, 133d; 106, mm. 186d, 200; 108, m. 53;

show a result did the plaintiff's suit on a prohibition bring him success.[25]

These laboriously collected figures may admit of some difficulties, and perhaps they do not rise to the level of statistics. But surely they furnish confirmation that the possible advantages to defendants inherent in wager were more than theoretical. They suggest that good reasons existed for the move to the second method of proof in prohibition cases, that which began with the possibility of submission of the general issue to a jury, a move which occurred, as Flahiff established, during the reign of Edward I.

II

TRIAL BY JURY

By the beginning of the fourteenth century, the use of juries rather than wager of law was the normal, though not the exclusive, way of trying the general issue in prohibition cases. In 1300, for instance, eleven of the fourteen cases pleaded to issue on the Common Plea rolls went to juries; only three were tried by wager of law.[26] The last use of wager found comes from 1335[27] and thereafter trial by jury is the only method so far found on the rolls, although surely a more dogged search would produce a few later cases of wager.

The evident advantage, at least to our eyes, of the end of wager was that it took the final determination out of the hands of the party with an interest in the outcome and put it into the hands of a more neutral body. The continued weakness of trial by jury was that it left the decision of the ultimate issue in the hands of a lay body, one which might or might not make its decision according to formal law. The general issue went to the jury in as blank a form as the general denial had put the question in wager cases; this meant that the jury could decide the underlying question of whether the original plea was within

---

113, mm. 36d, 74d; 115, mm. 185d, 200d; 118, mm. 51d, 68d; 123, m. 84d; 134, m. 58; 135, m. 164; 136, mm. 37d, 72d; 138, mm. 27, 27d; 139, m. 153d; 141, m. 57d; 145, mm. 152, 314d; 146, mm. 7d, 136; 149, m. 111; 151, mm. 168d, 207d; 153, m. 377d; 154, mm. 14d, 114; 155, mm. 126, 130, 159; 158, m. 231; 159, m. 5; 160, mm. 159, 203d; 171, m. 36; 173, mm. 284, 303; 176, m. 120; 178, mm. 41, 165, 246; 180, m. 231; 183, m. 169; 184, m. 164; 187, m. 234; 189, m. 383d; 193, m. 19; 195B, m. 60; 205, m. 145d; 211, m. 218d; 216, m. 170d; 219, m. 39; 220, m. 58d; 236, m. 329; 237, m. 158; 248, m. 189; 281, m. 19d; 288, m. 104; 292, m. 437d; 296, m. 408d (two cases); 300, m. 287. Also on the following JUST 1 rolls: Nos. 574, m. 7; 578, m. 11; 652, m. 38; 1089, m. 17.

[25] Cases counted for the plaintiff were found on the following CP 40 rolls: Nos. 69, m. 52d; 109, m. 81; 154, mm. 132, 236d; 171, m. 231d; 183, m. 287.

[26] Taken from CP 40/132-35; see also Flahiff 2. 274 n. 60.

[27] Letton v. Florence, CP 40/300, m. 287; the defendant successfully made his law.

spiritual or secular jurisdiction.[28] Its verdict may often simply have reflected community judgment on the question, and community judgment would of course have been formed as much by the influence of the parish church and by contemporary practice in the ecclesiastical courts as it would have been by the strictest royal view of the matter.

It is rare when one sees this in detail. But in a few cases where juries were questioned by the judge or where their verdict included the finding of facts we can see this community assessment at work, as in a 1296 case in which the jury apparently accepted the defendant's characterization of the underlying plea as involving sacrilege, not trespass,[29] or in a 1300 case from the Common Pleas in which the jury specifically found that the defendant had sued for tithes, not lay debts or chattels.[30]

Whether a plea belonged to ecclesiastical or lay jurisdiction was a question in which quite ordinary people might well have held a strong opinion. Besides their familiarity with ecclesiastical practice, they were often confronted with the same question in local courts. There, without the complicating factor of the royal writ of prohibition, were heard cases in which defendants were prosecuted for suing in Church courts over matters which could have been, and perhaps ought to have been, heard in the courts of manor,[31] borough,[32] or hundred.[33] Much skirmishing over jurisdiction went on at this local level – a

---

[28] See Flahiff 2. 273: 'This time the jury is going to answer directly about the very substance of the plea.' On the general subject see M. S. Arnold, 'Law and Fact in the Medieval Jury Trial: Out of Sight, Out of Mind', *American Journal of Legal History* 18 (1974) 267-80.

[29] St. George v. Prioress of Easebourne, CP 40/113, m. 58.

[30] Rex v. Richard parson of Drayton Beauchamp, CP 40/135, m. 262. A similar case is Rex v. Bray and Brian, CP 40/211, m. 51 (1315), in which the jury returned this verdict: '[P]redictus magister Willelmus non tenuit aliquid placitum in curia christianitatis de laico feodo Willelmi de Bikle nec idem Johannes secutus fuit idem placitum contra prohibicionem regiam. Dicunt enim quod predictus magister Willelmus tenuit quoddam placitum in curia christianitatis de decimis de quadam piro exeuntibus.' Judgment was entered for the defendant; this meant of course that the jury accepted the defendant's characterization of the goods as tithes.

[31] E.g., Wakefield Manor Court Rolls [Yorkshire Archaeological Society, Leeds] Md 225/1341-2, m. 7d (1342): 'Robertus Goldesmith et Willelmus de Sandale attachiati fuerunt ad respondendum Johanni de Gayrgrave de placito quare secuti sunt placitum contra eum in curia christianitatis de debito quod non est de testamento vel matrimonio contra prohibitionem et defensionem ballivorum per quod dictus Johannes suspensus fuit ab ingressu ecclesie.'

[32] E.g., Great Yarmouth Borough Court Records [Norfolk Record Office, Norwich] C4/18, s.d. Monday before Feast of St. Matthew (1297): 'Convictum est per inquisicionem in quam se posuerunt quod Rogerus de Leringsete clericus laboravit et maliciose fecit summoniri Thomam le Warrenner et Caterinam uxorem eius coram officiali Norwic' de debitis et catallis que non sunt de testamento vel matrimonio ad dampnum suum iii s.'

[33] E.g., Milton Hundred Records [P.R.O.] SC 2/181/76, m. 1 (1291): 'Gilbertus persona ecclesie de Milstode attachiatus per plegios quod sit ad proximum hundredum ad respondendum domino rege de placito quare traxit Johannem le Hewe in placitum in curia christianitatis et

fact worth emphasizing because it suggests that prohibition practice in the royal courts operated against a background of local habits and assumptions. The jury verdict was the means by which these were felt.

On the other hand, just as in wager cases, the plea rolls show that steps were taken to minimize the effects of leaving so much discretion in the hands of juries. Actual trials were not always so simple, it appears, as this outline suggests. The plea rolls give evidence of three ways this happened. First is by the introduction of evidence, which we must assume was open to evaluation and comment. The rolls contain references to documents introduced: to examination by the court of the original writ,[34] to inspection of appropriate writs of consultation,[35] and to production of other unspecified 'acts and instruments'.[36] We know also that witnesses were introduced in prohibition cases. The plea rolls record their presence,[37] Bracton mentioned them,[38] and churchmen challenged their suitability.[39] It is a good guess, for instance, that the well-nigh invariable practice of pleading the time and place of delivery of the writ, together with the names of at least two people who had been present,[40] had reference to verification by witnesses to be undertaken at trial. The testimony of two men was a familiar way of proving any fact. Why else were at least two identified men always mentioned in the pleading as having witnessed the crucial delivery if they were not meant to vouch for the fact at trial?

ipsum ibidem implacitavit de hoc quod ipse verberasse debuit quendam Henricum clericum suum.'

[34] E.g., Rex and Edmund earl of Cornwall v. Raymond chaplain of Egloshayle et al., KB 27/43, m. 16 (1279), a prohibition case in which the defendants demurred because the plaintiffs did not produce the writ of prohibition: 'Et predicti Raymundus et alii petunt iudicium si sine brevi originali debeant respondere.'

[35] E.g., Bentele v. Lacy, JUST 1/1089, m. 17 (1293): '... et profert predictam consultacionem que hoc idem testatur ....'

[36] E.g., Rex v. Archbishop of Canterbury and Sardene, CP 40/121, m. 285 (1297): 'Et profert quedam acta et instrumenta iudicialia.' See also the complaint of the clergy that the royal judges were requiring them to produce their *acta* before the royal court so that a decision could be made in prohibition cases (Provincial Council at London, 1257 no. 30 in *Councils and Synods with Other Documents Relating to the English Church II. A.D. 1205-1313. Part I. 1205-1265*, ed. F. M. Powicke and C. R. Cheney (Oxford, 1964), p. 544.

[37] E.g., Clarel v. William parson of Belton, JUST 1/454, m. 22d (1247): 'Et testes quos predictus Willelmus producit versus predictum magistrum Willelmum hoc idem cognoscunt et testificantur.'

[38] Bracton, fol. 410.

[39] See Provincial Council at London, 1257 no. 7, in *Councils and Synods* 1. 538; the clergy complain that they have been put to purgation in prohibition cases 'per testimonium duorum ribaldorum'.

[40] The pleading of delivery 'in the presence of X and Y and of others' was normal, although not absolutely invariable; e.g., Mateschale v. Shropham et al., CP 40/145, m. 152 (six named men); Lucy v. Bishop of Exeter and Briwelon, CP 40/160, m. 203d (no witnesses mentioned); Resham v. Wytham, CP 40/164, m. 66 (eight named men).

Second is the use of pleading containing statements of fact and characterizations of the underlying suit in a form beyond that necessary for framing the general issue. Both plaintiffs and defendants evidently enjoyed considerable freedom to put events and theories on the formal record to accord with their own view of the underlying matter, thus moving beyond the general issue to present each side's case more fully. We cannot speak with assurance about the nature of a medieval trial, but it is at least a reasonable supposition that this pleading was meant to have a use at trial. And when expanded pleading was used, its purpose seems likely to have been either to influence the jury's view of the facts or to invoke the help of the judge in determining the proper scope of ecclesiastical jurisdiction.

For example, a case from 1379: the plaintiff pleaded that the defendant had wrongfully sued him in Court Christian over lay debts and chattels, namely, for £ 10 in damages because the plaintiff had previously accused him of stealing some hay. Defendant answered with his own version of the same facts: he had sued for defamation, but only to clear his name; he had obeyed the writ of prohibition; he had obtained a writ of consultation; it was the plaintiff who had himself appealed to the Court of Arches; the plaintiff who had failed to show that the defendant was guilty of the theft and had been condemned to pay expenses of £ 10 by the ecclesiastical official acting *ex officio* and not at the instance of the defendant. The plaintiff's replication pleaded that the defendant had instigated every part of the prosecution in the Church court, and that the £ 10 represented damages, not expenses.[41]

It is impossible to be sure which side was right in this quarrel, although the jury apparently saw it the plaintiff's way because they brought in a general verdict for him. But the point is that the plea roll here and in like cases contained information which can only have been used to fill out the otherwise blank general issue.[42] It must have been meant for comment by judges and

[41] Colvyll v. Weston, CP 40/477, m. 414d. See the discussion on the general topic in James B. Thayer, *A Preliminary Treatise on Evidence at the Common Law* (Boston, 1898, rpt. 1969), pp. 114-18.

[42] This was perhaps most usual in cases in which the defendant alleged that tithes, not lay chattels, were the subject of the suit in the Church court; e.g., Rex v. Fraunceys, CP 40/164, m. 315 (1307), in which the defendant's answer reads: 'Et bene defendit quod ipse non tenuit aliquod placitum de laicis catallis ipsius abbatis sicut ei imponitur etc. Dicit revera quod quidam Adam de Osegoodby persona ecclesie de Goyngrave traxit predictum abbatem et conventum suum in placitum coram eo in prefata curia christianitatis super quibusdam decimis eidem persone subtractis per ipsum abbatem infra limites predicte ecclesie prout continetur in quodam libello ipsius persone quem profert, et quod quidem placitum post prohibicionem domini regis ei liberatam etc. tenuit ulterius per consultacionem a curia domini regis sibi directam etc. eo quod cognitio decimarum spiritualium etc. spectat ad curiam christianitatis et dum tamen decime ille non excedant quartam partem valoris ecclesie etc. unde dicit quod ipse nullum placitum tenuit de laicis catallis etc.' The issue went to a jury, but no verdict is recorded.

perhaps by the lawyers and for whatever influence a one-sided presentation of the case would have had on a jury.[43]

The third check on jury discretion was the use of detailed verdicts and of interrogatories which judges put to juries in order to clarify the nature of their general verdict. Similar to the detailed questioning of recognitors used in assizes of novel disseisin,[44] this practice evidently resulted from dissatisfaction with the lack of elaboration inherent in the simple 'guilty-not guilty' choice of the general verdict. Thus, for example, when the jury returned a verdict that the defendant had not sued in a Church court over a plea of trespass belonging to king's crown and dignity, the jurors were asked, what was the offense? They said, adultery. The judge then asked, was any money demanded? They said, no. Then, judgment for the defendant was entered.[45] Or, in a case where the attachment on prohibition was against ecclesiastical officials for holding a plea involving an advowson, when the jury found that the defendants had not done so, the judges asked, did the defendants, nevertheless, affix their seal to documents for an appeal to Rome? The jurors said that the officials had, adding that they had delivered the documents to the proctor of one of the parties.[46]

Similar to such questioning were verdicts which contained detail about the nature of the underlying suit in the Church courts, but which still included a general verdict on behalf of the jurors.[47] Not special verdicts in the sense that the jury found only the facts and left the application of legal principles to the judge, these not infrequent entries again suggest a dissatisfaction with the blankness of the general verdict.[48] And as M. S. Arnold has shown in a recent article, even when the plea roll records a simple general verdict, this may conceal greater discussion of fact and law at the trial level.[49] Therefore,

---

[43] See Arnold, 'Law and Fact' (above, n. 28), 274-77.

[44] See Donald W. Sutherland, *The Assize of Novel Disseisin* (Oxford, 1973), pp. 73-74, with citation to primary authorities. Neither this nor the fuller pleading referred to above was, of course, peculiar to prohibition cases. Questions put to the jury were in at least occasional use in trespass and other forms of action; e.g., Lanama v. Prior of St. Swithin, CP 40/92, m. 95 (1291); the jury was questioned about the authenticity of the seal of the Chapter of Winchester Cathedral in an action of debt on an annual rent.

[45] Rex and Faure v. Wynmundham et al., CP 40/105, m. 24 (1294): 'Et quesiti de huiusmodi transgressione etc. dicunt quod de adulterio. Et quesiti si aliquam pecuniam numeratam ab eis peciit dicunt precise quod non. Et ideo consideratum est quod predictus magister Simon eat inde sine die.' A similar example is Rex and Payne v. Leylond et al., CP 40/107, m. 55 (1295).

[46] Lovetot v. Romeyn et al., JUST 1/485, m. 1 (1281). No judgment is recorded on the roll.

[47] E.g., Honylane v. Arderne et al., CP 40/118, m. 68d (1297), a case which combined a detailed verdict with the use of interrogatories.

[48] Examples from the plea rolls: Rex v. Sprete, KB 27/49, m. 41d (1279); Lovetot v. Romeyn et al., JUST 1/485, m. 1 (1281); Rex v. Richard parson of Drayton Beauchamp, CP 40/135, m. 262 (1301); Chyld v. Wramplingham, CP 40/145, m. 279 (1303); Rex v. Bray and Brian, CP 40/211, m. 51 (1315); Hastyng et al. v. Lidgate et al., CP 40/440, m. 531 (1370).

[49] Arnold, 'Law and Fact' (above, n. 28), 273.

although one cannot be certain, probably the trial of many prohibition cases involved a responsibility shared between judge and jury and a use of judicial probing to lay open the facts in each case, with the judges nevertheless allowing (or rather insisting) that the verdict must ultimately be a general one and that the jurors must take responsibility for it.[50]

If this is so, it means that during the first part of the fourteenth century questions about the boundaries between the jurisdiction of Church and State were shared by judges and juries, but that ultimate responsibility fell to juries. This method of decision therefore gave considerable scope to shared community assumptions about the proper jurisdiction of the Church courts, and it did not guarantee that juries would not call close cases in favor of the Church. It could not result in strict vindication of the royal position. And it had the added disadvantage of uncertainty — not being able to predict whether many cases belonged to one forum or the other. That disadvantage, I think, was in part responsible for the shift to the third method of trial and decision, one which took place in the Chancery and which was determined largely by the libel from the Church Courts.

III

TRIAL BY CANONICAL LIBEL IN CHANCERY

During the thirteenth century, as Flahiff showed, writs of prohibition were issued by the Chancery of course, that is at the suit of the Church court defendant 'without any attempt ... to ascertain the true state of affairs.'[51] The new method allowed such an attempt to be made at some stage of Chancery proceedings.[52] It probably grew as part of the procedure for obtaining a writ of consultation.[53] Authorized from at least 1290, this writ allowed a party who

---

[50] E.g., Brun v. Dammas, JUST 1/740, m. 25d (1292), a case involving a writ of prohibition for suing over lay chattels: the jury gave a fairly detailed verdict to the effect that the suit was actually about the abetting of fornication, but the plea roll adds that the jury also found generally that the defendant was not guilty of suing contrary to the prohibition.

[51] Flahiff 2. 233.

[52] Thus the modern doctrine is that although a writ of prohibition is a writ of right, it is not a writ of course. H. R. Curlewis and D. S. Edwards, *The Law of Prohibition at Common Law and under the Justices Act* (London, 1911), pp. 11-12.

[53] See 'Statutum de Consultatione' (1289-90), 1 *Statutes of the Realm* (Record Commission; London, 1810), p. 108. Presumably the practice of issuing such orders antedates the so-called Statute of Consultation, since Bracton mentions the practice of consultation of the royal justices by ecclesiastical judges in cases of doubt. See Bracton, fols. 405b-406. Discussion of the nature of the writ of consultation is found in G. O. Sayles, Introduction to *Select Cases in the Court of King's Bench* 3 (Selden Society 58; London, 1938), pp. lxxiv-lxxv; G. D. G. Hall, Commentary to *Early Registers of Writs*, ed. Hall and Elsa de Haas (Selden Society 87; London, 1970), pp. cxi-cxiv.

had received a writ of prohibition, but believed that the original suit had been properly brought in Court Christian, to go before the Chancellor or Chief Justice, show his libel from the Church court, and upon a favorable ruling obtain a writ of consultation allowing him to proceed. In other words, the procedure authorized a fuller determination in Chancery of the jurisdictional question than had been possible before. Whether it occurred after or at the time the original writ of prohibition was issued, its essence was argument and substantive decision short of a jury trial.

Various sources make clear that decision in Chancery became the normal course in the later medieval period. A Yearbook case of 1422 reports that a plea involving tithes was 'debated at length in the Chancery.'[54] The Parliament rolls of 1414 contain a Commons petition mentioning the need to expedite process in Chancery in disputes over prohibitions and consultations.[55] A prohibition case heard in 1346 contains an order of supersedeas because of reasons proposed in Chancery.[56] An ecclesiastical court record of 1468 contains a prosecution of a litigant for having sent ecclesiastical documents to Chancery for use in a prohibition hearing.[57] And Chancery records themselves include files used in the hearing of prohibition cases.[58]

Probably the clearest piece of evidence of the shift to Chancery is the scarcity of pleaded prohibition cases on the plea rolls during the latter half of the fourteenth century. The new procedure meant that fewer genuinely disputed cases would appear as entries pleaded to issue in the records of the common law courts. More would be decided or settled in Chancery. The plea rolls show that this happened. The Common Pleas roll for Michaelmas term 1301, for example, has nine cases pleaded to issue;[59] the same roll for Michaelmas term 1370 has only one.[60] The change was not sudden or absolute. Throughout the century occasional entries in the old form of attachment on prohibition do

[54] '[U]n prohibitioun fut prie en le chauncerie, et la le mater fut longement debatu' (Y. B. Hil. 9 Hen. V, pl. 5, in *Year Books of the Reign of King Henry the Fifth: Year Books 9-10 Henry V (1421-22)*, ed. R. V. Rogers [1948], p. 46).

[55] The complaint was that the ecclesiastical court judges were refusing to grant a copy of the libel to the party seeking the prohibition (4 *Rotuli parliamentorum* 20a [no. 17]; see also 2 Hen. V, st. 1, c. 3).

[56] CP 40/346, m. 73. See also Prynne's *Records* 3. 1137-38, the record of a plea about the rightful possession of a cross heard before the Chancellor in 1306.

[57] Ex officio c. Thomas at Wode, Canterbury Act book Y.1.11, fol. 7v (1468) [Canterbury Diocesan Archives, Canterbury Cathedral Library].

[58] P.R.O. C 270/27 (temp. Ric. 2-Hen. 6).

[59] CP 40/135, mm. 72d (two cases), 164, 181, 262, 309, 335 (two cases), 363.

[60] Hastyng et al. v. Lidgate et al., CP 40/440, m. 531. I owe the reference to this roll and case to the kindness of Professor William McGovern, who examined it thoroughly. Professor Arnold and Dr. Robert Palmer have also confirmed that their work on fourteenth-century plea rolls substantiates this conclusion.

appear on the plea rolls. But if we think in terms of prevalence, it is clear that most substantive decisions about whether a prohibition lay took place in Chancery.

The result of this change was doubtless to minimize the problem of uncertainty and subjective interpretation inherent in wager and jury trial. However, it did not increase the effectiveness of the writ of prohibition as a curb on ecclesiastical jurisdiction. The Church court records give evidence of no diminution of activity in the disputed areas. In fact they show the reverse.[61] The culprit was, I believe, an unwillingness in Chancery normally to look beyond the ecclesiastical libel in deciding whether or not the prohibition was warranted.[62] And these libels were virtually worthless as indicators of the real nature of many suits in the Church courts. They disguised rather than revealed the underlying facts. The libel in a suit brought to enforce a promise to pay a debt, for instance, typically alleged only that the defendant had incurred the guilt of perjury by violating his oath and asked that he be punished by canonical sanctions for his guilt.[63] Only documents subsequently introduced in Church court practice would show that an ordinary commercial debt lay at the heart of the case.[64] Thus, if the libel alone were regarded, and if the Church were granted *any* jurisdiction over the sin of perjury, it would have been difficult to keep the Church out of cases involving promises to pay lay debts. That is exactly what happened.

This seems very hard to believe. That the royal officers should have hit upon a method for deciding cases of disputed jurisdiction which allowed one side to camouflage the true nature of prohibitable litigation seems unlikely. Even if we take account of possible favoritism by Chancellors who were themselves ecclesiastics, and of the formalism said to be characteristic of the fourteenth and fifteenth centuries,[65] the conclusion at least demands proof. However, there is proof.

For one thing, the records all speak of the libel as determinative. Under the Statute of Consultation, the Chancellor was to issue a writ 'having seen the

---

[61] The point is illustrated graphically in Woodcock. *Medieval Ecclesiastical Courts* (above, n. 4), p. 84.

[62] I am grateful to Mr. J. L. Barton, who first drew my attention to the importance of the libel in prohibition cases.

[63] The libel for a suit to enforce a contract set out in a fifteenth-century English ecclesiastical formulary (London, British Library Royal MS. 11.A.xi. fols. 5v-6), for example, asks only that the defendant be declared and pronounced a violator of his oath and perjuror and consequently be punished by canonical sanctions. It mentions nothing of the actual nature of the underlying contract or specific canonical penalty to be applied.

[64] On the subject generally, see my 'Assumpsit and Fidei Laesio *infra* 263-89.

[65] See Flahiff 2. 231.

libel'.[66] Defendants in common law courts also sometimes pleaded specifically that they had received a writ of consultation by showing their canonical libel in Chancery.[67] Libels with writs of consultation written on the dorse sometimes found their way into evidence in the royal courts,[68] and the Chancery records contain writs of consultation on the same membrane with the libel.[69] If we believe the records, that is, the libel is the document that counted.

Moreover, William Lyndwood, the fifteenth-century English canonist and dean of Arches, a man who must have known, in fact tells us that the method worked to secure ecclesiastical jurisdiction. Compose your libels without demanding payment of the debt, he advises ecclesiastical lawyers, and you will avoid a writ of prohibition — advice incompatible with anything but a procedure normally restricted to examination of the libel.[70] When the Commons complained to the king in 1333 that consultations were being granted all too easily, this procedure very likely lay behind their complaint.[71]

Most importantly, this method of decision fits and explains the circumstantial evidence. The decline in prohibition entries on the plea rolls, the habitual use of uninformative libels by the Church courts, and the ability of those courts to continue hearing cases which might have been prohibited had the facts been fully known, all these are explicable if we give credence to what the records say about the dominant importance of the libel. One need not imagine, of course, that prohibition cases never involved more than a hearing in Chancery based on the libel. That would be to deny the ingenuity and the efforts of litigants and their lawyers. Pleaded prohibition cases do occasionally appear on the plea rolls in the late fourteenth and the fifteenth centuries,[72] and attempts were made to

[66] See 1 *Statutes of the Realm* 108 (above, n. 53).

[67] E.g., Rex et al. v. Barnet et al., CP 40/462, m. 162 (1376): 'Et postmodum idem Robertus accessit ad cancellariam domini regis et monstravit ibidem libellum de prosecutione et habuit ibidem quoddam breve domini regis de consultacione super materia sua predicta.'

[68] E.g., Peres v. Pyrton and Poynz, CP 40/145, m. 135d (1302): 'Et profert quendam libellum qui testatur quod predictus Nicholaus in curia christianitatis, ..., qui quidem libellus consultatione predicta indorsatur et qui testatur quod procedendum est ad cognitionem huiusmodi mortuarii ....'

[69] C 270/27, passim. See also the ecclesiastical record nos. 125-127 (1377), in *John Lydford's Book*, ed. D. M. Owen (London, 1974), pp. 69-70. The libel is included in the consultation.

[70] *Provinciale (seu Constitutiones Angliae)* (Oxford, 1679), p. 315, s.v. 'perjurio': 'Ex praedictis colligi potest Practica libellandi in causa perjurii, ad evitandum prohibitiones regias.'

[71] *Rotuli parliamentorum Anglie hactenus inediti MCCLXXIX-MCCCLXXIII*, ed. H. G. Richardson and George Sayles (Camden Third Series 51; London, 1935), p. 226, no. 9: 'tiels consultacions sont ore grauntez trop legerement.' The petition for a remedy was unsuccessful (ibid., p. 229).

[72] E.g., Cawod v. Stokton, CP 40/464, m. 268 (1376).

circumvent the procedural obstacles of writs of prohibition.[73] As with trial by jury and wager of law, we must speak only of the predominant practice.

That it was the predominant practice, however, is shown also by the end of the story. When a serious attack on ecclesiastical jurisdiction was mounted in the 1490's and early 1500's, it was accomplished not through use of writs of prohibition, but through an expanded use of the Statute of Praemunire.[74] By reading that fourteenth-century statute to apply to Church courts within England as well as the Roman court, litigants brought actions based upon it which allowed them to plead all the facts which had occurred in the Church court. It permitted them to get behind the bare ecclesiastical libel and so put the real nature of the suit before the royal justices. It provided an 'end run' around the writ of prohibition.

IV

CONCLUSION

The necessity for circumventing the writ of prohibition reiterates, therefore, the conclusion drawn from the post-1285 plea rolls: that although the medieval writ of prohibition doubtless kept many litigants from pursuing Church court remedies, its formal availability was never the single determinative factor in deciding jurisdictional questions. Procedural obstacles stood in the way of effective vindication of royal claims. Trial and decision in prohibition cases involved three successive but overlapping methods: wager of law, trial by jury, and determination in Chancery based on the canonical libel. Each of these methods left room for variation, experiment, and argument. But each also contained procedural features which in practice allowed the Church to retain a good bit of jurisdiction denied to it in theory.

[73] E.g., Sturdy v. Richard parson of W., KB 27/393, m. 5 (1358), apparently an attempt to form an action on the case against one alleged to have sued over trespass and felony in a Church court; KB 27/381, Rex. m. 19 (1355), a criminal prosecution against the bishop of Hereford for violating jurisdictional rules in refusing to heed certain writs of prohibition against excommunicating trespassers in his woods and parks. See also Y.B. Mich. 9 Hen. VI, fol. 56, pl. 42 (1430).

[74] See J. H. Baker, Introduction to *The Reports of Sir John Spelman* (Selden Society 94; London, 1978), pp. 66-70; Ralph Houlbrooke, 'The Decline of Ecclesiastical Jurisdiction under the Tudors' in *Continuity and Change. Personnel and Administration of the Church of England 1500-1642*, ed. R. O'Day and F. Heal (Leicester, 1976), pp. 239-57, especially pp. 240-43; R. L. Storey, 'Clergy and Common Law in the Reign of Henry IV' in *Medieval Legal Records Edited in Memory of C.A.F. Meekings* (London, 1978), pp. 347-51; Michael Kelly, *Canterbury Jurisdiction and Influence during the Episcopate of William Warham, 1503-1532*, pp. 100-10 (unpublished Cambridge University Ph. D. thesis, 1964).

Of course, no one would argue that a way around these procedural obstacles was beyond the capacity of medieval men. The study of procedure cannot reveal the underlying reasons that contemporary society found tolerable the situation described in this article. But one cannot help speculating. That an effective curb on ecclesiastical jurisdiction was not found until the end of the medieval period suggests the existence of a widespread but unspoken consensus about the permissible role for the Church courts in medieval society, one wider than the strict royal position allowed.[75] It may have seemed unwise to push royal claims too far.[76] Community acceptance of the place of the ecclesiastical courts and generally shared agreement about the proper jurisdictional boundaries may have stood behind the procedural features which kept the writ of prohibition from being determinative. Theory was not abandoned. None of the methods of proof described involved ideological concessions. But theory was not pushed. A later age would look back, with William Prynne, and conclude that the ecclesiastical courts 'perpetually encroached [and] usurped upon the Temporal Jurisdiction ..., notwithstanding all Regal Prohibitions attachments Informations and Suits against them.'[77] A study of procedure can tell us how this happened. But the unarticulated consensus which made it possible, and even reasonable, we can only dimly perceive.

[75] Donahue, 'Stubbs vs. Maitland' (above, n. 4), 701 concludes that, viewed from the perspective of the ecclesiastical records at York, 'the prohibition system, ..., may be seen as the product of a working, probably tacit, compromise.' See also the remarks of C. R. Cheney, *From Becket to Langton: English Church Government 1170-1213* (Manchester, 1956), pp. 117-18.

[76] See also the warning of Sheehan, 'Canon Law and English Institutions' (above, n. 4), 394: '[T]he mere statement of law is not a satisfactory description of the social situation it regulates.'

[77] Prynne's *Records* 3. 1187-88.

5

WRITS OF PROHIBITION AND ECCLESIASTICAL

SANCTIONS IN THE ENGLISH COURTS CHRISTIAN

In medieval England the writ of prohibition, ancestor of the modern writ used to restrain an inferior court from exceeding its jurisdiction,[1] was most commonly used to restrain the courts of the Church, which administered the great body of canon law and stood independent of the jurisdiction of the King.[2] Prohibitions, normally issued on application to Chancery or the King's Bench, lay where the subject matter of the suit belonged to the "crown and dignity" of the King rather than to the jurisdiction of the spiritual courts.[3]

The writ was necessary because the medieval Church held a wider view of its sphere of subject matter jurisdiction than the King's government would allow. For example, the right to enforce contracts formalized by means of an oath was claimed by the English Church courts.[4] The English common law lawyers denied the claim.[5] They contended that unless the contract re-

---

1. *See generally* F. FERRIS, THE LAW OF EXTRAORDINARY LEGAL REMEDIES §§ 303-41 (1926); J. HIGH, A TREATISE ON EXTRAORDINARY LEGAL REMEDIES §§ 762-804 (2d ed. 1884); J. SHORTT, INFORMATIONS (CRIMINAL AND QUO WARRANTO) MANDAMUS AND PROHIBITION *426-98; Hughes & Brown, *The Writ of Prohibition*, 26 GEO. L.J. 831 (1938); Smith, *The Prerogative Writs*, 11 CAMB. L.J. 40 (1951). There are also several recent and useful articles on the writ in particular American jurisdictions. Boone, *Prohibition: Use of the Writ of Restraint in California*, 15 HASTINGS L.J. 161 (1963); Bosson & Sanders, *The Writ of Prohibition in New Mexico*, 5 N.M.L. REV. 91 (1974); Simko, *Mandamus and Prohibition in Idaho*, 4 IDAHO L. REV. 5 (1967); Note, *The Writ of Prohibition in Missouri*, 1972 WASH. U.L.Q. 511.
2. The most recent writer on English ecclesiastical law takes the position that the modern Church courts retain their independence and are "neither inferior nor superior" to the secular royal courts. E. MOORE, AN INTRODUCTION TO ENGLISH CANON LAW 125-26 (1967).
3. "[A]d coronam et dignitatem nostram." *See, e.g.*, H. BRACTON, DE LEGIBUS ET CONSUETUDINIBUS ANGLIAE, f. 402 (G. Woodbine ed. 1915-42) [hereinafter cited as H. BRACTON].
4. *See* Esmein, *Le serment promissoire dans le droit canonique*, 12 REVUE HISTORIQUE DE DROIT FRANCAIS ET ETRANGER, 3d ser. 248 (1888); Helmholz, *Assumpsit and Fidei Laesio*, infra 263-89.
5. *See* Constitutions of Clarendon, chs. 1, 15, in STUBBS' SELECT

lated to marriage or testaments, the ecclesiastical courts were without jurisdiction. They further insisted that those courts must not deal with lay contracts indirectly, by considering what amounted to a secular cause of action under a spiritual name.[6] Thus, while they admitted that the canon law could punish a man for perjury, they maintained that it had no jurisdiction to compel a man to comply with a simple contract he had sworn to fulfil. If the ecclesiastical court judges heard such suits, they and the party suing could be prohibited from continuing the suit, on complaint of the party aggrieved. And those who violated the writ of prohibition would suffer for it; they would be liable to imprisonment, fine, and (though this seems not to have been available in the earliest days) to damages in favor of the injured party.[7] The writ of prohibition was thus used to determine, and to enforce, the royal view of the proper boundary between the jurisdiction of royal and ecclesiastical courts.

Forty years ago, Professor Norma Adams published an article in this Review, entitled *The Writ of Prohibition to Court Christian.*[8] Professor Adams's article has stood up well in the intervening years, and its conclusions have been widely accepted. It has continued to be used and cited,[9] together with Flahiff's subse-

---

CHARTERS 164, 167 (9th ed. H. Davis 1921); Adams, *The Writ of Prohibition to Court Christian*, 20 MINN. L. REV. 272, 276 (1936) [hereinafter cited as Adams].

6. *See* 2 F. POLLOCK & F. MAITLAND, THE HISTORY OF ENGLISH LAW 201 (2d ed., reissued 1968). English canonists, on the other hand, suggest that such a purely formal variation in the remedy demanded was effective in practice to give the ecclesiastical courts jurisdiction. *See* William of Drogheda, *Summa Aurea*, in 2 QUELLEN ZUR GESCHICHTE DES ROMISCH-KANONISCHEN PROZESSES IM MITTELALTER 65, 67 (L. Wahrmund ed. 1913, reprint 1962); W. LYNDWOOD, PROVINCIALE (SEU CONSTITUTIONES ANGLIAE) 315 s.v. *perjurio* (1679). *See also* 3 ROTULI PARLIAMENTORUM 645-46 (no. 72 1410) [hereinafter cited as W. LYNDWOOD].

7. Adams, *supra* note 6, at 286.

8. Adams, *supra* note 6.

9. *E.g.*, S. Chrimes, *Introductory Essay*, in 1 W. HOLDSWORTH, A HISTORY OF ENGLISH LAW 66 n.8 (1966); F. LOGAN, EXCOMMUNICATION AND THE SECULAR ARM IN MEDIEVAL ENGLAND 88 n.93 (1968) [hereinafter cited as F. LOGAN]; S.F.C. Milsom, *Legal Introduction*, in NOVAE NARRATIONES cxcviii (80 Seldon Society 1963) [hereinafter cited as Milsom]; T.F.T. PLUCKNETT, A CONCISE HISTORY OF THE COMMON LAW 395 n.1 (5th ed. 1956); J. SAYERS, PAPAL JUDGES DELEGATE IN THE PROVINCE OF CANTERBURY 1198-254, 165 n.3 (1971) [hereinafter cited as J. SAYERS]; Dobbs, *The Decline of Jurisdiction by Consent*, 40 N.C.L. REV. 49, 51 n.9 (1961); Donahue, *Roman Canon Law in the Medieval English Church: Stubbs vs. Maitland Reexamined After 75 Years in the Light of Some Records from the Church Courts*, 72 MICH. L. REV. 647, 660 n.64 (1974) [hereinafter cited as Donahue].

quent and more extensive treatment.[10]   However, an important aspect of the topic was not covered by Professor Adams's article, nor have other commentators dealt with it.   This aspect is the receipt of the writ by the courts Christian and their treatment of cases involving conflicting claims to jurisdiction.   We know, it is true, that the bishops complained bitterly about the hardships caused to their courts by what they claimed was excessive use of prohibitions.   Their petitions for change in the system were frequent.[11]   But medieval petitions lent themselves to exaggeration.   Their object was redress of a grievance, not balanced presentation of fact.   A better, though not infallible, guide is provided by regularly compiled court records.   And here Professor Adams's article, like virtually all treatments of the subject, was based exclusively on royal records.[12]   Hence we know much more about the procedure for issuing writs of prohibition than we know about how the ecclesiastical courts reacted to them.   Our knowledge of the working and effectiveness of prohibitions is based on the records of the side that issued them, not on those of the side that received them.   For understanding the realities of legal relations between Church and State in pre-Reformation England, the testimony of both royal and ecclesiastical courts is equally important.[13]

The present article therefore treats writs of prohibition from the perspective of the reactions of the ecclesiastical courts. It is based on examination of most of the surviving records of England's ecclesiastical courts for the period prior to the Reformation.[14]   Unfortunately, only a small portion of these records

---

10.   Flahiff, *The Writ of Prohibition to Court Christian in the Thirteenth Century* (pts. 1 & 2), 6 MEDIEVAL STUDIES 261 (1944) and 7 MEDIEVAL STUDIES 229 (1945) [hereinafter cited as Flahiff].

11.   A comprehensive review is provided by Jones, *Bishops, Politics, and the Two Laws: The Gravamina of the English Clergy, 1237-1399,* 41 SPECULUM 209 (1966).   *See also* D. DOUIE, ARCHBISHOP PECHAM 113-22 (1952).

12.   The two exceptions known to me are B. WOODCOCK, MEDIEVAL ECCLESIASTICAL COURTS IN THE DIOCESE OF CANTERBURY 108 (1952) [hereinafter cited as B. WOODCOCK] and Donahue, *supra* note 9, at 665.

13.   This point is made clearly and at greater length in G. ELTON, ENGLAND, 1200-1640, at 114-15 (1969). For a general survey of the current state of knowledge, see Jones, *Relations of the Two Jurisdictions: Conflict and Cooperation in England During the Thirteenth and Fourteenth Centuries,* 7 STUDIES IN MEDIEVAL AND RENAISSANCE HISTORY 79 (W. Bowsky ed. 1970).

14.   For a summary description of the records and a description of the various types of courts, see D. OWEN, THE RECORDS OF THE ESTABLISHED CHURCH IN ENGLAND EXCLUDING PAROCHIAL RECORDS (1970).   A good example and a description of the records kept by the courts is found

has survived, much fewer than the number of the royal courts'
records. There are enough, however, to yield a significant sample. There are enough examples of prohibitions received and of
cases in which the Church dealt with questions of conflicting
jurisdiction to give some confidence in their representativeness,
even if they constitute only a statistically small part of the total
number of instances which must actually have occurred. Their
study fills out the history of the writ of prohibition and sheds
some new light on the history of legal relations between Church
and State.

I. RECEIPT OF ROYAL WRITS

For purposes of studying receipt of the writ, only cases in
which the Church court records show a prohibition introduced
into actual litigation are included. I have excluded second-
hand sources. For example, records of attachment on prohibitions from the plea rolls of the royal courts are not used. They
invariably suggest disobedience to the royal writ.[15] This, however, was a necessary part of the allegations, without which the
plaintiff could not have brought the action at all. It does not
prove actual disobedience. Also excluded are depositions from
the Church court records[16] and royal writs copied into formu-

---

in Donahue & Gordus, *A Case from Archbishop Stratford's Audience Act
Book and Some Comments on the Book and Its Value*, 2 BULL. MEDIEVAL
CANON L. 45 (1972). Citations to manuscript Church court records are
given hereinafter by diocese, rather than by present record repository.
The diocesan court records used, with corresponding repositories, are as
follows:

Canterbury	Library of the Dean and Chapter, Canterbury, and Lambeth Palace Library, London [Act book MS. 244].
Chichester	West Sussex Record Office, Chichester.
Ely	Cambridge University Library.
Exeter	Devon Record Office, Exeter.
Hereford	Hereford County Record Office, Hereford.
Lichfield	Joint Record Office, Lichfield.
London	Guildhall Library, London [MS. 9064 records] and Greater London Council Record Office [DL/C records].
Norwich	Norfolk Record Office, Norwich.
Rochester	Kent County Record Office, Maidstone.
York	Borthwick Institute of Historical Research [Cause Papers and A B Act Books] and York Minster Library [M 2 (1) Act Books].

15. In an attachment on a writ of prohibition, it was normally alleged that one party delivered the prohibition, but that the other, "spreta
regia prohibicione predicta nichilominus placitum illud ulterius secutus
fuit." *E.g.*, Public Record Office, London [hereinafter cited as P.R.O.]
C.P. 40/330, m. 275d (1342).
16. In a case heard in the Archbishop of Canterbury's Court of

laries or bishops' registers.[17] Some examples found among this excluded evidence have the ring of truth about them.[18] But too many are mere ex parte statements that we cannot verify. Rather than attempt, after centuries have passed, to sort out the reliable from the exaggerated, it seems safer to deal only with receipts of a writ in cases recorded in the regular course of Church court business. The scribe who compiled the court records had no reason to distort the truth. The canon law required that he make a true record.[19] He had nothing to gain by distortion or concealment of the facts.

Under this criterion, Church court records produce 52 cases of royal prohibitions received. They range in date from 1293 to 1501. The largest number come from the courts of two archiepiscopal sees, Canterbury and York. There are 23 cases from the former,[20] 14 from the latter.[21] Six other dioceses are also represented, however: Lichfield with seven;[22] Hereford with three;[23]

Audience and recorded in Canterbury Act book Chartae Antiquae A 36 IV, f. 15v (1340), for example, a witness testified that in a previous case in the same court, the archbishop had delayed the hearing after receipt of a prohibition until he could obtain a writ of consultation allowing the original case to proceed. Since I have been unable to trace the case referred to, I have not counted this instance.

17. Most bishop's registers contain one or more writs of prohibition, but not as a part of records of litigation. *See* 1 I. CHURCHILL, CANTERBURY ADMINISTRATION 528-34 (1933).

18. *E.g.*, 3 BRACTON'S NOTE BOOK, no. 1388 (1220) (F. Maitland ed. 1887), a case in which the defendant admitted continuing the case after receipt of a writ of prohibition, acting on the advice of the papal legate.

19. *Decretales Gregorii IX*, c. *Quonian contra falsam* (X 2.19.11), found in 2 CORPUS JURIS CANONICI, col. 313 (A. Friedberg ed. 1879). For a comment by a medieval canonist on the notary's duty, see, for example, HOSTIENSIS, LECTURA IN LIBROS DECRETALIUM, lib. 3, tit. *ne cler. vel. mon.*, ch. 8 (*Sicut te accepimus*) no. 4 (Venice 1581, f. 181A): "Primo, quod de his quae videbit et audiet et requisitus fuerit sine diminutione veritatis et commixtione falsitatis conficiet instrumentum."

20. Ecclesiatical Suit no. 54 (1293); Act book Lambeth Palace MS. 244, f. 4 (1304); f. 21r (1304); f. 25r (1304); f. 62r (1305); f. 68v (1305); f. 79r (1306); f. 93v (1308); f. 95r (1309); f. 96r (1309); f. 101r (1309); Canterbury Act books Chartae Antiquae II, f. 31r (1329); Chartae Antiquae IV, f. 34r (1340); Y.1.1, f. 40r (1373), f. 73v (1374), f. 75v (1374); Y.1.2, f. 27v (1397), f. 31r (1397), f. 117r (1398); Y.1.3, f. 42r (1418); Y.1.7, f. 156r (1463); Y.1.6, f. 205v (1467); Y.1.13, f. 378v (1483).

21. C[ause] P[apers] E 39 (1339), E 72 (1356), E 172 (1365); Act books M 2(1) b, f. 7r (1371), f. 9v (1371); M 2(1) c, f. 2v (1371), f. 3v (1371), f. 25v (1374); C.P. E 250 1383), E 141 (1385), E 217 (1395); Reg. Bowet I, f. 307r (1411); Act books Cons. A B 1, f. 65r (1418); A B 2, f. 56r (1425).

22. Act book B/C/1/1, f. 60v (1465), f. 161v (1467), f. 222v (1468); f. 252v (1469); B/C/1/2, f. 185r (1475), f. 259v (1476), f. 290r (1477).

23. Act books I/1, 204 (1495), I/2, 17 (1497), 54 (1498).

Rochester with two;[24] and London,[25] Ely,[26] and Bath and Wells[27] with one apiece. These ecclesiastical cases can be broken down by subject matter as follows:

Testamentary	16
Breach of Faith	6
Ecclesiastical Dues	6
Tithe	4
Defamation	4
Annual Pension	4
Spoliation of Benefice	1
Usury	1
Uncertain or Not Stated	10

The number of recorded cases is too small to be conclusive evidence concerning the areas actually in dispute. But, even admitting this, the relatively large number of testamentary causes is noteworthy. It is not surprising. The right of the executor to collect debts owed to the decedent and the right of the decedent's creditors to enforce their claims against the estate were, in the ecclesiastical view, a proper part of probate administration.[28] The Church courts were, therefore, open to suits between executors and debtors and between creditors and executors. Efficient administration required it. The royal courts viewed this as ecclesiastical encroachment on their jurisdiction. The executor should be no better off than the testator would have been himself. The testator, for most obligations, could only have sued at common law.[29] Therefore a prohibition lay to restrain the

---

24. REGISTRUM HAMONIS HETHE, DIOCESIS ROFFENSIS, A.D. 1319-1353, at 943 (1347) (C. Johnson ed. 48 & 49 Canterbury and York Society 1948) [hereinafter cited as REGISTRUM HAMONIS HETHE]; Act book DRb Pa 1, f. 133r (1440).

25. Act book DL/C/1, f. 994 (1501).

26. Act book EDR D/2/1, f. 86v (1378).

27. Act book D/D/C Al, 228, 230 (1461).

28. *See, e.g.,* COUNCILS AND SYNODS WITH OTHER DOCUMENTS RELATING TO THE ENGLISH CHURCH II, A.D. 1205-1313, at 958, 961 (F. Powicke & C. Cheney eds. 1964) [hereinafter cited as COUNCILS AND SYNODS]; Flahiff (pt. 1), *supra* note 10, at 277-79; Jones, *supra* note 13, 169-78. An example from the Church court records of suit brought by an executor is found in Chichester Act book Ep I/10/1, f. 43v (1508): the executor William Coklyn sued Thomas Gylly for 20 measures of barley, "quos debuit dicto defuncto."

29. COUNCILS AND SYNODS, *supra* note 28, at 875-77; ST. GERMAN'S DOCTOR AND STUDENT 232 (T. Plucknett & J. Barton eds. 91 Selden Society 1974). The remedies available at common law and the position taken as to the scope of the writ of prohibition in testamentary cases are slightly more complicated. For fuller accounts, see J. BARTON, ROMAN LAW IN ENGLAND 80-93 (Ius Romanum Medii Aevi V, 13a, 1971); R. GOFFIN, THE TESTAMENTARY EXECUTOR IN ENGLAND AND ELSEWHERE 37-57 (1901); McGovern, *Contract in Medieval England: Wager of Law and the Effect of Death,* 54 IOWA L. REV. 19, 38-48 (1968).

Church courts from giving the executor (or the creditor of the testator) a right that would not have existed had the testator been alive, namely the right to sue in a Church court. The persistence of the Church courts in maintaining their claim throughout the fourteenth and fifteenth centuries, together with the substantial amounts of money which must have been at issue in these cases, helps to explain the preponderance of prohibited testamentary causes.[30] We can only wonder that there were not more.

Equally noteworthy, but in the opposite way, is the small number of cases relating to ecclesiastical patronage. The right to present a cleric to the bishop for induction into a benefice was a valuable right in the Middle Ages.[31] Both canon law and royal law claimed the right to try disputes over it. To the Church it was a spiritual matter, heard under the heading of *jus patronatus*. To the King's court, on the other hand, the advowson, or right to present, was a lay possession. In no area of the law was the theoretical conflict between claims of the canon law and English law clearer,[32] but the number of cases relating to ecclesiastical benefices is very small in the remaining Church court records. Most of those did not encroach directly on the royal right to try all claims relating to advowsons.[33] Historians have generally concluded that the Church tacitly acquiesced in the royal claims to try questions of patronage in later medieval England.[34] The court records involving prohibitions do not contradict this conclusion.

---

30. Note, however, that the Church claimed jurisdiction by English custom, not because the subject matter was inherently spiritual; *see* W. LYNDWOOD, *supra* note 6, at 170 s.v. *insinuationem*. The English Act books also contain occasional testamentary causes remitted to secular tribunals by the Church court judges themselves; *e.g.*, Hereford Act book I/4, 122 (1511): "In causa testamentaria, . . . , iudex licenciavit eosdem ire ad consilium principis et sic partes dimisse [sunt];" Rochester Act book DRb Pa 1, f. 87v (1438): "Remittitur iuri communi;" 4 REGISTERS OF ROGER MARTIVAL, BISHOP OF SALISBURY 1315-1330, at 66-67 (K. Edwards & D. Owen eds. 141 Canterbury & York Society 1973-4).

31. 2 F. POLLOCK & F. MAITLAND, *supra* note 6, at 136-40.

32. Gray, *The ius praesentandi in England from the Constitutions of Clarendon to Bracton*, 67 ENG. HISTORICAL REV. 481 (1952).

33. *See* Donahue, *supra* note 9, at 661-63; O'Day, *The Law of Patronage in Early Modern England*, 26 J. ECCLESIASTICAL HISTORY 274 (1975); Plucknett, *Execrabilis in the Common Pleas: Further Studies*, 1 CAMB. L.J. 60 (1921).

34. *See, e.g.*, W. PANTIN, THE ENGLISH CHURCH IN THE FOURTEENTH CENTURY 86 (1962). The statistics supplied by Flahiff (pt. 1), *supra* note 10, at 310, are also illuminating. An excellent example of the attitude of an English bishop caught between royal and papal claims in matters

The writ of prohibition was introduced at various stages of the proceedings in the Church courts, from immediately after the first appearance by the parties,[35] to after definitive sentence by the judge.[36] When it came seems to have made no difference. This is what English common law would lead one to expect. Since a writ of prohibition was meant to protect the King's interest in his jurisdiction, the claim could not be waived by private parties.[37] They could not validly renounce their right to use the writ. They could not acquiesce in ecclesiastical jurisdiction if the subject matter of the quarrel belonged to royal jurisdiction. Therefore it would have made no difference at what stage of the suit in the Church court the prohibition was produced, and this is what one finds in the Church court records. In fact, we may say that the point of introduction seems dictated by the convenience of the party producing it, and that it had no apparent effect on the way the prohibition was received in the Church courts.

Two other general and useful conclusions can be drawn from this evidence by the legal historian. The first and most evident is the infrequency with which proceedings in the English courts Christian were interrupted by writs of prohibition. The Church courts apparently enforced the canon law unfettered by more than a very occasional prohibition. No precise figure for the total number of cases examined in all diocesan courts can be given. But it runs into several thousands. A total of 52 prohibited cases is a minute percentage of the total. To take a specific example, of the 102 cases heard in the diocesan court at Lichfield in 1476 only one was prohibited.[38] Of the slightly fewer than 300 cases recorded in the first court book from Bath and Wells, only one was subject to a recorded writ of prohibition.[39] Many, in fact most, of the remaining court Act books contain no recorded prohibitions at all.[40] The great legal historian F.W. Maitland described writs of prohibition as "always buzzing about the ears

---

of the patronage of ecclesiastical benefices is found in 10 REGISTRUM ROBERTI WINCHELSEY 1044-46 (R. Graham ed. 114 Canterbury & York Society 1942).

35. *E.g.*, Canterbury Act Book, Y.1.1, f. 31r (1397).
36. *E.g.*, York, C.P. E 72 (1356).
37. H. BRACTON, *supra* note 3, at f. 401b. *See also* Adams, *supra* note 5, at 283. *But cf.* Dobbs, *supra* note 9.
38. Act book B/C/1/1; the prohibited case is at f. 259v.
39. *See* Dunning, *The Wells Consistory Court in the Fifteenth Century*, in 106 PROCEEDINGS OF THE SOMERSETSHIRE ARCHAELOGICAL & NATURAL HISTORY SOCIETY 46, 55 (1962); note 27 *supra*.
40. *See generally* B. WOODCOCK, *supra* note 12, at 108.

of the ecclesiastical judges."[41] This description seems exaggerated.

It is certainly true, however, that not all writs of prohibition that were issued would find their way into the Church court records surveyed here. The writ did not have to be delivered in court to be effective.[42] It might be handed over to the judge and the opposing litigant out of court. And even if it were delivered in open court, we cannot be sure that the prohibition would have been mentioned specifically in the records. We may have, therefore, only a small sample of the total number of prohibitions actually used. On the other hand, there was no good reason for the scribe in the Church court to have omitted notation of the receipt of a prohibition. The fact that sometimes the introduction of the writ was recorded, coupled with the sheer volume of cases which were subject to being prohibited but which were in fact heard in the Church courts, does suggest strongly that writs of prohibition to the ecclesiastical courts were not frequently used. If this is so, the importance of prohibitions in daily practice was less than has been assumed.

The second conclusion to be drawn from the cases of receipt of prohibitions, to some extent inconsistent with the first, is that although there may not have been many prohibitions received and recorded, they were effective when used. When the writs were introduced, they were obeyed. Of the 52 cases noted above, not one was continued in the Act book after receipt of the prohibition. The case thereafter disappeared from the records. The court scribe made no entry in the case after introduction of the writ. Sometimes he made a marginal note—*prohibitum est*[43] or *prohibitio*[44]—to indicate the receipt of the writ. Other times he indicated the fact by a similar note in his record of the substance of the case.[45] In either situation, the following sessions of the court did not take up the prohibited case. It was dropped.

In a few of these 52 cases, the scribe made more than a summary record of the action taken by the judge in response to the prohibition. That action was never disobedience to the royal

---

41. 2 F. POLLOCK & F. MAITLAND, *supra* note 6, at 200.

42. At least in the thirteenth and early fourteenth centuries, however, it had in fact to be delivered somewhere. *See* Milsom, *supra* note 9, at cc. For a printed case in which the place of delivery was different from the ecclesiastical consistory, see Clerbek v. Lincoln, 26 Selden Society 98 (1301).

43. *E.g.*, Lichfield Act book B/C/1/1, f. 60v (1465).

44. *E.g.*, Canterbury Act book Lambeth MS. 244, f. 21r (1304).

45. *See, e.g.*, Donahue, *supra* note 9, at 669-70.

writ. For example, at Hereford in 1498, the scribe noted in one such instance that "the judge, having read the prohibition, desisted in the cause."[46] In a tithe case heard at Canterbury in 1373, when the judge received a writ of prohibition, he "declared that he was unwilling to proceed in the cause."[47] The judge of the diocesan court of Bath and Wells received a royal prohibition in a suit heard in 1461; the court scribe noted that the judge "was willing to comply with it in every particular."[48]

The ecclesiastical attitude towards the royal writs is particularly revealed by a case heard in 1306 before the Archbishop of Canterbury's Court of Audience. There were several defendants in the case. Some, but not all, of them delivered a writ of prohibition to the judge. He desisted as to those in whose name the prohibition ran. He proceeded as to the rest.[49] The judge would not extend the coverage of the writ of prohibition to all the defendants. But he would not violate it. The closest any of the 52 cases comes to suggesting disobedience to the royal writ is one from 1418 in which the record notes that one party delivered the writ. The court took no formal action against the defendant after he had delivered the writ, but the scribe noted that "nevertheless before his departure a compromise was reached."[50] Other than this, all the recorded writs were apparently effective.

One of the possible reasons that the writs of prohibition were so uniformly obeyed is that there was an avenue of redress for their misuse under English common law. If the prohibition had been wrongly obtained, the plaintiff in the court Christian could

---

46. Act book I/2, 54: "Dicta pars rea inhibuit iudici et exhibuit quandam prohibicionem impetratam a skaccario domini regis. Et iudex lecta prohibicione cessavit in causa." A similar entry in a prohibited case heard after the Act of Supremacy in 1535 is slightly, but not greatly, different. Act book I/6, 67 (1536): ". . . breve regium nobis prius exhibitum et transmissum, ob cuius reverenciam dicto breve prius perlecto iudex distulit et supersedebat."

47. Act book Y.1.1, f. 40r: the defendant, "porrexit unam regiam prohibicionem propter quam commissarius predictus protestabatur se nolle ulterius procedere in causa."

48. Act book D/D/C Al, 228: "Quo die adveniente prefatus dominus officialis recepit regiam prohibicionem pro eadem causa cui parere in omnibus voluit ut asseruit."

49. Act book Lambeth MS. 244, f. 79r: "Et demum quadam prohibicione pro Waltero Kough et Johanne filio et executore Walteri Kough in iudicio porrecto, unde decretum est quod supersedeatur in negocio memorato quo ad personas prenominatas et prefigimus aliis partibus terminum ad faciendum super excepcione proposita quod erit iustum."

50. Act book Y.1.3, f. 42r: "Ricardus Leek de parochia de Petham porrexit domino commissario unam prohibicionem in quadam causa

obtain a writ of consultation.[51]   Upon application to the royal
courts, and upon a showing that the true nature of the dispute
was within ecclesiastical cognizance, the aggrieved party could
obtain an order permitting the ecclesiastical judge to take up the
case again and the suit would proceed despite the prohibition.
Six of the 52 cases contain some kind of a reference to the pro-
curement of a writ of consultation. The records in three of these
cases demonstrate actual introduction of the writ.[52]   The records
in the other three merely indicate that one would probably be
sought, as in a case heard at Ely in 1378 in which the court scribe
recorded, "therefore we decree that the [cause] is to be suspended until we can obtain a consultation."[53]   These six cases
show, as does the aggregate of the 52, apparent obedience to the
royal writs and a willingness to accept the common law rules
rather than to attack them. To apply for a writ of consultation
was to work within the system of royal law. If it is true, as
suggested above, that writs of prohibition were infrequently introduced, it is not because they were disregarded by the Church
courts.

II. ECCLESIASTICAL SANCTIONS

The impression of ecclesiastical acquiescence in the claims of
the royal courts conveyed by the Church courts' reactions to royal
prohibitions is not, however, a complete picture. It is not wholly
accurate to say that the prelates were reduced to supplication
of the King for redress of their complaints about lay incursions
on ecclesiastical jurisdiction.[54]   The records of the Church courts
show that they had weapons of their own in the disputed areas
of jurisdiction.   Those weapons, although "purely spiritual" in
character, continued to be useful in the centuries prior to the

---

fidei lesionis et perjurii inter dominum Hugonem Mavys et ipsum; tamen
ante recessum eius a consistorio concordatum est cum parte et pars rea
est absoluta et dimissa."
    51. *See* Stat. Consultation, 18 Edw. I in 1 STATUTES OF THE REALM
108; 1 W. HOLDSWORTH, *supra* note 9, at 229.
    52. Canterbury Act book Y.1.13, f. 378v (1483); York C.P. E 141
(1385); York Reg. Bowet I, f. 307r (1411). Another instance, taken from
an actual case, is found in JOHN LYDFORD'S BOOK 69 (D. Owen ed. 1974).
    53. Act book EDR D/2/1, f. 86v: "Porrecta est regia prohibitio ideo
decernimus fore suspendendum quousque consultationem poterimus op-
tinere." The other two instances are found in Canterbury Ecclesiastical
Suit Roll, no. 54 (1293) and Act book Y.1.1, f. 40r (1373).
    54. *See, e.g.,* Jones, *supra* note 11, at 239. For the somewhat paral-
lel situation in France, see O. MARTIN, L'ASSEMBLEE DE VINCENNES DE
1329 ET SES CONSEQUENCES 172-74 (1909).

Reformation. There was, in other words, a positive defense of ecclesiastical claims to jurisdiction. The defense was not made by a direct attack on royal prohibitions. No spiritual sanctions were invoked against the King's government or the justices of the royal courts. But spiritual sanctions were invoked against those who *used* the machinery made available by royal courts. They were applied against litigants rather than against the Crown. It is doubtful, admittedly, that the existence of these sanctions can completely explain the infrequency of prohibited cases in the Church court records. But at least we are in a better position to assess the place of the writ in Church-State relations if we examine them.

It has long been recognized that the canon law contained penal sanctions against those who used secular power to hinder the Church from exercising its jurisdiction. Most notably in England, Archbishop Boniface's Council of Lambeth in 1261 promulgated a series of constitutions against lay encroachment on spiritual jurisdiction.[55] Not much attention has been paid to the effect of these measures in practice. It is true that the Pope, acting at the urgent request of Henry III, refused to confirm them.[56] Moreover, the English canonist William Lyndwood (d. 1446) later commented that they "were but little observed."[57] These facts, together with exclusive reliance on royal court records, have led some modern writers to disregard the penal sanctions.

However, as Professor Cheney has pointed out, the English constitutions defending the ecclesiastical jurisdiction did not need papal approval to be valid.[58] It is even possible that Lyndwood's remark meant only that the penalties actually used in practice were taken not from Archbishop Boniface's constitutions, but from the similar statutes of Archbishop John Stratford (d. 1348)[59] and from the law of the entire Western Church found

---

55. Councils and Synods, *supra* note 28, at 659-84.
56. *Id.* at 686. *See generally* O. Pontal, Les Statuts Synodaux 50 (Typologie des Sources du Moyen Age Occidental A-III.1 1975); Cheney, *Legislation of the Medieval English Church* (pt. 2) 50 Eng. Historical Rev. 385, 402-06 (1935); Jones, *supra* note 13, at 215.
57. W. Lyndwood, *supra* note 6, at 92 s.v. *contingit.* Maitland went too far, I believe, in suggesting that these were "useless canons," and that "the battle had been decided." *See* F. Maitland, *Church, State and Decretals,* in Roman Canon Law in the Church of England 61 (1898, reprint 1968).
58. *See* Councils and Synods, *supra* note 28, at 662.
59. 2 D. Wilkins, Concilia Magnae Britanniae at Hiberniae 702-09 (1737).

in the *Corpus Juris Canonici.*[60]   The Church court records suggest this possibility. Whenever they contain explicit reference to the source of the penalty it is to one of Stratford's statutes, called *Accidit novitate perversa,*[61] or to a canon found in Gratian's *Decretum* called *Si quis suadente.*[62]   Lyndwood included the former in his collection with no qualification on its usage. Thus, although the constitutions of Archbishop Boniface may not have been used in practice, their purpose was served by the use of other similar sanctions.   The Church courts were willing to take positive steps to enforce at least part of the canonical view of the jurisdictional boundary.   Evidence of effectiveness is difficult to assess.   But it would not be accurate to treat the disciplinary rules of the Church as a dead letter.   The court records suggest a continuing, sophisticated, and serviceable series of actions available to defend the ecclesiastical position.

The sanctions as enforced in the Church courts can be divided into two classes: first, disciplinary proceedings against parties who used the machinery of the secular courts, including writs of prohibition, to impede an ecclesiastical cause or judgment, and second, prosecution of persons who brought suits in the secular courts which belonged, because of their subject matter, to the Church courts.   The surviving records reveal a greater number of examples of the first practice than of the second. Most were brought ex officio.   That is, the ecclesiastical court itself prosecuted the suit.   They were sometimes brought specifically under the provincial constitution *Accidit novitate perversa* referred to above,[63] sometimes under the general rubric of con-

---

60. For brief descriptions of the standard corpus of the canon law, see R. MORTIMER, WESTERN CANON LAW 40-55 (1953); Donahue, *supra* note 9, at 648-49, nn. 10-14.

61. *E.g.*, Hereford Act book I/4, 104 (1510), in which Llewellyn ap Rees admitted to having caused the arrest of William Watkyns in a secular court because Watkyns had cited him before an ecclesiastical tribunal. The official of the diocesan court at Hereford then declared officially that Rees had incurred the "penam constitutionis que sic incipit *accidit novitate perversa.*"   Rees asked to be absolved and swore to obey the dictates of the canon law.   The constitution referred to is given by W. LYNDWOOD, *supra* note 7, at 260 and D. WILKINS, *supra* note 59, at 707.

62. *E.g.*, Exeter Act book Chanter MS. 776 s.d. 22 June 1518, in which William Blakmore was cited, "ad dicendam causam quare non debeat declarari pro excommunicato pro eo quod inciderit in canonem *si quis suadente* etc."   He submitted to the court.   The canon excommunicated those who "laid violent hands" on a cleric and was therefore appropriately used only in cases where the complainant was a cleric and there had been force.   It is found in the *Decretum Gratiani* (C. 17 q. 4 c. 29) 1 CORPUS JURIS CANONICI, *supra* note 19, at col. 822.

63. *See* note 61 *supra* and accompanying text.

tempt,[64] sometimes without any special designation.[65] All were aimed at disciplining the party who had made use of the secular legal process. All were aimed at undoing its effects. For example, at Rochester in 1321, Henry de Elham was cited for having laid violent hands on a cleric and for having made use of a royal prohibition in the dispute with him. Elham submitted to the judgment of the court, swore never to use a prohibition in an ecclesiastical cause again, and agreed to pay the aggrieved cleric four marks for the expenses he had incurred in the matter.[66] In 1443 at York, Cecelia Jackson appeared before the auditor of the Dean and Chapter to answer for having "impeded the ecclesiastical jurisdiction by arresting and unduly vexing by the temporal law" a certain Robert Clyse. Jackson "submitted herself to penance to be awarded and to the grace" of the court.[67] At Canterbury in 1399, Thomas Felton was summoned before the Church court and charged with interfering with its jurisdiction by using the secular courts to trouble the vicar of Eastchurch. Felton confessed and abjured further interference under penalty of 20 shillings.[68]

It is unfortunate that good statistics cannot be given for the number of these cases. The incomplete contemporary records of the Church's ex officio jurisdiction make it impossible to give any reliable figures. Most entries in the Act books state merely that a person was disciplined for wrongfully interfering with the jurisdiction of the ecclesiastical courts. Such entries sometimes mean no more than that the person involved had forcibly prevented the court's summons from being delivered.[69] We simply

---

64. London Deposition book DL/C/206, ff. 171r-173r, called *negotium contemptus.*

65. *E.g.,* Canterbury Act book Y.1.4, f. 98 (1422) in which John Odle was cited "super eo quod arrestavit sive arrestari procuravit rectorem de Hamme pro eo quod ipse rector prosequebatur dictum Johannem in curia christianitatis." Compare an entry in the same Act book, at f. 93r (1422), in which John Ashelsted was summoned to show cause why he should be declared to have incurred "penam illius constitutionis *accidit novitate perversa* pro eo quod fecit Thomam Ketyng arrestari." The Act book does not indicate why reference was made to the constitution in one instance but not in the other.

66. REGISTRUM HAMONIS HETHE, *supra* note 24, at 214-15.

67. Act book D/C A B 1, f. 104r. There is a printed example in W. HALE, A SERIES OF PRECEDENTS AND PROCEEDINGS IN CRIMINAL CAUSES, 1475-1640, at 32 (1973).

68. Act book Y.1.2, f. 131v.

69. York Act book D/C A B 1, f. 42r (1408), in which the accusation was that the defendant "insultum fecit Ricardo Lychefeld mandatorio venerabilis capituli pro eo quod idem Ricardus ipsum dominum Willelmum (the defendant) citavit, ipsumque Ricardum insequebatur cum arco

do not know, in many cases, if the interference involved the use of secular legal process. Sometimes we can be sure. Some of the entries specifically mention that there had been attachment or arrest by royal officials,[70] or that a writ of *capias* or prohibition had been used,[71] or that chattels claimed in an ecclesiastical suit had been seized by royal officers.[72] More often, however, we cannot tell.

It is also difficult to ascertain the way in which the disciplinary cases came to the attention of the judges in the ecclesiastical courts. Most prosecutions probably depended on a complaint, perhaps no more than an informal notice, given by the party against whom secular process had been invoked. In form and in theory the ecclesiastical proceedings were carried out ex officio, that is, at the suit of the judge.[73] No private party sued, but there must have been some way of bringing the matter before the judge. It is natural to think that it was done by one of the litigants, and that is what the records from the royal courts suggest. Occasionally the Church court records are full enough to suggest the same thing, as in a London prosecution from 1471 in which the case was dismissed when the parties involved reached an agreement.[74] Most of the records, however,

---

tenso et sagittis ac ad ipsum sagittavit." William confessed the attack, but alleged that he had mistaken Richard for someone else.

70. *E.g.*, Hereford Act book I/1, 75 (1493): "[P]rocuravit ipsum attachiari;" Canterbury Act book Y.1.3, f. 41v (1417): "[P]rocuravit dictum rectorem arestari." In the margin beside one such case, found in Canterbury Act book Y.1.5, f. 65r (1454), is a large hand pointing to the case. It was drawn by Francis Aldrich, registrar of the court in the late sixteenth century, evidently to support the post-Reformation court's claims to authority. I owe the identification of the scribe to Dr. William Urry, Reader in Paleography at the University of Oxford.

71. Canterbury Act book Chartae Antiquae A 36 IV, f. 90v (1347): "[I]mpetravit unum breve vocatum capias nomine vicarii;" Rochester, REGISTRUM HAMONIS HETHE, *supra* note 24, at 943 (1347): "[I]ncidisse in sentenciam excommunicationis majoris a jure latam, eo quod quandam regiam prohicitionem ad impediendum jurisdiccionem ecclesiasticam . . . impetrasti."

72. Rochester Act book DRb Pa 2, f. 108r (1439), in which the defendant was cited for causing the seizure of the horse of Richard Frowde because of a cause under litigation in the consistory court. In Canterbury Sede Vacante Scrapbook II, 71 (1294), the chattels at issue were alleged to be part of a legacy, and thus subject to the Church's jurisdiction. The defendant was alleged to have "caused them to be distrained by a lay court."

73. *See* A. LEFEBVRE-TEILLARD, LES OFFICIALITES A LA VEILLE DU CONCILE DE TRENTE 79-81 (1973); 8 J. WIGMORE, EVIDENCE IN TRIALS AT COMMON LAW § 2250 (McNaughton rev. ed. 1961); B. WOODCOCK, *supra* note 12, at 93-102.

74. Act book MS. 9064/1, f. 58v.

tell us nothing. The source and the factual details behind these
prosecutions are too often obscure. What *is* clear is their existence. Their use in practice as a means of defending the Church's
view of its jurisdiction is not open to doubt.

The principal remedy available under these ex officio proceedings was to require the person summoned to desist from
impeding the suit pending in the ecclesiastical court. That meant,
in a normal case, stopping the secular law suit. An order,
we may even say an injunction, "not to vex"[75] or "not to prosecute"[76] in the secular forum was therefore issued by the ecclesiastical judge. The offending litigant often took an express oath
to obey the injunction or to renounce further use of the secular
courts.[77] In appropriate cases the litigant was also obliged to
pay the expenses incurred by the person injured by the suit in
the royal courts.[78] Or he might have to undergo public penance.
That meant a public whipping, or marching barefoot and dressed
in penitential clothes in the parish procession before high Mass.[79]
Assessment of the appropriate penalty lay in the discretion of
the judge, and practice seems to have varied.[80] The essential
element, however, was to force the guilty party, under penalty

75. *E.g.*, Canterbury Act book Y.1.10, f. 314r (1477): "Deinde iudex
monuit dictum Thomam sub pena excommunicacionis quod non vexeret
ipsum in curia temporali."
76. *E.g.*, Norwich Act book ACT/1 s.d. 12 November 1509: "Dominus iniunxit Thome Balle de Bettler quod non prosequatur aliquam
accionem in curia seculari contra Gregorium Burnell . . . sub pena
excommunicacionis."
77. *E.g.*, Hereford Act book I/4, 104 (1510): "Et prestitit iuramentum de parendo iuri." *See also* J. SAYERS, *supra* note 9, at 255-57; Adams,
supra note 5, at 283 n.43.
78. Canterbury Act book Y.1.1, f. 105r (1375) (one mark expenses);
REGISTRUM HAMONIS HETHE, *supra* note 24. at 215 (four marks, reduced
from the eight claimed).
79. *E.g.*, York Act book D/C A B 1, f. 104r (1443): "Quo sic facto
dominus auditor iniunxit eidem quod tansiet coram processione in ecclesia cathedrali Ebor' per duos dies dominicales nudis tibiis et pedibus
tunicaque sua singulari induta more penitentiali, necnon cotidie in eadam
forma circa ecclesiam parochialem de Cave predicta." This penance was,
however, remitted *ex gratia*.
80. *See, e.g.*, JOANNES ANDREAE, NOVELLA COMMENTARIA IN LIBROS
DECRETALIUM, lib. 5, tit. *de poen. et remis.*, c. 3 (*Significavit*) (Venice
1581, f. 123): "Consideratis circunstantiis arbitraria poenitentia impone-
tur." With the penance mentioned in the text accompanying note 67 *supra*, compare a case recorded in Canterbury Act book Chartae Antiquae
A 36 II, f. 5r (1329); the offender was obliged to approach the shrine of
St. Thomas of Canterbury six times and make an offering of a candle of
a certain value. *See also* AN EPISCOPAL COURT BOOK FOR THE DIOCESE OF
LINCOLN, 1514-1520, at xv (M. Bowker ed. 61 Lincoln Record Society
1967).

of major excommunication, to undo the effects of his invocation of the secular jurisdiction to thwart proceedings in the ecclesiastical court.

The existence of these ecclesiastical sanctions and the use which the Church court records show was made of them in pre-Reformation England help to explain an apparent inconsistency in the record evidence. That is the disparity between the way writs of prohibition were actually treated in the Church courts and the way one finds them *described* as being treated in the plea rolls of the royal courts. No allegation appears more regularly on the plea rolls in cases involving prohibitions than disobedience to the writ.[81] The canon law judges were said to have spurned it. They "made light of" the royal writ. They "tore it up." They "threw it to the ground." They "fulminated" sentences of excommunication against the party introducing the writ.[82] The Church court records say just the opposite. They show that officials of the ecclesiastical courts obeyed writs of prohibition. This apparent inconsistency may be explained in some cases by the "two-stage" nature of the ecclesiastical reaction to the writs; that is, compliance with the writ, coupled with giving the party harmed the opportunity, in a separate hearing, to seek discipline in personam against the person who sued out the secular process. In the plea rolls, the two parts were alleged together. The "two-stage" ecclesiastical reaction was treated as a single transaction. Indeed its ultimate effect was single. If the evidence of the Church court records is considered in its entirety, the secular plea rolls may give an accurate picture of the reality.

The second situation in which the ecclesiastical courts acted affirmatively to defend their jurisdiction involved prosecutions brought against litigants who initiated in secular courts suits which belonged (according to the canonical view) to spiritual ju-

81. *E.g.*, P.R.O. C.P. 40/346, m. 73 (1346): "[E]t ipsum Ricardum causa liberacionis brevium predictorum excommunicavit;" C.P. 40/150, m. 25d (1304): "[D]ictum breve regium postquam illud admiserat a se contemptabiliter proiecit et illud inspicere vel a prosecutione sua in placito predicto . . . desistere penitus recusavit in Regis contemptum manifestum."

82. *E.g.*, P.R.O. C.P. 40/149, m. 195 (1304): "[C]um idem Henricus breve regium de prohibitionis ex parte domini Regis eidem Rogero porrexit . . . idem Rogerus mandatum Regis perinpendens in hac parte breve illud fregit et dilasteravit et ad terram proiecit et in ipsum Henricum racione brevis Regis sibi porrecti sentenciam excommunicationis sepius fulminavit et nichilominus placitum illud tenuit in curia Christianitatis."

risdiction. The offense alleged was not interference with an existing cause in the Church courts. It was suing in the wrong court. These prosecutions represent a rough ecclesiastical equivalent of royal writs of prohibition. For example, at Canterbury in 1456 Thomas Gylnot was summoned before the diocesan court "because he initiated and prosecuted a certain testamentary cause which belongs to the ecclesiastical forum in a secular court."[83] At York a prosecution was brought against a defendant because he had "impleaded [a cleric] in a secular court about a covenant breached [concerning] tithes."[84] In 1342 William Orable was prosecuted for withholding tithes and also for threatening to sue for the chattels involved in a secular forum.[85]

The result of such a prosecution was basically no different from that which followed most ex officio prosecutions for using the secular courts to impede ecclesiastical jurisdiction. In the 1456 case from Canterbury, for instance, Gylnot was ordered to withdraw the suit from the secular court under pain of excommunication and was directed to pay the other party's expenses.[86] Again it is impossible to tell how most of the cases came to the attention of the ecclesiastical court, except to suppose that many were initiated by a private complaint. In one case in 1471 the record specifically noted that the suit was prosecuted at the promotion of the monks of St. Augustine's Abbey, who were probably originally sued in the secular forum.[87]

It is worth pointing out that these ex officio prosecutions were far more efficient than royal writs of prohibition. The ef-

---

83. Act book Y.1.5, f. 109v: "Thomas Gylnot de parochia de Faversham ad dicendam causam quare puniri et excommunicari non debeat pro eo quod ipse Thomas Gylnot quandam causam testamentariam et ecclesiasticam que ad forum ecclesiasticum pertinet in foro seculari agite et prosequitur."

84. York Act book D/C A B 1, f. 13v (c. 1400): "[I]mplacitavit dictum dominum Johannem in curia seculari super convencione huiusmodi per ipsum dominum Johannem violata pro eo quod certas oves ad decimam quadragesimalem pertinencias . . . in curia seculari predicta obtinuit et recuperavit."

85. Canterbury Act book Chartae Antiquae A 36 IV, f. 57r: "Willelmus Orable parochianus dicte ecclesie de Cranebrok denegat solvere decimam silve sue cedue . . . asserens se velle fatigare abducentes huiusmodi decimas in foro seculari." He submitted and swore not to "fatigare" the vicar and to pay arrearages.

86. Note 83 *supra*: "Fatetur quod prosequitur et habet ad subtrahendum causam a curia seculari sub pena excommunicationis et satisfaciendum expensis." These expenses were taxed at 2s.

87. Canterbury Act book Y.1.11, f. 123v: "Johannes Pocul de Chartham notatur quod violavit libertates ecclesiasticas in tantum quod initiavit accionem spiritualem in temporalem; citat' per Nedam ad promocionem abbatis et conventus sancti Augustini."

fectiveness of the royal courts was considerably hindered by the procedure used there. Professor Adams' Article details the difficulties. For example, if the writ prohibited a plea of debt, whereas the real cause of action involved theft of chattels, a different but equally secular plea, the writ availed nothing.[88] There were many other such difficulties.[89] The ecclesiastical prosecution did not labor under them. It did not require delivery of a writ correctly describing the prohibited action. Its outcome did not depend on the vagaries of wager of law or jury trial. Rather, it was brought under a procedure which allowed the judge to interrogate the accused under oath to discover what he had done. If it turned out that the accused had brought a suit belonging to ecclesiastical jurisdiction in the royal courts, he had to withdraw it or suffer excommunication.

Even with these procedural advantages, however, the evidence of the court records suggests that this second sort of ecclesiastical sanction was not used as frequently as the first. There are fewer cases of ecclesiastical prosecution for bringing a spiritual plea in the secular court than there are prosecutions for using secular process to impede a case pending in the Church courts. There are more receipts of royal prohibitions recorded than there are instances of its spiritual counterpart. Those in which the subject matter is recorded cover only the tithe and testamentary causes. This suggests that if a litigant chose to bring a case involving a benefice or contract in the royal court, the ecclesiastical courts would not excommunicate him for doing so.[90] The Church courts might entertain such actions. They would not, in practice, interfere if a litigant went to the royal court instead.[91] Compared to the immediate problems raised by

---

88.   *See* Adams, *supra* note 5, at 283 n.49.

89.   *Id.* at 277-85; Flahiff (pt. 2), *supra* note 10, at 249-74. *But cf.* Milsom, *supra* note 9, at cc.

90.   A preliminary sample of cases on the late medieval royal court plea rolls also suggests that where any interference by canon law courts with royal court jurisdiction over advowsons was alleged, the interference was usually alleged to have taken place at the Roman court, not in England. *E.g.,* P.R.O. K.B. 27/342, Rex m. 29 (1345), in which the prebend of Hovedon was at issue, and in which it was alleged that James Multon, "machinans iudicium predictum in curia Regis predicta rite redditum et eius executionem enervare, . . . traxit in placitum extra regnum Regis Anglie et adhuc trahit in Regis contemptum ac iuris corone Regis Anglie preiudicium." *See generally* HEMINGBY'S REGISTER 14-36 (H. Chew ed. 18 Wiltshire Archaeological and Natural History Society, Records Branch 1962).

91.   *See* F. MAITLAND, *supra* note 57, at 64-65. The position taken

interference with suits already in ecclesiastical hands, this may have seemed a lesser problem. It was more theoretical, a matter of ideology, while interference with pending suits kept justice from being done. We can say only that there was a possibility of prosecution of litigants who brought in a secular court cases thought to belong in the ecclesiastical forum. How effective that possibility was in deterring litigants from doing so is a matter of speculation.

III. CONCLUSION

A summary of the evidence taken from the records of the Church courts relating to conflicts of jurisdiction is easily made. The canon law did not oppose the commands of royal justice directly. The Church courts obeyed a writ of prohibition when they received one. They did not excommunicate the King or his judges for hearing cases which belonged, according to the canon law, to spiritual jurisdiction. They did not impose interdicts on the lands of the King.[92] They did, on the other hand, make available remedies operating in personam against litigants who used the secular courts to interfere with the exercise of canonical jurisdiction.

We might analogize the situation to Chancery procedure where common law and equity conflicted. That is, Chancery made no attack on the common law rules. The Chancellor would not attempt to keep the common law judges from enforcing the restrictive rules of that law. He would, however, enforce a supplementary system which imposed a duty on one who sought to take advantage of a common law rule in order to work injustice.[93] Something like the same thing happened in the Church courts. A litigant might make use of the royal courts, but if he did so to frustrate justice as administered in the ecclesiastical courts, he could be proceeded against independently. He faced the added burden of excommunication. The effect of imposing this

---

by the French *Parlement* was analogous; *see* O. MARTIN, *supra* note 54, at 237-40.

92. An interdict was an order suspending participation in the sacraments by all Christians in a given area. It was subject, however, to a number of special rules and exceptions. *See generally* Gloss to Clem. 2.2.1, in CORPUS JURIS CANONICI (Rome 1582, cols. 90-91); Jombart, *Interdit*, in 5 DICTIONNAIRE DE DROIT CANONIQUE, col. 1464. The interdict was apparently used, at least occasionally, in France as part of ordinary canonical procedure. *See* O. MARTIN, *supra* note 54, at 243-47.

93. *See* J. BAKER, AN INTRODUCTION TO ENGLISH LEGAL HISTORY 42 (1971); Barton, *Equity in the Medieval Common Law*, in EQUITY IN THE WORLD'S LEGAL SYSTEMS 139, 150 (R. Newman ed. 1973).

on the litigant who used the secular courts was to blunt the force of writs of prohibition and other process of the royal courts.

But a hard question remains. Did the injunctions of the ecclesiastical courts have any force? The Chancery had considerable powers of enforcement behind it. The Church courts had only excommunication. Was this spiritual weapon effective? Unless it was, the sanctions described above were next to worthless. The court records supply no trustworthy answer to this hard question of effectiveness. Many of the entries in the Act books break off before conclusion of the suit. And even where the accused confessed and submitted to the court, we cannot be sure that he ultimately obeyed the court's injunctions. Perhaps he later had recourse to the royal courts to impede enforcement of the ecclesiastical sentence. There is no way to be certain.

At a distance of several centuries, it is difficult, perhaps impossible, to grasp the contemporary attitude towards excommunication. About its efficacy in medieval England opinions differ.[94] But there are two clear facts which suggest the utility of the ecclesiastical sanctions. One is that, even if the excommunicate did not fear the spiritual loss the sentence entailed, he was subject to a number of secular incapacities because of it. He was excluded from pleading in secular courts.[95] His company was to be shunned by all Christians.[96] In England he could be arrested and imprisoned if the bishop "signified" to the King that he had remained unrepentantly excommunicate for 40 days or more.[97] Excommunication was, in short, an unhappy position from which an ordinary man would seek to be released. The second fact is the real vitality of the Church courts in the late medieval period. Plaintiffs continued to use them to enforce their claims. The Church courts continued to exercise jurisdiction even in areas where prohibitions lay. The evidence from the Act books and several recent studies testify to this vitality.[98] This

94. *Compare, e.g.,* Hill, *The Theory and Practice of Excommunication in Medieval England,* 42 HISTORY 1 (1957) *with* Kelly, *The Submission of the Clergy,* 15 TRANSACTIONS ROYAL HISTORICAL SOCIETY, 5th ser. 97, 108 (1965).
95. H. BRACTON, *supra* note 3, at f. 426b.
96. *See, e.g.,* HOSTIENSIS, SUMMA AUREA, tit. *de sent. excom.,* no. 11 (Venice 1574, col. 1902): "Effectus autem maioris excommunicationis est, ut nullus Christianus cum tali participet."
97. *See generally* F. LOGAN, *supra* note 9.
98. *See, e.g.,* Bowker, *Some Archdeacons' Court Books and the Commons' Supplication against the Ordinaries of 1532,* in THE STUDY OF MEDIEVAL RECORDS 282 (D. Bullough & R. Storey eds. 1971); Donahue, *supra* note 9; Helmholz, *Canonical Defamation in Medieval England,* 15

must be taken as a sign of the effectiveness of the ecclesiastical sanctions. There is evidence to the contrary, but the evidence of the effectiveness of the Church courts should not be easily or completely disregarded.

In sum, the evidence suggests that the Church courts placed a real weapon in the hands of litigants whose interests coincided with the defense of the ecclesiastical jurisdiction. They were not helpless. The use made of the weapon must have varied considerably from case to case, according to the resources of the litigants and even according to the sentiment of the community. It may be that, in practice, customary rights of jurisdiction, dependent on what Professor Arnold has called "shared societal assumptions," had more to do with determining the boundary line between jurisdiction of Church and State than did the apparently peremptory commands of the writ of prohibition.[99] Of course, it is important to remember that there were many areas of harmony and cooperation between the two court systems. But even in terms of actual cases of conflict, writs of prohibition ought to be viewed as only one weapon used to determine particular disputes. They had a real force in the Church courts. That is evident. But the testimony of the court records indicates that the courts Christian had weapons of their own. They show how much room the resources provided by the two court systems left for harrassment, bargaining, and compromise.

The conclusions drawn from the record evidence do not diminish the value of Professor Adams' Article. They do supplement it. They fill out our knowledge of how writs of prohibition were treated in the Church courts themselves. And they suggest that it would be a mistake to draw too simple a picture of legal relations between Church and State in medieval England. All the advantage was not on one side. It is wrong to pretend that the writ of prohibition alone determined the jurisdictional boundary. A great deal depended on what use individual litigants chose to make of the resources provided by Church and King. If the resulting picture is confused, it accurately represents the reality. That the two court systems could have existed

---

AM. J. LEGAL HISTORY 255 (1971); Morris, *A Consistory Court in the Middle Ages*, 14 J. ECCLESIASTICAL HISTORY 150 (1973); Schoeck, *Canon Law in England on the Eve of the Reformation*, 25 MEDIAEVAL STUDIES 125 (1963).

99. *See* Arnold, *Law and Fact in the Medieval Jury Trial: Out of Sight, out of Mind*, 18 AM. J. LEGAL HISTORY 267, 279 (1974).

together for so long without greater friction and without reaching a final resolution of the question of jurisdictional competence is a tribute both to the weakness of all government in the Middle Ages and to the unwillingness on the part of either side to push theoretical claims to their logical conclusions.

6

EXCOMMUNICATION AS A LEGAL SANCTION:
THE ATTITUDES OF THE MEDIEVAL CANONISTS

One of Professor Kuttner's achievements has been to demonstrate the central place that the canon law occupied in medieval Europe. His work has shown that historians neglect at their peril the exacting study of canon law texts and canonistic commentaries. The present article attempts to provide an illustration of this theme by looking at the canon law of excommunication. Its argument is that the failure to appreciate the nature of the legal sanction of excommunication as understood by the medieval canonists has sometimes led historians to approach the history of the ecclesiastical courts with anachronistic assumptions. One of Professor Kuttner's essays touches upon this theme[1]), and it is the attempt of this article to sketch the canonistic treatment of the subject and set this treatment against the evidence of practice in the medieval ecclesiastical courts in England. Its purpose is to understand the nature of the sanction of excommunication as used in practice in the ecclesiastical tribunals.

The study of excommunication is particularly interesting from an historiographic point of view for a student of English history. English historians have very often asked the question: When did excommunication effectively lose its spiritual terrors? When did men cease to regard excommunication as a sanction to be dreaded, so that more drastic secular penalties had to be invoked to prevent the rending of the social fabric? The customary way of responding to this question has been to suppose a simpler, more obedient age somewhere in the past, a time

---

[1]) Stephan Kuttner, Harmony from Dissonance, Latrobe 1960, 44.

when men regarded the sanction with genuine spiritual horror. During that earlier period, the sanction "worked". However (so the analysis runs), with the misuse of excommunication for trivial or secular ends, with a decline in respect for the Church and clergy, or with a more general breakdown in societal order, the old system passed away and had to be replaced by sterner, secular sanctions. At that point excommunication ceased to be effective.

However, if this process occurred during some finite period, exactly when did it occur? The responses of English historians to this question have varied, and it is no great exaggeration to say that most have placed it in exactly the period they themselves had under investigation. Thus, the breakdown in respect for the sanction of excommunication has been located in the thirteenth century[2]). It has also been put in the fourteenth[3]). The sixteenth century has been cited as the pivotal period[4]). So has the seventeenth[5]). It has even been claimed that the eighteenth

---

[2]) Rosalind Hill, The Theory and Practice of Excommunication in Medieval England, History 42 (1957) 11: "... at last it degenerated from a tremendous spiritual sanction into a minor inconvenience." See also J. W. Gray, Canon Law in England: some reflections on the Stubbs-Maitland Controversy, in Studies in Church History 3 (C. J. Cuming ed. 1966), 63.

[3]) Mary Hume Maguire, Attack of the Common Lawyers on the Oath ex officio as administered in the Ecclesiastical Courts in England, in Essays in History and Political Theory in Honor of Charles H. McIlwain, Reprint New York 1967, 208: "By 1400 excommunication no longer inspired its former fears, and spiritual censures exercised little deterrent effect." See also J. Robert Wright, The Church and the English Crown 1305—1334, Toronto 1980, 222.

[4]) F. D. Price, The Abuses of Excommunication and the Decline of Ecclesiastical Discipline under Queen Elizabeth, English Hist. Rev. 57 (1942) 114: "When the censures of the church courts had lost their spiritual terrors, ...". See also Ralph Houlbrooke, Church Courts and the People during the English Reformation, Oxford 1979, 49. The author of this article himself pleads guilty to having given way to this temptation; see Support Orders, Church Courts, and the Rule of "Filius Nullius": a Reassessment of the Common Law, Virginia Law Rev. 63 infra 169-86. The habit is of course medieval; on the decline in respect for excommunication as compared with previous ages, see Joannes Monachus (Cardinalis), Glossa Aurea (Paris 1535) ad Sext 1. 2. 2 *(Ut animarum)* § *Et quia* no. 29 (f. 16).

[5]) Christopher Hill, Economic Problems of the Church from Archbishop Whitgift to the Long Parliament, Oxford 1956, 129: "The end of excommunication as an effective sanction was not one of the least significant consequences of the revolutionary period." See also I. M. Green, The Re-establishment of the Church of England, 1660—1663, Oxford 1978, 140—41.

century was the time when excommunication ceased genuinely to be feared[6]). In each instance, the century chosen as crucial has been that which the particular historian had under study. Always, so it seems, the "golden age" when excommunication was regarded with respect and awe had occurred about a century before.

Something is evidently wrong with a method of analysis which produces such results. The search for an antecedent period when excommunication worked effectively seems to lead into a blind alley. Perhaps a different question must be asked, and one logical alternative is to ask how the canonists themselves regarded the sanction of excommunication. What did they expect of it as a legal sanction? Here Professor Kuttner's insistence on the necessity for studying the works of the canonists may provide a better perspective, allowing us to approach the question of the effectiveness of excommunication in a more satisfactory fashion. If we know what the sanction was meant to accomplish, we shall be in a better position to evaluate the evidence from the records of the ecclesiastical courts about what it did in fact accomplish.

I.

Four principal themes emerge from an examination of the attitudes held by medieval canonists towards the effect of the sanction of excommunication. First, they regarded it as the most serious sanction of the canon law, one not to be invoked lightly. No more weighty sentence lay at the disposal of the judges of ecclesiastical tribunals. Second, it was a medicinal rather than a punitive sanction. Its purpose was to cure a spiritual disease, not to aggravate one. Third, it was not a final determination. Unjust sentences of excommunications were conceivable, indeed likely, but God would always reverse an incorrect earthly judgment. Fourth, excommunication should not ordinarily be used to impede the needs of society. Only in extreme cases should the effects of the sanction be carried far enough to risk upsetting public order.

The subject is undoubtedly a complex one, admitting of ambiguities and even contradictions. Others have well studied the nature and

---

[6]) Eric J. Evans, The Contentious Tithe (1750—1850), London 1976, 1, where the 18th century sanction is contrasted with "the fearsome weapon of the sixteenth century". See also Douglas Hay, Property, Authority and the Criminal Law, in Albion's Fatal Tree: Crime and Society in Eighteenth-Century England, New York 1975, 30.

development of the various forms and consequences of excommunication[7]), and this essay does not pretend to add anything substantial to their findings. Nevertheless, the canonists' attitudes towards the sanction may profitably be explored in connection with the actual use of excommunication in court practice. It is the question of what the canonists expected the sanction to accomplish which offers some aid in evaluating its effectiveness in practice. And therefore it is important that the canonists adopted a subtler and more modest view of the effects of excommunication than historians have sometimes assumed. The canonists were never blind to practical requirements imposed by the interworkings of what is now fashionable to call "law and society".

The first point is the gravity of the sanction. Throughout the writings of the canonists one finds statements reflecting the seriousness both of incurring and of issuing a sentence of excommunication. Panormitanus referred to it as the *maxima poena*[8]). The glossa ordinaria called it "the eternal separation of death"[9]). According to Hostiensis, excommunication's consequence was both to shut the person out of the Church and to hand him over to Satan[10]). The fifteenth century English canonist, William Lyndwood, styled the excommunicated person a "limb of the Devil"[11]). There was no graver penalty in the Church than major excommunication[12]). This was a canonistic commonplace.

These theoretical characterizations had concrete consequences. The

---

[7]) Modern scholarly work on the history of canonistic treatment of excommunication is extensive. See P. Huizing, Doctrina decretistarum de excommunicatione usque ad Glossam ordinariam Joannis Teutonici, Rome 1952; Josephus Zeliauskas, De excommunicatione vitiata apud glossatores (1140—1350), Zurich 1967; Br. Schilling, Der Kirchenbann nach canonischem Rechte, Leipzig 1859; Eugene Vernay, Le « Liber de excommunicatione » de Cardinal Berenger Frédol, précédé d'une introduction historique sur l'excomunication et l'interdit en droit canonique de Gratien à la fin du XIIIe siècle, Paris 1912; F. E. Hyland, Excommunication: Its Nature, Historical Development and Effects, Washington, D.C. 1928.

[8]) Commentaria in libros Decretalium (Lyons 1562) ad X 5. 39. 48 (*Sacro approbante*) no. 7 (f. 195).

[9]) Gl. ord. ad Extravagantes Johannis XXII: 14. 5 (*Quia quorundam*) s. v. *excludere debet a regno*.

[10]) Lectura in libros Decretalium (Venice 1581) ad X 5. 6. 6 (*Ita quorundam*) no. 8 (f. 31).

[11]) W. Lyndwood, Provinciale (seu Constitutiones Angliae) (Oxford, 1679) tit. *de immunitate ecclesiae*, p. 264 s. v. *reconciliationis*.

[12]) See C. 24 q. 3 c. 17 (*Corripiantur*).

primary among them was to hedge the imposition of excommunication round with procedural safeguards to keep it from being used inadvisedly — something like what modern lawyers call due process of law[13]). If excommunication were the Church's sternest sanction, it should not be imposed frivolously. Thus no person could be excommunicated except by a court with proper jurisdiction over his person. Only a person's judicial superior could excommunicate him in the external forum; otherwise the sentence was void[14]). Nor should one be excommunicated, except in special circumstances, without having been summoned by legitimate citation. There must be fair warning[15]) and an opportunity to respond. Judges issuing sentences of excommunication were also required to do so in writing. The person sentenced had the right to a copy of the sentence, and the sentence must express the cause of the excommunication[16]). It did not necessarily follow that all sentences issued contrary to these rules were null and void. They might simply give the party aggrieved the right to seek a remedy for their violation. The resulting situation is a measure of the canonists' desire to guarantee fairness in procedure while avoiding the other extreme of encouraging disrespect for the law's sanctions.

One particularly important example is the guarantee of protection for parties appealing a sentence of excommunication. Appeals from sentences challenged as unjust were protected; the person sentenced must suffer no prejudice as long as he prosecuted his appeal with dispatch[17]). From this followed the extensive development of absolution *ad cautelam*[18]). The

---

[13]) On this subject generally, see Clarence Gallagher, Canon Law and the Christian Community, Rome 1978, 154—62.

[14]) See Hostiensis, Summa Aurea (Venice 1574) V, tit. *de sent. excom.* no. 5 a (col. 1888): „... alii autem prelati omnes qui spiritualem iurisdictionem habent de consuetudine vel de iure communi ... excommunicare possunt etiam maiori excommunicatione." The diffusion of spiritual jurisdiction in medieval England and the necessity that all those who exercised it be able to impose proper sentences meant that excommunication could not be restricted in practice to those exercising episcopal office. The subject is treated in Eugene Vernay, Le « Liber de excommunicatione » du Cardinal Berenger, pp. xxiii—xxiv.

[15]) Gl. ord. ad Sext 5. 11. 3 *(Statuimus)* s. v. *monitionem canonicam*: „Hoc est regulare in excommunicatione hominis, ut semper procedat monitio."

[16]) See generally Sext 5. 11. 1 and especially gl. ord. ad id.

[17]) See Panormitanus, Commentaria ad X 5. 39. 48 *(Sacro approbante)* nos. 2—10 (fols. 194v—195).

[18]) See F. D. Logan, Excommunication and the Secular Arm in Medieval England, Toronto 1968, 116—20.

procedure maintained the theoretical force of excommunication while in
practice protecting the litigant's right to a full and fair hearing. Only if
he used appeal as a mere tactic of delay or appealed without colorable
claim of right were his rights to be cut off.

This point is connected with the view expressed by several canonists
that only the contumacious were to be excommunicated. Only those
who showed contempt for the courts or the law were to be punished, not
those who had indicated signs of willingness to comply with the law[19]).
Since excommunication was such a serious matter—cutting the excommunicate off from the fellowship of God and of his neighbors—it was
reserved for the offender against whom all else failed[20]). It must not be
used indiscriminately. And the person with a timely appeal must be
allowed to proceed with it. Only when he neglected to prosecute the
appeal did his conduct amount to the contumacy that the canon law
punished.

Second, and in some ways seemingly at odds with the first point,
excommunication was regarded by the canonists as meant for the
restoration to spiritual health of the person subject to it. It was not
primarily meant to punish. In the striking phrase used by Hostiensis,
"excommunication is medicine for the person excommunicated, not the
right of any one".[21]) Thus, in litigation between parties no plaintiff had
the unfettered right to insist that the defendant be declared excommunicate, even where the defendant was unquestionably liable to the plaintiff
or otherwise in the wrong. A good example is the case of the poor man
sued for a valid debt. If the poor man could not pay, he was not to be
condemned for the failure, although he would be obliged to swear an oath
to pay the debt when he returned to a prosperous state[22]). The creditor

---

[19]) E.g., Innocent IV, Apparatus in V Libros Decretalium (Frankfort 1570)
ad 5. 39. 6 *(Mulieres)* (f. 547v): „... cum excommunicatio non cadat nisi in
contumacem." Antonius de Butrio, Commentaria (Venice 1578) ad X 5. 39. 21
(A nobis) no. 9 (f. 121): „Et ratio, quia sententia excommunicationis non ligat
nisi ex contemptu." Angelus de Clavasio, Summa Angelica de casibus conscien-
tialibus (Venice 1569) s. v. *excommunicatio* I, no. 22 (f. 220): „Quare debet
quis excommunicari? Respondeo quod solum pro peccato mortali cui est annexa
contumacia."

[20]) Hostiensis, Lectura ad X 5. 40. 23 *(Ex parte)* no. 8 (f. 128): „... quia
nemo excommunicatur nisi pro mortali et qui aliter corrigi non potest."

[21]) Lectura ad X 5. 39. 40 *(Per tuas literas)* no. 5 (f. 118): „Est enim excommunicatio medicina excommunicati non ius alicuius."

[22]) Hostiensis, Lectura ad X 5. 40. 23 *(Ex parte)* nos. 10—11 (f. 128v):
„Caveat quod satisfaciat cum pervenerit ad pinguiorem fortunam ... et si non

could not insist that the poor man be excommunicated for non-payment, because excommunication was medicinal, not punitive, and its imposition against a debtor too poor to pay would have served no restorative spiritual purpose[23]).

This attitude towards excommunication had other legal consequences. The rule that a simple priest could absolve a dying man despite reservation of the function to a bishop or even to the pope was one[24]). The rule that no adverse consequences were to remain against the excommunicate after absolution was another[25]). Perhaps the most striking manifestation of the view that the sanction was primarily medicinal was the permission given to judges to lift it if it failed to achieve its proper end. Joannes Andreae, for instance, noted, "the prelate, as a doctor, who sees that the medicine of excommunication, even if justly imposed, is not helpful but rather deterimental, may discretely remove it even during contumacy, when he sees that this will be useful to the health of the person excommunicated"[26]). It is almost as if a modern injunction were to be lifted after a time if the person enjoined had refused to be guided by it[27]). Since a primary goal of the law was reconciliation, use of

---

potest aliam cautionem prestare, iuret." Antonius de Butrio held that a sentence of excommunication against a notoriously poor debtor was ipso facto a nullity. See Commentaria ad X 3. 23. 3 *(Odoardus)* no. 12 (f. 90).

[23]) Panormitanus put this point generally: Commentaria ad X 5. 39. 59 *(Si quem)* no. 3 (f. 197): „... sed excommunicatio non est proprie pena sed anime medicina ... unde eo ipso quod excommunicatus vult satisfacere obtinet absolutionem."

[24]) E.g., Panormitanus, Commentaria ad X 5. 39. 19 *(Tua nos)* no. 3 (f. 184): „... in articulo mortis ubi etiam incendiarius absolvi potest a sacerdote."

[25]) E.g., Innocent IV. Apparatus ad X 2. 20. 54 *(Testimonium)* no. 5 (f. 268v): „Excommunicatio non est culpa sed est medicina vel poenitentia ... et ideo ea cessante non debet aliqua infamia remanere."

[26]) Novella Commentaria in sextum Decretalium librum (Venice 1581) ad Sext 5. 11. 1. *(Cum medicinalis)* no. 1 (f. 157): „... quod prelatus medicus qui videt hanc medicinam excommunicationis etiam iuste latae non proficere sed officere illam discrete tollere potest etiam durante contumacia ex quo videt illius saluti sic expedire." See also the comments of the civilian Bartolus, Opera Omnia (Venice 1603) Commentaria ad Dig. 48. 1. 2 *(publicorum)* no. 7 (f. 139): „... quia illa pena non imponitur perpetuo sed ut a delicto desistat et emendetur quod facit."

[27]) This was put bluntly by Felinus Sandeus, Commentaria ad quinque libros Decretalium (Venice 1574) ad X 1. 29. 1 *(Quia quaesitum)* no. 16 (col. 921): „quod non debet imponi sentencia excommunicationis quoties non timetur."

the primary sanction of excommunication might appropriately be adjusted or even lifted to avoid frustrating that purpose.

There was bound to be some tension between this approach and the desire of the law to vindicate publicly the standards of the moral law—to avoid public scandal. But legal goals often come into competition in actual cases, and judges must make their choice of which is the more important in each instance. The canonists recognized the possible inconsistency, as is shown by their attempts to distinguish those situations in which excommunication served as a *poena capitalis* from those in which its role was instead purely medicinal[28]. In the end they said that excommunication should serve as a lasting punishment for the truly contumacious; for others its medicinal purpose was paramount. The distinction is admittedly difficult from a modern juridical point of view. It defines the purpose of a sanction in terms of actual effect on the particular person subject to the sentence. The prevalence of the distinction is therefore a good reminder of how far the terms of legal positivism are removed from the attitudes of the medieval canonists. The canonists did not expect that excommunication should work like a modern legal sanction.

Also alien to the norms of legal positivism was the third attitude of the canonists. They always recognized that earthly excommunication did not represent a final determination; it was always subject to reversal by God. Unjust sentences were inevitable[29]. As Hostiensis put it, although the sentence is medicinal, it may well be that the judge is "an unskilled doctor"[30]. And because the courts could only give judgment according to external proofs, incorrect judgments were bound to be made even by the most skilled judges. All canonists recognized this fact of legal life.

---

[28] E.g., Felinus Sandeus, Commentaria ad X 5. 1. 24 *(Qualiter et quando)* § *licet autem* nos. 51—52 (cols. 838—39); Philippus Decius, Repertorium aureum ad omnes lecturas super Decretalibus (1523) ad X 1. 5. 1 *(Ad haec in B. Petro)* no. 29 (f. 71).

[29] E.g., Panormitanus, Commentaria ad X 5. 39. 28 *(A nobis)* n. 2 (f. 187v): „Secundo nota quod quandoque ecclesia errat ligando non ligandum vel absolvendo non absolvendum hoc enim ideo procedit quia ecclesia non potest iudicare de occultis sicut ipse deus." See also G. Duranti, Speculum Iudiciale (Basel 1574) II, tit. *de positionibus*, nos. 42—43 (p. 595) distinguishing excommunications incurred *latae sentenciae* by violation of a canon from those imposed by judges on this basis.

[30] Lectura ad X 1. 31. 8 *(Ad reprimendam)* no. 13 (f. 162): „... quia posset esse medicus imperitus."

Their reaction to it took several forms. Safeguards for the appeal process, on the one hand. Unwillingness to treat a sentence of excommunication, even if unjust, as a nullity on the other. The first of these has been mentioned above. But the second is equally worth stressing, particularly because it is illuminating in its detail. The necessity of public respect for the judgments of the Church courts meant that determination of the validity of a sentence of excommunication could not be left to the unstable and self-interested interpretation of the person involved. An unjust sentence was not a nullity[31]). Thus the canonists found room for virtue even in unjust sentences of excommunication. The keys of the Church, wrote Antonius de Butrio, will be held in greater reverence where a man augments the merit of obedience through observance even of a sentence known to be unjust[32]). Hostiensis, among others, showed considerable ingenuity in finding ways in which a person excommunicated would be at a disadvantage before God compared to the equivalent but unexcommunicated sinner, unless the sentence were entirely without color of right. His guardian angel would work less diligently for him than for the other sinner. His prayers and good works would seem weaker[33]). The devil would drive him in the same way a peasant uses his donkey. Excommunication, whether just or unjust, was legitimately to be feared.

On the other hand, Hostiensis and the other canonists stressed that after all unjust excommunications, though valid on earth, did not bind in heaven[34]). They might subject the person sentenced to mundane inconvenience. But excommunication was no irreversible judgment. Thus the canonists could advise without hesitation that if it came to a choice between obedience to a sentence of excommunication and obedience to the law of one's conscience, one should choose the latter,

[31]) E.g., Antonius de Butrio, Commentaria ad X 1. 3. 43 *(Quia nonnulli)* no. 40 (f. 68): „Et nota quod excommunicatio iniusta, etiam a reo procurata, actorem repellit ab agendo."

[32]) Idem, ad X 1. 29. 36 *(Cum contingat)* no. 40 (f. 57).

[33]) Lectura ad X 5. 6. 6 *(Ita quorundam)* no. 11 (f. 31v): „Quod excommunicatus difficilius resurgit et gratiam dei recipit quam aliquis alius peccator non excommunicatus et quod orationes suae et alia opera de genere bonorum quae facit debiliora sint."

[34]) For Hostiensis' treatment, see Lectura ad X 5. 39. 40 *(Per tuas literas)* nos. 3—4 (f. 118).

patiently submitting to the earthly sentence[35]). And where a sentence of excommunication would upset the good state of the Church or lead to other evil consequence, the person should not obey it[36]). In the end, as one canonist put it, "the unjust sentence binds the excommunicator not the excommunicated."[37])

Given this view of excommunication, it perhaps comes as no surprise to find a general disinclination among the canonists to push doctrines associated with the subject to their logical conclusions where those conclusions might lead to substantial harm or inconvenience. This is the fourth point. The canonists adopted a sensible, not a strictly logical, approach to the extent of the effects of excommunication. They were particularly insistent that the theoretical exclusion of the excommunicate from society not be turned to the practical advantage of that person. But they went further, refusing to deny basic rights to him. Thus, for example, although the law held that it was wrong for anyone to associate with an excommunicate, there were exceptions made for family members, for servants, and for one's serfs[38]). In much the same way, although a person excommunicated was subject to the loss of many of his civil rights, the canonists conceded to him a considerable number of retained rights by way of exception. He could, for example, validly enter a contract of marriage[39]). Ordinary civil contracts entered into by an excommunicate were also valid under the canon law. They could be enforced against him even while the excommunication was in force, and he would be allowed to plead sub-

---

[35]) E.g., Panormitanus, Commentaria ad X 5. 39. 44 *(Inquisitioni)* no. 3 (f. 193v): „Tertio nota quod contra legem conscientie non est obediendum etiam pape." See also Hostiensis, Summa Aurea IV, tit. *de clandestina deponsatione,* no. 3 (col. 1288).

[36]) Panormitanus ad idem, no. 5 (f. 193v): „... nisi ex precepto pape vehementer presumatur statum ecclesie perturbare vel aliqua mala futura quia tunc non est sibi obediendum."

[37]) Antonius de Butrio, Commentaria ad X 1. 31. 5 *(Ex parte tua)* no. 8 (f. 72v): „Et potius ligat iniuste excommunicantem quam excommunicatum."

[38]) See, e.g., Panormitanus, Commentaria ad X 5. 39. 8 *(Nulli)* (f. 181v); see also the text of the Decretum authorizing this exception: C. 11 q. 3 c. 103. See also Angelus de Clavasio, Summa Angelica s. v. *excommunicatio* VIII, no. 6 (f. 246): „Item licite possum participare cum excommunicato pro salute animae meae et pro utilitate temporali puta querendo ab eo consilium cum alios peritos habere non possum."

[39]) See W. Lyndwood, Provinciale, 78 s. v. *actu legitimo;* Innocent IV, Apparatus ad X 2. 14. 8 *(Veritatis)* no. 2 (f. 240v).

stantive defenses by way of exception in the ensuing litigation[40]).
Such contracts could also be enforced in favor of the excommunicate
after the sentence had been lifted[41]). There was even support among
the canonists for allowing an excommunicate to enforce a contract
when he legitimately feared that irreparable harm would ensue from
delay, as in the situation where the debtor planned to flee before the
creditor could obtain absolution[42]).

Likewise, an excommunicated person could make a valid testamentary disposition of his property, according to the majority view
of the canonists[43]). This was a subject of some dispute, for it accorded
a considerable power to man under the Church's ban. But the opposite
result would have led to worse results, and the *communis opinio* recognized that fact. To take one more example, excommunication
ipso facto was the prescribed penalty for laying violent hands on a
cleric. But the canonists developed extensive exceptions to the rule,
as in the case of a cleric who bore no outward indicia of his status or
of a cleric who was subject to discipline at the hands of master or parent.
Hostiensis enumerated a total of twenty different exceptions, all of
which tempered the rule for essentially practical reasons[44]). The realities of life required them.

When one comes to places where the canonists commented expressly
on contemporary practice, therefore, it seems natural to read their
neutral observations about the ease with which permission was granted
to deal with excommunicated persons. "The pope daily concedes license
to communicate with excommunicates for various reasons," wrote

---

[40]) Philippus Decius, Repertorium Aureum ad X 2. 1. 7 *(Intelleximus)* no. 6
(f. 157v).

[41]) Hostiensis, Lectura ad X 2. 14. 8 *(Veritatis)* no. 11 (f. 65): „Hic autem
generaliter dicimus quod contractus initi cum excommunicato non solum igno-
ranter sed etiam scienter et excommunicatione durante tenerent." See also
Panormitanus, Commentaria ad X 5. 39. 34 *(Si vere)* no. 8 (f. 160v), noting
the existence of contrary opinion and commenting, „Et communiter moderniores
tenent oppositum dicentes contractum validum."

[42] Felinus Sandeus, Commentaria ad X 2. 25. 5 *(Cum inter priorem)* no. 16
(col. 42): „... ut si debitor suus fugitivus est quia audiretur super eius captura."

[43]) See Panormitanus, Commentaria ad X 2. 27. 24 *(Ad probandum)* nos
9—10; Felinus Sandeus, Commentaria ad id. no. 1 (col. 578), where the question
is described as „vetus querela". See also the discussion in Bartolus, Commentaria
ad Dig. 28. 1. 4 *(Si quaeremus)* no. 8 (f. 84), concluding, „in antiqua glossa non
determinabat, hodie in novella determinat quod possit facere testamentum."

[44]) Summa Aurea V, tit. *de sent. excom.* no. 4 (cols. 1884—86).

Innocent IV[45]). Panormitanus noted, with apparent approval, the papal practice of absolving ambassadors in order to receive them in formal audience, then reimposing the sentence once the audience had concluded[46]). In view of these comments and the large number of situations where commerce with excommunicates was permitted, it cannot have been shocking to contemporaries that excommunication did not effect the total exclusion of the person involved from human contact[47]). The canonists themselves would not have expected it. Indeed their efforts of interpretation were, in part, responsible for this result. The effects of the sanction would in many situations have depended upon a set of variables of considerable complexity. The attitudes of the canonists left room for this. They did not treat the sanction as if its force could be measured by the simple numerical test of how many people obviously dreaded its spiritual force.

II.

It is true enough that the writing of the canonists sometimes seems divorced from what actually went on in the Church courts. English historians may object that it is too theoretical to count for much, particularly since the question of principal interest to them has to do with the practical effects of the sanction of excommunication. A turn to actual litigation is therefore in order. It is not, however, an altogether easy transition. To turn from the pages of the canonists to the entries of a medieval English act book is to find oneself in a different world. The one is sophisticated and subtle; the other terse and inarticulate. Little but procedure was ordinaï'ly recorded, and nothing of the reasoning which moved the judges was set down by the court scribes. The move must nonetheless be attempted, because the relevant problem depends on the way excommunication worked in the

---

[45]) Apparatus ad X 5. 39. 8 *(Nulli)* (f. 547v): „Papa quotidie etiam ex variis causis multis concedit licenciam communicandi excommunicatis."

[46]) Commentaria ad X 5. 39. 41 *(Si aliquando)* no. 5 (f. 193): „Et ideo papa servat quod cum excommunicati ambasiatores petunt audientiam facit eos prius absolvi et explicata ambasiata reducit eos in pristinam excommunicationem."

[47]) Other notable doctrines permitted contact with the excommunicate in cases of necessity or when the contact was made for the sake of correction of the excommunicate. See X 5. 39. 54.

practice of the ecclesiastical courts. The writings of the canonists may suggest that excommunication should not be treated as a modern sanction, but unless this theory made a difference in practice it will not change the historian's estimate. Unless there are signs in the records of the ecclesiastical courts to suggest that the attitudes of the canonists were mirrored in court practice historians may continue to ignore those attitudes. Are there any such signs?

There are some. The records are neither free from ambiguity nor overwhelming in statistical terms; indeed, from the nature of record evidence one cannot expect to produce much evidence one way or the other. Records rarely tell the historian anything of the attitudes of the parties or the court officials to the sanctions at their disposal. The most that he can hope for is an occasional glimpse of the way in which the sanction was used. Hints are all he can expect. But such glimpses and hints as there are remain valuable, if they are treated carefully and with caution.

The act books clearly show that excommunication was not infrequent in English practice. It was not uncommonly invoked against those who had not responded to citations to appear before the ecclesiastical courts. If it was the most severe sanction of the canon law, it was nevertheless no rarity among the villagers of most parts of medieval England[48]). The frequency of its use to compel attendance by the contumacious must invite skepticism about the deliberation with which it was issued by the judges of the ecclesiastical courts, and it may suggest that the canonists' insistence on the seriousness of the sanction was accorded little weight.

However, this evidence does not by itself directly contradict the ideas put forward by the canonists. They stressed that excommunication was appropriate for the contumacious, and contumacy is exactly what refusal to appear before a consistory court entailed. The ease with which such sentences were lifted after appearance by the person who had been contumacious is exactly what the writings of the canonists would lead one to expect. No stigma remained. Likewise, the act books show that the courts respected the requirement of procedural regularity before imposing the sanction. Communication was almost invariably preceded by a lesser sanction, suspension *ab ingressu ecclesie*. And

---

[48]) See, for example, Brian W o o d c o c k, Medieval Ecclesiastical Courts in the Diocese of Canterbury, Oxford 1952, 99–102.

even that lesser sanction was preceded by legitimate citation, if the frequency with which court scribes recorded the fact can be trusted.

Moreover, if the procedure were irregular, the canon law gave the victim an opportunity to challenge it. The record evidence shows that this happened in practice. Separate actions attacking the legality of a prior sentence of excommunication could be, and in fact were, brought. A case heard before the consistory court of Rochester in 1451, involving the legality of a sentence promulgated *sine scriptis*, is one such example[49]. A case heard at Canterbury in 1294, in which it was alleged that the rector of the parish of St. Andrew, "wickedly intending and notoriously exceeding the bounds of his mandate, did maliciously and without care for justice excommunicate [the plaintiffsl]," furnishes another[50]. So too we find disciplinary proceedings undertaken *ex officio* by the consistory courts against lesser clerics for excommunicating laymen without express authority[51]. Proper judicial authority was a requisite to excommunication under the formal canon law, and judges of England's consistory courts enforced that requirement. Of course, it is true that the motivation for such proceedings may have been self-interest on the part of the judges initiating them. It would be foolish to ignore the possibility. But it would be just as wrong to ignore the evidence showing that the safeguards against frivolous use of excommunication were enforced in court practice. The due process that canonists insisted must accompany excommunication was not devoid of consequence.

---

[49] Rikerton c. Kesteven, Kent County Record Office, Maidstone, Act book DRb Pa 2, f. 152r: „... impetitus super eo quod ipse propria auctoritate dominum Johannem Rikerton pro oblacionibus subtractis publice excommunicavit sine scriptis."

[50] Noreis c. Gumbard, Canterbury Cathedral Library, Ecclesiastical Suit Roll No. 175i, Other examples: Hesswell c. Abbot of Werbergh (1428), Borthwick Institute of Historical Research, York, CP F. 167; Pocoke c. Grene (1527), Hants, Record Office, Winchester, Act book CB 5, f. 43r; Brochelle c. Archer, Canterbury Cathedral Library, Ecclesiastical Suit No. 134 (1293). See also Jane E. Sayers, Papal Judges Delegate in the Province of Canterbury, 1198 to 1254, Oxford 1971, 168—69.

[51] E.g., Ex officio c. Vicar of Halling, Kent County Record Office, Maidstone, Act book DRb Pa 2, f. 42v (1446). See also the ex officio prosecution 1475 against Isabelle Codrey of Lydden (Kent) for being „communis excommunicatrix vicinorum suorum" recorded in Canterbury Cathedral Library, Act book Y. 1. 10, f. 232v.

There are also indications scattered here and there among the act book entries that the judges of England's ecclesiastical courts paid heed to the medicinal nature of excommunication. They did not impose the sentence without considering its probable effects on the person subject to it. Thus one finds specific notations of the imposition of a sentence, "which [the party] accepted"[52]) or "which the aforesaid parties promised to obey."[53]) The most frequent entries suggesting the reality of the remedial approach are those in which the person subject to disciplinary action was given milder treatment because the judge apparently thought it would have greater positive effect than full sentence of excommunication. The act books contain many such dismissals *"sub spe beneficiandi"*[54]), or *"sub spe melioris vite"*[55]). Occasionally the offender was given the choice of leaving the parish and starting a new life in another location[56]). Perhaps his offense had warranted excommunication. But, as the canonists insisted, excommunication was meant to cure a spiritual sickness, not to make it worse, and if dismissal without penalty would work towards that end more effectively than the full rigor of the law, then a judge ought to opt for dismissal without penalty.

This attitude lies, at least in part, behind the common practice of commuting sentences of public penance to money fines. It often happened in English practice that parties subject to excommunication would petition to have the sentence lifted in return for a small money fine. Historians have sometimes regarded the practice as motivated solely by greed on the part of the ecclesiastical judges[57]). Perhaps in some

---

[52]) Rowley c. Rowley (1531), Joint Record Office Lichfield, Act book B/C/2/3, f. 167v: „sub pena excommunicationis quam iniunxionem acceptavit."

[53]) Foster c. Foster (1445), Kent County Record Office, Maidstone, Act book DRb Pa 2, f. 28r: „... quibus mandatis et iniunctionibus prefate partes obedire promiserunt et dimissi sunt."

[54]) Ex officio c. Freeman (1417), Norwich Record Office, Dean and Chapter Acta et Comperta 1, s. d. 3 November.

[55]) Ex officio c. Guilbrege (1457), Canterbury Cathedral Library, Act book X 1. 1, f. 125r.

[56]) E.g., Ex officio c. Elizabeth Ferrers (1521), Hertfordshire Record Office, Hertford, St. Alban's Act book, ASA 7/1, f. 28r: „Et monita est ut provideat de alia habitacione extra iurisdicionem sub pena publice penitencie."

[57]) The complaint is old; see the example from 1471 cited in Brian Woodcock, Medieval Ecclesiastical Courts in the Diocese of Canterbury, Oxford 1952, 99 n. 1.

measure it was, although there is no proof that the judges pocketed the fines for themselves. However, in the act books the remedial aspect of the practice appears predominant. A man, particularly a man of some standing in the local community, might find the prospect of public penance before his neighbors so humiliating that he would resist it, refusing reconciliation with the Church out of pride and fear of public ridicule. Composition gave him a way out. The initiative came from him, not from the court officials. As the writings of the canonists made evident, ecclesiastical discipline was not meant to punish offenders, as much as to restore them to spiritual health, and it was not meant to disrupt the requirements of ordinary life any more than was necessary to attain that goal. Commutation of sentences, as with the other practices which stopped short of full excommunication, was one way of accomplishing that goal. At first sight an admission of ecclesiastical impotence to bring the offender to condign punishment, such practices may instead reflect the canonists' view that excommunications should have a medicinal, non-disruptive effect.

This view is also consistent with the record evidence of the courts' use of the right to "signify" excommunicated persons to the royal chancery for caption. Under English law, any bishop could seek an order under which the sheriff would imprison persons who had stood excommunicate for more than forty days, thus forcing them to procure absolution[58]. The act books show, however, that this happened in an extremely small percentage of the cases where someone had been excommunicated[59]. The judges rarely made use of this harsh, secular sanction. It is very difficult to account for this reluctance if one supposes that the judges were primarily concerned about securing obedience to their decrees, and it makes more sense to account for the evidence by taking seriously the attitudes of the canonists. "Signification" was a disruptive, extreme remedy, not normally consistent with the restorative goals of the canon law. Most offenders against the norms of Church law ought to be treated with more nuanced sanctions. The act books show that this was the pattern in English litigation. Excommunication was not normally the occasion for a penal sanction.

---

[58]) The fundamental study is F. D. Logan, Excommunication and the Secular Arm in Medieval England, Toronto 1968.

[59]) See, e.g., R. H. Helmholz, Marriage Litigation in Medieval England, Cambridge 1974, 114 n. 6.

III.

There appears, therefore, a general congruence between the attitudes of the medieval canonists and the practices used in the ecclesiastical courts. To repeat, the writings of the canonists show at least four different attitudes towards the sanction of excommunication: it was the gravest sanction known to the canon law, requiring care and safeguards against improper imposition; it was a medicinal remedy, not to be used where it would frustrate the goal of bringing a sinner to contrition and reconciliation; it was an imperfect sanction in the hands of earthly judges, one always subject to overthrow by God's perfect judgment; and it was a weapon which should rarely be used to upset the working of society as a whole. While the evidence of the English court books does not provide a great deal of evidence to prove that these attitudes were dominant in the minds of the men who administered the courts, they do contain some suggestive evidence to that effect.

The evidence is, at any rate, clearly strong enough to show that the question: Did excommunication work in the Middle Ages? cannot be answered simply. The canonists did not envision that excommunication should have worked in the immediate sense of bringing all those sentenced to immediate and public obedience. The purposes of the sanction were too complex, and the exceptions to its effects too numerous and substantial for anyone to have supposed that it should have worked that way[60]). When the historian sees a case where a sentence of excommunication was disregarded or lifted short of full satisfaction, this may be because that is the way the remedy was supposed to work. The goals and effects of spiritual sanctions must necessarily be different from those of secular punishments. These differences, so apparent in the attitudes of the medieval canonists, ought not to be lost sight of by modern historians. The subject well bears out Professor Kuttner's insistence on the importance of working through the texts of the medieval canon law.

---

[60]) See the remarks on this subject in Robert E. Rodes, Jr., Ecclesiastical Administration in Medieval England: the Anglo-Saxons to the Reformation, Notre Dame 1977, 98—99; F. D. Logan, Excommunication and the Secular Arm, 15; Richard M. Wunderli, London Church Courts and Society on the Eve of the Reformation, Cambridge, Mass. 1981, 55—62; and Charles Donahue, Jr., Roman Canon Law in the Medieval English Church: Stubbs vs. Maitland Re-examined after 75 Years in the light of some Records from the Church Courts, Michigan Law Rev. 72 (1974) 707—08.

7

CRIME, COMPURGATION AND
THE COURTS OF THE MEDIEVAL CHURCH

The history of criminal law has claimed an increasing share of the attention of legal and social historians in recent years.[1] Undeterred by Professor Milsom's verdict that in the area of English criminal law, 'nothing worthwhile was created,'[2] historians have plunged into the study of doctrine and practice in the common law courts. The attractions of the source material are undoubtedly great. The law is relatively straightforward, at least compared to land litigation. The cases are interesting and sometimes sensational. The subject matter promises rewards in understanding the relationship between social change and legal development. And the study may even be immediately relevant, shedding light on current law enforcement problems.[3]

A troubling question, however, has been whether we have a sufficient understanding of the habits and attitudes surrounding the prosecution of crime in earlier centuries to draw sure conclusions. It is particularly important that we look at the question as unflinchingly as possible in evaluating what are undoubtedly the most ambitious of the studies of crime, the statistical analyses of court records.[4] Any new evidence which sheds light on the nature of criminal prosecution during the early period ought to be welcome, and it is the purpose of this article to contribute to the subject in a small way by opening up findings drawn from the archives of the medieval ecclesiastical courts.

The article has one subsidiary object: to add to our growing understanding of the place of ecclesiastical courts in English legal history. It shows

1. See L. A. Knafla, 'Crime and Criminal Justice: a Critical Bibliography,' in J. S. Cockburn, ed., *Crime in England 1550–1800* (Princeton, 1977) 270. A periodical devoted exclusively to the subject has also made an appearance; see *Criminal Justice History: An International Annual.*

2. S. F. C. Milsom, *Historical Foundations of the Common Law*, 2d ed. (Toronto, 1981) 403.

3. See, e.g., Alan Macfarlane, *The Justice and the Mare's Ale* (New York, 1981) 1: 'The apparently rising tide of physical violence . . . gives the historical study of crime and social control a special relevance.' Note also the conclusion of Carl Hammer, 'Patterns of Homicide in a Medieval University Town: Fourteenth-Century Oxford,' *Past and Present* 78 (1978) 23: '[T]he Oxford coroners' rolls do prove conclusively that a basically healthy and stable complex society can coexist with, perhaps even thrive in, an environment where violent death is common.' See also J. A. Inciardi and C. E. Faupel, eds., *History and Crime: Implications for Criminal Justice Policy* (Beverly Hills, 1980).

4. Much has been in the form of reviews of books whose authors have taken the statistical approach; e.g., J. B. Post, Review of J. B. Given, *Society and Homicide in Thirteenth-century England,* in *Archives* xiv (1979) 30. See also Lawrence Stone, *The Past and the Present* (Boston, 1981) 189–99. He dismisses the statistical approach in a short paragraph.

a hitherto unknown aspect of the jurisidiction of the Church courts during the medieval period, and is also broadly relevant to the general history of Western canon law. But its principal purpose is to contribute to the study of medieval crime by investigating the nature of the jurisdiction and the practices used in the ecclesiastical tribunals. The article is occasioned by the discovery that the medieval ecclesiastical courts regularly exercised jurisdiction over secular crimes like theft and murder. The secular courts apparently did not have a monopoly on the trial of criminals.

The Records

The evidence which makes the discovery of ecclesiastical jurisdiction over crime possible is contained in the *ex officio* Act books of Englands's ecclesiastical courts.[5] The courts of the Church, which enforced the canon law of the Western Church, long played an important role in the legal life of England. For centuries they exercised jurisdiction over wide areas of human life. The laws of probate, and of marriage and divorce, for example, were adminis-

5. The records used in the preparation of this article come from the courts of several English dioceses. They are today kept in various archives in England. Citation to these manuscript sources is given hereinafter by diocese and the following corresponding repositories:

Bath & Wells	Somerset County Record Office, Taunton.
Canterbury	Library of the Dean and Chapter, Canterbury.
Chester	Cheshire County Record Office, Chester.
Chichester	West Sussex Record Office, Chichester.
Ely	Cambridge University Library.
Exeter	Devon Record Office, Exeter.
Hereford	Hereford County Records Office, Hereford.
Lichfield	Joint Record Office, Lichfield.
Lincoln	Lincolnshire Archives Office, Lincoln.
Norwich	Norfolk Record Office, Norwich.
Rochester	Kent County Record Office, Maidstone.
St. Alban's	Hertfordshire Record Office, Hertford.
Salisbury	Wiltshire County Record Office, Trowbridge.
Winchester	Hampshire Record Office, Winchester.
York	Borthwick Institute of Historical Research, York.

tered by the English Church well into the nineteenth century. These canon
law courts have also left a considerable body of court records by which the
historian may judge the extent and effectiveness of ecclesiastical jurisdiction.[6] Among the most frequent survivals are *ex officio* Act books, which
contain records of prosecutions undertaken against alleged violators of the
canon law of the Church. Kept regularly by court scribes as memoranda of
past actions taken and as notations of future actions to be carried out, the *ex
officio* records (as opposed to 'instance' Act books) contain the records of
prosecutions undertaken officially by the court against those who had
publicly broken the norms laid down by ecclesiastical law.

Difficult to read and sometimes more difficult still to interpret, these Act
books have rightly been classed as 'among the more repulsive of all the relics
of the past' by a prominent modern historian.[7] Nevertheless, they are
proving to be useful. When approached with patience and used with
caution, they furnish information helpful in understanding the course of
legal development, secular as well as ecclesiastical. Examination of *ex officio*
cases involving secular crimes found in the Act books of the medieval
ecclesiastical courts demonstrates one instance of such usefulness.[8] First,
however, should come a brief treatment of the formal law and the legal
systems behind the cases: the canon law of the Church and the common law
of English royal courts. They lay the theoretical groundwork for understanding the cases.

The Canon Law

The law of the Western Church was contained in what is now called the
Corpus Iuris Canonici, a collection of texts gathered from the writings of
Church Fathers, from enactments of Church councils, and from legal deci-
sions of individual popes. The great bulk of the texts were collected by
Gratian in the *Decretum* (c. 1140) and by Raymond of Pennafort in the

6. See generally Dorothy M. Owen, *The Records of the Established Church in England
   Excluding Parochial Records* (London, 1974); and her 'Ecclesiastical Jurisdiction in
   England 1300–1550: The Records and their Interpretation,' in *Studies in Church History*
   11 (1975) 199; J. Purvis, *A Medieval Act Book With Some Account of Ecclesiastical
   Jurisdiction At York* (n.d.). Among recent book length works on the subject are: N.
   Adams & C. Donahue, eds., *Select Cases From The Ecclesiastical Courts of the
   Province of Canterbury: c. 1200–1301*, Selden Society, 95 (London, 1981); R. H.
   Helmholz, *Marriage Litigation in Medieval England* (Cambridge, 1974); Ralph Houl-
   brooke, *Church Courts and the People During the English Reformation 1520–1570*
   (Oxford, 1979); B. L. Woodcock, *Medieval Ecclesiastical Courts in the Diocese of
   Canterbury* (Oxford, 1952); R. Wunderli, *London Church Courts and Society on the
   Eve of the Reformation* (Cambridge, Mass. 1981).

7. G. R. Elton, *England 1200–1640* (Ithaca, 1969) 105.

8. There is a certain anachronism, of course, in the use of the phrase 'criminal law' to
   describe the medieval jurisdiction of the royal courts over pleas of the crown or felonies.
   See generally, A. Harding, *A Social History of English Law* (Baltimore, 1966) 61–76.
   The phrase is used here to refer to those activities which were the subject of indictment at
   common law.

Gregorian *Decretals* (1234).[9] Although not a Code in the modern sense, the *Corpus Iuris Canonici* furnished the legal texts that were the foundation of legal practice in the public courts—what the canon law called the external forum—of the medieval Church.

The *Corpus Iuris Canonici* contained a number of texts dealing with secular crimes.[10] They did not, however, unequivocally assert jurisdiction over such crimes committed by laymen. Most dealt with the crimes committed by the clergy, and no one questioned the Church's right to legislate for its own ministers. Commission of a secular crime, for example, clearly might bar a man from seeking ordination, and the canonical texts rightfully laid down this principle, together with accessory matters necessary to determine what sorts and degrees of crime stood as an effective bar. The texts of the canon law were susceptible of an interpretation limiting ordinary jurisdiction in criminal cases to clerical offenders.

On the other hand, the medieval Church could never have ignored the crimes of the laity completely, for crimes were also sins and must therefore have brought the sinner within the Church's admitted competence in the internal forum of the confessional. In addition, some of the canonical texts were susceptible of an expansive reading, one which would cover the crimes of all Christians even in the external forum of the ecclesiastical tribunals. In short, the texts were ambiguous. For their contemporary interpretation, one must turn to the commentators on these texts, the canonists. Their writings provide the best guide to the way in which the canon law was understood at the time.

A survey of the canonists yields an equivocal result. All agreed that the Church courts might take jurisdiction where it was allowed by local custom or where secular justice was not available to punish a crime.[11] These circumstances did not embrace most criminal cases, however, and they certainly did not reach the ordinary prosecution for crimes like theft or murder in medieval England. On this subject the canonists disagreed. The primary focus of this discussion of the subject was a decretal of Pope Alexander III (1159–81) called *Nos inter alios*.[12] The decretal directed a bishop to assign public purgation—that is an oath of innocence backed by oaths of several

---

9. For a concise introduction to the canonical texts, see E. W. Kemp, *An Introduction to Canon Law in the Church of England* (London, 1957); William W. Bassett, 'Canon Law and the Common Law,' 29 *Hastings Law Journal* (1978) 1383.

10. The fifth book of the *Decretales* of Gregory IX, for instance, contains titles dealing with homicide, theft, rape, arson and counterfeiting. See E. A. Friedberg, ed., *Corpus Iuris Canonici*, 2 vols. (Leipzig, 1879) 793–822. References to this collection will be given hereinafter to book, title, and chapter, e.g., X 5.12.1.

11. The opinion is clearly set out in Henricus Boich, *Commentaria in Libros Decretalium*, X 5.34.6 (*Nos inter alios*) no. 9 (Venice, 1576 ed.) 222.

12. X 5.34.6; two other canonical texts to which frequent reference was made were the decretal of Innocent III, *Novit*, X 2.1.13, on which see B. Tierney, *The Crisis of Church and State 1050–1300* (Englewood Cliffs, 1964) 134–35, 153 and the decretal of Lucius III, *Cum sit generale*, X 2.2.8.

neighbors to the same effect—to a member of his flock who was publicly suspected of having committed a crime. But this leaves an open question. Did this cover the laity, and did it reach secular, as opposed to spiritual, crimes? The decretal did not say.

One school of canonists, represented by the *Glossa Ordinaria* and by Innocent IV, held that it did not.[13] Because the Church, under this view, had no primary right to convict and to punish for secular crimes, neither should it have the right to assign purgation for the crime. In other words, the secondary matter (purgation) should follow the principal matter (adjudication and punishment). It was a commonplace of medieval juristic thought that the accessory should be determined by the principal, and this school of canonists held that the maxim should dictate the result in this situation.

The strength of this logic was buttressed by a more emotional argument: a contrary result might end by threatening the effectiveness, and even the legitimacy, of secular government. *Nos inter alios* could be interpreted to assert a 'triumphalist' claim to universal jurisdiction resting in God's representatives on earth, the clergy. It was one of those papal decretals which could be read to assert the Church's power in the most sweeping terms. This group of canonists was sensitive to the dangers inherent in such a reading. If the Church had a potentially unlimited jurisdiction over crime, what ultimate authority would the temporal sword of secular power have? Perhaps the result would indirectly undermine the legitimate punishment of crime by secular government. That danger must be avoided. It seemed most important, in this view, to support secular jurisdiction over crime by denying it to the Church.[14]

The other, and seemingly larger, group of canonists held that the Church might lawfully exercise jurisdiction over secular crimes. One reason cited, of course, has already been mentioned: crimes were also sins, and the correction of sin belonged to the Church.[15] However, this argument alone was not sufficient to found regular jurisdiction in the external forum, because of the possible conflict with secular justice, because the correction of sin might be accomplished in the internal forum alone, and because the canon law itself divided crimes into three sorts (ecclesiastical, secular and of mixed forum), not claiming the same authority over all. Hence these canonists distinguished between different purposes. If the purpose of the assignment of purgation were punishment, the Church lacked jurisdiction. But if the

13. X 5.34.6 s.v. *deficientibus*: '*Sed nunquid episcopus potest de quolibet crimine contra parochianum suum taliter procedere? Non credo.*' Innocent IV, *Apparatus in V Libros Decretalium*, X 5.34.6, no. 1 (Frankfurt, 1570 ed.) 538v: '*[S]i ergo coram eo prius non inducuntur probationes, quia non pertinet ad eum cognitio, quomodo indiceretur purgatio?*'

14. See H. Boich, supra note 11, X 5.34.6, no. 8: '*[A]lias frustra videretur commissus gladius domino temporali quia sic ratione cuiuslibet criminis tota iurisdictio ad ecclesiam pertineret.*'

15. See, e.g., Hostiensis, *Lectura in Libros Decretalium*, X 5.34.6, no. 2 (Venice, 1581 ed.) 90v: '*Nam generaliter de quolibet mortali peccato spectat cognitio et examinatio et correctio ad episcopum.*'

124   *Canon Law and the Law of England*

purpose were the correction and penance of the suspected criminal, the bishop could legitimately act.[16]

Two other arguments supported this conclusion. First, a 'plain meaning' argument that since *Nos inter alios* did not specifically exclude laymen, they were included on the face of the decretal.[17] Second, a more emotional argument that the clergy were in the end bound to account to God for the conduct of their flocks, and if they allowed a sinner to escape uncorrected they would themselves share some degree of his guilt. As one canonist put it, 'the bishop who does not correct the crimes of his subjects deserves the name of shameless dog rather than that of bishop.'[18]

Both the canonical texts and the canonical commentaries, therefore, revealed disagreement or uncertainty on the question relevant to the subject of this article: were ecclesiastical courts free under the canon law to proceed against secular criminals? The most that can be said with assurance is that such proceedings were not directly forbidden under the canon law, but that the canonists suggested a certain reserve in the exercise of whatever jurisdiction might be invoked in practice. At least, the Church must not make a primary claim to the trial and punishment of laymen accused of secular crimes.

The English Common Law

Whatever the canon law, it by no means follows that the Church courts were able to enforce it in England. The interests of the Crown and the integrity of royal justice might demand that the Church be restrained from the exercise of particular sorts of jurisdiction, and this might be true even where the conflict was indirect. In the case of crimes, it might seem imperative to assert royal rights even if the purpose of ecclesiastical jurisdiction was not aimed directly at punishment. We have learned in recent years that the rules of the royal courts did not always effectively limit the reach of the Church's jurisdiction.[19] However, those rules remain the starting point for

16. E.g., Antonius de Butrio, *Commentaria*, X 5.34.6, no. 7 (Venice, 1578 ed.) 101: '[P]redicta vera prout episcopus vult imponere penam temporalem et ad hunc finem inducere purgationem. Secus si velit procedure ad penam penitentialem quia quo ad istam quilibet subiectus est ecclesie.'

17. See, e.g., Panormitanus, *Commentaria in Libros Decretalium*, X 5.34.6, no. 2 (Lyons, 1562 ed.) 162: 'Item iste textus loquitur indistincte et intelligendus est ergo indistincte.' Guido de Baysio, *Rosarium Decretorum* at *Episcopus*, C 6 q. 2 c. 1 (Venice, 1481 ed.) n.p.: 'Sed littera textus istius decretalis facit pro primo dicto si bene videatur.'

18. Joannes Andreae, *Novella Commentaria*, X 5.34.6, no. 2 (Venice, 1581 ed.) 112v: '[E]piscopus qui subditorum crimina non corrigit magis dicendus est canis impudicus quam episcopus.'

19. See, e.g., J. W. Gray, 'The Ius Praesentandi in England from the Constitutions of Clarendon to Bracton,' *English History Review* lxvii (1965) 481; Charles Donahue, Jr., 'Roman Canon Law in the Medieval English Church: Stubbs vs. Maitland Re-examined after 74 years in Light of some Records from the Church Courts,' 72 *Michigan Law Review* (1974) 647; R. H. Helmholz, 'Debt Claims and Probate Jurisdiction in Historical Perspective,' *American Journal of Legal History* 23 (1979) : infra 307-21.

any statement of the jurisdictional boundaries between Church and State during the medieval period. They cannot be ignored.

Secular crime seemingly provided the clearest case in which the royal courts insisted on exclusive jurisdiction. From at least the days of King Henry II (1154 89), the direction of English law was towards assertion of sole jurisdiction in the Crown over serious crimes. The expansion of the King's peace and the elaboration of the pleas of the crown were part of the responsibility of the English kings to restore and to maintain public order. This required the end of habits of private settlement of criminal matters.[20] The Assizes of Clarendon (1166) and of Northampton (1176) were early steps in that direction.[21] In the thirteenth century, this principle was stated and enforced by royal writs of prohibition. The prohibition *de transgressione* was issued by the Chancery, and could be used to restrain a Church court from hearing any case which involved a trespass, as criminal proceedings necessarily would.[22] We know, of course, that the line between crime and trespass was not always distinct in thirteenth century England. But it is also clear that the stated rules of the royal courts demanded that the Church courts exercise no jurisdiction over ordinary secular wrongs under either rubric.

There were certain exceptions allowing jurisdiction to the Church even under the common law, several cases where an ecclesiastical court might lawfully proceed against someone guilty of a secular crime. The best known of these dealt with 'criminous clerks.' Under custom established in the wake of Henry II's quarrel with Archbishop Thomas Becket, a cleric convicted of a crime in the royal courts could be claimed by the bishop and 'handed over' to an ecclesiastical tribunal for canonical proceedings.[23] The cleric thus escaped secular punishment, but was subject to trial, which usually consisted of canonical purgation, and to canonical sanctions before an ecclesiastical court. A second class of exception was that dependent on the nature of the

20. See F. Pollock & F. W. Maitland, *The History of English Law Before the Time of Edward I*, 2d ed. 2 vols., (Cambridge, 1968) ii, 458 66. A recent example of the standard understanding of events, relevant to a topic of current interest, is Jacobs, 'The Concept of Restitution: an Historical Overview,' in J. Hudson and B. Galaway, eds., *Restitution in Criminal Justice* (Lexington, 1975) 45, 46 48.

21. See W. Stubbs, *Select Charters and Other Illustrations of English Constitutional History, From the Earliest Times to the Reign of Edward the First,* 9th ed., (Oxford, 1921).

22. See G. B. Flahiff, 'The Writ of Prohibition to Court Christian in the Thirteenth Century,' *Mediaeval Studies* VI (1944) 279 80. See also *Strange v. Forster* (King's Bench 1413 15), in R. L. Storey, 'Clergy and Common Law in the Reign of Henry IV,' in R. F. Hunnisett and J. B. Post, eds., *Medieval Legal Records Edited in Memory of C. A. F. Meekings* (London, 1978) 341, 377 81.

23. See L. Gabel, *Benefit of Clergy in England in the Later Middle Ages* (Northampton, 1929); J. R. Wright, *The Church and the English Crown 1305-1334* (Toronto, 1980) 217 22; R. B. Pugh, *Some Reflections of a Medieval Criminologist* (London, 1973) 9 10; W. R. Jones, 'Relations of the Two Jurisdictions: Conflict and Cooperation in England during the Thirteenth and Fourteenth Centuries,' *Studies in Medieval and Renaissance History* vii (1970) 178 92.

criminal act. Assaults upon clerics, for instance, could be tried in Church courts even under common law rules, an exception evidently carved out for the canonical category called *iniectio manuum violentarum* in contemporary practice.[24] Shedding blood in a churchyard and abstraction of church goods amounting to sacrilege were other exceptions allowed to the Church.[25] A third exception relied on the principle that accessory matters should be treated as the principal, so that where a cause legitimately before an ecclesiastical court involved a secular crime only incidentally, that court could proceed to investigate. Perhaps the clearest example is provided by ecclesiastical defamation for imputation of a secular crime. Since medieval common law conceded jurisdiction to the Church over all defamation, and since the truth of a defamatory statement could be put into issue in any such case, it was often relevant to know if a plaintiff in an ecclesiastical defamation suit had in fact committed the crime imputed.[26] This principle indirectly, but inevitably, involved the Church in determination of guilt or innocence of a secular crime.

In sum, the common law was prepared to grant jurisdiction to the Church in a limited class of criminal cases. For crimes without special characteristics the jurisdictional rules apparently excluded ecclesiastical jurisdiction, except in the 'internal forum' of the confessional. The secular courts must have exclusive jurisdiction. What happened in actual practice is, of course, another matter. The resolution and adjustment of jurisdictional conflicts did not always follow the formal rules of either canon or common law in medieval England. For practice we must turn to the Church's *ex officio* Act books.

Criminal Cases Heard

Virtually every medieval Act book surviving in English archives contains some *ex officio* proceedings involving what we think of as purely secular crimes. Men and women publicly suspected of crimes as varied as theft,

24. See the writ *Circumspecte Agatis* (1286), in F. Powicke and C. R. Cheney, eds., *Councils & Synods With Other Documents Relating to the English Church, A.D. 1205–1313*, 2 vols. (Oxford, 1964) ii, 974–75. The foundation of the canon law on the subject is found in a constitution of the Second Lateran Council (1139), *Si quis suadente* C. 17 q. 4 c. 29, in *Corpus Iuris Canonici*, i, 822.

25. The evidence from the royal courts on the first point is largely negative in character, that is, the absence of a specific writ of prohibition to cover it, the lack of litigated cases on the subject in the Yearbooks, and the stated assumption by the bishops to the king that they had valid jurisdiction over it. See, e.g., the Council of Merton and Westminister (1258), in *Councils & Synods*, supra note 24, 1, 573–74; Flahiff, supra note 22. The special status of property appurtenant to a church is, however, explicitly recognized in 44 Lib. Ass. 1. 29, no. 8 (1370); T. F. T. Plucknett & J. L. Barton, eds., *St. German's Doctor and Student*, Selden Society 91 (London, 1974) 323–24. On theft of ecclesiastical goods, see A. Fitzherbert, *Graunde Abridgement* (London, 1565) at Prohibition, no. 14. On the canon law, see, e.g., W. Lyndwood, *Provinciale (Seu Constitutiones Angliae)* (Oxford, 1679) 258 at *sacrilegi*; C. 17, q. 4 c. 21. (*Quisquis,*) in *Corpus Iuris Canonici* i, 820.

26. For an explicit holding from the royal courts, see 'W. de Merton's case,' in Dorothy M. Owen, ed., *John Lydford's Book* (London, 1974) 69–70.

murder, and assault were cited to appear before ecclesiastical courts and there assigned public purgation to clear themselves of the suspicion. This is true of every diocese which has court records surviving from the medieval period. The procedure used in practice apparently followed that prescribed by the expansive reading of *Nos inter alios*. The Act books show, in other words, that the canon law which granted possible jurisdiction over 'non-spiritual' crimes to the ecclesiastical tribunals was actually enforced. No objections to the jurisdiction were recorded in the Act books. Few writs of prohibition interrupted the ensuing cases.

In no instance, it should be said, did secular crimes constitute a large part of the overall number of *ex officio* prosecutions recorded in any Act book. The overwhelming majority dealt with sexual offenses.[27] Even in absolute terms, the number of proceedings involving secular crimes was never large. The diocesan court at Canterbury, for instance, dealt with an average of about three such cases per year between 1455 and 1457.[28] The Commissary court of the diocese of Hereford heard roughly one case a year involving secular crime in the 1440s,[29] and in a sample year (1470) London's Commissary court dealt with only four such cases.[30] The number of 'spiritual' crimes, like fornication or breach of the Sabbath, was vastly greater in every diocese. Cases involving secular crimes were everywhere regularly heard, but they were never heard in large numbers.

Of the secular cases heard in the ecclesiastical courts, most dealt with some form of theft. All but one of the nine Canterbury cases just mentioned, for example, were for theft. The allegations made in 1457 against John Steven of the parish of Faversham provide a not untypical instance. Steven was accused of having entered a common privy where he accosted a man commonly known as 'lame Wilbur.' There he had allegedly taken a sum of money by force from Wilbur.[31] The Act book portrays it as a simple robbery. We do not know what the outcome of Steven's case was. The Act book, as so often happens, is not complete enough to tell us. But it is clear that the accusation against Steven involved a purely secular crime. No cleric had been involved. The theft had not occurred on consecrated ground. No ecclesiastical goods had been taken.

A few examples from other dioceses and other parts of England may be worth citing to make the point clear that what the ecclesiastical courts were

27. E.g., J. Purvis, supra note 6, 4. Of the 3,640 offenses recorded in the York Act book of the Dean and Chapter's court, D/C A B 1 (1396–1485), 3,236 were sexual offenses. See also Dunning's Introduction to W. Hale, *A Series of Precedents and Proceedings in Criminal Causes, 1475–1640* (Edinburgh, 1973).

28. The cases are found in Canterbury Act book X 1.1, 99r, 100d, 113d, 118v, 121r, 121v, 123v, 126r, 126v and 128r.

29. Taken from Hereford Act books 0/2, 31; 0/3, 119, 163; 0/4, 44, 121, 123.

30. Taken from London Act books MS. 9064/1, 12r, 30v, 42r, 55r.

31. Canterbury Act book X 1.1, 118v: '. . . *quod intraret quandam communem cloacham infra libertatem de Fordesham et . . . hominem nomine Clays Torneluisson alias lame Wilbore a quo manu forti et furtive aufferret xx marcas in auro et argento.'*

hearing were cases involving ordinary types of theft. The charge against William Stretford heard at Hereford in 1442 was that he had stolen twelve sheep from William Bailey.[32] The accusation against Nicholas Cosyn at Norwich in 1435 was that he had stolen William Scheringham's horse.[33] The charge against Richard Swale at York in 1503 was that he had stolen linen cloth belonging to John Tramell.[34] These cases, and most others like them, involved determination of guilt or innocence of the simple crime of theft, one with no apparent ecclesiastical aspect. Most of the crimes would also have constituted felony at common law. The Act books do not always record the value of the goods or money stolen, but the majority of the cases with value indicated, as those mentioned above, concerned items clearly worth more than 12d.[35] The cases cannot be classed as mere misdemeanors.

Other criminal cases heard in the ecclesiastical courts covered a broad range. Persons accused of murder appeared before the courts.[36] So too did persons accused of counterfeiting,[37] of rape,[38] and of burglary.[39] The crimes of receiving stolen goods[40] and of assault[41] came before the ecclesiastical

32. Hereford Act book 0/2, 31: '. . . *commisit crimen furti videlicet quod felonice cepit xii oves de bonis predicte partis ree die martis proximo post festum sancti Bartholomei ultimo preteritum.'*

33. Norwich Acta and Comperta Roll 84: '*Nicholaus Cosyn de Hyndolveston notatur super crimine furti quod ipse furasset equum Willelmi Scheryngham.'*

34. York Act book Cons. A B 5, 14v: '. . . *diffamatur super eo quod ipse unum pannum lineum album Johannis Tramell nequiter et iniuste [cepit].'*

35. The largest amount found in a theft case is £25; London Act book MS. 9064 2, 265v (1488), brought against Richard Barker for theft of that amount in the county of Hertford.

36. Some of these were killings within the immediate family; e.g., Canterbury Act book Y 1.10, 30 (1469), in which '*Johannes Horne de Heth notatur quod occidit uxorem suam.'* These might possibly have been relevant to the decision of matrimonial causes. See Helmholz, *Marriage Litigation,* supra note 6, 94. However, this was not universally true, for there are instances where no such relationship apparently existed: Rochester Act book DRb Pa 2, 46r (1446), in which Nicholas Romeshed was accused of multiple killings, or Hereford Act book 0/3, 163 (1446), in which Nicholas Chynne was accused of the attempted murder of John Aylburton, or Canterbury Act book Y 1.10, 23v (1469), in which Clement Gyott was accused of 'being a homicide.'

37. London Act book MS. 9064 1, 12r (1470), an *ex officio* prosecution against Stephan Bray for '*fabricationem false monete et presertim false monete auree et quod ipsemet excambium fecit monete huiusmodi.'*

38. Canterbury Act book Chartae Antiquae A 36 iv, 105v (1318), an *ex officio* proceeding against Richard son of John Ponte.

39. Rochester Act book DRb Pa 2, 134v (1460), a prosecution against four men for breaking the house of H. Estall at night, coupled however with the commission of other crimes.

40. York Act book D/C A B 1, 115v (1451), the purgation of John Smyth for receiving stolen goods belonging to John Pluckett.

41. Rochester Act book DRb Pa 3, 343v (1458), a prosecution against John Hanschawe, who admitted the crime and was assigned public penance.

courts. Although the majority dealt with theft, therefore, this was not a product of any conscious limitation on the part of the ecclesiastical judges. They heard cases dealing with crimes of all sorts. The definition of crime under canon law was wide enough to cover virtually all acts made criminal by secular law.[42] Evidently the judges adopted the wide definition.[43]

Probably the most interesting substantively of the criminal cases heard by the ecclesiastical courts were those for which the royal courts provided an inadequate forum. Infanticide is the best example, for it has been suggested that, despite its theoretical criminality during the Middle Ages, the royal courts rarely prosecuted this act.[44] The ecclesiastical courts clearly did; the principal forum for cases of infanticide in medieval England may well have been that provided by the Church.[45]

Crimes in several other areas of substantive uncertainty under the common law also survive among the ecclesiastical court records. There were several cases revolving around attempts to commit a criminal act, as in a 1469 case at Canterbury for what amounted to attempted rape,[46] or one heard in 1465 for attempted murder.[47] The scarcity and the ambiguity of the early common law rules on the subject suggest both lack of settled doctrine and judicial hesitancy to punish any but completed crimes.[48] Here the ecclesiastical courts, perhaps more willing to deal with subjective questions of intent, may have filled the gap.

Other examples exist. Conversion of goods lawfully held by a bailee, long a debatable crime at common law, was the subject of a criminal case heard at Hereford in 1447[49] and one at London brought in 1490.[50] Extortion, also

42. See E. M. Elvey, ed., *The Courts of the Archdeaconry of Buckingham 1483-1523*, Buckinghamshire Record Society xix, (1975) 29.

43. See, e.g., the treatment and references in W. Lyndwood, *Provinciale*, supra note 25, 347 at *crimen*.

44. See Kellum, 'Infanticide in England in the Later Middle Ages,' *History of Childhood Quarterly* 1 (1974) 367; Hammer, supra note 3, 13; Cyril C. Means, Jr., 'The Phoenix of Abortional Freedom,' 17 *New York Law Forum* (1971) 335.

45. See R. H. Helmholz, 'Infanticide in the Province of Canterbury during the Fifteenth Century,' *History of Childhood Quarterly* 2 (1972) : infra 157-68.

46. Canterbury Act book Y 1.11, 11r (1469); Nicholas Whitfield was cited because '*vi voluit cognoscere carnaliter Benedictam at Walt.*' See also Rochester Act book DRb Pa 1, 49v (1446), an *ex officio* proceeding against Robert Bocheer who allegedly '*vires suos et operas dedit ad carnaliter commiscendum cum uxore Johannis Godebour.*'

47. Canterbury book X 8.3, 82v.

48. See Francis Bowes Sayre, 'Criminal Aspects,' 41 *Harvard Law Review* (1941) 821; J. F. Stephen, *History of the Criminal Law of England*, 3 vols. (London, 1883) ii, 221 25.

49. Hereford Act book O 4, 44: '. . . *crimen furti, videlicet quod ipsa furtive surripuisset iii flammeola de bonorum predicte Margarete locatorum.*' On the common law, see Stephen, supra note 48, i, 139 40; G. P. Fletcher, *Rethinking Criminal Law* (Boston, 1978) at 66 70, 83 6; Kathleen F. Brickey, 'The Jurisprudence of Larceny: an Historical Inquiry and Interest Analysis,' 33 *Vanderbilt Law Review* (1980) 1126.

50. London Act book MS. 9064/4, 61: '*Isabella Croste furtive abstulit serta (sic) bona Agnetis Effomato . . . quia dicta Isabella custodivit eadem tempore infirmitatis sue.*'

of questionable status at early common law, was dealt with by an ecclesiastical court in a 1515 prosecution at Rochester. The victim claimed to have lost over £5 as a result of the extortion practiced by George Walker.[51] The use of sorcery or magical practices to achieve illegal ends, again a subject of jurisdictional doubt in the fifteenth century, came within the cognizance of the Church courts on occasion.[52] In these cases the ecclesiastical courts may have acted when no regular prosecutions were undertaken by the secular law. The canon law held that ecclesiastical courts might assume jurisdiction in default of prosecution in the courts of primary jurisdiction.[53] That principle took concrete shape in these cases.

The majority of cases heard in the ecclesiastical courts, however, were not open to jurisdictional doubt. Most concerned matters that were clearly also crimes at common law. They would have constituted felony, and they were in no way disguised as 'mere sins' by the scribe who kept the Act books. Nor for the most part did they consist of the exceptional cases in which the royal courts granted jurisdiction to the Church. Not only did the Act books describe them as ordinary crimes, they also took care to note the special status of exceptional cases which did come before the ecclesiastical courts. Thus, where criminous clerks were being tried—an infrequent occurrence as most were dealt with by special commission[54]—the notation of the Act book recorded the nature of the case, usually also mentioning the prior proceedings in the royal court.[55] Where ecclesiastical jurisdiction was invoked because of an assault on a cleric or because sacrilege was involved, the Act book recorded the case's special status. The scribe used the phrase *iniectio manuum violentarum*,[56] or specifically styled the case one of sacrilege, usually giving details about the thing taken or the ecclesiastical property threatened.[57]

51. Rochester Act book DRb Pa 6, 132r (1515). On the common law, see Stephen, supra note 48, iii, 149.

52. See, e.g., the printed examples in *The Court of the Archdeaconry of Buckingham 1483-1523*, supra note 42, 23, 224, 291. On the common law, see J. G. Bellamy, *Crime and Public Order in England in the Later Middle Ages* (London, 1973) 62-3.

53. The principle was many times stated both in the canon law texts and by medieval canonists. See, e.g., the decretal *Ex tenore literarum comitis* (X 2.2.11), in *Corpus Iuris Canonici* ii, 251; Hostiensis, *Summa Aurea*, tit. *de foro competenti*, no. 11 (Venice, 1574 ed.) 461: '*Item quando iudex secularis iustitiam reddere negligit.*'

54. E.g., F. C. Hingeston-Randolph, ed., *Register of Walter De Stepeldon, Bishop of Exeter A.D. 1307-1326* (London, 1892) 3.

55. E.g., the papers from the diocesan court at Lincoln (Lincs. Archives, Box 80, 16th Century) invariably contain information about the secular procedure. The Act book for the archbishop of Canterbury's Court of Audience (Lambeth Palace MS. 244, 42v, 1305) contains one such case, but the circumstances of the secular court proceedings are fully set out. See also Owen, ed., *John Lydford's Book*, supra note 26, 60.

56. Hereford Act book I 1, 121.

57. Canterbury Act book Y 1.10, 259 v: '... *quod polluit cimiterium de Lympne predicta in percutiendo Johannem Clerk et sanquinem eius effundendo ibidem.*'

Only a few of the cases found in the Act books involved these exceptions. Normally the persons attacked were laymen, the places of disturbance were houses or fields, and the objects stolen were things like coins, woolen cloth or farm animals. Guilt or innocence of quite ordinary crimes was at issue. Despite the rules of the royal courts, therefore, England's ecclesiastical courts sometimes adopted the interpretation of the canon law that allowed them to take jurisdiction over secular crime. They were apparently not deterred by the rules of the royal courts which denied them jurisdiction.[58] Therefore, the cases clearly merit the attention of the historian interested in the reality of criminal jurisdiction in the period of the common law's early development. The best way to understand their meaning and importance is through examination of the way the cases were tried by the Church courts.

Compurgation

The normal method of trial in the criminal cases found in the Act books was by canonical purgation, the same procedure used in prosecuting offenders of specifically ecclesiastical offenses. This is what the formal canon law would lead us to expect. The right of the diocesan bishop to assign purgation in criminal cases had been the subject of the papal decretal *Nos inter alios*, the basis (according to most canonists) of the Church's jurisdiction over secular crime. Similar to wager of law in the secular courts, canonical purgation required the accused to take a formal oath that he was innocent of the crime and to find a number of compurgators who would support his oath by swearing that they believed he had sworn truly. The compurgators swore not to the truth of the underlying facts, but to their belief in the trustworthiness of the oath of the accused.[59] Although they were not simple 'character witnesses' as is sometimes said by critics of the ecclesiastical tribunals, compurgators were not required to know the underlying facts. It was enough that they could conscientiously swear to their belief in the oath of the accused. His character certainly entered into the picture. Medieval canonists devoted considerable attention to the procedures surrounding compurgation, and English Act books demonstrate general congruence between canon law theory and actual practice. What were the canonical rules, and how did they operate in the English courts?

The first requirement under the canon law was that there be pre-existing public fame that the accused had committed a crime. Without public fame, he could not be put to compurgation.[60] It is hard for those of us who live in a

58. See generally R. H. Helmholz, 'Writs of Prohibition and Ecclesiastical Sanctions in the English Courts Christian,' 60 *Minnesota Law Review* supra 77-99; and R. H. Helmholz, 'The Writ of Prohibition to Court Christian before 1500,' *Mediaeval Studies* xliii (1981) 297 : supra 59-76.

59. See the decretals *Quotiens Tridentinus*, X 5.34.5 in *Corpus Iuris Canonici* ii, 870, and *De testibus* (X 5.34.13) in *Corpus Iuris Canonici* ii, 875.

60. E.g., Panormitanus, *Commentaria*, supra note 17, at *Cum oporteat*, X 5.1.19, no. 2, 67: '*Nota quod licet per inquisitionem nihil sit probatum contra infamatum tamen simpliciter non absolvitur reus sed inducitur sibi purgatio propter infamiam.*'

crowded and mobile society to visualize how this requirement could have
had much impact in practice. Public fame, however, evidently was a
workable standard under medieval conditions. It provided the basis for early
presentment by English juries in the common law courts.[61] And the
medieval canonists clearly expected it to have a real effect in the ecclesiastical
forum. They did not treat it in a cursory fashion. They specified that the
suspicion must be held by good and substantial persons before further
proceedings could occur. The accused could not be put to compurgation if
his fame was impugned only by his enemies, or by untrustworthy men and
habitual perjurers.[62] They also excluded the case where suspicion was not
public, where it had not risen to the level of openly disseminated rumor.[63]
According to the canonists, a person cited before a court was even to be
afforded an opportunity to show the lack of public fame. He was entitled to
have a sworn inquest on that preliminary question.[64]

The Act books show that this requirement of public fame was followed at
least formally. Court scribes routinely noted the existence of public fame on
the formal record, as in this entry from the diocese of Exeter: 'James Borow,
detected of sorcery, . . . denied [the accusation], but because public fame
circulated against him the judge ordered him to undergo purgation.'[65]
Witnesses often testified to the existence of public fame, separating it from
their perception of the truth of the underlying matter.[66] Even the preliminary
inquest as to public fame was sometimes insisted upon in English practice.
Thus, for example, when George Fullbyke denied the existence of any public
fame within his parish of Lurgashall in Sussex that he had committed a
crime, the diocesan court at Chichester ordered an inquest. The inquest
reported that in fact no such public fame existed, and no further action was

61. See Assize of Clarendon, c. 1 (1166), in Stubbs, *Select Charters,* supra note 21, 170.
There are illuminating discussions in Milsom, supra note 2, 506–09, and Paul R. Hyams,
'Trial by Ordeal: the Key to Proof in the Early Common Law,' in Morris Arnold et al.,
ed., *On the Law and Customs of England: Essays in Honor of Samuel E. Thorne*
(Chapel Hill, 1981) 121–23.

62. Panormitanus, supra note 17, *Cum oporteat* (X 5.1.19), *rubr.,* 66v: '*non inimici vel
periuri sed idonei viri.*'

63. See, e.g., *Innocent IV, Apparatus,* supra note 13, at no. 1, 490v–491r: '*Item debent
adjicere, quod clamosa et non tacita est infamia, et est tanta, quod quasi facit manifestum crimen eius.*' Authorization for making this exception and forms for doing so is
found in an English formulary (15th century), British Library Royal MS. 11 A XI, 83.

64. See Panormitanus, supra note 17, ad id., nos. 8–10 67v. He goes on to note the '*questio
subtilis et notabilis et quotidiana*' of whether, the fame having been proved by the
preliminary inquest, the accused had the right to produce witnesses of his own to prove
that there was no such fame.

65. Exeter Act book, Chanter MS. 777. Thursday before Palm Sunday 1530 (7 April): '*Quo
die comparuit Jacobus Borow detectus apud officio de arte magica . . . respondebat
negative sed quia publica fama laborat contra eum iudex assignavit eidem ad purgandum
se quinta manu.*'

66. E.g., Lichfield Act book B/C/2/1, 65v (1525): the witness deposing to the article
relating to fame. '*Ad quartum dicit quod credit famam non laborare.*'

taken.[67] Presumably the matter then became one appropriate for the 'internal forum' of the confessional. The ecclesiastical courts dealt only with those crimes that were the subject of publicly held suspicion.

Publicity was likewise important in the second stage of procedure in the criminal cases, the provision for objection to be made against purgation by the accused. The canon law treated purgation as a subordinate form of proof, one to be used in default of the affirmative evidence provided by witnesses or documents.[68] It was natural, therefore, that interested parties should have had a chance to object to purgation if they wished, and to prove the crime if they could. A public proclamation in the parish church, to the effect that the accused would be admitted to purgation in the absence of any objection, was therefore routinely made.[69] Sometimes, seemingly when there was reason to think that objection was likely, the judges cited specific persons to appear as potential objectors before they allowed compurgation to go ahead. In cases where the offense was theft of another man's goods, for example, the supposed victim might be cited to appear before the court; he was then asked specifically whether he had any objection to purgation. Thus at Rochester in 1457 when Richard Colworth was cited for having stolen a sum of money from John Copdill, both Copdill and his wife were summoned to appear before compurgation could proceed.[70] Evidently, they were likely objectors, and there was good reason to have them participate in the proceedings.

There was no absolute requirement of interest in the underlying crime, although objectors were subject to punishment under the canon law for making purely malicious objections.[71] The ecclesiastical courts wanted to

67. Chichester Act book Ep 1/10/1, 34r (1507). Examples from other dioceses are: Rochester Act book DRb Pa 6, 146r (1516): '*Memorandum ad inquirandum de fama Katerine Bylton.*' St. Alban's Act book ASA 7/1, 6r (1516): '[*Iudex*] *decrevit descendendum fore ad inquirendum super fama et super veritate criminis.*' Salisbury Act book 3, 22v (1565): '. . . *unde dominus decrevit inquisitionem fieri ad inquirendum de fama predicta etc.*' An example of a record of the inquisition itself, apparently returned to the diocesan court, is found in Canterbury, Sede Vacante Scrapbook iii, 22 (1273).

68. E.g., Panormitanus, supra note 17, at *Accedens*, X 5.34.14, no. 4, 164r: '. . . *et existente vera probatione cessat purgatio.*'

69. E.g., Rochester Act book DRb Pa 2, 96r (1448): '*Et facta proclamatione ut moris est . . .*' Such a proclamation seems not absolutely to have been required under canon law, although the principle which underlay it was to be observed in some appropriate fashion. A judge was required to set a term for appearance by those who wished to object and to prove the crime. See Antonius de Butrio, supra note 16, at *Inter sollicitudines* (X 5.34.10) no. 21, 102r.

70. Rochester Act book DRb Pa 3, 323r. An example from the Northern Province, York D/C A B 1, 115v (1451) records the purgation of John Smyth accused of theft: '*et super hoc incontinenti purgavit se octava manu honestorum vicinorum suorum preconizatis primitus publice tunc ibidem omnibus et singulis interesse in hac parte se habere pretendentibus ac citatis specialiter in hac parte domino Willelmo Osgoodby capellano et Richardo Steresake ibidem etiam comparentibus et nichil contradicentibus.*'

71. See Antonius de Butrio, supra note 16, at *Quotiens*, X 5.34.5 no. 14, 100v: '[*T*]*amen denuncians si non probat, puniri debet extraordinaria pena arbitrio iudicis.*'

provide a chance for affirmative proof of the underlying crime and also to assure enough public knowledge of the forthcoming purgation to give objectors a chance to provide such proof. Every stage of canonical purgation was designed to be a public act.

These provisions against easy or clandestine purgation were more than theory in English practice. The proclamations were made. People did object. Objectors did assert that the accused person had committed the crime and that they were willing to prove the fact. For instance, at Chichester in 1520 after the proclamation had been duly made by the curate of Grinstead in the case of a man accused of buggary, Edmond Pynfold appeared to object and offered to prove the crime. The planned purgation was consequently suspended and Pynfold produced two witnesses to prove the guilt of the accused.[72] This was normal practice. In many dioceses it was common enough for the adoption of a regular name to describe the ensuing litigation: the *causa reclamationis contra purgationem,* that is, a case brought to make affirmative proof of the crime, one arising out of a contradicted offer of canonical purgation.

On the other hand, it is well to emphasize that the Act books show most criminal matters proceeding through to purgation. Cases where objection occurred were always in the minority, and in many instances where objections were raised, something happened to prevent further action or to allow purgation to proceed. Often the objector decided to withdraw when faced with the necessity of making affirmative proof of the fact of the crime.[73] It may have seemed easier to throw the burden of finding compurgators on the accused, particularly where witnesses to a crime were few, their agreement to appear reluctant, and their actual production costly. For several reasons, initial reclamations often did not end in a full trial of the crime.

Once the objection had been withdrawn, or when there had been none in the first place, purgation inevitably followed. Again, the canon law hedged this third stage of criminal cases around with safeguards. And again the canon law required that publicity attend the proceedings. Selection and production of the compurgators rested with the party accused, of course, but his choice was subject to control by the judges, who fixed the number of compurgators required and passed on their qualifications before admitting them to their oaths. According to the canonists, the number to be required was within the judge's discretion, to be exercised in light of the severity of the

---

72. Chichester Act book EP 1/10/2, 55r (1520). The entry from a Canterbury case put the procedure succinctly: Canterbury Act book X 1.1, 43v (1453); '*Quo die magister Johannes Bred contradicit purgationi dicti Edmundi [Broksall] et habet ad primo producendum.*' Other examples: Hereford Act book 0/2, 31 (1442); Rochester Act book DRb Pa 2, 96r (1448); London Act book MS 9064/1, 42r (1470); Ely Act book EDR D 2 1, 63r (1377); Winchester Court book 1, 122v (1517); York Act book D/C A B 1, 104r (1443).

73. E.g., Hereford Act book i 1, 178 (1493); John ap Jenner had reclaimed at the proclamation of the purgation of Elizabeth Lewys, but when appearing before the Consistory court, '*pars reclamans fatebatur quod reclamavit contra purgacionem nec tamen vult prosequi reclamacionem suam unde index imposuit eidem silencium.*'

offense and the character of the accused.[74] The judge had the opportunity to assess the situation through a preliminary examination of the accused under oath. The Act books show that such examinations took place in practice.[75] Although the large area left to judicial discretion removes most of the evidence from the scrutiny of the historian, it is at least likely that the judges exercised some control over this stage of compuration.

The records show such control, of course, only when something went wrong. Most often this happened when the compurgators offered were unsatisfactory. Canon law required several things of potential compurgators.[76] They had to be of good repute, free from public crime or *infamia*. They must be neighbors of the accused, familiar with his character. They must in appropriate cases be of equivalent status, a rule most notably observed for accused persons who were clerics. The Act books show that these devices of control were not dead letters. Proffered compurgators at Canterbury in an assault case of 1452 were challenged because they had allegedly been participants in the crime.[77] The successful purgation of John Honte was annulled at Hereford in 1454 because 'he did not purge himself with neighbors but with other strangers.'[78] At Rochester in 1445, the judge rejected proposed compurgators 'because they were not of the place where the offense was committed.'[79] It is true, on the other hand, that the official records may conceal negligence or corruption on the part of some judges. It would be foolish to ignore the possibility. But what little direct evidence there is suggests some vigilance on the part of the ecclesiastical officials to safeguard canonical purgation.

In practice, the publicity that attended compurgation was probably as important as these formal safeguards. Purgation was an open act, subject to the influences of public knowledge and social pressure. Compurgators had to live with their neighbors after the event. Canon law and English practice reflected the preference for publicity at this final stage of criminal cases. Court scribes routinely recorded the names of the compurgators in the Act

74. See, e.g., Antonius de Butrio, supra note 16, at *Inter sollicitudines*, X 5.34.10 no. 24, 102r.

75. This is fully spelled out in a sixteenth century entry from Winchester Act book 3, 113r (1567): '[*I*]*udex ad statim ad ipsius Simonis examinationem processit quo quidem Simon sic per iudicem examinatus respondebat dictis articulis prout in fine cuiuslibet articuli continetur et paulo post dominus assignavit eum ad purgandum se super per eum confessatis sua sexta manu honestorum virorum vicinorum etc.*'

76. See, e.g., the decretal *Cum P. Manconella* (X 5.34.7), in *Corpus Iuris Canonici* ii, 871. The canonical requirements are well set out in L. Gabel, *Benefit of Clergy*, supra note 23, 102-04.

77. Canterbury Act book X 1.1, 37r: '. . . *quod dicti compurgatores sunt participes eiusdem criminis.*'

78. Hereford Act book O 5, 139: '. . . *quod vir non purgavit se cum vicinis sed cum aliis extraneis.*'

79. Rochester Act book DRb Pa 2, 18v: '. . . *quia huiusmodi compurgatores non erant de loco ubi delictum fuit commissum.*'

books themselves, so that their oaths in favor of the accused were a matter of official record.[80] Moreover, the judges normally set the parish church of the accused as the place of purgation. For example, where Nicholas Romeshed appeared before the court at Rochester accused of theft and murder, the judge admitted him to purgation, and assigned his parish church at Tunbridge as the place and the vicar there as the officiant at the oath-taking itself.[81] Where the supposed offense had included 'pollution' of the church-yard, the place assigned for purgation was the church to which the church-yard belonged.[82]

The normal formula used in English practice called for purgation before the parish curate (*coram curato*.) Though the rule was not without excep-tion, for judges sometimes permitted purgation elsewhere,[83] purgation before one's neighbors was certainly the normal practice. It led, for instance, to annulling a proffered purgation at Canterbury in 1455 'because [the parties accused] wished to purge themselves in a different church and not in their own.'[84] The safeguard of publicity and attendant public opinion seemed worth insisting on in English practice. At least if we take seriously the Act book evidence, it appears that most of the safeguards the canon law required under the heading of canonical purgation were applied in court practice. It would be wrong to pretend that the system left no room for miscarriages of justice. The ecclesiastical judges were doubtless no freer from dishonesty than other men of their time. But at least insofar as the Act books recorded normal procedure, the assignment of public purgation permitted by the papal decretal *Nos inter alios* in cases of secular crime worked approximately as the canon law directed.

The Efficacy of Purgation

Despite the safeguards discussed above and despite the publicity that ensured a place for public opinion in the actual operation of canonical purgation, most modern commentators have taken a decidedly dim view of its efficacy. Their comments have ranged from critical to sneering. To Maitland purgation seemed 'little better than a farce.'[85] Others have drawn

---

80. E.g., Canterbury Act book X 1.1, 126r(1457): '*Thomas Smyth de parochia de Button Blen notatur quod ipse furatus fuit . . . comparet et purgatus est cum Thoma Denyngton, Willelmo Hull, Stephano Han, Johanne Heth, [et] Nicholao Fyssher.*' See also, F. G. Emmison, *Elizabethan Life: Morals and the Church Courts* (Chelmsford, 1973) 292.

81. Rochester Act book DRb Pa 2, 46r (1446).

82. Canterbury Act book X 1.1, 32v (1451).

83. E.g., Canterbury Act book X 8.3, 56r (1464); Bath and Wells Act book D/D/Ca 3, 68 (c. 1530): '. . . *legitime se purgavit in domo Roberti Roper de Crokhorne.*'

84. Canterbury Act book X 1.1, 105r (1455): '. . . *quia voluerunt se purgare in aliena ecclesia et non in sua.*'

85. Pollock & Maitland, *History of English Law*, supra note 20, i, 443. The classic treatment of the subject is H. C. Lea, *Superstition and Force*, 2nd ed. (New York, 1971) 1–84.

the same conclusion. It was a 'pantomime.'[86] It represented 'an easy option.'[87] It was a product of 'mere scandal and gossip.'[88]

The reason for these judgments and the proof of these assertions has rested in the low conviction rate that every test has found for the results of canonical purgation. Too many accused persons successfully underwent purgation for the method to inspire confidence as a fact-finding device. Recent studies of the Church courts in the sixteenth century have concluded that something like three-quarters of those who attempted to clear their names through canonical purgation were successful in doing so.[89] During the medieval period, the conviction rate for crimes in the Church courts was, if anything, even lower. Almost every person who came before the ecclesiastical courts accused of theft, murder or other secular offense, and who went on to purgation, did so successfully.[90] Where purgation failed, the assignment of public penance was the sanction imposed by the ecclesiastical courts. But this did not happen often in cases of secular crime, and those few who did not succeed at purgation more normally confessed their offense or disappeared from the court's jurisdiction at an early stage.[91] Therefore, it seems true that purgation was simply too easy for it to have been effective.[92]

As natural as such a conclusion is to modern minds accustomed to high conviction rates in criminal trials,[93] it does not necessarily follow for the medieval period. Recent research has shown that the conviction rate for criminal trials in the royal courts was not much higher than that for canonical purgation. For instance, the jury convicted only 14 accused felons tried before the royal justices at Cambridgeshire gaol deliveries between 1322 and 1334. Three times as many (42) were acquitted.[94] A study of gaol delivery rolls for the county of Norfolk between 1307 and 1316 has found a convic-

---

86. Emmison, *Elizabethan Life*, supra note 80, 294.

87. Bellamy, *Crime & Public Order*, supra note 52, 144.

88. Christopher Hill, *Society and Puritanism in Pre-Revolutionary England* (London, 1967) 310.

89. Emmison, *Elizabethan Life*, supra note 80, 296; Houlbrooke, *Church Courts*, supra note 6, 45.

90. Often the Act books simply do not record an outcome of the purgation, but, for example, of the seven cases of secular crimes entered in Canterbury Act book X 1.1 (1453-57) in which a result was recorded, all seven attempts at purgation were successful.

91. It was possible however, to fail. For instance, in 1420 at Canterbury, it was recorded that Thomas Moreys *'defecisse in purgatione'* in a case involving an accusation of theft of some cloth. (Act book Y 1.4, 26v)

92. See, e.g., the conclusion of L. Gabel, *Benefit of Clergy*, supra note 23, 104: 'The circumstance which perhaps more than any other discredits purgation is the fact that the records furnish so few instances of failure.'

93. See H. Kalven & H. Zeisel, *The American Jury* (Boston, 1966) 20.

94. Elizabeth G. Kimball, *A Cambridgeshire Gaol Delivery Roll 1332-1334*, Cambridge Antiquarian Records Society 4 (1978) 26.

tion rate of approximately 30% for larceny.[95] A thorough examination of medieval homicide cases recorded on the rolls of the justices itinerant has found that juries convicted only about 20% of all defendants.[96] Unless one is willing to dismiss jury trials in the royal courts as similarly farcical, there must be more than a low conviction ratio before one condemns the effectiveness of canonical purgation out of hand.

In fact, modern commentators have been far from uniform in condemning the effectiveness of medieval juries in the royal courts. To the contrary, many have praised them for refusing to be simple evaluators of evidence, and for bringing to their task local knowledge of details about the crime and the persons involved. The evidence of low conviction rates has itself been said to prove that juries acted humanely, mediating community values into the otherwise harsh world of medieval criminal law.[97] Clearly, this finding invites re-evaluation of the place of canonical purgation in the ecclesiastical courts. It suggests that there may be more to the story than simple determination of guilt or innocence in the records of secular crimes in the remaining Act books. It may be anachronistic to treat canonical purgation as we would a modern method of proving guilt or innocence. The reasons for the presence of secular crimes among the *ex officio* Act books may be more complicated than a simple assertion by the Church of jurisdiction in a disputed area.

The Role of the Courts in Cases of Secular Crime

The evidence from the Act books makes most sense if one thinks of purgation and the cases involving secular crime as serving a different function than bringing criminals to the bar of justice for trial and punishment. The Act books suggest that ecclesiastical jurisdiction was not being invoked primarily to try a question of fact. The cases, when carefully examined, suggest at least two alternative functions. First, a formal declaration of innocence in favor of a man publicly defamed of a crime was the primary reason that many of the cases were initiated. Publicity of innocence was the principal aim. Second, settlement of a quarrel through its exposition and mediation in a court with spiritual jurisdiction was the primary reason many others were begun. Peace was the paramount goal. This does not mean that guilt or innocence was irrelevant. Nor does it mean that the Church regarded

95. Barbara Hanawalt, *Crime in East Anglia in the Fourteenth Century*, Norfolk Record Society, xliv (Norwich, 1976) 20.

96. Thomas A. Green, 'The Jury and the English Law of Homicide, 1200 1600,' 74 *Michigan Law Review* (1976) 431. See also Bellamy, *Crime & Public Order*, supra note 52, 157 61; R. B. Pugh, *Medieval Criminologist*, supra note 23, 7; J. Given, *Society & Homicide*, supra note 4, 140; C. A. F. Meekings, *The 1235 Surrey Eyre*, Surrey Record Society xxxi (1979) 126.

97. See, e.g., Given, *Society & Homicide*, supra note 4, 105; Hanawalt, *Crime in East Anglia*, supra note 95, 20; Bellamy, *Crime & Public Order*, supra note 52, 161. But cf. G. R. Elton, *Policy and Police: The Enforcement of the Reformation in the Age of Thomas Cromwell* (Cambridge, 1972) 310, emphasizing the problems of prejudice and local influence which were equally at home with the system.

crime with indifference. But it does mean that trial and punishment of the guilty was not the principal goal of the Church's exercise of jurisdiction in most cases involving secular crime.

A public demonstration of innocence was exactly what canonical purgation provided. Publicity was essential at every stage of the proceedings. There was the initial requirement of public fame. There was the open proclamation providing for possible objections. And there was purgation itself, made solemnly before one's neighbors and with a certain number of them joining to vouch their belief in the veracity of the oath taken by the accused. The proceedings were public not just as a guarantee against legal impropriety, but also as a way of ending the public rumor that someone had committed a crime.

It is not difficult to imagine the utility of such a public demonstration in medieval England.[98] We need not equate the medieval English village with the world of aboriginal tribesmen to recognize that it was not an impersonal modern city. Even London was not a place where public scandal went unheeded. And the number of false accusations in open circulation would often have been substantial.[99] Any man would have found it difficult to carry on a normal life with a criminal reputation hanging over his head. Who would trust a man publicly thought to be a thief? Flight would have been his recourse. He needed a means of vindicating his reputation before his neighbors, and the Act books show that the Church courts provided him with one way of doing so.

This is not pure speculation. Besides the low 'conviction rate' of compurgation, the Act books provide several indications that this did occur. For one thing, under the canon law compurgation could be affirmatively demanded by a person defamed of a crime and the judge would award it to him.[100] This happened. For instance, at York in 1467, the Act book records that Hugh Reede and six other men appeared before the court, 'asserting that they were widely reputed as having stolen the geese and pigs of divers of their neighbors.'[101] They went on to 'urgently petition that a day be assigned to them to purge themselves of this crime.'[102] The judge granted the request, assigning purgation eight-handed in the cathedral church at York on a

98. There are instructive parallels with common law procedure noted in R. B. Pugh. 'The Writ de Bono et Malo,' 92 *Law Quarterly Review* (1976) 258.

99. See G. R. Elton, 'Introduction: Crime and the Historian,' in *Crime in England,* supra note 1, 13; M. Patricia Hogan, 'Medieval Villany: A Study in the Meaning and Control of Crime in an English Village,' in *Studies of Medieval and Renaissance History* ii. new series, ii (1979) 123; H. R. T. Summerson, 'The Structure of Law Enforcement in Thirteenth Century England,' *American Journal of Legal History* 23 (1979) 313.

100. See the decretal *Quum in iuventute,* X 5.34.12, in *Corpus Iuris Canonici* ii, 874.

101. York Act book D C A B 1, 180r: '... *graviter diffamati ut asseruerunt super eo quod ipsi falso nequiter et iniuste aucas et porcellos diversorum vicinorum suorum de Ricall predicta furtive ... cepissent et furati fuissent.*'

102. Ibid. '... *instanter petierunt a domino auditore diem sibi assignari ad purgandum se et eorum cuilibet.*'

following Wednesday, also citing a possible objector to be present at that same time. In other words, although this case was recorded in an *ex officio* Act book, the initiative behind it came from the persons accused. What they apparently wanted was the chance to make a formal demonstration of their innocence. In the event they did successfully undergo purgation on the day assigned.

The Act books give more detail about this York case than is usual, and it cannot be said that it represents every criminal case.[103] But initiative by the accused was not rare. Cases where a defamation plea followed immediately upon purgation in all likelihood were the product of the initiative of the person defamed.[104] Such a public demonstration of innocence may even have been a way of staving off a prosecution for crime in the royal courts.[105] Although it provided no legal bar there, the influence of canonical purgation on the opinions of presentment jurors who were drawn from the community cannot be discounted completely. Medieval jurors were expected to be familiar with the facts.[106] Purgation provided a means of influencing community opinion, and this might well influence the subsequent course of secular justice. Some men might therefore have had the strongest sort of incentive for seeking out canonical purgation.

The formal sentence of the ecclesiastical court in criminal proceedings reflected the concern for restoration of public reputation. A person who successfully underwent purgation was not formally acquitted of the crime. He was 'restored to good fame' or 'restored to his pristine reputation.'[107] He was also issued 'letters of purgation' or 'testimonial letters' as a continuing source of proof that he had cleared his name.[108] Sometimes to this was

---

103. There are several other examples where this was expressly stated: Lincoln Act book Cj/1, 13r (1498); Rochester Act book DRb Pa 2, 29r (1445); ibid, 42r (1446); St. Alban's Act book ASA 7/1, 22v (1520); York Act book Cons. A B 5, 14v (1503). A printed example from 1402 in which publicity of innocence of the charge complicity in murder and robbery was the apparent aim is found in W. E. L. Smith, ed., *The Register of Richard Clifford Bishop of Worcester, 1401–07,* (Toronto, 1976) no. 161. Such a case has also found its way into the archives of the royal Chancery; Public Record Office, London C 270/34/12 (1338) a case from the diocese of Coventry and Lichfield involving forgery.

104. See text accompanying footnotes 51-52.

105. See Jones, supra note 23, 202.

106. On the role of juries, see, e.g., Green, 'The Jury & the Law of Homicide,' supra note 96; Charles L. Wells, 'Early Opposition to the Petty Jury in Criminal Cases,' 30 *Law Quarterly Review* (1914) 97.

107. E.g., York Act book Cons. A B 5, 13r (1503); '[P]urgatus restitutus fuit ad suam pristinam bonam famam.' Canterbury Act book X 8.3, 94v (1466): '... quibus iuratis restituit ipsam pristine fame.'

108. E.g., Norwich Act book ACT 1, 3 December 1509: 'ideo dominus commissarius restituit eundem ad bonam famam in quantum de iure fieri poterit et decrevit eidem literas testimoniales super eisdem.' See also B. Woodcock, 'Medieval Ecclesiastical Courts,' supra note 6, 27. An actual certificate of purgation from the thirteenth century can be found in Canterbury *Sede Vacante* Scrapbook iii, no. 78 (c. 1293).

added an order for a public proclamation forbidding further accusations of the crime to be made against him.[109] Thus the relatively high success rate for canonical purgation may result not so much from its ineffectiveness as a way of proving guilt or innocence, but from its common use for a different purpose.

It is equally demonstrable that some of the *ex officio* criminal cases led to settlements of public quarrels through the mediation of the ecclesiastical courts. It may be that the Church courts' jurisdiction over some of the secular crimes was incidental to the goal of bringing disputants to concord, for it is quite understandable that quarrels between neighbors would have involved criminal accusations of some kind. Disputes over chattels, for example, naturally led to charges of theft. Because the canon law strongly affirmed the need for public peace,[110] it followed that the Church courts might occasionally investigate criminal matters in seeking to reach that goal.

Canonical purgation was not ill-suited to this task. The necessary inclusion of one's neighbors, the several delays for objection and for assembling compurgators, the local venue, the solemn occasion of the oath, all these worked as much for composition as for the ferreting out of the truth. A recent study of the ecclesiastical courts of two dioceses during the sixteenth century concludes that although purgation was an unreliable way of providing facts, it was nevertheless 'a useful means of avoiding conflict and maintaining social harmony.'[111] This may be the clue to the treatment of some criminal cases in the Act books. Successful purgation by a man accused of a secular crime marked not so much the proof of a fact, but the end of a quarrel.

Evidence from the Act books fits this explanation. It is no wonder, for example, that the judges attached such importance to the public proclamation calling for objections to the purgation and that they sometimes summoned individuals who might be interested in the matter to be present and to object if they wished.[112] Where theft was at issue, for instance, the underlying quarrel could be settled only with the co-operation, or at least the assent, of the person whose goods were in dispute. If peace were to be achieved, the disputants must be before the court. The Act books show the movement towards mediation and concord both impliedly and directly. Cases in which objectors were recorded as being present and expressly consenting to purgation's going forward probably resulted from a settlement of the underlying quarrel. Thus, at Hereford in 1442 William Stretford, accused of having stolen twelve sheep from William Bayly, was admitted to

109. E.g., Lincoln Act book Cj/1, 13r (1498): '. . . *mandando quod nullus eundem Willelmum super dicto crimine [theft] de cetero diffamet sub pena excommunicationis maioris.*'

110. See, e.g., Hostiensis, *Summa Aurea*, tit. *de officio iudicis* no. 3 (Venice, 1574 ed.) 343: '*Lites dirimere, . . . , Partes ad compositionem faciendam inducere.*'

111. R. Houlbrooke, *Church Courts*, supra note 6, 46; see also C. Hill *Society & Puritanism*, supra note 88, 310 11.

112. See text accompanying note 70.

purgation, the Act book carefully records, 'with Bayly expressly consenting.'[113] Whether there had been an 'out of court' compromise or whether Bayly simply wanted to satisfy himself that Stratford had not taken the sheep, we cannot tell. The Act book does not answer the question. What it does show is that the parties had reached the end of their quarrel.

In some instances the Act books note this directly. An entry for a case involving a charge of theft at Rochester in 1446 ends: 'And the parties compromised this and all other causes between them.'[114] One at Canterbury from 1465 in which the accusation was of attempted murder and which had been set for purgation was 'dismissed because the parties were agreed.'[115] A case involving the charge of extortion ended with the simple notation *Pax*, signifying the same thing.[116] Even a case where the crime included having castrated a cleric was settled by the victim's confession that '[the injury] had been satisfied and concord restored between them.'[117]

Not all the criminal cases in the Act books ended this way. It would not be safe to conclude that mediation was the sole task the Church courts undertook.[118] Neither it nor the public demonstration of innocence will explain every instance. But both happened often enough for us to infer legitimately that something other than simple prosecution of crimes was what led to the existence of many, and probably most, of the criminal cases in the Act books. The role of the ecclesiastical courts in treating matters involving secular crime cannot be reduced to a single formula. But the evidence suggests that we come closer to the truth if we emphasize their 'social' role in maintaining public peace than if we regard them primarily as triers of law and fact.

Conclusion

From this examination of the cases involving secular crimes heard in the medieval ecclesiastical courts two principal conclusions emerge. The first bears on the history of the canon law itself and on its place in English legal history. The second relates to our understanding of the nature of the history of the enforcement of English criminal law in the royal courts.

First, it is apparent that despite initial appearances, the criminal cases heard by the ecclesiastical courts signaled no claim by the canon law to regular jurisdiction over secular crime. The cases were too few in numbers,

113. Hereford Act book 0 2, 31: '. . . *et sic dicta pars actrix purgavit se ix manu rea expresse consentiente.*'

114. Rochester Act book DRb Pa 2, 42r: '. . . *et partes compromiserunt causam et omnes alias inter eas in* [named arbitrators].'

115. Canterbury Act book X 8.3, 82v: '[D]*imissa quia partes sunt concordes.*'

116. Rochester Act book DRb Pa 6, 132r (1515).

117. Rochester Act book DRb Pa 3, 519r (1466): '[*Fatebatur*] *sibi de lesione sua . . . videlicet castratione eiusdem fuisse et esse satisfactum et concordiam inter eos factam.*'

118. This is clearest in *ex officio* prosecutions for 'spiritual' crimes like adultery, where the Church courts held the principal responsibility for enforcement of contemporary moral standards.

and they too often served some purpose other than simple determination of guilt for them to be considered assertions of universal ecclesiastical jurisdiction. One school of canonical thought did permit purgation to be assigned to laymen accused of having committed secular crimes. But even this school felt a certain reserve about the implications of the Church's claim to jurisdiction, and the purposes of permissible intervention were limited as a result. The canonists' reserve about pushing the argument to its logical conclusions was mirrored in English court practice. The ecclesiastical courts asserted no claim to unlimited jurisdiction.

Instead, ecclesiastical jurisdiction over crimes seems to have been invoked only for special reasons, and normally at the request of private parties. The chief of these was that the justice offered by secular courts was inadequate to their perceived needs.[119] In areas where prosecution was doubtful in the royal courts, like infanticide or attempted crimes, the Church provided a forum. In cases where there was a need for a public demonstration of a person's innocence, canonical purgation furnished one. In cases where there was a quarrel to be settled, one which included a criminal act, the ecclesiastical courts could be used. It was the insufficiency of other courts that provided the reason for canonical intervention. Rather than evidence of 'triumphalist' claims to universal competence, the assertion of ecclesiastical jurisdiction over crime in medieval England points to the contemporary necessity to supplement deficiencies in existing practice in secular courts. Lawful under the canon law, ecclesiastical jurisdiction of criminal cases nevertheless depended on these deficiencies more than on expansionist notions of canonical theory.

Second, and despite the limited nature of ecclesiastical intervention in the criminal law, the evidence from the Act books casts doubt on the completeness of the royal courts' hold on criminal prosecutions. It lends support to the thesis that old patterns of private settlement of criminal matters persisted well beyond the time King Henry II asserted exclusive jurisdiction over crimes. The traditional view has been that the Anglo-Saxon habits disappeared in the twelfth century with 'a marvelous suddenness' and left the field to the royal courts.[120] Recent work has suggested, on the contrary, that 'an informal, extrajudicial system of monetary compensation long outlived the demise of the formal *wergeld* settlement.'[121] Under this view, crime's separa-

119. See note 53.

120. See Pollock & Maitland, *History of English Law*, supra note 20, ii, 458.

121. Thomas A. Green, 'Societal Concepts of Criminal Liability for Homicide in Mediaeval England,' *Speculum* xlvii (1972) 694. See also N. Hurnard, *The King's Pardon For Homicide Before A.D. 1307* (Oxford, 1969) 198–202; Michael Clanchy, 'A Medieval Realist: Interpreting the Rules at Barnwell Priory,' in E. Attwool, ed., *Perspectives in Jurisprudence* (Glasgow, 1977) 176; Barbara A. Hanawalt, 'Community Conflict and Social Control: Crime and Justice in the Ramsey Abbey Villages,' *Mediaeval Studies* xxxix (1977) 402; Joel T. Rosenthal, 'Feuds and Private Peace-Making: a Fifteenth-Century Example,' *Nottingham Mediaeval Studies*, xiv (1970) 84; Alfred Soman, 'Deviance and Criminal Justice in Western Europe, 1300–1800,' *Criminal Justice History* i (1980) 3.

tion from tort was a more gradual development than Maitland depicted it. We ought not to suppose, for example, that the rule against compounding for a felony has quite the impeccable common law pedigree sometimes ascribed to it,[122] for habits of private settlement long outlasted Henry II's reforms of the criminal law.

The ecclesiastical Act books show one way in which older habits survived. Compurgation, or wager of law, had been a way of deciding criminal matters in the twelfth century. It is supposed to have been swept away in the course of the thirteenth. In fact, however, it continued to be used, although it was increasingly restricted to the courts of the Church. Men used the Church courts and compurgation to settle criminal accusations long after historians have believed that the habit had disappeared. Whether money compensation changed hands between the parties we cannot tell. Nor can we be absolutely sure that the crimes were not prosecuted concurrently in the royal courts. But we do know that men did not think it inappropriate to raise a criminal matter in a court where any action must, strictly speaking, have been *coram non judice*. The details of consequent settlement we can rarely see. But the outlines are visible. Regular use of spiritual courts to deal with secular crimes shows something of the gulf that separates medieval attitudes towards crime from our own.

122. The modern relevance of this question, with citations to recent literature, is discussed in Randy E. Barnett, 'The Justice of Restitution,' 25 *American Journal of Jurisprudence* (1980) 119 20.

123. See, e.g., R. M. Perkins, *Criminal Law*, 2d ed. (Mineola, 1969) 518 22, giving the rule an Anglo-Saxon origin.

8

ABJURATION *SUB PENA NUBENDI*

IN THE CHURCH COURTS OF MEDIEVAL ENGLAND

Historians normally treat the canon law of marriage in the later Middle Ages as a unit.[1] The same law was applied in every country under papal jurisdiction. And from the publication of the *Decretals* in 1234 to the time of the Reformation and the Council of Trent there was no appreciable change in that law. The *Liber Sextus,* the *Clementines,* and the *Extravagantes* added virtually nothing to the canon law of marriage. Their sections on the subject are brief and devoid of innovation.

In the main, this unitary view is undoubtedly correct. Yet it is not the whole story. There was room for local variation.[2] And there was development in legal practice. Of this fact there is scarcely a better example, for England, than the existence and the fate of abjuration *sub pena nubendi*. This was the legal practice whereby couples convicted of fornication adjured sexual relations under penalty of being declared married for any subsequent offense. Its enactment by synodal statue, its application and enforcement by the courts, and its gradual abandonment under the pressure of multiple objections illustrate both local variation within the canon law and significant change over the course of time.

The subject has not as yet received much notice from historians. No doubt, this is largely due to the fact that the story can only be told from the surviving records of the ecclesiastical courts, which are scattered, unprinted, and only beginning to be studied. But both as a chapter in the history of canon law and as an indication of a gradually changing attitude towards marriage in the Middle Ages, abjuration *sub pena nubendi* merits the attention of ecclesiastical, legal, and social historians.

The custom itself is easily described. A man and a woman, convicted in a church court of fornication, were (in certain circum-

[1] The best treatment of the subject of the canon law of marriage is A. Esmein, *Le Mariage en droit canonique,* 2 vols. (Paris, 1891); See also: J. Duvillier, *Le Mariage dans le droit classique de l'église* (Paris, 1933); J. Freisen, *Geschichte des canonischen Eherechts* (Paderborn, 1893); G. H. Joyce, *Christian Marriage: An Historical and Doctrinal Study,* 2d ed. (London, 1948); T. A. Lacey, *Marriage in Church and State,* revised and supplemented by R. C. Mortimer (London, 1947).

[2] On this subject see: C. R. Cheney, "Legislation of the Medieval English Church," *English Historical Review,* 50 (1935), 193-224, 385-417.

stances) required to contract a conditional marriage. The man said, "Hic accipio te in uxorem meam si ex nunc cognoscam te carnaliter." The woman replied similarly. "Hic accipio te in virum meum si ex nunc cognoscas me carnaliter." Thus, under ordinary canon law principles, if they subsequently had sexual relations, they were instantly and automatically married. The condition was fulfilled. The words of present consent took immediate effect. There was, in theory, no need for a court action to enforce the marriage.

Abjuration *sub pena nubendi* was introduced into English practice by a series of synodal statues of the thirteenth century. It was not a feature of the *Decretals;* nor does it appear in Gratian's *Decretum.* And I have seen no canonist who commented on the custom. But Professor Cheney's recent edition of the enactments of English Church councils and synods gives examples of its adoption in the dioceses of Winchester, Coventry, Salisbury, Wells, London, and Exeter.[3] And court records show its use elsewhere. An early fourteenth century manuscript formulary from the Court of Arches, now in the Inner Temple Library, shows that abjuration was enforced there.[4] Act books and Cause papers produce examples of its use in the dioceses of Canterbury, Rochester, York, Ely, Lichfield, Norwich, and Hereford. It is safe to conclude that abjuration *sub pena nubendi* was adopted in all English dioceses. It was used and enforced throughout the English Church.

Not every couple charged and convicted of fornication was required to submit to this sort of abjuration. Some of the statutes adopted required that the fornication be public and "customary." Others restricted its use to third time offenders. The cases show that, in practice, there was variety and discretion in its application. Mechanical rules were not usually applied. But abjuration was normally confined to what might be called "aggravated fornication." For example, a man and a woman admitted before the Consistory court of Ely that they had lived together for three years, and that they had been "sepius multati per officialem domini archidiaconi."[5] They were required to abjure each other under penalty of marriage. In a York case of 1363, the woman cited for fornication also claimed

---

[3] F. M. Powicke and C. R. Cheney, *Councils and Synods with other Documents relating to the English Church, vol. ii: A.D. 1205-1313* (Oxford, 1964) I, 134-35, 213, 285, 410-11, 598, 631, 650, 707, II, 999. The practice was also given as one of the statutes of Archbishop Winchelsey in Wilkins, *Concilia Magnae Britanniae et Hiberniae A.D. 446-1717* (1737), II, 283. However, Professor Cheney has shown the ascription of those statutes to Winchelsey to be mistaken. See "The so-called Statutes of John Pecham and Robert Winchelsey for the Province of Canterbury," *Journal of Ecclesiastical History*, 12 (1961), 14-34.

[4] Inner Temple Library, Petyt MS. 511.3, fol. 33r; and see Canterbury, Dean and Chapter Library, Sede Vacante Scrapbook III, no. 348 (1294).

[5] Cambridge University Library, EDR D/2/1/, fol. 12r (1374).

that the man had made a clandestine contract of marriage with her. The man denied the contract, although admitted the fornication. Unfortunately, the woman had no witnesses to prove the contract. But the combination of a probable but unprovable contract with the man's admission of sexual relations was enough, so the judge felt, to impose abjuration *sub pena nubendi*.[6] A like penalty was applied in an Ely action of 1375, where there was an apparently technical flaw in the original contract which rendered it unenforceable. To the man's vows, the woman had answered only, "placet michi." She had not made any vow of her own. Thus, when she sued to enforce the contract of marriage, she was unable to allege the requisite *mutual* promises. The court could not, therefore, declare in favor of a valid marriage. But the judge did insist that the man abjure the woman under penalty of marriage.[7]

In some instances, the birth of children appears to have been the motive for application of abjuration *sub pena nubendi*. Two actions from the records in York specifically mention the birth of children as preceding the decision to impose the oath.[8] That this was the determining factor, we cannot be sure. But, it is one of the few times in which the existence of children is mentioned in the Church court records. Their existence and their interests played no apparent part in normal marriage litigation.

Occasionally, the idea apparently originated with the parties themselves. Faced with the prospect of a humiliating public penance, they chose to contract a conditional form of marriage instead. This happened in at least two actions for which records survived.[9] One cannot, of course, say that abjuration was used only in cases like these. Not least among the faults of the practice was the lack of firm guidelines for its application. Too much, perhaps, was left to the discretion of the cleric who administered it. But, where the evidence is full enough to give the details surrounding it, the fornication which resulted in abjuration *sub pena nubendi* was of an aggravated sort.

[6] York Minster Library M 2(1) f, fol. 6r.
[7] EDR D/2/1, fols. 39v-40r. The circumstances which led to another imposition of abjuration are given in the defendant's allegations in a York action: Borthwick Institute, R VII E 102 (1367): "Item ponit et probare intendit quod si idem Thomas aliquo tempore dixerat quod promisit dicte Margerie quod super bono gestu suo eam duceret in uxorem, . . . , quod nunquam dicta Margeria de preterito vel citra sic gessit vel habiut [se] quod aliquo tempore eam habere voluit in uxorem."
[8] R VII E 202 (1392-93); R 55, fol. 235r (1498).
[9] Ely, EDR D/2/1, fol. 72r (1377): "Et incontinenti ibidem dicti Johannes et Margeria de eorum mera et spontanea voluntate coram nobis pro tribunali sedente matrimonium adinvicem contraxerunt sub conditione . . ."; York M 2(1) f, fol. 6r (1363).

This, in brief, is the practice authorized by synodal statutes and adopted by English Church courts in the thirteenth century. It is impossible to speak with real authority about either the frequency or the over-all effectiveness of abjuration. We have, for the most part, only records of actions brought to enforce such contracts. The imposition we see only at second hand, and in cases where the original sanction has proved ineffective. Thus, no firm conclusions can be drawn as to how well the practice worked, although it should be noted that there is one indication that it was in regular use. It came to be described as *abjuratio sub forma communi,* or *sub forma ecclesie.*[10]

What we can see more clearly is the series of objections raised against abjuration over the course of time. In the first place, it was not a formal part of Western canon law. It does not appear in *Decretum* or *Decretals.* This is not to say that the English churchmen were intent on defying the common law of the Church by instituting the practice. The purpose was to strike at concubinage, to force men to give up their women or to marry them. This could be done within the canon law. But its local character may well have marked abjuration *sub pena nubendi* as something of a peculiarity, subject to special scrutiny as time passed. That scrutiny we can trace in the surviving records of the English Church courts, for abjuration caused serious practical problems.

First were the difficulties of evidence which necessarily surrounded proof of sexual relations subsequent to the abjuration. Historians have perhaps too often overlooked the importance of problems of proof in the operation of the canon law of marriage. The rules of evidence often made a tremendous difference. Nowhere more so than in the enforcement of these conditional contracts. Proof of subsequent sexual intercourse was the very foundation of most actions to enforce marriages under this heading. Understandably, it was often hard to come by. And it was hard to evaluate. What if a man, as in one case from Rochester, confessed that "cum eadem . . . nudus jacuit in uno lecto, set tamen eandem carnaliter non cognovit?"[11] Whether that admission, coupled with the woman's oath that there had been sexual relations, was enough to warrant a sentence in favor of marriage is a difficult question. In another case, from Canterbury, the man admitted that he had lain in the

---

[10] Ely, EDR D/2/1, fol. 55(A)r, (1376).
[11] *Registrum Hamonis Hethe,* ed. Charles Johnson (Canterbury and York Soc., 48), 922 (1347).

same bed with the girl after abjuration. "Sed an eam carnaliter cognovit, dicit se ignorare."[12] What of that?

In addition, we find cases where the woman deliberately set up a situation to take cynical advantage of the abjuration. A man at York claimed that a woman, whom he had abjured, twice came to his bed while he was asleep. Her idea was to spread false rumors about them. But his response (he said) was immediate flight. "Et quatenus novit vel scivit ipsam ibidem, incontinenti fugit a dicta camera."[13] In another action to enforce a contract of marriage, the woman presented evidence proving that she had been seen going into a man's house late one night. The woman alleged that this was in accordance with their plan. The man claimed that the visit came as an unwelcome surprise. "Dicit quod cepit eam per humeros et expulit a dicta domo et clausit hostium post eam."[14] In both these cases, the court held against the woman. The fact of sexual relations had not been proved. But a practice which gave rise to these situations was, at least, open to serious objection.

There were also cases in which subsequent intercourse, though admitted, did not in fact lead to marriage. They suggest a further weakness. The penalty was not evenly enforced. It could not be. For example, in a York case of 1387, a man told the court of having admitted a further offense to his confessor after abjuration. For it, he received "maior penitencia." But he was not condemned to marriage in the external forum of the Church. Although legally married, he was saved from its practical consequences by the woman's lack of independent proof and by the Church's rules about the sanctity of the confessional.[15] This difficulty was not peculiar, of course, to abjuration cases. The major problem of clandestine marriages, that is marriages contracted without witnesses, lay in difficulties

---

[12] Canterbury, Y.1.1, fol. 66 r (1374); in this case the judge ultimately decided in favor of a valid marriage (fols. 90v-91r). This was probably the correct result. See X 2.23.12, which sets up a strong presumption of sexual relations from such admitted facts.

[13] R VII E 191 (1393-94).

[14] York R VII E 211 (1394); the witnesses for the woman told this story "Dicta Alicia retulit isti iurato et Ricardo contesti suo quod ipsa convenit eadem nocte venire ad lectum dicti Johannis. Et infra noctis tenebras eiusdem diei, ipsa Alicia pulsante ad fenestram camere dicti Johannis, idem Johannes aperuit ostium camere sue et permisit eam intrare, videntibus isto iurato et Ricardo conteste suo qui fuerunt prope cameram ipsius Johannis ad explorand' eos."

[15] R VII E 135. And see York M 2(1) f, fol. 22r (1394), in which Robert Coupeland and Elena Comyn appeared before the capitulary court and confessed to fornication after having abjured each other *sub pena nubendi*. The judge's sentence appears to have given Robert a choice: "Et dominus auditor antedictus, attentis huiusmodi confessionibus, monuit dictum Robertum solempnizare matrimonium huiusmodi inter ipsum et Elenam citra primam diem dominicam Adventus proximi, alioquin proximo dominico sequente incipiat penitenciam suam." And in an action from the diocese of Lichfield the woman had not been present at the abjuration, so that although subsequent fornication was admitted, the abjuration had to be repeated, and no sentence of marriage could be given. Lichfield, Joint Record Office, Reg. Le Scrope, fol. 40v :1392).

of proof. If either party chose to deny the marriage, the Church courts could not enforce it. But abjuration raised a particularly difficult form of that problem.

A more interesting case, perhaps, is that of a man and woman who have abjured each other, and then had sexual relations while one of them was drunk. Does that make a valid marriage? The case arose at York in 1418.[16] Even assuming that a drunk cannot contract marriage, lacking the full use of his reason, this does not solve the legal question. The marriage had been contracted at the time of the adjuration. Only the removal of a condition took place during drunkenness. A fourteenth century treatise on ecclesiastical discipline, now in the Inner Temple Library, gives an answer to the problem. If the inebriation could be satisfactorily proved and if the person did not approve his action after returning to sobriety, the marriage was not valid. This was the result reached in the York case. The woman who had been drunk, "fecit finem; et composuerunt." That was, no doubt, a fair settlement. But it does point out again that abjuration *sub pena nubendi* brought with it special difficulties of proof and unevenness of enforcement.

The second problem which inevitably followed from the use of abjuration *sub pena nubendi* was this. It meant that inferior judges, who did not enjoy matrimonial jurisdiction, could in fact decide marriage cases. By the *ius commune* of the Church, jurisdiction in marriage actions was vested exclusively in the bishop of each diocese.[18] Canonists recognized that, by prescription or custom, competence could in fact be held by others, such as archdeacons, cathedral deans, or abbots.[19] Nonetheless, jurisdiction was restricted. Not every cleric with a court could validly hear marriage litigation. This rule was adopted because marriage cases required special expertise. The delicacy and closeness of the issues, together with the danger to men's souls, made it necessary. As Lyndwood wrote of marriage cases: "Periculosum est eas a simplicibus tractari."[20] Particularly important, it seemed, was the exclusion of rural deans. They were "communiter imperiti et iuris ignari," according to Lyndwood.[21]

[16] R VII F 78: The woman confessed the sexual relations, but "dicit tamen quod inebriata fuit illo tempore quod ipsam sic carnaliter cognovit."

[17] Petyt MS. 511.21, fol. 111r: "Dic quod non, si constiterit ecclesie de tali ebrietate, nisi quod fecit in tali ebrietate ratum habeat post ebrietatem."

[18] *Glossa ordinaria* ad X 5.31.12 s.v. *dignitatis.*

[19] *Ibid.* ad X 2.13.13 s.v. *in tua:* "In his enim consuetudo servatur quae dat iurisdictionem."

[20] *Provinciale* II, tit. 1, s.v. *ad infra* Oxford, 1679), 79. The English canonist William of Pagula wrote: "Per quos sunt cause matrimoniales tractande? Dic quod per iudices discretos qui habent potestatem et statuta canonum non ignorant." "Summa Summarum," tit. *de spons. et matr.*, Huntington Library EL 9/H/3, fol. 253v.

[21] *Ibid.* s.v. *audire praesumant.*

Ideally, then, marriage cases were handled by a small group of expert judges. However, purely corrective jurisdiction over sin was much more broadly spread. Every archdeacon, rural dean, and cathedral dignitary with a peculiar court had such competence. And as long as correction could lead to marriage by abjuration, minor clerics were able to impose sentences of marriage. Indeed, some of the synodal statutes assume that they will award abjuration. Of course, requiring abjuration is not exactly the same thing as hearing the merits of a full marriage case. But, since courts exercised discretion in imposing it, and since it was not automatic after a certain number of offenses, abjuration necessarily involved some of the same delicate questions. Practice also shows that the lower courts actually heard actions to enforce marriages under this heading. That is, having imposed abjuration, they later proceeded to hear and determine suits to enforce the conditional contract. This went directly against the Church's rule of limited competence in marriage cases.

To take one example, the receiver of the exchequer of the archbishop of York, as his title implies, primarily an accounting official. But he was sometimes granted corrective jurisdiction as well. Thus he came to award abjuration and to decide marriage actions when subsequent sexual relations were alleged. In an action of 1389, his authority to do so was challenged in the diocesan Consistory court.[22] But his right to jurisdiction over sins was shown in the court. And to the question: "An ille judex fuit iuris peritus ad cognoscendum in causis matrimonialibus," the answer was made: "Sic, et precipue in causis abiurationum in forma ecclesie." The Consistory court held this enough to validate the judgment of the receiver's court and to enforce the marriage. But as an authorization to hear marriage cases, it is not entirely convincing. The receiver was allowed to do by indirection what he was prohibited from doing directly. The same thing appears frequently elsewhere. In other cases, we hear of abjuration cases being heard before archdeacons without marriage jurisdiction, before prebendaries, before rural deans; one such case was apparently decided before a simple rector.[23]

A third objection raised against abjuration was more fundamental. It was that the practice used marriage as a penal sanction. Marriages ought to be freely entered into. "In matrimonio animus debet gaudere

---

[22] RVII E 150; for the receiver's jurisdiction, see: A. H. Thompson, *The English Clergy and their Organization in the later Middle Ages* (Oxford, 1947), 194-95.

[23] The archdeacon of Canterbury, Canterbury, Chartae Antiquae A 36, IV, fol. 54r (1341); the rural dean of Stafford, Lichfield, B/C/1/2, fol. 107r (1473); the rural dean of Bulmer, York, R VII E 211 (1394); the prebendary of Bugthrop, York R VII E 6/6 (1312); the rector of Godmersham, Canterbury, Sede Vacante Scrapbook III, no. 56 (1293).

plena libertate," was a commonplace of the canon law, and one
of its guiding principles. The canonists repeated the theme over
and over.[24] Thus the argument could be made that to force a man
and woman to enter into a contract of marriage, albeit a conditional
one, ran counter to the freedom which must inhere in marriage.
As a gloss to one of the synodal statutes specifically pointed out:
"Nota quod hec constitutio est contra iura et naturalem equitatem,
quia de iure libera debent esse matrimonia et sponsalia."[25]

It may be objected, in defense of abjuration, that the church courts
specifically enforced sworn espousals under threat of excommunication.[26] That is true, but the objection is insubstantial. It is
one thing to force a man to carry out a contract he has freely begun.
It is quite another to force him to make the contract in the first
place.

The cases show that this objection was raised in practice by attacks
on such conditional marriages as vitiated by force and fear. By
canon law, a marriage contracted under duress sufficient to sway
a "constant man" was invalid unless ratified. Abjuration *sub pena
nubendi,* the argument went, amounted to forcing men into marriage
by threat of excommunication. And this, it was claimed, was enough
to sway the constant man. In one York case, the defendant in an
action to establish such a marriage argued that the whole contract
was void because he had been obliged to make it "per metum qui
cadere potest in constantem ac sub pena legibus reprobata."[27] A
defendant in another case claimed that his marriage was invalid
because made "coactus et contra voluntatem suam, sed compul-
sus . . . per censuras ecclesiasticas."[28]

As a strictly legal point, there was some force to these arguments.
Canonists drew a distinction between just and unjust excommunication. If it could be shown that the original imposition of abjuration
was unjust, a question to be determined in each individual case,
then the marriage was voidable. At least this is the position arrived
at by the majority of later canonists. The earlier commentators had
generally held that even threat of unjust excommunication would
not invalidate a marriage. Such an unjust sentence did not bind a

[24] *Gl. ord.* ad C. 31 q. 2 c. 1, s.v. *quod autem;* X 4.1.17, X 4.1.29; See Hostiensis, *Summa Aurea* I, tit. *de his quae vi metusve cause fiunt,* no. 6 (Venice, 1574), col. 407; Durantis, *Speculum Iudiciale* IV, tit. *de sponsalibus,* no. 3 (Lyons, 1543), f. 315v.
[25] *Councils and Synods* II, 999, n. 4.
[26] See *gl. ord.* ad X 4.1.10 s.v. *compellas;* and note, for discussion of the problems caused by the inconsistency of the decretals *Ex literis* and *Requisivit* on the specific enforceabiliby of sworn espousals, Innocent IV, *Apparatus in V Libros Decretalium* ad X 4.1.10 (Frankfurt, 1570), fol. 464r.
[27] R VII F 150 (1480-81).
[28] York M 2(1) c, f. 23r (1375).

man before God. Therefore, it was not to be feared. It could not, as a consequence, count as a legitimate cause of force and fear.[29] Later commentators, Hostiensis, Johannes Andreae, and Panormitanus, were more realistic. They were also more insistent on the necessity for free consent in marriage. Pointing out the serious practical inconveniences of excommunication and emphasizing the fact that it was the Church's most powerful weapon, they reached a different result.[30] An unjust sentence of excommunication was enough to sway the constant man.

The attitude of the canonists, in other words, changed over the course of time on this point. It moved towards greater sensitivity to the necessity for free consent in marriage. This was precisely the point where abjuration *sub pena nubendi* was vulnerable. The later canonists opened up an argument against it which had not been available before. It is probably significant, therefore, that the cases in which this objection was raised come from the second half of the fourteenth and the fifteenth centuries. It should be said, however, that in neither York case was the argument accepted by the court. Both marriages were upheld. Doubtless the judge found that the original threat of excommunication had not been unjustly made. But there are signs that the judges were uneasy about the argument. The records sometimes stated specifically that the parties had been willing to accept abjuration. We find, for example, an action in which it was recorded that the defendant, "primo fuerat inditus per dictum magistrum Rogerum ad abiurationem huiusmodi supradictam sub pena excommunicationis, et postea idem Johannes dictam Aliciam abiuravit sponte et voluntate sua propria."[31] The obvious purpose of such an entry was to forestall a later objection that the contract was voidable because of duress.

Cases drawn from the Church court records thus show that abjuration *sub pena nubendi* was attacked on three counts. It was difficult to prove and sometimes conducive to fraud; it meant extension of matrimonial jurisdiction to clerics not entitled to it; and it violated the freedom from constraint that was one of the foundations of

---

[29] Geoffrey of Trani, *Summa super titulis decretalium* I, tit. *de his que vi metusve cause fiunt*, no. 3 (Lyons, 1519), f. 68: "Puto quod metus excommunicationis non excuset: aut enim est iniusta, et illa non liget quo ad deum." And see *gl. ord.* ad X 1.40.6 s.v. *violentia*. For discussion of the earlier view and further references, see Sanchez, *De Matrimonio*, 1.4, d. 5, nos. 17-18 (Venice, 1737), I, 253.

[30] Joannes Andreae, *Novella Commentaria* ad X 1.40.6, no. 9; Panormitanus, *Commentaria* ad *idem*, no. 6 (Paris, 1521), f. 149v: "Et communiter moderni distinguunt quod aut excommunicatio est iusta et non excusat ratione predicta, aut iniusta et excusat." Of excommunication, Panormitantus noted: "quod non est modica pena inter homines esse et hominum carere commercio." Hostiensis, *Summa Aurea* I, tit. *de his quae vi metusve cause fiunt*, no. 2, col. 403.

[31] York, E 150 (1389); York M 2(1), f. 6r (1363); and see above, n. 9.

marriage. It is hardly surprising, therefore, that the practice did not last. It was imposed with decreasing frequency as time went on. Court records from Canterbury and Rochester, for example, produce several examples from the thirteenth and fourteenth centuries. But none is forthcoming from the fifteenth, when the surviving records are in fact much more complete.[32] From Ely, where only one fourteenth century Act book remains, several examples can be drawn.[33] From London and Bath and Wells, where nothing survives from before the fifteenth, we find no examples of abjuration.[34] The Cause papers of the Consistory court at York tell the same story. There are nine cases raising the issue among the remaining fourteenth century papers. For the fifteenth, when more marriage cases survive in all, there are only two dealing with abjuration.[35]

Use of abjuration *sub pena nubendi* was, so far as the records allow for accurate generalization, used only fitfully in the fifteenth century. There is an example from Norwich in 1429, one from Hereford in 1455, and one from Lichfield in 1473.[36] The latest instance I have found comes from 1489, imposed by the court of the Dean and Chapter of York.[37] As in some other areas of marriage practice, the courts of York changed more slowly than did the courts of the Southern Province.[38] Probably I have missed a few late examples. But it is clear that by the end of the fifteenth century abjuration *sub pena nubendi* had virtually disappeared.

No one, I think, will lament the passing of the custom. Using marriage as a penalty for fornication is inconsistent, at bottom, with the principles of Christian marriage law. But the disappearances of abjuration *sub pena nubendi* is a real interest. The story of its abandonment is evidence of a matured thinking about the nature of marriage. Marriage was an institution which seemed, in the fifteenth century, to require a more truly free kind of consent than had been thought in the thirteenth. Abjuration was objectionable on several counts. But the compulsion to marry it entailed was

[32] Canterbury, Sede Vacante Scrapbook III, nos. 45 (1293), 55 (1293), 348 (1294); Y.1.1, fol. 66r (1374); Rochester, *Reg. Hamonis Hethe*, 922 (1347). For the fifteenth century records at Canterbury, see B. Woodcock, *Medieval Ecclesiastical Courts in the Diocese of Canterbury* (Oxford, 1952), 140-41.
[33] EDR D/2/1, fols. 12r (1374), 39v-40r (1375), 55(A)r (1376), 72r (1377).
[34] This statement is based on the examination, for the diocese of London, of the Liber Examinationum, 1489-1516, London Guildhall Library MS. 9065 and the Acta quoad correctionem delinquentium 1470-73 and 1489-91, MS. 9064 (i) and (ii); for Bath and Wells on the Consistory Court Act book (1458-98), Somerset Record Office, Taunton, D/D/C AL.
[35] R VII E 6/6, 102, 111, 114, 135, 150, 191, 202, 212; F 78, 150.
[36] Norwich Cathedral Archives, Acta et Comperta 6, s.d. 7 July 1429; Hereford Diocesan Archives, Act book 0/3, p. 35; Lichfield, B/C/1/2, fol. 107r.
[37] R 55, fol. 235r.
[38] For example, the courts in York adopted sequestration of parties during matrimonial actions after the practice had been taken up in the Southern Province.

by no means the least of these. Its enactment and use in the thirteenth and fourteenth centuries show one case where the canon law left room for local courts and churches to adopt special rules to deal with local problems. Its abandonment is the best example we have of change and growth in canonical marriage practice in later medieval England.

9

INFANTICIDE IN THE PROVINCE OF CANTERBURY

DURING THE FIFTEENTH CENTURY

Gratian's Decretum (1140) and the Decretals of Pope Gregory IX (1234) contained the basic law of the Church in medieval Europe. In both are texts devoted to the proper punishment of infanticide.[1] Synodal legislation from individual provinces and dioceses also includes provisions condemning those who took the life of an infant.[2] The existence of these laws suggests that ecclesiastical sources may provide solid evidence about infanticide in medieval Europe. The apparent absence of prosecutions for homicide of infants from secular jurisdictions similarly suggests that we look to ecclesiastical sources before concluding that evidence about it is beyond historical recall.[3] And, in fact, two recent articles in this journal have made excellent use of ecclesiastical records in probing the subject.[4]

This short article is meant to continue that process, by examining the surviving fifteenth century court records of one part of the Western Church, the Province of Canterbury. Much larger than the northern Province of York, the Province covered all of southern England and Wales. Generalizations based on the records of the southern Province do not necessarily hold for the northern. But at least the records are those of the courts which had jurisdiction over the great bulk of the English population during the fifteenth century.

1. C. 2 q.5 c.20; X 5.10.3. I have used the current system of citation to canonical texts throughout, as given in *Traditio* XV (1959) pp. 542-64, and the modern edition of the texts, *Corpus Juris Canonici*, ed. A. Friedberg, 2 vols. (Leipzig, 1879). Citations to the *glossa ordinaria* are taken from the edition printed in Rome, 1582.
2. *Councils and Synods with other documents relating to the English Church II: 1205-1313*, eds. F. M. Powicke and C. R. Cheney, 2 vols. (Oxford, 1964), pp. 32, 137, 183, 234-35, 274, 302, 351, 410, 432, 520, 590. For Italian parallels see Richard C. Trexler, *Synodal Law in Florence and Fiesole, 1306-1518* (Vatican City, 1971), pp. 126-27.
3. See Barbara A. Kellum, "Infanticide in England in the later Middle Ages," *History of Childhood Quarterly* I (1974), pp. 371-75, with references noted therein. On the possibilities for research into the field see Lloyd deMause, "The Evolution of Childhood," in *The History of Childhood*, ed. deMause (New York, 1974), pp. 1-73, esp. pp. 28-29, and Mary Martin McLaughlin, "Survivors and Surrogates: Children and Parents from the Ninth to the Thirteenth Centuries," *ibid.*, pp. 101-81, esp. pp. 120-22.
4. Kellum, "Infanticide in England," and Richard C. Trexler, "Infanticide in Florence: New Sources and First Results," *History of Childhood Quarterly* I (1973), pp. 98-116.

There are, it will be observed, several deficiencies in the provincial court records from the point of view of a modern historian. Not least of these is the scarcity and irregularity of their survival. The fifteenth century is the first for which substantial numbers of court records remain. But the records which have survived from this period do provide good evidence of the existence of infanticide. And they do yield some valuable evidence about the circumstances which surrounded both its commission and its punishment.

The relevant evidence comes largely from *ex officio* Act books. These books were the records, compiled in every diocese, of disciplinary proceedings brought against men and women accused of violating the Church's law. Sometimes combined with the records of instance causes, that is civil litigation between two parties, sometimes placed in separate Act books, *ex officio* proceedings make up a substantial part of the remaining records of the medieval and early modern Church courts.[5] And in the Act books, spread among the prosecutions for fornication and adultery, for laying violent hands on clerks, for conducting secular business on Sundays, are proceedings against men and women accused of infanticide. The entries do not tell us all that we wish to know. For example, we can seldom learn whether the child killed was legitimate or not. Nor is the motive of the killer ever apparent. And statistics drawn from the Act books must be treated with extreme reserve, as will be demonstrated below. But the records do normally give the name of the person summoned, the detailed charge against him or her, the person's answer (if he or she appeared), and the disposition of the cause, whether flight by the accused person out of the court's jurisdiction, denial and successful compurgation, or conviction and punishment. What do these records tell us?

To begin with, the records demonstrate the existence of infanticide in later medieval England beyond doubt. Successful prosecutions and the detail with which some of the deaths are recorded make this indisputable. Thomas Patrick and his wife, Denise, for example, were cited before the Consistory Court at Rochester in 1447. Thomas admitted killing their child by holding it under water until it drowned.[6] Stephen Colyn, appearing at Canterbury in 1470, threw his illegitimate son into a ditch, where the child died.[7] Agnes Coke of Malling allowed her child

---

5. A brief description of these records can be found in Dorothy M. Owen, *The Records of the Established Church in England excluding parochial records* (British Records Association, 1970).
6. [Kent County Record Office, Maidstone] Act book DRb Pa 2, f. 69r: "Et fatetur submersionem prolis sue in aqua."
7. [Dean and Chapter Library, Canterbury Cathedral] Act book Y.1.11, f. 84r: "Post partum huiusmodi prostravit puerum in quadam fossa aquosa." In Rochester Act book DRb Pa 2, f. 191v (1452), Agnes Hamond was summoned "quia proiecit puerum non baptizatum in sepe," but only the summons is recorded.

to be burned to death in a fire.[8] Joan Meller and her husband were convicted in 1448 of having left their child exposed, in consequence of which the child perished.[9] The Act books contain quite a few cases of killing by drowning, burning, or exposure. Even after the passage of centuries, they do not make pretty reading.

The Act books also contain several prosecutions for some kind of abortion. Most are cases in which a third party had caused the death of a fetus by his mistreatment of the mother. John Wren, cited to appear before the Commissary court of the diocese of London in 1487, was charged with having "wounded his wife during the time she was pregnant so that he killed the child in her belly."[10] Thomas Deneham of Minster in the diocese of Canterbury was prosecuted in 1471. Against him it was objected that, although he knew his wife to be pregnant, he "imposed such inordinate labors [on her] that she aborted."[11] George Hemery was charged by the judge of the Consistory court of Rochester in 1493 with placing medicines in a drink given to a woman "in order to destroy the boy he had procreated."[12] A few cases record prosecutions against a mother for causing an abortion herself. For instance, the servant of Joan Gibbes of the parish of Deal (also named Joan but with no surname given in the court record) was accused in 1469 of having "killed the infant lately in her womb by means of herbs and medicines."[13] Whatever the exact sort of abortion involved, however, these prosecutions were apparently treated together with conventional infanticide.[14] There is no indication that they were dealt with more or less

8. Rochester Act book DRb Pa 2, f. 74v (1447): "Notatur quod necglexit prolem in tanto quod periit igne." She admitted the charge and was assigned "solemn penance" in the cathedral. For French examples of similarly gruesome incidents, see Y.-B. Brissaud, "L'infanticide a la fin du moyen age, ses motivations psychologiques et sa repression," *Revue historique de droit français et étranger*, ser. 4, vol. 50 (June, 1972), pp. 229-56.
9. Rochester Act book DRb Pa 2, f. 91r.
10. [Guildhall Library, London] Act book MS. 9064/2, f. 179r: "Et eciam verberavit uxorem suam in tanto quod tempore quo impregnata est occidit puerum in ventre eiusdem uxoris sue." A similar case is recorded in Canterbury Act book Y.1.3, f. 12v (1416). The accused successfully underwent canonical purgation to establish his innocence, however.
11. Act book Y.1.11, f. 126r: "Sciens Hevelyng esse inpregnatam et gravidam imposuit eidem tales inordinatos labores quorum occasione peperit abortium."
12. Rochester Act book DRb Pa 4, f. 232v: "Administrat medicinas in potum ad distruendum puerum procreatum per ipsum." Hemery later fled the court's jurisdiction, apparently in preference to conviction and punishment.
13. Canterbuty Act book Y.1.11, f. 57r: "Per erbas et medicinas interfecit infantem nuper in utero suo." A later instance is recorded in Act book Y.2.10, f. 100r (1521).
14. See *glossa ordinaria* ad C. 2 q. 5 c. 20 s.v. *consuluisti:* "Tunc puniantur, quia sunt homicidae, cum homicida dicatur etiam qui conceptum in utero deleverit per abortum." The records show no evidence of dispute about the time of "quickening" of the fetus. See, for example, Glanville Williams, *The Sanctity of Life and the Criminal Law,* (New York, 1957), pp. 151-152; David W. Louisell and John T. Noonan, Jr., "Constitutional Balance," *The Morality of Abortion: legal and historical perspectives* (Cambridge, Mass., 1970), pp.223-6.

severely than killing a newly born infant. The same procedure and similar penances were used against offenders.

The largest part of the prosecutions recorded in the Act books were, however, for the suffocation of an infant. When a location was specified in the records, the suffocation usually occurred in bed. No doubt almost all of these were cases of overlaying, that is, of cutting off an infant's circulation by laying on top of the child. For example, Stephen Tiler and his wife Joan were cited before the Rochester court for having "smothered their daughter [who was] lying between them in bed."[15] Alice Michel of Hythe was accused of having "lain on top of her boy in bed until he was dead."[16] Numerous cases specify simply that the accused "suffocavit prolem."[17] The remaining records contain more such instances of infanticide than any other sort. They fully support the suggestion modern historians have drawn from ecclesiastical legislation that overlaying was the principal means of infanticide and the major problem for the Church courts.

It is noteworthy that these prosecutions for infanticide by overlaying contained no allegation of intent to kill. Nor did any of the defendants plead lack of volition to escape punishment. Purely accidental death of a child might not have been punishable. But accidental death which occurred because the accused had been careless or negligent was culpable. It was enough that the child had been killed through the fault of the accused.

This result in practice was in accord with the formal canon law. Under the canons, negligent infanticide was to be punished as well as intentional killing.[18] Lack of desire to kill was cause for mitigation in the degree of punishment, not reason for absolution. That this law was followed in practice is clear not only in the overlaying cases, but also in a

15. Act book DRb Pa 2, f. 234r (1454): "Filiam suam inter eos in lecto iacentem oppresuerúnt."
16. Canterbury Act book Y.1.10, f. 130r (1472): "Supraiecuit puerum suum in lecto usque ad mortem eiusdem."
17. [County Record Office, Hereford] Act book 0/14, f. 68r (1481); London Act books, MS. 9064/1, f. 38v (1470), MS. 9064/2, fols. 170r (1487); 173r (1487); Canterbury Act book X.1.1, fols. 69r (1454), 113r (1455); Rochester Act books DRb Pa 2, fols. 125r (1449), 215r (1453); DRb Pa 4, fols. 234v (1493), 274r (1495). See also Kellum, "Infanticide in England," pp. 369-71; McLaughlin, "Survivors and Surrogates," notes 102-107.
18. X 5.10.3: "De infantibus autem qui mortui reperiunter cum patre et matre et non apparet, utrum a patre vel a matre oppressus sit ipse vel suffocatus, vel propria morte defunctus, non debent inde securi esse parentes, nec etiam sine poena." The theme was discussed by medieval canonists. See, for example, Hostiensis, *Commentaria in Libros Decretalium* (Venice, 1581), who concludes ad X 5.10.3, no. 1: "Qui non adhibet omnem diligentiam quam potest in levi saltem culpa est." Lyndwood, *Provinciale* (Oxford, 1679), 307 s.v. *ne opprimantur:* "Si autem levis culpa praecesserit, poenitentia trium annorum est indicenda; ut d. c. ulti. Ubi autem nulla praecesserit negligencia vel culpa, non est aliqua poenitentia imponenda."

number of prosecutions in which the description of the death of the child was described in enough detail to make clear that only negligence was shown. In 1453, for example, the Consistory court at Rochester ordered penance by public whipping to be imposed on Thomas Bayware of the parish of Halling when it was found that Thomas had left his house with a fire lit, the doors closed, and his two children inside. The children, aged two and four, were killed when the house caught fire.[19] Of course, this result may possibly be what Thomas intended. But it is at least equally plausible that he had been merely negligent. The important point is that the court made no distinction between the two types of infanticide, except in the severity of the penance assigned.

The punishment of both negligent and intentional killing is a matter of more than strictly legal interest. It shows that the Church courts were not concerned solely with the sin of the parent. The safety of the child was also important.[20] Were the sin of the parent alone important, it would have made no sense to punish those who had done nothing *intentional* to harm the infant. Punishment of unintentional killing was meant to indicate to the parents that unless they took enough care with their children to keep them alive, they risked prosecution in the Church courts and consequent public penance.

Synodal legislation which forbade placing children in the same bed with adults shows the same concern. The danger to the infant lay in accidental, even more than in intentional, suffocation.[21] Such legislation is inconsistent with a desire solely to punish the sin of the killer. To require parents to be careful in the way they arrange for their children to sleep must represent a judgment that children are deserving of protection. The aim of the Church clearly extended beyond chastisement for sin. It extended to the protection of children's lives.

To return now directly to the evidence of the court records, it should be stressed that not all those who were accused of infanticide admitted the crime. Indeed, many did not. In cases of denial, the courts

---

19. Act book DRb Pa 2, f. 239v: "Compertum est quod due proles sue fuerunt cremate et destructe eorum culpa quia ipsi clausis hostiis dimiserunt proles in domo cum igne, unde tota domus combusta fuit et proles similiter." Another example of negligence only expressly recorded as having been alleged against the parent is found in the same Act book, f. 74v (1447). For a clear statement of the canonical principle, see *glossa ordinaria* ad C.2 q.5 c. 20 s.v. *homicidii:* "Non tamen punitur ratione homicidii, sed ratione negligentiae, . . ., minor etiam iniungitur poena sive poenitentia ab ecclesia pro negligentia."

20. For an appreciation of this point see John T. Noonan, Jr., *Contraception; a History of its Treatment by the Catholic Theologians and Canonists* (Cambridge, Mass., 1965), pp. 85-88. I am also grateful to Professor Trexler for raising this matter with me, and for helping me to think the question through, although I am not at all sure that he agrees with my position.

21. *E.g.* the diocesan statute of Exeter I begins: "Quia contingit interdum ibi perpetrari homicidium ubi nulla voluntas set casus mortis causam prestiterit, . . ." *Councils and Synods* I, 234.

of the Province of Canterbury assigned canonical compurgation as the method of proof. Infanticide is normally a secret crime, and any other sort of proof may well have been impossible. Compurgation required that the accused take a solemn oath of innocence before the court. And he had to find a specified number of neighbors as compurgators or oath helpers, who would swear that they believed his oath was true. They swore to their belief in the word of the accused, not to the truth of the underlying facts, which must often have lain outside their first-hand knowledge.[22] In a fairly typical entry from the Canterbury records, for example, Harriet Hadvarden of Lyminge, accused of destroying her child, denied the charge. She was assigned a day to purge herself *cum tercia manu,* that is, by means of her own oath and that of two compurgators.[23] She found two suitable compurgators, they took the oaths successfully, and Harriet was dismissed by the court.

Canon law allowed a considerable amount of discretion to the judge in the use of compurgation. He had, in the first place, to pass on the acceptability of those selected. And the number of compurgators assigned lay largely within the judge's control.[24] For example, the fifteenth century Rochester and Canterbury records show cases of the assignment of seven, five, and two compurgators in infanticide cases.[25] The records do not reveal any reason for the divergent numbers required. But no illegal action or abuse of discretion on the part of the judge was necessarily involved. In this instance, the law allowed him to assign a form of compurgation in accordance with his assessment of the persons and the crime involved.[26]

However, the existence of such wide discretion, together with the incompleteness of many of the final parts of Act book entries, does make it impossible to generalize confidently about the way compurgation worked or about its effectiveness in practice. It must be enough to say that canonical compurgation was used in almost all cases. The remaining Act books reveal a single case in which a special inquisition

22. X 5.34.13.
23. Canterbury Act book Y.1.10, f. 201v (1474).
24. See, for example, Hostiensis, *Summa Aurea* V (Venice, 1574), tit. *de purg. can.,* no. 4: "Sed certe hodie tenent omnes, quod numerus compurgatorum arbitrarius est."
25. Compare Act book DRb Pa 4, f. 234v (1493): eight handed compurgation, with idem, f. 232v (1493): six handed compurgation, and with Canterbury Act book Y.1.10, f. 130r (1472): three handed compurgation. Many of the entries do not specify the number to be used, reciting merely that the accused was given a day "ad purgandum se."
26. There were, however, some rules which were mandatory for accused persons, depending on their status, and for some crimes. The most important of the former was probably that the compurgators be *eiusdem ordinis* as the accused. See Hostiensis, *Summa Aurea* V, tit. *de purg. can.,* nos. 4-5.

was called to investigate a charge of infanticide.[27] It may be worthy of note that canonical purgation was the same method of proving guilt and innocence that was used in most *ex officio* prosecutions. Adultery, fornication, and infanticide were treated alike as far as concerned the method of proof.

If the accused admitted the charge of infanticide, or if he denied it but failed in the assigned canonical purgation, the Church court assigned a public penance.[28] The penance was apparently much like those Professor Trexler has unearthed at Florence, except that the English records do not ordinarily refer to the direct use of charitable payments as penance, which was apparently the practice in the Italian court.[29] To take one full example, Joan Rose was convicted at Canterbury in 1470 of killing her son. The judge ordered that Joan should dress in penitential garb and "go before the procession in the parish church of Hythe on three Sundays with a wax candle of half a pound in her right hand and the knife with which she killed the boy, or a similar knife, in her left."[30] She was also ordered to go twice around the markets of Canterbury, Faversham, and Ashford in a similar fashion. This was obviously meant as a humiliating public admission of guilt, and as a warning to others against the crime of infanticide.

The penance was not, however, equivalent to secular punishment for homicide. There is no sign that any punishment, beyond the sort detailed above, was imposed on infanticides. Once the penance had been performed the guilty person was quit of prosecution in the external forum. No referral was made to the secular arm. The evidence suggests that no independent secular prosecution was undertaken.[31] And a public penance, no matter how humbling, is a temporary thing. Of course,

27. Act book DRb Pa 2, f. 239v: "Et facta inquisicione per vicarium ibidem Johannem Turnour, Robertum Pathe et alios de parochia predicta Omnium Sanctorum compertum est quod due proles sue fuerunt cremate . . ."
28. The penance to be imposed when the accused failed in compurgation was the same which would be assigned for the crime itself. See Hostiensis, *Summa Aurea* V, tit. *de purg. can.*, no. 7: "Regulam trado tibi, quod sicut puniretur de crimine, de quod impetebatur, si convinceretur considerato modo agendi, sic punietur si in purgatione deficiat." The nature of the penance was, of course, also subject to judicial discretion. See, for example, Joannes Andreae, *Novella Commentaria in Libros Decretalium* (Venice, 1581) ad X 5.10.3, no. 1: "Hodie penitentiae sunt arbitrariae."
29. "Infanticide in Florence," pp. 108-09. On the discretion vested in the judge in assigning suitable penance see X 5.12.6.
30. Canterbury Act book Y.1.10, f. 42r: "Et iudex iniunxit eidem quod camisia tunica solummodo induta, . . . , procedat processionem in ecclesia parochiali de Hyth tribus diebus dominicis cum candela cerea dimidii libri in manu dextera et cultellum in sinistra cum quod occidit puerum vel similem cultellum et quod circuiat simili modo mercatum Cant' bis et simili modo bis circa mercatum de Feversham et bis circa mercatum de Asshford simili modo."
31. Barbara Westman, "The Female Felon in Fourteenth Century England," *Viator* V (1975), *passim;* Kellum, "Infanticide in England," pp. 372-73.

the Church courts had no power to shed blood. It can therefore be said that they imposed the maximum penalties their law allowed. But the fact that infanticide was regulated largely as a public sin by the Church, and that penances similar to those used for other wrongful conduct within ecclesiastical cognizance were thought suitable clearly supports Dr. Kellum's argument that infanticide was considered as "something less than homicide" in medieval England.[32]

Another piece of evidence which supports this argument is the extent of the penances awarded in practice. In 1481 before the Commissary court at Hereford, for instance, the suffocation of a child combined with fornication was punished by six public whippings. But in the same year and Act book, three public whippings were awarded for adultery and fornication, and six public whippings were awarded to a man who admitted fathering an illegitimate child, no suggestion of infanticide being recorded.[33] In other words, the treatment meted out to the person guilty of infanticide did not differ in kind, or even necessarily in degree, from that thought appropriate for sexual offenses. The most severe penance I have found called for public penance lasting over a seven year period. But this occurred in the case of drowning a boy who was almost seven years old.[34] Killing a child of a relatively advanced age must have seemed to call for more serious punishment than the killing of an infant. The evidence of the Act books, incomplete as it is, does tend to confirm the notion that infanticide was not considered as homicide, by ecclesiastical judges and by ordinary people alike.

The most disappointing aspect of using the Church court records to shed light on the subject of infanticide is the question of incidence. One wants inevitably to know, how much infanticide was there? And to this question the Act books give no reliable answer. The largest number of prosecutions for the crime I have found for any one year is four. This was the number recorded in the Commissary court of the bishop of London in 1487.[35] But one case a year is a more usual number for most courts surveyed, and in some years none at all was recorded. In fact, my search through the records at Lichfield produced no cases in any year for the Consistory court of that diocese.[36] But even if we could assemble some average figures, they would tell us little about actual incidence. This is true for two reasons.

---

32. "Infanticide in England," p. 375. See also Williams, *Sanctity of Life,* p. 25, who misrepresents the attitude adopted in practice as opposed to legal theory.
33. See Act book 0/4 (1481), pp. 68, 70, 71, 75.
34. Rochester Act book DRb Pa 4, f. 146v (1481).
35. Act book MS. 9064/2, fols. 168v, 170r, 173r, 179r.
36. However, the *ex officio* prosecutions found were included in the instance Act books. The number is too small to make possible any conclusive statements about practice in this diocese.

First, as Professor Trexler points out, there is no necessary relationship between the number of prosecutions and actual frequency of the practice.[37] Infanticide is a crime people try to hide. There is no guarantee that all instances of it would come to light, or even that any percentage of the total would appear in the Church records. And there are additional traps. Not all those prosecuted were necessarily guilty. Many of the accused denied the crime and successfully underwent compurgation. But even were we to exclude these, we should be little better off, since successful wager of law does not necessarily prove innocence. Until we understand more about this aspect of canonical practice, it would be wrong to make generalizations about how effective (or ineffective) canonical purgation was in the detection and punishment of crime.

Second, there is no diocese for which we have all the *ex officio* records. Jurisdiction over public sin was widely dispersed in medieval England. The courts of bishops, archdeacons, rural deans, capitular bodies, and some other ecclesiastical dignitaries possessed it in various places.[38] And in no part of the Province of Canterbury do enough *ex officio* records survive from the fifteenth century to cover all the courts which had jurisdiction in one entire area. Thus, even if we could determine what percentage of the total number of acts of infanticide committed was actually reported to the Church courts, and what percentage of those persons accused was in fact guilty, we would still not be able to give a reliable total for the number of cases in any particular area, as opposed to any particular court. There is, unfortunately, no escape from the reluctant generalization Professor Trexler made about Florence. The English records can properly be used only to indicate that the practice of infanticide "was common enough."

Of the sex of those involved in infanticide the Act books tell us slightly more. No evidence is forthcoming which bears on the thesis that female children were killed more often than male.[39] The Act books do record that the accused *suffocavit puerum* often enough to make it clear that not only girls were killed.[40] But normally they used the neutral word *proles*. The sex of the child is not given, so that we know simply that a child has been killed. No proportional figures can be given.

37. "Infanticide in Florence," p. 103.
38. See my *Marriage Litigation in Medieval England* (Cambridge, 1974), pp. 144-46.
39. For this subject, see Emily R. Coleman, "Infanticide dans le haut moyen age," *Annales* (1974), pp. 315-35, dealing however with an earlier period.
40. *E.g.* Canterbury Act book Y.1.11, f. 84r (1470); but the same Act book also used the terms *infans* and *proles* to describe the children (fols. 57v, 74v, 174v). I have found only two cases in which the scribe specifically used the word *filia* to describe the child killed; Canterbury Act book X.1.1, f. 69r (1454); Rochester Act book DRb Pa 2, f. 234r (1454).

There is, however, slightly better evidence on the sex of those accused of the crime. The English records suggest that more women than men committed infanticide (or at least were accused of having done so). But they also show it was by no means an exclusively female crime. For example, of the ten prosecutions recorded in the diocesan court at Canterbury between 1469 and 1474, eight were brought against women, two against men.[41] Between 1447 and 1455 at Rochester, there were thirteen prosecutions for infanticide. Of these five were against women, three against men, and five against a man and woman together.[42] It would therefore be wrong to conclude that in England at least, infanticide was committed exclusively by women.

Most of the infanticide prosecutions in the Church courts of the Province of Canterbury seem to have involved the parents of the child. At least this is a safe generalization if the sourt scribe used the adjective *suum* or *suam* correctly in preparing his record, since most entries use the possessive pronoun in describing the child killed. That is, they say that the accused had caused the death of *prolem suam* or *puerum suum*. Where the adjective was omitted, sometimes it is still likely that the infant was the child of the person accused, and that the scribe simply did not bother to include the fact of parentage. This was probably true in many prosecutions against a husband and wife together. In a few cases where the records make clear that the guilty person was not the parent, there was nevertheless a relation with the infant, as in the case of Agnes Turnour, prosecuted at Canterbury in 1474. She was the child's grandmother.[43] This still leaves, however, some entries unaccounted for. It is not a large number. But it may well be that these entries record prosecutions against persons other than the parents of the child. As is true for many questions of importance to modern historians, the Act books provide some evidence on this one, but no statistical conclusions.

This, in brief summary, is the evidence about infanticide in fifteenth-century England which can be drawn from the court records of the Province of Canterbury. One scarcely needs to suggest that it is evidence only. It is incomplete and often inconclusive. But it is surely evidence worth having, part of the picture historians must reconstruct. It shows clearly that infanticide occurred in practice, and that the Church courts undertook prosecution against it. What is harder to assess with accuracy is

41. Against men: Act book Y.1.11, fols 84r (1470), 126r (1471). Against women: Y.1,10, fols. 42r (1470), 130r (1472), 201v (1474); Y.1.11, fols. 57r (1469), 144r (1472), 175v (1472), 185r (1472), 322r (1474).
42. Against men: Act book DRb Pa 2, fols. 215r (1453), 239r (1453), 255v (1455); Against women: DRb Pa 2, fols. 74r (1447); 111v (1449), 125r (1449), 191v (1452), 228r (1453). Against both: DRb Pa 2, fols. 69r (1447), 91r (1448), 111v (1449), 234r (1454), 275r (1455).
43. Act book Y.1.11, f. 322r: "Notatur quod eius consensu interfactus erat infantulus cuiusdam filie eiusdem."

what the records prove about contemporary attitudes towards infanticide. If modern historians are correct that the secular courts did not in practice proceed against the crime of infanticide, certainly it is important that the Church, more than the royal courts, exercised regular jurisdiction over it. Certainly it is important that ecclesiastical penance, rather than secular punishment, seemed an appropriate way to deal with convicted infanticides. This, together with much of the evidence outlined above, gives support to the argument that infanticide was not considered the equivalent of homicide in medieval Europe.

It would be a mistake, however, to go much beyond this. It would be wrong to conclude that because infanticide was apparently treated as something less than homicide, it was therefore no crime at all. To speak, as some writers have done, about a "common law freedom of abortion" is unwarranted if the phrase implies that one could cause the death of a fetus with impunity.[44] The royal courts were courts of limited jurisdiction in medieval England. They assumed that local and ecclesiastical courts would take cognizance of a great deal of unlawful conduct.[45] It does not follow that because the royal courts did not regularly punish a particular type of conduct, the conduct was therefore permissible according to Common Law.[46] What it does show is that in contemporary eyes, jurisdiction over the crime was properly lodged outside the royal courts. Infanticide, in the present state of the evidence, appears to be one such crime. But the Church was a legitimate public authority in medieval Europe. Its role in punishing unlawful conduct deserves to be taken seriously. The fifteenth-century records of the Province of Canterbury do give reasons for thinking that medieval men did not regard infanticide with the horror we associate with premeditated homicide. But they do not show that society regarded the

44. See Cyril C. Means, Jr., "The Phoenix of Abortional Freedom," 17 *New York Law Forum* (1971), pp. 335-410. It is certainly permissible to argue, as Professor Means does, that American courts are not bound to accept the ecclesiastical law as part of the English Common Law as received in the United States. It is likewise permissible to argue (although it is conjectural) that crime crimes society considered as heinous were tried by the royal courts, so that the omission of a crime from royal jurisdiction indicates a lower degree of importance. What cannot be reasonably maintained is that any conduct not punished by the secular courts necessarily was legal. Professor Means comes close to falling into this position when he says, at p. 336, that "women enjoyed a common-law liberty to terminate at will an unwanted pregnancy, from the reign of Edward III to that of George III."

45. See G. O. Sayles, *The Court of King's Bench in Law and History* (London, 1959) p. 12; S. F. C. Milsom, *Historical Foundations of the Common Law* (London, 1969), p. 356.

46. Much the same could be said of heresy, for example. The most terrible punishment was imposed by the secular government for the latter crime, but the question of guilt or innocence could be tried only in the ecclesiastical courts.

fate of infants with indifference.[47] On the contrary, they show that some protection was afforded children against both intentional and negligent killing. Infanticide was a crime punishable by a regular system of public courts.

47. See for example the sentiment echoed in the *glossa ordinaria* ad X 5.10.3 s.v. *nec etiam sine poena:* "Si vero sponte hoc fecerunt, tunc gravissima poenitentia debet eis imponi, aliquantulum maior quam pro alio homicidio quia magis peccare videtur proprium filium occidendo."

10

SUPPORT ORDERS, CHURCH COURTS, AND
THE RULE OF *FILIUS NULLIUS*:
A REASSESSMENT OF THE COMMON LAW

IN 1973 the United States Supreme Court held that a state violated the equal protection clause by denying illegitimate children a right to parental support granted to legitimate children.[1]
Commentators have regarded that decision as a worthy departure
from the common law rule that denied illegitimate children any
right to support from their father. But, as those commentators have
noted, the decision simply forbade discrimination between legitimate and illegitimate children.[2] It stopped short of granting an absolute right to support. It did not challenge the widespread American rule, based on English common law, that in the absence of
statute an illegitimate child has no inherent right to parental support.

This article suggests that the approach of the American courts
rests on a misreading of the historical evidence. Admittedly, the
treatment of illegitimates at English common law is well established. "The common law of England," concludes a leading contemporary authority, "was ruthless in its denial of any rights to
children born out of wedlock."[3] He merely repeats what every
case,[4] every treatise,[5] and every law review article[6] states. The

---

[1] *See* Gomez v. Perez, 409 U.S. 535, 538 (1973).

[2] *See, e.g.,* Margolin, *Family Law; Rights of Illegitimate Children,* 1973/1974 ANN.
SURVEY AM. L. 233, 245-46; Shaw & Kass, *Illegitimacy, Child Support, and Paternity Test-
ing,* 13 HOUSTON L. REV. 41, 45 (1975).

[3] 1 S. SCHATKIN, DISPUTED PATERNITY PROCEEDINGS § 1.08, at 1-27 (4th ed. rev. 1975).

[4] *See, e.g.,* Baugh v. Maddox, 266 Ala. 175, 95 So. 2d 268 (1957); Schneider v. Kennat,
267 App. Div. 589, 47 N.Y.S.2d 180 (1944); Butcher v. Pollard, 32 Ohio App. 2d 1, 5, 288
N.E.2d 204, 207 (1972); Annot., 30 A.L.R. 1069 (1924).

[5] *See, e.g.,* P. BROMLEY, FAMILY LAW 592-93 (5th ed. 1976); H. CLARK, LAW OF DOMESTIC
RELATIONS § 5.1, at 155 (1968); W. HOOPER, THE LAW OF ILLEGITIMACY 135-36 (1911);
J. MADDEN, HANDBOOK OF THE LAW OF PERSONS AND DOMESTIC RELATIONS § 105, at 348
(1931).

bastard was *filius nullius,* a child without rights. According to traditional thought, only the passage of the Elizabethan Poor Law in 1576,[7] when the burden of supporting illegitimate children from parish funds had grown too great for men to bear with equanimity, fastened an obligation to support on the father. That statute, moreover, never formed part of the common law received by American courts. A strictly penal measure, meant rather to preserve parish funds than to protect infants, it allegedly left intact the fundamental proposition that the bastard was *filius nullius.*[8]

Initially, this proposition should arouse suspicion. The society that spawned the common law admitted no great disjunction between the teachings of morality and the dictates of law; and the duty to care for one's child, legitimate or not, was a part of the moral teaching of the time. This duty was enjoined on men by natural law.[9] The country that gave birth to the common law was also ruled by a succession of kings descended from an illegitimate sire.[10] American courts and commentators should have been skeptical of the proposition that such a society cast no enforceable obligation on the parent to care for his newly born infant.

In fact, the proposition is mistaken. The illegitimate child had an enforceable support right prior to 1576. True, the common law itself did not provide an action against the father of a bastard child. But the obligation to support was enforced in the courts of the English Church. The common law's apparent neglect of the child indicates only the jurisdictional boundary between the courts of Church and State, not a disregard of the illegitimate child.

---

6 *See, e.g.,* Stone, *Illegitimacy and Claims to Money and Other Property: A Comparative Study,* 15 INT'L & COMP. L.Q. 505, 507-08 (1966); Note, *Liability of Possible Fathers: A Support Remedy for Illegitimate Children,* 18 STAN. L. REV. 859 (1966); 6 BAYLOR L. REV. 520 (1954).

7 18 Eliz. 1, c. 3 (1576).

8 *See* 1 I. PINCHBECK & M. HEWITT, CHILDREN IN ENGLISH SOCIETY 206-14 (1969); Robbins & Deák, *The Familial Property Rights of Illegitimate Children: A Comparative Study,* 30 COLUM. L. REV. 308, 316-19 (1930).

9 Thomas Aquinas echoes the same Roman law text used by the canonists to show that the care of one's offspring is part of natural law. T. AQUINAS, SUMMA THEOLOGIAE 1a2ae.94,2 (28 Blackfriars ed. 83). *See also* text accompanying notes 18-20 *infra.* The right to existence and upbringing must, of course, be distinguished from the right to inherit from the parent.

10 2 F. POLLOCK & F. MAITLAND, THE HISTORY OF ENGLISH LAW 397 (2d ed. reissued 1968).

Proof of this assertion must rest in an examination of the canon law enforced in the English ecclesiastical courts.[11] This territory is unfamiliar for the legal historian as well as the lawyer. It calls for an investigation of proceedings not treated by most texts. But the development of the common law rules regulating domestic relations cannot be understood without it. Justice in England was not a unitary matter. Merchant courts, borough courts, and ecclesiastical courts all exercised jurisdiction over matters not covered, or only partially covered, by the royal courts. Whatever conflicts might have arisen among the various courts, all men assumed that each tribunal would carry out part of the total task of regulating men's behavior. Marriage, probate, and defamation, for example, all belonged to the jurisdiction of the ecclesiastical courts.[12] No one disputed this allocation. As this article will show, enforcement of a father's duty to support his illegitimate child also fell within the purview of the canon law. Only in this restricted sense did the common law deny the illegitimate child the support of his father.

I. THE CANON LAW

The law of the Western Church required the father to support his child, even if the child were born out of wedlock. The duty is a notable example of the twin influences of humanity and Christianity on the law. Classical Roman law had imposed no obligation on the father; the regime of *patria potestas* allowed him the power of life and death over any of his offspring.[13] Imperial legislation softened this regime by requiring the father to support children born of legitimate marriage or of the recognized Roman form of

---

11 In medieval England, every bishop and every ecclesiastical dignitary kept a regular court of law, in which his officials administered the canon law. These courts had jurisdiction over both clergy and laity, they met approximately every three weeks in regular session, and the main courts were staffed by professionally trained lawyers and judges. There were, in other words, few places in England without contact with the legal system of the Church. For a good description of the courts of one English diocese, see B. WOOD-COCK, MEDIEVAL ECCLESIASTICAL COURTS IN THE DIOCESE OF CANTERBURY (1952).

12 S. MILSOM, HISTORICAL FOUNDATIONS OF THE COMMON LAW 13-15 (1969).

13 W. BUCKLAND, A TEXT-BOOK OF ROMAN LAW FROM AUGUSTUS TO JUSTINIAN 103 (3d ed. rev. 1963). The scholarly literature on the subject in Roman law is extensive, and not free from disagreement. Two fairly recent articles containing reference to earlier literature are Lanfranchi, *Ius exponendi e obbligo alimentare nel diritto romano classico*, 6 STUDIA ET DOCUMENTA HISTORIAE ET IURIS 5 (1940) and Zoz, *In tema di obbligazioni alimentari*, 73 BULLETTINO DELL' ISTITUTO DI DIRITTO ROMANO 323 (1970).

concubinage.[14] But even under Justinianic law, the father had no duty to support spurious children.[15] That duty was added by medieval canon law. Pope Clement III's decretal letter setting forth the obligation was later incorporated into the Gregorian *Decretals* (1234), thereby becoming a standard text for the courts of the Western Church.[16] Parents had to furnish the necessities of life to all their children, according to the standard their means allowed. Even the child born of fornication or adultery had the right to this basic protection.

The medieval canonists and civilians who treated the question did not undertake as detailed and thoughtful an analysis of the support obligation as did the jurists of the 17th and 18th centuries.[17] But many canonists pointed out the distinction between Roman and canon law. They justified the latter as superior. Hostiensis (d. 1271), for example, distinguished the canon law rule from the "rigor and severity of the secular laws, . . . which nature neither moves nor softens." Children, he wrote, "are always to be nourished, according to the benevolence and equity of the canon law, natural law being considered." [18] Antonius de Butrio (d. 1408) defended canonical usage on several grounds: "And note that the Church intrudes itself into [questions of] providing sustenance to a son, and this because of the sin against the instinct of nature, or when

---

14 *See* 3 B. Biondi, Il Diritto Romano Cristiano 290 (1954); 1 P. Bonfante, Corso di Diritto Romano: Diritto di Famiglia 379 (1963) .

15 NOV. 89.15.pr. This text, from the Novels of Justinian, can be found in 3 Corpus Iuris Civilis (T. Mommsen, P. Krüger, R. Schoell, & G. Kroll eds. 1911) . There is a translation of the entire corpus of Roman law in The Civil Law (S. Scott trans. 1932).

16 X 4.7.5 (2 Corpus Juris Canonici, col. 688 (A. Freidberg ed. 1879)). A modern commentary which recognizes this in passing is Ayer, *Legitimacy and Marriage*, 16 Harv. L. Rev. 22, 23 (1902).

17 *Compare, e.g.*, Bartolus (d. 1357) , Commentaria at Digest 25.3.5.17, no. 1 (1580-81), *with* H. Grotius (d. 1645), De Iure Belli et Pacis lib. 2, c. 7.4 (1646) . Canonists were the academic writers on the law of the Church, civilians on the Roman (civil) law. For the most part their writing consisted of commentaries on the formal rules and enactments of the two laws. Perhaps because both canon and Roman law were based on official texts, rather than the system of case law precedent familiar to a modern American lawyer, the academic writers exerted a substantial influence over both court practice and legal education. For an introduction to the subject, see J. Clarence Smith, Medieval Law Teachers and Writers: Civilian and Canonist (1975).

18 Lectura in Libros Decretalium at X 4.7.5, no. 10 (1581): *"Solutio: illud secundum rigorem et subtilitatem legum secularium, ut ibi., quem nec natura movet nec mitigat, nam secundum benignitatem et aequitatem iuris canonici semper alendi sunt, considerato iure naturali."*

[sustenance] is denied for want of marriage, or when the Church fills a gap in the secular forum." [19] For him, like most canonists, the principles of equity and benevolence supplied sufficient reason to justify the canon law's deviation from the harsh Roman law rule.[20]

The divergence between the two forms of law, on the other hand, did not prevent the canonists from using the Roman law to justify and define the nature of the support obligation. They cited texts from the *Institutes*, *Code*, and *Digest*, virtually the whole of the Roman law, to show that natural law imposed a duty on all parents to nurture and support their children. They also borrowed the standards for determining the amount of support, for fixing the duration of the obligation, and for settling the means of proving paternity from the civil law. They saw no incongruity in using Roman law texts to shape an obligation towards illegitimate children, an obligation that Roman law itself denied.[21] This habit was not peculiar to paternity proceedings. It is found throughout medieval canon law.[22] This canonical borrowing, however, does highlight the often overlooked influence of the civil law upon English family law. Roman law, enforced first in the Church courts, later in the royal courts, helped to define the reach of the obligation to support.

The obligation to support adopted by the medieval canonists was a more extensive obligation than English or American law was to enforce subsequently. The duty was, in the first place, a

---

19 COMMENTARIA IN LIBROS DECRETALIUM at X 4.7.5, no. 6 (1578): *"Et nota quod super alimentis filio administrandis se intromittit ecclesia; et hoc propter peccatum contra instinctum naturae, vel quando denegantur propter defectum matrimonii, vel quando ecclesia supplet defectum fori secularis."*

20 *See also* BALDUS, COMMENTARIA at CODE 6.61.8.4d (1586): *"Hic dicitur quod pater debet alere filium non ratione ususfructus, sed ratione ipsius naturae . . . , quod est notabile dictum."* ("Here it is said that a father should support a son not by reason of [the son's] usefulness, but because of nature itself, which is a noteworthy statement.").

21 A clear example of this use of Roman law is the medieval *glossa ordinaria* at X 4.7.5 s.v. *secundum facultates*. Three principles are laid down: 1) that the support should be given according to the resources available, 2) that the child should be sustained with the mother before the age of three, after that with the father, and 3) that the obligation was reciprocal. The gloss supports all three points with citations from Roman law, principally from sections of DIGEST 25.3.

22 *See generally* Kuttner, *Some Considerations on the Role of Secular Law and Institutions in the History of Canon Law*, 2 SCRITTI DI SOCIOLOGIA E POLITICA IN ONORE DI LUIGI STURZO 349 (1953); Naz, *Droit romain*, 4 DICTIONNAIRE DE DROIT CANONIQUE 1502 (1949).

reciprocal one. Parents must support their children. Children must also support their parents.[23] Need and ability were the determinants. The duty also extended beyond parent and child. Grandparents, even aunts and uncles, could be required to support a child if the primary sources of support, the natural parents, were too poor.[24] The rights and duties of members of a family went a good deal further than they do today. The father's duty to nourish his illegitimate child was only one part of a much broader obligation.

II. THE ECCLESIASTICAL REMEDY

So much, of course, is only theory. The English Church courts did not put into practice every part of the medieval canon law.[25] If the duty of support were one of the parts they omitted, then the common law really did ignore the plight of the illegitimate child. Evidence of the conformity of English practice with medieval canon law must come from the contemporary Church court records.[26] Those records, unfortunately, are not easy to use or to

---

23 *See, e.g.,* HOSTIENSIS, LECTURA at X 4.7.5, nos. 7-9.

24 *See* BARTOLUS, COMMENTARIA at DIGEST 25.3.1 § *Item rescriptum,* no. 2; G. DURANTIS, SPECULUM IUDICIALE IV, tit. *qui filii sint legitimi,* no. 6; Joannes Andreae, COMMENTARIA at X 4.7.5, no. 7 (1581).

25 *See, e.g.,* Donahue, *Roman Canon Law in the Medieval English Church: Stubbs vs. Maitland Re-examined After 75 Years in the Light of Some Records from the Church Courts,* 72 MICH. L. REV. 647, 660-64 (1974).

26 These records, which are today kept in county and diocesan archives throughout England, are the basis of this article. The majority of the records which once existed has been lost over the course of the centuries, but the author has examined most of the surviving medieval and a large sample of the remaining 16th century records. Citation to these sources is given hereinafter by diocese. Those used, with corresponding modern archive, are as follows:

Canterbury	Library of the Dean and Chapter, Canterbury.
Chichester	West Sussex Record Office, Chichester.
Durham	Library of the Department of Palaeography and Diplomatic, University of Durham.
Hereford	Hereford County Record Office, Hereford.
Lichfield	Joint Record Office, Lichfield.
London	Guildhall Library, London [MS. 9064 records] and Greater London Council Record Office [DL/C records].
Norwich	Norfolk Record Office, Norwich.
Rochester	Kent County Record Office, Maidstone.
St. Albans	Hertfordshire Record Office, Hertford.
York	Borthwick Institute of Historical Research [Cause Papers and A B Act Books] and York Minister Library [M 2(1) Act Books].

interpret.[27] They survive in limited quantities, and the scribal habits of recording in the Act books often conceal more about the details of litigation than they reveal. Nevertheless, the available evidence is clear enough to show that the courts did enforce the obligation to support illegitimate children. The Act books demonstrate that the duty was not mere canonical theory.

Litigated cases imposing support obligations came before the Church courts in two ways: petitions by the mother on behalf of the child,[28] and prosecutions *ex officio* for fornication or adultery resulting in the birth of a child.[29] Either type of dispute could give rise to a support order entered against the putative father. A case heard in the diocese of York in 1371 furnishes a good example of a petition brought by an unwed mother. Emmota Ripon appeared before the official (the principal judge in the court) together with William of Hexham. She "humbly asked that the same William of Hexham be condemned, compelled, and coerced to contribute to the support" of the child she alleged he had fathered.[30] William disputed paternity. He "replied and said that he did not know whether the child was his or not." [31] He admitted sexual relations

---

[27] Act books were the official records of procedure taken in the ecclesiastical courts during each court session or consistory. In them, the court scribe recorded the names of the parties, the subject matter, the action taken (*e.g.*, the introduction of documents, the production of witnesses, or the delivery of sentence), and the terms assigned for the next hearing. They were unlike modern judicial opinions, in other words, in that they were normally confined to procedure. They were intended principally for future reference for internal court purposes. Fuller explanation of the nature of the court records can be found in D. OWEN, THE RECORDS OF THE ESTABLISHED CHURCH IN ENGLAND EXCLUDING PAROCHIAL RECORDS (1974); R. HELMHOLZ, MARRIAGE LITIGATION IN MEDIEVAL ENGLAND 7-11 (1974). An example of a particularly full record is transcribed in Donahue & Gordus, *A Case From Archbishop Stratford's Audience Act Book and Some Comments on the Book and its Value*, 2 BULL. MEDIEVAL CANON L. 45 (1972).

[28] Persons other than the mother could act for the child under the law. *See, e.g.*, BARTOLUS, COMMENTARIA at DIGEST 25.3.5.2, no. 3: "*Quaero an istud officium iudicis possit implorari ab alio quam a filio: Respondero quod sic quia consanguinei et alii admittuntur ad petendum alimenta pro filio.*" ("I ask whether the intervention of the judge can be sought by anyone but the son: I reply that it can, because blood relatives and others are admitted to seek sustenance for a son.") The mother was the person most closely concerned, however, and the English cases found were normally brought by the mother.

[29] BARTOLUS, COMMENTARIA at DIGEST 44.7.52, no. 1: "*Alimenta petuntur officio iudicis, quando non habet unde se alat.*" ("Sustenance is demanded by virtue of the judge's office, when [the child] does not have the means to support himself.")

[30] Act book M 2(1)c, f. 2r (1371): "*[I]psa Emmota peciit humiliter ab eodem domino officiali prefatum Willelmum de Hexham condempnari compelli et coherceri contribuere alimentacionem dicte prolis per eundem Willelmum ut ipsa asseruit de eadem suscitate.*"

[31] *Id.*: "*Willelmus respondit et dixit ipsum nescire an fuit proles sua vel non.*"

with her. But he suspected that someone else equally might be the father, "because he had been overseas and in other remote parts for a long time." [32] Like many such cases, this one came before the court only because the parties could not agree on the fundamental question of paternity. Emmota, however, swore a formal oath that William was the father. Having heard this, the official condemned William to pay two shillings for arrearages and to pay two pence weekly in the future toward child support. This was an interim order. The law required support to be paid until the question of paternity could be determined.[33] William was given an opportunity to prove that someone else was the father. The Act book, however, contains no further entry on the case. William may have acquiesced in the temporary order, or he may have settled the quarrel out of court. In either case, the court had acted to protect the child. It enforced the obligation of the putative father.

Ex officio prosecutions for sexual offenses provided the second forum for support orders in favor of illegitimate children. The statistical incidence of detection and prosecution of fornication and adultery in medieval England is unknowable, but pregnancies of unwed women must have brought to light many such affairs. When they did, the Church courts routinely required the father to support the child. For example, at Canterbury in 1465, Walter Tyler was prosecuted *ex officio* for fornication with Agnes Elys. He confessed. The court ordered him to undergo public penance, to provide a dowry for Agnes,[34] and to "cause the child to be nourished." [35] The Act book gives no details about what may have been a very complicated family matter. The possibility of marriage between Agnes and Walter is not mentioned; nor are the attitudes

---

32 *Id.*: "[D]ominus officialis interogavit ipsum Wellelmum an ipsa Emmota fuit cum aliquo alio homine diffamata, qui dixit quod nescivit quia fuit per longa tempora in partibus transmarinis et aliis locis remotis."

33 See the *glossa ordinaria* at CODE 5.25.4 s.v. *examinabit* (1582), which specifies summary procedure to determine the question of paternity but requires the father to provide interim support.

34 This may be a result of the civil law rule that a daughter could be disinherited and denied a dowry by her father if she committed fornication. *See* CODE 3.28.19; G. DURANTIS, SPECULUM IUDICIALE IV, tit. *qui filii sint legitimi*, no. 15. There are several orders to endow in the English court records, particularly in those at Canterbury, but not enough to say with any assurance how regularly courts required the guilty man to furnish a dowry for the woman he would not marry.

35 Act book X.8.3, f. 80r (1465) : "*Item quod dotat mulierem. Item quod nutriri faciat prolem etc.*"

of their parents, if they had living parents. The judge made no monetary award, perhaps leaving it to negotiation between the parties and their families. Clearly, however, the Church courts did not ignore the child. They routinely imposed the burden of support on the putative father. When the woman was pregnant at the time of the prosecution, the order specified that the obligation would attach "when the time comes." [36] A search that has been by no means exhaustive has produced examples of support orders for illegitimate children from the ecclesiastical courts of Canterbury,[37] Chichester,[38] Lichfield,[39] Lincoln,[40] London,[41] Norwich,[42] Rochester,[43] St. Albans,[44] and York.[45] This list includes virtually all dioceses where any medieval records remain.[46] The support obligation evidently was enforced throughout England.

Whoever initiated proceedings, paternity had to be established to warrant a support order; and paternity always has presented hard problems of proof. The medieval commentators recognized that proof of paternity was "difficult and almost impossible." [47] Following the outlines of Roman law, they therefore adopted a two step procedure weighted slightly in favor of the child. The first step was to be handled summarily.[48] If access was established

---

[36] Canterbury Act book Y.1.11, f. 217r (1473): *"Et iudex iniunxit eidem quod dotaret mulierem ac nutriri faciat puerum cum tempus advenerit."*

[37] *Id.*, ff. 225r (1473); 324v (1474). The largest number of support orders found in a single Act book comes from Canterbury Act book Y.1.10, ff. 180v (1473), 239v (1475), 244v (1475), 287v (1476), 291v (1477), 325c (1477), 334v (1478), 344r (1478).

[38] Act book Ep I/10/1, f. 92r (1509).

[39] Act book B/C/2/3, f. 74r (1529).

[40] 2 VISITATIONS IN THE DIOCESE OF LINCOLN, 1517-1531, at 15 (35 Lincoln Record Soc., A. Thompson ed. 1944).

[41] Act book MS. 9064/1, f. 40v (1470).

[42] Act book ACT/4b, f. 67r (1533).

[43] Act book DRb Pa 2, f. 58r (1446).

[44] Act book ASA 7/1, f. 8r (1516).

[45] Act book Cons. A B 1, f. 80r (1419). *See also* THE ROYAL VISITATION OF 1559, at 16, 88 (187 Surtees Soc., C. Kitching ed. 1975).

[46] The exceptions are Hereford and Durham, from which I have found no *ex officio* proceedings. The records from both do include support cases brought at the instance of private parties, however.

[47] 2 J. MASCⱭRDUS, DE PROBATIONIBUS, concl. 788, nos. 5-6 (1703).

[48] DIGEST 25.3.5.8; BARTOLUS, COMMENTARIA at *id., "In causa alimentorum proceditur summarie, et sentencia lata non facit praeiudicium in causa filiacionis ordinarie exercenda."* ("In a case about support, procedure is summary, and a sentence handed down does not create a prejudgment in a filiation case proceeding in ordinary course.") . *See also* B. BIONDI, *supra* note 13, at 295.

and the woman named the man as the father, he was required to support the child until full hearing and determination of the claim of paternity. The courts were to accept no defendant's protest or evidence of access by other men.[49] Theoretically, this initial order did not prejudice the second, full hearing on the question.[50] The order was intended to guarantee support for the infant once the woman had made a presumptive case.

In the second hearing, the medieval commentators called for further proof. But even at that hearing, in the nature of things, proof of paternity could never reach a high level of accuracy. As a result the jurists were prepared to sanction "proof by presumptions and conjectures." [51] They listed the facts tending to prove filiation. Of these, sexual relations, or at least the continued opportunity for sexual relations, naturally was the most compelling. Other factors to be considered were the common fame of the community, prior admissions against interest by the father, and care for the child as one's own, even if not coupled with a claim of paternity.[52] Antonius de Butrio concluded that "whenever treatment [as one's child] is coupled with the opinion and fame of the neighbors, this without doubt proves and concludes filiation." [53] But most jurists left much to the discretion of the judge. They were content to enumerate the factors he should consider. They never accepted what has become the American rule that proof of paternity must be "clear, convincing, and satisfactory." [54]

The scarcity and brevity of the remaining records make it impossible to determine with assurance how closely the English Church courts followed the elaborations of the jurists. What evidence there is suggests general congruence with medieval theory, with a greater use of compurgation than the medieval treatises

---

49 DIGEST 25.3.1.14; 37.9.1.14; CYNUS DE PISTOIA, COMMENTARIA at CODE 5.25.4, no. 4 (1578).

50 DIGEST 1.6.10; 25.3.5.9; BARTOLUS, *supra* note 48.

51 2 J. MASCARDUS, *supra* note 47, concl. 788, nos. 5-6; BALDUS, COMMENTARIA at DIGEST 1.6.10, no. 2. *See also* R. BARBARIN, LA CONDITION JURIDIQUE DU BATARD 33 (1960); L. CREMIEU, DES PREUVES DE LA FILIATION NATURELLE NON RECONNUE (1907).

52 HOSTIENSIS, SUMMA AUREA IV, tit. *qui filii sint legitimi*, no. 8 (1574); 2 J. MASCARDUS, *supra* note 47, concl. 790-92.

53 COMMENTARIA IN LIBROS DECRETALIUM at X 4.17.3, no. 10: *"Dico quod quandoque concurrit tractatus cum opinione et fama viciniae, et absque dubio hic probat filiationem et concludit filiationem."*

54 *See generally* 1 S. SCHATKIN, *supra* note 3, § 3.07.

would lead one to expect. Some Church courts clearly observed the division between the initial hearing for support purposes and the later full determination of paternity. They acted summarily in the initial hearing.[55] At Rochester in 1456, for example, Richard Bromlegh was prosecuted for fornication with Agnes Malemete, who had given birth to a child. He admitted fornication; he denied paternity. "And as for the procreation of the child, he said that the woman was defamed with other persons, and therefore he doubts the fathering." [56] The judge, noting this plea, nevertheless made a summary order. Bromlegh "was warned to pay two pence weekly for support of the child until it should be established [that there was] another father." [57] Such summary disposition was the pattern. The *exceptio plurium concubentium*, denying support where other men have had sexual relations with the mother, was not an absolute bar to support, as many American courts were subsequently to hold.[58] In some cases the woman was obliged to find compurgators, that is, neighbors who would swear they believed her oath, to support her claim.[59] But if she did, the court made the initial support order envisioned by Roman law and adopted by the medieval commentators.

About the second, full determination of paternity less can be said. Virtually all the evidence comes from the initial hearings. Only one case, a filiation proceeding from Lichfield in 1529, has survived to show that evidence of common fame and the man's treatment of the child as his own was introduced.[60] An initial

---

[55] The cases almost invariably reach a conclusion in one or at the most two court sessions; *e.g.*, Canterbury Act book X.8.3, f. 14r (1463), the record of a case in which the man was ordered to appear on July 4. He did not appear on that day but did appear on July 27, when a support order was entered against him.

[56] Act book DRb Pa 3, f. 521r (1456) : *"Et quoad prolis procreationem, dicit quod mulier est diffamata de aliis personis et ideo dubitat de genitura sua."*

[57] *Id.*: *"[T]amen monitus est quod solvat ad alimentationem prolis ii d. qualibet septimana quousque constiterit de alio genitore."*

[58] On this defense, see H. CLARK, *supra* note 5, § 5.3, at 167. Its checkered career in civil law countries is interestingly sketched in Scholtens, *Maintenance of Illegitimate Children and the Exceptio Plurium Concubentium*, 72 S. AFR. L.J. 144 (1955).

[59] Hereford Act book I/12 s.d. 22 March 1583; Lichfield Act book B/C/2/3, f. 74r (1529); Norwich Act book ACT/4b, f. 67r (1533); York Act book M 2(1)c, f. 2r (1371).

[60] Lichfield Act book B/C/2/3, f. 57r (1529), in which a master of a girl living in his house was said to have fathered her child. One of the questions put to the witnesses was whether the master had ever "caused the boy to be supported." There is also some evidence as to proof of filiation in CHILD-MARRIAGES, DIVORCES AND RATIFICATIONS, ETC.

hearing, followed by a realistic assessment of the situation and a compromise in light of that assessment, may have been all that was necessary in most cases. Much negotiation and discussion must have lain behind the bare notations of the Act books. The canon law permitted compromise of questions involving support, and the evidence suggests that judges and litigants took advantage of the permission.[61] Judges, in fact, allowed settlement of suits over child support often enough to imply that they actively promoted settlement, at least settlement under their broad supervision.[62]

Similarly, little can be discovered about the size and duration of the support order. But indefiniteness was the natural result of the law. So closely linked was the order to the needs of the child and to the ability of the father to pay, so hesitant was the law to set any minimum limit to the obligation, that few fixed rules could be enforced in practice.[63] The canonist Joannes Andreae (d. 1348), for example, noted only that the father must support the child according to his means, and that the obligation ceased when the child had means to support himself.[64] There was no fixed table of awards. What gloss civilians and canonists gave to the subject concerned the general types of expenses that the obligation encompassed. It included food, shelter, and clothing. But it did not include payment of the child's debts.[65] Whether it covered payment for medicine was open to academic controversy, the predominant

---

IN THE DIOCESES OF CHESTER, A.D. 1561-6, at 85-102 (108 Early Eng. Text Soc., F. Furnivall ed. 1897).

61 DIGEST 2.15.8. Compromise seems to have been allowed in Roman law even without the consent of the magistrate, except for future rights to *alimenta* bequeathed in a will. *See, e.g.,* G. DURANTIS, SPECULUM IUDICIALE IV, tit. *qui filii sint legitimi,* no. 27: *"Sed quaeritur utrum super alimentis transigi posset, et licet ista sint in Summa Azonis tacta, nota tamen quod de praeteritis potest transigi indistincte, . . . et etiam de futuris, nisi sint in ultima voluntate relicta."* ("But it is asked whether there can be compromise about support, and although these matters are dealt with in the Summa of Azo, note nevertheless that over past support compromise is always permitted, . . . and even over future support unless it has been left in a last will.") .

62 *E.g.,* Chichester Act books Ep. I/10/1, f. 140r (1511), a support case committed to arbitration; and Ep I/10/5, f. 37r (1534) , a support case in which formal proceeding was adjourned "in hopes of concord." (*"sub spe concordie"*) .

63 DIGEST 25.3.5.7; HOSTIENSIS, LECTURA at X 4.7.5, nos. 7-8. There is a fairly full discussion of the point in 5 ALEXANDER DE IMOLA, CONSILIA 55 (cons. 72, nos. 9-12) (1549).

64 COMMENTARIA at X 4.7.5, nos. 7, 9 (1581).

65 DIGEST 25.3.5.14-16; DIGEST 34.1.6; W. LYNDWOOD, PROVINCIALE SEU CONSTITUTIONES ANGLIAE 255 s.v. *alimenta* (1679). *See also* 1 P. BONFANTE, *supra* note 14, at 380; L. CREMIEU, *supra* note 51, at 45.

opinion apparently being that it did.[66] Baldus de Ubaldis (d. 1400) gave the broadest meaning to the obligation. "Let the term *alimenta* be [taken] liberally for all things necessary to life." [67]

Given this discretionary standard, the judges must have varied the size of their support orders to take account of individual circumstances, although in practice they rarely made large awards. The Act books do not suggest generosity. The amount of support varied from one penny per week (Rochester, 1347) [68] to six pence (York, 1374).[69] Two pence per week is the sum mentioned most often in the remaining records, and this amount even into the early sixteenth century.[70] Most entries, however, specified no exact amount at all. The order of the court, and the undertaking of the father, was simply to provide the child's sustenance.

The duration of the obligation also varied. The court records describe orders lasting until the child reached the age of three [71] and the age of seven,[72] but these may have been meant as interim orders subject to revision. Typically the entry required support "until [the child] should come to legitimate age." [73] A few cases may have adopted the civilian rule that a child was to be nourished by the mother until age three, by the father afterwards,[74] but the number does not establish a clear rule of practice. What the records do suggest is the exercise of judicial discretion and the use of

---

66 G. DURANTIS, SPECULUM IUDICIALE IV, tit. *qui filii sint legitimi*, no. 38: *"Sed nunquid is qui praestare tenetur alimenta praestabit et medicinas cum aegrotatur? Dicunt quidam quod sic, . . . alii distinguunt, . . . Sed primum verius."* ("But will one who is obligated to support also be obligated to supply medicine when there is illness? Some say that he is, . . . others make a distinction. But the first position is more correct.").

67 COMMENTARIA at Code 5.10.1, no. 9: *"[A]ppellatio alimentorum larga sit pro omnibus ad vitam necessariis." See* DIGEST 50.16.43.

68 REGISTRUM HAMONIS HETHE 951 (48 Canterbury & York Soc., C. Johnson ed. 1948).

69 Act book M 2(1)c, f. 18v (1374); another example is Chichester Act book Ep I/10/1, f. 92r (1509).

70 York Act book Cons. A B 6, f. 196v (1511); Norwich Act book ACT/1, f. 162v (1511). It is difficult to give an accurate assessment of the buying power of these sums. The average cost of a hen, for instance, was 1 5/8d. in 1347; 2d. in 1374, and 2 1/4d. for the period 1400-1540. But the cost of most agricultural products: wheat, barley, and the like, fluctuated greatly. *See* 1 J. ROGERS, A HISTORY OF AGRICULTURE AND PRICES IN ENGLAND 226-35 (1866 repr. 1963); 4 *id.*, 282-91.

71 Canterbury Act book Y.1.2, f. 103v (1398); Lichfield Act book B/C/2/3, f. 213r (1533).

72 York Act book M 2(1)c, f. 18v (1374).

73 *E.g.*, Lichfield Act book B/C/2/3, f. 38v (1528): *"usque ad etatem legitimam pervenerit."*

74 Canterbury Act book Y.4.1, f. 40v (1540); Norwich Act book ACT/1, f. 162v (1511); cases cited at note 71 *supra*.

private arrangement. Since the law envisioned an obligation co-
terminous with legitimate need, that is what we should expect.

If the available records are representative, inability to pay was
the only defense offered by fathers once the question of paternity
had been settled. Poverty was, of course, a possible plea under the
law. In 1374 a Canterbury judge accepted such a defense, presumably after determining its truth. He nevertheless ordered the
father to take up the obligation again "when he should come to
more plentiful fortune." [75] One case, heard at Rochester in 1463,
illustrates a court's readiness to provide support. Geoffrey Steyn
was convicted of fathering the illegitimate child of Agnes Jays. He
pleaded insufficiency of assets. "He had nothing in goods except
by the grace and will of his father." [76] The court accepted this plea,
but the judge "asked and induced Henry Steyn the father [of
Geoffrey] to provide for the care of the aforesaid child" until
better arrangements could be made.[77]

Seven years before the case involving Steyn, the Rochester
court had dealt with a similar situation. Apparently the father
could not pay; neither could the mother. But Joan Marot, the
sister of the mother, and her husband were "willing to take the
entire burden of maintenance upon themselves and to support the
child from their own resources." [78] The court approved the arrangement. Such entries reflect the only theme running consistently
through the cases: the concern that someone, and someone related
to the child, take up the obligation to support. Normally, responsi-

---

[75] Act book Y.1.1, f. 83r (1374). A slightly later *causa alimentationis prolis* from
Canterbury, recorded in Deposition book X.10.1, f. 33r (1413), includes a witness's description of the defendant: *"Habet ad sustentacionem suam vix valorem duarum marcarum
annuatim de bonis propriis; habuit tamen ad medium annum hinc elapsum et ea alienavit
matri sue."* ("Out of his own goods he has barely two marks a year for his sustenance;
however he had [goods] half a year ago and he alienated them to his mother.") .

[76] Act book DRb Pa 3, f. 466r (1463): *"Et vir dicit quod nichil habet in bonis nisi de
gracia et voluntate patris sui."*

[77] *Id.*: *"Et commissarius rogavit et induxit Henricum Steyn' patrem genitoris dicte prolis
ad disponendum pro conservatione prolis predicte quousque clarius constare et melius
poterit pro sustentatione eiusdem et exhibitione providere."* In a case recorded in Lichfield
Act book B/C/2/1, f. 74v (1526), the grandfather intervened, apparently voluntarily, to
take up his son's obligation.

[78] Act book DRb Pa 2, f. 282v (1456): *"[I]psi vellent totum exhibicionis onus in se
suscipere et dictum prolem exhibere sumptibus suis."* As part of the same proceedings,
Thomas Maynard and William Grenehill agreed not to attempt to draw the children
away from the house of Joan and her husband.

bility fell on the father. But if the father could not offer support, someone else should be found. This regime is the very opposite of the notion, so often said to have characterized medieval England, that the illegitimate child was *filius nullius*.

Identifying a person obliged to support a child, of course, was not always the end of the matter. Modern practice abundantly shows the difficulty of enforcing a continuing obligation that has no possibility of return.[79] The problem is not new. Many of the Act book entries involve claims for arrearages, fathers who had "fallen behind" in their payments. Perhaps encouraged by the canon law rule that relative need had a legitimate place in determining the scope of the obligation, the fathers had not met this obligation for long enough to bring the mother to the point of suing.[80] Suits occurred often enough to suggest that enforcement of support orders was a continuing problem.

The principal sanction available to the Church courts to secure enforcement was excommunication. In medieval society that spiritual penalty entailed a considerable loss of civil and religious rights.[81] Excommunication might even eventually result in a defaulting party's imprisonment.[82] But in assessing the nature of the enforcement in the Church courts, one should note that the judges did not rely on the threat of penal sanction alone. When a hearing was adjourned for attempts at arbitration and agreement, the ecclesiastical officials tried, whenever they could, to induce the defendant to agree voluntarily to pay support at a level acceptable to both himself and to the court.[83] Defendants often took solemn

---

[79] *See* W. GOODE, AFTER DIVORCE 221 (1956); Chambers, *The Child-Support Enforcement Process Study*, in C. FOOTE, R. LEVY & F. SANDER, CASES AND MATERIALS ON FAMILY LAW 850-56 (2d ed. 1976).

[80] *E.g.*, Canterbury Act book Y.1.2, f. 103v (1398), in which Nicholas Barbour was condemned to pay 9s.4d. *"pro custodia prolis per xxvii ebdomadas elapsas,"* ("for custody of the child for twenty-seven weeks past.").

[81] There is a summary of the disabilities in 1 W. HOLDSWORTH, HISTORY OF ENGLISH LAW 630-32 (7th ed. 1956).

[82] Imprisonment was possible through the use of the English Church's privilege of "signifying" an unrepentant excommunicate to the Chancery and requiring that the sheriff imprison him. I found one threat of signification in a *causa alimentationis prolis* in the remaining records: Canterbury Act book Y.1.1, f. 3v (1372). On the subject generally, see F. LOGAN, EXCOMMUNICATION AND THE SECULAR ARM IN MEDIEVAL ENGLAND; A STUDY IN LEGAL PROCEDURE FROM THE THIRTEENTH TO THE SIXTEENTH CENTURY (1968).

[83] *E.g.*, Canterbury Act book X.8.1, f. 33r (1401): *"Et monitus est ad concordandum cum matre pro invencione filii."* ("And he was ordered to reach agreement with the

oaths to fulfill the obligation, a practice indicating that the Church court judges wanted the obligation undertaken as willingly as possible.[84] Support of one's child was an essentially moral duty. Acknowledgement of the duty and agreement, even reluctant agreement, to fulfill it played a regular part in Church court procedure. The judges used both conciliation and penal sanction to enforce support orders for illegitimate children. That the combination did not always ensure continued payment is testimony to a stubborn and familiar fact of human nature.

III. CONCLUSION

The Elizabethan Poor Law of 1576 empowered Justices of the Peace to compel parents to provide for the sustenance of their illegitimate children. Reciting the burden to parish funds caused by illegitimates, the Statute allowed the Justices to require payment for child support "in such wise as they shall think meet and convenient." [85] The Statute traditionally has been treated as if it created a new duty.[86] That treatment is clearly incorrect. The Statute simply provided a new mechanism for enforcing a duty previously enforced only in the courts of the Church. The enforcement mechanism adopted by the secular courts did include some new features, suretyship guarantees to insure payment, for example. But much of the Statute merely provided for continuation in a new forum of earlier practice. The summary determinations of paternity and the immediate support orders, for instance, followed ecclesiastical procedure closely.[87]

The Statute, therefore, should be seen principally as part of the great movement of religious and social change in sixteenth century

---

mother for the support of the son."). Other instances: Canterbury Act book Y.1.4, f. 112r (1423); X.8.3, f. 14r (1463); Durham Act book III/1, f. 23 (1532); Rochester Act book DRb Pa 2, ff. 167r (1451); *id.*, f. 183r (1452); cases cited at note 62 *supra*.

[84] *E.g.*, Canterbury Act book Chartae Antiquae A 36 II, f. 28r (1329) : "*Willelmus Tenturer ad sancta dei Ewangelia corporale prestitit iuramentum quod solveret pro sustentacione Mariote filie sue . . . .*" ("William Tenturer swore an oath on the Holy Gospels to pay for the sustenance of Mariota his daughter . . . .").

[85] 18 Eliz. 1, c. 3, § 1 (1576).

[86] *See, e.g.*, 1 I. PINCHBECK & M. HEWITT, *supra* note 8, at 206; Robbins & Deák, *supra* note 8, at 317; Comment, *Support of Children Born out of Wedlock: Virginia at the Crossroads*, 18 WASH. & LEE L. REV. 343, 344 (1961) .

[87] *See, e.g.*, SUSSEX QUARTER SESSIONS ORDER BOOK, 1642-1649, at 85, 127 (54 Sussex Rec. Soc., B. Redwood ed. 1954).

England. That century redrew the boundary between the spheres of secular and spiritual obligation. To enforce a father's obligation to care for his illegitimate children by secular sanction, the result of the Statute, was to move the duty from one side of the boundary to the other and to recognize that an ecclesiastical remedy was no longer enough. A decline in the habits of obedience to the decrees of the Church courts required a new source of protection for the illegitimate child.[88] But the Statute marked no change in the substantive rights of that child. He had been entitled to support from his father as far back as the records yield reliable evidence.

The 1576 Statute itself did not restrict the Church's rights. It did not purport to oust ecclesiastical jurisdiction. Like much Elizabethan legislation, it merely offered an alternate remedy.[89] In fact, the Church courts continued to issue support orders at least for a time after 1576.[90] At some later point, however, the ecclesiastical remedy fell into desuetude. Only secular sanction was effective enough to be worth invoking. By Blackstone's day the secular action had become the sole remedy.[91] The old ecclesiastical jurisdiction was forgotten. Its disappearance left the impression that, prior to enactment of the Statute, an illegitimate child had no legal recourse against his father for support.

From this vantage point American lawyers drew the not unreasonable, but false, conclusion that at the time the common law developed, English courts imposed no legal duty on a father to support his illegitimate children. American courts therefore adopted what they supposed to have been the common law regime. Without the statute, the conclusion seemed inescapable. Unfortunately, this conclusion caused, indeed may continue to cause, a measure of hardship to illegitimate children. Of course, today American courts

---

88 *See generally* C. HILL, ECONOMIC PROBLEMS OF THE CHURCH: FROM ARCHBISHOP WHITGIFT TO THE LONG PARLIAMENT (1956); Houlbrooke, *The Decline of Ecclesiastical Jurisdiction Under the Tudors*, in CONTINUITY AND CHANGE 239 (R. O'Day & F. Heal eds. 1976).

89 Other examples: 1 Eliz. 1, c. 2, § 4 (1558-59) (church attendance) ; 5 Eliz. 1, c. 9, § 5 (1563) (perjury); 13 Eliz. 1, c. 8, § 8 (1571) (usury) . This fact may affect our estimate of the purpose of the Act, normally said to encompass only saving parish funds, not concern for the child's welfare. The desire not to challenge the rights of the Church directly may explain at least in part the Statute's failure to mention what had been the chief reason for the Church's jurisdiction, provision of support for the illegitimate child.

90 *E.g.*, Lichfield Act book B/C/2/26 s.d. 16 June 1590; Hereford Act book I/11 s.d. 25 July 1577.

91 *See* 1 W. BLACKSTONE, COMMENTARIES * 458.

and legislatures have in large measure granted to illegitimate children a legal right to parental support.[92] They have consciously, sometimes stridently, rejected the common law rule in order to reach that result. Ironically, in so doing, they have in fact adopted the regime of the age in which the common law was born.

---

[92] In 1966, one commentator noted that all but three states (Idaho, Missouri, and Texas) had provisions to compel a father to support his illegitimate child. Note, STAN. L. REV., *supra* note 6, at 860. After Gomez v. Perez, 409 U.S. 535 (1973), however, a state may not discriminate between legitimate and illegitimate children for purposes of support.

11

BASTARDY LITIGATION IN MEDIEVAL ENGLAND

Of the areas of conflict between Church and State in medieval England, not many present the apparent clarity of opposition that bastardy litigation does. Maitland described it as a "collision between the claims" of secular and ecclesiastical jurisdictions. The most famous instance of this collision, to which Maitland was in fact referring, is a familiar one. It is the story of the Council of Merton.[1] The bishops, anxious to bring English law into accord with what they conceived to be the clear dictates of religion, reason and civil law, urged upon the baronage the proposition that children born before the marriage of their parents should be counted as legitimate at English law. The barons refused. And their unanimous shout, "Nolumus mutare leges Angliae," has since been celebrated for more reasons than one.

The history of the dispute does not, however, end there. The legal issues involved are more varied, more complex, and more ambiguous than the incident at Merton alone suggests. And the response of the English courts to the problems created by the areas of disagreement was far from static. The more one examines the history of bastardy litigation, the clearer it becomes that the story cannot adequately be described strictly in the terms of a collision at Merton. Rather, one finds substantial areas of compromise and even of agreement, on the part of both sides. The purpose of this article is to explore the development of the handling of the disputed questions, both from the point of view of the canonists and from that of the English Common Law courts. Working through that development provides an instructive chapter in the history of legal relations between Church and State in the Middle Ages. It

---

* Department of History, University of California, Berkeley.
1. For a reconstruction of the chronology of the events surrounding this incident, see F. W. Maitland's introduction to *Bracton's Notebook* (London, 1887), 14-17. Maitland's more extended treatment of the conflict is in *Roman Canon Law in the Church of England* (London, 1898), 52 et seq. Felix Makower's *Constitutional History of the Church of England*, (London, 1895), 422-23 is also useful. The best, straightforward presentation of the English law on the subject is W. Hooper, *The Law of Illegitimacy* (London, 1911). See also J. D. White, "Legitimation by Subsequent Marriage", 36 *L. Q. Rev.*, 255-67 (1920).

also sheds light on an important aspect of the growth and maturing of the English Common Law in the fourteenth century.

It is well to start with the precise problem firmly in mind. No dispute between *regnum* and *sacerdotium* in the Middle Ages existed in a vacuum, dependent on rhetoric or theory alone, and this dispute was, if anything, more concrete than most. It turned around a precise legal issue, namely inheritance of real property. Whatever ideological problems bastardy litigation might ultimately raise, jurisdiction over land was always at its center. Now, land held in lay fee was within the cognizance of the secular courts. All sides agreed on that. It was equally agreed, however, that determination of a man's legitimacy belonged to the spiritual courts. As long as marriage, divorce and adultery were thought of as distinctly spiritual, this was perhaps natural. In concrete terms, the distinction meant that whenever an issue of bastardy was raised in the royal courts, the process there was suspended and a writ sent to the bishop, asking for a resolution of the bastardy issue. Not that the bishops had any very expert way of determining the question. Before the very end of the Middle Ages, there were no parish registers or other records to help them. In fact, the issue was usually determined by a sworn inquisition of neighbours, no more reliable and not at bottom much different from a Common law jury. The common fame of the country was the source of the verdict in both forums.[2] There was no intrinsic reason for having the Church decide the issue. But it seemed more fitting. After the ecclesiastical inquisition, the bishop or his officials certified the answer to the secular court, which could then finish the case accordingly.[3] In

---

2. The following extract from a case heard in the diocese of Canterbury and on this problem will perhaps make the point. Dean and Chapter Archives, Ecclesiastical Suit 310: ". . . . facta fuit inquisitio si ultimus partus dicte Johanne post formam factam procreatus esset partus dicti Ricardi. Dicebat inquisitio iurata quod fuerat partus dicti Ricardi et non alterius, quia de alio non fuerat defamata et talis est communis fama patrie." When witnesses were asked in the church courts about the source of their knowledge on legitimacy, their answers usually came down to this: "communis fama laborat quod dicta C. fuerat nata in legitimo matrimonio," or that the knowledge came "de relatu seniorum suorum qui habuerunt plenam noticiam;" Canterbury Consistory Court Deposition Book, X. 10.1, f. 47v (1420). An interesting side light on the ecclesiastical attitude comes from an attempt in 1294 to oust a clerk from his benefice for illegitimacy. He argued that he could not be illegitimate because his elder brother had succeeded as legitimate heir "secundum legem Anglie;" Sede Vacante Scrapbook III, no. 396.

3. A number of the king's writs with the episcopal returns from the 14th and 15th centuries are preserved in the Public Record Office, London, C.47/15/4 and E.135/7.

most cases, determination of the bastardy question would necessarily decide the outcome of the principal case.

The problems arose, as in the situation of the Statute of Merton, when Church and State did not apply the same substantive law. Whom one considers a bastard depends, after all, entirely on one's definition of legitimacy. When the two laws accepted definitions at variance with each other the question came down to this: would the secular courts be bound to follow the canonical definition of legitimacy because of the acknowledged principle that the subject lay within the Church's jurisdiction? Or would the ecclesiastical courts agree that the secular law should prevail because land was the subject of the action? It is worth pointing out that this was not a problem confined to England. Although Continental jurisdictions, following more closely the Roman Law texts, were closer to agreement with the canonical definition of bastardy, the definitions were not always identical.[4] The conflict was not a strictly insular one.

I

For canonists, the question of how bastardy should be settled could not be without some degree of ambiguity. On the one hand, a decretal of Alexander III (X 4.17.1) stated clearly that a prenuptial child was legitimate and could not be disinherited for that reason. On the other hand, no matter how one dissected the matter, it came in the end down to a question of real property. A man sued not to have his legitimacy publicly proclaimed, but to recover land he thought belonged to him. And here canonists had to deal with another decretal of Alexander III (X 4.17.7) which seemed to say that feudal law controlled. This decretal grew out of an English case in which papal judges delegate had adjudged possession of land to a man whose mother (through whom he claimed the land) was challenged as illegitimate. Henry II objected strenuously to this invasion of his rights. He was, in the decretal's words "motus et turbatus." Because of that objection, Alexander III ordered the case returned to the royal courts. The matter of legitimacy alone remained to the Church, "although," the decretal says, the double procedure "may seem incongruous." The decretal does not authorise the royal court to go ahead without the canonical determination of bastardy, but it was to acknowledge that on the fundamental

4. For example, at Roman Law the consent of the parents was required to legitimate the child (D. 1.6.11). On this subject see Constant Van de Wiel, *La Légitimation par mariage subséquent chez les romanistes et les décrétalistes jusqu'en 1650* (Antwerp, 1962). The author doubts, however, whether in practice the Roman law categories were always observed.

issue of what court should try ownership of the land, the secular court has jurisdiction. This the canonists themselves clearly perceived, as they showed by their efforts to distinguish it. One said that this second decretal applied only to cases of spoliation, not to claims for inheritance.[5] Another said that because the events which gave rise to the decretal occurred before John had granted and received back his kingdom as a papal fief, it was no longer good law for England.[6] But these convinced no one, not even their authors.

The canon law position had really to rest on the argument that the secular courts were *bound* to follow the canon law's determination of legitimacy for inheritance purposes, because of the inherent superiority of Church to State. This was the only clear way out of a logical impasse. Hostiensis took the occasion of commenting on the question to launch into the standard medieval comparison of the *sacerdotium* to the sun, the *regnum* to the moon, the obvious point being that the State, like the moon, was totally dependent for its light on the priestly sun.[7] In truth, the situation raised exactly that problem. If the king were really the moon, he had no choice but to let the light of canon law settle the determinative question of bastardy. If the pope were the sun, there could be no question that secular law was derivative, subject to correction by the pope's law. Accept the premise, and the logical problem is solved. The Church courts should determine legitimacy for inheritance purposes. Hostiensis put it with clarity: "in no way does it belong to the secular court to judge, but rather execution and admittance of the legitimate person belongs to it." [8]

In general, this was the position taken by canonists. There was, nonetheless, some appreciation for the arguments on the other side. Antonius de Butrio noted in his analysis of this problem

---

5. *gl. ord.* ad X 4.17.1 s.v. *hac occasione:* "Non est contra; ibi principaliter committitur causa super questione spoliationis, quae ad papam non pertinet inter eos qui non sunt suae iurisdictionis."

6. Joannes Andreae, *Novella Commentaria in Libros Decretalium* ad X 4.17.7 (Venice, 1581), ". . . . , sed hodie secus esset, cum postea Johannes rex Anglie filius Henrici maioris, quando Johannes successit in regno Ricardo fratri suo, recepit ab ecclesia Romana in feudum totum regnum."

7. *Summa Aurea*, t. *qui filii sunt legitimi*, c. 9 (Venice, 1574), col. 1385. And see Panormitanus, *Commentaria in quartum et quintum decretalium* ad X 4.17.5 (Lyons, 1555), f. 39*v*; Note also X 2.10.3.

8. *Summa Aurea*, col. 1386: ". . . . nullo modo ad secularem pertinet iudicare, sed bene pertinet ad eum executio et admittere legitimum, eo quod de legitimatione fuerit coram ecclesia facta fides." This theme is treated in the recent work by J. Watt, "The Theory of Papal Monarchy in the Thirteenth Century", *Traditio*, Vol. 20, 281 et seq. (1964) and also reprinted in book form (London 1965), 107 et seq.

that the Church should not disturb the jurisdiction of laymen, and that "it seems to detract from it to judge a case belonging to its judgement according to another law." [9] Joannes Andreae noted, though he did not unequivocally endorse, a more technical position favourable to secular jurisdiction. When, he wrote, bastardy was raised only "in the manner of an exception," the secular court could reasonably retain the case instead of sending it to the Church.[10] And Panormitanus, in the fifteenth century, held that a man legitimate for canon law purposes would not *ipso facto* be a legitimate heir, since the "custom of the country" might stand in the way.[11] Still, even for these writers, logic dictated that bastardy was a matter for determination by the tribunals of the Church.

The strongest sentiment mitigating the logic of the hierocratic point of view was the knowledge that, in the fact, it was not widely accepted. Joannes Andreae, after the passage just mentioned, went on to say that in principle the king's claims to jurisdiction over bastardy in inheritance cases might not be justified, but added that it was well to accept them, since "we do not wish to scandalize him." [12] And the marginal gloss to the standard *glossa ordinaria* noted, "But today in this kingdom the secular judge takes cognizance no matter what, and there is no remission to the Church." [13] As an appendage to his strong stand, Hostiensis wrote: "this, however, the legists hardly concede to us, but by strictness and natural reason I do not doubt that it is to be held." [14]

9. *Lectura super quarto decretalium* ad X 4.17.7 (Rome, 1474), f. 86*v*: "Nota quarto quod ad iudicium ecclesie non pertinet iudicare de temporalibus inter puros laicos et quod ecclesia non debet turbare iurisdictionem laicorum, quod detrahere videtur iuri alterius eo quod iudicat de causa ad eius non spectante iudicium."

10. *Novella Commentaria* ad X 4.17.5: "Verum tamen cum in modo exceptionis fuerit hoc oppositum coram iudice seculari, videtur quod sicut ipse cognosceret de exceptione que in suam jurisdictionem caderet sine libelli exceptione, sicut iudex ecclesiasticus qui in locum illius succedit sine libello procedere poterit." A useful discussion is contained in Innocent IV, *Apparatus super decretalibus* ad X 4.17.7 (Lyons, 1525), f. 183, noting disagreement among the canonists themselves.

11. *Lectura* ad X 2.10.3: "non sequitur est legitimus, ergo heres, quia posset obstare consuetudo patrie; ideo semper est hec questio remittenda ad secularem."

12. *ibid.* ad X 4.17.7: ". . . . asserit pertinere sibi; non tamen est ita in hoc casu, sed nolumus ipsum scandalizare."

13. See *gl. ord.* ad X 4.17.4: "Sed hodie in hoc regno indistincte iudex secularis cognoscit, nec fit remissio ad ecclesiam."

14. *Summa Aurea*, col. 1386: "Hoc tamen legistae vix concederent nobis, sed de rigore et ratione naturali non dubito sic tenendum." And see Raymond de Peñafort, *Summa de Poenitentia et Matrimonio* (Avignon, 1715), 431-32.

What had happened is that, on the Continent, the practice of sending questions of bastardy to the Church courts gradually disappeared.[15] Beaumanoir, writing in the 1280's, gave it as the rule that in inheritance disputes secular courts in his area might make their own determination of legitimacy.[16] The practice was not uniform in his day, but it was all but universal by the fourteenth century. The Church's theoretical rights were simply ignored. Canonists had little choice but to acquiesce in this decision and content themselves with the reminder that, by strict logic, the result ought perhaps to have been otherwise. Surely there were strong practical reasons for acquiescence. Reference to the ecclesiastical courts was time-consuming, necessarily irksome to the parties, and usually unnecessary. And when the subject of the ultimate dispute was, by the canon law's own principles, within the jurisdiction of secular law, the whole matter was not one in which the strictest sort of logic alone could control. This the canonists came close to admitting. They recognised the arguments on both sides and raised little objection to the fact that the "clerical" argument was not being followed.

In England, the Church certainly took this temperate position. Trial of bastardy in inheritance cases by the Church courts found few churchmen willing to lend it strong support. The very judges who insisted on the rights of the secular courts to determine the issue according to English law were, in the middle years of the thirteenth century, themselves clerics. It is interesting to note that Grosseteste, the leading figure among the bishops at the time of the Council of Merton, argued not that Church courts must decide the question, but that English law should be changed to accord with the only position, as he thought, in harmony with reason and divine law. Few men accepted more fully the hierocratic doctrines of subordination of secular to spiritual power than did Robert Grosseteste. In a letter he wrote to William Raleigh, then a royal judge, urging the legitimacy of children born before their parents' marriage,

---

15. For a more thorough modern treatment, see R. Génestal, *Histoire de la légitimation des enfants naturels en droit canonique* (Paris, 1905), 100 et seq.; A. Friedberg, *De finium inter ecclesiam et civitatem regundorum judicio* (Leipzig, 1861), 121; A. Esmein, *Le mariage en droit canonique* (Paris, 1891), Vol. 1, 31. The issue was not entirely an historical one for Charles Fevret, *Traité de l'abus* (Lyons, 1736), Vol. 1, 539 et seq. He discusses, and dismisses, the "distinctions subtiles des Ultramontains" on which, he claims, the ecclesiastical case depended.

16. Philippe de Beaumanoir, *Coutumes de Beauvaises*, ed. A. Salmon (Paris, 1899), no. 578, "Et pour ce que teus debas depent de l'eritage, convient il a la fois que juges seculiers s'entremete de connoistre la bastardie qui es proposee par devant li."

Grosseteste rehearsed these very arguments at length.[17] But even he did not say that only the Church could try the issue of bastardy. This is to admit, at least by implication, that the English courts might exercise that jurisdiction. If only they would do so in accord with the correct definition of bastardy.

What the bishops at Merton, following Grosseteste's lead, were unwilling to do, no matter whether they conceded that the royal courts could try bastrady, was to use their own courts to enforce the substantive position of English law. To sanction the use of their own courts to deny inheritance to a man who was canonically legitimate was quite a different matter from accepting, without great protest, that the English courts might do so. Practice prior to the Statute of Merton had required them to co-operate, in unmistakable fashion, in reaching that result. The writ from the royal justices asked them to specify whether the person had been born before or after wedlock.[18] To answer this made them co-workers in English legal practice, whereas if asked merely to determine bastardy in general terms, the bishop's court could follow its own law.

Where an answer to a specific question on the cause of alleged bastardy was demanded, and we shall see that it was demanded in other cases besides that of pre-nuptial children, the bishops baulked. But the long lists of clerical grievances surviving from the next two centuries after the Statute of Merton mention nothing of demands that jurisdiction should be returned to the Church in bastardy cases. I have found but one exception, and it is only apparent. During the reign of Edward II, attempts were made by some lawyers, through the use of changes in the wording of the pleadings, to deprive the Church courts of jurisdiction over even those bastardy cases where no substantive conflict between the two laws existed.[19]

---

17. *Roberti Grosseteste Epistolae*, ed. J. R. Luard (R. S., Vol. 35), 77 et seq. Grosseteste wrote that the ancient practice of England on children born before their parents' marriage had been in accord with the canon law. There does not appear to be any very positive evidence one way or the other on this point, but it is worth noting that Génestal concluded in his history of the subject (at 136) that legitimation by subsequent marriage was no part of Church law prior to the 12th century. The ecclesiastical writing he studied seemed, in fact, to assume that no legitimation would take place.

18. In Glanvill's day the bishop was asked to judge if the party "bastardus fuit natus ante matrimonium." *Tractatus de legibus*, ed. G. D. G. Hall (London, 1967), 87. Bracton argued that the bishops were still obliged to answer the specific question, and gave an expanded version of suitable writs, but it seems clear that by his time they were no longer co-operating with the English position. See *De legibus et consuetudinibus Angliae*, ed. G. E. Woodbine (New Haven, 1915-42), f. 419b.

19. See below.

The words used to make the claim of bastardy, it was argued, should control how the question should be tried. Here the bishops could answer the writ without difficulty; technicality alone robbed them of jurisdiction. But otherwise, Grosseteste had no successors. Even more than the canonists, the English Church was content to observe that practice did not conform to the ideal standard, to avoid direct involvement in reaching the result sanctioned by the English law, and to live, not unhappily, with the result.[20]

II

The bishops' refusal to answer writs on bastardy in accord with English inheritance law necessarily forced the Common Law justices to draw a line between those cases they would send to the Church and those they would not. Where the two laws had different views of bastardy, the question would have to be kept out of the bishops' hands. In the eyes of Bracton and those of following centuries, the date of the Statute of Merton was commonly regarded as the landmark date, one which forced on English lawyers a realization of the divergence of the laws of Church and State. In the Year Book case of 1338, for example, Scrope, J. remarked that "before the Statute if it was alleged that a man was born outside espousals, the practice was to send to the bishop to certify . . .; ever since the custom is not to inquire anything in those cases, except where bastardy is purely alleged." [21] Modern writers have generally adopted that description. Prior to Merton, the Church heard bastardy cases; afterwards only those where the law of bastardy was identical under both laws. Cases where there was a conflict were tried by assize as any other issue might be.

Investigation of the pre-1234 cases shows, however, that practice was not so uniformly in favor of ecclesiastical jurisdiction as Scrope's opinion indicates. Many cases of alleged bastardy went to the bishops which would afterwards have been tried by assize, that certainly is clear. But on the other hand, there are many which were being tried by assize even before that date. It seems impossible to explain the divergence of practice along any very consistent prin-

---

20. How unanimous in following Grosseteste's position the bishops were, or how consistent when it came to their own interest, is illustrated by a case in *Bracton's Notebook* (no. 1181) from 1237. The bishop of Carlisle sued Adam Wigenhale, arguing that Adam had no right to land in dispute, since his title descended through a man born before his parents had married. This was, of course, to stand with the barons. On the English clergy's attitude towards the whole problem see F. M. Powicke, *The Thirteenth Century* (Oxford, 1953), 70-71.

21. 11 Lib. Ass. no. 20, f. 32 (1337).

ciples. A possessory action in 1226 was determined by assize, resulting in a decision that the claimant was born before the espousal of his parents, and hence incapable of inheriting. Three years later, a similar case was sent to the bishop of Norwich.[22] In other cases we meet this same lack of consistency.[23] Probably the question of where to send the bastardy issue was settled case by case, considering the wishes of the parties. This almost certainly was the practice later on, for we find on the plea rolls cases in which the parties agree to trial by other than the usual method.[24]

It is one of Bracton's most impressive achievements to have taken the confused mass of English legal material and to have extracted from it generally consistent principles of law. When we consider the lack of legal handbooks and the miscellaneous recruitment of the English judges in the first half of the thirteenth century, it is no surprise that practice did not always conform exactly to what Bracton or other commentators wrote. Anything else would have been virtually impossible. But on this specific point of the decisiveness of the decisions of the Council of Merton, it is an exaggeration to say that the decision to try bastardy by assize was an innovation. The Common Law justices had submitted questions of bastardy to jurors before; thereafter they had merely to continue, and to extend, that practice. But they did have to be more careful. It had been pointed out in clear fashion that the bishops would refuse to co-operate in reaching a result they were bound to regard as iniquitous.

By retaining questions of bastardy for trial by assize, the royal justices took a course which in fact restricted the jurisdiction of the Church. And because that restriction went, as we shall see, beyond the case of pre-nuptial children, it is often cited as an area of struggle for jurisdiction between Church and State. Or at least an area of encroachment by the royal courts on ecclesiastical jurisdiction. The matter was, of course, entirely in the hands of the common law-

---

22. Compare *Bracton's Notebook*, no. 1879, with Curia Regis Rolls, XIII, no. 2133.

23. For pre-1234 cases in which bastardy was tried by assize, see *Bracton's Notebook*, nos. 227, 257, 1879; Curia Regis Rolls, IV, 16; VIII, 43; XII, no. 2075; XIII, nos. 211, 1339.

24. For example, P.R.O. K.B. 27/373 (Mich. 27 Edw. III) m. 46: "Et predicti Willelmus et Joannes Petche dicunt quod . . . . predicta Joanna bastarda est, ita quod nullius heres potest, et hoc petunt quod inquiratur per assisam. Et predictus Henricus dicit quod predicta Joanna legitima est et non bastarda, et paratus est verificare per assisam. Et predicti Willelmus et Johannes Petche similiter; ideo capiatur inter eos assisa." See also C.P. 40/121 (Mich. 25-26 Edw. I) m. 129d; K.B. 27/198 (Mich. 3 Edw. II) m. 126; C.P. 40/395 (Trin. 32 Edw. III) m. 458.

yers. After Grosseteste's protest, the Church did not raise objections on the matter, perhaps considering the ambiguity of its own law, and the royal courts were left to fix the line between spiritual and secular. Watching them fix that line shows something of their attitude towards Church-State relations. It is equally revealing in showing the growth of the English Common Law in the fourteenth century. We shall see that only in the middle of that century did the question of bastardy litigation reach a state of clear and consistent definition. That definition was not, we shall also see, achieved at the expense of ecclesiastical jurisdiction. As a way of tracing the development, let me take the specific instances of conflict beyond that of pre-nuptial children, one at a time. This requires delaying examination of the difficulties and changes in the fourteenth century, but it is necessary to appreciate the legal background from which they arose. Some have been well set out by Maitland and others, and require only statement. Some require more.

First, English law and canon law took quite different positions on the legitimacy of children born within wedlock but of adulterous liaisons. The reluctance of English law to bastardize any child born to a married woman goes back at least to the 12th Century.[25] But it was not until after the events surrounding Merton that the royal courts made consistent efforts to keep these cases out of the bishops' courts. A case from 1229 well illustrates the practice before that date. It arose in a writ of right for some land in Gloucestershire. To the claim the tenant answered, admitting the marriage on which the demandant's title depended, but saying that on the wedding night the bridegroom had found his new wife "gross and pregnant" and had expelled her from his bed.[26] He had had no access to her prior to the demandant's birth. Thus there could be, he argued, no question of inheritance of the land. The issue of bastardy, thus raised, was sent to the Church courts. Now this is just the sort of case the English courts had an interest in keeping out of the canon law system. Assuming the truth of the allegations of bastardy, the demandant would have

---

25. *Magna Vita Sancti Hugonis*, eds. D. L. Douie and H. Farmer (London, 1962) Vol. II, 20 et seq. A somewhat similar case is found in the Chancery Miscellaneous Records from 1390 (P.R.O. C. 47/15/4 no. 9). The wife of Ralph Basset had smuggled in the child of another woman and treated that child as her own. The true mother, some thirteen years later, the record asserts, admitted the fraud to a cleric, who urged that she seek "restitution" of the child. The whole matter came before the Chancery when the inheritance of Ralph was in dispute, but unfortunately, I have been unable to find any sign of the final result of the case.

26. *Bracton's Notebook*, no. 1229.

lost his case by canon law, and won it by English law.[27] Whether in 1229 the bishops were answering the writ in specific terms, allowing the courts to apply the English rule of refusing to bastardize adulterine children, as they did with pre-nuptial children, or whether the royal justices were simply not alert to the difference, does not appear from the record. We do not know. But cases after 1234 show that the difference was being taken into account.[28] Where bastardy because of adultery was alleged, the matter would not be sent to the bishop.

The reasoning used to justify the English law's unwillingness to bastardize children born of adultery is curious. Common lawyers were led to make some extravagant arguments in favor of a position which so clearly violated common sense. For instance, it was said that if a husband was in France at any time when conception could have taken place, the child was legitimate, no matter how clear the adultery. The reason: the husband might have slipped across the Channel at night. Only if he were as far off as the Holy Land was the result otherwise.[29] Finally, the even more mechanical test of the four seas, that is the limits of the kingdom, was settled on as the dividing line. And when called upon to produce an argument for legitimacy, the pleaders of the fifteenth century retreated to the homely analogy, "Whoso bulleth my cow, the calf is mine."[30] The "four seas" test was given up only in 1732, and then only (as Nicolas said) "on account of its absolute nonsense."[31] But even today, although perhaps for other reasons, the presumption that a child born in wedlock is legitimate is "one of the strongest and most persuasive known to the law."[32]

---

27. See Littleton's statement in Y.B. 18 Edw. IV, Hil. no. 28, f. 29 (1478), ". . . . si home espouse un feme grosment enseint ove un auter et deins iii jours apres ele est deliver, en nostre ley l'issue est mulier, et par le ley de seint Esglise bastard."

28. Y.BB. 2 Edw. II (Selden Soc. Vol. 19) 55 (1308-09); 39 Edw. III, Mich., f. 31 (1365); 44 Edw. III, Pasch. no. 21, f. 12 (1370). But see Y.B. 39 Edw. III, Pasch., f. 14 (1365), a case in which one party was obliged to petition Parliament for a remedy after the question of bastardy had been sent to the Church. For English law on this subject, see Harris Nicolas, *A Treatise on the Law of Adulterine Bastardy* (London, 1836).

29. Bracton, f. 418; Y.B. Hil. 32-33 Edw. I (Rolls Series), 63. A case from Hil. 35 Edw. I, in which it was held that even where the husband had been in the Holy Land, the child was held legitimate, is reported in the unprinted "Pleas at Law 1300-12", Brit. Mus. Add. MS. 35,116, f. 65v.

30. Y.BB. 43 Edw. III, Trin. no. 5, f. 19 (1369); 9 Hen. IV, Hil. no. 13, f. 9 (1407).

31. *Treatise*, 164. The rule was abrogated in *Pendrell* v. *Pendrell* 2 Stra. 925. See also Co. Lit. 244a.

32. 10 *Corpus Juris Secundum* 21 sec. 3.

Second, English law differed from canon law on the legitimacy of the children of divorced parents. The Church evolved a number of standards for judging the matter, the most important of which involved investigation of the formal correctness of the marriage and the good faith of the parents.[33] If they were innocent of wrongdoing and knowledge of the impediment which rendered their union unlawful, or at least if one of them was, their children were legitimate. Otherwise, the children were not. English law required a simpler rule, one easier to state, less difficult to prove, and not so open to fraud. By the reign of Edward III, this had been adopted: divorce for affinity or consanguinity did not bastardize the child, while divorce for pre-contract did.[34]

It seems obvious that the same rationale of visiting the parents' fault on their children lay behind both the English and the canonical rule. One may more easily believe that a person has ignored the extent of his kinship than that he has forgotten contracting marriage or professing monastic vows. Thus it seemed right to impose the penalty of bastardy more readily in the latter case. It may also be fair to think that the early English rule shows signs of a sensible dislike of the wide sweeping net of kinship disqualifications that complicate, and in a measure discredit, the medieval law of marriage. But, in any event, English substantive law took a different position from that of the canon law, and royal justices would, at least if one party demanded it, force the other to state the specific cause of divorce. If the cause was pre-contract, the ordinary writ would be sent to the bishop, since the substantive result would be the same under both laws. If it was consanguinity, that ended the matter. The court would not issue the writ, but would instead force the party to proceed to another issue or be non-suited. It is well to note, however, that this was true only when the case involved inheritance of real property. Where the issue was the marriage itself, the question of divorce went to the bishop, no matter what the cause for divorce was. If, for example, the question of the validity of a marriage were raised in a suit for dower, it was referred to the bishops. This without regard for the grounds of challenge, or the form in which it was made.[35] The point was to safeguard

---

33. X 4.17.2.

34. Bracton, f. 299, Y.B. Pasch. 11-12 Edw. III (R.S.), 480-87. The law was later changed to the even simpler rule of bastardizing even children born to parents divorced for affinity or consanguinity, although it is fair to say that the law continued to be uncertain on the subject. See Y.B. 18 Edw. IV, Hil. no. 28, f. 19 (1479), Hooper, *Law of Illegitimacy*, 51.

35. Y.BB. Hil. 32-33 Edw. I (R.S.), 4-7; Trin. 14 Edw. III (R.S.), 322-325; C.P. 40/115 (Mich. 24-25 Edw. I) mm. 40, 86; C.P. 40/129 (Trin. 27 Edw. I) m. 137d.

principles of English inheritance law, not to seize upon every excuse to exclude episcopal jurisdiction.

Common lawyers sometimes had harsh things to say about the handling of divorce litigation in the Church courts. A case from 1365 illustrates one reason. The bishop of Ely's commissary had, during his visitation, uncovered information showing that John T's father had been godfather to his wife's cousin. According to canon law rules, this relationship made marriage without grace of dispensation impossible, and the commissary, zealous for the rigor of the law, or wishing to harass the unfortunate John, proceeded to celebrate a divorce between John's parents. That those parents were themselves dead at the time was not a necessary canonical impediment to the divorce.[36] Subsequently, and perhaps inevitably, John was involved in litigation over his inheritance, and bastardy was objected against him. Whether or not he would have been held legitimate in the spiritual courts depends on factors not given in either the Year Book or the plea roll account of the case. But it was not impossible that he would have been held a bastard, and this the English courts would not admit. Thorp, J. expressed the opinion of the court when he said that if such questions were submitted to the Church, ". . . every Commissary could bastardize every man of the World without his even knowing about it, which would be great mischief." [37]

---

36. There was, it is true, some argument against these *post mortem* divorces, and Roman Church law today excludes them (*Corpus Juris Canonici* c. 1972). But it is not true, as is sometimes said, that they were canonically illegal in the Middle Ages. See the discussion in Antonius de Butrio's *Lectura* ad X 4.17.7, f. 87r. An example of such *post mortem* divorces, in the instance between a couple who had married seventy years before, can be found in the Dean and Chapter Archives, Canterbury, Sede Vacante Scrapbook, III, no. 396 (1294). The ruling that the action would be entertained was, however, vigorously contested and appealed to the Court of Arches.

37. Y.B. 39 Edw. III, Mich., f. 31 (1365); C.P. 40/421 (Mich. 39 Edw. III) m. 354. The English Common lawyers also complained with some frequency, and with some reason, about the long delays in the Church courts. In this same case, it was argued that bastardy ought not be submitted to the bishop because "il purra estre delay per ans per appeals." In another case, reported Y.B. 38 Edw. III, Mich., f. 27, a lawyer complained that the party "aura grands delais devant l'Evesqe. Et si l'Evesqe ne vient pas accepter les proves, le party suera per appel, et aura long proces." These two cases also illustrate the Church's unwillingness to submit the procedure in its own courts to English law. Bracton argued, at f. 420, that there could be no appeal of a judgement on bastardy from the bishop to whom the king's writ had been sent. But it is clear that this rule could not be enforced against the bishops, for they

Third, there were some other cases the royal justices refused to send to the church courts, although the two laws were not so clearly different in substance. If the bastardy of a dead man were alleged, the question was tried by assize, not sent to the bishop, without regard for the reason for the bastardy.[38] If the legitimacy of one who was not party to the action was questioned (as where the title to land descended through, and depended on, an alleged bastard), the issue likewise went to a jury.[39] In these instances, where no substantive difference in the two laws could affect the outcome, the English courts took a more restrictive view of ecclesiastical jurisdiction than principle alone warranted. The main reason they gave for the restriction was that non-parties would not be adequately represented before the Church court. In some ways, this seems more an excuse than a reason. The bishops could summon those who were alive, and the same problem of inadequate representation existed in trials by assize. It looks like a plain attempt to curtail ecclesiastical jurisdiction.

The Common lawyers had an answer to this charge. They said that in the royal courts, the bishops' certificates had a conclusive, pre-emptory force which jury verdicts did not.[40] That is, a certificate of legitimacy or bastardy coming from the Church could not be challenged in a subsequent lawsuit, even between different parties. The verdict of jurors bound no one beyond the individual parties. Thus it was essential to hedge recourse to the bishops with procedural safeguards. If a man's legitimacy could be conclusively settled by the bishops in a suit to which he was not a party, he might be

---

would not answer the writ if there were an appeal. In a case heard in the Common Pleas in 1277, the party who had appealed in the Church court was ordered to remit that appeal "si sibi videtur expedire ita quod episcopus procedere possit," C.P. 40/17 (Mich. 4-5 Edw. I) m. 144. But, as the cautious language suggests, it is not clear how far this remedy was enforced.

38. Bracton f. 269; Y.BB. 20 Edw. I. (R.S.), 172-73; 2 Edw. II (S.S., Vol. 17), 95; 39 Edw. III, Hil., f. 2 (1365). The situation did not in fact arise as frequently as it might have because of the exception made for the *bastard eigné*. If a bastard entered as son and heir, and held the land until his death, title based on his possession could not be challenged later. See F. E. Farrer, "The Bastard Eigné" in 33 *L. Q. Rev.*, 135-53 (1917) and Vol. 34, 27-34 (1918). The rule did not, apparently, hold against the king; K.B. 27/392 (Trin. 32 Edw. III) Rex m. 3.

39. Y.BB. 9 Edw. III, Trin. no. 4, f. 19 (1335), 17 Edw. III, Mich. no. 54, f. 59 (1343). That the rule was not in every case respected is indicated by *Rotuli Parliamentorum*, ii, 171a (1347), a complaint that a case of bastardy of a non-party had been sent to the Church, to his later prejudice.

40. See Y.B. 12 Ric. II (Ames Foundation), 74; *Rot. Parl.*, iii, 490a; Hooper, *Law of Illegitimacy*, 77.

deprived of the chance to bring forward all the proof he had. This is true because in a lawsuit in which he had no interest in the outcome, he would have little incentive to present his strongest case. Such, at any rate, was the lawyers' argument, and there is some cogency to it.

The argument depends, of course, entirely on the effectiveness of the bishops' certificates in the English courts. And although the rule of conclusiveness was often cited and mostly followed, a number of cases show an unwillingness by the judges to enforce it when injustice or fraud would result. The Common law justices were sometimes tied to mechanical application of technical rules in the fourteenth century, but on more than one occasion they dealt freely with this one. In a case from 1337, for example, it was pleaded that the plaintiff was a bastard by reason of birth before his parents' marriage. The plaintiff countered by showing record of a bishop's certificate from a previous decision testifying to his legitimacy. The court, however, refused to accept it as conclusive. As Shareshull, J. said, "I cannot have this answer because with it a man would gain inheritance against the law of the land." [41] Even where the situation was not so clearly that of the Council of Merton, the justices were willing on occasion to disregard the rule. In Trinity term of 1354, another litigant sought to introduce a bishop's certificate from a previous action of formedon and was driven to answer when the court again refused to accept it. [42]

A legitimate reason for the justices' disregard of the rule of conclusiveness was that it encouraged fraud on the English law. It was easy enough to set up one collusive lawsuit which raised bastardy without involving substantive conflict between the laws, get a bishop's certificate on the court records, then plead the certificate as conclusive when bastardy was raised in a subsequent dispute. It was a subterfuge, though not a particularly clever one. [43]

---

41. Y.B. Mich. 11-12 Edw, III (R.S.), 223-35.

42. 26 Lib. Ass. no. 64 (1352). A similar result was reached in Y.B. Mich. 18-19 Edw. III (R.S.), 32-41. And in a case heard as early as 1277, the Common Pleas refused to accept as proof of a valid marriage the letter of the archbishop of Canterbury certifying the legitimacy of one son for entry into a benefice. The ground given was that where there had been no former plea in the royal courts, no ecclesiastical certificate could have conclusive force; C.P. 40/17 (Mich. 4-5 Edw. I) m. 144.

43. It is interesting to note that Innocent IV was well aware of this abuse and sought to find a way to stop it; *Apparatus* ad X 4.17.7, f. 188 ". . . . nec debet quis admitti ad petendum se pronunciari legitimum nisi habet contradictorem et iustum, et si admissus fuerit, nulla est sentencia." But as a fictitious "contradictor" could be set up, and since the bishop's certificate was ordinarily conclusive once on the English court records, this solution did little good. Complaints in Parliament gave rise

To allow it defeated a strong policy of English law. The justices were sometimes, but not always, willing to disregard the procedural rule of the force of the certificate. They invoked it freely as an excuse for limiting the jurisdiction of the Church courts, but were less ready to apply it when it meant the application of canon law to questions of inheritance of English land.

The foregoing restrictions of the Church's jurisdiction to determine bastardy were probably less important than a fourth, the distinction between proprietary and possessory actions. Maitland has pointed it out: only when the action went to the right would recourse be had to the Church to determine legitimacy. Otherwise, bastardy would be tried "in what we may call a possessory spirit," that is by assize.[44] It is possible that this distinction was evolved after Bracton's time for there is no explicit mention of it in his discussion of bastardy, but it was an established part of English law by the end of the century.[45]

The justification for the rule is a familiar one, the same which had originally made possible the wide introduction of possessory assizes in the royal courts. Since it was theoretically always possible to follow a possessory action with a writ of right, no one could be obliged to have his legitimacy tried by assize. He could always sue later by an action going fully to the right, and the question would be sent to the bishop.

In this form, however, the argument is largely specious. The only class of cases which a party would especially want tried by the

---

to a poorly worded and ineffective statute designed to curb the abuse (9 Hen. VI, c. 11). In the 16th century Christopher St. Germain took note of it, but all he could suggest was a moral obligation on the part of the defrauder to return the property so acquired. *Doctor and Student*, Second Dialogue, c. 5 (London, 1721), 139. This is the weakest of solutions, obviously, for if such a man were minded to return the property, he would not have brought the fraudulent suit in the first place. No doubt, also, such a man would think it was the English law, not his collusive law suit, which was of dubious morality.

44. Pollock and Maitland, *History of English Law* (Cambridge, (1898), Vol. II, 380; Bastardy questions in writs of entry seem also to have gone to the country. C.P. 40/183 (Mich. 4 Edw. II) m. 111d; C.P. 40/216 (Mich. 10 Edw. II) m. 23.

45. Compare Bracton, f. 216b with Britton, f. 128. It is perhaps worth noting that support could be found for the English distinction in canonical-civilian theory, as set out in Guillelmus Durandus, *Speculum Iuris* t. *de ordine cognitionum* (Frankfort, 1668), II, 202. Durandus held that both when the spiritual question was prejudicial to the secular, as it always was in bastardy cases, the prejudicial question must be tried first, that is by the ecclesiastical court. He goes on to say, however, that this is true only for proprietary actions. "Si vero agitur possessorie et reus obiiciat preiudicialem exceptionem, secus est."

Church were those in which English and canon law were at variance. These, we have seen, it was the policy of the English courts to refuse to submit to the Church in the first place. Where the two laws were identical, it made little difference how the issue was tried. Thus, the result of the distinction between actions of right and of possession was, or ought to have been, to considerably restrict the number of cases which would be sent to the ecclesiastical tribunals. Actions of right were less frequent in the royal courts than possessory actions, so that the distinction, if rigorously followed, would have very largely removed bastardy litigation from the jurisdiction of the Church. We do know that it was not absolutely applied, for there were a few possessory actions which did in the event go to the bishops. But certainly, the distinction was very largely followed in the first half of the 14th century.[46]

To summarize briefly, the practice of sending questions of bastardy to the Church at the start of the fourteenth century was this. A number of specific situations had been developed in which the royal courts would not, unless the parties agreed otherwise, refer to the ecclesiastical forum. They were of two sorts. The first included cases where a substantive difference in the definition of legitimacy existed. Children of adulterous liaisons, those born before their parents' espousals, and those whose parents' marriage had been dissolved came under this heading. The second consisted of cases where the refusal was based on procedural grounds. Bastardy of dead men and other non-parties, and most importantly, possessory as against proprietary actions came under this second.

Retention for trial by jury, we noted above, was a necessary step in the first class, a step required to vindicate the principle that English law, not canon law, should determine inheritance of English land. As to the second group, reasons could likewise be given for each of its categories, but especially with the right-possession distinction, the result was not at all required by English law, in the same way that keeping cases of pre-nuptial or adulterous children out of the bishops' hands was. Retention of the cases in the second class was rather a slightly veiled attack on ecclesiastical jurisdiction than a vindication of English principles of inheritance. And it had one unfortunate result. The wide use of the second class focused attention almost entirely on the form in which the claim of bastardy had been raised. The essential question became, not what the reason for bastardy was, but how it had been raised. Whether or not the issue went to the Courts Christian depended not

---

46. K.B. 27/373 (Mich. 27 Edw. III) m. 45; Y.BB. 5 Edw. II (S.S. Vol. 33), 161-69 (1312); Pasch. 14 Edw. III (R.S.), 55 (1340); 26 Lib. Ass. no. 64 (1352), in which, however, Thorp, J. appears to have dissented.

on a question in which English inheritance law was at stake, but on a question of form.

It should not be totally surprising, then, that the end result of the possessory-right distinction in bastardy cases, and to a lesser extent that of the other procedural distinctions, was not a happy one. Theoretically, it should have been possible to keep all the cases straight. Mastery of technical pleading, we may say, was an essential part of an English lawyer's job; it was not a business for amateurs, and as long as the pleading reflected the real issues of conflict between Church and State, there need have been no difficulties. But in fact there were difficulties. The English lawyers were not the masters of pleading such distinctions required. In the first half of the fourteenth century, the emptiest of formalism seemed often to control, and the substance of English law was often sacrificed to considerations of pleading alone. Citation of a specific case may make this clear. *Le Fevre* v. *Sleght*, heard in 1313, was brought on a writ of right in which the demandant was challenged as being born before espousals, the classic Statute of Merton situation. But Scrope, for the demandant, argued: "This is a writ of right; judgement if such an answer should be allowed if you do not say simply bastard." This argument was accepted, and the court drove the tenant to allege general bastardy, which had to go to the Church for trial.[47]

It need hardly be said that this was bad law. *Le Fevre* v. *Sleght* raised exactly the issue which the events at Merton and after had made clear the royal courts had to retain for decision. Instead, that distinction was ignored. The distinction between writs of right and possessory actions and the technicalities of pleading had taken over and obscured the substantive issue of the inheritance claims of pre-nuptial children. But the same result was reached in other cases, notably one from 1334, in which the court sought to escape it by saying that it would accept a spontaneous finding of bastardy returned by the jurors, but that if bastardy were pleaded at all, the matter had to go to the bishop.[48] Confirmation of the unfortunate result comes from the Parliament records of 1327, when a petition complained that the bishops were hearing such bastardy cases and requested that henceforth the king's justices would themselves determine the issue by jury verdict.[49]

47. Y.B. 7 Edw. II (S.S. Vol. 36), 158.

48. 8 Lib. Ass. no. 5 (1334). See also K.B. 27/326 (Mich. 15 Edw. III) m. 165d; C.P. 40/195a (Mich. 6 Edw. II) m. 397; Y.BB. 6 Edw. II (S.S., Vol. 43), 72; 7 Edw. II (S.S., Vol. 36), 105-06.

49. *Rotuli Parliamentorum Anglie hactenus inediti*, eds. H. G. Richardson and G. Sayles (Camden Soc., 1935), Vol. II, 125: "Item pur ceo qe grant debate ad este entre frers dont lun nasquist devant les esposails et lauter apres, et grant delaye ad este en court cristien, qe desormes

Just as the right-possession distinction caused confusion, so the rule that the legitimacy of dead men would be tried by assize likewise gave rise to difficulty. We saw above that for procedural reasons, the legitimacy of non-parties was tried by assize. But we now begin to find the contention made that bastardy of living men could only be tried by Court Christian.[50] Also, we find cases in which it was said that the bastardy of a tenant of land in dispute could only be tried by the bishops.[51] Neither of these arguments made sense. The essential matter was to protect the English inheritance law, and these in fact thwarted it. They sent questions to the bishops which should have been retained. That the question of a dead man's legitimacy could not go to the bishops does not prove that a live man's must, for he may have been born of adultery or before his parents' espousals. That the law accorded some procedural advantages to the tenant as against the demandant is no reason to grant him trial of bastardy by bishop's certificate, for a tenant may be bastard by English law, legitimate by canon law as well as a demandant.

It is not always clear how far these arguments were adopted by the courts. The Year Book accounts concentrate on pleading rather than on judgements, so that we very often do not know how a particular case came out. But the plea rolls show that the court often did sanction a result contrary to English law. And when the arguments were repeated in case after case, over the course of years, and answered with neither good sense nor good law, it is clear that the law was in a confused state as regards trial of bastardy. And in the instances above the result of the confusion was to submit some cases of disputed inheritance to the jurisdiction of the Church, the exact opposite of what the barons at Merton had desired.

The conflicting results and confused arguments of the Year Book cases of the first half of the fourteenth century show that concentration on considerations of form and the lack of mastery of the art of pleading had confused the issue which had been more clearly drawn by Bracton. We have seen that this confusion led to

---

ne soit tiel delaye, mes qe les iustices pernent enqueste sil nasquist devant ou non et sur ceo face jugement."

50. See, for example, Y.B. 7 Edw. II (S.S., Vol. 36), 96, where it was objected, ". . . . la manere de vostre repouns est insufficient encountre cely qest en pleyne vie, qe ne put james estre bastard saunz certification del Evesqe." Or see Y.B. 9 Edw. III, Trin., f. 19 (1335).

51. Y.BB. 6 Edw. II (S.S., Vol. 43), 72-74; 9 Edw. III, Trin., f. 19 (1335). Bracton, at f. 418b, gave it as the rule that the burden of proof would be on the demandant, so that the tenant had this advantage, but there is nothing of the rule argued for in this Y.B. Case.

some cases being sent to the Church which should have been kept by the royal courts. But we should also note that it opened the way for attempts to avoid sending to the bishops cases which rightfully belonged to ecclesiastical jurisdiction. This was possible through a series of verbal tricks. It began to be argued that if one avoided using the actual word "bastard" in the pleadings, jurisdiction could be withdrawn from the Church. Thus, allegations in such forms as these appeared: the claimant was "not of the blood of," or "his father never married his mother," or "he was not the son of," his alleged ancestor.[52] Such pleadings neither raised any issue on which English law differed from canon law, nor amounted to anything more than a plain exception of bastardy. All they did was to avoid the use of the word "bastard," so that it could be argued that "special matter" had been introduced. This practice was senseless. The point of pleading special matter, as Bracton had explained it, was to determine whether the case was one in which English law and canon law were different, not to give the party raising the bastardy issue the choice of which forum he wanted.[53]

Of course, such "dodges" were not in every instance accepted. But it is clear that they sometimes were, and the testimony from the Church's side makes it obvious that these cases were not going unnoticed. Most of the examples of this sort of pleading that we have come from the first part of Edward II's reign. And the lone ecclesiastical complaint, of which we have record, against trial of bastardy in the royal courts comes from just that period. At the Council of London and Lambeth in 1309, a petition to the King was formulated, objecting that "certain justices of late, if the exception is proposed before them in this form, 'he is not legitimate,' take cognisance of it in fact." The bishops asked that "notwithstanding the variation of the words, the judges desist from hearing such cases." [54] We do not know what immediate effect the petition had. Perhaps very little. All the same, attempts to evade ecclesiastical jurisdiction by mere "variation of words" do very largely disappear from the Year Books after Edward II's reign.

We should note here that it was largely by the use of such purely formal variations that jurisdiction over bastardy was with-

---

52. Y.BB. 5 Edw. II (S.S., Vol. 31), 186-91, 7 Edw. II (S.S., Vol. 36), 105-107; 11 Lib. Ass. no. 20 (1337); "Pleas at Law 1300-1312", Brit. Mus. Add. MS. 35,116,f. 34r; C.P. 40/195a (Mich. 6 Edw. II) m. 92; C.P. 40/216 (Mich. 10 Edw. II) m. 122.

53. Bracton, f. 416: "sed quoniam ubi causa non adicitur sub tali responsione poterit esse obscuritas et incertitudo, quia cum sciri non poterit ad quod forum pertinere debeat cognitio . . ."

54. *Council and Synods with other Documents relating to the English Church II*, eds. F. M. Powicke and C. R. Cheney (Oxford, 1964), Pt. I, 1273.

drawn from the Church on the Continent. Rather than by frontal
attacks on the rights of the Church courts, Continental jurists used
indirect and technical distinctions to achieve the same result. Perhaps we should see in the English practices to which the 1309
Council objected the start of the same process in England. But,
in the event, it was a road the English lawyers did not take. Having
advanced some steps down it, the Common lawyers withdrew,
leaving the English Church's rights unimpaired. Whether they
did so because of the unfortunate results which had followed we
cannot be sure. But it is certain that most of the confusion in the
pleading which is found in the reign of Edward II on this issue had
disappeared by the middle of the century. It is difficult not to see in
this a growing understanding of the issues involved. And we must
note that in the process the justices rejected the method of restricting ecclesiastical jurisdiction through purely formal variation in pleading. Here, at least, they did not show themselves
jealous of the Church's jurisdiction.

If the Churchmen's protest, or judicial astuteness, gradually
eliminated this particularly obnoxious trick, the possession-right
distinction which had, by its emphasis on form, created a part of
the climate in which such confusion could flourish was left un-
touched. Though it had doubtless kept a large number of cases
out of the Church courts, the "possessory spirit" had led, like the
others mentioned, to difficulty and some confusion. Solution came
in 1364, in a case of novel disseisin from Surrey. It is worth setting
out the facts. The original holder of the land in dispute had had two
daughters. The plaintiff was the issue of one of them. The defendant had been enfeoffed with the entire piece of land by the other
daughter, and was in possession. One daughter had, in other words,
alienated the entire inheritance as if she held the fee, not simply
the half which came to her by English law. Thus the plaintiff had
a good claim to her mother's share of the inheritance, except that
the defendant objected that she was illegitimate. If that were
true, of course, none of the land could have descended to the plaintiff and the feoffment to the defendant was perfectly lawful.

For some reason, perhaps with prompting, the plaintiff asked
for a writ to the bishop of Winchester to try the bastardy. The defendant demanded trial by assize, "since that has been the use up
to now". Finch, J. agreed that this was the practice, but said he saw
no good reason for it. Since, in fact if not in theory, "blood will be
tried in a writ of assize for ever as well as in any other writ," the
distinction did not seem sensible to him. "There is," he said, "as
much good reason to send to Court Christian in this case as in any
other writ." [55]

---

55. Y.B. 38 Edw. III, Mich., f. 26: ". . . . mes jeo ne scay pas voier per

Finally, the matter was adjourned before the Court of Common
Pleas, where the justices said (in the words of the Year Book), "We
have taken advice of all our masters herein, and are all of one accord. As well in assizes as in other writs if bastardy is alleged
against a party, it will be sent to Court Christian." [56] With that,
they abolished a rule of practice which had been good law for at
least seventy-five years. Thereafter, there were some attempts made
by pleaders to get the justices to return to the old rule, but they
came to naught.[57]

The happy issue of this decision was to concentrate attention
once more on the substantive differences between English law and
canon law. If a child were said to be born before his parents' marriage, the royal courts kept the case, whatever the form of the action. If bastardy was alleged generally, without special matter,
then the issue was submitted to the bishops. In this decision lay
some of the means for clearing away the confusion which
clouded thinking on this issue of conflict between Church and
State. The Year Books of the later fourteenth and the fifteenth
centuries have little of the variety of treatment and disorder of argument about this subject which mark their predecessors. The readings at the Inns of Court and the treatises of Fortescue, Littleton,
and Coke are clear on the essential issue: the substantive differences in definition of bastardy by Church and State.[58] The refusal
to send allegations of bastardy of non-parties was retained, but the
reason que nous poiomes mults trier de bastardie in Assize que in auter
bref, car le sank sera try in ceo bref d'Assize pur toujours auxi bien
come in auter brief." Unfortunately, one of the few *De Banco* rolls missing from this period is this one from the Michaelmas term of 38 Edward
III.

56. *ibid.*, "Purque nous avons priz avis de touts nos Masters cyens, et
sumes tout d'un accorde; et auxy bien in Assise come in auter bref si
bastardie suit allege in cesty qui est party, home mandra au Court
Chrestien."

57. Y.B. 4 Edw. IV, Mich. no. 16, f. 34 (1464): "Et issint est de bastard,
l'issue pris sur ceo en action personel serra trie per le Evesque auxibien
come en le plea real, en uncore devant ceo temps en eigne temps le use
fuist auterment, scilicet en actions personel a trier per le pais, mes ore
change." Cf. also Y.B. 49 Edw. III Pasch. no. 11, f. 18 (1375); C.P. 40/458
(Pasch. 49 Edw. III) m. 395. Confirmation of the effectiveness of the ruling can be found in an unprinted Lincoln Episcopal Register, containing
a collection of royal writs from the late fourteenth century. It has three
judicial writs sent to the bishop to certify bastardy in possessory actions: Lincolnshire Archives Office, Reg. XIIb, f. 19*v* (1369); f. 48*r*
(1386); f. 73*v* (1396).

58. *Readings and Moots at the Inns of Court in the fifteenth century*,
ed. S. E. Thorne (S.S., Vol. 71), cxi-cxii; Fortescue, *De Laudibus Legum
Anglie*, ed. S. E. Chrimes (Cambridge, 1949), 99; Co. Lit. 245a.

possessory-right distinction made no further appearance. The 1364 decision was a sign, perhaps also a condition, of the maturing of one area of English Common law.

On the question of conflict between Church and State, the significance of that decision is that it was taken actually in favor of ecclesiastical jurisdiction. From the point of view of strict logic, the confusion might have as easily been cleared away by trying all bastardy cases by assize. This would have removed the problem entirely. And it was the attitude adopted in most Continental jurisdictions. Surely there was much to recommend it. But here, in the same year a Statute of Praemunire was adopted, the royal judges went out of their way to uphold, and in fact to increase, the extent of ecclesiastical jurisdiction. Whether they did so from conservatism, piety, or good sense, I do not know. But they must have realised that the real issue of conflict between Church and State was over inheritance of land by children of questionable birth, not one of competition between rival court systems. On the substantive issue, English law would not yield. But in this instance at least, the English justices showed themselves far from wishing to diminish the jurisdiction of the Courts Christian in their own favor.

In conclusion then, it can be said that the story of bastardy litigation in the Middle Ages is one in which there were very real elements of disagreement between Church and State, but that this disagreement is perhaps overshadowed by mutual accommodation and even harmony. The Church found, we saw in the first part of this paper, good reasons within its own law not to push the elements of disagreement. Where inheritance of lay fee was the basic issue, the canonists and churchmen recognized the force, if not perhaps the unimpeachable logic, of the secular jurists' arguments. And the English courts, for their part, rejected several precedents which allowed avoidance of ecclesiastical jurisdiction over bastardy cases by formal or procedural techniques. They abolished a long-standing rule of procedure so as to favor ecclesiastical jurisdiction.

In this, the Common law courts give evidence of an important growth in sophistication and control of pleading which took place in the middle years of the fourteenth century. Coke, who professed to be quoting a judge of the reign of Henry IV, wrote that, "In the reign of Edward the third, pleadings grew to perfection both without lamenesse and curiosity, . . . , for before that time the maner of pleading was but feeble in comparison of that it was afterward in the reign of the same king." [59] The source Coke claimed for this assertion has never been traced. But the history of bastardy litigation gives some warrant for accepting its substance.

---

59. Co. Lit. 304b.

III

The sequel to this account of bastardy litigation in the Middle Ages is perhaps worth telling. The English Reformation made no apparent changes in the practice. Questions of general bastardy still went to the bishops for decision. The system was still in operation in Blackstone's day, and it was only in the nineteenth century that bastardy jurisdiction was finally removed from the Church courts.[60]

The stand of the barons at the Council of Merton has had an even longer life. In the 1830's, the highest English courts found reason to again approve the rule, and in striking language. The rule, they said "is sown in the land, springs out of it, and cannot, according to the law of England, be abrogated or destroyed by any foreign rule of law whatsoever." [61] As in the Middle Ages, the outcome depended on land. It was only in 1920 by Act of Parliament, that the principle which had earned the unanimous and long-time disapproval of English barons was finally accepted. The Legitimacy Act of that year extended fully legitimate status to children born before their parents' wedlock.[62] It is difficult not to wonder what Grosseteste's reaction would be to the delay.

---

60. 3 *Bl. Comm.* 355; William Clerk's *The Trial of Bastardie* (London, 1594) gives instructions on how the process is to be carried out. And see Hooper, *The Law of Illegitimacy*, 76.

61. *Birtwhistle* v. *Vardill*, 2 Cl.-Fin. 571, at 579, 6 Eng. Rep. 1270 (1835), affirmed 7 Cl.-Fin. 895, 7 Eng. Rep. 1308 (1840).

62. 16-17 Geo. V, c. 60.

12

THE ROMAN LAW OF GUARDIANSHIP IN ENGLAND, 1300-1600

I. INTRODUCTION

The place of Roman law in the history of English law has long been a subject of interest and debate. At least since the seventeenth century, when James I's abortive union of Scots and English law sparked interest in the subject,[1] scholars have scrutinized the pages of Glanvill and Bracton, the procedures of Chancery, and the acts of Parliament to detect possible civilian influence.[2] The results have not been conclusive. Some writers have minimized the role of Roman law in English history.[3] Others have exaggerated its claims.[4] In the end, the question remains open:

The author would like to thank Professors Merton Bernstein, Charles Donahue, Jr., and Sue Sheridan Walker, who generously commented on earlier drafts of this article and suggested many useful changes.

1. *See* Levack, *The Proposed Union of English Law and Scots Law in the Seventeenth Century*, 1975 Jur. Rev. 97.

2. For informative modern studies on the subject, including references to past literature, see J. Barton, Roman Law in England (Ius Romanum Medii Aevi, Pars V) 13a (1971) [hereinafter cited as Barton]; J. Langbein, Prosecuting Crime in the Renaissance: England, Germany, France (1974); Plucknett, *The Relations Between Roman Law and English Common Law Down to the Sixteenth Century: A General Survey*, 3 U. Toronto L.J. 24 (1939) [hereinafter cited as Plucknett]; Turner, *Roman Law in England Before the Time of Bracton*, 1975 J. British Studies 1; *A Bracton Symposium*, 42 Tul. L. Rev. 455 (1968); Donahue, Book Review, 84 Yale L.J. 167, 178 (1974)[hereinafter cited as Donahue] (reviewing B. Levack, The Civil Lawyers in England 1603-1641: A Political Study (1973)).

3. *E.g.*, Plucknett, *supra* note 2, at 48.

4. *E.g.*, Sherman, *The Romanization of English Law*, 23 Yale L.J. 318 (1914).

What influence, if any, has Roman law had on the course of English legal development?

This article makes a small contribution to the subject by examining the use made of Roman law in the courts of the English Church. Focusing specifically on the law of guardianship of minor children, it explores a part of the history of that law that previously has been either ignored or unknown.[5] Based upon an examination of the surviving court records, the article attempts to show that the Church courts exercised a significant guardianship jurisdiction in England through application of Roman law. It then assesses the implications of the evidence for the history of the development of both canon and common law.

A.   The Common Law

The English common law of guardianship provides a necessary background for examination of Church court practice. Its outlines, of course, are well known. "[N]o part of our old law," wrote Maitland, "was more disjointed and incomplete than that which deals with the guardianship of infants."[6] It was disjointed because by 1600 English law recognized at least ten separate kinds of guardians.[7] It was incomplete because it provided permanent guardians for only a special class of fatherless children—heirs to real property that had been held by freehold tenure. Under the regime of primogeniture, when a father died leaving minor children the common law supplied a guardian for his eldest son alone; the younger children had no guardian. Even this very limited protection failed if the father held no freehold land. In that situation, the common law made no provision for the wardship of any of his children. Most infants, Maitland therefore concluded, were left "to shift for themselves and to get guardians as best they might from time to time for the purpose of litigation."[8]

---

5.   A standard work on the subject, for example, suggests that only feudal and borough guardianship were used in medieval and early modern England. H. Taylor, Law of Guardian and Ward (1935). *See also* P. Bingham, The Law of Domestic Relations § 8.4 (1968). Seventeenth century references to ecclesiastical guardianship can be found in E. Coke, The Compleat Copy-holder § 22 (2d ed. London 1650) (1st ed. London 1641); J. Godolphin, The Orphan's Legacy: or, A Testamentary Abridgement, pt. II, ch. 9 (London 1674); H. Swinburne, A Treatise of Testaments and Last Wills, pt. 3, §§ 7-14, at 263-97 (7th ed. London 1803) (1st ed. London 1590) [hereinafter cited as Swinburne on Wills].

6.   2 F. Pollock & F. Maitland, The History of English Law 443 (2d ed. reissued 1968) [hereinafter cited as Pollock & Maitland].

7.   A. Simpson, A Treatise on the Law and Practice Relating to Infants 183 (4th ed. 1926).

8.   2 Pollock & Maitland, *supra* note 6, at 444.

A special deficiency of the common law existed where an heir held land by military tenure. In such cases the common law treated guardianship as a lucrative right rather than as a trust for the child's benefit. The guardian could take the profits of the heir's lands, subject to a reasonable allowance for maintenance and education. He also could sell both the wardship and the marriage of the ward, tempting the purchaser to recoup the price from the heir's revenues.[9] Only where the heir held land by socage tenure was the guardian obliged to exercise his office for the benefit of the child.[10] Legal historians have commonly concluded, therefore, that guardianship in England was both deficient in coverage and open to abuse in application. This conclusion, however, is not entirely sound, since the royal courts did not have exclusive jurisdiction in guardianship matters. Professor Carlton has recently shown that the borough courts supplied some protection for orphans.[11] This article will show that some of the gaps in the common law were also filled by the courts of the Church through application of principles of Roman law.

B.   The Canon Law

The foundations for the Church's jurisdiction in guardianship matters were threefold. First, the Church claimed the right to exercise a general jurisdiction in favor of *miserabiles personae*, those who by reason of weakness or incapacity could not adequately protect their own rights.[12] Clearly, this jurisdictional claim could embrace fatherless children. Under canon law,

---

9. For the fullest treatments of the practice involved in secular wardships, see H. Bell, An Introduction to the History and Records of the Courts of Wards and Liveries (1953); J. Hurstfield, The Queen's Wards (2d ed. 1973); Walker, *Widow and Ward: The Feudal Law of Child Custody in Medieval England,* in Women in Medieval Society 159 (S. Stuard ed. 1976).

10.   This was by virtue of statute. Prov. of Westminster, c. 17 (1259) (1 Statutes of the Realm 10); Statute of Marlborough, c. 17 (1267) (1 Statutes of the Realm 24).

11.   C. Carlton, The Court of Orphans (1974). *See also* Gross, *The Medieval Law of Intestacy,* 18 Harv. L. Rev. 120 (1904).

12.   D.87 c.1; X 2.2.11; X 5.40.26. These references to the medieval canonical texts are found in Corpus Juris Canonici (A. Friedberg ed. 1879). All citations to the standard medieval gloss on these texts are taken from the edition printed in Rome in 1582 [hereinafter abbreviated *gl. ord.*]. The following system of citation to the texts is used herein:

D.1 c.1	*Decretum Gratiani,* Distincto 1, cap. 1.
C.1. q.1 c.1	*Decretum Gratiani,* Causa 1. quaestio 1, cap. 1.
X 1.1.1.	*Decretales Gregorii* IX, Liber 1, tit. 1, cap. 1.
Sext. 1.1.1.	Liber Sextus, Liber 1, tit. 1, cap. 1.
Clem. 1.1.1.	*Constitutiones Clementinae,* Liber 1, tit. 1, cap. 1.

Church courts shared this duty with the courts of the king, particularly when secular justice was inadequate.[13] Second, probate jurisdiction in England was lodged in the Church courts.[14] Medieval wills often contained legacies to minor children, who had a right, in some places at least, to a filial portion or *legitime*. In the absence of a valid will, they also had claims to an intestate share. It fell to the ecclesiastical courts to secure administration and distribution of these legacies and portions during the infancy of the child. Appointment of a guardian was a way to carry out that responsibility. Third, the Church exercised jurisdiction over many aspects of family law. Cases involving annulment of marriage or disputed paternity brought the Church courts into frequent contact with minor children.[15] Infants came naturally

---

13. *See gl. ord.* ad D.87 c.1 s.v. *plus tamen; gl. ord.* ad C.23 q.5 c.23 s.v. *oppressos. See also* B. Tierney, Medieval Poor Law 15-19 (1959). For the conflict growing out of this uncertain principle in France, see P. Fournier, Les officialités au moyen age 80-81 (1880) [hereinafter cited as Fournier]; O. Martin, L'Assemblée de Vincennes de 1329 et ses consequences 159 (1909) [hereinafter cited as Martin].

14. R. Goffin, The Testamentary Executor in England and Elsewhere (1901); M. Sheehan, The Will in Medieval England (1963). The most complete discussion of the practical operation of ecclesiastical jurisdiction is still Swinburne on Wills, *supra* note 5, first published in 1590. Jurisdiction was removed from the Church courts with the creation of the Court of Probate in 1857. Probates and Letters of Administration Act, 1857, 20 & 21 Vict., c. 77, § 4.

15. It was usual, for example, in the diocese of Canterbury for a man convicted of fathering a child to be compelled to provide a fund for the child's necessities and to endow the child's mother. *See, e.g.*, Canterbury Act Book Y.4.1, f. 40v (1540): *"quod exhibeat alimenta puero et dotaret mulieri x s. citra proximo et qualibet septimana puero per annum"* ("that he endow the woman with ten shillings and provide sustenance for the child before the next session and every week during the next year").

Citations to manuscript Church court records are given hereinafter by diocese, rather than by present archive. The diocesan court records used, with corresponding archives, are listed as follows:

Canterbury	Library of the Dean and Chapter, Canterbury.
Chichester	West Sussex Record Office, Chichester.
Durham	Library of the Department of Palaeography and Diplomatic, University of Durham.
Ely	Cambridge University Library.
Hereford	Hereford County Record Office, Hereford.
Lichfield	Joint Record Office, Lichfield.
London	Guildhall Library, London [MS. 9064 records] and Greater London Council Record Office [DL/C records].
Norwich	Norfolk Record Office, Norwich.
Rochester	Kent County Record Office, Maidstone.

under the jurisdiction of the courts that administered the law of domestic relations. Canon law therefore gave theoretical justification to, and English practice provided actual opportunity for, the ecclesiastical courts to appoint guardians as protectors of the interests of infants.

The law regularly applied in the ecclesiastical courts was, of course, the canon law of the Western Church. But the rules at the disposal of the English Church courts in exercising guardianship jurisdiction were drawn principally from the Roman law of *cura* and *tutela,* because the canon law contained no express law on the subject. Gratian's *Decretum* (c. 1140) and the *Decretales* of Pope Gregory IX (1234) provided the bulk of formal canon law. Neither included a section defining or regulating guardianship of infants. Where guardianship was mentioned, it was only with reference to an existing civil law institution.[16] The canonical texts accepted the civil law and tacitly approved it.[17] When medieval canonists treated the subject of guardianship, they almost always referred to appropriate sections of the Roman law *Code* and *Digest* for authority, not to canon law texts.[18] This is as true of the *Provinciale*[19] of the English canonist William Lyndwood as it is of the more numerous commentaries written on the Continent. Guardianship is thus an excellent example of the widely accepted

St. Albans (archdeaconry)	Hertfordshire County Record Office, Hertford.
York	Borthwick Institute of Historical Research, York [Cause papers and A B Act books] and York Minster Library[M 2(1) Act books].

16.   *See, e.g.,* D.87 c.5; C.20 q.2 c.2; X 1.19.1; X 3.26.16. On the subject of the status of children in medieval canon law, see Metz, *L'enfant dans le droit canonique medièval; orientations de recherche,* 36 Recueils de la société Jean Bodin 9 (1976)[hereinafter cited as Metz].

17.   The two laws did occasionally diverge. For example, canon law held that a monk could serve as a *tutor*; Roman law, that he could not. But minor details apart, the canon law received the Roman law of *cura* and *tutela. Compare* D.86 c.26 *with* Nov. 123.5.

18.   For example, to show that the judge could properly approve the appointment of a *tutor testamentarius,* but not a *tutor dativus,* without an inquisition into suitability and without *satisdatio,* the great canonist Hostiensis (d.1271) cited only Roman law texts: Institutes 1.13.5; Code 5.29.2; Code 1.4.27; and Institutes 1.24.pr. Henricus de Segusia, Lectura in Libros Decretalium ad X 2.28.67 [Ex parte M.], no. 9 (1581) (n.p.) [hereinafter cited by its usual medieval title, Hostiensis, Lectura, with reference to the text subject to the author's commentary]. This method of citation is followed throughout for medieval treatises on the civil and canon law.

19.   Provinciale (Seu Constitutiones Angliae) 176 s.v. *prius* (1679) [hereinafter cited as Lyndwood, Provinciale].

proposition that the canon law owed much of its procedure and some of its substance to the civil law.[20]

In this context, of course, civil law does not mean classical Roman law. It means the civil law found in the Emperor Justinian's *Corpus Juris Civilis* and interpreted by the medieval glossators and commentators. Many of the internal changes in the Roman law from the primitive to the postclassical periods were unknown or irrelevant to the commentators, who fixed their attention on the Justinianic texts. This article adopts the same view. In dealing with the impact of Roman law on the Church courts, this is the proper method. What must be meant by the reception of Roman law in medieval Europe is the reception of the only Roman law medieval men knew.

It does not necessarily follow, however, that the English Church courts actually made use of the civil law. Many parts of the canon law were not applied in practice. Local custom, pressure from the royal courts, and the urgent need to reach settlement of disputes, as Professor Donahue has recently demonstrated, meant that the courts could not invariably apply the formal law of the Western Church.[21] The important question must be: To what extent and in what manner was the Roman law of guardianship actually applied? To answer this question, we must look to the surviving court records.

C. The Church Court Records

Unfortunately, real difficulties confront the historian who undertakes research in these records, difficulties which affect the scope, or at least the certainty, of any conclusions drawn. The records have survived in very limited quantities and now lie scattered among various archives, almost entirely unprinted. Most importantly, Act books, that is, the day-to-day records of the procedural steps taken in litigation before the Church courts,

---

20. *Gl. ord.* ad X 5.32.1 s.v. *adiuvantur:* "*Dicas quod legibus utendum est in ecclesiasticis causis nisi canonibus contradicant.*" ("You may say that [Roman] laws are to be used in ecclesiastical causes unless they contradict the canons.") *See* Kuttner, *Some Considerations on the Role of Secular Law and Institutions in the History of Canon Law,* in 2 Scritti di sociologia e politica in onore di Luigi Sturzo 349 (1953) [hereinafter cited as Kuttner]; Merzbacher, *Die Parömie: Legista sine canonibus parum valet, canonista sine legibus nihil,* 13 Studia Gratiana 275 (1967); Naz, *Droit romain,* 4 dictionnaire de droit canonique 1502 (1949).

21. *See* Donahue, *Roman Canon Law in the Medieval English Church,* 72 Mich. L. Rev. 647 (1974); Ullmann, *A Decision of the Rota Romana on the Benefit of Clergy in England,* 13 Studia Gratiana 455 (1967).

constitute the principal available source. They normally set forth only rudimentary procedural information: the name and subject of each cause, the appearance by parties to it, the procedure taken on a particular day, and the term set for the next hearing. Except for chance survivals, mainly from York and Canterbury, we have lost the medieval Cause Papers that contained the substance of the law suits: the pleadings, the depositions, and the sentences. We therefore see inside the Church courts through a flawed medium, a record normally confined to the procedural steps taken.

This necessarily limits what can be known about the practice of guardianship jurisdiction. It means that the process of actual administration of the minor's property by guardians is largely hidden. The records do not reveal much about subjects such as how consciously the judges applied the formal law or how conscientiously guardians performed their offices. About these and other important questions the records provide only hints. They do show, on the other hand, a good deal about the appointment of guardians, the kinds of litigation in which they represented infants, and the use of formal checks on the qualifications and integrity of guardians. They reveal enough, in other words, to yield some reasonably reliable conclusions about the nature of the law of guardianship enforced by the ecclesiastical courts.

II.   CLASSIFICATION AND APPOINTMENT OF GUARDIANS

A.   *Distinction Between* Cura *and* Tutela

The Roman law of guardianship was neither simple nor free from internal ambiguity, but as understood by medieval jurists, it provided two basic sorts of guardian: The *tutor* and the *curator*. The former was given to a child in *pupillari aetate, i.e.,* one who had not yet reached puberty.[22] The *curator*, whose selection rested with the minor, represented the child till the age of twenty-five.[23] Of the two, the *tutor* was the more important. His duties em-

---

22.   Puberty was normally set at age 14 for boys and 12 for girls. Institutes 1.22. *See also id.* 1.13.3. On the subject of *tutela* in Roman law, see W. Buckland, A Text-book of Roman Law from Augustus to Justinian 142-73 (3d ed. 1963) [hereinafter cited as Buckland]; 1 P. Bonfante, Corso di diritto romano *Diritto di famiglia* 551-692 (1963) [hereinafter cited as Bonfante]; Solazzi, *Tutele et Curatele,* 53 Revista italiana per le scienze giuridiche 263 (1913); 54 *id.* at 17 (1914).

23.   Institutes 1.23; Hostiensis, Lectura ad X 1.19.1, no. 4: *"Nam tutor datur pupillo, curator adulto, et non pupillo."* ("For a *tutor* is given to a child below puberty; a *curator* to an adult and not to a child below puberty.") Problems of interpretation in classical and postclassical Roman law are treated in S. Solazzi, La minore eta nel diritto romano (1912).

braced protection of both the child's person and property.[24] The duties of the *curator* extended only to matters of property and litigation.

English practice reflected the difference between *cura* and *tutela*. For example, in a testamentary cause heard at London and appealed to Canterbury in the early 1290's, one question raised on appeal was whether a second guardian could properly be appointed for a child who already had a *tutor*.[25] The man who sought appointment as a second guardian did not state in his petition whether he was asking to be named a *tutor* or a *curator*. An exception was taken on the ground that "between a *tutor* and a *curator* wide difference and distinct effects exist, as appears evidently in many treatises of the law."[26] The petitioner's answer, that a *curator* could in some situations be appointed in addition to a *tutor*, and that the *tutor* already appointed should be removed for cause, was supported by citation from the *Digest*.[27] This case was clearly argued according to the Roman law of guardianship.

Unfortunately, this Canterbury case is one of the rare instances in which the remaining record indicates what legal arguments

---

24. Institutes 1.14.4; Azo, Summa Codicis V, tit. *de tut. test. (n.d.): "[S]ed persone datur eius universo patrimonio administrando."* ("But he is given to the person for administering his entire patrimony.")

25. Canterbury Ecclesiastical Suit Roll, no. 135. This case is to appear in a forthcoming volume of the Selden Society, edited by Professor Norma Adams with Professor Charles Donahue, Jr. Most medieval commentators held that in this situation a *curator* could be appointed if necessary for protection of the child's interests. *E.g.*, Baldus, Commentaria ad Digest 26.1.3.2 [*si pupillus*] (n.d.): *"Et ideo potest dici quod propter necessitatem sit adiungendus tutori curator, seu coadiutor generalis, per quem tutor poterit convenire et agere tuitorio."* ("And therefore it can be said because of necessity there may be joined to the *tutor* a *curator* or general coadjutor through whom he can act and sue as a *tutor*."); Azo, Summa Codicis V, tit. *in quibus causis tut. habenti* (n.d.): *"[U]bicumque autem dixi dari tutorem habenti tutorem ut ibidem iudex posset dare curatorem si viderit esse faciendum."* ("Wherever I have said that a *tutor* is given to one having a *tutor* as in that instance, however, a judge can give a *curator* if he shall deem [it] proper.") Placentinus (d. 1192) earlier took the view, however, that such a guardian could not properly be called either *tutor* or *curator*, suggesting the terms *auctor* or *administrator* instead. Placentinus, Summa Codicis V, tit. *in quibus causis tut. habenti* (1536) (repr. 1962).

26. *"[I]nter tutoren et curatorem longa sit differencia et effectus diversus sicut in multis iuris tractatibus evidenter apparet."* This plea seems to have failed, however, and in Ecclesiastical Suit Roll, no. 148, also relating to the same suit, Roger of Arderne is referred to as *tutor seu curator*.

27. Ecclesiastical Suit Roll, no. 135: *"Item suspectus est et inutilis in cuius loco alius datur quia debet alere pupillum ff. de susp. tu. 1. iii c. tutor et § si tutor* (Digest 26.10.3.12)." ("Item, he is suspect and useless, in whose place another is given because he must nourish the child.")

were used. Most surviving cases merely show enough use of civilian terminology to raise an inference that the Roman law distinction between *cura* and *tutela* was followed. For example, at Rochester in 1437 a small child named Thomas Chawnig was referred to correctly in the Act book as being *sub tutela*.[28] In a case heard at St. Albans in 1529, a girl of seven, Margaret Dyar, was rightly assigned a *tutor*.[29] And in a fourteenth century York case, a *curator* rather than a *tutor* served as representative of William, son of Galfred Smyth, described as *in minori etate*, the phrase used for a child who had passed puberty but not yet reached full majority.[30] At Canterbury in 1572, a girl of twenty-one or twenty-two was required correctly by the court to choose a *curator* in order to sue for a legacy allegedly left to her.[31]

These examples show knowledge and application of the Roman law distinction between *cura* and *tutela*.[32] Other cases, however, point in the opposite direction. They suggest a looseness in terminology and a blurring of the distinction between *tutor* and *curator*. The same person was named to serve in both offices simultaneously. In the York court records, for example, the guardian appointed was often called *tutor sive curator*.[33] At Ely

---

28. Rochester Act book DRb Pa 1, f. 31v.

29. St. Albans Act book ASA 7/2, f. 29r: *"Comparuit personaliter in iudicio Margareta Dyar filia ut asseruit Willelmi Dyar defuncti dum vixit parochie sancti Stephani etatis vii annorum vel circiter cui quidem Margarete propter ipsius minorem etatem dominus officialis assignavit Thomam Bamford parochie sancti Andree in tutorem."* ("Margaret Dyar, daughter as she says of William Dyar, deceased, during his lifetime of the parish of St. Stephen, appeared personally in court, and being seven years old or thereabouts the lord official assigned Thomas Bamford of the parish of St. Andrew as her tutor because of her minority.")

30. York CP.E.241r (1358): *"Petit Johannes de Stanton curator Willelmi filii Galfridi Smyth de Northburton puberis in minori etate existentis ad lites legitime deputatus nomine curatorio pro eodem . . . ."* ("John de Stanton, legitimately deputed *curator ad litem* of William, son of Galfrid Smyth of North Burton, seeks for him as his *curator* . . . .") A similar case is recorded in York Act book M 2(1)a, f. 5r (1316).

31. Canterbury Act book Y.2.29 s.d. 26 March 1572: *"Et deinde dictus Soppyn allegavit Margaretam Swetnam alias Swetman partem actricem presentem esse minorem xxi vel saltem xxv annis et eo nomine non habere legitimam personam standi in iudicio. Unde facta fide petit eandem Margaretam cogendam fore ad petendum sibi curatorem ad litem cui legata debita solvi possunt ex decreto."* ("And finally the said Soppyn alleged that Margaret Swetnam, alias Swetman, the present plaintiff, is less than twenty-one or at least twenty-five years and for that reason has no legitimate standing in court. Therefore, faith having been pledged, she asks that Margaret be compelled to seek a *curator* for herself to whom the legacies due can be disbursed by decree.")

32. It is possible, of course, that the Roman law term was used without carrying with it any of the substance. *See* R. Genestal, Etudes de droit privé normand I, La tutelle 58 (1930). The English evidence, given below, suggests by its contrast to feudal guardianship that at least some of the substance of the civil law was implied.

33. *See, e.g.,* CP.G.203b (1519); CP.G.421 (1550); Act book Cons. A B 6, f. 79v

in 1377, John Curteys was assigned as both *tutor* and *curator* for William, son of John Fulbourn.[34] In a 1533 case from the archdeaconry of St. Albans, the judge assigned two men without distinction as *tutores et curatores* for the children of William Heydon.[35] Thus, in practice the two offices were consolidated. Where a distinction was drawn, it was usually between care of the person of the child and administration of his goods: a *tutor* was placed in charge of the child's person, whereas a *curator* was placed in charge of the child's property. Thus, in a guardianship hearing at York in 1372, the judge set a term to appoint both *tutores personarum* and *curatores bonorum* for the children of Roger of Honyingham.[36]

Such a distinction had, of course, a certain congruence with the formal law.[37] A *curator* was appointed solely to protect the minor's property or to assist him in litigation. A *tutor,* at least as understood in the Middle Ages, was appointed in part to care for the child's person.[38] But neither classical Roman law nor medieval civilian jurisprudence limited a *tutor* to rights over the person, as the York case suggests. He had *administratio* of the child's goods.[39] The duty of *curator* and *tutor* was substantially identical

---

(1510). The phrase *tutor vel curator,* or a variant thereof, was found in the civilian texts. *See, e.g.,* Code 2.27.2; Digest 27.9.1; Nov. 72.2. It was used, however, because the same principle of law was applicable to both offices, not because there was no distinction between them, as happened in English practice.

34.   Ely Act book EDR D/2/1, f. 67r. The joint use of the terms was made at Ely in the sixteenth century. *See* Act book EDR D/2/12, f. 70v (1580), in which Robert Edward, son of Thomas Edward, asked that William Edward, *"patruum suum tunc et ibidem presentem sibi et omnibus et singulis bonis iuribus creditis et catallis suis atque in omnibus et singulis negotiis suis constitui tutorem atque curatorem donec ad legitimam etatem pervenerit"* ("his uncle then and there present, be constituted *tutor* and *curator* for him and for all his goods, rights, dues, and chattels until he comes of legitimate age"). A similar instance from the Canterbury records is found in Act book Y.3.21, f. 144r (1585).

35.   St. Albans Act book ASA 7/2, f. 79v (n.d.). This is an interesting case, brought into court by William Heydon and Thomas Heydon, alleging that John Ewer, executor of a testator also named William Heydon, was withholding legacies left to their sons. The court required them to find a *curator et tutor* to represent their own sons' interests. The record reads: *"Et dominus assignavit eisdem Willelmo et Thome ac eorum utrique ad comparendum cum pueris suis et uno viro honesto in curatorem et tutorem dictorum puerorum ordinando et deputando."* ("And the lord [official] assigned William and Thomas jointly and severally to appear with their children and one reliable man to be deputed and appointed *tutor* and *curator* to the said children.") In the same Act book, at f. 80r, Robert Long and John Heydon were duly appointed during a subsequent hearing, at which the children were also present.

36.   Act book M 2(1)c, f. 7r.

37.   *See* Institutes 1.14.4; Bartolus, Commentaria ad Digest 26.1.1, no. 5 (1580-1581).

38.   *See, e.g.,* Azo, Summa Codicis V, tit. *de admin. tut. vel cur.* § *debet gerere* (n.d.).

39.   Buckland, *supra* note 22, at 152-59, 169-73. *See also* note 24 *supra.*

in this respect. The difference was that the *curator* acted for a child past puberty, and the *tutor*, for a child who had not yet reached that age. Although medieval civilians carefully maintained this distinction,[40] practice sometimes employed a different one, depending on the function of the guardian rather than the age of the child.

In some recorded instances, court practice diverged even further from civilian usage, using terms quite foreign to Roman law. For example, at Rochester in 1439 the Act book styled a guardian acting for a child *curator et gubernator*.[41] The representatives in one instance from 1578 were designated *supervisores* of the children.[42] Sometimes no special description at all was given to the person acting for the child, as in a number of cases in which the Act book merely stated that the child's goods were to remain *in custodia* of a certain person.[43] In a few cases, the court records used the terminology of English common law. In an entry from 1564 at Chichester, the official records styled the court-appointed

---

40.   *See, e.g.*, Azo, Summa Codicis V, tit. *qui dare tut. vel cur.* § *potes autem* (n.d.): *"Ergo post pubertatem sibi alium curatorem debebit petere adultus."* ("Therefore, after puberty, the adult should ask for another *curator* for himself.")

41.   Act book DRb Pa 1, ff. 105v, 108v. This was a case apparently brought to recover the person of the child. It was called in the Act book *"causa subtractionis et alienacionis dicti pupilli contra formam decreti et commissionis officialis Roffensis."*
There are numerous other examples of court practice diverging from civilian usage. In a case recorded in Durham Act book III/4 s.d. 23 June 1581, there is a reference to James Slaiter, *"tutor, curator et gubernator Willelmi Slaiter et Ricardi Slaiter."* In another case, a suit was brought at Canterbury in 1418 (Act book Y.1.3, f. 48r) by Thomas Hather for a legacy allegedly owed to Alice, daughter of the testator, *"cuius gubernacionem habet uxor partis actricis."* The 16th century royal court records also contain a case brought by a guardian called *tutor testamentarius et gubernator assignatus* for the son and heir of John Sysours of London. Public Record Office, London, K. B. 27/1086 m. 73 (1533). The same terminology is used in a 1424 will found in 2 Register of Henry Chichele 277 (E. Jacob and H. Johnson ed. 1938).

42.   Rochester Act book DRb Pa 12 s.d. 4 March 1578, f. 83v. This may be a reference to the *supervisores* who were often appointed in probate matters to supervise the execution of a will, and it is noteworthy that in some cases, executors or administrators were called upon to act as apparent guardians of the children without express designation as *tutores* in the Act books. *See, e.g.*, York Act book M 2(1)c, ff. 29v-30v (1375); London Act book MS. 9064/11, f. 126v (1513). Medieval wills also sometimes specifically designated executors as guardians. *See, e.g.*, 5 Lincoln Record Society Publications, Lincoln Wills I, 1271-1525, at 22, 126 (C. Foster ed. 1914) [hereinafter cited as Lincoln].

43.   *See, e.g.*, Canterbury Act book Y.1.3, f. 67v (1418), in which John Frawnceys claimed to have been *"deputatus custos dictarum pecuniarum quousque idem Johannes pervenerit ad legitimam etatem"* ("deputed custodian of the said moneys until the same John shall reach legitimate age"). Other cases in which no formal designation was given in the record include Canterbury Act books X.1.1., f. 9v (1449); Chartae Antiquae A 36 I, f. 11r (1326); Chichester Act book Ep I/10/3, f. 35v (1524); Durham Act book III/1, f. 25v (1532); York CP.F. 259 (1479); and St. Albans Act book ASA 7/1, f. 46v (1527).

guardian as *custos*,[44] and in a 1512 London case, a child was described as being *in warda et tutela* of the guardian.[45] Occasionally the records produce an example of usage in direct conflict with the civil law rule, as in one York case from 1513 in which a boy of sixteen asked for both *tutor* and *curator*.[46] Theoretically, only a *curator* could be appointed because the boy had passed puberty.[47] Perhaps the combination of the two offices for children below puberty was so prevalent at York that it was carried over for one who had gone beyond the age of fourteen. It is difficult to be sure. In any case it is evident that, although the Roman law distinction between *cura* and *tutela* was known in England and sometimes invoked, more often than not the English Church courts used the terms without scrupulous concern for technical correctness.

B. Tutores

Roman law recognized three separate kinds of *tutela: Testamentaria, legitima,* and *dativa.*[48] The first term designated the guardian named in the parent's will; the second, the next of kin; and the third, the guardian appointed by the magistrate. Medi-

---

44. Cause Papers Ep I/15/1/118 s.d. 1564.

45. London Deposition book DL/C/207, ff. 98v-99r (1512). *See also* York CP.F.87 (1490): *"habentis tutelam et custodiam supradicti Alexandri"* ("having wardship and custody of the aforesaid Alexander"). In both of these cases, secular wardship seems to have been involved. In the first, in fact, the right had been purchased from the king. In a case recorded in Rochester Act book DRb Pa 2, f. 29v (1445), there is a reference to a five-year-old child being simply *"in potestate"* of the adult who received a legacy for the child. In Rochester Act book DRb Pa 3, f. 498r (1465), there is a reference to *"quatuor orphanis sub tutela et in custodia dicti Willelmi Bedill"* ("four orphans under the guardianship and in custody of the said William Bedell").

46. York Act book Cons. A B 7, f. 23r: *"Ricardus Seriantson filius Henrici Seriantson de Cawod defuncti xvi annorum etatis ut asseruit coram domino commissario personaliter comparuit et peciit Willelmum Johnson de civitate Ebor' sibi assignari in tutorem et curatorem persone sue et rerum ac bonorum suorum. Et dominus commissarius ad pecticionem dicti Ricardi decrevit ut peciit."* ("Richard Seriantson, son of Henry Seriantson of Cawood deceased, sixteen years of age as he asserts, appeared personally before the lord commissary and asked that William Johnson of the city of York be assigned to him as *tutor* and *curator* of his person and of his goods and possessions.") An apparently similar instance from the Southern province is Lichfield Act book B/C/2/10 s.d. 29 January 1572.

47. Azo, Summa Codicis V, tit. *qui dare tut. vel cur.* § *potest autem* (n.d.): *"Sed si detur tutor pueri ipso iure datio non tenet."* ("But if a *tutor* should be given to one past puberty, the appointment is invalid legally.")

48. *Id.*, tit. *de tutela test.*: *"et quia tutella alia testamentaria, alia legitima, alia dativa"* ("and because *tutela* is either testamentary, legitimate, or appointive"). *But cf.* G. Durantis, Speculum Judiciale I, tit. *de tutore,* § 4 (1574 repr. 1975) (adding fourth category, *tutela anomala,* to account for guardians that could not be fitted into other three categories).

eval jurists discussed all three as living institutions.[49] The law decreed that each was entitled to appointment in descending order of preference. The *tutor testamentarius,* if suitable, excluded all other claimants.[50] If he were disqualified or if no *tutor testamentarius* had been named, the *tutor legitimus* or next of kin served.[51] Although classical Roman law limited this class of tutors to agnates (relations on the father's side), the Emperor Justinian extended the law to include cognates. It was in this form that the institution was inherited by the Middle Ages.[52] Only in the absence of any suitable *tutor legitimus* would the magistrate appoint a *tutor dativus.*

Collections of medieval wills show that testamentary guardians were known in England. Parents sometimes named specific persons to care for their minor children and to take custody of the children's personal property.[53] The wills do not always use the Roman law term *tutor testamentarius* in making this appointment. But the law required no special form to create such a *tutor.*[54] And the functions normally mentioned in the wills were

---

49. The texts and commentators commonly mention a fourth type, *tutela fiduciaria.* *See* Institutes 1.19; Buckland, *supra* note 22, at 146-47. Medieval civilians debated the origins of the word *fiduciaria* and the possibility that *tutela dativa* had assimilated *tutela fiduciaria.* Cynus of Pistoia noted: *"Solet tamen quaeri, utrum ille titulus de fiduciaria tutela sit hodie correctus per 1. 12 tab. val per constitutionem novam . . . . De hoc est controversia: sed haec prolixae disputationis causa evitandae omitto."* ("It is usually asked whether this title of *tutela fiduciaria* is today corrected by the law of the Twelve Tables or new constitution . . . . There is controversy about this: but I omit it to avoid prolix disputation.") Commentaria in Codicem V., tit. *de legitima tut.,* 1. *frater,* no. 7 (1578) (repr. 1964). *See generally* Villata di Renzo, La Tutela 44-46 (n.d.) (noting common opinion that the institution continued to exist). English records, however, have produced no mention of *tutela fiduciaria.*

50. Baldus, Commentaria ad Digest 26.2rubr (n.d.); Cynus of Pistoia, Commentaria in Codicem V, tit. *de test. tut.,* no. 2 (n.d.).

51. Institutes 1.20.pr.; Cynus of Pistoia, Commentaria in Codicem V, tit. *de test. tut.,* no. 2 (n.d.).

52. Nov. 118.5; Azo, Summa Codicis V, tit. *di leg. tut.* § *itaque* (n.d.).

53. *See* Lincoln, *supra* note 42, at 22; 16 Somerset Record Society, Somerset Medieval Wills (1383-1500) 13 (F. Weaver ed. 1901); note 41, *supra,* at 109, 277. *See also* 10 Selden Society, Select Cases in Chancery, A.D. 1364 to 1471, at 100 (W. Baildon ed. 1896); 64 Surtees Society, Acts of Chapter of the Collegiate Church of St. Peter and Wilfrid, Ripon 85 (1875). In at least one case at York, the testament of the decedent was included in the file for the cause, doubtless for reference. CP.G.844 (1570).

54. Code 5.28.8; Swinburne on Wills, *supra* note 5, pt. 3, § 12, at 290: "It is not material by what words the tutor is appointed, so that the testator's meaning do appear; for they are nevertheless to be confirmed tutors." The rule in classical Roman law may have required formal words. Buckland, *supra* note 22, at 143-53. However, Gaius, upon whom Buckland appears to rely, seems to qualify this statement of formal requirement by the word *rectissime. See* 1 The Institutes of Gaius Bk. 1, § 149 (F. de Zulueta ed. 1946).

those of a *tutor*. It seems likely, therefore, that the testators had the civilian institution in mind.

The ecclesiastical court records confirm English familiarity with *tutela testamentaria* because the term *tutor testamentarius* was sometimes explicitly used.[55] In addition, it appears substantively in cases where the judge enforced the wishes of the testator in appointing guardians for a testator's children. In a case heard at Canterbury in 1452, for example, the judge put the specific question to witnesses: "Did the said Moses [the testator] order and specify in his last will that his children should be governed and supported by the feoffees of the said Moses?"[56] In a case three years earlier, the executors of William Colyn were cited *ex officio* by the diocesan court. The charge stated that they had "refused to permit John the son of William to be in the custody of John Trisham," who allegedly had been appointed in the father's testament to take charge of the child.[57] The result of an affirmative finding in both cases would be to uphold the appointment of a *tutor* appointed by testament.

Different in substance, but also indicative of a readiness to follow the directions of the testator, is a case heard at York in 1372. The widow of Nicholas Strensale had been named *tutrix testamentaria* in her husband's will on condition that she not remarry. She did remarry and consequently was removed from her office by the York court in favor of the man specified in the will as *tutor* in case of the widow's disqualification.[58] A more

---

55. *See, e.g.*, York Cons. A B 6, f. 49v, where a reference is made to Agnes While, *"tutrix testamentaria Roberti While filii naturalis et legitimi dicti Willelmi [While]"* ("testamentary tutrix of Robert While, the natural and legitimate son of the said William [While]"). She was also serving as executrix.

56. Act book X.1.1, f. 63r: *"Interrogatus an dictus Moises ordinavit et fecit in sua ultima voluntate quod filii eius essent gubernati et exhibiti per feoffatos dicti Moisi, dicit quod sic."* ("Asked whether the said Moses in his last will ordained and directed that his sons should be governed and cared for by the feoffees of the said Moses, he says that he did.")

57. Act book X.1.1, f. 9v. The entry did not specifically call John Trisham a *tutor testamentarius*, but the Act book recorded that the allegedly offending executors were initially assigned a term *"ad exhibendum testamentum et ultimam voluntatem dicti defuncti"* ("to show the testament and last will of the said deceased"). This suggests that the will would determine the outcome of the dispute over custody. Other custody cases include Rochester DRb Pa 1, f. 105v. (1439), and Canterbury Chartae Antiquae A 36 I, f. 11r (1326), where, however, it was the widow of the father who asserted the right as *curator* *"recipere dictum puerum et alere eundem pro lucro de dicti pecunia proveniente usque ad legitimam etatem eiusdem"* ("to receive the said child and to nourish him through the profit of the said money until his legitimate age").

58. Act book M 2(1)c, f. 8v. The disqualification was specified in the will, but it was

difficult case arose fifty years later at York. The question raised in litigation was whether a *tutor testamentarius* named in a father's will for the elder child had, by virtue of the appointment, the right to act as *tutor* for the child's younger brother if the elder child died. No result survives, however,[59] and the Roman law on the question is open to argument.[60] Both of these York cases do indicate, however, that the courts looked to the will of the parent in determining guardianship questions, as Roman law specified.

Second in the line of preference of appointment under Roman law was the *tutor legitimus,* the next of kin. The English court records do not provide conclusive evidence of compliance with this civilian rule. Only one possible reference to a *tutor legitimus* specifically so called has been found. In a case from 1509 at York, Roger Busshol was approved as *tutor et curator legitimus* to the children of William Godehap after he had proved that he was their uncle.[61] It appears that in practice, the *tutor dativus,* the guardian appointed by the magistrate, was normally used in default of a testamentary guardian. Judges appointed a guardian themselves if no *tutor testamentarius* had been named, despite the Roman law rule that a *tutor dativus* was to be appointed only if there were no qualified *tutor legitimus.*[62] Indicative of this approach are cases in which the ecclesiastical courts appointed someone to enforce a child's rights to a legacy.[63]

---

also in accord with the formal Roman law, which disqualified the widowed *tutrix* if she remarried. Code 5.35.2.

59. *See* Act book Cons. A B 6, ff. 49v, 50r, 58r, in which the judge *"decrevit fore deliberandum super ista peticione"* ("decreed that there should be deliberation on this petition").

60. The medieval commentators discussed only the question of how large an interpretation can be put on designations by class. *See, e.g.,* Bartolus, Commentaria ad Digest 26.2.6 [*Si quis filiabus*] (n.d.).

61. Act book Cons. A B 6, f.14v: *"[F]acta fide quod dictus Rogerus Busshol est avunculus eorundem liberorum, . . ., dictus vicarius generalis assignavit prefatum Rogerum in tutorem et curatorem legitimum dictorum liberorum Willelmi Godeknap."* ("[F]aith having been pledged that the said Roger Busshol was the uncle of the same children, . . . , the said vicar general assigned the aforesaid Roger as *tutor* and *curator legitimus* of the said children of William Godeknap.") In an earlier York cause, the representative of the children apparently claimed his office *"ut proximus agnatus liberorum"* ("as the nearest agnate of the children"), so that although no specific use of the term *tutor legitimus* was found in the record, the substance of the civil law seems to have been respected. York CP.F.128 (1420-1421).

62. There is a suggestion of this by at least one 13th century author. *See* Martinus de Fano, Formularium, c. 179, in 1:7 Quellen zur Geschichte des Romisch-Kanonischen Processes im Mittelalter 77 (L. Wahrmund ed. 1917)[hereinafter cited as Wahrmund]. For a later example, see 1 H. Grotius, The Jurisprudence of Holland 35 (R. Lee trans. 1926)[hereinafter cited as Grotius].

63. *See, e.g.,* Canterbury Ecclesiastical Suit, no. 315 (1291-1293), wherein a witness

Equally so are cases in which one of the lawyers attached to the court acted for the child.[64] In none of these cases does the record state that no *tutor legitimus* was available. The courts appointed *tutores dativi* instead of automatically allowing the next of kin to serve.

On the other hand, the English courts often considered the wishes of the family in appointing a *tutor dativus*. For example, at York in 1371 when naming a guardian of the children of Roger Honyingham, the judge first ordered the relatives of the children to be summoned in case they wished to participate in the appointment.[65] When several appeared, the judge chose two of them to serve as guardians. In a second case the appointment was made "by the common and express consent of all and singular cognates and agnates of the children,"[66] and in a third, the judge revoked his appointment of a guardian earlier thought to be related to the child after discovering that no kinship existed.[67]

Investigation of contemporary French court records has disclosed that some courts in France also convoked the kin of the child to participate in the designation of a *tutor*. Indeed, the practice was so prevalent that commentators have been able to speak of it as a *conseil de famille*.[68] They have cited it as evidence

was asked *"si dictus Rogerus sit tutor vel curator et si testamentarius vel dativus?"* ("if the said Roger is a *tutor* or *curator* and whether testamentary or appointive?"). He replied, *"quod curator est et dativus et per eundem magistrum Osbertum ut dicit"* ("that he is a *curator* and appointed by the same Master Osbert as he says"). In a case recorded in York Act book M 2(1)c, f. 26v (1375), there is citation of William Grynder, *tutor et curator* of the daughter of Philip Gourdemaker, *"auctoritate curie predicte legitime deputatus"* ("legitimately deputed by the authority of the aforesaid court").

64. St. Albans Act book ASA 7/2, f. 80r (1533); York CP.E241r (1358).

65. Act book M 2(1)c, f. 7r: *"citare et premunire omnes et singulos cognatos et amicos liberorum quondam Rogeri de Honyingham"* ("to cite and warn all and singular relations and friends and the children of the late Roger of Honyingham"). Cases in which the Act book records that the guardian chosen was related to the child are found in Chichester Act book Ep I/10/19, f. 91v (1593); Ely Act book EDR D/2/12, f. 70v (1580); Lichfield Act book B/C/2/26 s.d. 16 June 1590; Rochester Act book DRb Pa 1, f. 31v (1437); York Cons. AB 6, f. 14v (1509); Act book M 2(1)c, f. 19v (1374), CP.F.128 (1420-21), Exch. AB 5, f. 33r (1591); and St. Albans Act book ASA 7/2, f. 80r (1533).

66. York Act book M 2(1)b, f. 1v (1371): *"de communi consensu et expresso omnium et singulorum cognatorum et agnatorum liberorum."*

67. York Act book M 2(1)c, f. 14v (1374): *"Ac propter noviter comperta in iudicio quod non fuit eius consanguinea, dominus commissarius potestatem et curam ac literam curacie sibi factam verbotenus revocavit."* ("And because of matter newly discovered in court, to the effect that she was not his relation, the lord commissary orally revoked the right, power, and letter of *cura* issued to him.") There was, however, an appeal.

68. *See* P. Timbal, Droit romain et ancien droit français: regimes matrimoniaux, successions liberalités 110 (2d ed. 1975); M. Villey, Le droit romain 69 (1946); Levy, *L'Officialité de Paris et les questions familiales à la fin du XIVe siècle*, in 2 Etudes

of the way in which customary law influenced and changed the received Roman law in court practice. English evidence on the subject is less complete than the French, and it is impossible to speak about the practice as a fixed institution. But the similarity to French practice, even extending to the language used by the records,[69] may well be an indication of the same sort of adaptation of Roman law in light of customary usage. In any event, it seems certain that the courts did not observe strictly the Roman law preference for the *tutor legitimus*.

It does seem fair to point out, however, as the French commentators have not always done, that the use of a council of the family was not contrary to the underlying civilian principle, *i.e.*, representation and protection from the kinship group. Roman law preferred the family member, the *tutor legitimus*, to the *tutor dativus* for that reason. If English and French practice used the *tutor dativus* where the formal law would have used the *tutor legitimus*, that practice at least respected the principle of kinship selection behind the civil law preference.

In all, the evidence of the manner in which the ecclesiastical courts chose the *tutor* is insufficient to conclude certainly how far practice diverged from civilian rules. What evidence there is suggests an observance of the Roman law preference for the testamentary guardian, as well as a consolidation in practice of the *tutor legitimus* and the *tutor dativus*. The courts made the appointment themselves where no guardian was appointed by will. But the evidence, incomplete as it is, suggests that they did so with an eye to the wishes of the family.

C. Curatores

The second kind of guardian in Roman law was the *curator*, normally appointed for minors between puberty and the age of twenty-five. As a distinct office, *cura* played a smaller role in English practice than it had in Roman usage. As previously

---

d'histoire du droit canonique 1265, 1288 (1965); Richardot, *Tutelle, curatelle et émancipation des enfants légitimes en Forez au XIIIe siècle*, Revue historique de droit français et étranger, ser. 4, at 29, 39-40 (1945) [hereinafter cited as Richardot]. An apparently similar practice in Italy is noted in Viora, *Tutela e Curatela (Diritto intermedio)*, 19 Novissimo digesto italiano 919, 922 (1973).

69. Richardot, *supra* note 68, at 40: *"de communi consensu parentum impuberis et eciam amicorum"* ("by the common consent of the kin of the child and also of the friends"). *See* note 67 *supra*. A similar example is contained in the formulary of an Italian notary, Ars Notariae des Rainerius, c. 34, in 3:2 Wahrmund, *supra* note 62, at 42-43. *See also* 1 Grotius, *supra* note 62, at 37.

noted, the English courts frequently consolidated the office of
curator with that of the *tutor*.[70] Medieval canon law further diminished the role of the *curator* by allowing minors past puberty
to represent themselves in litigation involving "spiritual" causes
such as marriage, tithes, and Church office.[71] In some matters,
appointment of a *curator* was an option, not a necessity.

On the other hand, canon law and English practice did find
a place for the *curator*. Occasionally, they even consciously distinguished between *curatores ad litem* (or *ad lites*, as the records
more commonly state) and *curatores* with a continuing responsibility for administration of a minor's property.[72] This is clearest
in litigation in which the judge appointed one of the lawyers
attached to the court as *curator ad lites*.[73] It is difficult to believe
that continuing administration was envisioned for the lawyer,
who surely must have been meant to act only for purposes of
litigation. On the other hand, when the qualification *ad lites* was
not added, when the *curator* was related by blood to the minor,
and when he expressly swore to keep and preserve the child's
property, a *curator* with the full duties of his civilian counterpart
must have been meant.[74] The judge must have appointed a real
guardian to protect the minor's property during the period of
need.

Roman law had fewer formal rules about appointment of
curatores than it did for *tutores*. No *curator* at all had to be
appointed to protect the child's property rights unless the minor
requested one or a person entering into a contract with him demanded that one be appointed as protection against a later claim

---

70.   *See* notes 32-40 *supra* and accompanying text.

71.   Sext. 2.1.3; Metz, *supra* note 16, at 81.

72.   The origins of the distinction seem to rest in the rule that a particular *curator*
could not be assigned to an unwilling minor, except *ad litem*. Also, a *curator*, unlike a
tutor, could be assigned for a limited purpose. *See, e.g.*, Institutes 1.23.2; Digest 26.1.4
(both recognizing distinction).

73.   *E.g.*, Canterbury Act book Y.2.29 October 1572; Chichester Act book Ep 1/10/19,
f. 81r (1593); Durham Act book III/4 s.d. 9 June 1581; Lichfield Act book B/C/2/26 s.d. 12
May 1590; York CP.E.241r (1358), Act book M 2(1)c, f. 23v (1374).

74.   *See, e.g.*, Canterbury Act book Chartae Antiquae A 36 I, f. 11r (1326); York Act
book Cons. A B, f. 14v (1509). Even in this area, the courts did not maintain the separation
in every instance. In a Chichester case recorded in Act book Ep I/10/19 s.d. 22 December
1593, a *curator ad lites* was appointed to preserve property of two minor children until
they reached their majority: *"[A]ctui subsignavit necnon dimisit et scriptum suum obligatorium penes registrar' de resolvendo et satisfaciendo dicte Avitie predictam summam
xxx s. cum eadem Avitia ad suam legitimam etatem pervenerit."* ("The *curator* sub-
scribed to the record and left his written bond with the registrar to repay and to satisfy
with the said sum of thirty shillings the said Avitia when she shall reach legitimate age.")

that the transaction was invalid because the minor was not of age.[75] All *curatores* were *dativi, i.e.*, formally appointed by the magistrate. Where a *curator* had been named in a parent's will, however, the magistrate routinely approved the nomination.[76] Roman law also envisioned that the minor himself would suggest the *curator* to be appointed,[77] and this is the method usually specified in the Act books.

It is, in fact, impossible to read the records of appointment of *curatores* without seeing a real informality in the court proceedings. In a typical case, a child appeared in court to demand a legacy he believed was due him. Since he could not act in court without a guardian, he brought along someone willing to act for him. Seeing nothing wrong with the suggested appointment, the judge decreed as the minor requested. The suit then went forward. It was a simple, practical procedure. The ecclesiastical courts of Canterbury,[78] York,[79] Durham,[80] Ely,[81] and Lichfield[82] all contain records that suggest such informality. As with the consent of the family in cases of *tutores dativi*, social reality breaks through the formal record. The desires of the parties determined usage in the courts. Again the practice was in line with Roman law principles. And where the child was old enough to make a reasonable choice, as are most children between fourteen and twenty-five, no other practice made more sense. Only when the minor had no nominee of his own did the court itself find and appoint a *curator*.

In sum, English practice relating to the appointment of guardians followed a limited version of the Roman law categories. The consistency with which the courts of the northern province of York used civilian terminology was slightly greater than that of the courts of the sourthern province of Canterbury. Henry Swinburne, the York canon lawyer who wrote *circa* 1600, may

---

75.   The minor could not be forced to accept any particular *curator*, but could be compelled to name someone of his own choice. Digest 26.1.3.2; Azo, Summa Codicis V, tit. *de tut. test.* (n.d.).

76.   Institutes 1.23.1; Hostiensis, Lectura ad X 2.28.67 [*Ex parte* M.], no.8; Bartolus, Commentaria ad Digest 26.5. rubr.

77.   Code 5.31.6. *See generally* F. Schulz, Classical Roman Law 193 (1951) [hereinafter cited as Schulz].

78.   Act book Y.3.1, f. 68v (1575) (children aged 17, 15, and 11). This case, like the others following, was brought to recover a legacy.

79.   Act book Cons. A B 6, f. 15v (1509) (no age given).

80.   Act book III/4 s.d. 3 June 1581 (child aged 15).

81.   Act book EDR D/2/12, f. 70v (1580) (child described simply as *pubes*).

82.   Act book B/C/2/26 s.d. 12 May 1590 (no age given).

have meant to suggest this difference by purposely refraining from discussing more than guardianship in the courts at York.[83] But the evidence of differences between the north and the south is not absolutely conclusive, and even among individual jurists and commentators on Roman law there was uncertainty about which kind of *tutela* to use in describing a particular guardian.[84] If substance is taken as the test, it is clear that guardians were appointed in the south as well as in the north of England, and that they were sometimes more than guardians *ad litem*. Still, the English courts did not observe every distinction in terminology of the civil law; they did not follow every Roman law rule about the appointment of either *curatores* or *tutores*. But they did not ignore the law's substance.

III. DUTIES OF GUARDIANS

The classification and appointment of guardians show clearly the extent of English compliance with civilian categories. The question of how rigorously the Church courts enforced the duties of the Roman law *tutor* and *curator*, though a more complex subject legally, yields a conclusion roughly analogous to that relating to appointment, *i.e.*, use of Roman law without observance of all its features.

A. Preliminary Steps

The requirement of *satisdatio* provides a good example of this conclusion. Roman law required that the guardian produce surety of his faithful performance (*satisdatio* or *cautio*) in the form of a deposit of money or the production of personal guarantors before exercising his office.[85] The purpose of this requirement was protection against loss of the infant's property. English court records contain instances in which the courts adhered to this rule.

---

83. "But further, the customs of this realm are so divers and contrary one to another, which do concern this matter, that I might easily fall into divers errors." Swinburne on Wills, *supra* note 5, pt. 3, § 7, at 270-71. *See also* F. Clerke, Praxis in Foro Ecclesiastico, c. 214 (1666); 1 T. Oughton, Ordo Judiciorum, tit. 240-46 (1738). For other illustrations of variation in practice among the English dioceses, see Cheney, *Some Aspects of Diocesan Legislation in England During the Thirteenth Century*, in Medieval Texts and Studies 185 (1973).

84. One question frequently debated by commentators, for example, was whether a guardian invalidly appointed by will, but nevertheless confirmed by the court, should be called *tutor testamentarius* or *tutor dativus*. *See, e.g.*, Azo, Summa Codicis V, tit. *de confirm. tut. vel cur* (n.d.).

85. Institutes 1.24; Digest 46.6.4; Code 5.42.3. For a comprehensive discussion of the institution, see A. Guzman, Caucion tutelar en Derecho romano (1974).

In a testamentary cause heard in 1418 at Canterbury, for instance, the guardian suing to recover a legacy allegedly due to the child was first obliged "to produce sureties to safeguard the goods of the infant."[86] The terminology follows that of the civil law exactly. In numerous other cases the Act book specifically records a *cautio*'s or *satisdatio*'s being given.[87]

On the other hand, there are also cases in which no *satisdatio* was mentioned.[88] The formal law itself can explain some of these. It excused *tutores testamentarii* from this requirement on the ground that the testator's trust in their integrity provided a sufficient safeguard.[89] Although this sometimes may have accounted for omission of the *satisdatio*, neither this exemption nor that available where a *tutor legitimus* was found to be "an honest person, particularly if the child's fortune [was] of moderate size,"[90] will explain all the English cases in which no *satisdatio* was noted. Too many of them involved *tutores dativi*, for whom

---

86. Act book Y.1.3, f. 65v: *"In cause legati pupilli, . . . datur actrici ad producendum fideiussores res pupilli salvas fore in proximo."* ("In the cause relating to a minor's legacy, . . . the plaintiff is assigned the next session to produce sureties to guarantee the safety of the minor's goods.") *Compare* Digest 46.6.1.

87. Act book Cons. A B 6, f. 21v (1509): *"Et [dominus officialis] assignavit eidem ad ponendum securitatem et fideiussores sufficientes in scaccario domini archiepiscopi pro rebus huiusmodi pupillarum salvandis diem citra festum nativitatis sancti Johannis Baptiste."* ("And [the lord official] assigned them a day before the feast of the Nativity of St. John the Baptist to place security and sufficient sureties in the Exchequer of the Lord Archbishop in order to safeguard these goods of the children.") In a testamentary cause recorded in Canterbury Act book Chartae Antiquae A 36 1, f. 11r (1326), one party specifically alleged her willingness *"de cautione in hac parte prestanda"* ("to give surety in this matter"). This may have been an attempt to secure her right to guardianship by bringing herself under the rule that preferred a guardian willing to give security over one who was not. *See* Code 5.42.4. In St. Albans Act book ASA 7/1, f.45v (1526-1527), the court ordered the executors to return the decedent's property *"quousque providetur de securitate bonorum pupilli legatorum"* ("until security for the goods of the child left by legacy was provided"). Here, without formal designation, the executors were required to take the action of *tutores*.

88. Canterbury Act book Y.1.2, f. 97v (1398); Ely Act book EDR D/2/1, f. 67r (1377); Rochester Act book DRb Pa 1, f. 31v (1437); York Act book M 2(1)c, f. 7r (1372).

89. Code 5.42.4; Azo, Summa Codicis V, tit. *de tut. vel cur. qui satis.* (n.d.); Hostiensis, Lectura ad X 2.28.67 *[Ex parte* M.], no. 9.

90. Azo, Summa Codicis V, tit. *de leg. tut.* § *fi.* (n.d.): *"[S]i honesta sit persona remittatur eis* [sic] *satisdatio et maxime si substantia pupilli sit modica."* ("If they are honest of person, surety may be omitted, especially if the child's wealth is modest.") A similar example, in which Bartolus took the position that *satisdatio* might be omitted where the guardian was chosen *"electa industria personae,"* may be found in his Commentaria ad Digest 26.2.19.1 *[Hoc edictum]* (n.d.). In Ely Act book EDR D/2/1, f. 67r (1377), the guardian selected was described as *"virum providum et discretum."* This may indicate application of the exception.

no exemption was available.[91] The preliminary provision of sureties was therefore used, but was not required in every instance.[92]

One possible explanation for omission of the *satisdatio* may be the use in court practice of a formal oath taken by guardians to carry out their duties in the interests of the infant.[93] Apparently added to the classical law by the Emperor Justinian, this requirement no doubt reflects the great importance to the oath in the centuries after the establishment of Christianity. It is the best documented of the preliminary steps in the surviving English court records, which give more detail about its content than they do about the *satisdatio*. In one appointment at York, for example, the new guardians swore "corporally touching the Holy Gospels that they would in good faith keep and preserve the goods and persons of the said children during the time of their administration to the use and profit of the children and [that they] would do whatever was beneficial for the said children and would avoid what was harmful."[94] The "use" mentioned here was normal. The guardian typically swore to hold and administer the goods *ad usum filiorum* [95] or *ad usum orphanorum*,[96] one of the several

---

91. That a demand by the opposing party may have played a part in the decision is suggested by one case, in which the record mentions production of the *cautio* only after a demand. Canterbury Act book Y.3.1, f. 77r (1575): *"Tunc Patricius Smyth unus executorum predictorum peciit quatenus dictus Smyth* [the *curator*] . . . *ad prestandam sufficientem caucionem tam pro solucione dicte summe quibusdam Johanni Smyth, Agneti Smyth, et Agneti Smyth* . . . ." ("Then Patrick Smyth, one of the aforesaid executors, asked that the said Smyth provide sufficient surety for the payment of the said sum to John Smyth, Agnes Smyth, and Agnes Smyth . . . .")

92. Much the same can be said of the requirement that the guardian make an inventory of the infant's property. Code 5.37.24; Cynus of Pistoia, Commentaria ad Code 5.37.28.4, no. 1 (n.d.); Lyndwood, Provinciale 176 s.v. *prius* (1679). Sometimes the Church court records mention it; sometimes they do not. A later parallel from court practice in Holland can be found in Grotius, *supra* note 62, at 43.

93. Nov. 72.8; Cynus of Pistoia, Commentaria ad Code 5.37.28.4 (n.d.): *"Quarto debet iurare utilia facere et inutilia praetermittere."* ("Fourth, he must swear to do what is beneficial and avoid what is harmful.") Cynus cited only the Novels as authority, and no reference to the oath has been found in the Codex or Digest. Nor do most modern writers on Roman law mention it. A fuller form of the oath, similar to the one found in the English records may be found in gl. ord. ad Clem. 3.11.2 s.v. *tutorum et curatorum*.

94. Act book M 2(1)c, f. 7r (1372): *"iuramentis ad sancta dei evangelia corporaliter prestitis quod personas et res dictorum impuberum bona fide custodient et salvabunt durante tempore administrationis sue ad utilitatem et comodum impuberum eorundem, quecumque dictis impuberibus utilia facient et inutilia praetermittent."*

95. Chichester Act book Ep 1/10/3, f. 35v (1524). The Church court records consistently use the term *ad usum* rather than *ad opus*. They fully support Maitland's findings of the interchangeability of the two terms and of the dominance of the former in the ecclesiastical setting. See J. Bean, The Decline of English Feudalism, 1215-1540, at 105-19 (1968); 2 Pollock & Maitland, *supra* note 6, at 233-39.

96. London Act book MS. 9064/11, f. 126v. (1513). *See also* Chichester Act book Ep I/10/19, f. 123r (1593); Durham Act book III/4 s.d. 3 June 1581; Canterbury, Act books Y.1.2, f. 97v (1398); Y.2.10, f. 145r (1523); Lichfield Act book B/C/2/26 s.d. 22 September

ways in which the ecclesiastical courts employed the "use" normally associated with English land law.

One should not quickly discount the importance of this oath. It had both a moral and a legal force. The former was intangible, but not unreal. Medieval men accorded the oath a high place; witness the fact that it was the only preliminary step expanded beyond the Roman law texts. Its strictly legal force found expression in a legal remedy available for breach of the oath to protect the child's property. The guardian's oath was, therefore, in no sense an empty gesture. It occasionally may have satisfied judges that no *satisdatio* had to be produced.

B. Care of the Child's Person

Once formally qualified, the Roman law guardian had three principal duties: To provide for maintenance of the child,[97] to represent the child in litigation,[98] and to administer the child's property.[99] The English records contain examples of *tutores* and *curatores* carrying out all three of these functions. The duty of maintenance was normally inapplicable to the *curator,* who represented children old enough to shift for themselves.[100] It was, however, one of the primary duties of the *tutor.* And although of the three requirements, it has left the least evidence in the remaining Act books, clearly some medieval guardians undertook to care for the physical and educational needs of the infants committed to their charge. In a 1371 case from York, for example, the guardians chosen promised specifically "to provide for and educate [the children] until they reached puberty."[101] Fifty years earlier at Canterbury, the court had conditioned transfer of a child's legacy to his guardian on the latter's promise "to maintain [the child] from the profit stemming from the said money until

---

1590; York Act books M 2(1)b, f. 2r (1371); M 2(1)c, f. 28v (1375); Cons. A B 6, f. 79v (1510).

    97.   Digest 26.10.3.14, 27.2.3; Villata de Renzo, La Tutela 26 (n.d.).

    98.   Digest 26.7.1.2, 26.7.30.

    99.   Digest 26.7. *See also* Buckland, *supra* note 22, at 152-59. It is, of course, possible to divide the duties further. Azo separated them into eight categories, dividing the duty to care for the child's personal well-being, for example, into three distinct parts. *See* Azo, Summa Codicis V, tit. de *admin. tut. vel cur.* § *debet gerere tutor* (n.d.).

    100.   *See* notes 22 & 23 *supra. See also* Digest 17.2.3; Baldus, Commentaria ad *id.,* no. 1 (n.d.).

    101.   York Act book M 2(1)b, f. 1v (1371): *"[D]ecretum fuit per dictum dominum officialem quod predicte due libere sint in custodia prefati Thome qui, sumptibus ipsius Thome propriis, promisit dictas liberas durante earundem impubertate quousque puberes facte fuerint alimentare et educare."*

[he reached] legitimate age."[102] At Lichfield in 1590, one Act book entry records that the judge committed to the guardian "the protection and education [of the child]."[103] Not every entry of appointment of a *tutor* is so specific. Most reveal nothing at all about provision for care and maintenance. It is unclear whether the duty resting in the *tutor* was understood, or whether the care of the child's physical needs was left to informal resolution.

A second area of uncertainty, both under the formal Roman law and in medieval practice, concerns the right to custody of the infant. Roman law scholars do not agree on whether the *tutor* had control of the child's person in classical law. The answer apparently depends on whether the *vis et potestas* held by the Roman law *tutor* should be construed in a technical sense to include actual control.[104] It also depends on whether the texts assigning the *tutor* "to the person" of the child also imply control.[105] Professor Watson, for example, argues that the texts designating a *tutor* "to the person" of the child did not mean the *tutor* had any actual control over the child's person, but rather were intended simply to differentiate *tutores* from *curatores*. The *curator* could be assigned for one duty or for one item of property, whereas the *tutor* had authority over all the child's property. Therefore, a *tutor* was assigned generally "to the person," but did not have custody. Other scholars have interpreted the evidence literally, concluding that the *tutor* did have a right to custody.[106]

The English evidence on this point is conflicting. The disagreement apparently open under the civil law texts seems mirrored in English practice. There are cases in which, as part of his

---

102. Act book Chartae Antiquae A 36 I, f. 11r (1326), in which the guardian swore *"quod paratus fuit recipere dictum puerum et alere eundem pro lucro de dicta pecunia proveniente usque ad legitimam etatem eiusdem."* In a case recorded in Chichester Act book Ep I/10/2, f. 35v (1524), William Sanford received goods and 50s. owed to a child named Joan. At the same time, he *"accepit onus alendi filian ipsius Johanne predictan"* ("accepted the burden of supporting the aforesaid daughter of the same Joan"). William, however, was given no official designation as *tutor* for the child in the record.

103. Act book B/C/2/26 s.d. 6 June 1590: the diocesan official *"commisit educationem et tuitionem cuiusdam Henrici Bradshawe filii naturalis Johannis Bradshawe."* In an earlier Durham case, brought by a child who had reached majority, to recover an intestate share of his father's estate allegedly wasted by his guardian, the defendant guardian pleaded that whatever he had spent of the child's property had been "for sustaining the plaintiff during his minority." Act book III/1, f. 25v (1532). Unfortunately, no outcome of the case has been found.

104. *See* Digest 26.1.1; Institutes 1.13.2.

105. *See* Digest 26.2.14; Institutes 1.14.4.

106. A. Watson, The Law of Persons in the Later Roman Republic 108 (1967). *See* Schultz, *supra* note 77, at 173 (tutor's limited right over ward's person includes power to determine residence, education, and maintenance, but not power to give ward in adoption).

appointment, the guardian swore an oath to take custody of the child,[107] and there are other cases in which he did not.[108] Similarly, some cases indicate that the child's person was subject to control by the *tutor*,[109] while others show that the child was in the custody of someone else.[110] No sure explanation for this seemingly contradictory evidence can be given. Perhaps we can logically assume from the nature of the underlying disputes that most questions about custody were settled by private agreement among the families involved, which in turn would have led to diversity in the way children were provided for.

Even when actually brought before a court, custody cases are among the most difficult to decide by fixed rule. No judge who values the well-being of a child will grant custody to someone who does not care for the child. The preference of the child, the character of the candidates, and the wishes of the family all dictate variety in the results.[111] Perhaps this is why the Church court records do not furnish greater and clearer evidence about child custody. The judges normally did not give reasons for their decisions, and the Act books seldom hint at the human reality behind the procedure recorded. All one can say with assurance is that the records show the duty specified in Roman law to provide for the child being undertaken by some guardians. Occasionally, they also indicate that the child was in the guardian's custody.

C.   *Representation in Litigation*

The evidence relating to the guardian's second duty, vindication of the child's legal rights, is less ambiguous. Guardians clearly undertook this obligation. Appointments of *curatores ad litem*, whose function was to participate in a law suit on behalf of a minor, furnish one certain example.[112] Litigated cases in

---

107.   *See* note 94 *supra* and accompanying text.

108.   York Act book M 2(1)c, ff. 14r-14v: *"prestitoque iuramento per dictum dominum Johannem consueto de conservando res et bona, bona fide quousque dicta Johanna ad plenam pervenerit etatem"* ("and the accustomed oath of preserving the goods and effects until the said Joan shall reach full age having been taken in good faith").

109.   *See* Rochester Act book DRb Pa 1, ff. 105v, 108v, where a suit was brought to recover the person of the child and was styled a *causa subtactionis et alienationis dicti pupilli. See also* York Act book M 2(1)b, f. 1v (1371).

110.   St. Albans Act book ASA 7/2, ff. 79v. 80r (1533); Canterbury Act book Y.2.13, f. 221r (1536).

111.   *See, e.g.,* Note, *The Expanding Role of the Juvenile Court in Child Custody Disputes,* 63 Calif. L. Rev. 236 (1975). For later instructive examples from Chancery practice, see W. Forsyth, A Treatise on the Law Relating to the Custody of Infants in Cases of Difference Between Parents or Guardians 19-53 (London 1850).

112.   *See, e.g.,* Canterbury Act book Y.2.29, s.d. 29 October 1562: *"Quo die comparuit Bendicta Browne et spontanea voluntate elegit magistrum Ricardum Wallis et Willel-*

which the record specified that a *tutor* was acting for a child furnish another.[113] Instances of both occur in sufficient number to raise an inference that this part of the Roman law was applied throughout England. However, the evidence also suggests that the only regular court appearances by guardians occurred in probate matters, since all but two of the instances found come from testamentary causes. Typically, a *tutor* or *curator* sued to enforce the child's right to a legacy, an intestate share, or the portion of his parent's estate that fell to him under English inheritance custom. Most of these suits were brought against executors or administrators who had been unwilling to acknowledge, or at least to satisfy, the rights of the child.[114] The role undertaken by guardians in litigation was to secure and preserve the minor's testamentary rights to personal property.

Even in this testamentary litigation, however, the English courts did not invariably appoint a guardian to protect the infant's interests. Sometimes the executor or administrator performed informally whatever protective functions were in fact undertaken. The judge named no special guardian, and he fastened no extra designation of *tutor* or *curator* on one of the executors.[115] The executor, of course, always had a general responsibility to supervise distribution of legacies, which may have included a responsibility for making sure that the child's rights were fully protected.[116] However, the Act books do not specify this, and the

---

mum *Faryle in curatores ad lites etc.*" ("On which day Benedicta Browne appeared and of her free will chose Master Richard Wallis and William Farlye as *curators ad litem*.") In York Act book M 2(1)c, f. 23v (1374), John de Stanton was deputed *curator ad litem* to Thomas, son of William Wyte, at the same time that two other men were assigned as *tutores et curatores* for the child. Stanton was one of the regular staff of court proctors, doubtless the reason for the appointment.

113.   *See, e.g.,* Rochester Act book DRb Pa 1, f. 31v (1437): "*Johannes Novyn citatus est super eo quod detinet bona legata Thome Chownyng filio defuncti dicti sub tutela Willilmi Gode cognati eiusdem existenti ad promocionem eiusdem Willelmi Gode responsurus.*" ("John Novyn is cited at the promotion of William Gode to answer for detaining the goods left to Thomas Chownyng, the son of the said decedent, who is under the guardianship of William Gode.")

114.   Ely Act book EDR D/2/1, f. 67r (1377); Canterbury Act books Chartae Antiquae A 36 I, f. 11r (1326); *id.* Y.1.3, f. 65v (1418); *id.* Y.2.29 s.d. 26 March 1527. Such a suit probably lay behind Tooker v. Loane, 80 Eng. Rep. 338 (K.B. 1617). Dr. Charles Gray was kind enough to call my attention to this case.

115.   *See, e.g.,* London Act book MS. 9064/11, f. 123v (1513); St. Albans Act book ASA 7/1, f. 45v (1526-1527). The designation of executors and administrators as guardians was sometimes also mentioned in medieval wills. *See* note 42 *supra.*

116.   Thomas Ridley, the 16th century defender of the ecclesiastical courts against the Common Lawyers, noted that "Executors and Administrators do supply [the role of *tutores*] so far forth as they have the tuition and governance of minors during their underage." T. Ridley, A View of the Civile and Ecclesiastical Law 219 (London 1607).

interests of an executor and administrator were at times potentially antagonistic to those of the infant. Perhaps the English
judges made ad hoc judgments to appoint *tutores* whenever conflicts of interest occurred. Certainly the records contain cases in
which the Church court judges, acting on their own initiative,
ordered someone to hold a legacy for the benefit of a child.[117] Even
assuming, however, that this may have been a source of protection, these instances only emphasize the lack of a guardian with
full civil law powers and responsibilities. Moreover, not every
child had a guardian: *tutores* and *curatores* appeared in many,
but not all, testamentary causes involving children.

The absence of guardians from other litigation in the Church
courts contrasts markedly with their more frequent presence in
testamentary matters. Only two clear instances of representation
in other areas have been found, one in a matrimonial[118] and the
other in a contract case.[119] The English Church courts exercised
significant jurisdiction in both areas. And especially as to a
minor's contracts, Roman law assigned a significant place to the
tutor or *curator*.[120] Why do almost no *tutores* and *curatores* appear
in these areas? It is hard to be sure. The surviving records produce
no definitive answer, although their incompleteness may explain
much. But academic law does suggest a possible explanation for
both these omissions. Under the canon law of marriage, a child
had the right to renounce any marriage when he or she reached
the age of puberty. A child below puberty, therefore, would rarely
become involved in litigation. Little could be decided definitely
before then.[121] Nor did a child over the age of puberty need a
guardian in marriage cases, since his *curator* had authority only
over his property, and the child could therefore participate personally in marriage litigation. Significantly, the one marriage
case in which the court appointed a guardian involved a dispute

---

117. The judges in the following cases, apparently acting *sua sponte*, ordered money
to be held for the benefit of a child, no *tutor* or *curator* being named: Canterbury Deposition book X.10.1, ff. 106r-106v (1416); Act books Y.1.2, f. 97v (1398); *id.* Y.2.10, f. 145r
(1523); *id.* Y.3.1, f. 12v (1574); Rochester Act book DRb Pa 3, f. 345v (1458); London Act
book MS. 9064/2, f. 73v (1484); St. Albans Act book ASA 7/1, f. 19r (1518).
118. York CP.E.89 (1365). I am indebted to Professor Donahue for calling my attention to this case.
119. York Act book M 2(1)a, f. 5r (1315). With this absence of evidence, compare
the situation in the *Parlement* of Paris noted in Martin, *supra* note 13, at 314.
120. *See generally* Buckland, *supra* note 22, at 157-59, 170-73. The Church courts
in France appointed guardians for this purpose. Fournier, *supra* note 13, at 80-81.
121. *See* R. Helmholz, Marriage Litigation in Medieval England 98-99 (1974).

238 Canon Law and the Law of England

over the age of one litigant.[122] Where there was no dispute, guardians had no place.

As to contracts, litigation in the English Church courts involved obligations undertaken by means of an oath. "Breach of faith" was the rubric under which such cases were heard.[123] Medieval civil law treated sworn contracts differently from unsworn contracts; it regarded the former as inviolate. Therefore, if the minor had made the agreement with an oath, the law deprived him of the special protections extended under Roman law.[124] One of those protections was the need for a *curator* to allow him to contract more freely than he could without one. Since very small children would rarely make contracts, and since other children below age twenty-five could contract as adults by using an oath, there was no need for guardians in the sort of contract litigation heard by the English Church courts.[125] Thus, in the two areas of Church court jurisdiction where guardians might have served useful purposes, medieval law rendered their presence unnecessary.[126] Their role in litigation was therefore normally limited to participation in testamentary causes.

---

122. York CP.E.89. Perhaps significantly, the definitive sentence in the opinion includes reference to a *curator*, but the words have been crossed out. This may reflect the final decision of the court that the litigant was of age and needed no guardian *ad litem*. That a minor could act without a guardian in a marriage case was specifically recognized in X2.13.14. In Canterbury Act book Y.1.4, f. 125v (1423), there is a clear statement showing that no *curator* was present: *"Alicia Phillipp' de Herne etatis, ut dicit in ea parte interrogata, xvi annorum constituit M. Adam Body procuratorem suum in quadam causa matrimoniali."* ("Alice Phillipp of Herne, sixteen years of age as she says, being interrogated in this matter, constituted Master Adam Body her proctor in a certain matrimonial cause.")

123. *See* Helmholz, *Assumpsit and* Fidei Laesio, 91 Law Q. Rev. 406 : infra 263-89.

124. The Constitution *Sacramenta puberum* of Frederick I, laying down this rule for minors past puberty, was included in medieval copies of the *Codex Justiniani*. Code 2.28.1. For representative comments by civilians and canonists approving the rule, see Cynus of Pistoia, Commentaria ad Code 2.28.2, nos. 5, 10 (n.d.); Hostiensis, Lectura ad X 2.24.28, nos. 4-5; T. Sanchez, De Sancto Matrimonii Sacramento, lib. 6, disp. 38, no. 13 (1737) (n.p.) [hereinafter cited as Sanchez].

125. The rule of *Sacramenta puberum* was also extended to include children who were "nearly at the age of puberty." Sanchez defined this age as ten and one-half for boys and nine and one-half for girls; this would have covered almost all children likely to make agreements. *See* Sanchez, *supra* note 124, at lib. 6, disp. 38, no. 2; *id.* lib. 1, disp. 51, no. 24.

126. Sir Thomas Smith may have suggested as much, writing that as soon as children reach puberty, they are of age, and "[t]hat which is theirs they may give or sell, and purchase to themselves either lands and other moveables." T. Smith, De Republica Anglorum, lib. 3, c. 7 (London 1583).

D. Administration and Accounting

Under Roman law, administration of the child's property was the most important and extensive function of the *tutor*. He was required to administer the assets for the exclusive benefit of the infant. Unlike the common law of feudal guardianship, Roman law made him a trustee. Civilians fashioned complicated rules regulating what acts the *tutor* or *curator* could perform in the interests of the child. They fastened liability for violation of these rules squarely on the guardian.[127]

English Church court records contain clear references to *administratio* being undertaken by the guardians of infants.[128] The office carried with it the duties of a trustee (in theory at least), for the guardians assigned by the courts were always ordered to hold the property for the use of the child,[129] not for their own enrichment. In English practice, however, *administratio* must have been a much simpler task than that undertaken by the Roman law *tutor*. The medieval guardian had only a limited form of property to administer. The duties of the *tutor* were normally exercised in this area, as in litigation, only within the Church's probate jurisdiction. They were restricted, therefore, to chattel interests. More specifically, the court decrees transferring property to the *tutor* mention only simple pecuniary legacies. There may have been exceptions, such as cases involving leases, but the records examined produced no cases of assets requiring continued management, such as a business or even a herd of animals, falling into the hands of the *tutor*. In the one case where stock animals were part of a minor's intestate share, the animals were sold immediately to an agent of a neighboring abbey.[130] The guardian then held the money for the child. Bequests to children occasionally included valuable personal items, such as a silver bowl.[131] But preservation of a bowl requires little management. In the normal situation the restricted nature of the property assigned to the care of the *tutor* simplified his task. He had only money to preserve.

---

127. *See* Buckland, *supra* note 22, at 154-59.

128. *See, e.g.,* Chichester Act book Ep I/10/3, f. 35v (1524), where a reference is made to a sum of money that *"dominus assignavit inter filios ut patet ex dorso inventarii, deinde commisiit administracionem Thome Myles . . ."* ("the lord [official] assigned among the sons as appears on the back of the inventory, of which he committed the administration to Thomas Myles . . .").

129. *See* text accompanying notes 95 and 96 *supra*.

130. York CP.F. 259 (1479).

131. Chichester Act book Ep I/10/3, f. 35v (1524); York Act book M 2(1)c, f. 17r (1374).

Administratio in England was further simplified because the medieval guardian was not required, like his Roman predecessor, to lend an infant's money at interest.[132] No doubt he had to stand accountable for whatever profits were actually made, after deducting a legitimate amount expended for the child. But this was a different matter from requiring him to make usurious use of the fund.[133] Although there were means of avoiding the Church's prohibitions against usury, the *tutor* was not obliged to embrace them. The English records use words like *conservare*,[134] *custodire*,[135] and *redeliberare*[136] when defining the task of administration of the fund. If these words were used precisely, the guardian must have had to keep custody of the money and hand it over to the child when he came of age. More than that he need not have accomplished. As a result, English *administratio* was a much less involved task than that detailed in the civil law texts. Compared to the *administratio* undertaken by the Roman *tutor*, or by the guardian at common law, administration by the canonically appointed *tutor* was a slight burden.

The last act required of the *tutor* was to make an accounting of his administration.[137] This ended the formal relationship. There are clear indications in the English records of observance of this final step, both in the initial oath taken by guardians to account and in actual court terms scheduled for the accounting.[138] Thus, at Chichester in 1565, Roger Cutsolde was assigned a day in court "for rendering an account of the portion of the boy" whose property he had held.[139] After the hearing, the guardians apparently turned the property over to the former ward and obtained a formal acquittance from the court.

Classical Roman law contained a number of remedies available where guardians had not carried out their duties properly.

---

132. *See generally* Villata di Renzo, La Tutela 259-70 (n.d.).
133. For a discussion of this point, see Cynus of Pistoia, Commentaria ad Code 5.37, c. *novissime* (n.d.).
134. York Act book M 2(1)c, f. 14r (1374).
135. Canterbury Act book Y.1.3, f. 67v (1418).
136. Rochester Act book DRb Pa 2, f. 286r (1456). The French evidence from the *pays du droit écrit* indicates a much fuller kind of management responsibility. *See* Richardot, *supra* note 68, at 55-59.
137. Digest 27.3.1.3; Baldus, Commentaria ad *id.* (n.d.).
138. *See, e.g.,* York Act book M 2(1)c., f. 7r (1372), in which the *tutores*, as the final part of the oath, swore that "*administracionis sue tempore finito ordinarion qui protempore fuerit racionem de eis reddent plenarie et fidelem*" ("at the end of the period of their adininistration, they [would] render a full and faithful account to the ordinary of the place at that time").
139. Act book Ep. I/10/12, f. 37v: "*ad reddendum compotum de porcione pueri.*"

Removal of a suspect *tutor* was the primary remedy during the period of guardianship.[140] Liability in favor of the child could later be asserted under three or four different forms, depending on the nature of the offending act.[141] English practice clearly knew the remedy of removal. Instances of it have survived.[142] Cases were also brought against guardians for violation of their oath to administer faithfully.[143] Presumably, restitution to the child followed successful prosecution of such a suit. But there is no surviving evidence to suggest any sophistication or differentiation in remedy against defaulting *tutores*. The English records show no sign of any of the four distinct ways in which a former ward could theoretically seek redress under the civil law. Of the *actio rationibus distrahendis* or the *actio tutelae utilis*, the English courts knew, or at least enforced, nothing.

IV. CONCLUSION

The examination of Church court records accomplishes basically three things. It demonstrates how Roman law principles were used in English practice. It shows something about the extent to which the Church courts supplied the need for guardians not met by secular courts. And it suggests a possible significance of ecclesiastical practice in tracing the development of the common law.

First, guardianship jurisdiction enforced by the English ecclesiastical courts was a limited form of that found in the *Corpus Juris Civilis* and expounded by medieval civilians. The consolidation of the offices of *tutor* and *curator,* the preference for the *tutor dativus* chosen with the advice of the family, the relatively simple

---

140. Institutes 1.26; Digest 26.10. The reasons for removal were broad. *See, e.g.,* Azo, Summa Codicis V, tit. *de suspectis tutoribus* no. 1 (n.d.).

141. Baldus, Commentaria ad Digest 27.3.1.21 [*in tutela*]: *"Et nota hic quod si tutor furatur pecuniam pupilli ex hoc facto resultant quatuor agendi formae."* ("And note here that if the *tutor* steals the child's fund, from this deed four forms of action can result.") *See generally* Schulz, *supra* note 77, at 178; H. Weymuller, Contribution a l'histoire de l'actio tutelae (1901).

142. *E.g.,* York CP.E.32 (1337). *See also* note 58 *supra.*

143. *E.g.,* London Act book MS 9064/11, f. 114r (1513): an action brought against Elizabeth, widow of Thomas Kymberell *"alias iurata de conficiendo et exhibendo verum inventarium . . . quod quidem inventarium alias per ipsam exhibitum est falsum . . . cuius pretextu reatum periurii se incurrere recognovit"* ("sworn at another time to make and exhibit a true inventory . . . which inventory exhibited by her is false . . . by reason of which she makes recognizance that she had incurred the fault of perjury"). And in York CP.E 32 (1337), the court specified that removal was warranted because of violation of the guardian's oath.

nature of *administratio* undertaken by English *tutores*, and the disregard of the four separate remedies against defaulting guardians all lead to the conclusion that there was selective enforcement of the Roman law categories, even in ways one would not expect from reading contemporary jurists. Practice moved further towards simplicity than Roman law and its medieval commentators provided.

Modern French writers, noting a similar phenomenon in the courts of their country, have suggested that this pervasive simplification represents a compromise with, or perhaps an enrichment by, customary practice.[144] This is a plausible suggestion for England as well. There are cases, for example, in which the Church courts followed the secular law in setting the majority of a minor at the age of twenty-one rather than at twenty-five, as specified by Roman law.[145] There is equivalent evidence of their use of a "family council" not found in Roman law.[146] These examples suggest, and indeed compel, a conclusion that the canon law was not a closed system; it was open to outside influence.

The difficulty with this conclusion is that it is not possible to find a customary source for every ecclesiastical variation from the Roman law.[147] A slightly different explanation may better fit the evidence. It is that the Church courts discarded those parts of Roman law that no longer made practical sense in light of the conditions of medieval and early modern society. Consolidation of the offices of *tutor* and *curator* is a good example of this process. Originally, *tutela* had been a right granted for the benefit of the *tutor*; *cura* had always been meant for the minor's protection. But by the time of Justinian, the powers and duties of the two offices had become virtually indistinguishable.[148] Imperial

---

144. *See* notes 68-69 *supra* and accompanying text.

145. *E.g.*, Canterbury Act book Y.3.21, f. 134r (1585), in which the intestate shares were ordered distributed *"filiis dicti defuncti cum venerint ad seperales etates xxi annorum et filiabus dicti defuncti cum venerint ad suas etates xvii annorum vel in dies maritagii"* ("to the sons of the said decedent when they come severally to the age of twenty-one and to the daughters of the said decedent when they come severally to the age of seventeen or on the day of their marriage"). *See also* Canterbury Act books Y.3.1, ff. 132r-132v (1575); Y.2.29 s.d. 26 March 1572; York CP.G. 844 (1570).

146. *See* notes 65 & 67 *supra*.

147. Variation and simplification in the guarantees of faithful performance by the *tutor* actually required in court practice furnish a good example of this point. *See* text accompanying notes 85-92 and notes 140-43 *supra*.

148. There is a full discussion of the development of the powers and duties of the two offices in 2 B. Biondi, Il Diritto Romano Cristiano 229-40 (1952). *See also* 1 Bonfante, *supra* note 22, at 552-55; Buckland, *supra* note 22, at 172; Levy, *Vulgarization of Roman Law in the Early Middle Ages*, 1 Medievalia et Humanistica 14, 31-32 (1943).

legislation had fastened the same protective function on each. The one major difference lay in the age of the child protected, but that is a formal difference only. In practical terms, the distinction made no sense. Medieval commentators, who were tied to the texts, maintained it. But in contemporary legal practice it had long since ceased to have real significance.[149] All guardianship was one. This fact may explain why the English Church courts so frequently disregarded the distinction between *cura* and *tutela*. More generally, it may also explain the other areas of selective enforcement of the civil law categories. The Act books make clear that the canon law courts used the Roman law of guardianship. They did so, however, with an eye to the habits and the needs of contemporary practice. They discarded purely formal, archaic elements of the Roman law of guardianship.

Second, the Church courts regularly provided guardians only for minors with rights, or at least potential rights, to part of a decedent's estate. A legacy, a filial portion, or an intestate share was a prerequisite for the appointment of a *tutor* or *curator*. The evidence supporting this conclusion largely depends on an argument from silence: the Act books contain so many instances of guardians acting in testamentary causes that their virtual absence from other areas makes this conclusion probable. But if true, the conclusion means that in England guardianship was normally exercised as part of the Church's probate jurisdiction, rather than as part of the canon law's wider responsibility for *miserabiles personae*. The Church courts, in other words, did not provide a guardian for all orphans. They filled some gaps in the English common law of guardianship, but not all. The Church, therefore, made no systematic effort to remedy the defects in the secular law.[150]

This conclusion should come as no surprise. Social historians have taught us that the Middle Ages paid little heed to the special needs and status of children.[151] It may even be true that in

---

149. The distinction was apparently dropped in other parts of Europe and abandoned by the commentators in the 16th and 17th centuries. *See* H. Jolowicz, Roman Foundations of Modern Law 119-20 (1957).

150. This conclusion does not necessarily show that the Church did not provide some support for children in other ways, as, for example, poor relief. See the document recorded in J. Pound, Poverty and Vagrancy in Tudor England 110 (1971).

151. P. Ariés, Centuries of Childhood (1962); F. Du Boulay, An Age of Ambition: English Society in the Late Middle Ages 116-20 (1970); I. Pinchbeck & M. Hewitt, Children in English Society (1969) (2 vols.). Recent work on the subject is reviewed in Berkner, *Recent Research on the History of the Family in Western Europe,* 35 J. Marr. & Fam. 395 (1973).

any age most orphans do not need guardians, except in special circumstances. Our own society, despite its greater solicitude for children, has not taken the step of requiring the appointment of a guardian in all cases.[152] Medieval society left less place than does our own for intrusion into family affairs by public courts. More was left to private resolution. That the Church courts did not provide every orphan with a *tutor* or *curator* is therefore no cause for wonder.

Finally, the enforcement of Roman law principles of guardianship in the English Church courts raises the possibility of influence on the development of the common law. Three changes in the common law illustrate this point. First, whereas the early law allowed the guardian in socage to profit from his office at the expense of the ward, two thirteenth century statutes changed this policy by requiring an accounting at the end of the guardianship. What had been a profitable right to exploit became a trust.[153] Second, during the fifteenth and sixteenth centuries, the Court of Chancery began to appoint guardians in order to protect the property of infants. The Chancellor's jurisdiction, according to most commentators, was "very similar to that exercised over guardians by the Roman *Praetor*."[154] Third, a post-Restoration statute made it possible for a father to dispose of the custody and tuition of his children by will.[155] Guardianship of heirs in socage previously had passed automatically to the nearest relative who could not inherit from the child. After 1660, to the extent that informal practice had not anticipated statutory change, the father could exclude this relative by appointing a testamentary guardian.

---

152. The matter is not free of controversy. *See, e.g.,* Bersoff, *Representation for Children in Custody Decisions: All That Glitters Is Not* Gault, 15 J. Fam. L. 27 (1976); Fratcher, *Toward Uniform Guardianship Legislation,* 64 Mich. L. Rev. 983 (1966); Hansen, *Guardians ad Litem in Divorce and Custody Cases: Protection of the Child's Interests,* 4 J. Fam. L. 181 (1964). For English law, see the instructive opinion of Mr. Justice Bennett in *In re* D. (An Infant), [1943] 1 Ch. 305. He was puzzled by the "well-established practice of making a nominal settlement on an infant when it is desired to make that infant a ward of court." *Id.* at 306. The practice may be a purely formal continuation of the medieval practice. *See also* James, *The Legal Guardianship of Infants,* 82 Law Q. Rev. 323 (1966).

153. *See* note 10 *supra.*

154. Scrutton, *Roman Law Influence in Chancery, Church Courts, Admiralty, and Law Merchant,* in 1 Select Essays in Anglo-American Legal History 208, 220 (1907). *See also* 1 G. Spence, The Equitable Jurisdiction of the Court of Chancery 608-14 (London 1846); Cogan, *Juvenile Law, Before and After the Entrance of "Parens Patriae,"* 22 S.C.L. Rev. 147 (1970); Kuttner, *supra* note 20, at 352.

155. 12 Car. II, c. 24, § 8 (n.d.).

That these three instances of change all approximated the Roman law rules of guardianship requires no demonstration. That these rules were applied in the ecclesiastical courts is equally sure. Can we make a connection between the two? Can we speak of a "legal transplant"?[156] It is hard to be sure. There were differences between the Roman law and the practices adopted by English law. Also, Professor Plucknett was certainly correct to point out that any suggestion of influence must "rest on inference rather than strict proof."[157] But the similarities are very striking. And not every inference is wrong. To exclude the possibility that the influence of Roman law principles came through the courts of the Church seems as incautious as to adopt the idea automatically once the similarities are noted.[158]

This article began by asking how large a role Roman law has played in the history of English law. It has answered that question only in a limited area, but within that compass the place of Roman law has been substantial. Enforced in simplified form within the courts of the Church, civil law principles and practices not only supplied some of the deficiencies in the English common law of guardianship, they may also have shaped the course of development of the common law itself. Not least among the contributions of the Church courts to English legal development has been the introduction of Roman law principles. The Church's jurisdiction over guardianship illustrates this point with particular clarity.

---

156. *See generally* A. Watson, Legal Transplants (1974).

157. Plucknett, *supra* note 2, at 48.

158. For a recent review of the literature and perceptive comments on the question of Roman law influence on English law, see Donahue, *supra* note 2, at 174.

13

LEGITIM IN ENGLISH LEGAL HISTORY

I. INTRODUCTION

The history of a child's right to a share of his or her parent's estate and (its opposite) the parent's right to dispose of the estate free from any filial claim except a moral one, occupies a place in almost every account of English legal history.[1] The importance of the child's right, known from Roman law terminology as the *legitim*, has required some notice by conscientious historians. But they have taken it up gingerly. The English evidence shows that the *legitim* probably was enforced at an early date in medieval history, and that it had largely disappeared by the seventeenth century. In the interval, however, the evidence is slight. The common law courts dealt with the right in a fashion which can only be called confused, contradictory, and half-hearted.

More importantly, historians have had to leave blank half of the story of the *legitim*. That is the ecclesiastical half. Because primary probate jurisdiction rested with the courts of the church from the Middle Ages until the nineteenth century, and because the same tribunals largely controlled the devolution of moveable property at death, it follows that much of what we can know about the subject of the *legitim* must come from ecclesiastical sources. The great legal historian F.W. Maitland, writing almost ninety years ago, and after laying out the admittedly unsatisfactory secular evidence, concluded that the full story could not be told without investigation of "whatever records there may be of the ecclesiastical courts . . . ."[2] There the study has remained since. Later writers have added little.

This article seeks to fill this gap in our knowledge.[3] Considerable

---

1. *See* J. BAKER, AN INTRODUCTION TO ENGLISH LEGAL HISTORY 321-22 (2d ed. 1979); 3 W. HOLDSWORTH, A HISTORY OF ENGLISH LAW 550-56 (3d ed. 1923); T. PLUCKNETT, A CONCISE HISTORY OF THE COMMON LAW 743-46 (5th ed. 1956); 2 F. POLLOCK & F. MAITLAND, THE HISTORY OF ENGLISH LAW 348-56 (2d ed. 1905); Cooper, *Patterns of Inheritance and Settlement by Great Landowners from the Fifteenth to the Eighteenth Centuries*, in FAMILY AND INHERITANCE 192, 225-26 (1976); Keeton & Gower, *Freedom of Testation in English Law*, 20 IOWA L. REV. 326, 337-40 (1935).

2. *See* 2 F. POLLOCK & F. MAITLAND, *supra* note 1, at 352.

3. This is the fourth of five articles by the author devoted to the history of rights of children

numbers of records of the ecclesiastical courts do in fact survive, although most of them have remained in manuscript repositories in England's local archives. The article surveys the evidence on the subject found in them, after outlining the formal law of the *legitim*. Regrettably, these records will not answer every question the legal historian would like to put to them, including the most important questions of exactly how and why the right disappeared. In some sense, the story they tell is as difficult of interpretation as the story the common law sources have produced. But the evidence is worth having, and it is also illuminating for what it reveals about the more general question of the role of the canon law in English legal history.

II. THE ROMAN-CANON LAW

To understand the role of the *legitim* in English law, the historian must begin with formal law, and the exact starting place must be Roman law. Despite a natural assumption that because the church courts enforced the law of the church, the canon law, rather than the civil law inherited from the Roman Empire and found in the *Corpus Iuris Civilis*, it is to the law of Rome that one must look. The medieval church borrowed both procedure and substance from Roman law where these were not contrary to principles of Christianity, and one good example of such borrowing is this rule of succession. The canon law had no separate law on this subject. The church in effect canonized the civilian principle that a child had a *de iure* share in the estate of his or her parent.[4]

The Roman law texts inherited by the Middle Ages explicitly stated the principle of entitlement, although they left some room for argument about details and allowed for some variation in actual application. The rule was, of course, only one of several restrictions on freedom of testation found in the civil law. Probably the most notable restriction was the *lex Falcidia*, under which the testator's designated heir had to be given at least a quarter of the estate.[5] The purposes of these two restrictions were quite different in origin,[6] but they often coincided in effect because the decedent's heir was normally also his

---

in the English Church courts. *See* Helmholz, *The Roman Law of Guardianship in England, 1300-1600,* 52 TULANE L. REV. 223 (1978); Helmholz, *Support Orders, Church Courts, and the Rule of Filius Nullius: A Reassessment of the Common Law,* 63 VA. L. REV. 431 (1977) [hereinafter cited as Helmholz, *Support Orders*]; Helmholz, *Infanticide in the Province of Canterbury During the Fifteenth Century,* 2 HIST. CHILDHOOD Q. 379 (1975). The last article will deal with relationships within the family. See above, chapters 9 (pp. 157-68), 10 (pp. 169-86), and 12 (pp. 211-45).

4. *See* DECRETALES GREGORII IX, GLOSSA ORDINARIA X 3.26.16 (book 3, title 26, chapter 16) (Venice 1572) (marginal gloss s.v. Trebellianum: "[E]t multae ipsius leges sunt canonizatae.").

5. *See* INST. JUST. 2.22; DIG. JUST. 35.2.3. *See also* 2 P. VOCI, DIRITTO EREDITARIO ROMANO 755-89 (2d ed. 1963).

6. In the civil law, the heir performed the functions of a modern executor, and in order for a testament to be fully valid the heir named in the testament had to be willing to serve. It naturally happened that heirs who received nothing from the testator refused to serve as executors; hence, the *lex Falcidia*. Its purpose was to avoid intestacies.

child. Thus, medieval jurists sometimes treated the two restrictions together; occasionally they even referred to the children's share as the *quarta Falcidia*.[7]

The classical rule held that the children were entitled to a fourth of the estate. If unjustly disinherited, a child could invalidate the will by means of an action called *querela inofficiosi testamenti*.[8] By virtue of a later imperial constitution, if the testator had left less than the fourth part to his children, they also had a separate action *ad supplendam legitimam* against the heir.[9] This action allowed them to recover their share without invalidating the testament, although they also retained the older *querela*. The Emperor Justinian made a number of changes in this regime, the most significant of which increased the children's portion to one-third of the estate if there were four children or fewer, and to one-half if there were five or more.[10] This more generous treatment was the rule taken over by the medieval canon law.

Two decretals, that is, papal decisions defining principles of canon law, explicitly recognizing and enforcing the *legitim*, were included in the official collection of Decretals issued in 1234 by Pope Gregory IX.[11] This collection, along with the earlier Decretum Gratiani (c. 1140) provided the bulk of the canon law applicable throughout Latin Christendom,[12] and the two decisions it contained involved the church in defining and upholding the child's right. The medieval canonists, the contemporary commentators whose discussion of the texts provides the best guide to understanding the law, also spoke emphatically on the point. For example, Antonius de Butrio (d. 1408), glossing one of the decretals in question, told his readers: "You should recognize that a child has the remedy of a *querela inofficiosi testamenti* against the will of his father when he is disinherited unjustly."[13] Or as Hostiensis (d. 1271) had earlier put it, much of testamentary law could be left to local custom or to individual choice, but "in the *legitim* [the child] could in no way be injured."[14]

The canonists advanced several justifications for canonical

---

7. *See, e.g.*, Antonius de Butrio, Commentaria in libros decretalium X 3.26.18, nos. 7-18 (Venice 1578) [hereinafter cited as de Butrio].

8. *See generally* W. Buckland, Text-book of Roman Law from Augustus to Justinian 327-33 (rev. 3d ed. 1963).

9. Code Just. 3.28.36.

10. Nov. 18.1.

11. *See* 2 Corpus Iuris Canonici, X 3.26.16, 18, cols. 544-45 (A. Friedberg ed. 1881).

12. Although the relevant literature on the subject of the medieval canon law is immense, there is no comprehensive work in English. For two brief introductions, with special reference to the canon law in England, see E. Kemp, An Introduction to Canon Law in the Church of England (1957); R. Mortimer, Western Canon Law (1953). For a more recent useful introduction see Bassett, *Canon Law and the Common Law*, 29 Hastings L.J. 1383 (1978).

13. de Butrio, *supra* note 7, at X 3.26.16, no. 20. His text reads: "Vos debetis scire quod filius habet contra testamentum patris quando est exheredatus iniuste remedium querelae inofficiosi testamenti." *Id.*

14. Lectura in libros decretalium X 3.26.16, no. 71 (Venice 1581). The text reads: "In legitima enim gravari non potuit ullo modo." *Id.*

enforcement of this rule. One was that the rule stemmed from the "office of piety."[15] Another held that it was required by principles of "canonical equity."[16] A third, the most substantial and frequently repeated, was that the *legitim* formed part of natural law. Fathers were bound *ex iure naturae* to provide for their children.[17] When they disregarded that duty, the law should step in to make good their omission or their wrong. Although the canonists did not claim exclusive jurisdiction for the courts of the church in enforcing the right, they nevertheless held that where the matter did come before a canonical tribunal, the tribunal ought to uphold the right of the children.

The principle behind the rule appears relatively straightforward. Its implementation, however, was not. The legal rules relating to the *legitim* that emerged from the commentators' treatment of the subject would eventually fill a treatise of 730 folio pages, divided into two hundred separate *quaestiones*.[18] Some of these *quaestiones* were the sort of academic exercises the Middle Ages prized, questions raised because of the demonstration of learning they facilitated rather than because they raised genuinely difficult, disputed, or important points of law. But most were not. A sixteenth century writer prefaced his discussion by terming the material "useful, extremely frequent in practice, and delightful."[19] He meant "delightful" in the sense of the pleasure one derives from solving difficult problems to which one needs to know the answer.

Some of those difficult problems with the rule that a parent must provide for his children arose out of exceptions to the rule's full enforcement. The share was computed after payment of the testator's legitimate debts, and the computation also required taking account of any advancements made to the children during the lifetime of the testator.[20] A child's renunciation of the right during the parent's lifetime could also eliminate the child's right, or at least complicate its subsequent enforcement.[21] Moreover, there could be valid reasons for the

15. *See, e.g.*, DECRETUM GRATIANI, GLOSSA ORDINARIA, Dist. 9 c. 7 (Distinctio 9, canon 7) (Venice 1572) (s.v. *officiosa*). The text reads: "sicut inofficiosum testamentum quod est contra officium pietatis."

16. *See, e.g.*, DECRETALES GREGORII IX, GLOSSA ORDINARIA, *supra* note 4, at X 3.26.16, s.v. *legitimam*. The text reads: "Et ita tenendum est secundum canonicam equitatem."

17. *Id.*, s.v. *Trebellianum* which stated: "Nota ergo quod quartarum alia est debita iure naturali." *See also* DE BUTRIO, *supra* note 7, at X 3.26.16, no. 23.

18. JOANNES ANTONIUS MANGILIUS, DE IMPUTATIONIBUS ET DETRACTIONIBUS IN LEGITIMA TREBELLIANICA . . . TRACTATUS (Venice 1618) [hereinafter cited as MANGILIUS]. *See also* CLAUDE DE BATTANDIER, TRACTATUS LIBERORUM PARENTUM AC FRATRUM . . . LEGITIMARUM MATERIAM CONTINENS (Lyons 1560).

19. M. CRASSUS, TRACTATUS DE SUCCESSIONE 415 (Venice 1584) in which the author said: "Haec materia legitimae iucunda, utilis, et in foro frequentissima est."

20. For discussion and medieval references, see *id.*, Quaesta 1, no. 3; MANGILIUS, *supra* note 18, Quaest. 49, no. 8.

21. The canon law required a sworn renunciation. *See* MANGILIUS, *supra* note 18, Quaest. 91, nos. 9-10. Mangilius said, "[R]enunciatio etiam generalis cum iuramento sufficit ad excludendum filium a legitima." *See also* Cooper, *supra* note 1, at 266.

parent's having disinherited the child; for instance, the "vice of ingratitude."[22] If a son physically attacked his father[23] or if a daughter married contrary to her father's expressed wishes,[24] these children not only incurred social stigma, they also forfeited, at least according to some views, their rights to the *legitim*. The canonists and civilians expected that hard questions of fact would arise in practice about whether or not the *legitim* would be due.

The commentators also discussed difficult and disputed legal questions that might arise in practice. For example, suppose a man had five sons, and one of them had been disinherited for good cause. Should the share due to the others be calculated on the basis of the man's having five or four children?[25] If the former, they were entitled to half the estate; if the latter, they were limited to a third. On the one hand, the one-third share seemed correct since the reason behind the distinction was that larger families required a larger overall share in order to provide more than a pittance for each child. On the other hand, the texts themselves were explicit that if a parent had more than four children, the *legitim* was one-half. However you looked at it, the man in question still had five children. This "plain meaning" approach was not without its adherents, and it was further buttressed by the argument that where a child predeceased the parent, the child's estate did not necessarily forfeit his right to *legitim*. This question was, in other words, one of the inevitable matters of detail that were the source of work for medieval lawyers, just as they are for lawyers today. The child's right to set aside the will of the parent raised many such questions.[26]

In all the discussion of detail, however, the canonists and civilians never lost sight of larger principles. The fundamental reasons behind the obligation recurred throughout their discussions. Nowhere is this more evident than in their treatment of the question of whether a statute or custom could abridge or abrogate the right. The question was much disputed. A sixteenth century commentator remarked: "It is the great question, and one of the more difficult that exists in the law, . . . on the truth of [which] *doctores* have contended for two hundred years

---

22. *See* DECRETALES GREGORII IX, GLOSSA ORDINARIA ad X 3.26.16, s.v. *legitimam*.

23. *See* G. DURANTIS, SPECULUM IUDICIALE (Basel 1574) IV:4 tit. *De natis ex libero ventre*, no. 13, containing a libel alleging that these acts gave rise to a cause of action against the son for ingratitude.

24. HOSTIENSIS, SUMMA AUREA (Venice 1574) IV, tit. *de matrimoniis*, no. 27. Hostiensis says: "[Q]uicquid leges dicant, incurrit tamen filia vitium ingratitudinis nisi voluntati patris consentiat, et propter hoc exhaeredari posset."

25. *See* BARTOLUS, COMMENTARIA (Venice 1570-71) at Authenicum, Collatio iii, tit. *de triente et semisse* (*Iam quidem*), no. 9.

26. An interesting example, on which canonists and civilians apparently disagreed, occurred where the father entered a monastery, the equivalent in some sense of "civil death." Canonists generally held that the children were entitled to the *legitima pars* at once, whereas civilians held that the children must wait until the natural death of the father. *See* M. CRASSUS, *supra* note 19, Quaest. 12, no. 6.

and more."[27] It could be said, for instance, that because a statute (the imperial constitutions) granted the right, a statute could equally revoke it.[28] To this, it could be objected that the statute was declaratory of natural law, and that since the obligation rested on natural law, neither custom nor statute could abrogate it.[29] This objection could, in turn, be met by the argument that texts declaring that the obligation arose from natural law meant only that it proceeded *ex instinctu naturae* or *ex cursu naturae*. In other words, the commentators could say that the *legitim* had simply grown up from men's natural inclinations to favor their children, and did not have its source in immutable right.[30]

A second approach looked to the basic reason for the right. This too led to subtlety and equivocation. Parents had an unquestioned duty to support their children in the basic necessities of life (*alimenta*), and in some sense the *legitim* resembled the right to *alimenta*.[31] However, what if the child were rich? Then he needed no support, and the canon law held he had no enforceable right to *alimenta* if this would merely require his parents to add to his riches. In some ways, the *legitim* seemed an easier case than *alimenta* for allowing the rich child to be deprived lawfully of part of his parent's assets, which might otherwise go to pious or at least more useful social purposes. The *legitim* partook of the characteristics of mere bounty, so that where no actual need existed, it might be said that the parent's obligation ceased. There was an answer to this analysis.[32] However, the analysis did demonstrate that the obligation was not always absolute. Hence, it could be used in argument to support the proposition that statute or custom that abridged the right was not necessarily invalid.

After all the argument, the medieval consensus reached something of a compromise. A statute or custom might validly diminish, but it could not entirely abrogate, the child's right. Certainly, no statute or custom could eliminate the *legitim* unless the child were rich. There was a fourteenth century decision of the Roman Rota, the regular papal court of appeal, approving this limited power of statute or custom. Antonius de Butrio, professor of the canon law successively at Florence and Bologna, noted the decision, and remarked with casual

27. *Id.*, Quaest. 42, pr. The original text read: "Maxima quaestio est, una de difficilioribus quae sit in iure . . . ita quod asserverat Socinus circa veritatem huius quaestionis Doctores pugnasse a ducentis annis citra."

28. *See, e.g.*, BARTOLUS, *supra* note 25, at no. 1. Bartolus says, "Nam legitima debetur filio iure civili . . . ergo potest tolli per aliud ius civile scilicet per statutum."

29. *See, e.g.*, PANORMITANUS, COMMENTARIA at X 3.26.16. Panormitanus says, "quod potest diminui non autem in totum tolli quia esset contra equitatem naturalem."

30. *See, e.g.*, BARTOLUS, *supra* note 25, tit. *de triente et semisse*, no. 1. Bartolus says, "ex quodam instinctu naturae."

31. *See* PANORMITANUS, *supra* note 29, at X 3.26.16; M. CRASSUS, *supra* note 19, Quaest. 42.

32. The answer was that for many purposes *legitim* and *alimenta* were not identical; for example *alimenta* required a "needs test," while *legitim* was figured by percentage of the estate. This difficult balance has to some extent been repeated by the provisions of the English Inheritance (Family Provision) Act of 1938. *See generally* P.M. BROMLEY, FAMILY LAW 622-36 (5th ed. 1976).

authority, "The opinion has always been to my liking."[33] This became the *communis opinio*.

III. THE ENGLISH EVIDENCE

Historians should certainly expect the *legitim* to have played a part in English history. Bede mentions the divisions of a man's estate into thirds as the customary rule,[34] and the treatises ascribed to Glanvill and to Bracton in the twelfth and thirteenth centuries, respectively, also speak of the third part reserved to the children.[35] Because the royal courts virtually withdrew from the field of succession to movables under Edward I (1272-1307), these early statements might count for little during the latter Middle Ages, but since the church courts occupied the area, one should expect continued enforcement of the substance of the right to *legitim* in those courts. The canonized Roman law outlined above should have come regularly into play in the testamentary causes heard in the church courts.

When one looks at the records for answers to questions about actual enforcement, it is immediately apparent that the records leave much to be desired. They are much more complete for the fifteenth and sixteenth centuries than for the thirteenth and fourteenth, so that conclusions are surer for the later period than for the earlier. They are also unlike modern case reports in that they almost never reveal any substantive reasons for the judge's decisions. The historian's conclusions must always remain tentative or rest on reasonable inferences drawn from the accumulation of evidence.

Nevertheless, even with these caveats, two conclusions about the *legitim* during the later Middle Ages emerge from an examination of the record evidence. First, there was a time when the right was known and enforced, probably throughout England. However, the right was principally thought of as a matter of custom, not a right guaranteed by the statute law of the church. Second, from at least the end of the fourteenth century, testators in most parts of England acted as if they had freedom of testation. With the possible exception of children with a real need for subsistence, few English children enjoyed a right to the *legitim* after 1400.

The first of these conclusions rests on slightly more satisfactory documentary evidence. Wherever records mention *legitim* or the *legi-*

---

33. DE BUTRIO, *supra* note 7, at X 3.26.17, no. 23. Antonius de Butrio said: "Et ita decidunt domini de Rota et semper mihi placuit haec opinio."
34. *See* BEDE'S ECCLESIASTICAL HISTORY OF THE ENGLISH PEOPLE 488-89 (B. Colgrave & R. Mynors eds. 1969). Professor Bruce Mann kindly provided me with this reference.
35. *See* 2 H. BRACTON, ON THE LAWS AND CUSTOMS OF ENGLAND 178-81 (fols. 60b-61) (G. Woodbine ed. & S. Thorne trans. 1968); TREATISE ON THE LAWS AND CUSTOMS OF THE REALM OF ENGLAND COMMONLY CALLED GLANVILL Book VII, ch. 5, 80 (G.D.G. Hall ed. 1965). *See generally* 2 F. POLLOCK & F. MAITLAND, *supra* note 1, at 353-55; M. SHEEHAN, THE WILL IN MEDIEVAL ENGLAND 292-95 (1963).

tima pars bonorum, they refer to the right as a customary one. A single possible exception is a reference to the *lex Falcidia*, found in a 1306 record from Canterbury. But this record may refer to the rights of the heir or the executor, not to those of the children. And in any case this particular ecclesiastical cause stopped short of actual enforcement. The *lex Falcidia* was noted only as a possible objection that someone might have raised against a testament.[36] It is a thin piece of evidence when contrasted with the many documents which treat the right as customary.

The records produce several cases from the fourteenth century specifically enforcing the right on the basis of long established custom. A clear statement from the same Canterbury act book of 1306 noted that the third part was due "according to the custom of England."[37] A 1365 reference from York described the portion as due "by the English custom."[38] Existing precedent books, drawn up for use in the ecclesiastical courts, also described the right as customary, although they occasionally added that the right was owed *de iure* as well. One from the diocese of Salisbury, for example, contains a form setting out the right as a custom "laudable and ancient, observed throughout the realm from 10, 20, 30, 40, 50 and 60 years and more, from time whereof the memory of man runneth not to the contrary."[39] That was the normal way of pleading a valid customary right in English canonical practice, and it suggests the contemporary understanding of the source of the *legitim* as one resting ultimately on custom.

The conclusion is enforced by examination of the *Provinciale* of William Lyndwood, the fifteenth century English canonist and judge of the Court of Arches. He clearly knew that such a thing as the child's portion existed in the law books. But he had little to say about its obligatory character in England. What he said instead is this: "For this *portio*, recourse should be had to the custom of the place."[40] He noted that there was no single custom throughout the realm, but rather various customs. "[T]here may be," he wrote, "a general custom of any province, and likewise of any city, territory, or place. The custom of

---

36. Waleys c. Waleys, Lambeth Palace (London) MS. 244, fol. 49r. The executors were ordered to pay to the plaintiffs the sum demanded, presumably a legacy, "nisi locus appareat legi falsidie (sic)."

37. Bonn c. Felingham, Lambeth Palace (London) MS. 244, fol. 17v. The manuscript says "terciam partem bonorum dicti defuncti ipsam dominam Johannam iuxta consuetudinem anglicanam existentibus liberis." For two similar references from 1313, see 1 REGISTRUM PALATINUM DUNELMENSE 369, 385 (Rolls Series 62:1, T. Hardy ed. 1873).

38. Borthwick Institute (York), D/C H 1/2, fol. 112/1 [The Institute is the record repository for the diocese of York.]. The manuscript says "de iure vel consuetudine anglicana." *See also* SELECT CASES FROM THE ECCLESIASTICAL COURTS OF THE PROVINCE OF CANTERBURY c. 1200-1301, at 138-39 (N. Adams & C. Donahue eds. 1981) [95 Selden Soc.].

39. *See* Wiltshire Record Office (Trowbridge) Salisbury Precedent Book 1, fols. 1655v-1656r; British Library (London), Harl. MS. 6718, fol. 35.

40. W. LYNDWOOD, PROVINCIALE (SEU CONSTITUTIONES ANGLIAE) 178, s.v. *defunctum* (1679).

the location or region is to be attended to diligently."[41]

A number of ecclesiastical court records do contain references to the *portio legitima* due to children, without stating explicitly the source of the obligation. However, some of these cases probably involved the intestacy of the parent,[42] and if we follow the understanding of Lyndwood and the sense of the entries more fully spelling out the source of the obligation, these cases probably also have depended on the existence of custom. Although the English ecclesiastical lawyers must have been familiar with the canonical texts enforcing the right, when that right was fully articulated in contemporary practice, it was treated as one dependent on customary observance.

The second conclusion suggested by the court records is that by the end of the fourteenth century, the *legitim* had been reduced to the level of a local rather than a national custom, and had largely ceased to be in force outside the Northern Province of York. The Canterbury cases cited above, which invoked the "custom of England," come from the first decade of the fourteenth century. The last surviving Canterbury case in which the right was clearly enforced in the case of testate succession comes from 1375. A fifteenth-century case from the City of London, where the *legitim* was long retained, attributed the right "to the custom of the City of London" rather than to any wider English custom.[43] It looks as though the right had fallen out of general observance by 1400.

Much of the other available evidence fits this picture of relegation to the status of a local custom, enforced only in the North and in a few places in the South of England. The fifteenth-century records of ecclesiastical courts are relatively abundant, but they contain a striking lack of litigation on the subject. The matter seemingly did not arise in practice. Although this is merely an argument from silence, it is enough to suggest that the custom had died out in most places. The law on the subject was complicated. It should have produced legal disputes. However, such disputes do not figure in the surviving records.[44]

In the Northern Province of York, where the custom remained in force until 1679, the situation is quite different. The right to *legitim* has left considerable evidence in the surviving court records. For example,

---

41. *Id.* at 172, s.v. *consuetudinem patriae.*

42. Wynstall c. Wynstall, Canterbury Cathedral Library, Diocesan Act book Y.1.1, fols. 102r, 104v, 107v (1375); Ex officio c. Jakys & Edwardes, Cambridge University Library, Ely Diocesan Records, Probate Liber B, fol. 33v (1468); Chaydok c. Tyldesley, Cheshire Record Office, Chester Archdeaconry Records, EDC 1/1, fol. 7b (1502); Shepard c. Mason & Gretton, Joint Record Office (Lichfield) Act book B/C/2/3, fol. 51r (1529); Aldred c. Aldred, Lichfield Act book B/C/2/3, fol. 68v (1529).

43. Hall c. Walpole, London Guildhall Library Act book MS. 9064/2, fol. 147v (1486). The manuscript says "terciam partem bonorum iuxta consuetudinem civitatis London."

44. This statement is based on the author's examination of most of the surviving fifteenth-century records of the Province of Canterbury. *See* R.H. HELMHOLZ, MARRIAGE LITIGATION IN MEDIEVAL ENGLAND 233-35 (1974).

the records contain references to the invalidation of testaments as *contra officium pietatis*,[45] or *inofficiosa*.[46] Both phrases were those used where it was necessary to set aside a will as inconsistent with the child's right to *legitim*. The records also contain cases in which questions of law relating to the right were raised in the course of litigation. In *Colynson c. Godesburgh*, for example, a suit heard in the consistory court at York in 1427,[47] one litigant raised the question of what effect the remarriage of a father had on his children's right to the third part of his goods. Did the children's share include property acquired and held in common during the second marriage? Or was it limited to property held by the parent during the marriage of which the child was an issue? In *Hodgeson c. Richardson*, heard at Durham in 1532, the principal issue litigated was the propriety of expenditures by the plaintiff's guardian during his minority.[48] What effect did these have on the *legitim* remaining to the child when he reached majority? Should they be deducted from the share? Unfortunately, the incompleteness of the case records prevents discovery of the answers to the questions. But at least we know that they were litigated. From the Southern Province of Canterbury there is no comparable evidence. Such absence is striking. The most satisfactory explanation for it is that the custom had disappeared there by the end of the fourteenth century.

Moreover, there is more positive evidence. Many of the act book[49] entries make little sense without the assumption that by 1400, a parent had the power to disinherit his children in most parts of England. For instance, in a Rochester case from 1467, a disinherited daughter sued to upset her father's will on the ground that he had been *non compos mentis*.[50] If the daughter had a right to *legitim* at the time, she very likely would have had no need to undertake the burden of showing testamentary incapacity to secure her third part of his estate. In a sixteenth-century case from Winchester, two daughters accused the executor of their father's estate of fraudulently inserting a clause in the testament by which they were deprived of the use of £20 willed to them.[51] Had the daughters enjoyed the right to elect against the will, surely they

---

45. Pye c. Baledon, Borthwick Institute CP.G.444 (1529).

46. Toppam c. Hodshon, Borthwick Institute D/C.CP.1563/8 (1563).

47. Borthwick Institute, CP.F.163 (1427). This cause was still being litigated in early 1430. It was complicated both by the widow's claims and by an allegation of prior satisfaction. Unfortunately no sentence has survived. Other suits at York involving, at least *inter alia*, the recovery of the child's portion, are Wilson v. Belwoode, CP.G.365 (1547); Polyngton c. Polyngton, CP.G.18 (1503-04); Clerk c. Executors of Rede, CP.F.128 (1420); Holme c. Holme, CP.F.18 (1402).

48. Durham Diocesan Records (Dept. of Paleography, University of Durham), Act book III/1, fol. 25v.

49. Act books were the official day-by-day records of procedure taken in all cases heard by the ecclesiastical courts.

50. *In re* Testament of Richard Austyn, Kent County Archives (Maidstone), Rochester Diocesan Records, Act book DRb Pa 3, fol. 548v. The court ultimately referred the case to arbitration.

51. *In re* Estate of William Wigmore, Hampshire Record Office (Winchester), Diocesan Records, Act book 3, fol. 97v (1525).

would have done so rather than raising the difficult allegation of tampering with their father's testament.

Reliance on the exact terms of bequests in the parent's last will is normally unnecessary if the child has a right to *legitim*, and such reliance appears over and over again in the records of the Southern Province in England. Children in the Southern Province brought many actions to enforce specific legacies contained in their fathers' testaments.[52] It makes most sense to suppose that they did so because by the fifteenth century the children no longer had a right to anything else. A right to *legitim* no longer formed part of the customary law in most of Southern England.

Surviving post-1400 testaments also suggest freedom to disinherit children. In some of these testaments, fathers mentioned their children but bequeathed less than a third share of the estate to them. The freedom of testation assumed in these wills is particularly impressive in contrast to the few testaments from special places where the *legitim* survived. For instance, in 1416, a testator from Grimsby in northern Lincolnshire left his daughter Alice £40 as well as a remainder interest in land; but he added that if she were not content with the £40, and chose instead to take her *portio* against the will, she should forfeit the remainder interest in the land.[53] The testator assumed, that is, that his daughter had the right to set aside part of his will, and he made the best provision he could for the eventuality. The absence of such provisions from most English wills is therefore doubly probative. In them the drafters assumed that the *legitim* did not exist.[54]

None of this should imply that parents regularly disinherited their children in southern England. Such treatment would be contrary to what we know about the ties of kinship in the Middle Ages and afterwards. It would also be contrary to much evidence in actual wills; indeed, some fathers expressly left the "third part of their goods" or the *portio* to their children.[55] Even in the South, division of an estate into thirds as a proper form of bequest remained a living idea well into early modern times. But the cumulation of evidence suggests that by 1400 this division represented the testator's choice rather than a legal obligation.

To this general regime of testamentary freedom one slight qualification exists: when the child was in need of the basic necessities of life,

---

52. *See, e.g.*, Pratt c. Pratt, West Sussex Record Office (Chichester), Diocesan Records, Act book Ep I/10/4, fol. 29r (1527). The child alleged that "defunctus legavit in testamento suo dicte Johanne filie sue xl s. quam summam dicti executores solvere recusant."

53. *See* the Testament of William Alcok in *Register of Bishop Repingdon, 1405-19*, in 74 LINCOLN REC. SOC'Y 218 (M. Archer ed. 1982) (no. 407).

54. *See, e.g.*, the Testament of Edward Coudray (1428), in 3 REGISTER OF HENRY CHICHELE, ARCHBISHOP OF CANTERBURY 1414-1443, at 374 (E. Jacob ed. 1938). The testator left only a small legacy to his daughter Joan. Possibly, in this and other such cases, the parent had advanced the daughter's share, for example in a marriage portion.

55. *See, e.g.*, 2 F. POLLOCK & F. MAITLAND, *supra* note 1, at 354.

the church courts provided some protection. They regularly enforced a father's duty to support his minor children, even illegitimate children.[56] The courts enforced trusts established for children, interpreting and even modifying them then "for the comfort and utility" of the child.[57] In addition, a few entries in the records suggest that provision for children with special needs was also sometimes made as part of probate proceedings. For example, John Hull at Canterbury left a residuary legacy to his children. In making the distribution, the court gave one child a share ten times that allotted to the other children "because he was sickly."[58] Need counted. Although the discretionary nature of the ecclesiastical remedies has removed most of the evidence from the historian's scrutiny, the records suggest that the church courts did not adopt a wholly heartless regime even while they did increasingly permit testamentary freedom. The reader may recall that in discussing whether or not custom might validly abrogate the right to *legitim*, the medieval canonists were most insistent that the right be preserved for the child who could not otherwise support himself. Although the records do not show that the courts enforced this rule uniformly, they do suggest that its spirit was not a dead letter.

IV.   POSSIBLE EXPLANATIONS FOR THE DEMISE OF THE *LEGITIM*

Except for special situations and except for particular parts of England, therefore, the story of the *legitim* during the later Middle Ages is one of decline and disappearance. From a general rule corresponding to the provisions of the Roman-canon law, it had become a custom enforced only in the North of England and a few places in the South by the end of the fourteenth century. The records themselves show this happening.

Exactly how and why the *legitim* dropped out of general use are, unfortunately, not questions to which the ecclesiastical court records provide exact answers. However, several possible explanations may be advanced. The first explanation is essentially procedural. It takes an internalist approach to legal change. The practical difficulties of enforcement of the right to *legitim* in the church courts must sometimes have been very great. The possibility of *inter vivos* conveyances made calculations difficult. The lack of control of questions involving inheritance of land made full enforcement of the *legitim* impossible. The English church courts were never in a position where they could enforce the full civil law system into which the *legitim* fit, if only because they held a limited jurisdiction. Enough examples of the inherent diffi-

---

56.   The evidence on this point is laid out in Helmholz, *Support Orders*, supra 169-86.

57.   Canterbury Cathedral Library, Act book Y.1.2, fol. 97v (1397). The record describes an undertaking by Thomas Neve, rector of Kingsdown, to administer a trust "ad commodum et utilitatem" of Katherine, daughter of John Otebred.

58.   Canterbury Cathedral Library, Act book Y.3.2, fol. 361 (1600). The court allocated £5 to Cales Hull, as opposed to 10s. given to each of the other three children "quia est morbosus."

culties have survived in the records to suggest that the church courts
never overcame these problems,[59] and this difficulty in enforcement
may have contributed to disappearance of the right.

The historian who finds policy explanations more plausible may
suggest a second possibility: that a growing sentiment in favor of testamentary freedom influenced practice in the church courts. The sentiment is readily observable in the law relating to real property; the
popularity of the use and the ability to bar entails during the later Middle Ages in England reflected testators' natural desires to pass title to
land free from the shackles of strict inheritance rules.[60] The success of
these devices shows which way the tide ran. The policy against re-
straints on alienation had its birth in the common law courts of the
Middle Ages, and it is not beyond thinking that the judges of the
church courts were subject to something like the same influences.

The historian more doctrinally inclined may point to a third possibility. The controversy among medieval commentators as to whether
the *legitim* could be abrogated by statute or custom suggests that the
complex English situation simply mirrored the attitudes of the canonists.[61] It is certain that the enforcement of the *legitim* did not rank as a
high priority in the medieval canon law. Although included in its texts,
the canon law never ascribed such weight to the *legitim* that the canonists felt required to treat it as beyond debate. This uncertain status may
well have affected actual practice. The judges may not have been sure
enough about it to enforce it as a matter of strict right. The *legitim* was
not a rule beyond doubt.

Each of these explanations makes sense.[62] The principal draw-
back to each is that none is supported by demonstrable evidence of
causation. They cannot be proved, because no actor ascribed the disappearance of the *legitim* to any of these three factors. Indeed, no actor
in the story has left any indication whatsoever of motivation. Although
there are entries in the surviving church court records which are consistent with each of these explanations, none of the entries rises to the
level of proving a connection. Consistency, not proof, is what they
offer. Moreover, each possible explanation fits poorly with the counter
examples of the Province of York and the City of London, the one the

59. *See, e.g., In re* Testament of Wynbussh, Rochester Diocesan Act book, DRb Pa 2, fols. 79r, 81v, 84v, 86r (1447). One of the children, who the court cited for impeding his father's testament by withholding goods, answered, "quod bona que habuit erant ei data per patrem suum dum vixit et manualiter liberata et hoc offert se probaturum." *Id.* at fol. 79r ["that the goods which he had were given to him by his father during his lifetime, and manually delivered. And he offered to prove this"]. Commentators admitted that the *legitim* excluded perfected *inter vivos* gifts. *See, e.g.,* MANGILIUS, *supra* note 18, Quaest. 10. This exclusion inevitably led to some of the same techniques for "avoiding probate" known to modern lawyers; for example, the life estate followed by remainder, as in a case involving the Estate of William Pyndfold, Canterbury Cathe-dral Library, Act book Y.1.3, fol. 180r (1422).
60. *See generally* J. BEAN, THE DECLINE OF ENGLISH FEUDALISM (1968).
61. *See supra* notes 27-33 and accompanying text.
62. *See also,* 3 W.S. HOLDSWORTH, *supra* note 1, at 554-56.

most traditional, the other the most economically "advanced" area of England.[63] In both places the custom of *legitim* survived the Middle Ages. It is hard to see why this survival should have occurred in both places on the basis of any of the arguments advanced above.

Although none of the possible explanations is analytically unassailable, they do nevertheless show the compatibility of this custom with change and communal choice.[64] This is a point worth making. The *legitim* was part of a complex system of inheritance derived ultimately from Roman law. The Roman law system was in widespread use on the Continent, but little of it obtained in England. English law divided testamentary succession between two court systems: secular courts for devolution of real property, and ecclesiastical courts for succession to chattels. Even in the ecclesiastical tribunals the civil law system of universal heirship was only partly enforced. Such a partial civilian regime naturally left greater leeway for change and for variation. The *legitim* was isolated from the regime which gave it birth, and knowledgeable men must therefore have seen it as a simple customary right rather than as an integral part of a functioning system of succession. This left it more vulnerable to challenge in England than on the Continent, where the *legitim* largely survived. If we cannot quite trace the motives of the English actors who retained the custom in some places but not in others, we can nevertheless show that an isolated customary right like the *legitim* was subject to change, perhaps even to rational debate.

V. STUBBS-MAITLAND CONTROVERSY

One additional point ought to be made. It relates to the authority of the canon law in medieval England. The question has long been dominated by the old controversy between F. W. Maitland and Bishop Stubbs.[65] Stubbs initially held to the view that, even before the Reformation, the English church courts were free to pursue a path independent of foreign, and particularly papal, direction. The canon law of Rome, Stubbs wrote, "although always regarded as of great authority in England, was not held to be binding on the courts."[66] Maitland found this argument contradicted by the available evidence. In a series

---

63. *Compare* 3 H. SWINBURNE, TREATISE OF TESTAMENTS AND LAST WILLS 997-1001 (1640) (no. 18) (York) *with* 11 Geo. I, ch. 18 (date) (London) *and* C. CARLTON, THE COURT OF ORPHANS 47 (1974) (London).

64. For remarks on the place of custom, with accompanying references, see B. TIERNEY, RELIGION, LAW, AND THE GROWTH OF CONSTITUTIONAL THOUGHT 1150-1650, at 56-57 (1982). *See also* J. GILISSEN, LA COUTUME (1982).

65. *See generally* Jones, *The Two Laws in England: the Later Middle Ages*, 11 J. CHURCH & ST. 111 (1969); Donahue, *Roman Canon Law in the Medieval English Church: Stubbs v. Maitland Re-examined After 75 Years in the Light of Some Records from the Church Courts*, 72 MICH. L. REV. 647 (1974).

66. 1 ECCLESIASTICAL COURTS COMMISSION, REPORT OF THE COMMISSIONERS INTO THE CONSTITUTION AND WORKING OF THE ECCLESIASTICAL COURTS, at xviii (1883).

of lively and critical essays he attacked Stubbs' position, maintaining that the "papal law books" were in fact regarded as binding statute law in England. Although the strong hand of the English kings kept some parts of the canon law from being enforced in England, Maitland said, for Stubbs' view to carry the day, "[w]e must see an ecclesiastical judge whose hands are free and who has no 'prohibition' to fear, rejecting a decretal . . . ."[67] That he could not find.[68]

If Maitland had looked to the law of *legitim*, he would have found exactly that example. The rule was "not held to be binding on the courts" even though ecclesiastical judges were entirely free to enforce it. No part of the English common law, no writ of prohibition, would have stopped them. And the decretal law supported by the great majority of the canonists called for them to do so. However, except for special local custom, the English church courts did not enforce the right. If put to choose between Maitland and Stubbs on the basis of this evidence, therefore, we should have to embrace the view of Stubbs.

However, so stark a choice need not be made. The Stubbs-Maitland controversy took too "modern" a view of the history of the canon law, and it is important to approach the question from the appropriate perspective. The history of the *legitim* provides an excellent corrective. First, the controversy treated the canon law too simply. Not all parts of the law were of the same character. Rules about heresy or simony, for example, had greater importance for the medieval church than did rules about inheritance. Not all papal decretals were meant to have the force of "binding statute law" in a modern sense. Some were. Some were not. *Legitim*, and most inheritance questions, fell into the latter group. The Stubbs-Maitland controversy must therefore be broadened to allow for the variety of rules found in the "papal law books." Not all were meant to be treated alike.

Second, the controversy was anachronistic in reading into the Middle Ages the tenets of legal positivism. Local custom, of which the *legitim* in England is only a small example, played a much greater role in the legal practice of the ecclesiastical courts than modern statute law would allow.[69] It is of course true that some local customs were illegitimate under the medieval canon law and not to be allowed in practice. But many more were tolerable, though they might qualify or even contradict a papal ruling. What was missing from the Stubbs-Maitland controversy was a recognition of the wide scope that the medieval

---

67. F. MAITLAND, *Church, State, and Decretals*, in ROMAN CANON LAW IN THE CHURCH OF ENGLAND 51, 84 (1898).

68. *Id.*

69. *See* Ourliac, *La juridiction ecclésiastique au Moyen-Age*, 34 MÉMORIES DE LA SOCIÉTÉ POUR L'HISTOIRE DU DROIT ET DES INSTITUTIONS DES ANCIENS PAYS BOURGUIGNONS, COMTOIS ET ROMANDS 13, 17 (1977). Ourliac says, "C'est la coutume qui détermine, en chaque lieu, la compétence de l'officialité . . . même contre les décrétales pontificales, mais dont il est bien difficile de saisir les nuances." *See also* Southern, *Outlines of a National Church in the Thirteenth Century*, [1983] REP. FRIENDS LAMBETH PALACE LIBR. 11.

canon law left for local variation. The medieval canonists often approached the rulings found in the official texts with a freedom that modern lawyers may find daring. This freedom allowed them to modify and even sometimes to disregard the clear import of the text. This same freedom is found in the local variation permitted within the canon law. Of the inappropriateness of dealing with the medieval canon law as if it were "binding statute law," the history of the *legitim* in England provides a perfect illustration.

VI. CONCLUSION

This article has sought to fill a long-standing gap in the history of English law by describing the evolution of a child's right to *legitim* in the church courts between the thirteenth and seventeenth centuries. The courts enforced that right as a matter of general English custom at the start of the period. By about 1400 they had ceased to do so. *Legitim* had become a local and noteworthy custom.

Whether this change came about because the English church courts had only a partial probate jurisdiction and lacked power to use the civilian system upon which true enforcement of the *legitim* depended, or because progressive sentiment in favor of freedom of testation came to dominate the minds of ecclesiastical lawyers in most parts of England, are questions that have proved impossible to answer with any assurance. The evidence is too scanty. But in any case, freedom of testation had largely carried the day by the fifteenth century. The church courts had showed themselves open to this legal change. Although free to follow the law found in papal decretals and endorsed by medieval commentators, the courts nevertheless responded to stronger forces and abandoned the *legitim*. If the exact reasons for the change have proved elusive, the fact and timing of change have both emerged clearly from a survey of the surviving records.

14

ASSUMPSIT AND *FIDEI LAESIO*

Causa fidei laesionis seu perjurii was the name given in the records of the medieval English Church courts to a suit brought to enforce a sworn promise. Typically, the promise at issue was to pay a simple debt for goods purchased. The seller, alleging that the buyer had promised with an express oath to pay the money owed for the goods, sued to enforce this sworn undertaking. The Church's general jurisdiction over the sins of laymen gave rise to this litigation. It was a sin to violate one's sworn promise.[1] And the canon law held that one could be obliged, under pain of excommunication, to complete his promise.[2] There was controversy among canonists about whether a simple promise, *nudum pactum*, gave rise to an action.[3] But a sworn undertaking was always understood to be enforceable by the ecclesiastical censures the Church courts had at their command.

Not much has so far been discovered about the way the courts Christian exercised this jurisdiction.[4] But we do know today what was not known to historians of the law of contracts fifty years and more ago, namely that these causes were staple parts of the business brought before the English Church courts during the fifteenth and

1 The canon law texts used to found this jurisdiction, and upon which canonists most frequently commented, were C. 22 q. 5 c.12, X 1.35.1, X 2.24.35, Sext 2.2.3, and Sext 2.11.2. [All citations to canonical texts are taken from *Corpus Juris Canonici*, ed. A. Friedberg, 2 vols. (Leipzig 1879). Citations to the medieval *glossa ordinaria* are taken from the edition printed in Rome, 1582.] See also W. Lyndwood, *Provinciale (seu Constitutiones Angliae)* (Oxford 1676), 315 s.v. *perjurio*: " Et quod super juramento cognoscit judex ecclesiasticus, . . ., et est ratio quia perjurium directe concernit dei irreverentiam, quae propriae est religioni Christianae contraria."

2 *Gl. ord.* ad Sext 2.11.2 s.v. *licet*: " Nota finaliter quod quis praecise compellitur servare iuramentum licitum et obligatorium." The matter is discussed at length in J. Roussier, *Le fondement de l'obligation contractuelle dans le droit classique de l'Église* (Paris 1933). The history of the Church's jurisdiction is covered in A. Esmein, " Le serment promissoire dans le droit canonique," (1888) 12 R.H.D. 3d ser., 248.

3 The canonists' treatment of this question is dealt with in F. Spies, *De l'observation des simples conventions en droit canonique* (Paris 1928), 35–138. There is also a useful summary in E. W. Kemp, *An Introduction to Canon Law in the Church of England* (London 1957), 21–23.

4 Short printed notices about the *fidei laesio* jurisdiction can be found in J. L. Barton, *Roman Law in England, Ius Romanum Medii Aevi* V, 13a (Milan 1971), 54–5; Charles Donahue, Jr., " Roman Canon Law in the Medieval English Church: Stubbs v. Maitland Re-examined after 75 years in the light of some records from the Church Courts," (1974) 72 Michigan L.R. 647, at 660–1; Brian Woodcock, *Medieval Ecclesiastical Courts in the Diocese of Canterbury* (Oxford 1952), 84, 89–92; and F. Pollock, " Contracts in Early English Law," (1893) 6 Harvard L.R. 389, at 403–404.

into the sixteenth centuries.[5] In the diocesan court at Canterbury, for example, 84 of a total of slightly fewer than 200 causes heard in 1416 concerned breach of faith. At the end of the fifteenth century hundreds of these causes were being heard every year at Canterbury.[6] In the Consistory court at Hereford, a more typical court than the one at Canterbury, 72 of these causes were introduced in 1472, out of a total number of 101.[7] At Lichfield, 44 of the 172 causes introduced in 1467–68 were *fidei laesio* suits.[8] It is no exaggeration to say that these suits were frequent in all the ecclesiastical courts for which medieval records remain. Court books from York, Chichester, Ely, Exeter, London, Rochester, and Bath and Wells all demonstrate the substantial proportion of the Church courts' business *fidei laesio* represented.[9]

Some of these causes may well have been brought in the nature of debt recognisances. Buyer and seller chose to register their transaction in the ecclesiastical court records for future security, resembling what was called in France *juridiction gracieuse*.[10] But this will not explain every case. Many of the causes were contested. Many went to the stage of proof by witnesses and of final sentence.

Henry II's Constitutions of Clarendon (1164) forbade the Church to hear these causes where the underlying transaction was a debt.[11] The Yearbooks contain much dicta to the same effect.[12] But the rule and the availability of writs of prohibition made little apparent difference to actual Church court practice in the fifteenth century. The Courts enforced sworn promises largely unmolested. This means that far from being a " recollection " in the late fifteenth

---

5 The older view, that *fidei laesio* jurisdiction had been effectively removed from the Church courts by the fifteenth century is found in James Barr Ames, *Lecturers on Legal History* (Cambridge, Mass. 1931), 125–128.

6 The figure for 1416 is taken from Canterbury [Library of the Dean and Chapter] Act book Y.1.3. A graph showing the incidence of breach of faith causes at Canterbury is given in Woodcock, *Medieval Ecclesiastical Courts*, 84.

7 Taken from Hereford [County Record Office] Act book I/1. This is, however, a temporary classification. All Act books are to be placed under a new HD/11/A class.

8 Taken from Lichfield [Joint Record Office, Lichfield] Act book B/C/1/1.

9 On the incidence of *fidei laesio* causes in these dioceses, see below *passim* and esp. nn. 86–89.

10 See Paul Fournier, *Les Officialités au moyen âge* (Paris 1880), 291.

11 Cap. xv: " Placita de debitis quae fide interposita debentur, vel absque interpositione fidei, sint in justitia regis." *Stubbs' Select Charters*, 9th ed. rev. by H. W. C. Davis (Oxford 1921), 167. The writ *Circumspecte Agatis* (1286) allowed the Church courts to assign penance in cases of breach of faith, but forbade the giving of a secular remedy. Note the purely formal compliance with this rule apparently urged by Lyndwood, *Provinciale*, 315 s.v. *perjurio*.

12 See Y.BB. Mich. 2 Hen. IV, pl. 45; Trin. 11 Hen. IV, pl. 40; Pasch. 38 Hen. VI, pl. 11, Mich. 20 Edw. IV, pl. 9; Trin. 22 Edw. IV, pl. 47; Trin. 12 Hen. VII, pl. 2. On the writ of prohibition see G. B. Flahiff, " The Writ of Prohibition to Court Christian in the thirteenth century " (1944–45) *Medieval Studies*, VI, 261 and VII, 229.

and early sixteenth centuries, as Ames and others thought, causes arising under a theory of *fidei laesio* had both a long history and a regular and important place in contemporary legal practice. They would have been familiar to anyone who had any contact with the ecclesiastical courts.

It is the contention of this article that there is a connection between the *causa fidei laesionis* and the early history of assumpsit in the royal courts. The connection can only be made out for the early period, roughly between the 1520s and 1560s. The subsequent evolution of assumpsit through *Slade's Case* and beyond is accounted for by developments within the Common Law itself.[13] But during the early years of assumpsit, when the promise was genuine and when, in theory and in fact, assumpsit was distinct from the action of debt, the record evidence suggests a real connection. The legal elements requisite in pleading the undertaking were remarkably alike. The kinds of obligations enforced through the two actions were similar. And the coincidence in time between the rise of assumpsit and the disappearance of *fidei laesio* was strikingly close. There were significant differences in the nature of the damages and in the remedy available. But in the principal elements of the contracts at issue, assumpsit and *fidei laesio* appear much alike. And this similarity appears closer than that which previous writers have suggested may exist between the rise of assumpsit and the Chancellor's enforcement of parol contracts during the fifteenth century.

The evidence which makes a detailed comparison possible is provided by the records of the Church courts, set against the plea rolls of the royal courts. The Act books and cause papers of the ecclesiastical courts have survived from the fifteenth and early sixteenth centuries in sufficient quantities to demonstrate a good deal about the nature of the *causa fidei laesionis*. The academic canon law is also helpful at points, although much of the canonists' treatment of contracts was taken up by the question of the propriety of enforcing simple promises, of whether an action arose from a *nudum pactum*. This problem did not arise in the English practice, if the surviving records tell an accurate story. The presence of an

---

[13] The problem lay, as Professor Milsom writes, in " accommodating [the] idea within the framework already established." *Historical Foundations of the Common Law* (London 1969), 295. It is around this problem that most scholarship about assumpsit has centred. The present article makes no pretension to dealing with it beyond giving a certain amount of documentary support to the conclusion that there was a real, not simply a conceptual, difference between the action of debt and early assumpsit.

oath took an agreement out of the area of the *nudum pactum*. And in practice an oath to fulfil the promise was always alleged.[14]

I

Examination of the plea rolls and the Church court records shows, in the first place, a similarity in the kinds of promises which were enforced in practice. Assumpsit and *fidei laesio* were both remedies used to enforce oral, as against written, agreements.[15] And the sums at issue in both were relatively small. For assumpsit, this fact is explained by the unavailability of wager of law in an action of debt brought on a sealed instrument. Where the transaction was large enough and where the parties were experienced enough to use a sealed instrument to record the obligation, typically the conditional defeasance bond for twice the amount of the debt, the defendant could not wage his law when sued on the bond.[16] Since the reason for using assumpsit was precisely to oust wager, assumpsit was used only for lesser transactions. Its need was to cover promises where the underlying obligations had been too informal or too small for the parties to have used a sealed instrument.

Like assumpsit, the ecclesiastical *causa fidei laesionis* dealt with oral, relatively informal, promises. There was no competing action in the Church courts which restricted breach of faith causes to small sums and to oral agreements. But almost all the ecclesiastical causes were for small sums of money. Most of the causes heard in the Church courts would not have met the 40s. jurisdictional limit of the royal courts. For instance, at Canterbury the average size of money claims in 1463 for causes in which the Act book gives a figure was approximately 8s. 6d., the highest being 40s., the lowest 12d.[17] In London's Commissary court for 1484, the average figure was a similar 8s. 1d.[18] In the Consistory court at Hereford in 1492, the

---

[14] *Infra*, nn. 53–58. Canonists, while conceding that the man who broke his simple promise committed a sin, also held that the addition of an oath to the promise created a stronger obligation. See, for example gl. ord. ad C. 22 q. 5 c. 12 s.v. *distanciam*: " Magis tamen peccat peierando quam mentiendo, solidius subsistit ubi iuramentum interponit." And to the same effect see gl. ord. ad X 2.24.35 s. v. *quod promisit*.

[15] See, for example, the report of *Slade's Case*, in which reference is made to the fact that " an *assumpsit* is called a parol covenant," in J. H. Baker, " New Light on Slade's Case," [1971] C.L.J. 51, at 61, and *ibid*. 213, at 229.

[16] See A. W. B. Simpson, " The Penal Bond with Conditional Defeasance," (1966) 82 L.Q.R. 392; S. E. Thorne, " Tudor Social Transformation and Legal Change," (1951) 26 New York U.L.R. 10, at 19–21.

[17] Taken from Act book X.8.3. It may be important to note that the recording of each cause in the Act book did not always specify the sum involved, so that this figure does not include all cases heard. Any distortion produced probably reduces the average figure, since larger claims seem more likely to have been disputed.

[18] Taken from Act book MS. 9064/2; 37 causes are included.

average amount was 13s.[19] The relative insignificance of the obligations at issue is doubtless the practical explanation for the absence of written contracts in *fidei laesio* suits. Where a writing was introduced, as one was in a 1474 cause heard at Lichfield, the record specifically referred to it as being merely *in subsidium probationis.*[20]

There was, however, a part of the litigation in the Church court which dealt with larger obligations. The largest claim found in the court records was for £20, in a cause brought at Hereford in 1493.[21] Quite a few other breach of faith suits involved sums well over the 40s. figure. Claims for £6, for £14, for £4 12s., for £6 11s. 8d., are examples appearing in the Act books.[22] Of the six *fidei laesio* causes surviving today among the York Cause papers of 1510–25, the sums at issue were the following: 5 marks; £5; 18s. 10d.; £12; £10 11s. 4d.; £8.[23] The large figures for York are probably accounted for by the nature of the court, which was the court of appeal for an entire province, and by the greater likelihood of survival of Cause papers in a suit involving a large sum than a small sum. But, for purposes of this article, the essential fact is that there was a part of the Church court jurisdiction over *fidei laesio* which extended to promises to pay more than 40s. The larger amounts at issue in some of the ecclesiastical causes would have been cognisable in assumpsit.

The records also show a similarity in the great variety of agreements which could be the subject of both actions. Neither assumpsit nor *fidei laesio* was restricted to situations where there had been a promise to pay money. Both were used to remedy the breach of many kinds of promises.[24] Agreements to deliver goods,[25] to convey

---

19 Taken from Act book I/1; 22 causes are included.
20 Act book B/C/1/2, f. 186v; it apparently detailed a prior concord and agreement between the two parties. Another cause in which a written instrument was introduced is York [Borthwick Institute of Historical Research] C[ause] P[apers] G 100 (1520–1); the document had been drawn up by a London notary public.
21 Act book I/1, p. 105.
22 Causes recorded, respectively, in London [Guildhall Library] Act book 9064/1, f. 18r (1470); Canterbury Act book Y.1.6, f. 46v (1464); Lichfield Act book B/C/1/1, f. 157v (1467); Hereford Act book 1/1, p. 71 (1493).
23 Taken from C.P. G 48 (1510); F 311, 321 (1511); G 106–7 (1512); G 118 (1518); G 100 (1520–21); and G 123 (1521).
24 See generally H. K. Lücke, " *Slade's Case* and the Origin of the Common Counts," (1965) 81 L.Q.R. 422, 539; (1966) 82 L.Q.R. 81; Ames, *Lecturers on Legal History*, 129–148; A. K. R. Kiralfy, *The Action on the Case* (London 1951), 143–150, 158–163.
25 *e.g.,* London Act book MS. 9064/3, f. 118v (1485): non-delivery of two yards of woollen cloth and [Public Record Office, London] K.B. 27/1152, m. 133d (1549): non-delivery of ten pieces of woollen cloth.

land,[26] to do construction work,[27] to give marriage portions,[28] are all found both in the records of the Church courts and on the plea rolls. Promises to accept arbitration awards,[29] contracts of bailment,[30] and suretyship agreements [31] all appeared as the subjects of both *fidei laesio* and assumpsit.

The ecclesiastical cause did have a disciplinary side which was absent from the royal courts. The Church would punish (normally by means of a public penance) the violator of an oath even where there had been no damage to a promisee. The canon law held that the violation of one's oath was punishable as a spiritual offence even without an agreement running between two parties. So, for example, it was possible to invoke this jurisdiction against a man who had broken his oath to observe the statutes of a London guild.[32]

---

[26] See, for example, the language of an ecclesiastical cause brought to enforce a promise to convey; Canterbury Act book Y.1.7, f. 219v (1463); " Actor petit deliberacionem sive seisinam in certarum terrarum (*sic*). Reus fatetur quod promisit sibi fide media deliberare seisinam in tribus peciis terre in parochia de Holyngbourne.'' Compare the substance of C.P. 40/1127, m. 593 (1546): " Et licet idem Henricus statum possesionem et seisinam eidem Johanni de clauso predicto habendo sibi heredibus et assignatis suis infra certum tempus iam preteritum faciend ' cum prefato Johanne convenisset et super se assumpsisset, predictus tamen Henricus. . . .''

[27] Compare, for example, Canterbury Act book Y.4.3, f. 32r (1500), in which the promise was to build a house, and C.P. 40/1139 (1549), in which it was to build a wall.

[28] Compare, for example, York C.P. F 294 (1499) brought for a promise to pay £4, and K.B. 27/1192, m. 178 (1559), brought for £20.

[29] See Kiralfy, *Action on the Case*, 195, 197, for a table of incidence. An interesting example from the Church courts is York C.P. F 210 (1455), brought to enforce an award about a dispute originally brought " in quadam causa sive materia debiti in wapentagio de Hertill'.'' In Canterbury Act book Y.1.1, f. 105r (1375) the original law suit was brought in the royal courts. The award was that one party " haberet dictam domum bene in pace pro perpetuo et unam marcam pro expensis quas idem Johannes fecerat per iniustam fatigacionem dicti Roberti in curia regis.'' In Rochester [County Record Office, Maidstone] Act book DRb Pa 2, f. 294v (1456) the original dispute had been brought " in curia civitatis.'' All three causes were brought on the basis of the defendant's sworn promise to obey the arbiters' award. .

[30] London Act book MS. 9064/1, f. 63r (1471): " Margareta famula Walteri merceris fregit fidem Alicie Barden' pro certo scerica quod recepit a dicta Alicia et promisit per fidem reportare.'' In Canterbury Act book Y.1.6, f. 40v (1464), the plaintiff asked for " restitutionem duarum bestiarum.'' In Canterbury Act book Y.2.13, f. 67v (1531) the allegation was that the defendant " violasse promissum in non solvendo sive liberando parti actrici summam quinque marcarum quam recepit ab eodem ad custodiendum ad usum suum.'' On baliment contracts and assumpsit, see Kiralfy, *Action on the Case*, 158–163.

[31] On the use of assumpsit, and its early acceptability because debt did not lie for suretyship agreements, see Lücke, " Origin of the Common Counts,'' 423–425. An example of the ecclesiastical cause in Hereford Act book I/1, p. 22 (1492): " Pars rea fatetur quod promisit fide sua media ad salvandam dictam partem actricem indempnem penes quendam Johannem Robertis quo ad summam quatuor nobilium.'' In London Act book MS. 9064/3, f. 210v. (1476) it was similarly alleged that the defendant " fecit fidem eidem quod salvaret eum indempnem pro solucione dictarum pecuniarum.'' Other examples: Chichester Act book Ep I/10/1, f. 60v (1506); York C.P. F 251 (1470); London MS. 9064/2, f. 9r (1483).

[32] London Act book MS. 9064/2, f. 163r (1486): " Stephanus Kyng notatur officio quod incuruit periurim infrangendo statuta fraternitatis molendinariorum

It is impossible to tell in such a case how the matter came to the attention of the Commissary court in London. It was brought as an *ex officio* prosecution, and unless the Act book records that the case was promoted by a private party there is no way to discover who reported the breach of the oath. It was, in any event, treated as a disciplinary matter. Assumpsit, on the other hand, was always brought for damages by an injured promisee. Simple punishment of perjury was outside its scope. To this extent the ecclesiastical remedy covered a broader range of obligations.

The disciplinary side of the Church's jurisdiction should not, however, be overemphasised. Most breach of faith causes involved a broken promise between two contracting parties, as in assumpsit. And the great majority involved a promise to pay money. They alleged promises to discharge an ordinary debt: for the price of a horse or cow sold,[33] for grain delivered,[34] for curing a man of illness,[35] for cloth dyed,[36] or for a simple loan.[37] Most of the causes recorded in the Act books do not specify the subject of the original debt. But of those which do, by far the greater part arose out of a promise to pay an ordinary commercial or personal debt. The same is true of assumpsit. By the time assumpsit appears in significant numbers on the plea rolls, it was normally brought to remedy an alleged failure to pay money. Of the 98 assumpsit entries appearing on the King's Bench plea rolls for 1559, for example, 78 were for money promised.[38] Although *fidei laesio* and assumpsit could be and were in fact used to deal with many sorts of broken promises, most often both came to be used when the underlying transaction was a simple debt. An analysis of the sorts of contracts enforced by assumpsit in the 1540s and 1550s is thus remarkably similar to the sorts of contracts the Church courts entertained 50 years before. Anyone who moves from one class of records to the other cannot help feeling that he is in the same world.

ad quorum observanciam iuratus est." There are also, in the London act books, a number of *ex officio* prosecutions alleging that the defendant was " communis violator fidei." For example, MS. 9064/8, f. 251r (1500).

[33] Hereford Act book I/1, p. 29 (1492); the promise was to pay 13s. 4d. " pro quodam equo." In Canterbury Act book X.1.1, f. 135v (1457) the promise was to pay 6 marks and 4s. for eight cows.

[34] York C.P. F 266 (1484); Canterbury Act book X.1.1, f. 80r (1452).

[35] Canterbury Act book Y.1.1, f. 32v (1373). The defendant " fatetur quod convencio fuit inter dictum magistrum Johannem et ipsum quod idem curaret dictum magistrum de quadam infirmitate quam patitur et quod idem Thomam solveret eidem magistro Johanni cum principio v s. et cum curaverit illum de infirmitate huiusmodi alios quinque s." In London Act book MS. 9064/2, f. 51v (1484) the suit was for " v s. quos dictus dominus debuit sibi pro medicinis et aliis necessariis sibi ministratis tempore infirmitatis."

[36] York C.P. F 23 (1402), in which the debt was for 7s. " pro tinctura panni."

[37] Ely [Cambridge University Library] Act book EDR D/2/1, f. 88v (1378), in which the promise was to pay 8s. " ex causa puri mutui."

[38] *Infra*, n. 90; Milsom, *Historical Foundations*, 292–304.

II

The parol nature of the contracts, their relatively small size, and their similarly broad variety do not, however, demonstrate any necessary connection. The similarities in circumstance may be important for social historians, but they need reflect no legal relationship between the royal court action and *fidei laesio* in the courts Christian. It is possible, however, to tell if there is anything more than a superficial similarity by comparing the elements alleged in pleading the two actions. The plea rolls of the royal courts, together with the early reports, make this feasible for assumpsit. And the ordinary elements of *fidei laesio* cause can be traced in the Act books and Cause papers.

The closest equivalent in the ecclesiastical court to the entries on the plea rolls is probably the document called positions. Positions, introduced after the opening libel in an ecclesiastical cause, alleged separately each element of the plaintiff's case. The defendant, either personally or through his advocate or proctor, was required to respond to each position separately. The purpose of the introduction and the answers was to frame the issues for proof.[39] Here is a fairly typical set of positions from a *fidei laesio* cause, one which comes from the York records of 1511. It was brought by George Chart to recover £5, which Oliver Foster had promised to pay for stock animals delivered to him.

> *Imprimis* the said proctor intends to prove that the aforesaid Oliver Foster, at a time before the feast of St. Laurence recently past, bought and received from the aforesaid George Chart forty sheep, forty lambs and twenty hogs worth £6 6s. 8d.
> *Item* that the same Oliver on the day of delivery and receipt of the said sheep, lambs and hogs, paid 26s. 8d. in part payment of the said sum of £6 6s. 8d.
> *Item* that the same Oliver by his oath faithfully promised the same George to pay £5 the rest of the same £6 6s. 8d. on a certain day now past.
> *Item* that the aforesaid George by himself and his men long before the present suit duly requested the said Oliver to pay to the same George the said £5, the rest of £6 6s. 8d.
> *Item* that the aforesaid Oliver, thus requested as is aforesaid, has delayed and refused to pay or deliver to the same George the said £5, just as he delays and refuses at the present time.

---

[39] Willielmus Durantis, *Speculum Iudiciale* (Lyons 1543), II tit. *de positionibus*; William of Drogheda, *Summa Aurea* in *Quellen zur Geschichte des Römisch-kanonischen Prozesses im Mittelalter*, ed. L. Wahrmund (Innsbruck 1907–28) II:2, 201–203.

Item that the aforesaid are true, public, notorious, and manifest etc.[40]

With this, compare a typical claim made in assumpsit. It comes from an action brought in the King's Bench in 1549. Richard Fisher sued Gerard Power for non fulfilment of a promise to pay for stock animals worth £4 6s. 8d. which Fisher had delivered to Power.

> Richard Fisher complains of Gerard Power in custody of the Marshal of the Marshalsea of our lord King that whereas the aforesaid Richard, on 20 October in the 35th year of the reign of King Henry VIII at Warwick in the aforesaid county, at the instance and special request of the aforesaid Gerard delivered to the same Gerard two cows and two pigs worth £4 6s. and 8d., and upon the same delivery the same Gerard then and there faithfully promised to the same Robert and took upon himself that the same Gerard would well and faithfully acquit and pay the same Richard the aforesaid £4 6s. and 8d. whenever requested, nevertheless the aforesaid Gerard, heedless of his promise and undertaking, and scheming craftily and falsely to deceive and defraud the aforesaid Richard of his £4 6s. and 8d. has not paid the same £4 6s. and 8d. according to his promise and undertaking to the same Richard, although often requested etc., by which the same Richard is hurt and damaged in his credit towards many of the subjects of the lord King, and especially towards Nicholas Johnson and Ralph Pratt to whom the said Richard had promised to acquit and pay the same £4 6s. and 8d. on the faith of the faithful performance of the aforesaid promise and undertaking. And he has damage to the amount of £10.[41]

Examination of these two documents shows at a glance that except for one or two places there is no exact correlation in language. No one would argue that the royal courts took *fidei laesio* whole from the Church courts and called it assumpsit. It is nonetheless clear that there are three real similarities. The consideration, the express promise, and the breach of the promise are all set down in similar fashion.

First, both began with a recital of the transaction which lay behind the promise. In the two examples given, it consisted of a simple sale of goods. This, as shown above, is typical of both assumpsit and *fidei laesio*. The consideration for the promise to pay

---

[40] C.P. F 321.
[41] K.B. 27/1151, m. 30; see also Milsom, *Historical Foundations*, 299; A. K. R. Kiralfy, *A Source Book of English Law* (London 1957), 198–200.

was an ordinary business transaction between buyer and seller. It was set out at the start of the pleading, and it introduced the recital of the promise to pay. For the ecclesiastical courts, it is clear that consideration must be understood in the sense of the civilian *causa*. The canon law and the Church court records make clear that what was stated in the first position was not the *quid pro quo* of the classical Common Law action of debt, but the existence of an honest, possible and lawful cause for the promise.[42] In fact, the records frequently abbreviated this opening statement by noting only the existence of a *causa honesta et licita* as supporting the later promise.[43] Because the formal records and the Act books recorded the essential elements of causes heard by the courts, repeated use of this phrase clearly indicates that what the court required was the civilian motive or inducement, not the bargain of the later history of consideration.

Where, in the Cause papers and deposition books, fuller statement of the transactions behind the promise is found, the consideration recited always falls in this category. And it is worth noting that the surviving documents in the Church courts always allege a real transaction of some sort. Simple love and affection were not set out as supporting a promise. Whether or not the Church courts would have enforced a wholly gratuitous promise under the rubric of *fidei laesio* is now impossible to tell. Too many of the medieval records have perished to allow for confident statement. But it is clear that the records which remain all speak to the sort of inducement which would later support an action of assumpsit. The pre-existing debt,[44] the giving of a marriage portion,[45] the

---

[42] Canonists usually stated the doctrine negatively; all promises were enforceable unless they were illicit. *e.g.*, Hostiensis, *Lectura in libros Decretalium* (Venice 1581) ad X 1.31.1, no. 6: " Pacta custodiantur, . . . dummodo non sint contra leges, vel contra bonos mores, et nisi dolo fiant."

[43] *e.g.*, Hereford Act book I/3, p. 48 (1500); York C.P. F 174 (1430). The defendant could, however, object to the vagueness of this statement; *e.g.*, Hereford Act book I/2, p. 89 (1499): " Et dictus procurator partis ree peciit licitam convencionem sibi in libello fore declarand'. Et procurator partis actricis declaravit quod pro xl, etc. dicta pars rea alias fide sua media se astruxit."

[44] This is particularly clear where there was dispute about the original debt, but the promise to pay all or part of it was made by way of settlement of the controversy. For example, in a cause recorded in Canterbury Deposition book X.10.1, fols. 91v–92r (1415), the full subject of the original debt was not given in the depositions. But the threat to sue, the plaintiff's forbearance to do so, and the promise to pay by the defendant are all clearly stated by the witness: " Qui quidem J. Edmund supplicavit eundem quatinus concederet sibi dies solucionum de dicta summa et quod non implacitaret eundem; et sic dicens J. Garden' concessit sibi, . . . pro quibus solucionibus fideliter faciendis temporibus antedictis dedit idem J. Admund fidem suam in manibus dicti Johannis Garden tunc ibidem."

[45] York C.P. F 311 (1511), containing much interesting information about local customs regarding the marriage portion. The Church courts did not always follow the Common Law rule that *maritagia* could be recovered only if not

payment of a decedent's debts by his executor,[46] the release of a debtor from gaol by payment of outstanding debts owed to third persons [47]; these were all honest and licit causes underlying a promise. They were all frequently alleged in the Church courts. They would not fit a strict " bargain theory " of consideration. But they were real transactions which imposed an obligation on the promisor and furnished a good reason for his promise to pay.[48]

Of the early history of consideration in assumpsit it is impossible to speak with assurance. The printed reports are in many ways ambiguous or confusing. Modern historians have not solved all the problems they raise, although most recent writers on the subject have treated consideration in early assumpsit as equivalent to the civilian *causa*.[49] It is, however, certain that the consideration alleged in assumpsit was not identical to the *quid pro quo* of debt. It is also clear that there is a strong similarity in the nature of considerations *actually* alleged in assumpsit and in breach of faith causes. As it appears on the plea rolls, the consideration pleaded in early assumpsit was very like the lawful inducement of *fidei laesio*, taken over and added to the delictual side of the action as it already existed. The bill or the count set out the true inducement: the antecedent debt, the sale of goods, the suretyship agree-

---

involving land (See Bracton, f. 407b). Canterbury Deposition book X.10.1, f. 83r (1414), for example, involved a promise by Thomas Petyman to convey two acres of land, along with money, to the plaintiff and his wife in consideration of their marriage.

[46] *e.g.*, London Act book MS. 9064/2, f. 177r (?1487): " Gye Asswell executor testamenti Beatricis Elys defuncte recusat solvere v marcas Isabele Whith, quam summam promisit eidem Isabelle satisfacere ex bonis dicte Beatricis." The ability to sue an executor for the debts of the decedent was, of course, one of the advantages of using assumpsit. See William McGovern, " Contract in Medieval England: wager of law and the effect of death," (1968) 54 Iowa L.R. 19. It seems clear that prior to the rise of assumpsit, such suits were routinely brought in the Church courts, either as *fidei laesio* or as testamentary causes. How long such jurisdiction was exercised in practice by the ecclesiastical courts is explored infra 307-21.

[47] *e.g.*, London Act book MS. 9064/2. f.9r (1483): " Robertus Caper promisit fide sua quod si Henricus Brewster relaxaret condempnacionem suam erga Ricardum Strekely incarceratum et condempnatum et permittere eum liberari a carceribus quod videret . . . ad solucionem debiti." Similar assumpsit actions have rather more elaborate statements, alleging the great friendship between the gaoled debtor and the promisor and the promisor's special request that the debtor be released in return for his promise. But the substance, in terms of consideration, was no different.

[48] See the discussion in J. L. Barton, " The Early History of Consideration," (1969) 85 L.Q.R. 372.

[49] *Sidenham and Worlington's Case* (1585) 2 Leo. 224; and see the cases in Dyer 272a note. See also the modern discussion of the cases in A. W. B. Simpson, " The Place of *Slade's Case* in the history of Contract," (1958) 74 L.Q.R. 381; Kiralfy, *The Action on the Case*, 172–173; Lücke, " The Origin of the Common Counts," 444; P. Vinogradoff, " Reason and Conscience in Sixteenth-Century Jurisprudence," (1908) 24 L.Q.R. 373, at 381; Holdsworth, *History of English Law*, VIII, 2–8; Grant Gilmore, *The Death of Contract* (Columbis, Ohio 1974), 18–34.

ment, then added to it allegations of deceit, forbearance to sue, special requests and the like. But the underlying inducement was the same as that alleged in breach of faith causes. The developed English doctrine of consideration was arrived at by explaining and by limiting what had already been done.[50]

There was, however, some hesitation and uncertainty about the adequacy of the civilian *causa* as consideration right from the start. Although the inducement was invariably alleged in early assumpsit, it was normally followed both by language importing deceit and by the recitation of another consideration which might also support the promise to pay and which might technically fit a " bargain theory " of consideration. Sometimes this was a forbearance to sue. Frequently it was the giving of a few pence to the defendant by the plaintiff in return for the fresh promise to pay. That is, the pleading alleged first the existence of the true inducement for the promise, then added that the defendant *pro duodecim denariis pre manibus solutis* made the promise on which the action was grounded.[51] It certainly may be that these nominal considerations were in fact paid in many cases as a way of binding the promisor. But the small sum quickly came to be fictitious. There is no evidence that it could be traversed.[52] And it gradually dropped out of the pleading during the course of the sixteenth century. The most likely possibility is that it is a sign of caution on the part of the lawyers using the new remedy. In the climate of uncertainty about the avail-

---

[50] See Barton, " The Early History of Consideration "; C. H. S. Fifoot, *History and Sources of the Common Law: Tort and Contract* (London 1949), 395–443; Milsom, *Historical Foundations*, 309–315; Professor A. W. B. Simpson's article " The Equitable Doctrine of Consideration and the Law of Uses," (1965) 16 U. of Toronto L.J. 1, treats the development of the doctrine in Chancery prior to the rise of assumpsit and suggests a connection between the two.

[51] In the following entry, for example, John Wryley the defendant is alleged to have promised to pay a debt owed to the plaintiff Simon by Richard Paddock. The bill reads: " Pro eo videlicet quod cum quidem Richardus Paddock vicesimo secundo die Januarii anno regni Henrici octavi . . . tricesimo septimo apud Lychefeld in comitatu predicto indebitatus fuit predicto Simoni in summa 46s. et 8d. ac pro vera solucione et contentacione eorundem 46s. et 8d. pro duodecim denariis per prefatum Simonem eidem Johanni Wryley ad tunc et ibidem pre manibus solutis prefato Simoni ad tunc et ibidem fideliter promisit et super se assumpsit . . . " K.B.27/1140, m. 70 (1546). In K.B. 27/1190, m. 14d. (1559), the entry recites after the prior indebtedness: " pro et in consideracione duodecim denariorum legalis monete Anglie . . . in manibus solutorum. . . ."

[52] It was, however, the subject of a *protestando* in at least one case, K.B. 27/1112, m. 32 (1542): " Et idem Willelmus Fyndern' defendit vim et iniuriam quando etc. Et protestando quod narracio predicta minus sufficiens in lege ad quam idem W. F. necesse non habet nec per legem terre tenetur respondere protestando eciam quod predictus W. F. non recepit de predicto Willelmo Pynnok predictos duodecim denarios in forma qua predictus W. P. superius versus eum queritur; pro placito tamen idem W. F. dicit quod ipse non assumpsit modo et forma prout predictus W. P. superius versus eum narravit. Et de hoc ponit se super patriam."

ability of assumpsit, it may well have seemed prudent, even if not absolutely essential, to add to the count this nominal consideration which could be represented as a true *quid pro quo*. The use of additional language, added out of caution, has been a characteristic of lawyers in many ages. It does not mean that the recitation of the true underlying consideration for the promise was irrelevant. In this recitation, as in the sorts of considerations alleged, assumpsit was very close to the canonical *fidei laesio*.

The second element of similarity of pleading, evident in the two examples given above, is the centrality of the express promise. In both it was alleged that the defendant *fideliter promisit*. A promise to pay or to fulfil some other obligation, undertaken by means of an oath, was an essential part of the *causa fidei laesionis*.[53] It was invariably alleged.[54] And it was a real promise. The surviving depositions of witnesses make clear that the promise was an actual one, and that it was separate from the underlying transaction in fact as well as in legal theory. Witnesses often told enough about the details behind the ecclesiastical cause to say this with some assurance. For example, in a cause brought by John Palmer against Christopher Manser before the London Consistory court in 1487 to enforce a promise to pay an antecedent debt, Roger Copynt, one of the witnesses, testified that Palmer " asked the said Christopher when he would deliver the money which he owed him." Christopher said he did not have the money at hand, but offered some grain in part payment, and then " swore by the faith of his body that the same John Palmer would have [it] within a week or so." [55] Palmer accepted this plan, although he was apparently sceptical, since the

---

53 This is especially clear in comparing breach of faith causes with other causes brought in the Church courts for money. Compare for example the language used in Hereford Act book I/3, p. 17 (1499), a *causa subtractionis iuris ecclesiastici*: " Dicta pars rea fatetur se debere . . . xis s.," with a similar entry in a breach of faith cause in Act book I/3, p. 21 (1499): " Fatetur se alias promississe fide sua media ad solvendum parti actrici xvii s." Examples from dioceses not already illustrated are: Chichester [County Record Office] Act book Ep I/10/1, f. 37v (1508): " Actor allegavit viva voce quod pars rea violavit fidem eo quod promisit sibi fidem de solvendo actori xx s." Ely Act book EDR D/2/1, f. 67v (1377): " Dicta Cristina tenetur eidem Andree in vii s. v d. argenti quos eidem iuravit solvere." Exeter [County Record Office] Deposition book MS. Chanter 854/1, pp. 124–125 (1517): " Dictus dominus Michaelis tunc et ibidem promisit se sua fide media." Rochester Act book DRb Pa 1, f. 228r (1441): " Et libellato viva voce quod idem Benedictus promisit fide media ad deliberandum dicto Thome. . . ."
54 This fact differentiates the causes heard by the Church courts from those oral contracts enforced in Chancery and in most of England's local courts. See R. L. Henry, *Contracts in the Local Courts of Medieval England* (London 1926); W. T. Barbour, *The History of Contract in Early English Equity* (Oxford 1914), 117, 135, 138.
55 Liber Examinationum MS. 9065, fols. 13v–14r: " Christopherus iuravit per fidem corporis sui quod eadem septimana vel proxima sequente idem Johannes Palmer haberet ab eodem. . . ."

witness noted that Palmer remarked that he " well remembered
the promises Christopher had made in the past." In the event, the
scepticism was probably warranted, since the law suit was brought
later to enforce this violated promise.

The point of reciting the facts of this cause is to show that the
promise to pay was clearly separate in reality from the antecedent
debt which served as its inducement. In this cause, in fact, the
circumstances surrounding the original debt are as unknowable as
they would be in the later *indebitatus* assumpsit. But the existence
of a pre-existing debt was important only as inducement for the
promise in the Church courts. Like assumpsit, the breach of faith
suit need not specify all the details surrounding the original debt or
other obligation. The cause was brought for the breach of the
promise to pay, not for the debt.

There also are distinct signs in the depositions of a quasi religious
seriousness with which many of the promises were made. Here are
two examples: " By my faith I shall faithfully observe the agreement which I made with you if God gives me life." [56] And " By
my faith I shall faithfully pay the said sum before the feast of
Michaelmas next." [57] Often the promise was made with a pledge
of faith *in manum dexteram* or *in manibus* of the promisee.[58] The
promise was a real one in the Church courts. And *fides* was not
necessarily a fiction.

This importance of the promise is clearest in those ecclesiastical
causes in which the defendant admitted the existence of a debt but
denied having promised to pay it. The outcome of the cause
depended on the latter point. So, for instance, when William
Hyham, before London's Commissary court in 1481, confessed that
he owed Roger Constabill 21s. 10d., but showed that he had not

[56] Canterbury Deposition book X.10.1, f. 23r (1410): " Per fidem meam illam
convencionem quam tecum feci fideliter observabo si deus dederit mihi vitam."
Note that under the canon law the *fidei datio* was equivalent to an oath taken
on a sacred object. *e.g.*, Lyndwood, *Provinciale*, 110 s.v. *et inspectis*:
" Juramentum obliget ipsum jurantem, sive fiat per Deum, sive per librum
sacrorum Evangeliorum, . . . vel cum fidei interpositione: nam per fidei
interpositionem obligatur sic jurans."
[57] *Ibid.* f. 115r (1418): " Per fidem meam fideliter vobis solvam citra festum
sancti Michaelis proximum dictas pencunias." Other examples: Exeter
Deposition book MS. Chanter 854/1, p. 124 (1517): " Promisit se sua fide
media et in verbo sacerdotis se observaturum et perimplementurum per omnia
huiusmodi convencionem." London Liber Examinationum MS. 9065,
fols. 13v–14r (1487): " Qui accipiens per manum dexteram juravit per fidem
suam quod dictum promissum vellet fideliter perimplere." York C.P. G 100
(1520–21): the defendant " dyd swere upon a boke that he shuld pay. . . ."
[58] *e.g.*,York C.P. F 58 (1410): " fideliter promittere et per fidem suam iurare
manu sua dextera extensa." Other examples where physical action is
specifically stated: Canterbury Deposition book X.10.1, f. 23r (1410); fols.
86r–86v (1415); fols. 91v–92r (1415); Rochester Act book DRb Pa 2, f. 294v
(1456); York C.P. F 210 (1455).

pledged his faith to pay the sum, he was dismissed.[59] In a York cause of 1521, when the witnesses testified that Simon Weldon had received a black gelding from John Milley, but could not testify to any express promise by Simon to pay for the gelding the judge held for the defendant.[60] The obligation could not be enforced in the Church courts without an actual promise to pay and a giving of faith. The promise was the essence of the *causa fidei laesionis*.

The nature of the promise alleged in early assumpsit seems very like that of the ecclesiastical causes. The action could not be maintained without an express promise. Whatever the theory of damages, assumpsit proper could not be brought without it.[61] And, if the thesis of this article is correct, the evidence of the reality of the sworn promise in *fidei laesio* illuminates some of the darkness surrounding the growth of assumpsit. There is general agreement today that, at first, there was a substantive as well as a formal difference between debt and assumpsit. " The claim on the assumpsit was somehow different from the claim to the debt recited," as Professor Milsom put it. [62] The Common Pleas required the promise to be a real one throughout the sixteenth century. In the King's Bench the promise was real at first, then gradually became fictitious in the second half of the century. It was around this dispute between the courts that *Slade's Case* turned. Looking back from the vantage point of that case, which determined that assumpsit would lie as an alternative to debt and that the promise need not have been a real one, the earlier distinction seems artificial. But the distinction was not necessarily artificial in the middle of the sixteenth century. Looked at forwards, from the point of view of lawyers more familiar with *fidei laesio* than with *Slade's Case*, the distinction makes good sense. It seems entirely natural that contemporaries should have regarded an action grounded on breach of a promise as different in kind from an action grounded on failure to deliver money owed.[63]

[59] London Act book MS. 9064/3, f. 42r. In Canterbury Act book Y.1.5, f. 125r (1456), the defendant admitted " quod emit equum pro marca, de qua solvit vii s., negat tamen fidem se fecisse pro dimidia marca." In York C.P. G 7 (1503), the defendant answered the position which alleged that he had faithfully promised to observe the compromise award to be made: " Credit compromissum et negat fidei dationem." In Rochester Act book DRb Pa 1, f. 112r (1439), the defendant " dicendo et litem contestando negat quod nunquam prestitit sibi fidem ob aliquam causam."

[60] C.P. G 123 John Nowson, one of the witnesses, deposed that he "bene novit quod dictus magister Simon rector habuit et occupavit unum equum nigrum vocatum spadonem qui fuit dicti domini Johannis, sed an promisit solucionem, quantum vel ad quem terminum, nescit deponere."

[61] Ames, *Lectures* 149.

[62] *Historical Foundations*, 300–301; See also Hans Julius Wolff, " Debt and Assumpsit in the Light of Comparative Legal History," (1966) 1 Irish Jurist [n.s.], 316.

[63] *Brooke's Abridgement*, s.v. *accion sur le case*, no. 5: " Un home est endetted a moy et il promes de payer davant Michelmas ieo puis aver accion de det

It is not clear, however, that assumpsit ever required the *fidei datio* which was a necessary part of the ecclesiastical cause. Certainly there is no evidence to suggest that an unsworn promise was treated differently from a sworn promise. Pleading in assumpsit did, however, always include an allegation that the defendant *fideliter promisit*. This phrase was added to the simple allegation that the defendant *super se assumpsit* of pre-1500 delictual assumpsit.[64] They were used together. The " faithful promise " was an invariable part of assumpsit as soon as that action began to be used regularly to enforce promises. It was also, as shown above, common form in the Church courts.[65] Whether or not there was any truth behind the use of the word *fideliter* in assumpsit, as there was in the Church courts, is now impossible to say. The reality is hidden behind the general issue. There is no secular equivalent to the depositions used in the ecclesiastical courts to tell us. But the identity of language is clear. If we subtract the *super se assumpsit* from the pleading in the royal courts, the promises look much the same.

The third aspect of similarity between pleading in assumpsit and in *fidei laesio* is the allegation of the plaintiff's request to the defendant to fulfil the obligation and of the defendant's express refusal to do so. The breach was set out in the same way. In a typical case brought to enforce a promise between buyer and seller, the defendant was described as having been *sepius requisitus* to pay by the plaintiff. And the pleading specified that the defendant *recusavit*. Too much, probably, should not be made of the use of the same words. Similar language was used in other actions in the royal courts. And it is not certain that the actual making of the request and the refusal were prerequisites to bringing either assumpsit or a *causa fidei laesionis*. Witnesses in the Church court were sometimes asked whether or not the request had been made, but it is hard to find any evidence beyond this to suggest that it was legally required.[66] And the formal sentences hide by their

sur le contract ou accion del case sur le promise et issint ceo est in divers respects, car sur le promyse ne gist accion de det."
[64] Kiralfy, *Action on the Case*, 166, where *promisit* is described as " an old mercantile form."
[65] It is probably the most common language used in the surviving depositions and positions, but the phrase *promisit fide sua media* was also often used. Sometimes they were used together; *e.g.*, York C.P. G 7 (1503): " fide sua media fideliter promiserunt et iurarunt."
[66] *e.g.*, Canterbury Act book X.1.1, f. 79r (1452), in which part of the deposition of Thomas Baron reads: " Interrogatus an dictus Willelmus Gold requisivit dictum Johannem Danyell ad observandum fidem suam et solvendum dictam summam, dicit quod sic. Interrogatus quomodo scit quod requisivit eum, dicit quod presens erat quando interpellavit eum, et iste Johannes Danyell recusavit et sic credit quod violavit fidem suam." In a cause recorded in London MS. 9065, fols. 166v–167r (1493), one witness testified that "dictus

blankness the actual reason for the judge's decision. A sentence for the defendant in a Church court normally said only that the plaintiff had failed in proving his case, not the specific element which had not been proved.[67] The reason for a judge's decision was not made part of the record. The evidence on this point is also unclear for early assumpsit.[68] The similarity in the form of the pleadings, however, is undeniable.

III

In these three ways of pleading the agreement assumpsit and *fidei laesio* suits were the same in substance. Two things principally distinguished them: the nature of the damage alleged and the remedy available. It is well known that when assumpsit began to be used in cases of nonfeasance in the sixteenth century, the allegations of deceit and tortious damage used in medieval assumpsit and appropriate in cases of misfeasance, did not drop out of the pleadings.[69] They continued to be used alongside the newer elements. The pleadings thus commonly alleged that the defendant had acted " heedlessly of his promise and undertaking, and falsely and craftily scheming to deceive and defraud." Where appropriate the deceit included alienation of the subject matter of the promise, thus compounding the fault and rendering it impossible for the defendant to carry out the promise. Most assumpsit actions also included the allegation of lost reputation and profits. The plaintiff's reputation was " hurt and damaged in various ways towards divers of the king's subjects." This credit was especially damaged with one of his creditors to whom he had promised the money owed on the faith that the defendant would faithfully carry out his promise. He was commonly said to have lost " divers gains, profits and benefits in buying, selling and lawfully bargaining." There was some variation

---

Willelmus Plumbe requisivit dictum Ricardum de satisfaciendo promissum suum." But in a breach of faith cause brought by Laurence Ashford against Henry Crouche in the Commissary court at Canterbury the depositions show no sign that the witnesses were examined about the request. Deposition book X.10.1, f. 23r (1410).

[67] *e.g.,* York C.P. G 123 (1512). The formal sentence reads simply: " In dei nomine amen. Quia per acta inactitata deducta preposita exhibita allegata confessata et probata, invenimus et comperimus evidenter predictam partem actricem intencionem suam in iudicio deductam sufficienter [non] fundasse et probasse ac predictam partem ream fidem sive iuramentum suum in hac parte [non] violasse, idcirco . . ."

[68] See *Banks* v. *Thwaits* (1578) 3 Leo. 73, where it was held that the request was traversable, and *Estrigge* v. *Owles* (1588) 3 Leo. 200, where it was held that in indebitatus assumpsit the request was necessary " as the request is not any cause of the action."

[69] See S. F. C. Milsom, "Not Doing is No Trespass " [1954] C.L.J. 105; Ames, *Lectures on Legal History,* 129–148.

in the way in which these tortious elements were stated.[70] And most quickly became, if they were not already by mid-sixteenth century, largely fictitious. But the allegations continued to be made. The defendant's conduct in assumpsit was said to have been intended to deceive and harm the plaintiff. The damages alleged to have been suffered were secular, and usually financial.

Neither of these was true in *fidei laesio*. The language about wicked conduct and deceitful intent, which sounds ecclesiastical in tone, was not found in *fidei laesio*. The allegations of damage in the libels used in ecclesiastical causes were general and compressed compared to assumpsit. The only wording close to the allegations in assumpsit about the defendant's wickedness was a general statement that he had imperilled his soul. The defendant was commonly said to have acted " to the grave danger of his soul and the pernicious example of many others." [71] The emphasis was, in other words, placed on the spiritual dangers to the defendant inherent in breaking his sworn promise. No intent to deceive or to defraud was alleged. *Fidei laesio* jurisdiction, it should be remembered, existed under the canon law because it was a sin to violate one's oath. This continued to be stated in court documents, even where what seems to us to have been at issue in a cause was a simple commercial obligation.

Pleading in *fidei laesio* did, however, include an allegation of harm to the plaintiff. He was commonly said to have suffered " great prejudice, damage and grievance " as a consequence of the defendant's non-performance.[72] But this statement was always brief and formally stated. It incorporated no allegation that the defendant had intended any fraud or deceit. And the detailed recitation of harm to the plaintiff's reputation and his loss of profits was never a part of the ecclesiastical cause. Emphasis in *fidei laesio* was, in other words, placed on the promise, not on the fraudulent conduct of the defendant. To put the matter in more modern terminology, the *fidei laesio* cause concentrated on the formation and non-fulfilment of the contract. Assumpsit always incorporated these when used to enforce obligations in the sixteenth century. But it also incorporated express allegations of tortious conduct and secular damages, often set out at great length. The

---

[70] Kiralfy, *Action on the Case*, 89.

[71] The allegation was not necessarily regarded as untrue. In York C.P. F 23 (1402), the deposition of one witness records that "dicta Alicia fidem suam erga dictum Thomam in magnum dampnum et preiudicium ipsius Thome temere et notorie scienter violavit in anime sue grave periculum ut dicit iuratus iste in suo iuramento." Lyndwood, *Provinciale*, 110 s.v. *et inspectis*, also treats breach of the promise as a real danger to one's soul.

[72] York C.P. G 123 (1521): " ... ac supradicti domini Johannis preiudicium dampnum non modicum et gravamen."

plaintiff in a breach of faith cause alleged only the violation of a spiritual obligation and the presence of injury to the plaintiff.

The greatest theoretical contrast between assumpsit and *fidei laesio* lay, of course, in the remedy available. Assumpsit offered damages consequent upon the defendant's non-performance of his promise. *Fidei laesio* offered specific performance of the sworn promise and, if appropriate, public penance. A fairly typical Act book entry from Hereford ends: " And the judge ordered [the defendant] to observe this promise and faith before the aforesaid day under pain of major excommunication." [73] A defendant at York who disputed the obligation was given a day to show cause " why he should not be compelled to observe the agreement." [74]

Public penance also was in routine use in the Church courts in breach of faith causes. In another cause from Hereford, for example, the defendant confessed the breach of his sworn promise and was assigned four public whippings as penance.[75] In another York cause, a defendant was ordered to march in the parish procession on three successive Sundays wearing penitential garb and carrying a candle, which he was to offer on the high altar.[76] But it is impossible to be sure why public penance was ordered in some instances and specific performance in others. Woodcock's explanation that penance was used as an experiment at Canterbury between 1500 and 1511, with specific performance always being awarded before and after that period will not hold up in other dioceses.[77] Both were used during the same periods.[78] The nature of the promise, the defendant's own willingness or ability to fulfil an order of specific performance, and the discretion of the judge may well have been the determinants.[79] On a rare occasion, it is

---

[73] Act book I/2, p. 49 (1497): " Et iudex precepit eidem observare huiusmodi promissionem et fidem citra predictos dies sub pena excommunicationis maioris una cum expensis." This result was clearly one sanctioned by the canon law. See *gl. ord.* ad Sext 2.11.2 s.v. *licet.*

[74] Act book Cons. A B 6, f. 86r (1510): " quare non debeat compelli ad observacionem dicte composicionis." See also Edward Fry, " Specific Performance and *Laesio Fidei*," (1889) 5 L.Q.R. 235, at 241.

[75] Act book I/4, p. 7 (1508).

[76] C.P. F 210 (1465).

[77] *Medieval Ecclesiastical Courts in the Diocese of Canterbury*, 90–1. But *cf.* Canterbury Act book Y.1.17, f. 27r (1497), in which there was actual performance specified, and *ibid.* f. 35v (1497), in which it was public penance. This seems to me to throw some additional doubt on Woodcock's explanation.

[78] *e.g.*, compare Chichester Act book Ep I/10/1, f. 3r (1506), in which public penance was awarded, and *ibid.* f. 12r (1506), in which there was an order to fulfil the promise to pay.

[79] That the defendant's own attitude played a role is occasionally suggested by the language of the records; *e.g.*, Rochester Act book DRb Pa 1, f. 342v (1443), where the defendant was "monitus ad solvendum . . . sub pena excommunicacionis maioris, quod facere sponte promisit et iuravit." Ely Act book EDR D/2/1, f. 67v (1377), in which after the order, the sentence adds " ad quam solucionem bene et fideliter faciendam tactis sacrosanctis dicta Cristina corporale prestitit iuramentum."

possible to suggest a reason. In a cause heard at Chichester in 1506, the promise was that the defendant would act as a servant for the plaintiff for an agreed salary.[80] The award of public penance which was made in this case may have reflected a court's reluctance to enforce specifically a contract of personal service. But this explanation has, perhaps, too modern a ring. And in most instances it is simply impossible even to hazard a guess since the formal sentences, as opposed to the Act books, never themselves made clear what the remedy would be. They state only that the defendant was " to be punished as a perjurer." [81] The Act books alone show the availability of specific performance. But the contractual nature of the remedy in most *fidei laesio* causes, and the basic difference in theory between them and assumpsit is clear.

It is, however, questionable how important the difference would have been to most prospective litigants. Usually the plaintiff was a seller of goods. He wanted the buyer to pay what he had promised to pay, plus expenses. If, as seems to have been the case, the measure of damages in assumpsit was normally close to the agreed purchase price then it would have made little difference in practice which remedy was used.[82] The Church courts awarded expenses to a victorious plaintiff. Sometimes these expenses amounted to significant sums, as in a Lichfield cause of 1467 in which £4 was awarded.[83] Sometimes the size of expenses actually exceeded the amount of the debt, as in a Canterbury cause heard in 1461 in which only 18d. was at issue, but the expenses were taxed at 3s.[84] Where this was true, an order to pay the amount of the original debt, plus a not insignificant sum as expenses, may well have been very close to the normal amount of damages in assumpsit.

IV

Examination of the court records thus shows that in framing his claim a plaintiff in both assumpsit and a breach of faith cause alleged a consideration, a promise, and a breach which were sub-

---

[80] Ep I/10/1, f. 3r.

[81] *e.g.*, at Canterbury where, as Woodcock shows, the order to fulfil the promise was used, a formal sentence still reads: " Nos commissarius antedictus prefatum N. fidem suam et iuramentum suum prestitum temere violasse et periurium incurrisse et pro suo periurio et fidei lesione canonice puniri pronunciamus et declaramus, ipsumque N. sic ut premittitur periurium et fidei sue violatorem denunciandum fore decernimus ..." (Taken from Act book Y.1.5, f. 40r (1454). The caution of the language may result from the desire to avoid writs of prohibition. See Lyndwood, *Provinciale*, 315 s.v. *perjurio*.

[82] Kiralfy, *Action on the Case*, 167–168.

[83] Act book B/C/1/1, f. 136v.

[84] Act book Y.1.7, f. 104r; on the other hand a cause in which the promise was to pay 40s. had expenses taxed at 10d. in *ibid.* f. 148v (1462).

stantially similar. The plaintiff's allegation of damage and the remedy he demanded were different. Assumpsit resembled *fidei laesio*, in other words, in its contractual side. It was unlike the ecclesiastical cause in containing elements of tort.

Apart from formal similarity, there is also a striking connection between the incidence of the two actions in actual court practice. In looking at the sorts of promises involved in assumpsit and *fidei laesio*, we noted that although most of the causes brought in the Church courts concerned sums of money too small to have been cognisable in assumpsit, some of them were large enough to have been brought in the royal courts. Most breach of faith causes were brought for less than 40s. But some were brought for promises to pay amounts of up to at least £20.[85] And most assumpsit actions dealt with similarly small amounts of money. As to a small but real part of the breach of faith causes brought in the Church courts, therefore, the sums at issue were very like the typical sums at issue in assumpsit in the royal courts.

The hypothesis that a part of the breach of faith litigation in the Church courts could easily have been brought under assumpsit is borne out by the following tables of incidence of the two actions in the ecclesiastical and royal courts. The first table shows the number of *fidei laesio* causes brought in the consistory court of the five dioceses for which the records are complete enough to yield more than isolated statistics. All figures are for a one-year period, although the nature of the records has made it necessary to start in the middle of the year in some dioceses. Where feasible more than one year is included and an average figure has been used.[86]

YEAR(S)	BREACH OF FAITH CAUSES PER YEAR	TOTAL CAUSES PER YEAR
	Canterbury	
1495	200	350
1528	41	161
1534	9	105
1545	4	77
1551	0	160
	Hereford	
1497–98	49	88

[85] *Supra*, nn. 18-23; see also J. L. Barton, *Roman Law in England*, 94–95.
[86] With the exception of the 1495 total from Canterbury, which is taken from Woodcock, *Medieval Ecclesiastical Courts in the Diocese of Canterbury*, 84, all figures have been drawn from my own counting in the relevant Act books. Only causes introduced in a year are included, not the total number of causes in which any part of the process occurred during that year.

Year(s)	Breach Of Faith Causes Per Year	Total Causes Per Year
	Hereford—cont.	
1509–10	9	66
1536–37	2·5	89
1552–53	0	120
	Lichfield	
1476	27	102
1531	3	68
1547	0	60
1561	0	151
	Chichester	
Oct. 1506–Oct. 1507	38	78
Jan. 1524–Jan. 1525	11	53
Jan. 1535–Jan. 1536	2	21
Oct. 1556–Oct. 1557	1	55
Jan. 1565–Jan. 1566	0	63
	Exeter	
Sept. 1513–Sept. 1517	11	65
Nov. 1533–Nov. 1534	3	75
Sept. 1561–Sept. 1562	0	unavailable

The figures tell a remarkably similar story for every diocese. *Fidei laesio* reached (or retained) a high level of use in the late fifteenth century.[87] By the second decade of the sixteenth century, there had been a marked decline, but breach of faith causes were still being heard. By the 1550s and 1560s the Church's jurisdiction over these causes was gone. There is no guarantee, of course, that the above figures are representative of all English dioceses. In fact, there is reason to believe that breach of faith disappeared earlier from the Norwich Act books.[88] But the dioceses taken as a sample do not represent only one region of England. And the records of other dioceses, although less complete, are generally consistent with

[87] Incomplete evidence suggests that the jurisdiction grew considerably in the fifteenth century. See Woodcock, *ibid.* 84; Donahue, " Roman Canon Law in the Medieval English Church," 660; and the Ely Act book EDR D/2/1 (1374–82), which contains a smaller proportion of *fidei laesio* causes than most books of the next century. Unfortunately, no fifteenth century records survive for Ely.

[88] R. A. Houlbrooke, " Church Courts and People in the Diocese of Norwich, 1519–1570," (unpub. Oxford D. Phil. thesis 1970), 45. There is a breach of faith cause recorded in Norwich [Norfolk Record Office, Norwich Public Library] Act book ACT/1, f. 254v (1512). But the Norwich Act books do not always contain the subject of the causes introduced there so that a generalisation about incidence is questionable.

the story told by the figures given above. The last breach of faith cause found at York, for example, comes from 1542.[89] It seems fair to conclude that, as a practical matter, the Church's jurisdiction over *fidei laesio* was in serious decline by the 1520s and had disappeared by 1550.

Figures drawn from the plea rolls of the Court of King's Bench are not quite the reverse of the downward curve in the Church's jurisdiction. But they are not far from it. Below is a table of the number of assumpsit actions brought in the Court of King's Bench.[90] Again, all figures are either for a one year period or are the yearly average.

YEAR(S)	ASSUMPSIT ENTRIES	NUMBER FOR MONEY
1490	0	0
1525–29	6·6	1
1536–40	14·2	9·2
1549	45·0	21·0
1559	98·0	78·0

Too much should not be claimed for these figures. They do not show the rise in total number of actions of all sorts brought. And they do not include litigation in the Common Pleas, in which assumpsit was less frequent.[91] But they are good enough, I believe, to show the growth of assumpsit as a regular means of enforcing informal promises. By 1560, the number had not reached uncountable proportions. But assumpsit was in regular use. 30 years before it had been an occasional thing. And 30 years before that it had been a rarity. The exact opposite is true of *fidei laesio* in the Church courts. There was a period, during the late 1520s and the 1530s, when the Church courts' jurisdiction had declined seriously and when assumpsit was not yet established in the King's Bench as an ordinary remedy. But, if that be taken as a " transitional period," it is literally true that assumpsit rose while *fidei laesio* fell.

---

[89] C.P. G 306. The records for Rochester are not complete enough to give accurate figures, but the Act books of the fifteenth century all include breach of faith causes. The Act book containing the record of 1579 (DRb Pa 12), however, contains none. The same is true of Ely, where there is a gap in the Act books between 1382 and 1580 (Comparing EDR D/2/1 with D/2/12).

[90] I am indebted to Dr. J. H. Baker for the figures from 1525–29 and 1536–40, as well as for several helpful talks about the subject of this article. The other figures have been taken from the following plea rolls: K.B. 27/914, 915, 916, 917; K.B. 27/1149, 1150, 1151, 1152; and K.B. 27/1189, 1190, 1191, 1192. Again, only the total number of cases introduced, not total number of entries, has been used. K.B. 27/1183 (Trin. 1557), however, produced 45 nonfeasance entries, a higher number than any of my figures. See Milsom, *Historical Foundations*, 287.

[91] Milsom, *Historical Foundations*, 287; Kiralfy, *Action on the Case*, 195–196.

V

This is the evidence which suggests a connection between *fidei laesio* and assumpsit. A few comments may be appropriate in conclusion. The strongest piece of evidence is probably the last presented: the fact that *fidei laesio* disappeared at the same time assumpsit began to be commonly used in the royal courts. The other evidence might be the product of chance, caused by the limited number of ways in which all contracts are entered into and by the few appropriate forms in which suits for their breach can be pleaded. But that some of the amounts claimed in breach of faith causes were large enough to have been brought in the royal courts, coupled with this coincidence in time, suggests strongly that claims on broken promises which would have been brought in the Church courts in the 1490s were being brought in the royal courts by the 1550s. This cannot be proved beyond doubt. But it seems very likely.

If this is true, then the similarity in pleading between assumpsit and *fidei laesio* may be more than simple coincidence. It is at least possible that the Common lawyers were influenced by the way in which the ecclesiastical cause was formulated when they drew up the bills by which assumpsit was most commonly brought in the King's Bench. The ecclesiastical cause set out the contractual side substantially identically with the way it would be pleaded in assumpsit. It was the contractual element of assumpsit that was new in the sixteenth century.[92] The older delictual assumpsit, which stretches back to the *Humber Ferry Case*, did not emphasise, or even contain, the elements of the contractual side of assumpsit. The introduction of the emphasis on contract in the assumpsit of the early sixteenth century may reflect a borrowing from the canon law of an already existing theory of the enforcement of promises. It cannot have been a lifting whole. The language used in pleading was not identical. But the theory was there, enforced in the practice of every consistory court in England. Is it not natural to think that it played some part in the rise of assumpsit?

This argument is, to be sure, conjectural. However, it is slightly less conjectural than the connection which has been suggested between assumpsit and the Chancellor's willingness to enforce informal agreements in the fifteenth century. The argument, advanced by several writers, but most thoroughly and persuasively by W. T. Barbour, is that the clerical Chancellors asserted " the power of which they had been shorn as ecclesiastics " by enforcing

There was a jump from 19 to 42 in number of assumpsit entries on the King's Bench plea rolls for one term between 1559 and 1566, however.
[92] Ames, *Lectures*, 129–166.

contracts under principles derived ultimately from canon law.[93] The Common Law courts took over the jurisdiction in the expansion of the contractual side of assumpsit during the sixteenth century. There was, in other words, an " indirect reception " of the canonical *fidei laesio* coming through the Chancery.

This argument may be correct. It is inherently more probable that the Common lawyers would have taken models from the Court of Chancery in which many of them practised, than from ecclesiastical courts, in which they did not. But the argument does not take into account the continued vitality of the Church's jurisdiction over breach of faith well into the sixteenth century. Barbour thought that *fidei laesio* had long since disappeared from the ecclesiastical tribunals by the late fifteenth century. He had, therefore, to discount any but an indirect connection. But the continuance of the Church's jurisdiction and coincidence in time between the decline of *fidei laesio* and the rise of assumpsit makes it possible that the connection was a direct one. As long as the Common lawyers had any knowledge of the existence and nature of breach of faith causes in the Church courts, any influence need not have been mediated through the Chancery.

Also, Barbour's argument does not recognise that assumpsit paralleled *fidei laesio* in form more closely than it did the contracts enforced in Chancery practice. This is clear from the Act books surveyed in this article and from Barbour's own research. First, the petition in Chancery could be identical with an action of debt. The power of the defendant, or the poverty of the plaintiff served as a reason for jurisdiction, even if the claim was formally identical with an action of debt.[94] Second, written obligations were often introduced in suits brought in Chancery. The contracts enforced there are not in practice limited to parol agreements.[95] Third, and most important, no express promise had to be alleged in Chancery. That the defendant *fideliter promisit* was a necessary allegation only in assumpsit and *fidei laesio*, not in Chancery practice. Relief there was granted because the conduct of the parties had made it unfair not to redress an inequity between them.[96] " Reason and conscience " provided the foundation for relief, not the existence of a

---

[93] *The History of Contract in Early English Equity*, 163–168; O. W. Holmes, " Early English Equity," (1885) 1 L.Q.R. 162, at 173–174. It was this view of " indirect reception " that Ames attacked. See *Lectures*, 124. The state of the question has not been materially altered since 1914, although Dr. Helmut Coing has added to it. See "English Equity and the Denunciatio Evangelica of the Canon Law," (1955) 71 L.Q.R. 223. See generally Fifoot, *History and Sources of the Common Law*, 301–307.
[94] Barbour, *History of Contract in Early English Equity*, 78, 98–100.
[95] *Ibid.* 84–97.
[96] *Ibid.* 107: " The promise is implied from the circumstances of the case." See also Ames, *Lectures*, 126.

promise. None of these characteristics was found in the pleading of early assumpsit. Although many of the claims enforced in Chancery were in fact identical to those enforced in assumpsit, the invariably close parallel between pleading in a breach of faith cause and in assumpsit did not exist. The Chancellor's jurisdiction in the fifteenth century was broader and less closely tied to the contractual elements which are identifiable in every action of assumpsit and in every *causa fidei laesionis*.

The evidence seems therefore to point to a more direct connection between the canon law and the growth of assumpsit than has previously been thought. The transition to which Ames pointed many years ago whereby assumpsit, originally sounding only in tort, came " by a natural transition " to be regarded as arising *ex contractu* may owe something to the breach of faith causes heard in the ecclesiastical courts.[97] It is well to echo here the words of Barbour. The connection is " not demonstrable with mathematical precision." There is no *direct* evidence to prove it. It depends on the comparison of similarities in surviving records. But examination of the records makes it very likely that such a relationship existed.

The transition from *fidei laesio* to assumpsit is a matter of more than strictly legal history. It is an instance of the secularisation in men's attitudes which occurred during the late fifteenth and sixteenth centuries. What had created a religious obligation as late as 1500 gave rise to a secular cause of action by the time of the breach with Rome. This fact is of real consequence for our understanding of the nature of the English Reformation; the secularisation in attitude towards obligations occurred prior to the Henrician reforms in Church and State. The decline of vitality of *fidei laesio* in the ecclesiastical courts happened before the years when direct pressure was put on the Church by Henry VIII's government. The loss of the Church's jurisdiction was not the consequence of an Act of State. Rather, it reflected a natural decline. The transition to assumpsit may then have been the work of lawyers confronted with the problem of enforcing obligations, and faced with a situation in which *fidei laesio* jurisdiction was a less acceptable means of enforcing them than it had previously been.

This theme of social and religious history is, of course, a different story from the argument advanced by this article. It must be taken up elsewhere, when other evidence from the Church court records and from the plea rolls can be used and when its implications

---

[97] Ames, *Lectures*, 144; the argument of this article is, of course, incompatible with Ames' position. See *Holmes-Pollock Letters*, 2nd ed. (Cambridge, Mass. 1961), I, 144–146.

can be considered in more detail. For the moment, the evidence suggests that the growth of the Common Law represented by the development of assumpsit for nonfeasance was accomplished through assimilation by the royal courts of a remedy once available in another jurisdiction. This is not a new theme. But it is surprising to find that the evidence points so directly to an ecclesiastical source.

15

BANKRUPTCY AND PROBATE JURISDICTION BEFORE 1571

I. INTRODUCTION

For a student of the law of probate and legal history, an invitation to contribute to a volume of essays in honor of Professor William F. Fratcher is hard to decline. Few scholars have moved as easily and as successfully between current problems relating to the devolution of property at death and their historical antecedents. Professor Fratcher has also illuminated, on more than one occasion, the role that the English ecclesiastical courts have played in the development of modern probate law.[1] This Article attempts to carry this work forward by investigating the earliest kind of English bankruptcy, that first exercised within the probate jurisdiction of the ecclesiastical courts. It is based primarily on examination of the surviving manuscript records of these courts, records which are teaching us a great deal about the place of probate jurisdiction in the development of modern law.[2]

---

1. *See, e.g.*, Fratcher, *Fiduciary Administration in England*, 40 N.Y.U. L. REV. 12, 67-71 (1965); Fratcher, *Sovereign Immunity in Probate Proceedings*, 31 MO. L. REV. 127, 135-36 (1966).

2. The diocesan court records examined in the preparation of this Article consist principally of act books, i.e., official records of procedure in every cause that came before each consistory court. Those examined, with corresponding modern archives, are the following:

Canterbury	Library of the Dean and Chapter, Canterbury.
Chichester	West Sussex Record Office, Chichester.
Ely	Ely Diocesan Records, The University Library, Cambridge.
Gloucester	Gloucestershire Record Office, Gloucester.
Hereford	Hereford County Record Office, Hereford.
London	Guildhall Library, London.
Norwich	Norfolk Record Office, Norwich.
Rochester	Kent County Record Office, Maidstone.
St. Alban's	Hertfordshire Record Office, Hertford.
Winchester	Hampshire Record Office, Winchester.

Those records show conclusively that English bankruptcy practice has antecedents and perhaps even roots in the canon law administered by the Church courts. Although none of the standard accounts of the subject recognizes the relevance, or even the existence, of the jurisdiction of ecclesiastical courts,[3] examination of the records of those courts demonstrates that essential aspects of the law of bankruptcy were in use in England before the first secular legislation on the subject was enacted in the sixteenth century. All current treatments of the subject begin with the Tudor statutes,[4] principally the statute enacted in 1571. In fact, however, there was something worthy of note before then.

That no legal historian has ever raised the possibility that probate bankruptcy jurisdiction was exercised by the ecclesiastical courts may be cause for mild surprise. It is a reasonable assumption that the Church might have developed rules for dealing with estates of men who died with assets insufficient to pay their debts. Not only did the Church long exercise probate jurisdiction in England, but the ecclesiastical courts also once dealt with all sorts of debt claims brought by and against the estates of decedents.[5] Prior to the sixteenth century, they were accustomed to evaluating and settling the rights of creditors against executors and administrators. Since the royal courts in practice conceded this probate jurisdiction to the Church courts, there was no impediment to the development of rules for insolvent estates.

Moreover, it is also a reasonable assumption that the lack of any secular law of bankruptcy prior to the Tudor period would have augmented the number of insolvencies to be settled on death. Probate courts would inevitably have had to deal somehow with sorting out the resulting claims. Even the social attitudes of an earlier day might have suggested the appropriateness of the Church's jurisdiction over bankrupt estates. In medieval England, a man's death bed was often a place for reckoning up what he owed and what he was owed. Anxiety about one's fate in the next world often led men to want their debts clearly set down and to ensure that payment was

---

For purposes of this Article, each case is referred to under the name of the decedent, i.e., "Estate of *N.*" This terminology is modern, and it is adopted here only as a convenience to the reader in locating and making reference to the original documents. A printed edition of one of the act books of the kind used in this Article is THE COURTS OF THE ARCHDEACONRY OF BUCKINGHAM, 1485-1523 (19 Buckinghamshire Record Society, E. Elvey ed. 1975). *See also* B. WOODCOCK, MEDIEVAL ECCLESIASTICAL COURTS IN THE DIOCESE OF CANTERBURY (1952).

3. *See* 1 W. HOLDSWORTH, A HISTORY OF ENGLISH LAW 470-73 (7th ed. 1956); W. JONES, THE FOUNDATIONS OF ENGLISH BANKRUPTCY: STATUTES AND COMMISSIONS IN THE EARLY MODERN PERIOD (1979); J. MACLACHLAN, HANDBOOK OF THE LAW OF BANKRUPTCY § 26, at 20 (1956); Levinthal, *The Early History of Bankruptcy Law*, 66 U. PA. L. REV. 223 (1918).

4. 34 & 35 Hen. 8, ch. 4; 13 Eliz. ch. 5, 7.

5. The evidence on this point is laid out infra 307-21.

made as fairly as their assets permitted.[6] What the records of the ecclesiastical courts reveal about the existence of probate bankruptcy jurisdiction should therefore come as no great surprise.

II. INITIATION OF BANKRUPTCY PROCEDURE

The evidence clearly shows the existence of probate bankruptcy before enactment of the Tudor legislation. Its frequency is less easy to estimate with confidence. The records are insufficient here, and at several other points, to yield unimpeachable conclusions. But one piece of evidence does suggest the prevalence of probate bankruptcy: the frequency with which executors named in the testaments of decedents disclaimed their executorships. Executors were subject to at least the possibility of being held personally liable for the debts of the man whose estate they administered,[7] and when they feared an excess of claims over available assets the safest course appears to have been to refuse the office. So, for example, in 1473 before the consistory court of the diocese of Rochester, John Turk, the executor nominated in the testament of Stephan Brown, "refused to take upon himself the burden of execution of this testament out of fear of the creditors, because the goods were insufficient for payment of the debts."[8]

Working through the act books of the Church courts produces many such entries. An executor at Lichfield in 1540 renounced his responsibility "because the decedent was and is greatly weighed down by debt."[9] A London man refused executorship in 1512 "because of the excessive debts in which the same decedent was indebted at the time of her death."[10] Some entries verge on the colorful, such as the executrix who refused to act "be-

---

6. This assertion is based on the examination of numerous depositions in testamentary causes. They often record the circumstances surrounding the making of testaments, e.g., Estate of John Pope, Canterbury Deposition book X.10.1, f. 69v (1415), in which a witness deposed that the scribe "scripsit certa debita dicti Pope tempore mortis sue aut modicum ante."

7. *See generally* R. GOFFIN, THE TESTAMENTARY EXECUTOR IN ENGLAND AND ELSEWHERE 52-55 (1901); A. SIMPSON, A HISTORY OF THE COMMON LAW OF CONTRACT 559 (1975).

8. Estate of Stephen Brown, Rochester Act book DRb Pa 4, f. 16r (1473): ". . . recusavit onus executionis huiusmodi testamenti in se suscipere propter metum creditorum quia bona non sufficiunt ad solucionem debitorum."

9. Estate of Gregory Fyderne, Probate Act book B/C/10/2, f. 63r (1540): ". . . quia predictus Gregorius defunctus erat et est ere alieno multum aggravatus et aliis legitimis causis."

10. Estate of Agnes Elham, London Probate Act book MS. 9168/4, f. 1r: ". . . propter excessiva debita in quibus idem defuncta mortis sue tempore etc. fuerat indebitata expresse renunciavit etc." For the diocese of London generally, see R. WUNDERLI, LONDON CHURCH COURTS AND SOCIETY ON THE EVE OF THE REFORMATION 115 (1981).

cause of the cruelty of the creditors,"[11] or the executors who renounced their position because of the "multitude"[12] or even the "uncertainty"[13] of the existence of creditors with claims against the estate. No reason for refusing executorship appears more often in the remaining act books than this one. Although not invariably followed by actual bankruptcy, that likelihood dominated the minds of enough executors to have left a significant mark in the records.

The consequence of these disclaimers was normally less in practice than might be thought. Evidently designed to prevent even the possibility of personal liability, disclaimer usually changed only the form of the administration. Technically, the decedent was declared intestate, since a willing executor was necessary for testation, but in practice administration was conceded to carry out the decedent's last wishes insofar as possible. Modern administration c.t.a. is a descendant of medieval practice. This meant another grant of administration, even if in a slightly altered form, and the actual testament was followed as closely as the claims against the decedent's estate would allow. The ecclesiastical officials very often committed administration to the same person who had just disclaimed formal executorship. A typical entry reads, "The executors of the testament of John Hevyn . . . refused to assume the burden of execution of the testament etc., nevertheless to them is committed administration of all goods of the said decedent, dying intestate."[14] Here only the name "executor" was refused; administration would proceed normally.

What renunciation did principally was set the stage for bankruptcy of the estate. The last wishes of the decedent expressed in his testament could not be carried out under the canon law if this meant the defrauding of creditors. This principle resulted in several variations from normal probate practice.

First, the oath sworn by the personal representative took a slightly different form. All men and women who administered estates in whatever capacity were required to swear a formal oath to administer faithfully, i.e.,

---

11. Estate of Peter Bolcham, Rochester Act book DRb Pa 2, f. 164r (1451): ". . . propter crudelitatem creditorum et insufficienciam bonorum."

12. Estate of Roger Chip, Rochester Act book DRb Pa 2, f. 96v (1448).

13. Estate of Margaret Crofton, London Probate Act book MS. 9168/1, f. 93v (1498).

14. Estate of John Hevyn, Hereford Act book 0/13, p. 187 (1479): "Elizabeth relicta eiusdem et Ricardus filius dicti defuncti comparuerunt et recusarunt expresse subire onus execucionis testamenti etc. tamen commissa est eis administracio etc. omnium bonorum dicti defuncti ab intestato decedentis in forma iuris etc." A succinct example from the diocese of Chichester is Estate of William Gysbourne, Act book Ep. III/4/1, f. 99r (1500): "Hac die comparuit Margeria relicta Willelmi Gysbourne et exhibuit testamentum eiusdem Willelmi et renunciavit administracionem eiusdem testamenti et acceptavit in se onus administracionis bonorum dicti defuncti."

to pay the debts and legacies of the person they represented.[15] But when bankruptcy was feared, to this oath was added the proviso, "insofar as the goods may suffice,"[16] or "as far as the goods extend,"[17] or "according to the quantity of the inventory."[18] A late sixteenth century entry from the diocese of Salisbury spelled out this modification fully. The official "charged . . . [the executors'] consciences that if and insofar as sufficient goods shall come into their hands, they should pay" the debts according to the schedule.[19] Their duty was limited accordingly.

Second, the sequestration of the decedent's assets was routinely ordered for bankrupt estates. The evident notion was that in case of insolvency the assets were subject to special risk and required special protection.[20] The act books yield examples of up to three sequestrators being named to protect the goods pending full settlement of the estate,[21] and they also yield *ex officio* prosecutions against persons charged with having violated the order of sequestration.[22] Seemingly no special place or means of sequestration was involved. None is mentioned in the records, and one defendant pleaded that he had no knowledge of the sequestration, suggesting that no physical signs of sequestration had been evident.[23] But some publicity may have been achieved by the order, and the sentence of excommunication which its knowing violation entailed may have provided a safeguard worth having.

Third (though not always limited to cases of insolvency), the ecclesiastical officials required that a public proclamation be made, calling for all creditors of the decedent to appear at a specified time to file their claims.

---

15. *See* the account of ordinary procedure in Jacob, *The Archbishop's Testamentary Jurisdiction*, in MEDIAEVAL RECORDS OF THE ARCHBISHOPS OF CANTERBURY 45-46 (1962). *See generally* M. SHEEHAN, THE WILL IN MEDIEVAL ENGLAND (1963).

16. Estate of John Tebold, Rochester Act book DRb Pa 3, f. 312v (1457): ". . . ad solvendum debita et quatenus bona sufficiant legata in testamento predicto."

17. Estate of Elena Gorwell, Canterbury Act book Y.4.2, f. 102r (1487): "Et iuratus de fideliter administrando quatinus bona extendunt."

18. Estate of John Dawson, Gloucester Vicar General's Act book DLC 330, f. 45r (1523): ". . . solvendoque debita et legata dicti defuncti iuxta vires inventarii."

19. Estate of Raoul Pearce, Office Act book 4, f. 15v (1599): ". . . onerando tamen eorum conscientias si et in quantum bona sufficientia ad eorum manus pervenerint dicti defuncti ad quem pertinebant eandem ratam solvere etc."

20. *E.g.*, Estate of Thomas Dixson, London Probate Act book MS. 9168/9, f. 37v (1539): "Adeo quod dicta Frideswida non audet assumere in se onus executionis dicti testamenti unde dominus ne bona interim pereant etc. sequestravit eadem."

21. *E.g.*, Estate of John Chambyr, Rochester Act book DRb Pa 2, f. 24r (1445).

22. Estate of Laurence Waren, Chester Archdeaconry Act book EDC I/4, f. 80r (1530); Estate of Edward Deux, London Act book MS. 9064/2, f. 245v (1488); Estate of William Gore, Rochester Act book DRb Pa 2, f. 109r (1449).

23. Estate of Edward Deux, London Act book MS. 9064/2, f. 245v (1488): ". . . asserens se non novisse ea fuisse sequestrata." *See also* R. HOULBROOKE, CHURCH COURTS AND THE PEOPLE DURING THE ENGLISH REFORMATION, 1520-1570, at 94 (1979).

For example, this entry from the diocese of Norwich in 1510: Richard San-dryingham, curate at Great Yarmouth, certified that he had, in the parish church, publicly required that "all and singular creditors to whom the . . . [said decedent] stood indebted should appear before his lordship, the official, on . . . [a certain] day to receive their share according to the schedule of goods of the said decedent."[24]

Standard procedure called for three separate proclamations to be made.[25] Normally they occurred in the parish church of the decedent, sometimes also in neighboring parishes, sometimes in the public market, or (in a London case of 1539) at Paul's Cross.[26] As in the Norwich entry, the curate who made the proclamation was required to send certification of the performance of his duty to the official of the consistory court, and, in theory at least, those creditors who failed to appear were foreclosed from making any claim against the estate in the ecclesiastical forum.[27] Thus modern "non-claim" statutes have an evident antecedent in medieval practice. How effective they were—and, in particular, whether they kept creditors from suing the executor separately in a secular court—are not questions to which the surviving records provide even a hint of an answer.[28] We are left to conjecture. What the remaining records do make clear, on the other hand, is the regularity of the proceedings to cite creditors with claims against estates and to protect the assets when there was reason to fear that they would be insufficient to meet the claims.

III. Treatment of the Claims of Creditors

Whatever the practical effect of the foreclosure of further claims after the last proclamation, the next step—the actual filing of creditors' claims with the Church court officials—was a regular and apparently effective pro-

---

24. Act book ACT/1, s.d. 15 January 1509/10: ". . . quod omnes et singuli creditores quibus dicti Willelmus et Robertus indebitati existent quod compareant coram domino officiali istis die et loco suas porciones iuxta ratam bonorum dictorum defunctorum percepturos."

25. *E.g.*, Estate of William Austen, Canterbury Act book Y.4.2, f. 104r (1489) (first proclamation made January 13, the second March 11, and the third March 31). Intervals between the proclamations were normally short.

26. Estate of John Turpyn, London Probate Act book MS. 9168/9, f. 103r (1540): "apud crucem divi Pauli."

27. *E.g.*, Estate of Robert Copratt, Chichester Act book Ep I/10/2, fols. 43v-44 (1520): "Dominus pronunciavit omnes alios non comparentes aliquid de bonis defuncti vendicare contumaces et in penam contumaciarum suarum decrevit eos ulterius non fore audiendos et bona distribuenda inter dictos comparentes iuxta ratam etc."

28. The executor could plead *plene administravit* to a suit on a debt brought in the royal courts, but it is by no means certain that this sufficed to bar the action. The Church courts themselves did not apply the rule inflexibly. In Estate of John Spencer, Chichester Act book EP I/10/2, f. 119r (1520), a new debt claim was entered after formal preclusion of further claims.

cedure. It has left considerable evidence in the surviving records, generally
in the form of lists of claims against the estate. Often they were accompa-
nied in the record by notation of the disposition of each claim. In some
cases the procedure seems to have been extremely simple. William Sevan,
for instance, was the only creditor of the estate of Margery Cherch, who
died in 1460 within the diocese of Rochester. His claim was for 35s., but
when probate and funeral expenses were deducted only 12s. was left in her
estate. This sum was turned over to Sevan.[29] In other cases, however, the
procedure was considerably more complex. When Robert Copratt died
within the diocese of Chichester in 1520, he left at least forty creditors with
aggregate claims of almost £300 against his estate. All their names and the
nature of their claims were entered in the appropriate act book. The assets
available to meet them came to only about £22, and about £13 once necessary deductions had been made. The creditors had to prove their claims,
and even those who did so successfully received only a ratable award of 10d.
on the pound.[30]

A necessary preliminary to the equitable division of assets was, of
course, their collection. Here bankruptcy posed the special problem of
transfers made in fraud of the rights of creditors. The English Church
made special provision for the problem. A provincial constitution, or statute, made in 1343 and known by its first words *Cordis dolore*, declared excommunicate those who participated in such fraudulent transfers.[31] To
avoid the consequences of excommunication and to merit absolution, trans-
ferees were required to return the fruits, i.e., the amount they had received
without giving adequate consideration, to the decedent's estate. *Cordis
dolore* also punished, by denial of Christian burial, the decedent who had
alienated his own property in order to deceive his creditors. One example
of an exhumation order in such a case has survived in the act books.[32]

Cordis dolore covered both outright gifts and transfers made in the form
of a sale but without adequate consideration.[33] The evidence, however,
does not suggest that as part of probate practice the ecclesiastical officials
undertook a scrutiny of the fairness of all the transactions entered into by
the decedent. They avoided it. The act books contain almost no disputed

---

29. Rochester Act book DRb Pa 3, f. 418v (1460): ". . . unde funeralibus
deductis parum remanebat unde officialis assignavit ei bona in dicto inventario pro
satisfactione sua."

30. Estate of Robert Copratt, Chichester Act book Ep I/10/2, fols. 43v-44
(1520).

31. It is found, with medieval gloss, in W. LYNDWOOD, PROVINCIALE (SEU
CONSTITUTIONES ANGLIAE) 161-65 (1679).

32. Estate of William Warner, St. Alban's Act book ASA 7/1, f. 24r (1520).

33. A distinction was made, however, which required that the transferee by
sale have known of the fraud on creditors. Donees, on the other hand, were covered
whether they had knowledge or not. See W. LYNDWOOD, *supra* note 31, at 164 s.v.
recipientes.

cases of sales,[34] and elsewhere within ecclesiastical jurisdiction the courts regularly enforced sworn contracts without apparent examination of their fairness.[35] Whether this unwillingness stemmed from conviction about the sanctity of obligations freely entered into or from reluctance to enter a tangled thicket of claims is impossible to say at this distance. But the unwillingness to entertain such claims seems fairly clear.

There is, on the other hand, considerable evidence that *Cordis dolore* was put into effect against genuinely gratuitous transfers. Standard procedure called for the express citation of donees, who were required to show cause why they should not be declared to have incurred the penalties of the constitution. Some of the persons cited did in fact present affirmative defenses at the ensuing hearing. One, for example, alleged that the transfer had been part of a contract to maintain the decedent during his old age.[36] Most gratuitous transferees, however, submitted to the court's jurisdiction and tendered the goods. Typical are the transferees at Rochester in 1465 who are recorded as admitting receipt of all the goods of John Pycot "long before his death . . . by grant for certain necessary causes, nevertheless, having no wish to occupy those goods in fraud of creditors," they offered to surrender them.[37] One man at London in 1497 ingeniously justified receipt of the decedent's goods by saying that his father had given them to him during his lifetime specifically in order to satisfy his debts.[38] Probate avoidance is evidently no invention of the twentieth century.

The ecclesiastical courts frequently dealt with such difficult cases by appointing the donee as administrator of the estate.[39] The donee himself then had to pay the debts of the decedent out of the assets already in his

---

34. Only one apparent exception has been found, and in it the disparity between the purchase price and the value of the two oxen in dispute (7s. 8d. as against 18s.) was considerable. Estate of Thomas Braibroke, Rochester Act book DRb Pa 2, f. 53r (1446).

35. At least the author has not found substantive unfairness as a defense in any of the *cause fidei lesionis* in the remaining records. *See* Helmholz, *Assumpsit and Fidei Laesio*, 91 L.Q. REV. 406 (1975); supra 263-89.

36. *Ex officio* c. Pyndfold, Canterbury Act book Y.1.3, f. 180r (1422): ". . . fatetur quod prefatus Jacobus Hendeman donavit sibi omnia bona sua inter vivos ea intencione ut ipse Jacobus haberet a prefato Ricardo sustentacionem suam et quod dictus Ricardus exhiberet sibi necessaria sua quamdiu viveret." *See also* Clark, *Some Aspects of Social Security in Medieval England*, 16 J. SOC. HIST. 307 (1982).

37. Rochester Act book DRb Pa 3, f. 492v (1465): ". . . diu ante obitum suum dedit eis bona sua per cartam ex certis necessariis causis ipsi tamen nolentes huiusmodi bona occupare in fraudem creditorum."

38. Estate of James Day, London Probate Act book MS. 9168/1, f. 13r (1497).

39. *E.g.*, Estate of William Sutton, London Probate Act book MS. 9065J/1, f. 48r (1519). Thomas Chycheley was first cited for "detaining" the goods of the decedent. He appeared in court and was almost immediately assigned the task of compiling a list of the debts owed by the decedent. The practice survived at least to the end of the end of the sixteenth century, *e.g.*, Estate of John Beton, Ely Act book

hands. If goods remained after all claims had been satisfied, so much the better for him. If not—if the estate were truly bankrupt—the donee was bound to satisfy the claims insofar as his assets allowed. Nothing would remain in his hands after the satisfaction of legitimate claims. This practice was certainly not ideal. It put administration into the hands of the person who stood most to gain by the rejection of claims against the estate. He was obliged to render an account of his administration, and creditors were always given the chance to prove their claims before the court. But these are measures of last resort in probate. Surely it would have been fairer to appoint a disinterested administrator. The ecclesiastical courts frequently resorted to a shorter, and doubtless easier, compromise with the problem of fraudulent alienations than modern standards of impartiality demand and even than the strict tones of *Cordis dolore* suggest.

The records make certain, moreover, that the dangers were more than theoretical. Administration under the canon law required evaluation of claims by the administrator of the estate. The schedules of debts found in the remaining act books sometimes record the acceptance, the refusal, or the compromise of claims against estates. The evidence given in support of each claim was also sometimes noted: a debt book,[40] a written obligation,[41] a tally,[42] or an oath supported by compurgators.[43] An entry from the diocese of Salisbury, for example, noted that John Follyot appeared during probate of the estate of Edward Adlambe. He "laid a claim to 21s., but he had no specialty."[44] This notation probably was made necessary by the rule, adopted as early as the sixteenth century, that debts evidenced by a writing were to be preferred to those that rested on simple contracts.[45]

The court records themselves do not make clear much beyond the fact that the nature of each debt claim was examined by the administrator and, sometimes, by court officials. During the Middle Ages, the Church courts provided a regular forum for the trial of testamentary debt cases, but it abandoned this contentious jurisdiction during the reigns of the first two

---

EDR D/2/18, f. 176v, in which the son of the decedent alleged the inter vivos gift and was assigned the duty of administration.

40. Estate of William Milde, Gloucester Act book GDR 17, p. 150 (1560): "Deinde comparuit quidam Thomas More et allegavit dictum defunctum debuisse ei tempore mortis sue xiii s. ad quod probandum produxit librum suum mercatoris etc."

41. Estate of William Bayly, Salisbury Act book 2, f. 85r (1562), called *bille obligatorie*.

42. Estate of Clerk, London Probate Act book MS. 9168/1, fols. 35v-36r (1497): "Johannes Grove petit vii li. x s. quam summam petit per tallios."

43. Estate of Whetstone, Canterbury Act book Y.4.4, f. 91r (1529).

44. Estate of Edward Adlambe, Salisbury Office Act book 2, f. 44v (1585): "Comparuit etiam Johannes Follyot et nomine Johannis illius vendicavit xxi s. sed nullam habet specialitatem."

45. J. GODOLPHIN, THE ORPHAN'S LEGACY, OR A TESTAMENTARY ABRIDGEMENT PT. 2. at 217 (4th ed. 1701).

Tudor monarchs. If there was a law suit, it occurred in a secular forum.[46] Nonetheless, then as now, most debt claims were settled well short of trial. The court records suggest that discussion and settlement of claims continued to occur under the umbrella of the Church's probate jurisdiction even after the ecclesiastical courts ceased to hear such cases formally.

The early rules governing the order of payment of claims against an insolvent estate are difficult to determine from the Church court records. After the late sixteenth century, the English Church courts adopted a detailed system of priorities among creditors.[47] Some were based on the creditor's status, some on the nature of his claim. But it may be that these had their origins in the royal courts.[48] The medieval and early sixteenth century ecclesiastical records, as well as the fifteenth century commentary by William Lyndwood, do not provide a comparable system, but they do show that some claims were satisfied before others. The expenses of administration—things like the cost of making an inventory and even paying for the proclamation calling for creditors, in addition to regular court fees—were everywhere payable before the claims of creditors.[49] So were funeral expenses.[50] One of the common complaints leveled against the Church courts was their excessive probate fees, and practice in bankruptcy cases shows something of the reason.[51] The Church took its share at the expense of prior creditors.

The position of the wife's portion, her right to the equivalent of a forced share of her husband's estate, is also not entirely clear. Was it given priority over the claims of creditors? Two cases show that it was.[52] But this is a small number upon which to base a firm conclusion, and both cases

---

46. *See* Helmholz, infra 316-19.

47. *See* H. SWINBURNE, A TREATISE OF TESTAMENTS AND LAST WILLS PT. 6, at 269-71 (2d ed. 1641).

48. For example, many of the citations given in support of the rules given by Swinburne's work come from English common law sources.

49. *E.g.*, Estate of Robert Copratt, Chichester Act book Ep I/10/2, fols. 43v-44 (1520).

50. *E.g.*, Estate of William Blakbourne, Chichester Act book Ep I/10/1, f. 64v (1506) (the debts owed were 62s. 7d., but nothing was left to meet them after the court had deducted what the Act book records as "expense funerales" and "alie expense curie" as well as "alie expense necessarie pro esculentis et poculentis curati et appreciatorum"); Estate of Nicholas a Doith, London Probate Act book MS. 9068/4, f. 10a (1513) ("Item funeralibus expensis iii s. Item ordinariis expensis ii s. vii d. Et sic remanent inter creditores x s. vi d.").

51. *See* Bowker, *Some Archdeacons' Court Books and the Commons' Supplication Against the Ordinaries of 1532*, in THE STUDY OF MEDIEVAL RECORDS: ESSAYS IN HONOUR OF KATHLEEN MAJOR 282, 296-302 (D. Bullough & R. Storey ed. 1971).

52. Estate of John Blake, Chichester Act book Ep I/10/4, f. 15v (1527); Estate of William Skyner, Chichester Act book Ep I/10/5, f. 19r (1533). There is also one Rochester entry which suggests, but does not clearly state, the same disposition: Estate of William Frawnces, Rochester Act book DRb Pa 5, f. 60r (1499).

come from the same diocesan court. Surprisingly, the prior creditor most often noted in the remaining records is the decedent's landlord. Where the decedent had leased the property in which he lived, the general creditors were paid their share only after the landlord had been paid in full. The records show that this at least was the rule within the dioceses of London,[53] Chichester,[54] and Rochester.[55] There is just a trace of suggestion that this may have been recognition of the landlord's ability to physically seize the decedent's goods.[56] It may also be that the king occupied a position as prior creditor in medieval practice. He clearly did later on,[57] although the two remaining lists of creditors containing debts to the crown do not show any sign of special treatment.[58]

The whole area of priorities in claims is admittedly obscure. The act book evidence is good enough to show only that not all creditors were invariably treated alike, and it may be that ecclesiastical practice clothed the executor with enough discretion to prevent the development of fixed rules.[59] There is a suggestion of this in the treatment by Swinburne, the late sixteenth century canon lawyer whose treatise on the law of wills is the standard authority for our knowledge of early English probate law.[60] There are also cases in the court records which contain divisions of assets that are difficult to account for on any principle other than that of discretion vested in the administrator.[61] No recognizable order of priorities emerges from the folios of many of the surviving act books.

---

53. *E.g.*, Estate of John Phipps, London Probate Act book MS. 9168/4, f. 17v (1513): ". . . de quibus debet iii libras domino fundi et sic nichil remanet inter creditores."

54. *E.g.*, Estate of Carpenter, Chichester Act book Ep I/10/5, f. 54r (1534), the landlord being the prior of Boxgrove.

55. *E.g.*, Estate of Richard Bregge, Rochester Act book DRb Pa 3, f. 511r (1465): "Postea exhibito computo de administracione et nichil remanente in manibus quia dominus fundi habuit omnia pro debitis eiusdem."

56. *Id.* A note records that "W. Downer dominus domus omnia bona arestavit pro arregiis firme." In Estate of Thomas Hyott, London Probate Act book MS. 9168/1, f. 142r (1499), there is also a note to the effect that "domina Jane vicompta Lyell domina domus arestavit pro reditu huiusmodi domus omnia bona."

57. *See* J. GODOLPHIN, *supra* note 45, at 216; M. SHEEHAN, *supra* note 15, at 223.

58. The king appears listed among ordinary creditors in the following two places: Estate of John Rith, Winchester Act book 4, f. 64r (1527); Estate of John Royse, Chichester Act book Ep I/10/3, fols. 4r-4v (1524).

59. *See* Kitching, *The Prerogative Court of Canterbury from Warham to Whitgift*, in CONTINUITY AND CHANGE: PERSONNEL AND ADMINISTRATION OF THE CHURCH IN ENGLAND 1500-1642, at 207 (R. O'Day & F. Heal ed. 1976).

60. H. SWINBURNE, *supra* note 47, at 270: "And if there be divers obligations, then it seemeth to be in the power of the executor, to discharge which obligation and to gratifie which of the creditors he will."

61. *E.g.*, Estate of Carpenter, Chichester Act book Ep I/10/5, f. 54r (1534). After full payment of the landlord, the servants of the decedent and the Earl of

Payment of general creditors followed satisfaction of whatever preferred creditors there were. Sometimes nothing was left. Where there was, a ratable award, called a *rata bonorum* or *defalcatio* in the act books, normally followed.[62] As in modern bankruptcy practice, this entitled each unsecured creditor to a percentage of his claim. Thus, at Gloucester in 1561, each creditor of the estate of William Milde received 6s. in the pound.[63] In an insolvent estate administered at Chicester in 1533, the ratable award was 4s. for each pound claimed, a percentage of one fifth.[64] In one case from the diocese of Winchester in 1527, it was only 8d. in the pound, a mere thirtieth of the amount owed.[65] The unsecured creditor, then as now, had little to hope for where he had to seek satisfaction from the assets of a bankrupt estate. Creditors of men who died insolvent had the right to a share of the estate, enforceable before the tribunals of the Church. But what evidence is left shows that it often turned out to be a small share.

IV. CONCLUSION

The foregoing has described the outlines of bankruptcy practice in the ecclesiastical courts before 1571. What the records show is far from modern bankruptcy. Of that there is no doubt. It is one thing to provide for the orderly division of assets that once belonged to a man who died insolvent. It is quite another to provide a living person with a fresh start. We cannot pretend that the medieval ecclesiastical practices adopted a "modern" outlook on the problem of bankruptcy.

We can say, on one hand, that there were similarities between the

---

Arundell received larger shares, although not their full claims, while the other creditors were paid only *secundum ratam*.

62. The actual amounts of the awards are not normally found in the Act books, which were used at the time to record what was to be done in the next court session and which therefore did not need to record fully the final act of each case. However, assignments to award the ratable are found in most diocesan books examined: Canterbury, Estate of Nicholas Mount, Act book Y.2.10, f. 121v (1522) (*secundum ratam porcionem*); Chichester, Estate of Robert Copratt, Act book Ep I/10/2, fols. 43v-44 (1520) (*iuxta ratam*); Gloucester, Estate of William Milde, Act book GDR 17, p. 150 (1560) (*pro qualibet libra vi s.*); Lichfield, Estate of Richard Grene, Probate Act book B/C/10/1, f. 13r (1533) (*iuxta ratam bonorum*); London, Estate of Daniel Fulcum, [Greater London Record Office] Vicar General's Act book DLC 330, f. 11v (1521) (*iuxta ratam inventarii*); Norwich, Estate of William Base, Act book ACT/1, s.d. 15 January 1509/10 (*iuxta ratam bonorum*); Rochester, Estate of John Dovill, Act book DRb Pa 2, f. 164v (1450) (*facta est defalcatio*).

63. Estate of William Milde, Gloucester Act book GDR 17, p. 150 (1561).

64. Estate of John Cocke, Chichester Act book Ep I/10/6, f. 12v (1533).

65. Winchester Act book C B 5, f. 34v (1527). Other fully documented examples of ratable awards are found in Estate of Nicholas Mount, Canterbury Act book Y.2.10, f. 121v (1522) (7s. 3d. in the pound); Estate of Robert Copratt, Chichester Act book Ep I/10/2, fols. 43v-44 (1520) (10d. in the pound); Estate of Robert Blake, Chichester Act book Ep I/10/5, f. 52v (1534) (3s. 2d. in the pound).

Tudor legislation on the subject and the prior canonical practice. A modern view of the plight of the bankrupt is conspicuously absent from the early statutes. The road to modern bankruptcy has been neither short nor straight.[66] The Tudor legislation, for example, provided no discharge of the insolvent debtor. It left no room for voluntary bankruptcy. The statutes envisioned a limited sort of bankruptcy, one in which the protection of creditors and the fair division of assets rather than the rehabilitation of the over-extended debtor furnished the principal provisions. In this, the legislation resembled prior practice in the ecclesiastical forum.

On the other hand, there were dissimilarities between prior ecclesiastical practice and the Tudor legislation. The most notable innovations were those required by the change to permitting bankruptcy for a living person. The definition of an "act" of bankruptcy—long a troublesome but necessary part of the initiation of the secular process—was one such. The Church courts had needed no comparable trigger, for death initiated their procedure. Other differences went beyond what the nature of the change in jurisdictions required. Most notably, the English law provided bankruptcy only for merchants and traders. The Church provided it for anyone who died insolvent and subject to its probate jurisdiction. There were also differences in detail. For example, the 1571 statute imposed fines and double penalties on those who fraudulently withheld the assets of the bankrupt from the commissioner.[67] Ecclesiastical practice had contained no equivalent feature.[68] Many, perhaps most, of the detailed features of the bankruptcy regime initiated during the sixteenth century differed from earlier practices of the Church courts. They were the result of innovation, or at least they were closer to prior secular practices in other areas of the law.

The relevant evidence thus shows both similarities and differences, and in making connections it may be unwise to go beyond that evidence. Nevertheless, three questions remain which should be raised, even if none can be answered satisfactorily. First, in what measure, if any, was the Tudor and early Stuart bankruptcy legislation consciously modeled upon ecclesiastical probate bankruptcy? Second, why did introduction of the secular bankruptcy procedure occur when it did? And third, did knowledge of Roman bankruptcy procedure play any part in the evolution of English law on the subject?

The first question, that of the conscious adoption of ecclesiastical rules by the Tudor legislators, should be the easiest to answer. But it is not. The genesis of the Tudor legislation is impossible to reconstruct from Parliamentary sources, and, as noted above, the dissimilarities between the procedures

---

66. The development is well traced by W. JONES, *supra* note 3.

67. 13 Eliz. ch. 7.

68. *Cordis dolore* in fact mentioned no sanction other than excommunication; it was only indirectly, i.e., in order to have the sentence of excommunication lifted, that the donee in fraud of the rights of creditors was made to give up the property alienated.

spelled out in the secular legislation and the ecclesiastical antecedents are as great as the similarities. Still, the suggestion of influence is not implausible. No Englishman of any experience with the world could have been wholly ignorant of probate bankruptcy in the sixteenth century. Every consistory court in the country would have been enforcing its rules. And the men who enacted the secular laws came from the class of men who would certainly have had experience with wills. They would have known the ecclesiastical procedures. It makes sense to suppose that when they thought about what a bankruptcy regime should consist of, they might naturally have turned to what they knew already. Of course supposition, even likely supposition, is not proof. We lack any direct proof. Perhaps it is best to leave the question of conscious imitation open, noting simply that the congruence in essential features and the assured fact of familiarity make the possibility a lively one.

Second, even if we accept the ecclesiastical pedigree of the Tudor adoption of bankruptcy, what *did* cause the undoubted changes that the secular legislation entailed? Why did the developments occur when they did? Put another way, why did probate bankruptcy no longer suffice in sixteenth century England? Contemporary commentators attributed the necessity for legislation to an increase in the numbers and influence of foreign traders and to a general decline in the standards of honesty and frugality among all merchants.[69] Profligate habits, borrowed from abroad, inevitably led to bankruptcy on a level that the common law had to address. Modern commentators have naturally found this sort of explanation simplistic.[70] It cannot be shown that the Tudor Age witnessed any considerable rise in commercial dishonesty, and it is not even entirely clear that there was any marked overall rise in commercial activity during the period.[71]

Knowledge of the ecclesiastical antecedents therefore suggests a possible answer to this second question. We know that the Tudor Age redrew the boundary lines between the secular and the religious spheres of life. Obligations that had once been enforced by religious sanction were increasingly taken over into the secular sphere.[72] In this context, then, the enactment of bankruptcy legislation is simply one part of a much more fundamental change in English habits of mind. It was one consequence of the English Reformation. This is not a complete explanation, if only because of the differences between ecclesiastical bankruptcy, which was limited to decedents' estates, and the new secular procedures. It may well be that economic developments in fact had something to do with the introduction of secular bankruptcy. But at least the ecclesiastical evidence sets the

---

69. *See, e.g.*, E. COKE, THE FOURTH PART OF THE INSTITUTES OF THE LAWS OF ENGLAND *276-77.

70. W. JONES, *supra* note 3, at 51.

71. *See* S. JACK, TRADE AND INDUSTRY IN TUDOR AND STUART ENGLAND (1977).

72. *See* A. DICKENS, THE ENGLISH REFORMATION 325 (1964).

sixteenth century developments more accurately into their historical context.

Third, did the relatively sophisticated Roman law system of bankruptcy play any role in the law administered in the Church courts and in the Tudor changes? Insolvency in Roman law—in particular the *cessio bonorum*, under which a living person could avoid the penalties of the law by surrendering his property for the common benefit of his creditors—resembled and could well have provided some impetus for the new secular legislation.[73] We know that the sixteenth century was a period of resurgence of study of Roman law. Indeed, it once seemed to scholars that the future of the English common law was threatened by civilian learning under the Tudors.[74] It therefore seems natural to assume that civilian influence may have played some part in the foundation of English bankruptcy law. Proof of this assumption, however, is another matter. There were considerable differences between the early English statutes and the Roman law, not the least being that the former permitted no voluntary initiation of the process by the insolvent debtor. And, as with the suggestion of ecclesiastical influence, the suggestion lacks affirmative proof. Nothing like legislative history suggests conscious imitation. We must, it seems, treat it as a possibility only.

What *is* clear is that the history of bankruptcy in England did not begin in 1571, or even 1542. In its essence, bankruptcy was no new thing. The most recent student of the subject has defined the essence of bankruptcy as the "notion that creditors shared a community of interests," which community entailed collection of all the debtor's assets and "distribution *pro rata* of the proceeds."[75] All these things the ecclesiastical courts had been putting into practice well before 1571. The secular legislation on the subject did not copy all the details of probate bankruptcy procedure. But the legislation was not without precedent. The ecclesiastical courts had enforced its important features long enough and regularly enough to require recognition of the early existence of probate bankruptcy jurisdiction.

---

73. *See* 2 W. BLACKSTONE, COMMENTARIES *472 (suggestion that the English legislators "attended to the example of the Roman law"). For the Roman law of bankruptcy, see 4 S. SOLAZZI, IL CONCORSO DEI CREDITORI NEL DIRITTO ROMANO (1943).

74. The classic statement of this position is F. MAITLAND, ENGLISH LAW AND THE RENAISSANCE (1901); it is, however, no longer generally thought that there was any real threat to the position of the common law. *See, e.g.*, Baker, *Introduction* to THE REPORTS OF SIR JOHN SPELMAN 23-51 (J.H. Baker ed., 94 Selden Soc. 1978).

75. W. JONES, *supra* note 3, at 18.

16

DEBT CLAIMS AND PROBATE JURISDICTION

IN HISTORICAL PERSPECTIVE

By all accounts the separation of probate jurisdiction from jurisdiction over claims in favor of and against a decedent's estate is an ancient one. Wills are proved in a probate court. Debt claims are litigated in a court of general jurisdiction; this being a continuation of early English practice under which, in the absence of special circumstances, debt claims fell outside the probate jurisdiction of the Church courts.[1] Maitland said it well. When in the reign of Edward I (1272-1307), the king's justices had "thrown open the doors of their court to the executor, he could there sue the debtor, he could there be sued by the creditors. Such suits were not 'testamentary causes'."[2] They were cognizable only in secular courts, not in the tribunals of the Church, and a Church court which attempted to hear such a claim would be restrained by issuance of a royal writ of prohibition.[3] That testamentary debt was not a part of early probate jurisdiction has become the settled opinion.[4]

---

1. *E.g.*, T. Atkinson, *Law of Wills* § 127, at 704 (2d ed. 1953): "At common law claims against a decedent's estate were not established in the court of probate."

2. 2 F. Pollock & F. W. Maitland, *History of English Law*, 348 (2d ed. reissued 1968).

3. *See* the royal response to the bishops' petition of 1285 in 2 *Councils and Synods with Other Documents Relating to the Engish Church II, A.D. 1205-1313*, at 958 (F. Powicke and C. R. Cheney eds. 1964). On the writ of prohibition generally, *see* N. Adams, "The Writ of Prohibition to Court Christian," 20 *Minn. L. Rev.* 272 (1936); G. Flahiff, "The Writ of Prohibition to Court Chris-

The opinion became settled, however, before anyone had looked seriously at the records of the Church courts. It has always rested on the rules of the secular courts, not on investigation of the ecclesiastical court records themselves.[5] Research in recent years has shown that the rules developed by the royal justices are not always reliable guides to medieval practice,[6] and in fact, Maitland's statement of the relative jurisdictional competence of Church and State will not survive an examination of actual practice in the Church courts. Suits concerning the debts of decedents, brought both by and against executors are found in significant quantities in the medieval Act books of the Church courts. This article is intended to demonstrate this fact, to describe briefly the nature of the litigation, to establish when the Church courts lost their jurisdiction over testamentary debt, and to assess the importance of the evidence for legal history generally.

---

tian in the Thirteenth Century [pt. 1]," 6 *Medieval Studies* 261 (1944) and *idem* "[pt. 2]," 7 *Medieval Studies* 229 (1945); R. H. Helmholz, "Writs of prohibition and Ecclesiastical Sanctions in the English Courts Christian," 60 *Minn. L. Rev.* 1011 (1976): supra 77-99.

4. *See* James Barr Ames, *Lectures on Legal History* 95 (1913); R. Goffin, *The Testamentary Executor in England and Elsewhere* 46-7 (1901); 3 W. Holdsworth, *A History of English Law* 585-95 (5th ed. 1942); T. F. T. Plucknett, *A Concise History of the Common Law* 741-2 (5th ed. 1956); M. M. Sheehan, *The Will in Medieval England* 227-28 (1963); A. W. B. Simpson, *A History of the Common Law of Contract* 559-60 (1975).

5. These records are the sources for this article. Consisting principally of Act books, that is, official records of the procedure taken in every cause which came before a Consistory court, the diocesan court records examined, with corresponding modern archives are the following:

Canterbury	Library of the Dean and Chapter, Canterbury.
Chichester	West Sussex Record Office, Chichester.
Durham	Library of the Department of Palaeography and Diplomatic, University of Durham
Ely	Ely Diocesan Records, The University Library, Cambridge.
Exeter	Devon County Record Office, Exeter.
Hereford	Hereford County Record Office, Hereford.
Lichfield	Joint Record Office, Lichfield.
London	Guildhall Library, London.
Norwich	Norfolk Record Office, Norwich.
Rochester	Kent County Record Office, Maidstone.
St. Albans	Hertfordshire Record Office, Hertford.
York	Borthwick Institute of Historical Research.

For a description of these records, together with the use to which they can be put, see Dorothy M. Owen, *The Records of the Established Church in England Excluding Parochial Records* (1974); B. Woodcock, *Medieval Ecclesiastical Courts in the Diocese of Canterbury* (1952).

6. *See,* for example, Charles Donahue, "Roman Canon Law in the Medieval English Church: Stubbs vs. Maitland Re-examined After 75 Years in the Light of Some Records from the Church Courts," 72 *Mich. L. Rev.* 647 (1974).

I. THE CANONICAL REMEDY

A. *Suits by the Executor*

The remaining records of the Church courts show that executors sued frequently to recover property owned by the decedent and money owed to him. The ecclesiastical courts' refusal to observe the royal rules can be seen easily from two unexceptional examples. In 1377 the executor of Alexander Hall sued John Stryk of Chesterton before the bishop's Consistory court at Ely for ten marks Stryk had allegedly owed to Hall. Stryk appeared before the court. He did not contest the court's jurisdiction. He did not introduce a royal prohibition, as he was entitled to do under common law. Instead he admitted the debt, and when at a later date he still had not paid, he pleaded only "that he was poor and stricken with poverty so that he had been unable and still was unable to pay out the aforesaid sum."[7] At Rochester in 1439 the executors of William Clyft of Offham sued John Palmer before the Consistory court on a simple debt which Palmer had owed to Clyft. Palmer defended by alleging payment in the testator's lifetime. At least at first he did; the cause was later compromised.[8] The essential point is that neither defendant made the response which the royal court rule would lead us to expect. Both apparently accepted that the ecclesiastical courts had jurisdiction over the claims in favor of the decedent's estate.[9]

It is impossible to give reliable figures for the number of such suits heard by the medieval Church courts. Act books, which furnish the only surviving record of litigation in most dioceses, were basically records of procedural steps taken in each matter coming before the courts, and they normally described each case only in general terms as a "testamentary cause." Besides a testamentary debt case, the term was sometimes used to refer to a dispute over a testament's validity, a claim for a legacy, or other matter falling within probate jurisdiction. Only when the court scribe set down some of the details of litigation can one be sure of the underlying nature of the suit. Fortunately this happened often enough to show that testamentary debt was a common subject of litigation. Of the twenty-eight testamentary causes heard at Canterbury in 1517, for example, five clearly concerned testamentary debt, although most of the rest cannot be

---

7. Rede c. Stryk, Ely Act book EDR D/2/1, fols. 67r, 77r, 130r: "Pars rea allegat et proponit quod est inops et paupertate gravata adeo quod non potuit solvisse nec adhuc potest summam predictam."
8. Rochester Act book DRb Pa 1, f. 104r (3s. 4d.)
9. William Lyndwood, the fifteenth century English canonist, refers to it in respect to goods as *practica communis*. *Provinciale (seu Constitutiones Angliae)* 175 s.v. *effectum* (1679) [hereafter cited as Lynwood, *Provinciale*].

described.[10] Recognizable suits brought by executors to recover money owing to the decedent also appear in the records of the dioceses of Chichester,[11] Ely,[12] Hereford,[13] Lichfield[14] London,[15] Norwich[16] Rochester,[17] and York.[18] That is every diocese with surviving medieval records examined in the preparation of this article.

In theory, of course, the underlying nature of all these suits made them subject to a royal writ of prohibition. But few were in fact prohibited. Whether through technical problems inherent in the writ itself,[19] acquiescence by both parties in the Church's jurisdiction,[20] or the threat of counter sanctions by the ecclesiastical courts,[21] few defendant-debtors invoked the secular remedy. By at least the middle of the fourteenth century, testamentary debt had become a staple part of medieval probate jurisdiction.

The normal elements of a suit by the executor on the decedent's claim were the following: he alleged 1) his appointment as executor of the testament, 2) the commission of administration to him by the Church court, 3) the transaction which created the debt in the testator's lifetime, 4) his request for payment by the debtor, 5) the debtor's refusal to pay, and 6) his consequent inability to carry out

---

10. Taken from Act book Y.2.6, fols. 30v-65r; the five causes are found at fols. 33v, 59v, 61r, 61r, and 63v.

11. *E.g.,* Belchambyr c. Moundevyle, Act book Ep I/10/1, f. 99v (1507). The amount claimed was £4.

12. *See* Rede c. Stryk, *supra* note 7. The Ely Act book which covers the years 1374 to 1382, has the fewest recognizable testamentary debt cases of the Act books examined. The reasons for this fact are unclear to me. No Ely court records survive from the Middle Ages except this single book.

13. *E.g.,* Bole c. Smyth, Act book 0/3, 41 (1445). The amount claimed was 6s. 8d.

14. *E.g.,* Executors of Sternesdale c. Wodshawe, Act book B/C/1/2, f. 155r (1474). The amount claimed was £3.

15. *E.g.,* Executors of Helmych c. Spynell, Act book MS. 9064/2, f. 24r (1483). The amount claimed was £8 11s.

16. *E.g., Ex officio* c. Burman, Act book ACT/1 s.d. 2 December 1510. The amount claimed was 20s.

17. *E.g.,* Totesham c. Bysshop, Act book DRb Pa 1, fol. 55v, 61r, 66v (1438). The amount claimed was 7 marks.

18. *E.g.,* Tydd c. Eley, CP.F.264 (c. 1481). The amount claimed was £7 3s. 10d.

19. The principal weakness of the medieval writ of prohibition, as developed in the course of the fourteenth century, seems to have been an unwillingness by Chancery to look beyond the canonical libel in deciding whether or not the writ was warranted. I am indebted to Mr. John Barton for initially calling this point to my attention, and I hope to return to the subject of how the issue was tried in medieval prohibition cases in a later article.

20. *See,* e.g., D. Dobbs, "The Decline of Jurisdiction by Consent," 40 *N. Car. L. Rev.* 49 (1961).

21. *See* Helmholz, "Writs of Prohibition," *supra* 87-93.

fully the last will of the decedent.[22] No allegation of an oath to pay by the debtor, such as the Church Courts normally required before they heard contract disputes between living parties, was necessary to found the action.[23] It sometimes happened, of course, that the decedent had contracted the debt by sworn oath; the pleading often reflects this by calling the suit a *causa testamentaria et fidei lesionis*.[24] But the oath was not legally required.

Nor do the remaining records produce only cases where the debt had been recognized or reduced to judgment during the testator's lifetime, cases in which Bracton conceded that the executor might sue in a Church court.[25] Neither the pleading nor the depositions of witnesses ever mention this exception as a possible source of ecclesiastical jurisdiction. The debts subject to probate jurisdiction need be no more than obligations to pay for goods delivered, loans made or services performed, that is, simple debts for money owed.

Proof of the debt (or of its absence) was made either by witnesses or by oath of the party supported by compurgators, the canonical equivalent of wager of law. How the choice of method was made is now difficult to say. One can reasonably think that the discretion of the judge, the choice of the plaintiff, and the availability of witnesses played a role, but until there has been a more thorough investigation of methods of proof actually used in the Church courts, little can be said with confidence. Apparently similar cases in the same set of Act books could call for either form of proof.[26] If there was a guiding principle other than individual choice at work, the record does not state it.

---

22. Taken from the plaintiff's "positions" or statement of claim in York CP.F. 264. It does not vary significantly from other causes, at least those heard at York. York is the only diocese from which substantial numbers of cause papers, as distinct from Act books, remain.

23. *See* R. H. Helmholz, "Assumpsit and Fidei Laesio," 91 *Law Q. Rev.* 406 (1975): supra 263-89.

24. *E.g.,* Executors of Backer c. Sevyngham et al., Canterbury Act book Y.1.2, f. 111v (1398), styled a *causa testamentaria sive fidei lesionis et periurii*.

25. *See* 4 H. Bracton, *De Legibus et Consuetudinibus Angliae*, f. 407b (G. Woodbine ed., S. Thorne trans. 1968-77, at 267). I have been unable to find any authority for this exception apart from Bracton and query its continued vitality in the fourteenth and fifteenth centuries.

26. Compare, *e.g.,* Watyrfeld c. Lende, Chichester Act book Ep I/10/1, f. 83v. in which proof was by oath, with Wyllet c. Smyth, Chichester Act book Ep I/10/1, f. 31r, in which proof was by witnesses. That the choice rested with the plaintiff is suggested by Frawnceys c. May, Canterbury Act book Y.1.3, f. 68r (1418); after the defendant's denial of the claim, the court scribe recorded: "Ex delacione actoris datur eidem parti ree iurandum quarta manu. . . ."

Once the debt was proved, the judge ordered the debtor to pay, under threat of excommunication. The debtor was considered an "impeder" of the decedent's testament. The theory was that his detention of the decedent's assets (the money owed) made full administration of his estate impossible.[27] For this reason, the Church courts drew no clear distinction between recovery of the testator's chattels and recovery of debts owed to him.[28] Also for this reason the Church enjoined the frequent reading in parish churches of the Provincial Constitution excommunicating all those who impeded the last wishes of decedents, including the decedent's debtors.[29] Surviving depositions show that this was no empty injunction. The parish clergy in fact read the Constitution publicly.[30] To carry out fully the last wishes of the decedent, the Church courts had to retain some jurisdiction over testamentary debt. As a contemporary clerical spokesman put it, "The final expediting of a testament ought to be one and undivided."[31] So it seemed at any rate to many Churchmen and litigants in the later Middle Ages.

---

27. *E.g.,* Canterbury Ecclesiastical Suit Roll, no. 140 (1293); the document specifies that all those who impede last wills and testaments, "sunt auctoritate concilii excommunicationis sentencia involuti et contra ipsos tanquam ecclesiasticarum libertatum violatores per censuram ecclesiasticam procedi debeat." In an early fifteenth century suit against an executrix, the plaintiff's witness was asked specifically whether she was impeding the decedent's last will; he said that she was and that he knew it because "irascitur cum parte actrice in eo quod petit dictam summam." Northwode c. Hakenblen. Canterbury Deposition Book X.10.1, fols. 109-109v (1417). For contemporary commentary, see Lyndwood, *Provinciale* at 175 s.v. *effectum;* he deals with the case where the assets in the executor's hands are sufficient to pay all specific legacies even without payment of the debt, and manages to bring even that case under the Constitution by stressing that the residuary legatees or the takers under intestacy will be deprived of their proper share unless the Constitution is invoked against the debtor. *See also* M. M. Sheehan, *supra* note 4, at 226-7.

28. *E.g.,* Wynstall c. Wynstall, Canterbury Act book Y.1.1, f. 99v (1375); the defendant was ordered "quod restituat eidem executori omnia bona mobilia que fuerunt dicti defuncti dum vixit." In Mercaunt c. Mercaunt, Norwich Act book ACT/1, s.d. 21 October 1510, the judge warned the defendant "quod restituat et adducat bona per eum subtracta ad locum in quo reposita erant." The causes do not differ from testamentary debt except that goods were involved.

29. The text of the Constitution is given in Lyndwood, *Provinciale* 171-9.

30. *E.g.,* Deposition by John Engham, a witness in Broke c. Wallys, Canterbury Deposition book X.10.1, fols. 62v-63r (1415): "Interogatus an impedientes ultimas voluntates defunctorum sunt excommunicati, dicit quod sic et audivit sic sepius publicatum in ecclesia parochiali ubi moram trahit et aliis locis convicinis."

31. *See Registrum Johannis de Pontissara, Episcopi Wyntoniensis* 773 (19 Surrey Record Soc., C. Deedes ed. 1923): "Preterea cum una et indivisa esse debeat finalis expedicio testamenti." *See also* the clergy's response to the king's refusal to grant their request of 1285, in 2 *Councils & Synods, supra* note 3, at 961.

There was, of course, some justification for this belief. Enforcement of testamentary debt claims within probate jurisdiction had practical advantages. To take one example, in a 1374 cause from Canterbury, the executor of Alice Baker sued William Williams on a debt owed to Alice. William's defense was that Alice's last will and testament required him to spend the sum of the debt on the repair of roads in Herne. The executor claimed that Alice had revoked that part of the will, and that the debt was therefore still owing.[32] This was not, of course, an insoluble problem under the divided system of courts which came to be the rule. Proof of the will and decision of the question of revocation in one court and enforcement of claims in favor of the estate in another court could ultimately accomplish full administration. But the divided system did cause and has continued to cause practical problems. It gives rise to uncertainty about where to sue in some cases, and it can cause delays in the collection of assets.[33] As an original proposition it made sense for one court to handle all disputes arising over a debt like the one owed to Alice Baker at Canterbury. This was possible under the system enforced by the Church courts in medieval England.[34]

B. *Suits against Executors*

The same considerations of convenience apply to the reverse situation, suits against the personal representative by creditors of the decedent. These were also a regular part of medieval ecclesiastical jurisdiction, although there are fewer recognizable in the remaining court records than suits brought by executors. Consider, for example, a fifteenth century case from the diocese of Rochester. Denise Stephen had three claims on the estate of the decedent, her former employer

---

32. Canterbury Act book Y.1.1, f. 71 v.

33. *See* generally 3 W. Page, *Treatise on the Law of Wills* § 26.17, at 54 (Bowe-Parker ed. 1961).

34. These remarks should not be taken to imply that the Church courts enforced, or even desired, exclusive competence over testamentary debt. By canon law and secular law both, the Church's probate jurisdiction was based on custom, not divine imperative. *See Lyndwood, Provinciale* 170 s.v. *insinuationem;* Y.B. 11 Hen. 7, f. 12, pl. 1 (1496). The royal court plea rolls for the medieval period are also full of debt actions brought by executors against debtors. Likewise, local and manorial courts heard suits involving testamentary debt. For example, Dr. Elaine Clark has found that 12.6 percent of the debt actions in the Essex manor of Writtle involved executors or administrators. *See* Debt Litigation in Medieval Essex and Norfolk, 1270-1490 (unpublished paper delivered at American Hist. Assoc. Annual Meeting, Dallas, Dec. 30, 1977). In some courts the royal court rule requiring a specialty to sue an executor may have been applied. At the manor court for Sutton, Lincs., an executrix demurred to the creditor's plea in a debt action, "eo quod non monstrat nullum speciale factum quod potest eos executores ligare." Public Record Office, London [hereafter cited as P.R.O.] DL 30/86/1170, m. 2 (1335).

Thomas Hermon: a legacy, a debt for past services, and what amounted to a tort claim, because (as the record laconically states) Hermon "carnally knew her and for other reasons."[35] Of these, the first and third were within the Church's jurisdiction. What sense did it make to require that a suit for the second, the debt, be brought in a secular court? Of course, if the second went forward in the Church court, the plaintiff would have gained a choice of forum denied her had Hermon lived. Thereby royal jurisdiction was theoretically infringed; a prohibition lay. But from a practical point of view, it made sense for the ecclesiastical court to hear all three claims. That is what the Consistory court at Rochester in fact did.

The argument of convenience appears all the stronger when one considers that prior to the rise of assumpsit for money in the sixteenth century, a creditor could not sue the executor at all in the royal courts unless he had a specialty.[36] Commentators explained this result by saying that one of the rights of defendants in actions of debt was the right to wage their law. The executor, who might have no personal knowledge of the debt, could not without risk of perjury wage his law, as the decedent could have done had he been alive.[37] Therefore, it was a safer course to forbid the suit entirely. Hard things can be said about this rule.[38] Whatever its merits may be, from a practical standpoint the situation demanded a remedy. Should the man with a valid debt but no specialty be cheated of a legitimate claim by the accident of death? Surely one reason the common law rule was tolerable is that the creditor had an alternative forum.[39] As the Act books demonstrate, in practice the creditor had the alternative of suing in the Church courts.

The common law did permit suit in the Church courts under one condition. They might hear the claim of a creditor if the testator had specifically directed in his testament that the executor pay his debts.[40] The claim could then be treated as a legacy. However, this

---

35. Rochester Act book DRb Pa 3, f. 462v (1463); the claim was successful, and the executor was ordered to pay the former servant 5 marks and 10s. worth of goods.

36. *See* W. McGovern, "Contract in Medieval England: Wager of Law and the Effect of Death," 54 *Iowa L. Rev.* 19, 41-44 (1968).

37. Y.B. Trin. 41 Edw. 3, f. 13b, pl. 3 (1367); Y.B. Trin. 12 Hen. 4, f. 23, pl. 3 (1411).

38. *See* G. D. G. Hall's remarks in *Glanvill, Tractatus de Legibus et Consuetudinibus Regni Angliae* 191 (1965); A. W. B. Simpson, *supra* note 4, at 559.

39. The creditor also had the option, in places at least, of suing in a local court. *See* note 34, *supra;* M. M. Sheehan, *supra* note 4, at 229. Why there should earlier have been more suits brought by executors than against executors in the Church courts, in view of the lacuna in secular remedy, is puzzling.

40. *Bracton's Note-Book,* no. 162 (1222) F. W. Maitland ed. 1887; A. Fitzherbert, *New Natura Brevium* *44B (1677).

exception will not explain the many suits against personal representatives remaining in the Act books. Many wills contained no direction to pay debts,[41] and some of the claims were brought in cases of intestacy, where by definition there could have been no direction to pay debts.[42] In fact, none of the remaining records in suits against executors mentions a direction to pay debts, either as part of the preliminary pleading or as a defense by the executor. The records suggest, on the contrary, that the executor was bound by virtue of his office. In a cause heard at York in 1517, for instance, John Symson sued the executor of James Fawcett to recover £5 6s. 11d. allegedly owed for grain received by Fawcett during his lifetime. The plaintiff's pleading does not allege a direction to pay debts, and in fact examination of Fawcett's testament, which happened to be included in the cause file, shows that it contained no such direction. What the pleading does contain is the allegation that the executor "was sworn upon the Holy Gospels, corporally touched by him, by the ordinary of the place at the time administration was committed to him to pay the [testator's] debts."[43] The executor's status as personal representative, his oath to pay the testator's legitimate debts, and his possession of sufficient assets of the decedent were the foundation of his liability. As with debt claims brought by the executor, it was the integrity of the process of probate administration which seemed to require the extension of ecclesiastical jurisdiction to the decedent's creditors.

In sum, the record evidence shows that disputed claims over debts owed by and to decedents continued to be heard regularly by the ecclesiastical courts long after the royal courts offered a remedy to the executor and long after writs of prohibition were available to

---

41. Wills included in the episcopal register of Archbishop Chichele without directions to pay debts outnumber those with directions, by a margin of 34 to 21, for the first four years of his episcopate (1414-17). 2 *Register of Henry Chichele* 1-137 (E. F. Jacob & H. Johnson eds. 1938). The pre-1510 wills without directions outnumber wills with directions by a margin of 29 to 4 in 1 *Lincoln Wills, A.D. 1271 to A.D. 1526,* at 1-44 (5 Lincoln Record Soc., C. Foster ed. 1914). Buckinghamshire testaments registered between 1483 and 1491 have no directions in 43 of 51 instances. *Courts of the Archdeaconry of Buckingham, 1483-1523,* at 1-104 (19 Buckinghamshire Record Soc., E. M. Elvey ed. 1975).

42. Examples are found in London Act book, MS 9064/2, f. 51v (1484); Rochester Act book DRb Pa 2, f. 53r (1446); St. Albans Act book ASA 7/1, f. 37r (1525). The nature of the records often makes it impossible, however, to tell whether the decedent had died testate or intestate, since the terms administrator and administration were used in both situations.

43. York CP.G.85 (1517): "Ricardus Fawshede executor testamenti dicti Jacobi patris sui ad solucionem debitorum eiusdem erat per loci ordinarium tempore administracionis sibi commisse in forma iuris ad sancta dei evangelia per ipsum corporaliter tacta iuratus."

prevent them. The claim could be made in either jurisdiction, and the choice of where to sue in an individual case must have depended on convenience and local circumstance. During the last century many American jurisdictions and the framers of the Uniform Probate Code have opted for a system of concurrent jurisdiction.[44] Within the confines of the constitutional guarantees to jury trial, the plaintiff has his choice of forum. Although there are many differences in detail, that decision restores something like the situation which existed in medieval England.

II. DISAPPEARANCE OF THE CANONICAL REMEDY

When did the Church lose its jurisdiction? When and how did testamentary debt come to rest solely within secular jurisdiction in English practice? Unfortunately the question admits of no easy answer, because of the nature of the record evidence and the absence of contemporary commentary. Nonetheless, what evidence there is suggests that the change took place gradually, without appreciable struggle by the Church, and that it occurred during the last years of the fifteenth century and the first decades of the sixteenth.

In the records for 1483-84 from the Commissary court at London, for example, there are causes recognizably about testamentary debt. The Act book for the same court from 1514, on the other hand, contains none.[45] The fifteenth century Rochester court records produce numerous suits over debts brought by and against executors. But the same records from 1527-28 produce none.[46] At Chichester, the Consistory court was clearly hearing litigation over testamentary debt in 1506-07. However, the Act book from 1526-27 contains only three testamentary causes, and all three concern the payment of a legacy.[47] None concerns a testator's debts.

In two dioceses, Hereford and Canterbury, where we cannot penetrate beyond the general rubric, the records are consistent with the same conclusion. At Canterbury the number of testamentary causes dropped from 31 in 1476 to 18 in 1527.[48] At Hereford the drop was from an average in excess of 18 between 1509 and 1513

---

44. *Uniform Probate Code* § 3-105.

45. Comparing Act book MS. 9064/2, fols. 19r, 24r, 43r, 51v, with Act book MS. 9064/11, fols. 146-208.

46. Comparing Act book DRb Pa 1, fols. 49r, 55v, 82r, 104r (1438) with Act book DRb Pa 12, which covers the years in the 1520's, and contains a number of actions for money allegedly owed by a decedent to a parish church, but none certainly involving testamentary debt.

47. Comparing Act book Ep I/10/1, fols. 2r, 58r, 58v, 66v, 71r, 83v, 98v with Act book Ep I/10/4.

48. Comparing Act book Y.1.12 with Act book Y.2.12.

to an average of 10 between 1536 to 1538.[49] Although this proves
nothing conclusively, it is at least reasonable to suppose that the decline in total numbers reflects the dropping out of litigation about
debts from the courts' testamentary jurisdiction.

There is no reason to suppose that the disappearance must have
occurred in every place at exactly the same time. Suits over testamentary debt may well have ceased in the dioceses of Norwich and
Winchester,[50] for instance, while the Consistory court at Lichfield
was still hearing them.[51] But taken together, the evidence from seven
or eight dioceses suggests that the disappearance had occurred by the
second decade of the sixteenth century. That is, the common law
position that debts owed to and by testators were not testamentary
causes, and were not cognizable in the courts of the Church, had come
to describe the true state of affairs by the late 1520's.

Exactly how this change occurred must remain, at least for the
present, a matter of some uncertainty. There is no sign of a fundamental shift in the royal position. It had long held that suits over
testamentary debt belonged to secular jurisdiction, even though, as
noted above, writs of prohibition had not been effective to prevent
the Church from hearing testamentary debt claims.

However, there is one sign of change in the records of the royal
courts: during the last decade of the fifteenth century and increasingly
in the early years of the sixteenth, the plea rolls of the Court of
King's Bench contain private actions, based on the Statue of *Praemunire,* against litigants who had sued in the ecclesiastical courts over
matters belonging to royal jurisdiction.[52] Some of these actions concerned testamentary debt.

The Statute itself was not new.[53] It dated from the fourteenth
century. There has been scholarly uncertainty about the original moti-

---

49. Comparing Act book I/4 with Act book I/6; the figure for testamentary
causes in 1520, however, is 20 (Act book I/5).

50. Dr. R. A. Houlbrooke's forthcoming study (Oxford U. Press) of the
courts of Norfolk and Winchester indicates that claims over testamentary debt
were not heard in the 1520's.

51. Again it is impossible to speak with certainty, but 14 causes involving probate were introduced in the court at Lichfield in 1529. Two years later there
were only four, three of which were brought for "subtraction" of a legacy (taken
from Act book B/C/2/3).

52. *See generally* 2 *Reports of Sir John Spelman* 66-8 (94 Selden Soc., J.
Baker ed. 1978); Michael Kelly, "Canterbury Jurisdiction and Influence during
the Episcopate of William Warham, 1503-1532," 100-10 (unpublished Cambridge Univ. thesis, 1964).

53. 16 Ric. II, c. 5 (1392-3); other earlier similar statutes, also occasionally
used in plea rolls entries, are 27 Edw. III, st. 1, c. 1 (1353); 38 Edw. III, st. 2,
cc. 1, 2 (1364).

vation of the Statute, but its professed aim was to deter the hearing of litigation which touched the King's regality in the papal court.[54] The Statute laid heavy penalties on anyone who sued process in a matter belonging to the King's jurisdiction "in the Roman court or elsewhere." During the fifteenth century the phrase "or elsewhere" was interpreted to include pleas within as well as outside the realm of England,[55] and hence it became possible to invoke the stringent procedures and penalties of the Statute of *Praemunire* to punish litigants in the Church courts in a way which had not been feasible with a writ of prohibition.[56] That is, a person sued in a Church court could bring an action based on the Statute, alleging that his opponent had incurred its penalties and must answer for his offense before the King's Bench.

Thus, to take an example involving testamentary debt, the plea roll for Easter term 1506 contains an action brought by John Sackvile against the three executors of the testament of William Rosse.[57] The plea begins by setting out the terms of the Statute and by stating the principle that pleas of lay debt belong to the court of the lord King and not to the ecclesiastical forum. It continues by alleging that the defendants, heedless of the Statute and scheming to deprive the king of his rights, had sued Sackvile for 53s. 4d. allegedly owed to Rosse before the Archbishop of Canterbury's Court of Audience and had caused various kinds of process and sentences to be "fulminated" against him in that court. It ends by asking that he be warned by the sheriff to appear to answer for these actions. It is a typical example of many entries on the plea rolls. Its availability provided litigants with a weapon for use in hindering the claims of executors. Its use brought new pressure to bear on the ecclesiastical courts to conform to the rules of secular law.

---

54. *See* E. B. Graves, "The Legal Significance of the Statute of Praemunire of 1353," in *Anniversary Essays in Mediaeval History by Students of Charles Homer Haskins* 57 (C. Taylor ed. 1929); W. T. Waugh, "The Great Statute of Praemunire," 37 *English Historical Rev.* 173 (1922).

55. Y.B. Mich. 5 Edw. 4, f. 6, pl. 7 (1465). An earlier attempt to use a Statute of *Praemunire* to cover actions within England had been met with a demurrer: "Dicit quod per eadem non supponitur ipsum Willelmum aliquam sectam seu prosecutionem extra regnum Anglie fecisse nec aliquid in aliena curia extra idem regnum in preiudicium domini Regis attemptasse . . ." Rex. v. Corby, P.R.O. C P. 40/479, m. 511 1380). No result is recorded, however. A similar attempt, again without result is Mercer v. Nasserton, C.P. 40/598, m. 441 (1410).

56. *See* notes 19-21, *supra.*

57. P.R.O. K.B. 27/979, m. 23; the case also appears at K.B. 27/978, m. 26. *See generally* R. Brooke, *Grande Abridgement, Praemunire* *144b (1573).

Actions of *praemunire* were not unknown on the plea rolls of the King's Bench from before the last years of the fifteenth century.[58] However, it was only in the years around the turn of the sixteenth century that they began to appear in considerable numbers.[59] Their appearance did not signal the immediate collapse of the Church's jurisdiction. The same Church courts which had had their actions subjected to *praemunire* actions heard cases apparently violating the secular rules afterwards.[60] But, as noted above, the Church's jurisdiction gradually shriveled. And although the process by which the Church courts lost their jurisdiction is not yet fully understood, it is likely that the actions brought on the Statute of *Praemunire* played a role in it. Litigants may simply have felt that the risks of incurring the penalties of the Statute were too great to make it worth resorting to the ecclesiastical forum.

III. CONCLUSION

Several conclusions can be drawn from this brief history of the Church's jurisdiction over testamentary debt. First, and most certain, the principles of the secular law do not tell the whole story, or even the correct story, about the extent of the probate jurisdiction of the medieval Church courts. Writs of prohibition would stop a single testamentary cause.[61] They did not determine the scope of ecclesiastical jurisdiction. The effective separation of probate jurisdiction from jurisdiction over disputed claims for and against a decedent's estate must therefore be moved forward from the reign of Edward I to sometime around the turn of the sixteenth century.

---

58. The plea rolls from 1468 (K.B. 27/827-30), produce one action of *praemunire*, Sharp v. Tempyn, K.B. 27/830, m. 128. The same rolls from 1481 (K.B. 27/877-80) again produce only one such action, which was not pleaded to issue; Prior of Wenlock v. Prior of Dudley, K. B. 27/879, m. 7d. *See also Calendar of Patent Rolls*, 1408-13, at 27; *Calendar of Patent Rolls*, 1422-29, at 400; Waugh, *supra* note 54, at 199.

59. *See generally* 2 *Reports of Sir John Spelman, supra* note 52, at 66-8.

60. Compare Newman c. Executor of Fawcett, York CP.G.85 (1517), a suit for £5 6s. 10d. allegedly owed for grain delivered to the decedent, with Constable v. Holme, K.B. 27/931, m. 41d and K.B. 27/934, m. 26 (1494), an earlier royal court case in which the plaintiff had been sued before the court at York as executrix of her husband's testament for 7 marks allegedly owed by the husband. The record of the ecclesiastical court for this case has coincidentally survived, and it shows that (according to the royal court rules) the complaint was well justified. Holme c. Constable, CP.F.304 (1492), was a suit before the court at York for the 7 marks. For some reason this particular suit in the royal court was brought on a writ of prohibition.

61. The evidence for this is set out in R. H. Helmholz, "Writs of Prohibition," *supra* 85-7.

Second, the disappearance from the Church courts of testamentary debt left a gap in remedies available to litigants with legitimate claims. It particularly hurt the decedent's creditor who had no written obligation, for as noted above, without it he could not sue the executor at all in debt.[62] Occurring prior to the time assumpsit for money came into common use, this disappearance of the ecclesiastical remedy left him with no recourse outside Chancery.[63] The executor with a claim against a debtor was better off, since he could bring debt; however debt could be met by wager of law on the defendant's part, and the executor with witnesses to the contract may well have been better off in the Church courts, where he could prove it by witnesses.[64]

This dilemma was ended, as legal historians have often noted, by the expansion of assumpsit during the course of the sixteenth century. Assumpsit allowed the creditor to sue the debtor's executor. It allowed the creditor's executor to sue the debtor and have the issue tried by jury.[65] In light of the evidence from the Church court records, perhaps it was no accident that the expansion of assumpsit to include promises to pay money occurred when it did. The expansion was the work of men, not a matter of any inherent necessity, and the practical problems facing litigants with valid claims but no satisfactory remedy outside Chancery may have provided some impetus for attempts to stretch assumpsit to cover the situation.[66] As long as the Church courts provided adequate recourse, common law rules like the one which kept debt on an oral contract from being brought against an executor were tolerable rules. Once the Church had lost its jurisdiction, they were harder to live with. The resources inherent in the secular law had to be exploited to fashion a remedy.

Third, the decline in ecclesiastical jurisdiction must be tied to the fundamental religious changes of the sixteenth century. It is particularly noteworthy that the decline occurred gradually, and that it happened mostly prior to the Henrician Reformation. In the broadest sense, the decline therefore reflects a basic shift in attitude towards

---

62. *See* notes 36 and 37 *supra*.
63. The Chancellor's jurisdiction over contract is studied in W. Barbour, *The History of Contract in Early English Equity* (1914).
64. *See* note 26 *supra*.
65. *See* J. H. Baker, "New Light on Slade's Case: Pt. II," 1971 *Cambridge L. J.* 213, 228-30; McGovern, *supra* note 36, at 48-57.
66. This suggestion is also made by S. F. C. Milsom, "Sale of Goods in the Fifteenth Century," 77 *Law Q. Rev.* 257, 265 (1961). The generally accepted explanation for the rise of assumpsit in the common law courts has been the fear of competition from Chancery. See, for example, A. W. B. Simpson, *supra* note 4, at 561. The explanation suggested above is, of course, a different one, but it is not intended wholly to exclude the influence of Chancery. Both may have been at work.

the proper role of the Church in men's lives. It points to a gradual change of mind about what things belonged to the spiritual side of life and what things to the secular. The medieval Church could not have maintained its testamentary jurisdiction over debt without some kind of consensus that it was proper. When that consensus disappeared, so did the jurisdiction.

Even if the decline occurred partly in response to actions of *praemunire,* as suggested above, that does not fundamentally alter this conclusion. The Statute had been available for more than 100 years when it began regularly to be exploited in the King's Bench to restrict ecclesiastical jurisdiction. No technical improvements in its coverage under Henry VII have been discovered. The legal expansion to include pleas heard within England had occurred decades previously. The Statute may therefore have furnished part of the means for the change. But we ought not to confuse the means with the cause. The cause must be seen more broadly; it is as much a matter of social and religious change as of a political or legal innovation.

One of today's leading Reformation historians has characterized the most important development in the thought of the period as a "change of viewpoint concerning the nature and functions of religion."[67] Exactly that change of viewpoint is evident in the end of the enforcement of debt claims within the English Church courts. In historical perspective, the effective separation of debt claims from probate jurisdiction is at bottom a product of this secularizing change.

67. A. G. Dickens, *The English Reformation* 325 (1964).

17

USURY AND THE MEDIEVAL ENGLISH CHURCH COURTS

Historians of medieval England have devoted little sustained attention to the law of usury, and what attention they have paid to the subject has not been focused on the law's enforcement in court practice. A common assumption has been that one could not go much beyond academic treatises and legislative enactments in studying the subject. This has left an undeniable gap, one which English historians have not made as much progress in filling as have Continental historians.[1] In dealing with enforcement of the law of usury in medieval England, therefore, most general treatments have had either to make reasonable guesses from secondary evidence or to be silent.

This article fills a part of the gap.[2] It collects the evidence relating to the subject of usury found in the surviving records of the English church courts.[3] In some measure, the approach is purely descriptive, bringing to light evidence not previously available. However, insofar as the records permit, the article also attempts to interpret and explain the evidence. Regrettably, the attempt cannot wholly succeed. The records that survive are far from complete, and the information they contain is often unsatisfactory, leaving many questions unanswered. However, the records do contain useful and sure information about the church's attempts to enforce its usury prohibitions in medieval England. They further allow the historian to compare canon law theory with practice and to suggest tentative reasons for the shape that medieval practice took.

The author of this article wishes to acknowledge the helpful criticism of Professors John F. McGovern, Norman L. Jones, James A. Brundage, and John T. Noonan, Jr. They read all or parts of previous drafts, correcting the author's understanding and improving his presentation.

[1] E.g., Richard C. Trexler, *Synodal Law in Florence and Fiesole, 1306–1518* (Vatican City, 1971), pp. 105–12; Bernard Schnapper, "La repression de l'usure et l'evolution economique," *Tijdschrift voor rechtsgeschiedenis* 37 (1969), 53–57; Julius Kirshner and Kimberly lo Prete, "Peter John Olivi's Treatises on Contracts of Sale, Usury and Restitution: Minorite Economics or Minor Works?" *Quaderni fiorentini* 13 (1984), 233–86; see also works cited in nn. 56–58 below.

[2] Among the general treatments consulted in the preparation of this article are T. P. McLaughlin, "The Teaching of the Canonists on Usury" (part 1), *Mediaeval Studies* 1 (1939), 82–107, and (part 2), ibid. 2 (1940), 1–22; Benjamin N. Nelson, *The Idea of Usury* (Princeton, 1949); John T. Noonan, Jr., *The Scholastic Analysis of Usury* (Cambridge, Mass., 1957); Raymond de Roover, *La pensée économique des scolastiques* (Montreal, 1971).

[3] Some account of the character of the records of the church courts, together with bibliographical references, may be found in G. R. Elton, *England, 1200–1640* (Ithaca, N.Y., 1969), pp. 102–7.

THE ENGLISH BACKGROUND

From at least the twelfth century, prosecution of living usurers in England belonged to the church. Glanvill, author of the earliest systematic treatise on English law, denied any jurisdiction to the royal courts except at the usurer's death, when the king would be entitled to the usurer's chattels and the feudal lord would be entitled to his lands.[4] The twelfth-century *Dialogue of the Exchequer* gave a similar account of English practice.[5] The church was entitled to hear all pleas concerning usury during the lifetime of offenders, and to determine them freely according to the canon law. This remained the basic jurisdictional rule until the Tudor era. Although medieval parliaments passed occasional statutes marginally affecting the enforcement of the law of usury,[6] they left principal regulation of the subject to the canon law.

This rule was consistent with the canon law itself. The medieval church claimed exclusive jurisdiction to determine what conduct amounted to usury.[7] The church did not, however, claim exclusive jurisdiction to *punish* proven usurers. At least some canonists allowed secular courts to undertake prosecution and enforcement of the law against usury, provided that enforcement followed the church's definition, and provided also that cases of doubt about the usurious nature of any specific transaction would be referred to a church court. English medieval common law was, therefore, slightly more favorable to the rights of the church than the canon law itself required, because until 1485 the royal courts declined to exercise any jurisdiction at all over usury except at the usurer's death.

The canon law to which the English common lawyers conceded jurisdiction was strict in definition. It defined usury as "whatsoever is taken for a loan beyond the principal."[8] Any gain stemming from a loan, no matter how small, was considered usurious and unlawful. The law was also strict in sanction. Offending usurers were subject to ipso facto sentence of excommunication. This entailed exclusion not only from the church's sacraments, but also from the normal company of other Christians — a real and considerable penalty under medieval conditions.[9] Convicted usurers were required to make restitu-

---

[4] See *The treatise on the laws and customs of the realm of England commonly called Glanvill*, ed. G. D. G. Hall (London, 1965), p. 89; see also Felix Makower, *Constitutional History and Constitution of the Church of England* (London, 1895), pp. 440–42.

[5] *Dialogus de Scaccario*, ed. Charles Johnson (London, 1950), pp. 99–100.

[6] 15 Edw. III, st. 1, c. 5 (restating the jurisdictional rules); 3 Hen. VII, c. 5 (condemning "bargayns groundyt in usurye" and subjecting makers to a penalty of £100 in addition to ecclesiastical sanctions).

[7] E.g., Panormitanus, *Commentaria in libros decretalium* (Venice, 1589) ad X 2.2.8, no. 17, distinguishing two canonistic opinions on the point, but stating that given in the text as the *communis opinio*. For modern treatment, see McLaughlin, "Teaching of the Canonists" (part 1), pp. 18–21.

[8] *Decretum Gratiani*, ed. A. Friedberg (Leipzig, 1879), dictum post C.14, q.3, c.4: "Ecce evidenter ostenditur, quod quicquid ultra sortem exigitur usura est."

[9] See, for example, the statement of the penalties in the work of the thirteenth-century canonist Hostiensis, *Summa aurea* (Venice, 1574), 5, tit. *de usuris*, no. 10. For a modern discussion, see McLaughlin, "Teaching of the Canonists" (part 2), pp. 1–12.

tion of the usury to the victim or (if the victim were unavailable) to charitable uses.[10] Unrepentant usurers were denied Christian burial, and a variety of ecclesiastical decrees struck at those who aided and abetted usurers.

In England, as in most parts of western Europe, local church councils adopted specific legislation to implement and supplement this law. For example, the incumbent of every English parish was enjoined to make a public statement three or four times each year in his church declaring all usurers excommunicate.[11] Episcopal visitations of English dioceses were to search out and correct cases of usury.[12] William Lyndwood, the great English canonist, discussed usury's meaning and noted its illegality in commenting on the constitutions of the province of Canterbury.[13] If fully implemented, therefore, the canon law of usury would have been both widely known and strict in effect. It would have put severe obstacles in the way of anyone wishing to lend or borrow money at even low rates of interest.

The church's law of usury was also technically complex. Transactions that were not loans — such as annuities, shared risk contracts, or penal bonds to guarantee payment of a debt — were held to fall outside the prohibitions of the law. Only a contract classified as *mutuum* fell within. This definitional complexity might seem to have left room for evasion of the law; however, it was balanced by the rule that a transaction not formally a *mutuum* nevertheless fell afoul of the prohibitions if the transaction served merely as a cloak for usury.[14] Thus, if a man sought to borrow 100s., and the lender agreed only if the borrower would purchase a hat from him that was worth 2s. for the sum of 25s., this amounted to usury. It was a fraud on the prohibition against usury, because the sale of the hat served only to permit the loan to be made without formal interest. In short, it was a mere subterfuge. This "cloaked" usury is a simple example of the many transactions that might come within the church's ban because they were made in an attempt to evade the law's prohibitions.

The resulting intricacies of the medieval law of usury are not within the scope of this article except as they affected court practice shown in the surviving records. Nonetheless, it is useful to look at the subject of contemporary practice with an appreciation both for the strictness of the law's standards and

---

[10] *Glossa ordinaria* ad X 5.19.14 (Lyons, 1566) s.v. *restituerit:* "Non enim excusatur usurarius si nullus repetat ab eo vel si denuntiet, immo etiam tenetur usuram restituere saltem pauperibus si nullus apparet cui restituat; aliter non liberatur a peccato." For modern discussion, see Karl Wienzierl, *Die Restitutionslehre der Frühscholastik* (Munich, 1936).

[11] E.g., synodal statute c. 62 (1222–25), in *Councils and Synods with Other Documents Relating to the English Church*, 2: *A.D. 1205–1313*, ed. F. M. Powicke and C. R. Cheney (Oxford, 1964), pt. 1, pp. 150–51 and index, s.v. Usury.

[12] See, e.g., the visitation for the diocese of Hereford, in A. T. Bannister, "Visitation Returns of the Diocese of Hereford in 1397," *English Historical Review* 44 (1919), 279, 444.

[13] *Provinciale (seu Constitutiones Angliae)* (Oxford, 1679), p. 161, s.v. *usura est.*

[14] On contracts *in fraudem usurarum*, see McLaughlin, "Teaching of the Canonists" (part 1), pp. 112–24.

the intricacy of many of its provisions. The combination of these two characteristics has caused some modern writers to conclude that the academic law on
the subject bore little relation to the course of most men's lives. The law of
usury, critics say, was "remote from the practical conduct of affairs." In practice, therefore, it must have been "largely evaded or ignored."[15] Against this
sort of unfavorable but not implausible judgment, the evidence drawn from
the surviving records should be evaluated.

EXTENT OF ENFORCEMENT

Cases involving usury have been found in the early court records of the
dioceses of Canterbury, York, Bath and Wells, Chester, Chichester, Ely,
Hereford, Lichfield, Lincoln, London, Rochester, Salisbury, and Winchester.
This list includes virtually all the dioceses for which medieval court records
have survived. It seems fair to say that usury cases formed a regular part of
ecclesiastical jurisdiction throughout England. One cannot always be sure that
the church's jurisdiction was successful simply because cases were introduced
and heard. Sometimes offenders ignored citations and disobeyed decrees.
However, prosecutions were undertaken and carried forward widely enough
that one can fairly conclude that the canon law of usury was by no means the
dead letter in England that critics have sometimes assumed.

Some of the examples found in the records were instance causes, that is,
suits brought by the debtor to secure restitution of the usury paid as well as
punishment of the usurer. Such a suit, normally styled a *causa usurarie
pravitatis* in the records, could entail long judicial process. It could call for
repeated court sittings, documentary evidence, and testimony by witnesses.[16]
Complicated legal points might arise, and there might have been good reason
both for delay and for consultation among legal experts to decide such cases.
Instance usury cases, in other words, could and in fact sometimes did fully
occupy the energy of English ecclesiastical lawyers.

Most of the cases discovered, however, were not instance causes. They were
criminal prosecutions, begun and carried forward *ex officio* by the court itself.
Brought against men and women[17] who had attracted public notoriety as
usurers, these cases were dealt with summarily, normally in one or two court
sessions. The records normally style the defendants in these cases as "public"[18]

---

[15] H. G. Richardson and George Sayles, *Law and Legislation from Aethelberht to Magna Carta*
(Edinburgh, 1966), p. 85. For similar judgments, see, e.g., F. R. H. Du Boulay, *An Age of
Ambition: English Society in the Late Middle Ages* (London, 1970), p. 59.

[16] For a printed example, see Elcok c. Springman (1348), in *Registrum Hamonis Hethe*, ed.
Charles Johnson, Canterbury and York Society (1948), pp. 1001, 1005, 1017, 1023, 1028–29,
1041.

[17] There are cases in which women appear accused of usury in the remaining records: e.g., Ex
officio c. Mariona Turboll, diocese of Salisbury, Subdean's Act Book 1 (Wiltshire Record Office,
Trowbridge), fol. 9v (1477).

[18] Mariona Turboll, in the Salisbury case just cited, for instance, was described as "publica
usuraria" in the act book.

or "common"[19] or "manifest"[20] usurers. This phraseology did not necessarily signify that the person accused was a person who made a career out of lending money at interest. The canon law[21] and the evidence of the records themselves[22] make it clear that the "manifest" character of the usury had to do with public knowledge of the act of usury. The act's repetition, although naturally leading to public knowledge, was not what made a man a "public" usurer.

If usury prosecutions were a routine part of the business of a medieval English church court, they were never a large part. Most courts heard few such cases each year. In the commissary court for the diocese of Canterbury, for example, only five usury causes were heard during the two-year period 1373–74.[23] Almost a century later, for 1453–54, the total for the same court came to a similarly small figure of four.[24] The greatest incidence found comes from the diocese of Lichfield, where seven instance causes were introduced in 1477.[25] But that figure is exceptional. One, two, or perhaps three cases per year was the norm in the diocesan courts.

Sometimes the annual records of a particular diocesan court contain no usury cases at all. For instance, Rochester's consistory court for 1445–46[26] and London's commissary court for 1513–14[27] apparently heard none. Such total absence is unusual, but not unparalleled. It would be fair to say that although it never comes as a surprise to find a usury prosecution in one of the remaining court books, it is unusual to find many of them undertaken in any one year. Because most of these diocesan courts were dealing with something like a hundred cases each year,[28] the appearance of usury cases can be character-

---

[19] Ex officio c. Discott, diocese of Hereford, Commissary Court Act Book (Hereford County Record Office, Hereford) O/13, p. 73 (1480): "est communis usurarius."

[20] Ex officio c. Taillour, diocese of Ely, Consistory Court Act Book (Cambridge University Library) EDR D/2/1, fol. 78 (1377): "tanquam usurarium manifestum."

[21] One sense in which this phrase was used by the canonists was that of "manifesti per famam tantum." See Hostiensis, *Summa aurea* V, tit. *de usuris*, no. 10; this was insufficient to establish guilt, but was sufficient to require him to deny the charge on oath. Another sense of "manifest" required a judicial declaration of guilt. It is clear that the English records use the terms in the former sense. See generally McLaughlin, "Teaching of the Canonists" (part 2), pp. 12–13.

[22] This is shown by cases in which only one act of usury was noted and nevertheless was treated as being sufficient to give rise to a charge of "common" usury. E.g., Ex officio c. Tente, diocese of Canterbury, Commissary Court Act Book (Canterbury Cathedral Library) X.1.1, fol. 7v (1449): "Ricardus Tente de Dodington notatur quod est communis usurarius pro eo quod mutuavit c s. cuidam Jacobo Lydingden de eadem et recepit ultra sortem."

[23] Taken from Act Book Y.1.1, fols. 27v–109.

[24] Taken from Act Book X.1.1, fols. 64v–98v.

[25] Taken from Act Book (Joint Record Office, Lichfield) B/C/1/2, fols. 227v–263v.

[26] Based on examination of the Consistory Court Act Book (Kent County Record Office, Maidstone) DRb Pa 2.

[27] Based on examination of the Commissary Court Act Book, London, Guildhall Library, MS 9064/11. See also Richard M. Wunderli, *London Church Courts and Society on the Eve of the Reformation* (Cambridge, Mass., 1981), pp. 127–28.

[28] Examples can be found in R. H. Helmholz, "Assumpsit and Fidei Laesio," *Law Quarterly Review* 91 (1975), 425–27 : supra 282-4.

ized as regular but infrequent, a distinctly minor part of the business of an ordinary English ecclesiastical court.

From this relative infrequency few far-reaching conclusions can be drawn. The records are insufficient to prove either the overall prevalence of usury or the effectiveness of the church's prohibitions. Even leaving aside the question of the force of the church's sanctions, two insuperable barriers stand in the way. First, despite the absence of royal court jurisdiction, other lesser courts did undertake prosecution against usurers during the Middle Ages. Manor courts prosecuted them in places.[29] So did the courts of cities and boroughs, most notably London, where the mayor and aldermen heard usury cases from at least the fourteenth century.[30] The infrequency of usury cases in the records of the commissary court for the diocese of London, the place in England where one would have expected the highest incidence of usury, probably occurred because the local secular courts heard most cases. Legal jurisdiction in medieval England did not break down into a neat pattern. There were many courts with conflicting, and sometimes competing, claims to jurisdiction. Usury was one of the subjects they shared. On a local level, therefore, the canon law's claim to exclusive jurisdiction over usury was not observed as it was on the royal court level. This fact makes conclusions about the extent of usury impossible to draw on the basis of the evidence surveyed.

Second, even had there been no overlapping jurisdiction, the records of the church courts could not furnish an accurate picture of the extent of canonical enforcement. They tell us nothing about enforcement undertaken in what the canon law called "the internal forum," that is, the confessional. As noted above, the diocesan courts dealt only with "public" or "manifest" usurers. This excluded cases where the fact of usury was known only to the parties involved. And in the nature of things, then as now, much usury is not made public. Many debtors will not bring the matter into the open. They may be wary of implicating themselves in the crime (a possibility the canon law left open).[31] They may count the attendant shame a greater cost than the usury paid. They may want to protect future sources of credit. The canon law itself recognized these difficulties and therefore assigned much responsibility for searching out

---

[29] E.g., Wakefield Court Roll (Yorkshire Archaeological Society, Leeds) 1336/7, m. 3: "Adam del Brighous de Elfloburgh est communis usurarius ideo in misericordia"; Hundred of Appletree Court Roll (Public Record Office, London) DL 30/45/523, m. 8 (1389): "Agnes de Tyso est usurarius."

[30] See the *Judicium contra usurarios* (1377), in *Liber albus*, ed. Henry T. Riley, Rolls Series (London, 1859), 1:394–401; and see generally William Holdsworth, *A History of English Law*, 8, 2nd ed. (London, 1937), pp. 102–3; Sylvia L. Thrupp, *The Merchant Class of Medieval London [1300–1500]* (Chicago, 1948), pp. 175–77; Wunderli, *London Church Courts and Society on the Eve of the Reformation*, pp. 127–28.

[31] See X 5.19.4, and canonists ad idem. The distinction came down to the difficult questions of the degree of need of the borrower and the possible fraudulent intent of the parties.

cases of usury to the parish priest in the confessional. Contemporary confessor's manuals show this plainly.[32] So do the canon law texts themselves.[33]

The seal of the confessional, therefore, and the shared nature of jurisdiction over the crime of usury stand in the way of firm conclusions about the incidence of usury or the efficacy of its detection. And there is of course the difficulty of knowing whether or not the courts were able finally to enforce the canon law's sanctions. What one can say with more confidence is that on regular, though not frequent, occasions the courts of the church did undertake public enforcement of the canon law against usury. The possibility existed, and it was used. The further question that can usefully be addressed is: How closely did actual litigation in the church courts follow the formal canon law on the subject?

Nature of the Cases

The records show that the substantive canon law was in fact applied in the cases and that the problems raised in academic treatises on the law of usury were relevant to what happened in the courts. There was correspondence between law and practice. However, there were limits to it. The records show that few large loans were attacked as usurious; they strongly suggest that only substantial rates of interest were punished as usurious; and they demonstrate conclusively that the rules against "indirect" participation in usurious transactions were not put into practice. The English church courts prosecuted only public lenders, lenders who had entered into relatively small transactions, and at relatively large rates of interest.

Correspondence between law and practice is found in the nature of the transactions the English courts treated as usurious. The centrality of the loan, *mutuum*, for the canon law's definition of usury has already been noted. The records are in accord with this. The scribes who kept the records often took care to note specifically that the prosecution was for usury *pro mutuo*[34] or *pro mutuatione*,[35] or that the defendant *mutuavit* a sum of money and received *ultra sortem* for it.[36] The language used, in other words, tracks that found in the formal law so closely that the historian may fairly assume that the court officials had the formal categories in mind. This correspondence is not surprising. It is what was supposed to exist under the canon law system, and it occurred in other areas of the canon law applied in the English courts. How-

[32] E.g., Thomas de Chobham, *Summa confessorum*, ed. F. Broomfield (Louvain, 1968), pp. 515–16.

[33] X 5.19.10.

[34] E.g., Ex officio c. Baker, Rochester Act Book DRb Pa 3, fol. 346 (1458): "Alicia Baker super crimine usure reddendo viii d. de Ricardo Hidemont pro mutuo xl d."

[35] E.g., Ex officio c. Parke, Canterbury Act Book X.1.1, fol. 4v (1450): "pro mutuacione xx s. cuidam Carpenter de Radmersham receperat iiii nobiles."

[36] E.g., Ex officio c. Phelpot, Hereford Act Book O/22, p. 200 (1502): "mutuavit Johanni Phelpot xx s. et recepit ab eodem in certis terminis xxv s. per annum et sic ab eodem habet ultra sortem principalem v s. nomine usure annuatim."

ever, the correspondence between law and practice remains a point worth making, because it did not exist in *every* area of church court practice.[37] Where it does, the historian should take note. It means that the academic law was not in fact entirely out of touch with the realities of legal practice.

Moreover, correspondence with the law found in academic writing exists in the many cases of allegedly "cloaked" usury that came before the ecclesiastical judges. The law held that if the purpose of entering into a more complicated transaction was merely to disguise a usurious loan, the transaction was fully as unlawful as the simple receipt of a sum beyond the principal of a loan would have been. These more complicated cases of alleged fraud arose in practice. One found in the surviving records is the simulated contract of sale. For example, at York in 1397, John Domins was accused of usury for contracting to purchase a quantity of grain from Henry Andrew and John Burnman on August 15, and to resell the grain to them on November 11.[38] The price to be paid by Domins on the former date was 25s. The agreement was that he would sell the grain back to them on the latter date for 40s. The result of such a contract amounted to usury because it was in effect a loan of 25s. to Andrew and Burnham. That sum would be repaid at the end of the three months together with interest of 15s. Domins would be richer by that amount after the three-month period. That it was formally disguised as a sale of grain should not alter its substance.

Regrettably, it is not possible to probe much further into the legal issues raised in the case, and they might in fact have been considerably more complicated. This analysis assumes that the value of the grain would remain essentially the same during the three-month period. However, if there had been a risk of market fluctuation in the interval between August and November, and Domins had agreed to share in this risk, the legitimacy of the transaction could have been defended under canon law. Thus, it is cause for legitimate regret that the court record is not complete enough to show whether any such legal argument was in fact made. All we know is that in this case, and in several like cases,[39] a contract of sale allegedly *in fraudem usurarum* was attacked in a church court.

---

[37] See Charles Donahue, Jr., "Roman Canon Law in the Medieval English Church: Stubbs vs. Maitland Re-examined after 75 Years in the Light of Some Records from the Church Courts," *Michigan Law Review* 72 (1974), 647–716; R. H. Helmholz, "Legitim in English Legal History," *University of Illinois Law Review* (1984), 659–74 : supra 247-62.

[38] Act Book (York Minster Library) M 2(l)f, fol. 27v (1397): "Dominus Johannes Domins comisit usuram gravem emendo a Henrico Androwe et Johanne Burnman de Coton x quarteria ordei emendo quarterium pro ii s. vi d. circa festum Assumptionis beate Marie et vendendo eisdem dictum ordeum circa festum sancti Martini proxime sequens ultimo preteritum viz. unum quarterium pro iiii s. dictis viris."

[39] Other cases involving allegedly fraudulent sales are: Ex officio c. Makkanhull, York Act Book (Borthwick Institute, York) D/C AB 1, fol. 174 (1465); Ex officio c. Mannyng, London Commissary Court Act Book MS 9064/4, fol. 301v (1491); Ex officio c. Somer, London Commissary Court Act Book MS 9064/6, fol. 77v (1494); Ex officio c. Hogham, London Commissary Court Probate Act Book (Guildhall Library, London) 1496–1500, fol. 38v (1498).

A second kind of "cloaked" usury found in the records involved the mortgage or pledge. At Rochester in 1447, for instance, John Medeherst was cited for making a usurious loan of six marks (80s.) to Stephan Yonge to enable Yonge to purchase land from him for that price. Under the terms agreed upon, Medeherst was to retain formal title to the land until the six marks had been fully paid. But at the same time he also leased the identical land to Yonge for 6s. 8d. a year.[40] This was, in effect, a mortgage. Yonge would pay off the loan in installments, together with 6s. 8d. "rent" each year for four years, until the purchase price had been paid. At that time, the land would be fully his. Under the canon law, the 6s. 8d. represented a usurious payment, because it served no function other than paying for the original loan of the land's purchase price. In effect the money had been given for deferring payment of the principal. That the transaction formally left title in Medeherst for the interim period, and called the 6s. 8d. rent, should not disguise that fact. In substance there had been a loan, coupled with an interest payment.[41]

This Rochester case shows clearly that the canon law of usury was being put into practice, because Medeherst raised an affirmative defense to the charge. He answered that Yonge enjoyed an unconditional right to pay the six marks at any time during the year term.[42] He brought a written indenture to that effect into court. This should mean, he argued, that the 6s. 8d. truly represented rent for the land, of which Yonge was enjoying the fruits. Since the six marks could be paid at any time, there was, in substance as well as form, no *mutuum* involved. Hence there could be no usury.

Under the canon law, the outcome of such a dispute turned as much on the intent and understanding of the parties as on the terms of the indenture itself. If the written terms alone controlled, the prohibitions against usury could be too easily evaded. And, in fact, Medeherst's case was handled in just this way. He was required to swear a formal oath that no fraud on the usury laws had existed in the transaction and to find nine "oath helpers," neighbors who would swear to their belief in his oath. In the event, Medeherst successfully underwent this process, called canonical purgation. He was consequently dismissed by the Rochester judge.

A third form of "cloaked" usury, the gift in return for a loan, appears less

---

[40] Act Book DRb Pa 2, fol. 75: "Johannes Medeherst de Kyngesden citatus est per A.C. super crimine usurarie pravitatis recipiendo pro mutuo de Stephano Yonge pro vi marcis ad emptionem unius mesuagii mutuati per annum xx s."

[41] Other cases attacking allegedly fraudulent mortgages or pledges are: Schotynden c. Barthelot, Canterbury Act Book Y.1.1, fol. 17 (1373, involving a cow pledged); Ex officio c. Rolf, Canterbury Act Book X.8.3, fol. 49v (1464, involving land); Ex officio c. ap Jeynkyn, Hereford Act Book O/13, p. 22 (1480, involving land); Pravit c. War, Rochester Act Book DRb Pa 4, fol. 303v (1496, involving land); and Fryingham c. Rosse, Hereford Act Book I/5, p. 432 (1523, involving land).

[42] Rochester Act Book DRb Pa 2, fol. 75: "Interrogatus dicit quod comparavit de predicto Stephano Yonge unam peciam terre pro vi marcis et concessit et tradidit ei terram predictam ad firmam pro vi s. viii d. annuatim per tres annos et quod convenit et concessit ei quod si solveret ei interim predictas vi marcas rehaberet predictam terram."

frequently than either of the other two mentioned. Such cases did, however, occur. At Chichester in 1508, Thomas Fowler was sued for receiving a silver spoon for a loan of 8s. previously made to Richard Sawton, the plaintiff.[43] Fowler's defense was that Sawton had "freely given" him the spoon; that it had nothing to do with the loan.[44] Again, this case seemingly rested on the difficult question of whether the parties had intended to evade the prohibition against usury. The judge postponed the hearing, the record noted, "because it was arduous."[45] Thereafter it disappeared from the act book. Like many such cases, one learns only that a transaction allegedly *in fraudem usurarum* was attacked, not what the eventual outcome was. Points from the canon law of usury were raised. To suppose that they were argued according to the formal law would be a reasonable, but not a provable, assumption. Correspondence between theory and practice is, at least, positively suggested.

On the other hand, it would not be reasonable to assume that the courts enforced the canon law rule defining usury as the taking of *any* amount above the principal. In practice, only loans at "immoderate" rates of interest seem to have been subject to prosecution. The act books strongly suggest this important limitation on the law's enforcement. The evidence to prove it is unfortunately imperfect. Many of the act book entries record no more than that a named person had been cited as a common usurer. And even in fuller cases, where a complicated transaction was involved, it becomes difficult to calculate the effective rate.[46] However, where the record does give the facts about a loan fully and clearly, the case involved a usurer prosecuted for taking more than a small amount beyond the loan's principal.

Examination of the records has turned up twenty-eight cases where the yearly rate of usury alleged can be calculated with reasonable certainty. Figuring on the basis of simple interest, the mean rate of usury alleged for these cases is 16⅔%.[47] The highest rate found was 50%, alleged both in a Canterbury case of 1471 and in a Rochester case from 1456.[48] The lowest was 5½%, from an Ely case of 1380, in which the defendant was acquitted "because [the

---

[43] Chichester Act Book (East Sussex Record Office, Chichester) Ep I/10/1, fol. 106v: "et actor allegavit viva voce quod pars rea recepit et adhuc habet de actore unum cocliarium argenteum pro modo usure pro mutuo viii s."

[44] Ibid.: "et pars rea negat sed dicit quod actor libere dedit sibi dictum cocliarium."

[45] Ibid.: "Et quia causa est ardua ideo iudex respectavit causam usque proximum."

[46] They were not, however, necessarily complicated. Where a lender took goods or crops as usury, it is impossible to be exact about the rate and they have not been included. E.g., Ex officio c. Cece, diocese of Hereford (1397), in A. T. Bannister, "Visitation Returns of the Diocese of Hereford in 1397," *English Historical Review* 44 (1929), 453: "mutuavit cuidam Jak atte Hulle xii s. quos recepit integros una cum iiii bussellis frumenti pro dilacione."

[47] Three such causes were found: Ex officio c. Taillour, Ely Act Book EDR D/2/1, fol. 78 (1377); Ex officio c. Fauxton, Canterbury Act Book Y.1.11, fol. 28v (1468); Ex officio c. Somer, London Commissary Court Act Book 9064/6, fol. 77v (1494).

[48] Ex officio c. Mychell, Canterbury Act Book Y.1.10, fol. 93v; Ex officio c. Burgh, Rochester Act Book DRb Pa 2, fol. 293v. Both involved very small loans (3s. 4d., and 4d.)

charge] was not fully proved against him."[49] Apart from this somewhat equivocal Ely case, the rate in all the rest was higher than 7½% a year, and the great majority clustered between 12½% and 33⅓%.[50] Although it is possible, therefore, that the church courts would entertain a *causa usurarie pravitatis* where only a small amount had been taken in excess of a loan's principal, the evidence suggests that normally they did not.

This finding is not wholly unexpected. Contemporary civilians, that is, commentators on Roman law, followed the texts of the *Corpus iuris civilis* in permitting interest under certain conditions.[51] One of the texts found in the *Novellae* permitted a moderate rate of interest to be stipulated in a loan.[52] The civilians endorsed its wisdom. Thus, the distinction between moderate and immoderate rates of interest, with only the latter being considered unlawful, was a living idea at the time of the litigation described here. Many English ecclesiastical lawyers would have been familiar with it.

The canonists also dealt with the possibility of adopting this lenient understanding of usury in commenting on a canon of the Fourth Lateran Council (1215) that condemned *graves et immoderatas usuras*.[53] This text could be used to argue that the canon law condemned not simply all usury, but *only* immoderate usury. The canonists ultimately rejected this understanding of the text, holding that the canon law prohibitions necessarily prevailed over the lax Roman law on the subject.[54] However, their writings show that the distinction had practical force and even appeal at the time. Arguments were advanced in its favor, such as the modern-sounding notion that if a moderate rate of interest were allowed, this would keep borrowers out of the clutches of truly rapacious lenders.[55]

Even more than academic opinion, however, evidence from parts of the Continent renders the English situation less surprising than it might otherwise be. Scholars have shown that late medieval practice, often resting on local

[49] Wardale c. Bytering, Act Book EDR D/2/1, fols. 126, 128v; the instance cause seems to have been settled by agreement between the parties; the pendent *ex officio* matter allowed to go to purgation "quia non est clare probatum contra dictum dominum Ricardum."

[50] Records of the cases counted, apart from those noted above, are found in: Canterbury Act Books Y.1.1, fol. 17 (1373), 15+%; Y.1.3, fol. 80 (1418), 23⅓%; X.1.1, fol. 18 (1450), 12½%; Y.1.11, fol. 64v (1470), 10%; Y.1.11, fol. 93v (1470), 35%; Y.1.11, fol. 107v (1470), 7½%; Y.1.10, fol. 93v (1471), 50%; Y.1.10, fol. 245 (1475), 8⅓%; Y.2.10, fol. 1v (1515), 13⅓%; Rochester Act Books DRb Pa 2, fol. 75 (1447), 25%; DRb Pa 2, fol. 293v (1456), 30%; DRb Pa 2, fol. 293v (1456), 50%; DRb Pa 3, fol. 346 (1458), 20%; Leicester (Archdeaconry) Act Book, Lincs. Archives Office, Lincoln, Viv/2, fol. 29 (1489), 33⅓%; London Act Books 9064/6, fol. 194 (1497), 35+%; 9064/8, fol. 230 (1499), 25%; Hereford Visitation Book, in *English Historic~' Review* 45 (1930), 460 (1379), 33⅓% (two cases); Hereford Act Books O/13, p. 274 (1480), 38%; O/22, p. 195 (1501), 8+%; O/22, p. 200 (1502), 20%; I/5, p. 432 (1523), 13⅓%.

[51] See generally G. Cassimatis, *Les interêts dans la legislation de Justinien et dans le droit byzantin* (Paris, 1931).

[52] Nov. 34.1.

[53] X 5.19.18.

[54] E.g., *Glossa ordinaria* ad idem: "Ergo moderatas videtur permittere, a contrario sensu. . . . Quod non est verum."

[55] See McLaughlin, "Teaching of the Canonists" (part 1), pp. 92–95.

statutes, permitted the taking of moderate rates of interest in locations as disparate as Venice,[56] Aragon,[57] and parts of northwestern Europe.[58] Usury was apparently thought of in something like the modern sense, as an exorbitant rate of interest. A distinction between high and low rates of usury was apparently accepted in fact, if not in canonical theory, in many parts of Europe. What makes the English evidence striking is that the church courts themselves, the institutions most closely tied to the formal canon law, seem to have accepted the distinction. Whatever the theory, in fact their records suggest that they did not undertake prosecutions against "moderate" usurers.

Equally absent from the surviving records are cases brought to enforce the canonical penalties against those who cooperated with usurers. The canon law contained some sweeping, even extravagant, provisions aimed at discouraging usury. For instance, clerics who granted Christian burial to or received alms from impenitent usurers were to be suspended from their clerical office.[59] Likewise, a cleric or even a layman who leased property to someone who practiced usury on the premises might himself be excommunicated.[60] However, neither of these proscriptions has left any trace of actual enforcement in the surviving records. If they were applied in practice, it was only in the forum of the confessional. Cases found in the surviving act books were brought only against direct participants in usurious transactions and, as noted above, only when that transaction had involved more than a low rate of usury.

In one additional respect the law applied by the church courts seems to have been restricted in practice. That is in the amount of the loans attacked as usurious. Very few involved large sums of money. The largest instance discovered in the surviving act books was for slightly more than £24.[61] The smallest involved a loan of only 4d.[62] The great majority of cases dealt with loans of 40s. or less. Cases brought over loans in amounts between 10s. and 20s. are the most common found. Large lenders, at least if the surviving records are representative,[63] escaped the nets of the church courts.

Why these limitations were observed in English practice is not always easy to

---

[56] Gino Luzzatto, "Tasso d'interesse e usura a Venezia nei secoli XIII–XV," in *Miscellanea in onore di Roberto Cessi* (Rome, 1958), 1:191–202.

[57] See Christian Guillere, "Les visites pastorales en Tarraconaise à la fin du moyen-âge (XIVe–XVe siècles): L'example du diocese de Gérone," in *Mélanges de la Casa de Velazquez* (1983), 19:155; Marjorie Grice-Hutchinson, *Early Economic Thought in Spain 1177–1740* (London, 1978), p. 41.

[58] Raymond de Roover, *Money, Banking and Credit in Medieval Bruges* (Cambridge, Mass., 1948), pp. 104–6; and see generally John Gilchrist, *The Church and Economic Activity in the Middle Ages* (New York, 1969), p. 114.

[59] Sext 5.5.2.

[60] Sext 5.5.1.

[61] Ex officio promoto c. Holnehurst and Blechyndon, Canterbury Act Book Y.1.3, fol. 80 (1418); the loan was for 28 marks, and (at least in the defendant's submission) a lease of real estate, with no usurious motive, was involved.

[62] Ex officio c. Burgh, Rochester Act Book DRb Pa 2, fol. 293v (1456): "pro mutuo 4 d."

[63] It is possible that fuller record survival would reverse this conclusion; the medieval records of the Court of Arches (the provincial court of appeal) and the consistory court of London have virtually all disappeared.

determine. No external pressure from the royal courts to limit the scope of prosecutions or to conform to a lax definition of usury existed. No English statutes restricted the right of church court judges to follow the letter of the canon law. Can it be that virtually no borrower at less than a modest rate of interest complained during the many years of litigation covered by the surviving records? Or that no official had the energy to prosecute those who aided manifest usurers? Or that no victim of usury in a large-scale loan had incentive enough to complain? These possibilities seem implausible. But they are apparently the fact.

To a large extent, the searcher in the records of the church courts can only describe the situation as it existed. In the nature of things, the records cannot provide a satisfactory explanation, because they do not record any motivation or reasoning on the part of either judges or litigants, and we have little but record evidence from which to judge. At most, examination of the procedure used in usury cases will provide suggestions and perhaps some clues to the meaning of the evidence.

PROCEDURE AND PROOF IN USURY CASES

In most respects, practice in usury cases did not differ from that used in other litigation in the English church courts. When a cause was begun at the instance of a private party, the responsibility of proving the usurious character of the transaction was left to that plaintiff. If the defendant denied the allegation, the plaintiff had the burden of producing witnesses or written documents to prove that the transaction was usurious. A few records from actual litigation have survived to show that this happened in practice.

By far the greater number of usury cases, however, arose from *ex officio* prosecutions. Unlike instance causes, they were brought in the name of the court itself to vindicate the public law of the church. In such cases, if the person accused denied the charge of usury, he was required to swear a formal oath that he was innocent and to find oath helpers or "compurgators" who knew him and could conscientiously swear to their belief in his oath.[64] Successful purgation led to acquittal and a public declaration of the defendant's innocence. Unsuccessful purgation (or failure to find a sufficient number of compurgators) led to conviction and punishment, normally by undergoing public penance in the parish church before the congregation assembled on a succeeding Sunday.

Both forms of procedure contained possibilities of mitigation. There were ways in which factors that were not strictly legal could have shaped the nature of litigation. No doubt, certain of the cases that came before the church courts would have been quite clear-cut. Simple loans of money in return for a promise to pay a greater sum raised a straightforward question of fact: Had the loan been made on the terms alleged? However, when the underlying transac-

---

[64] E.g., Ex officio c. Baker, Rochester Act Book DRb Pa 3, fol. 346 (1458): "Alicia Baker super crimine usurarie . . . , negat et habet ad purgandum se coram vicinis.

tion was more complicated, as it often was, both forms of procedure left room for mitigation in some of the law's strictness.

In instance causes, this could have occurred in two ways. First, the courts required proof that usury had been paid for a loan. They would not give sentence on a debtor's word or simply because of public suspicion. The necessity for proof normally required that the plaintiff bring witnesses to testify, and many a witness had a mind of his own about the subject. They also had a chance to express their views. They were routinely asked to testify whether or not a transaction had been usurious, and they were free to say what they thought. One witness, testifying at Canterbury in 1292, remarked that the defendant could not be a usurer because "he did nothing else than was commonly done in the parish of Aldington in selling oxen and sheep."[65] Another added (perhaps sarcastically) that the defendant "took less than the archbishop takes from his debtors."[66] In the face of such attitudes and in light of the relative complexity of the canon law of usury, the church court judges would have had to overcome lay attitudes to enforce the rules as rigorously as the formal law required.

Most judges did not make that attempt. This is one reason the law's strictness was subject to mitigation. In practice, the judges routinely permitted, and seem even to have encouraged, compromise and private settlement of usury cases. Far from giving evidence of judicial efforts to impose a strict definition of usury on the laity, the court records repeatedly show the judges allowing the parties to settle their own quarrels. Notations such as *Pax est*[67] or dismissals *sub spe concordie*[68] are frequent in the act books. The court record simply states that the parties had reached an agreement.

This characteristic of usury cases is not unusual; it occurred throughout the litigation heard in the English church courts.[69] However, it does suggest a way in which the rules about usury might have been tempered in practice, and one possible explanation for the restricted nature of the prosecution undertaken. The judges permitted litigants to settle the cases themselves, or to do so with the help of neighbors who had taken an interest in the restoration of concord between them. There was little that was inquisitorial about instance jurisdiction over usury. It left room for the parties to set aside some of the harsher canonical rules.

In *ex officio* cases, the possibility that procedural and attitudinal factors

[65] Ex officio c. Hamdenum, Ecclesiastical Suit Roll 92: Matthew Frauncey testified, "quod alio modo non fecit quam communiter efficitur in parochia de Aldenton vendendo boves et oves."

[66] Ibid., John Bere testified that no usury intervened, "... hoc adiiciendo quod minus accepit ab isto teste ut dicit quam archiepiscopus accepit a suis debitoribus."

[67] E.g., Ex officio c. ap Goth, Hereford Act Book O/5, p. 16 (1454): "Postea vero pars rea comparet et absoluta est quia dicit quod pax est."

[68] E.g., Barbowe c. Fauconer, diocese of Chester, Consistory Court Act Book (Cheshire Archives, Chester) EDC 1/6, fol. 9v (1533): "Stet sub spe concordie."

[69] See R. H. Helmholz, *Marriage Litigation in Medieval England* (Cambridge, Eng., 1974), pp. 135–38.

shaped usury jurisdiction is likewise evident. Both in the inception and the termination of these prosecutions, the community played a role as important as that of the judges. First, most *ex officio* cases came before the courts as a result of local initiation. Presentment by the parish churchwardens or other appointed "questmen" normally brought suspected usurers before the courts,[70] rather than an officially sponsored investigation. Doubtless there is something to the common allegation that the church courts permitted abusive summoners to ferret out offenses of the laity. But that was the exception, an abuse of canonical procedure. Normally, *ex officio* cases arose because there was local presentment of the offense by representatives of the parish church.

These representatives, or "questmen," were laymen drawn from the community. They were appointed to carry out local ecclesiastical duties and to serve (on a smaller scale) the same function a grand jury served in secular criminal practice. They were specifically assigned to report matters that were amiss in their parish, including the existence of public usurers. It may be that some of the prosecutions were brought to the attention of the courts by disgruntled debtors,[71] but presentment by these laymen was the chief source of *ex officio* prosecutions. The church lacked a functioning and inquisitorial bureaucracy ready to search out cases of usury. Much depended on local and private initiative, and to this extent the strict law of usury was subject to mitigation by the mechanism of failure to present anyone except the creditor who took immoderate usury. Insofar as the men and women of any parish found only gross usury offensive, they were free to translate that sentiment into action by presenting only immoderate usurers.

Mitigation could also have occurred at the proof stage. Compurgation, the method of proof used in *ex officio* cases, depended on the conscience of both the defendant and his compurgators. The defendant's oath required him to swear that he had not committed the crime of usury. The oath of the compurgators asked them to swear that they believed the person accused had sworn truly.[72] Neither was asked to swear to a simple question of fact: Did you lend ten marks and receive back twelve? It was a more complicated inquiry. Because the usurious character of many transactions actually depended on whether the transaction had been made in fraud of the usury laws, intent was a relevant factor. Compurgation was therefore not an inappropriate method of fact-finding. It tested whether or not there had been fraud. It also left room for some moderation of the law's definition of what constituted punishable usury.[73] Much depended on the conscience and understanding of the

---

[70] E.g., Ex officio c. Cressy, archdeaconry of St. Alban's (Hertfordshire Record Office, Hertford) ASA 7, fol. 6 (1515): "Testes sinodales et inquisitores jurati in eadem parochia dicunt et presentant. . . ."

[71] It is possible to suspect this where the debtor also appeared in court: e.g., Ex officio c. Rolf, Canterbury Act Book X.8.3, fol. 49v (1464); Rolf was accused of committing usury in a loan to Richard Aleyn, who is recorded as appearing personally in court.

[72] X 5.19.5, 13.

[73] See the judicious remarks in Ralph Houlbrooke, *Church Courts and the People during the English Reformation 1520–1570* (Oxford, 1979), pp. 45–46.

parties involved. This may help to explain why the English church courts undertook such restricted enforcement of the law of usury. Procedure influenced substance.

On the other hand, it would be mistaken to suppose that the procedure outlined here adequately explains the failure of the English church courts fully to implement the canon law of usury. Nothing in the records proves that the judges abdicated control of litigation to the judgment of the community. It would be strange if they had. Nor is there much positive evidence (except the result) for supposing that medieval Englishmen considered the taking only of immoderate rates of usury as wrongful. In fact, we can only guess at the attitudes of the judges and the laymen involved in litigation. We are dealing with reasonable conclusion, not proof. With this caveat, however, it remains clear that the procedure used in the courts left room for mitigation of the law. The possibility is there.

FATE OF ECCLESIASTICAL JURISDICTION

The Reformation did not bring the demise of the English church's jurisdiction over usury. In fact, the first English canonical treatment of the subject was written in 1569 and published in 1572.[74] It states the traditional law on the subject, citing the medieval canonists in profusion.[75] The temporal law also permitted the continuation of the church's jurisdiction. Both the statute of 1545 and the more important enactment of 1571 which created a common-law offense of usury contained "savings clauses" to preserve the rights of the ecclesiastical courts.[76] Parliament did not intend to oust the church's jurisdiction, but to add secular jurisdiction to it.

The church courts in fact took advantage of those "saving clauses." Records from after 1571 continued to contain both *ex officio* prosecutions brought against usurers and instance causes brought by debtors. They were little changed in form from those brought prior to the Reformation.[77] The numbers were reduced, as might be expected, but the old forms were maintained by the Elizabethan church courts.

The most revolutionary feature of the Tudor legislation, historians have always assumed, was its distinction between rates of interest in excess of 10% per annum and those below. Although the latter was not made legal, the law's

---

[74] Thomas Wilson, *A Discourse upon Usury,* ed. R. H. Tawney (London, 1925).

[75] Wilson cites Panormitanus (p. 318), Hostiensis (p. 328), Guido de Baysio (Archidiaconus) (p. 290), Franciscus Zabarella (Cardinalis) (p. 329), Joannes Andreae (p. 329), Joannes de Imola (p. 329), Petrus de Ancharano (p. 329), and Willelmus Durantis (p. 329).

[76] 37 Hen. VIII, c. 9, repealed by 5–6 Edw. VI, c. 20, and 13 Eliz. c. 8, made perpetual by 39 Eliz. c. 18. The allowable rate was reduced to 8% by 21 Jac. I, c. 17.

[77] Ecclesiastical records after 1571 have been examined less fully than those for the earlier period; there is a real need for more work here. However, the records so far explored do reveal the existence of usury cases: Kyrwoode c. Jauncye, Hereford Act Book I/11 s.d. 23 Feb. 1576; Ex officio c. Turner, Canterbury Act Book Y.3.16, fol. 290v (1579); Ex officio c. Somefeld, Lichfield Act Book B/C/3/1, s.d. 19 May 1591. See also the valuable discussion in Richard L. Greaves, *Society and Religion in Elizabethan England* (Minneapolis, 1981), pp. 596–611.

full force was directly against only the former. Taking interest at less than 10% was not punishable except by forfeiture of the interest, and it soon became apparent that in practice this would be interpreted to allow rates below that figure. This development normally has been seen as an express rejection of the medieval canon law on the subject, in favor of a more "Calvinist" doctrine that restricted illegal usury to the taking of high rates of interest.[78] In one sense, it was exactly that. The Elizabethan statute did set aside the law of the church that defined usury as the taking of any rate of interest, no matter how small. It did adopt a position something like that advocated by John Calvin.

However, in a more immediate and probably also more accurate sense, the new legislation built upon what had been long-time fact in English legal practice. The distinction between "petit usury" and "grand usury" was not radically new. Evidence from the medieval records shows that the distinction came close to practice that the English church courts had long made familiar. In this way the canon law not only provided much of the legal substance behind the new secular legislation and the common law cases that built upon it; the canon law as enforced in the medieval church courts also provided a practical precedent for the new definition of what rates of interest were usurious enough to call for the full sanctions of the law.

[78] See William Holdsworth, *History of English Law*, 8:109; Peter Ramsey, *Tudor Economic Problems* (London, 1965), pp. 152–53; C. G. A. Clay, *Economic Expansion and Social Change: England 1500–1700* (Cambridge, Eng., 1984), 1:150–51; 2:232–33.

18

THE EARLY ENFORCEMENT OF USES

As a means of avoiding feudal incidents and of evading the common law rule prohibiting devises of freehold land, the feoffment to uses, ancestor of the modern trust, enjoyed a popularity at least from the reign of Edward III (1327-1377).[1] The holder of freehold land—the feoffor—would convey land during his lifetime to feoffees to uses. They in turn held it for the benefit of the feoffor, or sometimes of a third party—the cestui que use—under instructions to convey the land to persons to be named in the feoffor's will.[2] Enforcement of the feoffor's directions, however, long posed a problem. What of the feoffee who refused to carry out those directions after the feoffor's death? What of the situation where the directions were ambiguous or contradictory? Except in special circumstances, the common law courts would neither enforce nor interpret the use,[3] and the Chancery's jurisdiction over uses developed only gradually during the second quarter of the fifteenth century.[4]

How can so important and so widespread an institution have existed without legal sanction? Can its effectiveness really have rested solely on the conscience and good sense of the feoffees prior to the time the Chancellor began to intervene? This seems implausible. Yet it is the answer that historians of the law have had to give. Professor J.M.W. Bean, the latest and most thorough investigator of the medieval use, suggests some informal checks on the potentially dishonest feoffee, but in the end he is obliged to leave the

1. J.M.W. BEAN, THE DECLINE OF ENGLISH FEUDALISM, 1215-1540, at 120 (1968); F. MAITLAND, EQUITY 23-42 (1909); T. PLUCKNETT, A CONCISE HISTORY OF THE COMMON LAW 578 (5th ed. 1956); Fratcher, *Uses of Uses*, 34 Mo. L. REV. 39 (1969).
2. The essence of the "use" was the separation of legal title to land from its beneficial enjoyment. Since the common law prohibitions, like the rule against devises of land, applied only to the legal estates, the "use" enabled landowners to treat the land as their own but to avoid the restrictions and penalties associated with legal title. Thus forfeiture for treason, the feudal incidents of wardship and marriage, the demands of creditors, and the Statute of Mortmain could all be avoided. It was common to convey to several feoffees jointly to protect against the legal restrictions being applied to any of them individually, and additional feoffees could be named as time went on. The Statute of Uses, 27 Hen. 8, c. 10 (1536), was passed specifically to put an end to these evasions of the common law. The ability to devise lands was quickly restored, because of pressure from the land-owning classes, in the Statute of Wills, 32 Hen. 8, c. 1 (1540).
3. Y.B. Pasch. 4 Edw. 4, pl. 9 (1464) *per* Moyle. *See generally* J. BAKER, INTRODUCTION TO ENGLISH LEGAL HISTORY 212 (2d ed. 1979); A. SIMPSON, AN INTRODUCTION TO THE HISTORY OF THE LAND LAW 164 (1961).
4. A commons petition of 1402 assumes that no remedy was then available in Chancery. 3 ROTULI PARLIAMENTORUM 511. The most recent and thorough accounts of the rise of the Chancellor's jurisdiction over uses are Avery, *An Evaluation of the Effectiveness of the Court of Chancery Under the Lancastrian Kings*, 86 L.Q. REV. 84 (1970); Avery, *History of Equitable Jurisdiction before 1460*, 42 BULL. INST. HIST. RESEARCH 129 (1969). Avery's conclusions have since been challenged by Nicholas Pronay: *The Chancellor, the Chancery and the Council at the End of the Fifteenth Century*, in BRITISH GOVERNMENT AND ADMINISTRATION: STUDIES PRESENTED TO S. B. CHRIMES 87 (H. Hearder & H. Loyn eds. 1974). However, his principal point concerns the representativeness of Avery's geographical sample and consequent assessment of the reasons for the rise of the court of Chancery. They affect the point of this Article, the development of the enforcement of uses, only marginally.

question of legal sanctions unresolved.[5] Others have found themselves in the same quandary, compelled to leave a large gap in time between the rise of uses and the possibility of their enforcement.[6]

A possible solution to the puzzle is that early uses might have been enforced by the courts of the Church. Maitland suggested it long ago.[7] The suggestion has since found few adherents, however, for two fundamental reasons. First, a rule of the royal courts prohibited the Church's tribunals from taking jurisdiction over cases touching freehold land; and second, there has been no positive evidence in favor of the suggestion. The force of the first reason has been diminished in recent years; research has shown beyond doubt that the medieval Church exercised jurisdiction in several areas forbidden to it by the common law, despite the threat of royal prohibitions.[8] However, the second reason remains. The possibility has rested on speculation alone.[9]

In fact, good evidence to support the suggestion does exist: the court records from the ecclesiastical courts of the dioceses of Canterbury and Rochester contain many cases involving feoffments to uses. The records are in manuscript. They are hard to read, and often difficult to interpret.[10] As a consequence, until recent years they have been left largely unexplored. However, the records furnish the best test of the actual scope of the Church's jurisdiction, and although they do not allow for absolutely confident generalization, they tend to prove that some English Church courts regularly enforced feoffments to uses. Because of the light they shed on the early history of the use, their evidence merits presentation and assessment.

Ecclesiastical Enforcement of Uses

From the last quarter of the 14th century, when the earliest surviving Canterbury Act books begin, up through the middle of the 15th century,

---

5. J.M.W. BEAN, *supra* note 1, at 156: "Of all the precautions . . . none was absolutely effective."

6. *E.g.*, 4 W. HOLDSWORTH, A HISTORY OF ENGLISH LAW 432 (3d ed. 1945) ("In early days the relation between the feoffee to uses and the feoffor or cestuique use was of a strictly personal character."); T. PLUCKNETT, *supra* note 1, at 578 ("So far, the cestui que use had no legal protection."); 1 A. SCOTT, THE LAW OF TRUSTS § 1.3, at 14 (3d ed. 1967) ("[U]ses were mere honorary obligations resting upon the good faith of the feoffee."). *See also* A. KIRALFY, POTTER'S HISTORICAL INTRODUCTION TO ENGLISH LAW 606 (4th ed. 1958); J. AMES, *The Origin of Uses*, in LECTURES ON LEGAL HISTORY 233, 236-37 (1913); Barton, *The Medieval Use*, 81 L.Q. REV. 562, 569 (1965); Cook, *Straw Men in Real Estate Transactions*, 25 WASH. U.L.Q. 232, 233 (1940); Hargreaves, *Equity and the Latin Side of Chancery*, 68 L.Q. REV. 481, 489 (1952).

7. 2 F. POLLOCK & F. MAITLAND, HISTORY OF ENGLISH LAW 232 (2d ed. 1898, reissued 1968): "Some of them may have been enforced by the ecclesiastical courts."

8. *See, e.g.*, B. WOODCOCK, MEDIEVAL ECCLESIASTICAL COURTS IN THE DIOCESE OF CANTERBURY 92 (1952); Donahue, *Roman Canon Law in the Medieval English Church: Stubbs vs. Maitland Re-examined after 75 Years in the Light of Some Records from the Church Courts*, 72 MICH. L. REV. 647 (1974); Helmholz, *Debt Claims and Probate Jurisdiction in Historical Perspective*, 23 AM. J. LEGAL HIST. 68 (1979): supra 307-21.

9. S. MILSOM, HISTORICAL FOUNDATIONS OF THE COMMON LAW 171 (1969).

10. G.R. Elton has described them, for example, as "among the more strikingly repulsive of all the relics of the past." G. ELTON, ENGLAND, 1200-1600, at 105 (1969).

cases involving uses appear as regular parts of the business of the diocesan courts there and at Rochester. The records leave little doubt that quite ordinary feoffments to uses were involved. For example, in 1375 the feoffees to uses of a certain John Roger were cited to appear before the court at Canterbury for violating the directions given to them by their feoffor. Upon interrogation, they confessed that they had received ten and three quarters of an acre of land, a windmill, and a grange under Roger's instructions that they convey it to his wife Margery after his death.[11] They admitted violation of this instruction by alienating half the land to a certain Hugh Pryor, but maintained that they had only done so out of compulsion and fear of Hugh. The judge, apparently after a brief hearing, held that the alleged fear had been "empty and insufficient to move a constant man," [12] and that the feoffees must suffer the canonical penalties for failing to carry out their duty.[13]

Seventy-five years later, at Rochester, the feoffees to uses appointed by Robert Wode appeared as defendants before the consistory court. Wode had declared in his nuncupative will that he wished his feoffees to hold his lands and tenements for the use of his son until the son reached the age of 21, then to convey to the son. If the son died before that age they were to sell the land and to apply a designated part of the proceeds to his widow and the rest "in the best manner to benefit the health of [Wode's] soul and to please God." [14] Remainders, even contingent remainders, were no strangers to the ecclesiastical officials when created in connection with a use. The cestui que use who held such an interest evidently had a right in the Church courts to enforce it against the feoffees.

The Basis of Jurisdiction Under the Canon Law

What justification in law can be given for the existence of such cases in the records of the Church courts? The records themselves articulate no reasons, but it is clear as an initial matter that no "special factors" can

---

11. *Ex officio* c. Smyth & Holyngbroke, Canterbury Act book Y.1.1, f. 94v (Diocesan Archives, Canterbury Cathedral Library. All subsequent references to Canterbury manuscript material refer to this archive repository.). A full list of Canterbury Act books is found in B. WOODCOCK, *supra* note 8, at 140.

12. This was the standard test of the canon law. 2 CORPUS JURIS CANONICI, col. 220 [X 1.40.4] (A. Friedberg ed. 1879).

13. They were excommunicated. What action they had to take to have the sentence lifted, and whether or not they took it, unfortunately does not appear in the surviving records.

14. Rochester Act book DRb Pa 2, f. 214r (1453) (Kent County Archives, Maidstone. All subsequent references to Rochester material refer to this archive repository.). The actual entry reads: "Thomas Filpot et Willelmus Barker feoffati existunt usque ad etatem filii sui xx annorum et quod tunc remaneat heredibus suis et si contingat heredes suos obire infra etatem predictam quod tunc terras et tenementa venderent et dicta Johanna habeat inde x marcas et quod residuum disponatur per eosdem feoffatores et executores suos meliori modo quo viderint anime sue salutem proficere et deo complacere." ("Thomas Filpot and William Barker are enfeoffed until the twentieth year of his son, and then the lands are to remain to his heirs; but, if it should happen that his heirs die before the aforesaid age, then they should sell the lands and tenements and the said Joan should have ten marks therefrom and the residue should be disposed of by the same feoffees and executors in the best manner that shall appear to profit his soul and to please God.")

explain their presence. The feoffees in the two cases above, for example, were laymen. Clerical status of the defendants could therefore not have been the reason for the Church's jurisdiction.[15] Nor can the land involved in such cases have been held by burgage tenure, which might have come under the Church's probate jurisdiction because it was devisable by custom.[16] Medieval boroughs were small in area, and in many cases too much land was involved for this exception to have given jurisdiction.[17] Moreover, where the scribe noted the parish of the feoffor, it was often a rural parish.[18]

Nor can leasehold, which was for many purposes treated as a chattel interest and was therefore subject to the Church's testamentary jurisdiction, offer a good explanation for the presence of these cases in the court records.[19] The cases involving uses never mentioned the existence of a lease. A direction that the feoffee should sell the land in certain circumstances was mentioned often enough that the feoffor's interest must have been a fee. Furthermore, had the land involved in the cases been devisable in the first place it is hard to see why a feoffment to uses would have been necessary at all.[20] Therefore, the cases found in the remaining records must have been just what they seem: disputes over quite ordinary uses. They were not special cases in which the English common law conceded jurisdiction to the Church.

On the other hand, the surviving cases suggest one limitation on the Church's jurisdiction. The cases found in the records all dealt with a use established by someone who was dead at the time of the suit. In none was a living feoffor seeking to enforce a use against his feoffees. Of course, too many records have disappeared over the course of centuries to permit a categorical assertion that the Church courts never enforced a use where the feoffor was still alive. Theoretically, such a suit was possible under the canon law, which claimed jurisdiction over obligations undertaken under oath.[21] Because feoffees often swore formally to fulfil the grantor's directions as part of the original enfeoffment, it would have been possible for

---

15. This has been suggested as a possible source of jurisdiction over some uses. *See* J.M.W. BEAN, *supra* note 1, at 154; Barton, *supra* note 6, at 566.

16. Burgage tenure was the tenure by which most land in ancient boroughs or towns was held. It was subject to many local customs, one of the most frequent of which was devisability. The right was not, however, unlimited or everywhere in effect. *See* M. BATESON, *Introduction* to 2 BOROUGH CUSTOMS (21 Selden Soc. xcii 1906); M. HEMMEON, BURGAGE TENURE IN MEDIAEVAL ENGLAND 130-44 (1914).

17. *See, e.g.,* Luke c. Austyn, Canterbury Act book Y.1.3, f.20 (1416), in which three virgates of woodland (*tres virgate bosci*) was the subject of a suit in the Church court.

18. *E.g.,* Canterbury Act book Y.1.3, f. 62v (1418) (the decedent-feoffor had lived in Reculver); *Ex officio* c. Symond, Rochester Act book DRb Pa 3, f. 337v (1457) (the decedent-feoffor had lived in Hadlow). Neither is listed as a borough in M. BERESFORD & H. FINBERG, ENGLISH MEDIEVAL BOROUGHS: A HAND-LIST 128-31 (1973).

19. *See* A. SIMPSON, *supra* note 3, at 131.

20. This point was made long ago by William Somner in A TREATISE OF GAVELKIND 152-53 (1726).

21. *See* Esmain, *Le serment promissoire dans le droit canonique,* 12 REVUE HISTORIQUE DE DROIT FRANCAIS ET ETRANGER 248 (3d serv. 1888); Helmholz, *Assumpsit and Fidei Laesio,* 91 L.Q. REV. 406 (1975): supra 263-89.

a living feoffor to have sued them before an ecclesiastical tribunal. However, if the surviving records are representative, this did not happen. The cases that appeared before the Church courts all involved probate jurisdiction, either directly or indirectly.

This limitation indicates the reasons for and the nature of ecclesiastical intervention. As is well known, the English Church exercised probate jurisdiction throughout the Middle Ages, and even afterwards. One of the responsibilities attendant upon that jurisdiction, in the eyes of the men who exercised it, was the duty to secure a person's final wishes.[22] Since testators frequently put instructions to feoffees into their last will and testament, documents involving uses of land inevitably came before the ecclesiastical courts. Although a strict separation between land and movables could have been made, the medieval Church regarded such a division as artificial; it sought to enforce all of the decedent's final wishes where it could.[23] The enforcement of uses, according to this view, seemed a legitimate part of the Church's probate responsibility. Where the feoffees were not carrying out the feoffor's instructions, they became in effect "impeders" of the decedent's will,[24] and so the court records style them.[25]

There was a second reason favoring intervention where the feoffor was dead. A principle of canon law held that the courts of the Church should provide justice whenever secular law was inadequate.[26] Although the English Church courts did not always act on this potentially sweeping principle, they did not ignore it completely. A living feoffor normally had a remedy at common law: he could enter for breach of the condition.[27] The cestui que use, however, could not, and since after the death of the original feoffor he alone would have any incentive to complain, there was no other

---

22. The most useful account of the functioning of the probate jurisdiction of the Church court is still H. SWINBURNE, TREATISE OF TESTAMENTS AND LAST WILLS (1st ed. 1590-1591). The growth and history prior to 1300 is well covered in M. SHEEHAN, THE WILL IN MEDIEVAL ENGLAND (1963). *See also* R. GOFFIN, THE TESTAMENTARY EXECUTOR IN ENGLAND AND ELSEWHERE (1901).

23. *See* REGISTRUM JOHANNIS DE PONTISSARA, EPISCOPI WYNTONIENSIS 773 (19 Surrey Record Soc., C. Deedes ed. 1923): "una et indivisa esse debeat finalis expedicio testamenti" ("the implementation of the testament should be one and undivided"). *See also* Jacob, *The Archbishop's Testamentary Jurisdiction*, in MEDIAEVAL RECORDS OF THE ARCHBISHOP OF CANTERBURY 35, 47 (1962).

24. *See* Archbishop Stratford's Provincial Constitution *Caeterum contingit interdum* (1343), given in W. LYNDWOOD, PROVINCIALE (SEU CONSTITUTIONES ANGLIAE) 171-79 (1679). Lyndwood's gloss, at 169 s.v. *residuis*, cites approvingly the opinion of the Continental canonists Hostiensis and Innocent IV, "qui dicunt, quod quaelibet voluntas testatoris rationabilis dici potest pia, et servari debet" ("who say that any sort of rational will of the testator can be called pious and should be complied with").

25. *E.g.*, *Ex officio* c. Smyth & Holyngbroke, *supra* note 11, in which the defendants were held to have incurred "sentenciam maioris excommunicationis a sanctis patribus contra impedientes ultimas voluntates decedencium in hac parte latam" ("the sentence of major excommunication imposed by the holy fathers against impeders of the last wills of decedents in this regard").

26. 2 CORPUS JURIS CANONICI, cols. 250-51 [X 1.2.10, 11]. For a modern commentary on the principle involved, see Tierney, *"Tria Quippe Distinguit Iudicia"* . . . *A Note on Innocent III's Decretal Per Venerabilem*, 37 SPECULUM 48 (1962).

27. *See* T. LITTLETON, TREATISE OF TENURES § 355 (1841 ed. re-issued 1978); Barton, *supra* note 6, at 566.

way in which the use could be enforced prior to the rise of the Chancellor's jurisdiction. Because of this gap in secular remedies, enforcement of uses by the Church as part of its probate jurisdiction fit neatly with the canon law's injunction. Without this remedy, a decedent's final wishes would have been legally unenforceable.

Nature of the Cases Heard and Remedies Given

Most litigated cases in the surviving records seem to have dealt not with the outright dishonesty of the feoffees but with uncertainty engendered by contradictory instructions from the original feoffor. An illustrative example is a 1465 *ex officio* prosecution from Rochester. The decedent's will apparently contained directions contrary to those the feoffees had received as part of the original feoffment.[28] Were the first instructions binding or were they subject to change by will? The feoffees claimed that they were genuinely uncertain about what to do. A second example is a Canterbury case from 1398, where the feoffees of Thomas Manndenyle were sued by his executor. They had evidently refused to obey the testamentary direction, but they "exhibited judicially a certain condition" containing a contradictory direction.[29] They did not know which direction bound them, and they had refrained from acting for that reason.[30]

A firm line between dishonesty and honest perplexity is, of course, hard to draw, particularly on the basis of record evidence. Defendants, even dishonest ones, almost always have an excuse. The devisee in one case, for instance, claimed that the original grant had been made to such uses as the feoffor should designate; the feoffees replied that it had been to such use as they themselves should select.[31] In another case one party maintained that the land granted was to be disposed of for the soul of the grantor; the feoffees maintained that the grant had been unconditional.[32] It is difficult to determine whether these were honest justifications, or only excuses. In an age when the grant of land need not have been by deed, and in which the Church courts would enforce the wishes of a dying man with no requirement of a testamentary writing, there was inevitably much room for uncertainty and disagreement. The merits of most resulting quarrels are now past

---

28. *Ex officio* c. Watsone, Rochester Act book DRb Pa 3, f. 506r. The feoffee claimed that the testator "non potuit disponere de ii acris in testamento eo quod ipse et socius erant feoffati ad aliud usum" ("could not dispose of the two acres in his testament because he and his companion were enfeoffed to a contrary use").

29. Stace c. Frend & Godard, Canterbury Act book Y.1.2, f. 136v: "dicti vero feoffati exhibuerunt iudicialiter certam condicionem cuius quidem condicionis commissarius decrevit partibus copiam" ("the said feoffees exhibited in court a certain condition, a copy of which the Commissary decreed to the parties").

30. In neither of these two cases does the record contain a decision of the court. We cannot even know with certainty what principles of interpretation the courts used.

31. *In re* Testament of Richard Middleton, Rochester Act book DRb Pa 3, f. 481 v. (1464). One witness testified that he had heard the grantor say "quod feoffavit eos ex confidencia ad usum suum et non ad usum illorum" ("that he enfeoffed them out of trust to his [own] use and not to their use"). The feoffees maintained the opposite.

32. Herford c. Fen, Canterbury Act book Y.1.4, f. 107v (1423).

untangling. But while one may admit existence of the problem of dishonesty among feoffees, the evidence suggests that disputed cases stemmed from lack of clarity more than from conscious impeding of a decedent's declared wishes. The Church provided a necessary forum for the interpretation of contradictory directions.[33]

Once the directions had been determined, the remedy normally available in the Church court was an order against the feoffees to fulfil the terms of the feoffment. For example, in a suit brought at Canterbury in 1416 against Henry Austyn, the feoffee to uses of William Germyn, the Act book records that "the aforesaid Henry was ordered to restore the three virgates of woodland" which should have been held for the feoffor's sons.[34] In a Rochester case from 1438 the record reads simply that after the will and testament had been read, the feoffees "being warned in court to carry out this last will, withdrew." [35]

The records unfortunately supply no evidence on what remedies the Church courts offered in more complicated cases, if indeed any was available. Where the feoffees had alienated the land to a purchaser, we cannot be sure whether the remedy would extend to action against the alienee. Nor is there any sign of the recovery of money damages from defaulting feoffees. So far as the records reveal, an order for specific performance was the sole remedy available. The records are likewise unclear about other complexities of the law surrounding uses. There is no evidence, for example, regarding a problem that later vexed the Court of Chancery, whether action could be taken against the heirs of the feoffees.[36]

The records provide some, but not conclusive, evidence on other points of importance in the history of the use. Most uses were declared in favor of members of the feoffor's family, although uses in favor of religious purposes do appear, particularly where part of the land was to be sold and applied as the feoffees should determine best for the feoffor's soul.[37] One case from Canterbury shows incidentally that the feoffees were paid for their services.[38] Other cases show that there could be a continuing use established to cover chattels as well as land.[39] But these may

---

33. The situation was apparently the same later in Chancery. *See, e.g.*, The Case of the Sub Poena in Chancery (1459), in SELECT CASES IN THE EXCHEQUER CHAMBER 173 (51 Selden Soc. 1933). *See also* S. MILSOM, *supra* note 9, at 183.

34. Luke c. Austyn, Canterbury Act book Y.1.3, f. 20: "Et monitus est dictus Henricus ad restituendum tres virgatas bosci." Evidence from this case is also found in Deposition book X.10.1. fols, 106-106v.

35. Fraunceys c. Rede, Act book DRb Pa 1, f. 49v: "Et moniti ad perficiendum ultimam voluntatem huiusmodi in iudicio recesserunt."

36. Y.B. Pasch. 22 Edw. 4, pl. 18 (1492); Keilwey 42b (pl. 6), 72 Eng. Rep. 199 (1502).

37. *See, e.g.*, note 14 *supra*.

38. Canterbury Deposition book X.10.1, f. 112b (1417): One witness, Thomas Reynold, deposed that the direction had included "quod quilibet feoffatorum haberet pro labore suo xl denarios" ("that each of the feoffees should have 40d. for his labor").

39. *E.g.*, Comubere c. Executors of Brode, Canterbury Deposition book X.10.1, f. 137v. The plaintiff there was described as "unus feoffatorum bonorum dicti Johannis Brode et supervisor bonorum suorum" ("one of the feoffees of the goods of the said John Brode, and [also] supervisor of his goods").

be isolated cases, and it is impossible to generalize from them. Unfortunately, no learned commentary on the subject exists. William Lyndwood, the only contemporary canonist who might be expected to speak about the subject because of his familiarity with English court practice, was silent.[40] Thus it is regrettably true that we must leave most questions of legal and social detail unanswered.

The Extent of Ecclesiastical Enforcement

In evaluating the evidence in the surviving records the most perplexing problem is to determine whether or not enforcement of uses was general throughout the English Church. The cases discussed in the Article some from only two dioceses, Canterbury and Rochester, both of which lie within the county of Kent. Medieval England contained seventeen dioceses, of which two others—Ely and York—have regular court records surviving from the period before the Chancellor began regularly to intervene.[41] Neither seems to contain cases involving uses.

There is, however, a not insignificant possibility that this absence of York and Ely cases is simply a product of chance. Both dioceses have only partial court records surviving. York has no systematic Act books recording litigation heard before the consistory court.[42] Ely has a single Act book, covering the years 1374-1382.[43] The records at Rochester and Canterbury are much fuller; both have many Act books surviving. The lack of evidence of actions brought against feoffees to uses from other English dioceses may therefore reflect no more than the accident of survival. If so, the Church courts held jurisdiction over uses, just as they did over other aspects of medieval jurisdiction that ran counter to common law rules.[44]

Nevertheless, the fact that all the evidence comes from the two English dioceses that lay within the county of Kent is undeniably troublesome. The pre-eminent influence there of the archbishop of Canterbury, not only England's most powerful churchman but also a powerful secular landlord within the county, suggests at least the possibility of a special place for the Church courts in his diocese.[45] Not every man would question the rights of an archbishop who happened also to be his lord.

The existence in Kent of a special custom of inheritance, called gavelkind, also suggests a possible explanation for the predominance of cases involving uses there. Under this customary system, all male children shared

---

40. W. LYNDWOOD, supra note 24, at 166-79.
41. There is a list of most of the surviving medieval court records in R.H. HELMHOLZ, MARRIAGE LITIGATION IN MEDIEVAL ENGLAND 233-36 (1974).
42. See Donahue, supra note 8, at 656-57.
43. Act book EDR D/2/1, Ely diocesan archives, Cambridge University Library. There are, of course, also scattered records of judicial proceedings in Church courts, e.g., 4 REGISTERS OF ROGER MARTIVAL, BISHOP OF SALISBURY 1315-1330 (68 Canterbury & York Soc. 1975) [hereinafter cited as REG. MARTIVAL]. In the absence of sustained records, however, it seems impossible to draw conclusions from them except as to the cases that actually appear in them.
44. See works cited in note 8 supra.
45. See generally F. DU BOULAY, THE LORDSHIP OF CANTERBURY (1966).

equally in a decedent's lands, unlike the system of primogeniture that largely prevailed elsewhere.[46] One would not initially think that gavelkind promoted feoffment to uses. Provision for equal inheritance seems to demand a feoffment to uses and subsequent division by will less than the system of primogeniture. On the other hand, the researches of Avery and Pronay have shown how prominently Kentish feoffments figured in the rise of the Chancellor's jurisdiction.[47] The later records of Chancery indicate that the feoffment to uses was particularly prevalent in Kent,[48] or at least that Chancery litigation over uses was particularly prevalent there. It may be that the uncertainty of gavelkind (*i.e.,* which child would get what land) made uses that allowed the devise of land, and disputes over them, especially common in Kent. If this is true, then one would expect uses to appear frequently in the Canterbury and Rochester records and not in the less complete records of the courts at Ely and York, not because the ecclesiastical courts there would not entertain them, but because there were fewer disputes over uses within these dioceses and because their surviving records are not abundant enough to show the smaller number of cases heard in them.

The reasons for the restriction of the existing evidence to Canterbury and Rochester, and the possibility that courts of other dioceses heard suits brought to enforce uses, are questions that must, in the end, be left open. Although matters of legitimate speculation, in the present state of research there appears to be little direct evidence one way or the other. No court records survive. It is only from the last third of the fifteenth century that court records from dioceses other than Canterbury and Rochester survive in quantities significant enough to inspire confidence in conclusions drawn from them.[49] By then, however, even the records from Canterbury and Rochester contain no cases involving feoffments to uses. The ecclesiastical jurisdiction of those courts over uses had disappeared.

Disappearance of Ecclesiastical Jurisdiction

Cases involving feoffments to uses cease to appear in the court records after the middle third of the fifteenth century. The last unambiguous example found comes from 1465,[50] and they probably had been gradually declining in numbers long before. By that date, of course, the jurisdiction of Chancery over uses had been established. If not the major proportion of the Chancellor's jurisdiction, suits involving uses were at least established

46. *See* 3 W. HOLDSWORTH, HISTORY OF ENGLISH LAW 260-63 (5th ed. 1942); T. ROBINSON, COMMON LAW OF KENT; OR, CUSTOMS OF GAVELKIND (2d ed. 1858).
47. *See* works cited in note 4 *supra.* I am indebted to Dr. J.A. Guy for this point.
48. However, it does not appear that Professor Bean noticed any particular prevalence of Kentish uses. *See* J.M.W. BEAN, *supra* note 1.
49. *See* R.H. HELMHOLZ, supra note 41, at 233-35.
50. *Ex officio* c. Watsone, Rochester Act book DRb Pa 3, f. 506r. The last case found at Canterbury is Glastonbury c. Newman & Newman, Canterbury Act book Y. 1.6, f. 28v (1464), although it is not entirely clear from the entry that the feoffees were being called upon to do more than produce the decedent's will.

as normal parts of Chancery business.[51] The evidence of the Church court records is consistent with the natural supposition that ecclesiastical jurisdiction declined as the Chancellor's jurisdiction grew.

The Church courts put up little apparent fight to retain their jurisdiction over uses. The ecclesiastical officials were certainly capable of sustained efforts to protect jurisdictional rights they considered important,[52] but neither the court records nor other contemporary evidence suggests that the loss created a stir of any kind. Such a graceful surrender made sense, of course, even under the Church's own law. Canon law did not consider testamentary jurisdiction to be exclusively spiritual in nature, as it did some other parts of ecclesiastical jurisdiction, marriage for example.[53] Lyndwood, the most famous fifteenth century English canonist, clearly directed that the secular laws on the subject of inheritance were to be deferred to.[54] The Church court records for testamentary causes unrelated to uses also show that this was not a merely theoretical injunction; the judges in practice looked to local custom and to English secular law.[55] More important, by the time the Church had lost its jurisdiction over feoffees, the Chancery regularly offered the cestui que use a remedy against a feoffee.[56] Since one of the reasons that Church courts took cognizance of uses in the first place was the lack of an adequate secular remedy,[57] there was no longer the same need for canonical intervention.

In the eyes of most contemporaries, the end of ecclesiastical intervention against feoffees to uses and the rise of the enforcement of uses by Chancery must have seemed a natural development. Although in form the Church courts merely exercised in personam jurisdiction over feoffees, title to freehold land was ultimately at issue, and the royal courts had long since declared a special interest in all disputes over freehold.[58] Extension of protection to a previously unprotected aspect of the devolution of land was therefore a natural result both of this principle and of the medieval notion that the King had a residual responsibility to do justice. The Chancery in the late Middle Ages was the court where this responsibility took concrete shape.[59]

---

51. *See* the articles by Avery, *supra* note 4.
52. Helmholz, *Writs of Prohibition and Ecclesiastical Sanctions in the English Courts Christian*, 60 MINN. L. REV. 1011, 1021-30 (1976) : supra 77-99.
53. *E.g.*, 3 HOSTIENSIS, COMMENTARIA IN LIBROS DECRETALIUM 74 [at X 3.26.3, no. 7] (Venice 1581).
54. W. LYNDWOOD, *supra* note 24, at 172 s.v. *mobilibus. See also* M. SHEEHAN, *supra* note 22, at 120-38.
55. *See, e.g.*, REG. MARTIVAL, *supra* note 43, at 66 (1322), a case in which the ecclesiastical judges refused to probate a will because of possible royal interest in the decedent's chattels. They delayed "until [they] should be fully informed by experts in the law of the realm."
56. *See* note 4 and accompanying text *supra.*
57. *See* note 26 and accompanying text *supra.*
58. R. GLANVILL, TREATISE ON THE LAWS AND CUSTOMS OF THE REALM OF ENGLAND, bk. XII, c. 25 (G. Hall ed. 1965); Constitutions of Clarendon, cap. 9 (1164), in W. STUBBS, SELECT CHARTERS 165-66 (9th ed. 1921); R.C. VAN CAENEGEM, ROYAL WRITS IN ENGLAND FROM THE CONQUEST TO GLANVILL 212-31 (77 Selden Soc. 1959).
59. *See* J. BAKER, *supra* note 3, at 84-93; J. BARTON, ROMAN LAW IN ENGLAND, 50-71, esp. 69-70 (Ius Romanum Medii Aevi, V 13a 1971).

equally in a decedent's lands, unlike the system of primogeniture that largely prevailed elsewhere.[46] One would not initially think that gavelkind promoted feoffment to uses. Provision for equal inheritance seems to demand a feoffment to uses and subsequent division by will less than the system of primogeniture. On the other hand, the researches of Avery and Pronay have shown how prominently Kentish feoffments figured in the rise of the Chancellor's jurisdiction.[47] The later records of Chancery indicate that the feoffment to uses was particularly prevalent in Kent,[48] or at least that Chancery litigation over uses was particularly prevalent there. It may be that the uncertainty of gavelkind (*i.e.*, which child would get what land) made uses that allowed the devise of land, and disputes over them, especially common in Kent. If this is true, then one would expect uses to appear frequently in the Canterbury and Rochester records and not in the less complete records of the courts at Ely and York, not because the ecclesiastical courts there would not entertain them, but because there were fewer disputes over uses within these dioceses and because their surviving records are not abundant enough to show the smaller number of cases heard in them.

The reasons for the restriction of the existing evidence to Canterbury and Rochester, and the possibility that courts of other dioceses heard suits brought to enforce uses, are questions that must, in the end, be left open. Although matters of legitimate speculation, in the present state of research there appears to be little direct evidence one way or the other. No court records survive. It is only from the last third of the fifteenth century that court records from dioceses other than Canterbury and Rochester survive in quantities significant enough to inspire confidence in conclusions drawn from them.[49] By then, however, even the records from Canterbury and Rochester contain no cases involving feoffments to uses. The ecclesiastical jurisdiction of those courts over uses had disappeared.

Disappearance of Ecclesiastical Jurisdiction

Cases involving feoffments to uses cease to appear in the court records after the middle third of the fifteenth century. The last unambiguous example found comes from 1465,[50] and they probably had been gradually declining in numbers long before. By that date, of course, the jurisdiction of Chancery over uses had been established. If not the major proportion of the Chancellor's jurisdiction, suits involving uses were at least established

---

46. *See* 3 W. HOLDSWORTH, HISTORY OF ENGLISH LAW 260-63 (5th ed. 1942); T. ROBINSON, COMMON LAW OF KENT; OR, CUSTOMS OF GAVELKIND (2d ed. 1858).

47. *See* works cited in note 4 *supra*. I am indebted to Dr. J.A. Guy for this point.

48. However, it does not appear that Professor Bean noticed any particular prevalence of Kentish uses. *See* J.M.W. BEAN, *supra* note 1.

49. *See* R.H. HELMHOLZ, supra note 41, at 233-35.

50. *Ex officio* c. Watsone, Rochester Act book DRb Pa 3, f. 506r. The last case found at Canterbury is Glastonbury c. Newman & Newman, Canterbury Act book Y. 1.6, f. 28v (1464), although it is not entirely clear from the entry that the feoffees were being called upon to do more than produce the decedent's will.

as normal parts of Chancery business.[51] The evidence of the Church court records is consistent with the natural supposition that ecclesiastical jurisdiction declined as the Chancellor's jurisdiction grew.

The Church courts put up little apparent fight to retain their jurisdiction over uses. The ecclesiastical officials were certainly capable of sustained efforts to protect jurisdictional rights they considered important,[52] but neither the court records nor other contemporary evidence suggests that the loss created a stir of any kind. Such a graceful surrender made sense, of course, even under the Church's own law. Canon law did not consider testamentary jurisdiction to be exclusively spiritual in nature, as it did some other parts of ecclesiastical jurisdiction, marriage for example.[53] Lyndwood, the most famous fifteenth century English canonist, clearly directed that the secular laws on the subject of inheritance were to be deferred to.[54] The Church court records for testamentary causes unrelated to uses also show that this was not a merely theoretical injunction; the judges in practice looked to local custom and to English secular law.[55] More important, by the time the Church had lost its jurisdiction over feoffees, the Chancery regularly offered the cestui que use a remedy against a feoffee.[56] Since one of the reasons that Church courts took cognizance of uses in the first place was the lack of an adequate secular remedy,[57] there was no longer the same need for canonical intervention.

In the eyes of most contemporaries, the end of ecclesiastical intervention against feoffees to uses and the rise of the enforcement of uses by Chancery must have seemed a natural development. Although in form the Church courts merely exercised in personam jurisdiction over feoffees, title to freehold land was ultimately at issue, and the royal courts had long since declared a special interest in all disputes over freehold.[58] Extension of protection to a previously unprotected aspect of the devolution of land was therefore a natural result both of this principle and of the medieval notion that the King had a residual responsibility to do justice. The Chancery in the late Middle Ages was the court where this responsibility took concrete shape.[59]

---

51. *See* the articles by Avery, *supra* note 4.
52. Helmholz, *Writs of Prohibition and Ecclesiastical Sanctions in the English Courts Christian, supra* 77-99.
53. *E.g.,* 3 HOSTIENSIS, COMMENTARIA IN LIBROS DECRETALIUM 74 [at X 3.26.3, no. 7] (Venice 1581).
54. W. LYNDWOOD, *supra* note 24, at 172 s.v. *mobilibus. See also* M. SHEEHAN, *supra* note 22, at 120-38.
55. *See, e.g.,* REG. MARTIVAL, *supra* note 43, at 66 (1322), a case in which the ecclesiastical judges refused to probate a will because of possible royal interest in the decedent's chattels. They delayed "until [they] should be fully informed by experts in the law of the realm."
56. *See* note 4 and accompanying text *supra.*
57. *See* note 26 and accompanying text *supra.*
58. R. GLANVILL, TREATISE ON THE LAWS AND CUSTOMS OF THE REALM OF ENGLAND, bk. XII, c. 25 (G. Hall ed. 1965); Constitutions of Clarendon, cap. 9 (1164), in W. STUBBS, SELECT CHARTERS 165-66 (9th ed. 1921); R.C. VAN CAENEGEM, ROYAL WRITS IN ENGLAND FROM THE CONQUEST TO GLANVILL 212-31 (77 Selden Soc. 1959).
59. *See* J. BAKER, *supra* note 3, at 84-93; J. BARTON, ROMAN LAW IN ENGLAND, 50-71, esp. 69-70 (Ius Romanum Medii Aevi, V 13a 1971).

Even in the eyes of ecclesiastics, the development was not necessarily cause for complaint or discouragement. No doubt the loss of jurisdiction caused some diminution in fees to the lawyers practicing in the courts at Rochester and Canterbury. But cases involving uses never formed more than a small part of the total cases heard there, and during the years when the jurisdiction over uses was disappearing any "slack" was more than taken up by the rise in ecclesiastical jurisdiction over sworn contracts.[60] Moreover, we should not exaggerate the extent of ideological disagreement between churchmen and common lawyers.[61] The canon law granted primary jurisdiction over questions of feudal tenure to secular courts and, as noted above, it never held that testamentary jurisdiction was its exclusive right.[62] Some canonists might even have seen the growth of Chancery jurisdiction in a positive light, as an affirmation of the canonical principle that in the absence of special circumstances the wishes of a dead man should be enforced by legal sanction.

Conclusion

The evolution of the enforcement of uses from ecclesiastical to Chancery jurisdiction serves as an example of the role that canon law has played in the growth and development of our common law. Modern students of legal history may regard it as part of the long continuing absorption into the secular law of remedies once available only in the courts of the Church.[63] The rise of the Chancellor's jurisdiction over feoffees to uses is not, therefore, the story of the creation of a legal remedy where previously there had been none. Rather it is the story of continuing enforcement in a new setting.

This understanding of the early enforcement of uses is suggested, though it is not conclusively proved, by the records at Canterbury and Rochester. It is well to re-emphasize the limited geographical scope of the evidence. But the evidence of regular ecclesiastical intervention prior to the rise of the Chancellor's jurisdiction, at the very least, makes it possible to think that the Church courts played an important role in the growth and enforcement of uses. It becomes more than the purely speculative possibility it has hitherto been.

---

60. B. WOODCOCK, *supra* note 8, at 84.

61. *See* Jones, *The Two Laws in England: The Later Middle Ages,* 11 J. CHURCH & STATE 111, 113-14 (1969).

62. *See, e.g.,* the papal decretal *Per venerabilem,* 2 CORPUS JURIS CANONICI col. 714 [X 4.17.13]. Its effect limited the ecclesiastical rights to confer legitimacy of birth to spiritual matters; absent special circumstances this would not affect rights in inheritance. *See also* note 26 and accompanying text *supra.*

63. *See generally* Sheehan, *Canon Law and English Institutions,* in PROCEEDINGS OF THE SECOND INTERNATIONAL CONGRESS OF MEDIEVAL CANON LAW 391 (S. Kuttner & J. Ryan eds. 1965); Bassett, *Canon Law and the Common Law,* 29 HAST. L.J. 1383 (1978).

INDEX

abbots, as judges delegate, 22, 31n
abortion, 159–60, 167
absolution
 ad cautelam, 105
 of the dying, 107
 requirements for, 297, 324–5
 see also sanctions, ecclesiastical
academic jurists *see* canonists
acceleration *see* litigation
accidit novitate perversa, 89, 90n
accounting, by fiduciaries, 240–1, 256
act books *see* records, ecclesiastical
actio iniuriarum, 9
Adams, Norma, 1, 78–9, 95, 98
administration, of estates, 13–14, 239–40, 294–7,
 301, 310–12
administrators *see* intestacy; executors
adoption, consequences of, 29
adultery
 as disqualification, 26, 196–7
 jurisdiction over, 142n, 188, 314
 prosecutions for, 70, 142n
 see also sexual offences
advancements, 257
advocates
 absence from diocesan courts, 43
 disqualification for interest, 30
 fees of, 46–7
 professional standards of, 42–57
 see also proctors
advowsons, disputes over, 65, 70, 83, 95n
affection, as judicial disqualification, 30
affinity, as judicial disqualification, 29; *see also*
 consanguinity
Alexander III, Pope, 122, 189
alimenta, obligation to provide, 172–4, 214n, 252,
 257–8
ambassadors, rights of, 112
Ames, James Barr, 264–5, 288
Ancharano, Petrus de, 29
Andreae, Joannes, 17, 27, 29, 31, 107, 153, 180,
 191
apostoli, 45n
appeals
 abuse of, 43
 right to, 105–06
 to papal court, 3, 22, 25, 70, 252, 318
 to provincial courts, 51, 69, 199n, 218, 267

arbitration
 delay for, 183
 enforcement of awards, 268
 in choice of judges delegate, 24–5, 38
 see also compromise
archdeacons, jurisdiction of, 146, 151, 165
Arches, Court of, 69, 146, 199n, 254, 334n
Arnold, M. S., 70, 98
arrest *see* sanctions, temporal; signification
articles, canonical, 45, 48–9
assault, 128, 159; *see also si quis suadente*
assumpsit, 263–89, 314, 320
attachment *see* prohibitions
auctoritate dei patris, 9
Audience, Archbishop's court of, 80n, 86, 130n,
 318
Audiencia litterarum contradictarum, 23–4
avarice, and lawyers, 43–5

bailments, 129, 268
Baker, J. H., 9n, 185n, 305n
Baldus, de Ubaldis, 181
bankruptcy, 11–15, 291–305
Barbour, W. T., 286–7, 320n
bastardy *see* illegitimacy
Bath and Wells, nature of litigation at, 84, 154
Bean, J. M. W., 341, 349n
Beaumanoir, Philippe de, 192
Becket, Archbishop Thomas, 125
Bede, the Venerable, 253
benefit of clergy *see* criminous clerks
bishops
 attitudes towards canon law, 6, 194
 attitudes towards royal courts, 79, 192–5, 199–
 200
 canonical rights of, 105n, 107
 certificates of, 188, 193, 200–01
 enforcement of royal court orders, 6–8
 gravamina of, 79, 206, 307n
 material interests of, 31, 83n, 194n
bonds, penal, 266; *see also* suretyship
Boniface VIII, Pope, 25
Boniface, Archbishop, 88–9
borough courts *see* local courts
Bracton, Henry of, 21n, 32n, 63, 68, 71n, 205–06,
 211, 253
Brentano, Robert, 37
bribery, 24, 31–2